Contents

Introducing Cultural Studies

Elaine Baldwin

Brian Longhurst

Scott McCracken

Miles Ogborn

Greg Smith

The University of Georgia Press
Athens

Published in the United States of America in 2000 by the University of
Georgia Press, Athens, Georgia 30602
First published in Great Britain by Prentice Hall Europe

This edition is published by arrangement with Pearson Education
Limited

Typeset in 9.5/12 pt New Baskerville by Fakenham Photosetting Ltd
Printed and bound in Great Britain by Redwood Books

04   03   02   01   00   P   5   4   3   2   1

Library of Congress Cataloging-in-Publication Data for this edition
available on request. The European edition was cataloged as follows:
Introducing cultural studies/Elaine Baldwin ... [et al.].
    p.   cm.
   Includes bibliographical references and index.
   ISBN 0–13–433301–2 (alk. paper)
     1. Culture—Study and teaching.   I. Baldwin, Elaine.
  HM101.I578   1998
306'.071—dc21   98-27056

ISBN 0–8203–2245–8

British Library Cataloguing-in-Publication Data

A catalogue record for this book is available from the British Library

7 Cultured bodies

8 Subcultures: reading, resistance and social divisions

List of Key Influence boxes

List of Defining Concept boxes

Preface: A User's Guide

We think that cultural studies is one of the most stimulating areas of activity in intellectual life. It is also something that is studied at different levels, forming an important part of the profile of many university courses. There are many books on cultural studies. However, as we have found in our own teaching, there is no introduction to the field that seeks to offer an overview and exploration of some of the most important avenues of research in the field – hence this book, which deliberately and very consciously sets out to be a textbook for students who are studying cultural studies as part of a university course.

In seeking to write an introduction we have not attempted to be completely comprehensive. We think that we cover the most important aspects of cultural studies, but ultimately this can only be our interpretation of the field, written from particular standpoints. We have organised the book into nine chapters divided into two parts. Part I, on cultural theory, contains three chapters. In the first we introduce some different meanings of the concept of culture and the issues arising from these meanings. This leads us to point to the importance of cultural studies as an activity that produces knowledge that separate disciplines cannot. Our own disciplinary training and affiliations vary, taking in anthropology, sociology, geography and English, and we continue to work in university departments that reflect disciplines. However, we would all attest to the ways in which our contacts with cultural studies have changed the ways in which we think, teach and research.

In Chapter 2 we examine some important aspects of communication and representation, introducing critical issues of language and meaning. This is followed by a chapter concerned with multiple dimensions and theories of power and inequality. Together the three chapters in Part I address important general issues and debates in cultural studies and provide a map around them. In these chapters, and in the rest of the book, we are particularly concerned with the division of culture along the lines of class, race and gender.

Part II of the book contains six chapters which examine in some detail different dimensions of culture. One of the most significant developments in the humanities and social sciences in recent years has been the increased attention to the importance of space and time. Indeed, we would argue that cultural studies has been an important impetus behind such developments. We reflect these concerns in Chapters 4 and 5, which point to the ways in which contemporary culture cannot be understood without significant attention to space, place, conceptions of time and social change. Of course these academic developments are contextualised by the increased pace of contemporary life and the ease of communication and travel which are producing new experiences of time and space.

Another important shift in contemporary culture and the study of it has been a redefinition of politics. Often arising from the new social movements of the 1960s and after, there is now an understanding of the way in which politics, as activity concerned with power, is all around us. In Chapter 6 we address a number of issues raised by this expansion and change in the meaning of politics.

Another significant area of concern in contemporary life is the body. We are all aware of the state of our bodies and the forms of treatment for them when they are not functioning adequately. Moreover there is increased debate around new technologies of healing and body alteration. Again, cultural studies has been in the vanguard of consideration of some of these issues – a concern reflected in the subject matter of Chapter 7.

Culture can often be seen as all-encompassing in that many things and activities are seen to be part of a culture. However, cultures are also divided along the lines of class, race, gender and age and, as we have suggested, by space and time. One important way of discussing and characterising such divisions is through the concept of subculture. Chapter 8 is devoted to this area. In particular it examines work on youth subcultures.

The final chapter of the book returns to some of the issues of representation outlined in Part I. Using ideas about technological change and broad shifts in culture, we address important developments in visual culture. Part of our concern here is to locate forms of visual representation and the visual aspects of everyday interaction historically and spatially.

That is the outline of the structure and content of our book. We expect that you will read those chapters that most interest you or will be of most use at any one time for a particular purpose. To facilitate the use of the book, we have further divided all the chapters into sections. You will find extensive cross-referencing between chapters and sections, but it is also important that you use the table of contents and the index for these purposes as well. The sections of chapters can be read on their own, but you will also find that they fit into an argument that is developed through a chapter.

We have included other types of devices to convey our ideas: figures, diagrams, cartoons, photographs of buildings, monuments or paintings discussed in the text and tables. We have also included three types of box: Key Influences, Defining Concepts and Extracts. You will find concepts and people who are boxed highlighted in bold in the text, for example **Donna Haraway**. Defining Concept boxes provide an overview to help generate a basic understanding. Extract boxes include material that is often then discussed in the text, but which we think also repays more detailed study on your part. Key Influence boxes address the most salient aspects of the life and work of some of the major thinkers in cultural studies. We have tried in these to include three different types of writer: first, those who have been particularly important in the development of cultural studies (examples include Richard Hoggart, E.P. Thompson and Raymond Williams); second, those authors who historically initiated important general approaches that have subsequently been developed or influential in cultural studies (examples here are Karl Marx, Michel Foucault, Max Weber and C.L.R. James); finally, there are those who are currently participating in the redevelopment of cultural studies as it becomes more attentive to issues of gender, 'race', postcolonialism, cultural hybridity and so on, such as Judith Butler, Angela McRobbie, Paul Gilroy and Edward Said.

This approach means that the majority of our Key Influence boxes represent white men, some of whom are long dead. This in itself reflects the development of the field and the power struggles that shape it. We wish that the situation were otherwise. However, it is perhaps of some significance that even many of the white men were marginal to mainstream academic life. We are also conscious of some of the names that are missing (for example Derrida, Lyotard, Jameson), which may mean little to you at the moment, but which you will come across in this book and others you read. However, we have tried to box those people whose ideas are most used in the book, reflecting the sense that this is our version of cultural studies.

All the Key Influence and Defining Concept boxes contain further reading that can be used to deepen the understanding of the concepts, approaches and people they contain. We have also included a guide to further reading for the rest of the book at the end of each chapter.

Acknowledgements

All books are the products of a number of influences. Textbooks are even more so. Many people over more years than we would care to remember have affected this book. We would like to begin by acknowledging this general debt. We are also particularly grateful to the anonymous referees for their helpful comments.

Elaine Baldwin would like to thank her colleagues for their contribution to the writing of the book.

Brian Longhurst would like to thank the students who have worked with him on the material in this book. Particular thanks are due to Julie Weir for permission to use her excellent photographs. As always his biggest debts are to Bernadette Oxley, James Oxley-Longhurst and Tim Oxley-Longhurst for sharing it all.

Scott McCracken would like to thank for their contributions and enthusiasm, the students on English and Cultural Studies, on Sociology and Cultural Studies and on the MA in Cultural Studies at the University of Salford. Particular thanks go to Georgina Waylen for her support.

Miles Ogborn would like to thank Phil Crang, John Gould, Catherine Nash, and the second and third year Cultural Geography students at Queen Mary and Westfield College for their comments on earlier versions of chapter 4.

Greg Smith would like to thank Julie Jones for comments on an early draft of Chapter 7 and Jason Rutter for assistance with Chapter 3.

Grateful acknowledgement is made to the following sources for permission to reproduce material in this book. Every effort has been made to trace copyright holders, but if any have been inadvertently overlooked the publisher will be pleased to make the necessary arrangement at the first opportunity.

Box 2.4: reproduced by permission of Secker & Warburg, and Curtis Brown on behalf of David Lodge. Box 2.5: reproduced by permission of Marion Boyars Publishers. Box 2.7: reproduced by permission of British Sociological Association. Figure 2.3: figure from 'Myth Today' from Mythologies by Roland Barthes, translated by Annette Lavers; translation copyright © 1972 by Jonathan Cape Ltd; reprinted by permission of Hill and Wang, a division of Farrar, Straus & Giroux, Inc., and Random House. Figure 2.4:

reproduced by permission of Jackie Fleming. Figure 2.5: reproduced by permission of Routledge & Kegan Paul. Figure 2.6: reproduced by courtesy of the Trustees, The National Gallery, London. Figure 2.8: © 1998, The Art Institute of Chicago; reproduced by permission.

Box 3.2: reproduced by permission of Cambridge University Press. Box 3.3: extract from 'Illiteracy spells misery for 2 million' by Donald MacLeod, 1 July 1997; © *The Guardian*, 1997.

Figures 4.1 & 4.2: © John Leighly, 1991. Figure 4.4: reproduced by courtesy of the Trustees, The National Gallery, London. Figure 4.5: © *Good Housekeeping*; reproduced by permission of The Hearst Corporation. Figures 4.6 & 4.7: reproduced by permission of The National Gallery of Ireland. Figure 4.8: reproduced by permission of the Musée du Louvre.

Table 4.1: reproduced by permission of Arnold.

Figure 5.1: reproduced by permission of The Museum of Modern Art, New York; Abby Aldrich Rockefeller Fund; © 1998 The Museum of Modern Art, New York. Figures 6.1, 6.2 & 6.3: reproduced by permission of PA News. Figure 6.7: reproduced by permission of the Musée Carnavalet, Paris.

Box 8.1: reproduced by permission of Routledge & Kegan Paul. Box 8.2: (text) reproduced by permission of Routledge & Kegan Paul; (photographs) reproduced by permission of Getty Images. Box 8.3: reproduced by permission of Routledge & Kegan Paul. Box 8.4: reproduced by permission of Blackwell Publishers. Figure 8.1: reproduced by permission of Verso. Figure 8.2: reproduced by permission of Blackwell Publishers. Figure 8.3: reproduced by permission of Blackwell Publishers. Figure 8.4: reproduced by permission of Routledge & Kegan Paul. Numbered list on p. 324: reproduced by permission of Blackwell Publishers.

Box 9.3: reproduced by permission of Duke University Press.

Box 9.4: reproduced by permission of MIT Press. Figure 9.1: reproduced by permission of Penguin Books; © Alan Sheridan, 1977. Table 9.3: reproduced by permission of Sage Publications and J. Urry. Table 9.4: reproduced by permission of Blackwell Publishers. Numbered list, p. 401: © British Sociological Association; reproduced by permission of Cambridge University Press.

part 2

Cultural theory

Culture and cultural studies

1.0 | Introduction

Cultural studies is a new way of engaging in the study of culture. Many academic subjects have long brought their own disciplinary concerns to the study of culture; chief among them are anthropology, history, literary studies, human geography and sociology. However, over the past two decades or so there has been a renewed interest in the study of culture which has crossed disciplinary boundaries. The resulting activity, cultural studies, has emerged as an intriguing and exciting area of intellectual activity which has already shed important new light on the character of human cultures and which promises to continue so to do. While there is little doubt that cultural studies is coming to be widely recognised as an important and distinctive field of study, it does seem to encompass a potentially enormous area. This is because the term 'culture' has a complex history and range of usages, and thus it has provided a legitimate focus of inquiry for several academic disciplines. In order to begin to delimit the field which this textbook considers, we have divided this chapter into four main sections:

1.1 A discussion of some leading *definitions* of culture.

1.2 An introduction to the *core issues* raised by the definitions and study of culture.

1.3 An analysis of some of the *principal accounts* offered to date which address these core issues.

1.4 An outline of *our view* of the developing field of cultural studies.

By commencing our book in this manner, we hope to show the complexity of the field of culture and to begin to provide a map of the important issues. We shall consider some of the ways in which these issues have been addressed in studies of culture in order to define and explicate the new and developing field of cultural studies.

Learning objectives

▪ To learn the different definitions of the concept of culture.

■   To identify the principal issues in the study of culture.
■   To learn about some of the leading theoretical perspectives in cultural studies.

1.1 | What is culture?

The term 'culture' has a complex history and diverse range of meanings in contemporary discourse. Culture can refer to Shakespeare or Superman comics, opera or football, who does the washing-up at home or the organisation of the office of the President of the United States of America. Culture is found in your local street, in your own city and country, as well as on the other side of the world. Small children, teenagers, adults and older people all have their own cultures; but they may also share a culture.

Given the evident breadth of the term, it is essential to begin by trying to define what culture is. Culture is a word that has grown over the centuries to reach its present broad meaning. One of the founders of cultural studies in Britain, **Raymond Williams** (p. 5), has traced the development of the concept and provided an influential ordering of its modern uses. Outside the natural sciences, the term 'culture' is chiefly used in three relatively distinct senses to refer to: the arts and artistic activity (1.1.1); the learned, primarily symbolic features of a particular way of life (1.1.2); and a process of development (1.1.3).

1.1.1 | Culture with a big 'C'

In everyday talk, culture is believed to consist of the 'works and practices of intellectual and especially artistic activity', thus culture is the word that describes 'music, literature, painting and sculpture, theatre and film' (Williams, 1983b: 90). Culture in this sense is widely believed to concern 'refined' pursuits in which the 'cultured' person engages.

1.1.2 | Culture as a 'way of life'

In the human sciences the word 'culture' has achieved wide currency to refer to the creation and use of **symbols** (p. 288) which distinguish 'a particular way of life, whether of a people, a period or a group, or humanity in general' (Williams, 1983b: 90). Only humans, it is often argued, are capable of creating and transmitting culture and we are able to do this because we create and use symbols. Humans possess a symbolising capacity which is the basis of our cultural being.

What, then, is a symbol? It is when people agree that some word or drawing or gesture will stand for either an idea (for example a person, like a pilot), or an object (a box, for example), or a feeling (like contempt). When this has been done, then a symbol conveying a shared idea has been created. These shared ideas are symbolically mediated or expressed through symbolism: for example, by a word in the case of 'pilot', or by a drawing to convey the idea of a box, or by a gesture to convey contempt; and it is

Key influence **1.1**

Raymond Williams (1921–88)

Raymond Williams was a Welsh cultural analyst and literary critic. His 'serious' attention to 'ordinary culture' was a key influence on the development of the idea of cultural studies, of which he is normally seen as a founding figure.

Born into a Welsh working-class family, Williams studied at Cambridge before serving as a tank commander in the Second World War. He returned to Cambridge after the war to complete his degree. He taught for the Workers' Educational Association during the 1950s, before returning to Cambridge to take up a lectureship in 1961. He was appointed Professor of Drama in 1974.

Williams's earliest work addressed questions of textual analysis and drama and can be seen as reasonably conventional in approach, if not emphasis. His influence was enhanced and reputation made by two key books: *Culture and Society* (1963) and *The Long Revolution* (1965). The former re-examined a range of authors to chart the nature of the formation of culture as a response to the development of industrialism. The latter pointed to the democratic potential of the 'long revolution' in culture. Williams distanced himself from the elitist and conservative perspectives of F.R. Leavis and T.S. Eliot in arguing for both socialist transformation and cultural democracy. Williams emphasised these themes in *Communications* (1962) which also contained some proto-typical media analysis. Television was the subject of the later *Television: Technology and Cultural Form* (1974) which introduced the concept of 'flow'. From the 1960s on, Williams's work became more influenced by Marxism, resulting in *Marxism and Literature* (1977) and *Culture* (1981). His *The Country and the City* (1973a) greatly influenced subsequent interdisciplinary work on space and place. His vast corpus of work (including over thirty books) also addressed drama, cultural theory, the environment, the English novel, the development of language, leftist politics and, in the period before his death, Welshness. He was also a prolific novelist.

The impact of Williams's rather dense and 'difficult' writings was often in terms of his overall approach, cultural materialism, and emphasis rather than in the detail of his analyses. His lifelong commitment to socialism, combined with the desire for cultural communication and democracy, was greatly attractive to a generation of leftists. His current status is enhanced by the use of his concept of structure of feeling to study various phenomena from literary texts to urban ways of life.

Further reading

Williams wrote a vast amount, so much so that his identity has been seen as that of 'writer'. The first reference is a revealing set of interviews, which combine the life and work.

Williams, R. (1979) *Politics and Letters: Interviews with New Left Review*, London: New Left Books.
Eldridge, J. and Eldridge, L. (1994) *Raymond Williams: Making Connections*, London: Routledge.
Inglis, F. (1995) *Raymond Williams*, London: Routledge.

these meanings that make up a culture. A symbol defines what something means, although a single symbol may have many meanings. For example, a flag may stand for a material entity like a country and an abstract value such as patriotism. To study culture is thus to ask what is the meaning of a style of dress, a code of manners, a place, a language, a norm of conduct, a system of belief, an architectural style, and so on. Language, both spoken and written, is obviously a vast repository of symbols but there are any number of things that function as symbols: flags, hairstyles, road signs, smiles, BMWs, business suits – the list is endless.

Given the way that we have discussed culture so far, it might be thought that culture is everything and everywhere. Indeed, some approaches to the study of culture take such a position, especially, for instance, those coming at the topic from a more anthropological point of view. Thus, the nineteenth-century anthropologist Tylor (1871: 1) gave the following definition of culture as 'that complex whole which includes knowledge, belief, art, morals, law, customs, and any other capabilities and habits acquired by man [sic] as a member of society'. This definition points to the pervasiveness of culture in social life. It emphasises that culture is a product of humans living together and that it is learned. A similar sort of approach informs the description of the English way of life by the American poet and critic T.S. Eliot as including

> [A]ll the characteristic activities and interests of a people. Derby Day, Henley Regatta, Cowes, the 12th of August, a cup final, the dog races, the pin table, the dart board, Wensleydale cheese, boiled cabbage cut into sections, beetroot in vinegar, 19th Century Gothic churches, the music of Elgar ... (Eliot, 1948, as quoted by Hebdige, 1979)

Other approaches have tended to argue that some areas of social life are more properly thought of as political or economic than cultural and thus can in some fashion be separated from culture. Thus, those who would define culture in sense 1.1.1 (arts and artistic activity) would tend to exclude some institutions and phenomena which those accepting and using definition 1.1.2 (way of life) would see as part of culture. There is little consensus on this matter but it is clear that it will be an issue in this book.

Culture in the sense of way of life, however, must be distinguished from the neighbouring concept of society. In speaking of society we refer to the pattern of social interactions and relationships between individuals and groups. Often a society will occupy a territory, be capable of reproducing itself and share a culture; but for some (especially large-scale modern) societies it may make more sense to say that several cultures coexist (not always harmoniously) within the society.

1.1.3 | Process and development

The earliest uses of the word 'culture' in the late Middle Ages refer to the tending or cultivation of crops and animals (hence agriculture); a little later the same sense was transferred to describe the cultivation of people's minds. This dimension of the word 'culture' draws attention to its subsequent use to describe the development of the individual's capacities and it has been extended to embrace the idea that cultivation is itself a general, social and historical process (Williams, 1983b: 90–1).

The different senses in which the concept of culture can be used are illustrated in the following examples. A play by Shakespeare might be said to be a distinct piece of cultural work (sense 1.1.1: culture with a big 'C'), to be a product of a particular (English) way of life (sense 1.1.2: culture as a way of life) and to represent a certain stage of cultural development (sense 1.1.3: culture as process and development). Rock 'n' roll may be analysed by examining the skills of its performers (sense 1.1.1); in terms of its association with youth culture in the late 1950s and early 1960s (sense 1.1.2); and as a musical form, looking for its origins in other styles of music and also seeing its influence on later musical forms (sense 1.1.3).

In this book we shall consider all three of these different senses of culture. However, it is important to note that these definitions and their use raise a number of complex issues and problems for the analysis of culture which we introduce in the next part of the chapter.

1.2 | Issues and problems in the study of culture

The three senses of culture identified in the previous part of this chapter have tended to be studied from different points of view. Hence, artistic or intellectual activity (sense 1.1.1) has commonly been the province of the humanities scholar. Ways of life (sense 1.1.2) have been examined by the anthropologist or the sociologist, while the development of culture (sense 1.1.3) might seem to be the province of the historian using historical documents and methods. These disciplines have tended to approach culture in different ways and from different perspectives. However, as we shall demonstrate in this chapter, the central importance of a distinct cultural studies approach is that it facilitates the identification of a set of core issues and problems which no one discipline or approach can solve on its own. Let us explain what we mean through the identification and exemplification of these core questions. As you will see, they both start and finish with the issue of the relationship between the personal and the cultural.

1.2.1 | How do people become part of a culture?

Culture is not something that we simply absorb – it is learned. In anthropology this process is referred to as acculturation or enculturation. In psychology it is described as conditioning. Sociologists have tended to use the term 'socialisation' to describe the process by which we become social and cultural beings. The sociologist Anthony Giddens (1989: 87) describes socialisation as the process whereby, through contact with other human beings, the helpless infant gradually becomes a self-aware, knowledgeable human being, skilled in the ways of the given culture and environment. Sociologists have distinguished two stages of socialisation. Primary socialisation usually takes place within a family, or family-like grouping, and lasts from birth until the child participates in larger and more diverse groupings beyond the family, usually beginning with school in Western societies. Primary socialisation involves such elements as the acquisition of language and a gendered **identity** (p. 224); secondary socialisation refers to all the subsequent influences which an individual experiences in a lifetime. Psychology and its subdisciplines like **psychoanalysis** (p. 8) pay particular attention to childhood and the conditioning that relates to the acquisition of a gender and a sexuality. Gender refers to the social roles that different societies define as masculine or feminine. Sexuality refers to the desires and sexual orientation of a particular individual. The founder of psychoanalysis, **Sigmund Freud** (p. 8), argued that masculinity and femininity and the choice of a sexual object are not directly related to biology, but are a result of conditioning. Feminists have used Freud's theories to oppose the idea that men are naturally superior, even though Freud himself was not particularly sympathetic to **feminism** (p. 120). The concepts of acculturation and enculturation, conditioning and socialisation draw attention to the many and various social arrangements which play a part in the ways in which humans learn about meaning.

Defining concept **1.1**

Psychoanalysis

Psychoanalysis is the name given to the method developed by Sigmund Freud (1856–1939). Freud himself used his interpretative technique to analyse literature and art. Psychoanalytic theory has subsequently developed into a number of different schools, some of which have influenced **feminist** (p. 120), **Postcolonial** (p.189), **Marxist** (p. 97) and **postmodernist** (p. 400) cultural criticism. Critics who have used psychoanalytic ideas include members of the **Frankfurt School** (p. 109), **Julia Kristeva** (p. 232) and **Judith Butler** (p. 231).

Freud's method of interpretation is first developed in *The Interpretation of Dreams* (1900). He describes how symbols in dreams represent condensed or displaced meanings that, when interpreted, reveal the dreamer's unconscious fears and desires. In *The Psychopathology of Everyday Life* (1901), he showed how slips of the tongue and the inability to remember words are also symptoms of unconscious mental processes. Condensation, displacement and 'symptomatic' methods of interpretation have been deployed by critics to decode cultural texts. Psychoanalysis has been particularly influential in film criticism. Freud developed a tri-partite theory of the mind: the id or unconscious; the ego, which adjusts the mind to external reality; and the super-ego, which incorporates a moral sense of society's expectations. Perhaps his most important work was on a theory of sexuality. The psychoanalytic concept of sexuality posits a complex understanding of desire. The fixed binarism of masculine/feminine given by earlier biologistic theories of sexual difference tended to assume an equally fixed desire by men for women and by women for men. In psychoanalysis, there is no presupposition that sexual desire is limited to heterosexual relations. Rather, the adaptable nature of desire is stressed and an important role is given to fantasy in the choice of sexual object. Freud's work was still partially attached to a theory of biological development. The

→

influential psychoanalytic critic, Jacques Lacan, argued that the unconscious is structured like language. In other words, culture rather than biology is the important factor. Lacan's work has been important for feminist critics, who have developed an analysis of gender difference using Freud's Oedipus complex. According to feminist psychoanalytic criticism, the context in which feminine sexuality develops is different to that of masculine sexuality. Men and women enter into different relationships with the symbolic order through the Oedipus complex. The Oedipus complex arises through the primary identification of both boys and girls with their mother. Paradoxically, it is the mother who first occupies the 'phallic' position of authority. The discovery that the mother does not hold as powerful a position in society as the father (it is the father who symbolises the phallus) creates the crisis through which the boy and the girl receive a gendered identity. The boy accepts his 'inferior phallic powers', sometimes known as 'the castration complex', but with the promise that he will later occupy as powerful a position in relation to women as his father does. The girl learns of her subordinate position in relation to the symbolic order, her castration complex, but for her, there is no promise of full entry to the symbolic order; consequently her feeling of lack persists as a sense of exclusion (Mitchell, 1984: 230).

In cultural studies the theory of the unconscious has allowed a more subtle understanding of the relationship between **power** (p. 94) and the formation of subjectivity. While psychoanalysis has been found wanting in that it suggests but does not actually show how the social relates to the psychic, that suggestion has been the starting point for some of the most fascinating investigations in cultural studies.

Further reading

Weedon, C., Tolson, A. and Mort, F. (1980) 'Theories of language and subjectivity', in *Culture, Media, Language*, London: Unwin Hyman.
Mitchell, J. (1984) *Women: The Longest Revolution, Essays in Feminism, Literature and Psychoanalysis*, London: Virago.

1.2.2 | How does cultural studies interpret what things mean?

Anthropology and some forms of sociology see meaningful action, the understandings that persons attribute to their behaviour and to their thoughts and feelings, as cultural. This approach to culture refers to the shared understandings of individuals and groupings in society (or to sense 1.1.2 of culture – way of life). Some sociologists, for example Berger and Luckmann (1966), stress that human knowledge of the world is socially constructed, that is, we apprehend our world through our social situations and our interactions with other people. If it is the case that our understanding is structured by our social situations, then our views of the world may be partial. Although there may be a real world, we can only view it from certain angles. Thus, our knowledge of the world is inevitably perspectival. This view complements the issue of cultural relativism (see section 3.4). Here the emphasis is on the way that social roles and relationships shape the way we see and give meaning to the world, whereas cultural relativism stresses the way that habitual, taken-for-granted ways of thought, as expressed in speech and language, direct our understandings. An example of perspectival knowledge is the differing accounts of the dissolution of a marriage given by those involved and affected by it. The explanation given for the break-up of a marriage by one partner will rarely coincide with the explanation given by the other (Hart, 1976).

The sociology of knowledge, as this approach to understanding is known, suggests that the sense that we make of the world can be made intelligible through the examination of our social situation. For example, it is sometimes proposed that one's view of the world is linked to class position, so that working-class people will have a different view of the world from upper-class people. Sociologists of knowledge do not propose that our beliefs can always be reduced to, or simply read off from, our social situation, but they do suggest that these world-views are cultural, and that culture has to be studied in relation to society. Moreover, the interpretation of culture in relation to social situation introduces further issues of evidence and relativism. If knowledge is socially constructed, can there be such a thing as 'true' knowledge? If perceptions and beliefs are always relative to social situation, then why should we believe any particular view, even the view of the person asserting this statement, since it too will be influenced by the person's situation? In seeking to interpret a way of life of a different society or a different group in our own society, why should we believe one interpretation rather than any other? If we are to begin to adjudicate or evaluate different interpretations then we will need to consider the types of evidence offered for the particular interpretation. Interpretation of meaning is therefore a core issue in cultural studies, and it relates to how we understand the relationship between the past and the present (see Chapter 5).

1.2.3 | How does cultural studies understand the past?

One hears much talk in England of the traditional nature of culture (see Box 1.1); England is seen by some to have a culture that stretches back over a thousand years. Within this context, culture in English studies has often been conceived in terms of influence and tradition. For T.S. Eliot (1932: 15), for example, 'no poet, no artist of any art, has his complete meaning alone. His significance, his appreciation is the appreciation of his relation to the dead poets and artists'. More recently, English studies has begun to question the values of the canon, that is, those written texts selected as of literary value and as required reading in schools and universities. Texts that have been previously neglected have been introduced into school and university syllabuses. More women's writing, writing by minority groups in British society, non-British writing and popular fiction have been included in the canon. For example, the poems of Derek Walcott (St Kitts, Caribbean), the novels of Chinua Achebe (Nigeria) and those of Alice Walker (USA) are now regarded as deserving literary consideration. English studies has widened its outlook beyond the influence of other poets and writers to look at social and historical factors affecting the production of texts. It is now common for critics to look at, for example, the position of women in the nineteenth century when considering the novels of the period. Critics like **Edward Said** (p. 168) and Gayatri Spivak have also looked at the history of European imperialism and asked how that history manifests itself in literature.

Box *1.1*

Tradition and traditional

Derived from the Latin verb *tradere* meaning to pass on or to give down. Commonly used in cultural studies to refer to elements of culture that are transmitted (e.g. language) or to a body of collective wisdom (e.g. folk tales). As an adjective (traditional) it implies continuity and consistency. Traditions and traditional practices may be seen positively or negatively. Where the past is venerated, traditions may be seen as a source of legitimacy and value; in revolutionary situations the past may be viewed with contempt and seen as a brake upon progress.

The term 'tradition' has a number of different meanings, all of which are central to how culture is understood. It can mean knowledge or customs handed down from generation to generation. In this sense the idea, for example, of a national tradition can have a positive sense as a marker of the age and deep-rooted nature of a national culture. On the other hand, the adjective 'traditional' is often used in a negative or pejorative sense from within cultures like those of North America or Western Europe which describe themselves as modern. Here 'traditional', when used to describe non-European cultures and societies, can mean 'backward' or 'underdeveloped', terms that assume that all societies must modernise in the same way and in the same direction. Cultural studies is always critical of this kind of imposition of the standards of one culture upon another to define it as in some way inferior. 'Traditional' can also refer to social roles in society which are often taken for granted, but which might be questioned in cultural studies: for example, what it is to be a mother or a father.

This particular example from the discipline of English shows that traditions are not neutral and objective, somehow waiting to be discovered, but are culturally constructed. In being constructed and reconstructed some things are included and others excluded. This reflects, according to many writers, patterns of the distribution of **power** (p. 94) in society. Let us attempt to clarify some of these points through another example.

The kilt and Highland dress are presented, both in Scotland and outside, as Scottish traditional costume. This garb is one of the most recognisable and visible components of Scottish culture and is worn by Scottish people at a variety of special occasions. It is thus presented to the non-Scots world as a component of Scottishness – the attributes of a particular place. It also functions in this manner for many Scots who consider the wearing of the tartan to be a method of identification with their cultural heritage. However, it appears that the kilt as a traditional cultural form has been constructed and repackaged to meet some historically specific needs. David McCrone (1992: 184) has suggested that 'a form of dress and design which had some real but haphazard significance in the Highlands of Scotland was taken over by a lowland population anxious to claim some distinctive aspect of culture at a time – the late nineteenth century

– when its economic, social and cultural identity was ebbing away'. Thus a widely accepted and representative cultural form is shown to have been far from universal but rather associated with a particular group at a specific moment in time. Furthermore, this means that the meaning of the kilt is constantly changing within Scottish society. For example, in the 1950s wearing a kilt was thought effeminate by certain sections of the younger generation; however, since the recent increase in Scottish nationalism the kilt has come back into fashion, and is often worn at occasions such as weddings.

1.2.4 | Can other cultures be understood?

An issue of reliability of evidence is also raised through this example as it may be difficult to know precisely who wore the kilt and when. Further, it raises the problem of what has been termed 'historical relativism'. What this draws attention to is the extent to which we, as contemporaries of the last decade of the twentieth century, dwell in a world that is sufficiently different from the worlds of our predecessors, so much so that it may be very difficult for us to understand those worlds in the way that they did. How well can we understand what was in the middle-class, lowland Scots person's mind when he or she adapted and adopted Highland dress? There are some similarities between the issues raised under this heading and others thought more often to be associated with cultural relativism which we discuss next.

Further to the difficulty of studying culture across history, there is the parallel problem of interpretation of cultures from different parts of the world or in different sections of our own society. Is it possible for us to understand the cultures of other peoples in the way they do themselves, or will our understanding inevitably be mediated via the distorting prism of our own cultural understandings? These problems have always confronted anthropologists in their attempts to interpret the other worlds of non-European societies. Is it possible to convey adequately the evident seriousness that the Azande accord to the consultation of oracles (see Box 1.2) or the conceptions of time held by Trobriand Islanders (see Box 1.3), in texts designed for consumption by Western audiences who hold very different temporal conceptions and ideas about magic and witchcraft? Novelists, sociologists and journalists also face this problem in describing the ways of life of different groups in their own society. Many quite serious practical difficulties can arise from this problem. For example, one influential study of conversation (Tannen, 1990) suggests that the many misunderstandings that arise between men and women do so because what we are dealing with is an everyday version of the difficulties of cross-cultural communication. In the USA 'women speak and hear a language of connection and intimacy while men speak and hear a language of status and independence' (Tannen, 1990: 42). Differing conversational practices are employed by men and women. Tannen observes that in discussing a problem, women will offer reassurance whereas men will seek a solution; women tend to engage in 'rapport-talk' while men are more at home lecturing and explaining; men are poorer listeners than women. According to Tannen, women engage in more eye contact and less interruption than men in conversation. Her argument is that men and women employ distinct conversational styles which she labels 'genderlects'. These are

> ## Box *1.2*
> ## Azande
>
> The Azande, an African people, live around the Nile–Congo divide. The classic work on their belief systems is *Witchcraft, Oracles and Magic among the Azande* by E.E. Evans-Pritchard, published in 1937. The Azande believe that many of the misfortunes that befall them are caused by witchcraft (*mangu*). *Mangu* is inherited; the Azande believe that it has the form of a blackish swelling in the intestines, and it is this substance that, when activated, causes harm to others. Even though individuals may have inherited *mangu* they do not necessarily cause harm to others because it is only bad, anti-social feelings that set off witchcraft. As long as a person remains good tempered they will not cause witchcraft. Since witchcraft is the product of bad feelings, then a person who suffers a misfortune suspects those who do not like her or him and who have reason to wish harm. The first suspects are therefore one's enemies. There are five oracles that a Zande (singular of Azande) may consult in order to have the witch named. After an oracle has named the witch, the person identified is told that the oracle has named them and she or he is asked to withdraw the witchcraft. Usually named people protest their innocence and state that they meant no harm; if they did cause witchcraft it was unintentional. Evans-Pritchard states that Azande do not believe that witchcraft causes all misfortunes and individuals cannot blame their own moral failings upon it. Azande say that witchcraft never caused anyone to commit adultery. Witchcraft is not the only system of explanation among the Azande; they do recognise technical explanations for events: for example, a man is injured because a house collapses, but witchcraft attempts to answer the question of why *this* house collapsed. All systems of explanation involve the 'how' of events and the 'why' of events; the house collapses because the wooden supports are rotten – this is the technical 'how' of explanation – but why did it collapse at a particular time and on a particular man?
>
> The 'why' of explanation deals with what Evans-Pritchard calls the singularity of events: 'why me?', 'why now?' Religious explanations offer the answer that it was the will of God; scientific explanations speak of coincidences in time and space; agnostics may see the answer in chance; the Azande know that it is witchcraft. Evans-Pritchard comments that while he lived among the Azande he found witchcraft as satisfactory a form of explanation for events in his own life as any other.

sufficiently different from each other that the talk between men and women might be appropriately regarded as a form of cross-cultural communication (see section 2.4.4).

Hollis and Lukes (1982) include both historical and cultural relativism under the broad heading of 'perceptual relativism' and argue that there are two different dimensions to be examined. First, there is the degree to which seeing or perception is relative;

Box **1.3**
Trobriand Islanders

The Trobriand Islands are politically part of Papua New Guinea. The best-known works on the Trobriand Islands are by Malinowski but E.R. Leach has written on Trobriand ideas of time in 'Primitive calendars' (*Oceania* 20 (1950)), and this, along with other work, is discussed in *Empires of Time: Calendars, Clocks and Cultures* by Anthony Aveni, 1990.

The Trobriand calendar is guided by the moon: there are twelve or thirteen lunar cycles but only ten cycles are in the calendar; the remaining cycles are 'free time' outside the calendar. The primary event of the Trobriand calendar is the appearance of a worm which appears for three or four nights once a year to spawn on the surface of the water. There is a festival (*Milamak*) in this month which inaugurates the planting season. The worm does not appear at exactly the same time every year and planting does not take place at exactly the same time every year so there is sometimes a mismatch between worm and planting. This situation is exacerbated because the Trobriand Islands are a chain and the worm appears at the southern extremity of the chain, so news of its appearance takes time to communicate. The consequence is that the festivals, and so the calendar, vary greatly in the time of their celebration from island to island. When the discrepancies are felt to be too great to be manageable there is a realignment and the calendar is altered to achieve consistency.

Trobriand reckoning of time is cyclical, associated with the agricultural year. Lunar cycles that are not connected to this activity are not recognised so there is time out of the calendar; a difficult notion to grasp in modern industrial societies where time is believed to be a natural and inevitable constraint upon activity. The Trobriand language has no tenses; time is not a linear progression that, once passed, cannot be regained; in the Trobriand system, time returns. Trobriand ideas of the nature of existence are not set in time but in patterns; it is order and patterned regularity that locates events and things, not time.

that is, when we look at something or seek to understand it, do we actually see the same thing as another person looking at it? Second, there is the extent to which perception and understanding rely on language. These questions about perception remind us that, as students of culture, we must constantly think about who we are – where we come from and what our 'position' is – in order to understand who and what we are studying.

1.2.5 | How can we understand the relationships between cultures?

This question of position raises another problem in terms of how we understand the relationships between cultures. One conventional way of understanding this is to see cultures as mutually exclusive block which intersect, interact and interface along a boundary or 'zone of contact'. For example, it would be possible to consider the interactions between the Trobriand Islanders or the Azande and the Europeans who arrived as part of the process of **colonialism** (p. 189) (including, of course, the anthropologists who studied them and wrote about them). This way of thinking about culture often describes these relationships in terms of 'destruction' of cultures or their 'disappearance' as one culture 'replaces' or 'corrupts' another. A good example would be the fears of Americanisation as McDonald's hamburgers, Coca-Cola and Levi's jeans spread to Europe, Asia and Africa through processes of **globalisation** (p. 159).

However, this point of view is limited in certain ways. First, it is impossible to divide the world up into these exclusive cultural territories. As we have pointed out, culture is also a matter of age, gender, class, status – so that any such cultural bloc, defined in terms of nation, tribe or society, will be made up of many cultures. This means that we will also be positioned in relation to not just one culture but many. Second, culture does not operate simply in terms of more powerful cultures destroying weaker ones. Since it is a never-ending process of socially made meaning, cultures adapt, change and mutate into new forms. For example, the Trobriand Islanders took up the English game of cricket, but they did so in terms of their own war-making practices. So cricket did not simply replace other Trobriand games, it was made into a new **hybrid** (p. 159) cultural form which was neither English cricket nor Trobriand warfare. Finally, it might be useful to think about the relationships between cultures in terms of a series of overlapping webs or networks rather than as a patchwork of cultural 'territories' (see, for example, Chapter 8). This would mean that understanding the meaning of any cultural form would not simply locate it within a culture but would look at it in terms of how it fitted into the intersection between different cultural networks. For example, Coca-Cola has taken on different meanings in different parts of the world: signifying **neo-colonial** (p. 189) oppression in India (and being banned for some time), while it signifies freedom and personal autonomy to British–Asian young people in London. Its meanings cannot be controlled by the Coca-Cola company, although they try through their advertising campaigns. Neither do their meanings simply involve the extension of an 'American' culture. Instead these meanings depend upon the location of the product in a complex network of relationships which shape its significance and value to differently positioned consumers.

1.2.6 | Why are some cultures and cultural forms valued more highly than others?

In English studies, literature has traditionally been seen as part of high culture (sense 1.1.1: arts and artistic activity). Certain literary texts have been selected as worthy of study, for example the novels of Charles Dickens or the plays of Shakespeare. This process of selection has meant the simultaneous exclusion of other texts, defined as non-literary. It has also led to an emphasis on writing, to the detriment of other, more modern forms of cultural activity, for example film and television. In a further step such forms of literature or high culture are regarded by some to be culture itself. Other excluded forms of writing or texts are defined as simply rubbish, trash or, in another often derogatory phrase, as mass culture. This entails a judgement of value, which is often assumed to be self-evident. Thus some forms of culture are to be valued and protected and others written off as worthless and indeed positively dangerous. However, as we have already seen, such canons or traditions are themselves constructed. Furthermore, as Hawkins (1990) has maintained, things that are thought to be high culture and those defined as mass culture often share similar themes and a particular text can be seen as high culture at one point in time and popular or mass culture at another. The example of opera may be used to illustrate this point. In Italy opera is a popular and widely recognised cultural form, singers are well known and performances draw big audiences which are knowledgeable and critical. In contrast, opera in Britain is regarded as an elite taste and research shows that typically audiences for opera are older and are drawn from higher social classes than other forms of entertainment. Yet in 1990, following the use of *Nessun Dorma* from the opera *Turandot*, sung by Pavarotti, to introduce the BBC television coverage of the 1990 World Cup Finals, opera rocketed in public popularity in Britain. In addition to increased audiences at live performances in opera houses, there were large-scale commercial promotions of concerts of music from opera in public parks and arenas. Television, video and compact disc sales of opera increased enormously and an album, *In Concert*, sung by Carreras, Domingo and Pavarotti, was top of the music charts in 1990 (Cultural Trends, no.7, 1990). The example illustrates the point that it is often empirically difficult to assign cultural practices to neat conceptual divisions.

The question of boundaries between levels of culture and the justification for them is an area of central concern for cultural studies. Pierre Bourdieu (1984) (see Defining Concept 8.1, p. 355) has maintained that the boundaries between popular and high art are actually in the process of dissolving. Whether or not one accepts this view, it is clear that the study of boundaries and margins may be very revealing about cherished values which are maintained within boundaries. The relationships between cultural systems are a fruitful area for the study of the processes of boundary maintenance and boundary change, linked as these topics are to issues of cultural change and cultural continuity (sense 1.1.3: culture as a process of development).

Within social anthropology there is an established practice of demonstrating the value and viability of cultures that are often regarded by the relevant authorities as poor and impoverished or as anachronisms and, as such, ripe for planned intervention to bring about change. Studies by Baxter (1991) and Rigby (1985) have argued that nomadic pastoralism, that is a way of life in which people move with animals and in which animal products are the staple diet, is a wholly rational and efficient use of resources. Such peoples are able to live in inhospitable areas where cultivation is not possible and enjoy a rich cultural, social and political life. Despite this evidence there is pressure from development planners to enforce change through land policies that compel pastoralists to give up their traditional way of life and become settled cultivators or wage labourers. Similarly, Judith Okely in her study of gypsies (1983) has shown the complex richness of gypsy cultural beliefs and practices, identifying a set of core principles around which gypsy life is articulated and which gives meaning to all activities. Gypsies, like pastoralists, are under pressure to settle down and to conform to prevailing ideas about a proper and fitting way of life. Both these examples draw attention to the issues of power and inequality in cultural and social life to which we turn in the next section of the chapter.

1.2.7 | What is the relationship between culture and power?

Implicit in our discussions so far has been the issue of **power** (p. 94). Since it is a product of interaction, culture is also a part of the social world and, as such, is shaped by the significant lines of force which operate in a social world. All societies are organised politically and economically. Power and authority are distributed within them, and all societies have means for allocating scarce resources. These arrangements produce particular social formations. Cultures are affected by the interests of dominant groups in societies, which seek to explain and validate their positions in particular structures.

One of the ways in which groups do this is through the construction of traditions and their promulgation through the population. Thus it might be argued that the idea of a tradition of British Parliamentary democracy excludes other ideas of democracy and social organisation that are against the interests of the powerful. Likewise, tradition in English literature excludes and marginalises other voices. The definition of trash or mass culture might be seen to negate forms of culture that are actually enjoyed by oppressed groups.

However, another way of looking at this suggests that such mass or popular forms are actually used by those in power to drug or indoctrinate subordinate groups. Forms of popular culture can in this view be seen to be like propaganda. For example, one commentary on modern culture, that of the **Frankfurt School** (p. 109) of critical theory, argues that the culture industries engender passivity and conformity among their mass audiences. For example, in this type of analysis the relationship between a big band leader and his fans could be seen to mirror the relationship between the totalitarian leader and his followers; both fans and followers release their tensions by taking part in **ritual** (p. 288) acts of submission and conformity (Adorno, 1967: 119–32).

Whatever view is adopted, it is clear that power and culture are inextricably linked and that the analysis of culture cannot be divorced from politics and power relations. Indeed, we would argue that this is a very important reason for studying culture and for taking culture seriously. However, the precise way in which forms of culture connect to power remains an issue to be studied at greater length.

1.2.8 | How is 'culture as power' negotiated and resisted?

Given the perspectival nature of society, it is inevitable that cultural attitudes will always be in conflict. Thus, the process of negotiation is endemic to, and cultural **resistances** (p. 258) occur in many domains of life. Four key areas of struggle and negotiation that have concerned cultural studies are around gender, 'race', class and age (for more on these categories see section 1.3.1 and Chapter 3). These concepts define social relationships which are often fraught. To take one area as an example, the concept of gender encompasses both how masculinity and femininity are defined (see section 1.2.1) and how men and women relate to one another. Gender definitions are points of struggle in many societies since what it is to be a man and what it is to be a woman are never fixed. Indeed, these definitions themselves are, in part, the product of a power struggle between men and women.

Feminist writers have been most influential in gender studies. Feminist discussion of gender might be divided broadly into arguments for equality, for commonality or universality, and for difference. The argument for equality emphasises the political idea of rights. Equality between men and women is defined by abstract rights, to which both sexes are entitled; inequality can be defined by women's lack of rights, for example to vote or to equal pay. Negotiation here is around the concept of women's rights. The argument for commonality or universality stresses that although women may belong to very different social, geographical and cultural groups they share common or universal interests because of their gender. Negotiation here is around the fundamental inequality of women because of their subordination in all societies. The argument for difference is more complicated; it rejects both ideas of simple equality and universality. Instead, it argues that the differences between men and women and between different groups of women mean that a concept of gender can never be abstracted out of a particular situation. Negotiation, therefore, while not denying inequality, will be around the specificity of differences. Critics of gender divisions struggle to redefine cultural constructions of gender. Women's movements, but also campaigns for lesbian and gay rights, seek to redraw the cultural boundaries of men's and women's experience. Such political movements are often drawn into conflict with the law and social and political institutions like religious organisations and political parties which do not wish the cultural support for their dominance to be eroded or destroyed. In this example it can be seen that the wider frameworks of society (power and authority structures) influence and impose themselves on cultural belief and practice to affect outcomes. We have already introduced a number of other areas where culture can in some sort of way be held to be connected to relationships and patterns of power.

1.2.9 | How does culture shape who we are?

The above examples demonstrate that struggle and negotiation are often around questions of cultural **identity** (p. 224). An example that gives the question of identity more prominence is the way in which the origins of English studies in the nineteenth century were closely linked to the growth of universal education. As a discipline English was, in the view of many commentators, designed to give schoolchildren a sense of a national culture (Batsleer *et al.*, 1985, as discussed in Ashcroft *et al.*, 1989). Literary texts were used to instil this sense. Consequently, although English literature was often presented as a proper study in itself, the way it was taught was often designed, consciously or unconsciously, to encourage a particular national identity, a sense of what it meant to be British. In teaching this sense of British identity, other national cultures or identities within Britain were either treated uncritically as part of English culture, or were left out of the canon.

Another effect of this process, which some writers have detected, was to infuse a

Box 1.4

Conrad on Africa

The prehistoric man was cursing us, praying to us, welcoming us – who could tell? We were cut off from the comprehension of our surroundings; we glided past like phantoms, wondering and secretly appalled, as sane men would be before an enthusiastic outbreak in a madhouse. We could not understand because we were too far and could not remember because we were travelling in the night of first ages, of those ages that are gone, leaving hardly a sign – and no memories.

The earth seemed unearthly. We are accustomed to look upon the shackled form of a conquered monster, but there – there you could look at a thing monstrous and free. It was unearthly, and the men were – No, they were not inhuman. Well, you know, that was the worst of it – this suspicion of their not being inhuman. It would come slowly to one. They howled and leaped, and spun, and made horrid faces; but what thrilled you was the thought of their humanity – like yours – the thought of your remote kinship with this wild and passionate uproar. Ugly. Yes, it was ugly enough; but if you were man enough you would admit to yourself that there was in you just the faintest trace of a response to the terrible frankness of that noise, a dim suspicion of there being a meaning in it which you – you so remote from the night of first ages – could comprehend.

Joseph Conrad, *Heart of Darkness* (1898); quoted in Chinua Achebe (1988: 6)

pride in the British Empire. For example, the Nigerian writer and critic Chinua Achebe has criticised the way that the novel *Heart of Darkness* by Joseph Conrad is still often presented as a great example of English culture. The novel describes a nightmarish encounter with Africa from the European point of view (see Box 1.4). However, Achebe has demonstrated that the representation of African culture that it contains is partial, based on little knowledge and is thus grossly distorted. Consequently, to read the novel as an English or even a European (Conrad was Polish in origin) work of art is to receive a very one-sided view of European imperialism in Africa. Through such processes an English national identity was constructed which involved constructing African identities in particular ways: as irrational and savage 'others'.

Identities are very often connected to place both locally and more widely. We may feel that we identify with a particular local area, a city, a region and a country and that the extent to which we place emphasis on one of these may depend on a context, for example, who we are talking to at any particular time. However, it is clearly the case that these identities can cause conflict and disagreement and that important issues in the study of culture concern the way in which such identities are constructed and how they reflect and inflect particular distributions of power.

1.2.10 | Summary examples

In order to examine some of the ideas contained in section 1.2, two short examples are given below: the family and Shakespeare.

Example 1: The family

An examination of family life reveals some of the issues that we have identified in the study of culture. For instance, within a family adults have great power over the lives of children because human infants are dependent on adults for their survival for relatively long periods of time. One way of understanding family life is to examine relationships and processes in terms of dominant and subordinate cultures. This approach has been used extensively by many feminist writers who have used the concept of patriarchy to refer to the assemblage of cultural and material power that men enjoy *vis-à-vis* women and children (Campbell, 1988; Pateman, 1989). The period of dependence of children varies from culture to culture, both historically and contemporaneously, and a number of writers have commented that the Western notion of childhood is a relatively recent concept (Aries, 1962; Walvin, 1982). Further, in many parts of the contemporary world it is a mistake to think of the lives of children in terms of childhood as it is understood in the West; this period of growth and learning is seen quite differently from that in Western societies. Caldwell (1982), writing of India, remarks that in Indian rural society there is the cultural belief and practice that wealth flows from children to parents as well as from parents to children. He comments that, typically in Western society, resources flow in a one-way direction from parents to children and parents do not expect young children to contribute to the material wellbeing of the family of origin. However, in many parts of the world children are valued, at least in part, for the contributions that they make to the domestic economies of family and household; there is what Caldwell calls a 'reciprocal flow' of goods and services between parents and even quite young children. For example, toddlers can join in gathering firewood and this is a valuable contribution in economies where this is the only fuel available for cooking and boiling water. This cultural view of children is significant in understanding responses to family planning projects. Caldwell argues that all too often Western cultural assumptions about family life and desirable family size direct the policy and goals of these projects. Looking beyond the English family to families in other parts of the world reminds us of the heterogeneity and diversity of culture and alerts us to the dangers for under-standing in assuming that cultures and cultural meanings are the same the world over.

Indeed, even in Western societies there is much cultural diversity. Novels and academic studies point to the effects of class and power on family life. In the recent past criticisms have been levelled against some traditional reading for children because it portrays a middle-class view of family structures and relationships which is far removed from the experiences of many children. Accusations of sexism and racism in literature for children have also been made. These criticisms again draw our attention to the relationships between general, diffuse cultures and local, particular cultures. Although we may identify an English culture as distinct from, say, a French culture, it cannot be assumed that all English families have identical cultures. This opens up the challenging issue of how particular local cultures relate to the broader, more general ones of which they may be thought to be a constituent part.

It is also clear that family structures and organisation change over time, not just chronological, historical time, but also structural time, that is as relationships between family members change as a consequence of age and maturation. In all societies, as children grow to adulthood the power of other adults over them diminishes. This occurs both as a result of physiological change (children no longer depend on their parents for food) and also as a result of cultural expectations about the roles of parents and children. These cultural expectations may be gendered; for example, the English idiom that describes adult children as 'being tied to their mother's apron strings' can be read as a general disapproval of adults who do not leave the immediate sphere of their mother. Yet this idiom is overwhelmingly applied to adult male children and thus expresses a view about the proper, expected relationships between adult males and their mothers. Men are expected to be free from the close influence of their mothers, whereas there is often felt to be an identity between adult women and their mothers. Variables such as the sex of children, the number of children and the age of the parents when children are born, all affect the course of family life. In Victorian England, when family size was bigger and life expectancy less than now, some parents had dependent children for all their lives – there was no time in which all their children had grown up and left home. These demographic and social factors greatly influence the course of family life and demonstrate not only the heterogeneity of culture but also the malleability of culture. All cultures are reproduced in specific circumstances; ideas and values are interpreted and understood in the light of local conditions. This last point brings us back to the issues of judgement and relativism in the understanding of cultural practice that we raised earlier in this section. A cultural approach to a common institution, in this case the family, demonstrates the power of cultural studies to generate a wide range and number of potential areas of investigation. Some of these have been alluded to in this example but you will be able to identify more.

Example 2: Shakespeare

The study of Shakespeare has always been central to English studies and to some constructions of English **identity** (p. 224). Traditionally, in English studies, Shakespeare's plays and Shakespeare's language have been presented as the essence of Englishness. They have been made to serve as the defining features of a homogenous and unchanging culture. Subsequent authors have often been judged in terms of how they fit into that tradition. Because of this connection between Shakespeare and national identity the position of these plays in schools has become an important issue. The argument is put forward that children must read Shakespeare in order to learn English and Englishness. Shakespeare's plays become valued over and above other forms of cultural production. As a result the teaching of Shakespeare, and English history, was also a part of **colonialism**'s cultural project (p. 189).

However, cultural studies asks rather different questions about Shakespeare. Instead of taking Shakespeare's position for granted, it asks what the social position of the theatre was in Elizabethan times. Further, it asks how plays were written and produced in the sixteenth and seventeenth centuries. Evidence that shows a high degree of collaboration between playwrights and adaptation of plays on the stage changes the conception of Shakespeare as individual genius; he appears as part of a wider culture. Shakespeare is then placed historically rather than his plays being seen as 'timeless' or 'eternal'. The question of the audience is addressed both in the sixteenth and seventeenth centuries and now. This gives a sense of who the plays were intended for and how they have been received, further challenging the conception that his work is universal: that is, for everyone, all of the time. We might ask what groups of schoolchildren make of Shakespeare's plays depending on class, race and gender, or whether they have seen the plays in the theatre or in versions made for the cinema.

The timeless nature of Shakespeare can also be challenged by studies that show that the texts have been altered considerably over the years; and that he was not always considered as important as he is now. Cultural studies looks at the changing conceptions of Englishness – and its relationships to the rest of the world – that caused Shakespeare to be rediscovered in the eighteenth century as the national poet. This extends from studying different versions of the plays to looking at the tourist industry in Stratford-upon-Avon. It can also involve studying the versions of Shakespeare that are produced in other parts of the world. These do not simply show the imposition of English cultural meanings, but the complex processes of negotiation within networks of cultural interaction which mean that Shakespearean history plays were vehicles for discussing political authority in the Soviet Union, and which recently brought a Zulu version of *Macbeth* from post-apartheid South Africa to the reconstruction of Shakespeare's Globe Theatre in London.

All of these processes of questioning and negotiation are of course political; they show that the interpretation of Shakespeare is a matter of power. This was clearly shown by Margot Heinemann (1985) in her essay 'How Brecht read Shakespeare'. She gave the example of Nigel Lawson, Chancellor of the Exchequer in the late 1980s, who quoted from Shakespeare's play *Troilus and Cressida* (1601–2). Lawson used the quotation 'Take but degree away, untune that string/And hark what discord follows' to argue that Shakespeare was a Tory. However, as Heinemann pointed out, the character who makes the speech, Ulysses, is in fact a wily, cunning politician, who is using the threat of social disorder to attain his own ends (see Box 1.5).

All of these questions and issues derive from adopting a rather different approach to the study of culture to that represented by English studies in its more conventional guises. They are the sorts of questions posed by those adopting a cultural studies perspective and are shaped by the core issues that we have identified. However, they also involve asking questions which lead us on to examining the theoretical perspectives used within cultural studies: what is the relationship between the social position of the audience (e.g. race, class and gender) and the interpretation of the text? How can we understand the ways in which the meanings of Englishness (and their link to Shakespeare) and the meanings of Frenchness become defined as opposites? What

Box **1.5**

Troilus and Cressida

But when the planets
In evil mixture to disorder wander,
What plagues and what portents, what mutiny!
What raging of the sea, shaking of earth!
Commotion in the winds! frights, changes, horrors
Divert and crack, rend and deracinate
The unity and married calm of states
Quite from their fixure! Oh when degree is shak'd,
Which is the ladder of all high designs,
The enterprise is sick. How could communities,
Degrees in schools, and brotherhoods in cities,
Peaceful commerce from dividable shores,
The primogenity and due of birth,
Prerogative of age, crowns, sceptres, laurels,
But that degree stand in authentic place?
Take but degree away, untune that string,
And hark what discord follows. Each thing meets
In mere oppugnacy: the bounded waters
Should lift their bosoms higher than the shores,
And make a sop of all this solid globe;
Strength should be lord of imbecility,
And the rude son should strike his father dead

Troilus and Cressida I.iii.94–115

ideas and methods can we use to interpret plays in their historical context or the contemporary meanings of Shakespeare within schools? In the next section we examine some of the most influential ways of theorising culture.

1.3 | Theorising culture

This section introduces theories of culture which attempt to address the issues and problems set out above and to unite them within frameworks of explanation. The bringing together of diverse issues and problems into a single form necessarily involves a process of abstraction. Theorists move away from the detail of particular instances and look for connections in terms of general principles or concepts; the consequence of this for the student is that theories are often difficult to grasp at first sight, couched as they are in abstract language. It may help you to think of issues and problems as the building blocks of theories; but there is no escaping the fact that the language of theory is abstract, and you may well find it difficult on first reading.

General theories of culture address one or more of the following questions:

1. What is the relation of culture to 'social structure'?

2. Which ideas and methods of investigation offer the most promising prospects for interpreting culture?

3. How is meaning organised and patterned?

In addressing each of these in turn we will move through a range of theoretical approaches. Broadly – and this is a caricature that can be filled out by looking at examples in the rest of the book – we start with functionalist and **structuralist** (p. 24) forms of understanding which suggest clearly defined, and often rather rigid, relationships. From these we move on to theoretical approaches (which sometimes might still be called structuralist and are often influenced by **Karl Marx** (p. 97) that place emphasis on the understanding of culture and meaning through thinking about their relationships to political economy (for example, class structures, modes of production, etc.) and their importance within conflicts between differently positioned social groups. Finally we stress what are often called **poststructuralist** (p. 24) or **postmodern** (p. 400) theoretical approaches which retain a concern with politics (and some concern for economics) in explaining culture (see Chapter 6), but use a much more flexible sense of how cultures and meanings are made.

Defining concept **1.2**

Structuralism and poststructuralism

Structuralism was an intellectual approach and movement which was very influential in the social sciences and the arts in the 1960s and 1970s. The basic idea of structuralism is that a phenomenon under study should be seen as consisting of a system of structures. This system and the relationship between the different elements are more important than the individual elements that make up the system.

The Swiss linguist de Saussure is regarded as the founder of structuralism. In his study of language, he drew attention to the structures (langue) that underpin the variation of everyday speech and writing (parole) and analysed the sign as consisting of a signified (concept) and signifier (word or sound), founding **semiotics** (p. 34) as the science of the study of signs. The emphasis on the structure to be found below or behind everyday interaction, or the variety of literary texts, was taken up by a number of (mainly French) writers working in different areas of the social sciences and humanities. Examples include: Lévi-Strauss (anthropology) in studies of kinship, myth and totemism; Lacan (psychoanalysis) who re-worked Freud, arguing that the unconsciousness is structured like a language; **Barthes** (p. 52) (literary studies), who examined the myths of bourgeois

→

societies and texts; **Foucault** (p. 28) (history and philosophy) who pointed to the way that underlying epistemes determine what can be thought in his archaeological method; and Althusser (philosophy), who drew on Lacan's re-working of Freud in a re-reading of **Marx** (p. 97) which emphasised the role of underlying modes of production in the determination of the course of history. Debate around Lacan was influential on the work in feminism of writers like **Kristeva** (p. 232) and Irigaray.

Poststructualism developed partly out of critique of the binary divisions so often characteristic of structuralism. So, for example, it criticised the idea that there is actually a distinct structure underlying texts or speech, blurring such distinctions. Moreover, it is critical of some of the scientific pretensions of structuralism. Structuralism tended to work on the premise that the truth or the real structure could be found. Poststructuralism is more concerned with the way in which versions of truth are produced in texts and through interpretation, which is always in dispute and can never be resolved. Post-structuralism therefore tends to be more playful in practice if not outcome. The work of Derrida and Baudrillard exhibits some of these poststructuralist ideas. Derrida shows how texts subvert themselves from within and Baudrillard explodes the neat oppositions of sign and signifier, use and exchange value.

Examples of structuralist and poststructuralist analyses can be found in cultural studies. More formal structuralist analyses have sought to find the hidden meanings of folk tales (Propp), James Bond (Eco), the Western film (Wright) and romantic fiction (Radway). Poststructuralist influence is more diffuse, but can be found especially in more literary forms of cultural studies, where the complexities of texts and their multiple meanings are interpreted.

Further reading

Hawkes, T. (1991) *Structuralism and Semiotics*, London: Routledge.
Wright, W. (1975) *Sixguns and Society*, Berkeley, CA: University of California Press.

1.3.1 | Culture and social structure

Sociologists often use the term 'social structure' to describe 'the enduring, orderly and patterned relationships between elements of a society' (Abercrombie *et al.*, 1984: 198). A common way of describing the structure of a particular society is to focus upon its main lines of cleavage. In Western societies social scientists most commonly identify these as class, age, gender and ethnicity. In this tradition the realms are seen as interconnected and interacting but essentially unequal as forces for change. Where the prime realm is that of social structure, culture is treated as a derivative of structure. This is clearly the case in functionalism.

Functionalism

One influential formulation of the relationship of culture to social structure can be seen in the work of the American sociologist Talcott Parsons. Parsons treats culture as necessary for the proper functioning of society. In general terms culture – that is, values, norms and symbols – provide the linchpin of Parsons's solution to the problem of social order. This problem is an analytical issue concerning the sources of the enduring quality of social life – how is the regularity, persistence, relative stability and predictability of social life achieved? Parsons maintains that culture is the central element of an adequate solution to this problem because it provides values, the shared ideas about what is desirable in society (perhaps values like material prosperity, individual freedom and social justice), and norms, the acceptable means of obtaining these things (for example, the idea that honest endeavour is the way to success). Culture also provides language and other symbolic systems essential to social life. Parsons further maintains that culture is internalised by personalities and that individual motivation thus has cultural origins. Moreover two of society's basic features, its economy and its political system, are maintained by culture. Hence there is an important sense in which culture 'oils the wheels' of society. In the functionalist view of Parsons, society, culture and the individual are interrelated, each interpenetrating the other, but culture occupies a central place because on the one hand it is internalised by individuals and on the other it is institutionalised in the stable patterns of action that make up the society.

Social structure and social conflict: class, gender and 'race'

The separation of culture and social structure is not limited to functionalist theorists. It appears also in the work of theorists who argued that conflict is at the core of society and who understand culture in terms of the structured relationships of politics and economics (or political economy). **Karl Marx** (p. 97), the nineteenth-century philosopher and revolutionary, and the social theorist **Max Weber** (p. 243) treated beliefs, values and behaviour as products of social and economic inequalities and power relationships. Although Marx's ideas are very complex, some of his followers have argued those who hold the means of production in society will control its ideas and values. The ruling ideas of a society (its forms of law, politics, religion, etc.) will be those of the dominant class. These ideas will be used to manage and perpetuate an unequal and unjust system. In this scheme, culture serves as a prop to the social structure, legitimising the existing order of things.

Feminist (p. 120) theorists have also seen culture as a product of social conflict; but whereas Marxists see social conflict as between classes, feminists see gender relations as just as important. Two key terms in feminist theory are 'subordination' and 'patriarchy' (see Box 1.6). Both these terms describe how men have more social and economic power than women. Feminist theory focuses on the political and economic inequalities between men and women. However, because women have often been excluded from the mainstream of political and economic life, feminists have also emphasised the importance of studying culture as the place in which inequality is reproduced. Because it is within culture that gender is formed, feminists have studied culture in order to examine the ways in which cultural expectations and assumptions about sex have fed the idea that gender inequality is natural.

Culture and conflict are also linked in the study of 'race' and racism. The concept of

Box **1.6**

Subordination and patriarchy

Subordination of women: a phrase used to describe the generalised situation whereby men as a group have more social and economic power than women, including power over women (Pearson, 1992). Men are dominant in society and masculinity signifies dominance over femininity in terms of ideas.

Patriarchy: originally an anthropological term that describes a social system in which authority is invested in the male head of the household (the patriarch) and other male elders in the kinship group. Older men are entitled to exercise socially sanctioned authority over other members of the household or kinship group, both women and younger men (Pearson, 1992).

Patriarchy has been criticised by some feminists as too all-embracing a term to describe the different forms of male dominance in different societies.

'race' is often put in inverted commas because 'race', like gender, is also a social rather than a biological category. Although people are often differently defined by 'racial' characteristics, there are always as many differences within a defined 'racial' group as between 'racial' groups (Fields, 1990: 97). Fryer (1984) has argued that racial prejudice is cultural in the sense that it is the articulation of popular beliefs held by a people about others who are felt to be different from themselves. Racism, however, articulates cultural difference with structured inequality, using perceptions of these differences to validate oppression. The argument is that cultural domination is an essential element of economic and political control. Just as feminists contend that the cultural roles assigned to women (gendered roles) serve to account for their separate and unequal relationship with men, so critics of racism argue that prejudicial values and attitudes towards colonised peoples developed as European imperialists slaughtered them, took their lands and destroyed their cultures (Richards, 1990).

Culture in its own right and as a force for change

However, culture need not be seen as dependent upon and derivative of the economic or any other dimension of social structure. The celebrated case here is **Max Weber**'s (p. 243) account of the part played by the Protestant ethic in explaining the origins of modern capitalism. Weber argues that the beliefs of the early Protestant sects played a key causal role in the establishment of the 'spirit' or culture of capitalism, and thereby contributed to development of the capitalist economic system. Many of the early Protestant groups subscribed to the teachings of Calvin's doctrine of predestination which maintained that the believer's eternal salvation was determined at birth and that no amount of good works could alter God's decision. This placed a tremendous psychological burden on believers who had no way of knowing whether they numbered among the Elect (those who achieve eternal salvation in the life hereafter). The practical solution offered by the Protestant religion to the anxiety thus generated lay in the notion of vocation: the believer was instructed to work long and hard in an occupation in order to attest his/her confidence and conviction that Elect status was assured. Later, the doctrine was relaxed so that systematic labour within a vocation and the material prosperity that accompanied it came to be seen as a sign of Election. The consequences of these beliefs and related restrictions on consumption and indulgence was (a) to introduce a new goal-orientated attitude towards economic activity to replace the diffuse attitudes that had persisted through the Middle Ages, and (b) to facilitate the process of capital accumulation. Weber of course was well aware that a number of factors other than the cultural contributed to a phenomenon as complex as capitalism (Collins, 1980). His intention was to show how ideas can be 'effective forces' (Weber, 1930: 183) in the historical development of societies. Culture (here in the form of religious ideas) can shape as well as be shaped by social structure.

A more interwoven view of the relationship between culture and society is shown in the work of Mary Douglas and **Michel Foucault** (p. 28). They both stress in their writings that our understanding of particular objects relates as much to the way we think about those objects as to any qualities those objects may have in themselves. There is a reciprocal relationship between thought and the object(s) of thought: a two-way process where objects have qualities that make an impression upon us, but that impression is influenced by the ways in which we have been conditioned to think about that object. Thought and object are, then, inseparably linked but this does not mean that we always

Key influence **1.2**

Michel Foucault (1926–84)

Michel Foucault was a French philosopher and historian – indeed these two categories or identities become blurred together in his writing and thought – who has had a dramatic and far-reaching impact on cultural studies through his work on the connections between **power** (p. 94), knowledge and subjectivity.

Foucault's varied career took him through several disciplines – including philosophy and psychology – and various countries – he worked in France, Sweden, Poland, Tunisia and Germany before taking up a position at France's premier academic institution, the Collège de France, in 1970. Significantly, his job in Paris was, at his suggestion, a professorship in History of Systems of Thought and in this we can trace the themes of much of the work that he undertook from the 1950s through into the 1980s.

Foucault's early work traced changing modes of thought in relation to 'psychological' knowledges. His book *Madness and Civilisation* (1961) traced the relationship between madness and reason; reading the changing reactions to madness, and the incarceration of the mad, in terms of thinking about rationality as they changed from the medieval period, through the Enlightenment's Age of Reason, and into the nineteenth century. The issues that it raised were explored in varied and changing ways in his subsequent work. Careful attention to the

→

changing patterns of knowledge produced *The Birth of the Clinic* (originally published in French in 1963), *The Order of Things* (French original 1966) and *The Archaeology of Knowledge* (French original 1969). Indeed, he used the term 'archaeologies' to describe all these projects. The connections between knowledge and power which the treatment of the insane had revealed were further explored in relation to other marginalised groups in his *Discipline and Punish: The Birth of the Prison* (originally published in French in 1975), his edited editions of the lives of the murderer Pierre Rivière (1975) and the hermaphrodite Herculine Barbin (1978), and his three books on *The History of Sexuality* (originally published in French: Volume I 1976, Volumes II and III 1984). In all of these studies – which he called genealogies – he used theories of **discourse** (p. 30) to trace the changing ways in which power and knowledge are connected in the production of subjectivities and **identities** (p. 224).

Foucault's impact has been academic. He has changed the ways in which we think about power, knowledge and subjectivity, encouraging us to look at the ways in which they are connected and the ways in which they change from context to context. In emphasising that 'Nothing is fundamental. That is what is interesting in the analysis of society', he has encouraged us to think about the ways in which things – power relations, ways of thinking, and ways of understanding ourselves and others – could be different. This means that his influence has also been political. His attention to the forms of power which shape institutions and subjectivities has been influential in, for example, campaigns over prisoners' rights and gay rights.

Further reading

Foucault, M. (1980) *Power/Knowledge: Selected Interviews and Other Writings 1972–1977*, ed. Colin Gordon, Brighton: Harvester Press.
Kritzman, L.D. (ed.) (1988) *Michel Foucault: Politics, Philosophy, Culture. Interviews and Other Writings 1977–1984*, London: Routledge.
Rabinow, P. (ed.) (1984) *The Foucault Reader*, Harmondsworth: Penguin.

think in the same way about things and that ideas never change. It does mean that change is the outcome of reciprocal relationships, not a uni-directional causality from structure to culture. This means that culture may influence structure, as well as structure influencing culture. The recognition that culture is a force for change (not simply the object of change) leads to the belief that culture can be examined as a system in its own right. For example, in *Purity and Danger* Mary Douglas (1966) argues that ideas about dirt and hygiene in society have a force and a compulsion, not simply because they can be related to the material world through ideas about contamination, germs and illness, but because they are part of a wider cosmology or world-view. Dirt and hygiene are understood within a culture not just in terms of their relation to disease, but also in terms of ideas of morality, for example moral purity versus immoral filth. Thus, a cultural understanding of dirt will have to take into account the meaning of dirt in more than just a medical sense. It will have to understand dirt's place historically, within a specific culture. The ordering and classifying of events which result from ideas about the world gives meaning to behaviour. The state of being dirty is thus as much the product of ideas as it is of the material world.

In turn, Foucault argues that social groups, identities and positions – like classes, genders, races and sexualities – do not pre-exist and somehow determine their own and other cultural meanings. They are produced within **discourses** (p. 30) which define what they are and how they operate. So, for Foucault, even though there have always been men who have sex with men, there was no 'homosexual' identity, and no 'homosexual sex' before that identity and the figure of the 'homosexual' were defined in medical, psychological and literary texts at the end of the nineteenth century. That those discourses about homosexuality both produced moves to regulate male sexuality – and therefore defined more clearly a group of homosexual men – and provided the basis for positive identification with that term on the part of some of those men, meant that 'homosexuality' came to have a significant place within the social structure. In Foucault's version of things there is no determinate relationship between social structure and culture. Instead there is a flexible set of relationships between **power** (p. 94), discourse and what exists in the world.

Defining concept **1.3**

Discourse

Discourse is a way of thinking about the relationship between **power** (p. 94), knowledge and language. In part it is an attempt to avoid some of the difficulties involved in using the concept of **ideology** (p. 84). It is a way of understanding most associated with the work of the French philosopher and historian **Michel Foucault** (p. 28).

For Foucault a 'discourse' is what we might call 'a system that defines the possibilities for knowledge' or 'a framework for understanding the world' or 'a field of knowledge'. A discourse exists as a set of 'rules' (formal or informal, acknowledged or unacknowledged) which determine the sorts of statements that can be made (i.e. the 'moon is made of blue cheese' is not a statement that can be made within a scientific discourse, but it can within a poetic one). These 'rules' determine what the criteria for truth are, what sorts of things can be talked about, and what sorts of things can be said about them. One example that Foucault uses which can help us here is the imaginary Chinese encyclopaedia about which the Argentinian writer Jorge Luis Borges has written a short story. Foucault uses this to challenge our ideas about the inherent truthfulness and rationality of our own classification systems and scientific discourses. In the encyclopaedia:

> [A]nimals are divided into: (a) belonging to the Emperor, (b) embalmed, (c) tame, (d) sucking pigs, (e) sirens, (f) fabulous, (g) stray dogs, (h) included in the present classification, (i) frenzied, (j) innumerable, (k) drawn with a very fine camelhair brush, (l) *et cetera*, (m) having just broken the water pitcher, (n) that from a long way off look like flies.   (Foucault, 1970: xv)

Foucault's aim is to problematise the relationship between words and things. He suggests

→

that there are lots of ways in which the world can be described and defined and that we have no sure grounds to choose one over the others. In turn this also means that he is dedicated to recovering those ways of knowing that have been displaced and forgotten.

Discourse is also about the relationship between power and knowledge. Foucault (1980) argues that we have to understand power as something productive. For example, it is not in catching a criminal that power lies but in producing the notion of 'the criminal' in the first place. As he says: 'There is no power relation without the correlative constitution of a field of knowledge, nor any knowledge that does not presuppose and constitute at the same time power relations' (Foucault, 1977: 27). To continue the example, it is the body of knowledge – the discourse – that we call 'criminology' that produces 'the criminal' (and, in the past, now forgotten figures like 'the homicidal monomaniac') as an object of knowledge, and suggests ways of dealing with him or her. The criminal, the criminologist, the policeman and the prison are all created together 'in discourse'.

This does not mean that the world is just words and images. Foucault is keen to talk about the institutions and practices that are vital to the working of discourse. If we think about medical discourse we soon realise that the forms of knowledge and language that make it up are inseparable from the actual places where these discourses are produced (the clinic, the hospital, the surgery) and all the trappings of the medical environment (white coats, stethoscopes, nurses' uniforms) (see Prior, 1988).

Further reading

Foucault, M. (1980) *Power/Knowledge: Selected Interviews and Other Writings 1972–1977*, ed. Colin Gordon, Brighton: Harvester.

Purvis, T. and Hunt, A. (1993) 'Discourse, ideology, discourse, ideology, discourse, ideology . . .', *British Journal of Sociology*, 44, 473–99.

In considering culture and social structure we have demonstrated the rigid determinism of the functionalists; the strong connections between cultural struggles and the social relations of class, race and gender made by Marxists, feminists and anti-racists; and the importance of culture in reciprocally shaping social structures and social positions and identities. We can take these theories further by considering how cultural critics approach the patterning and organisation of meaning.

1.3.2 | The organisation of meaning

Raymond Williams (p. 5) argues that the patterning of meaning is a crucial starting point for cultural analysis:

> [I]t is with the discovery of patterns of a characteristic kind that any useful cultural analysis begins, and it is with the relationships between these patterns, which sometimes reveal unexpected identities and correspondences in hitherto separately considered activities, sometimes again reveal discontinuities of an unexpected kind, that general cultural analysis is concerned.   (Williams, 1960: 47)

However, there are many different ways in which this search for patterns of meaning can proceed.

Speech, language and text

Two key concepts in the theories of meaning are intention and reception, neither of which can be understood in a common-sense way. For example, it can be argued that there is never perfect communication between speaker and audience, not least because a speaker may conceal meaning (intentionally or unintentionally). None the less, speech acts do contain clues to the intentions of speakers. The tone of voice may 'speak' about the relationship between speaker and audience, so one may not be wholly dependent upon the content of the speech act. In listening to speech one learns about the wider cultural values which are implicit in speech.

Speech and language have proved to be rich fields for analysts of the transmission of culture. **Semiologists** (p. 34) have argued that all cultural products should be seen as texts. A cultural product may not be actually written but it still consists of signs (see Chapter 2) whether visual, aural or even tactile (e.g. sculpture, which may be touched) which can be 'read' or interpreted. An example of this would be a flag which stands for a particular country. Semiotics assumes standard associations that are well known, an established part of the cultural repertoire, and so can be readily and easily called upon. There is no single, natural meaning of any sign. Its value or meaning can only be determined in relation to other signs, which in turn requires searching out oppositions and differences. In the field of semiotics it is important to remember that there may be many associations for a specific cultural item and they may, when grouped together, appear conflicting or contradictory. The situational and contextual nature of meaning must be stressed but the notion of contextually dominant meanings does not rule out the presence of other meanings. In the case of the flag which represents a country, we can see that to one group of people this flag may have the meaning of patriotism and shared history, but to a different group of people this same flag may represent oppression and injustice: for example, the British flag is used patriotically in some parts of Britain, but in Ireland is sometimes referred to as 'the butcher's apron' because of its connotations with bloody repression. The sense of oppression or injustice is less likely to be recognised by the first group, if they represent a dominant social group, but this does not mean that this sense is not present. This search for interpretation can be more or less ordered through the conventions of structuralism.

Structuralism and the order of meaning

Structuralists see culture as an ordered system or structure. Culture is presented as a system of coded meanings which are produced and reproduced through social interaction. Their interest is in how participants in interaction learn and use the codes of communication. A number of perspectives has been brought to this issue.

Certain theories of linguistics, for example those of Ferdinand de Saussure and Noam Chomsky, state that there is a universal structuring principle in all human language: that of binary oppositions. Binary oppositions consist of two opposing terms; for example, black and white, man and woman, high and low. Lévi-Strauss (1966) argues that these oppositions are not amenable to direct observation or analysis. Instead, they operate at a level that is not conscious, a level sometimes described as that of deep structure. The study of culture, according to structuralists, consists of an examination of cultural forms. These cultural forms are the result of the human mind being brought to bear on particular environments. Lévi-Strauss argues that the resultant cultural forms all exhibit the same pattern, that of binary oppositions. The content of particular cultures may be different but this is the result of different environments. What is significant is not the different contents, but the identical patterning of cultural forms. Working from the assumption that cultural forms consist of identical patterns, Lévi-Strauss says that individuals have an innate biological capacity, what he calls a 'bio-grammar', which they use to 'decode' or interpret codes of cultural information. Codes are cultural in the sense that they are the expression of a people's shared conventions at a particular time. Acculturated members of a society know the codes for their society. Codes are culturally specific, but the ability to decode is universal and innate.

This means that everyone makes sense of the world at two distinct levels which take place simultaneously. The first is at the level of deep structure where the binary oppositions operate. The second is at the surface level of contemporaneous activity where knowledge of a cultural code allows sorting and classifying to operate and meaning to emerge. Lévi-Strauss likens this thinking to what we engage in when we listen to music. We hear both the melody and the harmony, but in order to achieve an understanding of the music we have to integrate them. It is the whole that gives us the message, and so it is both surface and deep structure that gives us our understanding of cultural messages. Lévi-Strauss worked out these ideas through the analysis of myth, which he argues is one of the clearest forms of cultural expression of a society's view of itself.

Mary Douglas (1966) and Edmund Leach (1970) adopt a similar stance to that of Lévi-Strauss towards cultural understanding and the reception of cultural messages. They both agree that meaning arises out of patterning and order, but they differ from Lévi-Strauss in locating the source of order in the social world and not in physiology. It is the social and cultural contexts and the agreed meanings of shared experience through interaction that allocate and set meanings. Leach, for example, illustrates his case with colour classifications. In English culture there are customary associations made between colours and fact and feeling – thus red is the colour of danger, red is also associated with pomp, it is the colour of the British Labour Party and it is a term used to describe members of the Communist Party. A native user of English is aware of some if not all of the repertoire of available meanings and on hearing the word 'red' will decide, according to context, which meaning is appropriate. This will be the meaning that makes sense to the hearer and gives a message. This sociocultural explanation of culture and communication also pays attention to other features of conventional cultural systems, such as gesture, dress, physical appearance, volume and tone of communication. The standardised meanings that cluster around each cultural item provide support and evidence for situationally preferred readings. Semiotics and structuralism are discussed further in Chapter 2.

Defining concept 1.4
Semiology and semiotics

The study or science of signs, known in Europe as semiology (a term coined by Saussure) and in North America as semiotics (a name devised by C.S. Peirce (1839–1914) for his independently developed philosophical system which shared many common premises with de Saussure's).

Ferdinand de Saussure (1857–1913), a Swiss linguist, saw language as a system of signs whose meanings are arbitrary. His most influential ideas were set out in lectures given between 1907 and 1911 and published posthumously in 1916 as *Cours de Linguistique General*, edited from Saussure's papers and his students' notes. Saussure emphasised that what a sign stands for is simply a matter of cultural convention, of how things are done in a given culture – it has nothing to do with what the sign refers to in the world or the sign's history. He suggested that 'the linguistic sign unites, not a thing and a name, but a concept and a sound-image.' Signs comprised two elements: a signified, a concept or idea, which is materialised in a signifier, a sound-image such as an advertising hoarding or a newspaper text. The meaning of signs must be sought in the relations (of similarity, contrast, etc.) between signs. For Saussure, the cardinal principle was 'that nothing can ever reside in a single term'.

A further influential distinction suggested by Saussure is between language as a patterned system (*langue*) and language as embodied in actual speech (*parole*). The study of language was itself located as part of a larger science devoted to 'the study of the life of signs within society' which Saussure named semiology.

Semiologists maintain that it is possible to discern certain logics or structures or codes which underpin the multiplicity of cultural life as we experience it. Saussure's ideas have been developed especially effectively in the broader sphere of culture by **Roland Barthes** (p. 52). His writings explicate the latent meanings – the myths and codes – that inform such diverse cultural phenomena as guide books, steak and chips, electoral photography, all-in wrestling, margarine, and the Eiffel Tower.

If the sign is arbitrary, then its meaning can only be established by considering its relation to other signs. It is thus necessary to look for the differences and oppositions between signs. These are classified in two broad ways:

- Syntagmatically – the linear or sequential relations between signs (thus traditional English meals consist of a main course which follows a starter, and a dessert which follows the main course).

- Paradigmatically – the 'vertical' relations, the particular combination of signs (thus soup or melon but not apple pie for starters).

The meaning of signs may not be readily apparent. Semiologists speak of different levels of signification. The skilled semiologist can proceed from the level of denotation, the obvious meaning of the sign (e.g. a photograph of a black soldier saluting the flag), to the connotation of the sign, its taken-for-granted meaning (e.g. colonialism must be right

→

– there are people that it supposedly oppresses who are perfectly willing to die for it). In this way the ideological functions of signs can be exposed. Certain cultural forms can be seen as myths which serve to render specific (often bourgeois) values as natural, universal and eternal.

Further reading

Barthes, R. (1973) *Mythologies*, London: Paladin.
Gottdeiner, M. (1995) *Postmodern Semiotics*, Oxford: Blackwell.

Hermeneutics and interpretation

Another significant tradition in the social sciences concerned with interpretation is hermeneutics. Derived initially from debates in German-speaking countries over the interpretation of the Bible, this approach has become increasingly concerned with wider issues of interpretation and with philosophical debates over the connections between meaning and existence. Hermeneutics argues that it is impossible to divorce the meaning of a text from the cultural context of its interpreter. In order to interpret any text the interpreter necessarily and unavoidably brings to the text certain prior understandings or fore-understandings from his/her own culture. The interpreter's fore-understandings facilitate the process of interpretation and are themselves worked upon (i.e. confirmed, modified, refuted, amended, etc.) in the course of interpretation. This conversation-like process is sometimes described by the term 'the hermeneutic circle' (Gadamer, 1975: 235–45). Advocates of the hermeneutic circle maintain that interpretation is not a simple one-way transmission of ideas from text to reader but it is rather an interactive process in which the reader's fore-understandings are required for any further understanding of the text to be possible. Thus, when we read Shakespeare's *Hamlet* (1600–1), or watch a performance of it, we bring to bear our present-day cultural understandings about filial duty, jealousy and revenge, sexual propriety, etc., and these understandings are elaborated and modified in consequence of our reading of this play. The notion of the hermeneutic circle has fed into many theories of culture in the social sciences and humanities. One of its central implications is to underscore the absence of any privileged position or Archimedean point for the interpretation of cultural phenomena – knowledge of a culture, to paraphrase the American sociologist Harold Garfinkel, is always knowledge 'from within' a culture.

One example of the development of a sociological approach to interpretation influenced by the hermeneutic tradition can be found in the work of the Hungarian sociologist of knowledge Karl Mannheim. Mannheim argues that a cultural act or text contains three levels of meaning: objective, expressive and documentary. Mannheim uses the hypothetical example of a friend giving alms to a beggar to bring out the differences between these three layers of meaning. The objective meaning of the act or product inheres in the act itself, and in this example it is assistance. The second level, expressive meaning, involves the consideration of what an actor intended or wishes to express by any particular act. Mannheim's friend may have been wishing to convey sympathy to the beggar through his act. The third layer of meaning is the most important for Mannheim as it links the act to wider contexts. The act can function as a document of the friend's personality and could be seen to document hypocrisy if, for example, the friend was a multi-millionaire who made his money by making the beggar redundant from a job in the first place. However, to formulate this interpretation we have to know the wider context of the act, for example, that its author was exceptionally wealthy. This connection to wider contexts establishes, in this case, links between the act and the political economy within which it takes place. In the next section we discuss political economy and the importance of **ideology** (p. 84) as a way of understanding patterns of meaning.

Political economy, ideology and meaning

An interest in political economy means an interest in issues of power and inequality that are associated with the allocation of resources and the formation of wealth. The ideas of political economy have had a widespread value and application in social science and in disciplines such as history and English studies because they have proved fruitful in the investigation of patterns of meaning. To relate political economy to culture is to prompt some of the following questions. What are the connections between ownership and control of the media and cultural transmission? What is the role of the economic infrastructure in the dissemination of ideas? What are the links between technology transfer and the transfer of knowledge? In all these areas of investigation a relationship is sought between politics, economics and culture.

An example of this approach would be an analysis of newspaper content to see if a connection can be established between the ownership and control of the newspaper and the type and character of news printed. In simple terms, it suggests considering the extent to which the owner's views and interests are reflected in the content of the newspaper. Newspaper coverage of the news has been found to be overwhelmingly pro-capitalist, pro-*status quo* in character. The question then becomes: how is this coincidence with owners' interests to be explained? One explanation points to the concentration of ownership and control of British newspapers (85 per cent of all newspaper circulation is controlled by seven large companies). Newspaper proprietors have mutual interests in other financial and industrial undertakings, and also have an upbringing and lifestyle in common; in short, they have shared economic interests and a shared culture. Thus it is hardly surprising that the press's coverage is biased in favour of the interests and values of private enterprise. An alternative explanation draws attention to some different features of the political economy of newspaper production. Here emphasis is placed on the prevailing logic of the market in which newspapers are presently produced. The commercial survival of newspapers depends upon advertising revenue which in turn generates a pressure to maintain a newspaper's circulation. To retain a large readership newspapers give people what they are believed to want – human interest stories, crime, sex, sport and scandal. Entertaining the readership comes to take precedence over providing information about significant world events and educating the public in the ways of responsible citizenship. Material documenting cultural difference and ideological diversity tends to get squeezed out of newspapers, leaving only a relatively narrow middle ground.

Analyses using the assumptions of political economy can also be linked to issues of what ought to be. For example, there is a widely accepted belief that says that 'more means worse'. More channels, more programmes and more broadcast hours of radio and television designed to appeal to a mass audience will lead to a lowering of the quality of service (see section 1.2.6). Some trends in cultural studies, discussed in Chapter 2, have voiced fears about the corrupting nature of mass media for audiences.

A more sophisticated way of connecting the concerns of political economy and questions of cultural meaning are through the concept of **ideology** (p. 84). Ideologies can be of various sorts. **Antonio Gramsci** (p. 38) divided up ideologies into three categories. The first is that of common sense. Common-sense ideas are those we all take for granted. Common-sense ideas and values are part of everyday life. They form the bedrock of our understanding of the world; but when examined closely they may appear to be either contradictory or very superficial. An example of a common-sense ideology is given in the phrase 'Boys are better at football than girls'. This expresses a widely held idea, commonly held to be true. A closer examination of this 'truth', however, might question its validity by asking 'Are boys encouraged to be more physically active than girls?' or 'Are girls allowed to participate in football or are they excluded at home, at school, or at club level?' If the answer to these questions is yes, then the common-sense idea that boys are better at football than girls is shown to be true only because of particular circumstances (see section 7.1.2).

Gramsci's second category of ideology is that of a particular philosophy. This means not so much the thought of a particular philosopher but of a particular group of people in society who put forward a reasonably coherent set of ideas. These people Gramsci calls intellectuals; and he includes both traditional intellectuals such as priests, and intellectuals who emerge from social movements, like trade unionists or political activists. Thus, examples of ideologies that are philosophies are Roman Catholic teachings or the ecological ideas of Greenpeace or the beliefs of Right to Life anti-abortionist groups. Gramsci's third category is that of a dominant or **hegemonic** (p. 106) ideology, that is one that has a leading role in society. An example of a hegemonic ideology in a particular society might be the dominance of one person's ideas, for example in a dictatorship. Or it might be the description of a society as capitalist or individualistic, whereby ideas (or ideologies) like 'the primacy of monetary profit' or 'the survival of the fittest' are the dominant ideas.

An understanding of how these three different categories of ideology may interrelate can be gained by thinking about the ideology of racism. In the first category, 'common-sense' racism might consist of phrases like 'The English are cold', or 'Black people are natural athletes'. These phrases express everyday prejudices as common sense. They do not, on their own, express anything more than the individual prejudice of the speaker. If, however, these common-sense ideas become part of a coherent system, then they enter Gramsci's second category of a philosophy. Nineteenth-century anthropologists classified the 'races' of humanity, placing Europeans at the top of a purportedly evolutionary ladder with Orientals and Africans coming further down; this is plainly an

Key influence 1.3

Antonio Gramsci (1891–1937)

Antonio Gramsci was an Italian political activist and writer who was influential in the development of **Marxist** (p. 97) cultural theory. He aimed to develop concepts that would enable the understanding and transformation of twentieth-century political and economic structures and social and cultural relations. He is best known for his work on the idea of **hegemony** (p. 106).

Gramsci was born in Sardinia and was educated in Turin where he joined the Italian Socialist Party, and worked as a journalist. In 1921 he was a founder member of the Italian Communist Party (PCI) and, after a visit to Moscow, was elected to the Italian Parliament. He later became leader of the PCI and, in 1926, was sentenced to twenty years' imprisonment by Mussolini's Fascist government. At his trial the official prosecutor demanded of the judge that 'We must stop this brain working for twenty years!' However, during his imprisonment Gramsci wrote his most famous works, published as *Selections from Prison Notebooks* (1971), which combined studies of politics, philosophy, history, literature and culture. He died shortly after being released from prison.

Gramsci is important to cultural studies because of his attempts to develop the connections between class relations, culture and **power** (p. 94) without reducing issues of culture and meaning to a superstructure determined by an 'economic base'. His concept of hegemony aimed at understanding how dominant classes could organise their rule through consent when their political and economic power was not in the interest of those they subordinated. However, this was not a static situation within which the ideas of the powerful went unchallenged. Gramsci used the metaphor of a 'war of manoeuvre' to suggest that political struggles were continually being fought in a whole variety of arenas: political, economic and cultural. In turn this meant conceptualising the role of the intellectuals who were part of fighting these 'wars'. Through his notion of the 'organic intellectual' he argued that everyone who used ideas was an intellectual – it was not just a label for a small professional group – and that these 'thinkers' and their ideas were organically tied to particular class interests. It can be argued that it is Gramsci's ideas that form the basis of the notion of 'cultural politics', due to the ways in which they were taken up and reworked by those working in the Birmingham **Centre for Contemporary Cultural Studies** (p. 327) in the 1970s.

Further reading

Gramsci, A. (1971) *Selections from Prison Notebooks*, London: Lawrence and Wishart.
Gramsci, A. (1985) *Selections from Cultural Writings*, London: Lawrence and Wishart.
Joll, J. (1977) *Gramsci*, London: Fontana.

example of a racist philosophy. The Nazi and Fascist beliefs about Aryan racial superiority are of the same type. Racism becomes a dominant or hegemonic ideology when it is used within a particular society to legitimate the social divisions and organisation of that society. So, for example, the use of racist ideas to justify the European colonisation of India and Africa or to exclude black people from housing or particular jobs is an example of a hegemonic ideology. In practice, these three categories are often combined. Thus, a common-sense racist remark is often made in the context of an accepted knowledge of available racist philosophies and of racism as a hegemonic ideology.

Poststructuralism and the patterns of meaning

Thinking through the concept of ideology means considering a whole range of social groups and their relationship to ideas and cultural meanings. In the structuralist version these meanings are strictly patterned according to specific structures and systems such as binary opposition. In the political economy view there are more or less strong links between the different groups and the ideas and meanings that they hold and propound. Poststructuralism has questioned the nature of the connections that are made in both of these other theoretical approaches.

First, it questions what are seen as the rigidities of structuralist systems of thought. Instead of binary oppositions it suggests that there are much more complicated and ever-changing systems of meaning which need to be understood in their particular contexts. Thus, the meanings that things have are not fixed – they are fluid and changing. As in our Shakespeare example, the meanings of the plays are not defined by fixed systems of signs – for example, thinking about the relationships between harmony and disharmony or order and disorder in the comedies – but are dependent on the contexts in which they are written, enacted, consumed and interpreted. Thus Shakespeare's understandings of race and money – in a play like *The Merchant of Venice* – can be interpreted in terms of contemporary discourses of economics and morality. This need not be based upon direct knowledge that Shakespeare had, but a set of interlocking cultural codes. As Stephen Greenblatt argues, dealing with the correspondences between medical texts and Shakespeare's texts:

> [T]he state of Shakespeare's knowledge of medical science is not the important issue here. The relation I wish to establish between medical and theatrical practice is not one of cause and effect or source and literary realization. We are dealing rather with a shared code, a set of interlocking tropes and similitudes that function not only as the objects but as the conditions of representation.   (Greenblatt, 1988: 86)

It is not, therefore, the systems and structures of meaning that are important but the ways in which more diffuse patterns of meanings intersect in particular situations.

Second, poststructuralists question the solidity of the relationships that the political economy approach argues exist between economic relationships and cultural meanings. Instead of asserting that there are ideologies appropriate to classes, they argue that the relationships are both contingent and contextual. Again, classes, genders and races are, in part, formed through the ideas, ideologies and discourses that are used about them and that they use in their struggles; and these will differ depending on the time, the place, the nature of the struggle, and the history of that struggle. Thus the patterns of meaning cannot be traced back to underlying political and economic structures; they are related to them but in ways that are ever-changing and which must be explored and interpreted by the cultural analyst. Thus, Shakespeare does not always define English-ness for a certain class, but is taken up in that way in particular battles over education, status and **cultural capital** (p. 355). All of this puts much more of a burden on our own interpretations of culture.

A central element of poststructuralist thought is the idea that culture – in all its forms – is a 'text' which can be 'read'. This theoretical move towards 'textuality' shifts the focus of the study of culture. What is studied is not so much cultural forms or representation as the text itself. Whereas before it has been assumed that it might be possible to gain knowledge by the study of cultural form, poststructuralist theorists (**Barthes** (p. 52), **Foucault** (p. 28), Jacques Derrida) have questioned the search for meaning and coherence. Jacques Derrida has argued that the texts that make up culture can never be pinned down. Instead of yielding meaning and knowledge to the student of culture, they defer it. The task of students of culture is not, therefore, to look for explanations, but to 'deconstruct' meaning in culture. Students of culture should not look for systems, structures and ideologies but should look at the gaps, dis-continuities and inconsistencies in texts. Followers of this approach contend that there is always partiality and subjectivity in understanding; culture consists of multiple realities which are never understood in their entirety either by the sender or the receiver of information. Texts are always subject to interpretation, doubt and dispute, whatever the attempts of authors to exercise control.

One older version of poststructuralism does attempt to relate textuality back to social factors. The '**Bakhtin** School' (p. 202), and particularly V.N. Volosinov, argues that the sign is a site of social contestation. This means that different groups within society struggle, argue and dispute over the meanings of different signs. In *Marxism and the Philosophy of Language* (1973) Volosinov argues that it is class conflict that conditions the struggle over signs. Bakhtin's idea that any text contains 'multiple voices' within it has been developed by **Julia Kristeva**'s (p. 232) influential concept of 'intertextuality'. This idea concerns the relation of a given text to other texts. Any text, it is argued, can be analysed in terms of the other texts that it has absorbed and transformed. Thus intertextuality embraces various forms of textual borrowing and echoing, such as allusion, parody, pastiche and quotation. The concept allows us to appreciate how a science fiction movie like *Blade Runner* draws on 1940s 'hard-boiled' detective stories and *film noir* as intertexts (*The Maltese Falcon*, *The Big Sleep*, etc.). What we see in *Blade Runner* is the incorporation and transformation of these intertexts in a futuristic setting (the movie is set in 2019). Most of the action takes place in shadowy rooms or after dark in poorly lit public places; the film's hero makes a living out of a technologically advanced parody of the classic gumshoe role; the heroine dresses in 1940s retro style; like many *film noir* movies, the development of the plot is at times opaque and, also like many movies of this genre, in the original version of *Blade Runner* the hero provides 'voice-over' to link scenes (see also section 4.3.4). By deconstructing *Blade Runner* in terms of its intertexts it becomes possible to realise one poststructuralist premise, 'the death of the author'. What this means is that the author's intentions are adjudged irrelevant to the interpretations of the text; the text is a separate and autonomous entity. Thus, instead of studying the influences on the author and the sources s/he drew upon in authoring the text (a notoriously contentious interpretive strategy), the interpreter is left instead to consider the intertexts figuring in a given text.

1.4 | Cultural studies

What, then, is cultural studies? Throughout this chapter we have stressed the linkages between something that we have called cultural studies and the disciplines of sociology, history, geography, English and anthropology. We have discussed a set of foci for these disciplines, arguing that, given their common interests in culture, there are issues and problems that they all must address. These foci we call the core issues and problems in the study of culture. It is the shared interest in the topic of culture and the recognition of common themes that has brought practitioners from different disciplines together in the belief that it is through cooperation and collaboration that understanding and explanation will develop most powerfully. This clustering of different disciplinary perspectives around a common object of study offers the possibility of the development of a distinctive area of study characterised by new methods of analysis. It is this configuration of collaborating disciplines around the topic of culture that we see constituting both the substance and the methods of cultural studies. The arena in which this takes place is labelled an 'interdiscursive space', capturing the fluidity and focus that characterise cultural studies and contrasting the emergent, innovatory themes in substance and method which arise out of collaboration with the traditional, evolutionary themes of single disciplines. The metaphor of space also draws attention to the permeable nature of cultural studies: there are no fixed boundaries and no fortress walls; theories and themes are drawn in from disciplines and may flow back in a transformed state to influence thinking there.

Richard Johnson (1986) has pointed out the dangers of academic codification in regard to cultural studies, suggesting that its strength lies in its openness and hence its capacity for transformation and growth. He argues that cultural studies mirrors the complexity and polysemic qualities of the object of its study, culture. The power of culture arises from its diffuseness: the term is used where imprecision matters, where rigidity would destroy what it seeks to understand. Consciousness and subjectivity are key terms in Johnson's portrayal of cultural studies. Consciousness is used in the Marxist sense of knowledge and also in a reflexive sense to give the idea of productive activity. Subjectivity is used to refer to the construction of individuals by culture. Combining these two concepts leads Johnson to describe the project of cultural studies as being to 'abstract, describe and reconstitute in concrete studies the social forms through which human beings "live", become conscious, sustain themselves subjectively'.

This project has been interpreted in cultural studies in terms of three main models of research: (a) production-based studies; (b) text-based studies; (c) studies of lived cultures. As you can see, there is a close correspondence here with the three senses of culture which we elaborated earlier in this chapter. Each one of these areas has a different focus; the first draws attention to processes involved in and struggles over the production of cultural items; the second investigates the forms of cultural product; the third is concerned with representation. Johnson points to the necessarily incompleteness of these ventures; like the wider arena in which they operate, they are fed by interactive communication. Each one gives to and takes from the others.

In summary, we suggest approaching cultural studies as an area of activity that grows from interaction and collaboration to produce issues and themes that are new and challenging. Cultural studies is not an island in a sea of disciplines but a current that washes the shores of other disciplines to create new and changing formations.

Re-cap

- In cultural studies the concept of culture has a range of meanings which includes both high art and everyday life.
- Cultural studies advocates an interdisciplinary approach to the study of culture.
- While cultural studies is eclectic in its use of theory, using both structuralist and more flexible approaches, it advocates those that stress the overlapping, hybrid nature of cultures, seeing cultures as networks rather than patchworks.

Further reading

Although they are not always easy reading, the best place to begin exploring the issues raised in this chapter is to look at the acknowledged early 'classics' of cultural studies: Richard Hoggart's *The Uses of Literacy* (1958), Raymond Williams' *Culture and Society 1780–1950* (1963) and E.P. Thompson's *The Making of the English Working Class* (1968). Each of these works has had a profound influence over the subsequent development of cultural studies. Graeme Turner's *British Cultural Studies: An Introduction* (1990) plots the institutional development of cultural studies while Fred Inglis's *Cultural Studies* (1993) offers some singular interpretations of its history. Important stocktakings of the field's development are Lawrence Grossberg's *Marxism and the Interpretation of Culture* (1988) and the substantial collection edited by Grossberg, Cary Nelson and Paula Treicher, *Cultural Studies* (1992). John Storey's *An Introductory Guide to Cultural Theory and Popular Culture* (1993) connects debates about popular culture to the concerns of cultural studies. Richard Johnson's 'What is cultural studies anyway?' (1986) critically charts the possibilities of three models of cultural studies (production-based studies, text-based studies and studies of lived cultures). The collection edited by Jessica Munns and Gita Rajan, *A Cultural Studies Reader: History, Theory, Practice* (1995) attests to the diversity of cultural studies in the 1990s. For original recent work in cultural studies, the reader may wish to consult the following journals: *Cultural Studies, New Formations* and *Social Text.* You will probably need access to a university library to read these periodicals.

Communication and representation

2.0 | Introduction

In this chapter we explore a number of important aspects of communication and representation. The idea of representation immediately raises a number of issues that have been the subject of much philosophical debate over the centuries. Many of these will be addressed as this chapter progresses. However, it is important to be aware of some of the dimensions of this debate immediately. Thus, it can be suggested that we are all familiar with the idea of representation in what might be termed a photographic sense (see further Chapter 9), where the image is a representation which seems to capture the whole of what is framed. The picture is thought to be a copy of what exists in some form. In this sense language might be seen as a representation of what already exists in that it describes or copies it in some way. For instance, it is often thought that the language of natural science captures the nature of the world in this sense. The example of the photograph immediately introduces a difficulty in that photographs can be cropped or framed to re-present the world. Representations, then, do not simply copy the world, they produce a *version* of it. Consequently, representations are involved in the *production* of a version of the world, they do not simply copy it. A further position is reached when it is maintained that the representation is centrally involved in the *construction* of the world. At the extreme, such positions imply that the world is that which is captured in language. Thus, returning to the idea of the relation between science and the world, it can be suggested that scientific language does not simply represent in the sense of describing the world, or capturing certain features of it, but that the natural world is actually defined through the language and concepts used to discuss it. For example, because we have a concept of 'radioactivity' in our language, we are able to perceive risks that in a real sense did not exist for people lacking the concept.

To consider these issues and others, we begin with a discussion of the centrality of language to human culture and society as it is through language that we communicate. In section 2.1 we consider the main attributes of language and examine debates on cultural relativity of language and thought. This is followed by section 2.2 which focuses on the important approach known as semiotics which examines the construction of signs and meaning in language. This approach has been very influential in cultural studies, in particular in the analysis of advertising which is discussed in section 2.3. These sections on semiotics, signs and advertising raise a number of important issues concerning the relationship between language, representation and power. These are addressed more specifically in the next section, where the dimensions of class, race and gender are emphasised. This section also considers some of the discussions of the ethnography of speaking. After this the chapter moves to consider a specific instance of communication and representation through a discussion of art. Again, the dimensions of power, class and gender are addressed. Finally, we explore some dimensions of representation in the most important contemporary cultural medium: television. This discussion will lead to consideration of the complexities of contemporary representations and **discourse** (p. 30). All through the chapter we shall be pointing to the importance of representation and communication to relationships of power, but also to their problematic nature.

The learning objectives for this chapter are to:

- introduce key debates concerning language, communication and meaning;
- examine different ways of studying representations;
- explore particular dimensions of representations in different media.

2.1 | Language, communication and representation

All human societies have language, and so intimately connected are the requirements of society with the features of language that it is difficult to imagine how a society might exist without it. As a minimum condition for existence human society requires ordered and regular relationships between individuals, the recognition of shared meaning and the ability to transmit knowledge and information among a population. These fundamental features of society depend upon a means of constituting the objects and events of human experience and conveying their meaning in an efficient and effective way. Overwhelmingly, though not exclusively, it is language that fulfils these requirements.

2.1.1 | The attributes of language

Linguistic analysis has identified that all human languages are built upon combinations of sounds named *phonemes*; the patterning of sounds, the attribution of meaning to these patterns and the recognition of certain patterns as words are all culturally specific processes, as is the *syntax* of a language – the conventions about how sentences or phrases are constructed. The cultural attribution of meaning is the outcome of events and processes in particular social settings, and although meanings are standardised and conventional, they do change over time as a result of the action of social and cultural forces. Sometimes this change is very rapid, at other times it can be very slow.

However, all language use and meaning changes over time as a result of the changed environments in which they operate. For example, the language of Chaucer or of Shakespeare is different from the language of late twentieth-century Britain, even though they are all labelled 'English'. To take another example, contemporary English

---

Box **2.1**

Achievements based on semantic universality

- To share information.
- To learn the accumulated knowledge of their community without having to experience things at first hand.
- To make both specific and abstract statements.
- To speak in the present about events in the past or to anticipate events in the future – the 'displacement feature' of language.

Gaisford (1981)

---

usage has been very much influenced by the specialised language of computer technology: an example of this is the widespread use of the letter 'K' to mean one thousand and the use of 'input' as both a noun and a verb. These changes are learned by members of a language community as they acquire conventional language from infancy through the process known as socialisation or acculturation. The knowledge of meaning and of conventional usage in a language community is the taken-for-granted knowledge of the native user. The conventional standardised features of language, the so-called *semantic universality*, enable members of a language community to develop the abilities listed in Box 2.1.

The knowledge and information that is communicated in language is an artifact of language itself since language is constituted to identify and give meaning to human experience. Thus the events, objects, persons, emotions and so on that the language identifies are not discrete entities in human experience awaiting a label to be attached to them; they are constituted through language and the meaning given in language. In this way language stands for or **represents** (p. 61) that which it names. Since language is cultural, the product of human interaction, then it can be said that it is through language that humans define themselves and their world (Gaisford, 1981).

2.1.2 | Language, culture and thought

If language represents the world as defined by humans, can language then be seen as the representation of human thought – are language and thought one and the same thing? Interest in the relationship between language, culture and thought has a long history; Aristotle (384–322 BC) saw words as expressions of mental experiences and so for him thought came before words in apprehending the world. The Austrian philosopher Ludwig Wittgenstein (1889–1951) puzzled about the links between individual thought, private language and the language of the public realm, concluding that 'the limits of my language are the limits of my world' (Wittgenstein, 1981).

Anthropologists in their studies of 'other cultures' have reported the existence of highly elaborated lexicons to describe important aspects of social experience. In contemporary Western societies a similar feature has been documented, particularly with reference to subcultures (see Chapter 8) and to professional groups (see below section 2.4.1 and Chapter 3). These and similar findings have prompted questions about whether language is constitutive of thought and perception: can we know how people think from the language they use? Does language represent and communicate thought? Some introduction to these issues can be found in Box 2.2 on cattle, sport and language.

Box 2.2
Cattle, sport and language

The Nuer are cattle-keeping people studied by the anthropologist Evans-Pritchard in the 1930s in what was then the Anglo-Egyptian Sudan. Evans-Pritchard (1960: 18–19) argues that:

> We have seen in a brief survey of some Nuer institutions and customs that most of their social behaviour directly concerns their cattle. A fuller study of their culture would show everywhere the same dominant interest in cattle, e.g. in their folklore. I used sometimes to despair that I never discussed anything with the young men but livestock and girls, and even the subject of girls led inevitably to cattle. Start on whatever subject I would, and approach it from whatever angle, we would soon be speaking of cows and oxen, heifers and steers, rams and sheep, he-goats and she-goats, calves and lambs and kids. I have already indicated that this obsession – for such it seems to an outsider – is due not only to the great economic value of cattle but also to the fact that they are links in numerous social relationships. Nuer tend to define all social processes and relationships in terms of their cattle. Their social idiom is a bovine idiom.

From this quotation it can be seen that cattle are the core of this society. Evans-Pritchard further describes how poetry, songs, love making, marriage and family, religion and spirituality, dispute and killing, life and death, are all expressed and encompassed in the imagery of cattle. The vocabulary for the colours and marking of cattle, the position of horns on the head, the range and length of horns, and the size and shape of cattle is extensive and complex.

It can be suggested that the language and imagery of sport is similarly pervasive in contemporary American and British societies. For example, Ferraro *et al.* (1994: 296) detail a long list of expressions from baseball taken from Hickerson (1980: 118) which feature heavily in everyday American language:

▪ He made a grandstand play

▪ She threw me a curve

→

- She fielded my questions well
- You're way off base
- You're batting 1,000 (500, zero) so far
- What are the ground rules?
- I want to touch all the bases
- He went to bat for me
- He has two strikes against him
- That's way out in left field
- He drives me up the wall
- He's a team player (a clutch player)
- She's an oddball (screwball, foul ball)
- It's just a ballpark estimate

The language of football and cricket is similarly pervasive in British society, evident in such everyday expressions as:

- Moving the goal posts
- Establishing a level playing field
- Given the red card
- Taking an early bath
- Being a safe pair of hands
- Playing a straight bat

Lexicons burgeon to capture significant cultural events and because of their pervasiveness they are used idiomatically to capture and convey the sense of quite different realms of experience. For example, the language of sport, particularly of football, is widely used in the sphere of politics. This may be an attempt by politicians to convey political argument through popular expression; it may be an attempt to associate sectional interests with mass popular culture; it is also the use of language from a predominantly male sphere to capture national issues and as such it may reveal the masculinist assumptions of politicians about what the world is like and how best to convey that message. This point is elaborated later in the chapter in the section on gendered language. You might like to think about other expressions from different areas of life that operate in the way of sport in this example.

2.1.3 | The Sapir–Whorf hypothesis

An explicit attempt to account for the relations between language and thought is the *Sapir–Whorf* hypothesis which bases its proposals on the existence in all languages of specialised and elaborated lexicons dedicated to the description and understanding of important features of social and cultural life. It is primarily concerned with the grammatical rules and constraints upon thought and perception. Benjamin Lee Whorf, who was an engineer by profession, became interested through his work in the ways that specialised groupings used language – an interest that developed more abstractly into a consideration of the connections between language use, cultural meaning and ways of thinking. In the 1920s the American anthropologist Edward Sapir had written that the development of specialised languages resulted in the creation of language communities which inhabited distinct worlds, not merely the same world as everyone else with different labels attached to events and objects, as some had suggested (Sapir, 1929). Whorf drew on this work for his researches among the Hopi, a native American people. Unlike mainstream American culture which expresses the understanding of time in spatial metaphors – for example, one may say 'it is a *long time* since . . .' or 'it will happen in a *short time*' – the Hopi expressed events as happenings taking place in a state of *being*, a condition that does not lend itself to being categorised in the same way as mainstream American notions of time. Similarly the tenses of the Hopi language did not correspond with American customary notions of past, present and future. The work on the Hopi, together with Sapir's earlier analysis, contributed to the formulation of the Sapir–Whorf hypothesis which states that language creates mental categories through which humans make sense of the world. The proposition is that the world is filtered through the conceptual grids produced by language and the routine and regular use of particular languages produces habitual thought patterns which are culturally specific. It is these culturally specific thought patterns that Sapir and Whorf refer to as *thought worlds*. Whorf expresses the idea in the following way:

> We dissect nature along lines laid down by our native languages. The categories and types that we isolate from the world of phenomena we do not find there because they stare every observer in the face; on the contrary, the world is presented in a kaleidoscopic flux of impressions which has to be organized by our minds and this means largely by the linguistic systems in our minds. We cut nature up, organize it into concepts, and ascribe significances as we do, largely because we are parties to an agreement to organize it in this way – an agreement that holds through our speech community and is codified in the patterns of our language. The agreement is, of course, an implicit and unstated one. *But its terms are absolutely obligatory;* we cannot talk at all except by subscribing to the organization and classification of data which the agreement decrees.   (Carroll, 1956: 212–14, in Black, 1972: 97)

The culturally specific nature of thought, language and action, which the Sapir–Whorf hypothesis proposes, raises questions about the possibility of understanding and representing the meanings of other cultures. How can we represent the thought of others when that thought is expressed in a language that is not our own and which has its own (different) mental categories? Similarly, how does one translate an elaborated semantic domain in one language (culture) to another language (culture) that does not have such elaboration? Questions about the translation and interpretation of culture are very important in the practice of cultural studies since these processes bear directly on the issue of *meaning* – the meaning that people give to action and the meaning attributed by cultural analysts – a key concept in cultural studies, as we have seen in Chapter 1.

The connections between language and conceptual thought that are expressed in the hypothesis are widely accepted by cultural analysts. However, there is less agreement about the causal relationship between them; some question whether there is a direct unilateral relationship between language and thought or, vice versa, between thought and language. Others question whether it is possible to distinguish thought from language.

Some structuralists (see further section 2.2) contend that it is impossible to locate forms of thought from spoken or written language since these are simply local (culturally specific) manifestations of the process of the mind working on environments. In this approach the categories of thought are latent, they are located in the workings of the human mind. In this respect they are subconscious, and as such they are incapable of direct observation or analysis through surface phenomena. From this point of view language is a context-specific (cultural) representation of the way that hidden thought processes act upon environment; one may learn about particular environments but nothing about the way the mind works; that analysis lies in the field of natural science, probably in the discipline of biochemistry.

Social and cultural analysis takes the stance that careful scrutiny of social and cultural phenomena is revealing about forces that shape and change social life. The argument is that major principles of social and cultural organisation are given expression in and through language so the study of language behaviour is both rewarding and instructive. In this sense language can be said to **represent** (p. 61) social and cultural constructs. The field of study known as *sociolinguistics* is concerned with the broad area of the connections between language use and social relations, while the area of study known as the *ethnography of speaking* looks at speech acts in specific settings.

2.1.4 | Sociolinguistics

An underlying assumption of sociolinguistic analysis is that languages are culturally specific phenomena and that language is grounded in social and cultural experience. It is these characteristics that make language a valuable source of cultural and social analysis. Sociolinguistic analysis employs *semiotic* analysis; a method of analysis that is possible because language in its grammar (syntax) and vocabulary (lexicon) is conventional and indeed must be so for it to be an effective means of communication. Standardised messages are given in language because there are well-known associations for words, metaphors and forms of speech and writing. In this way language represents the significant features of social and cultural experience that are regularly and routinely communicated among speakers and writers. This is explained by the English literary and cultural critic F.R. Leavis in Box 2.3. Leavis in his writing sought to emphasise the organic development of society up to industrialism's rupture with the traditional. This led him to certain conclusions about language which have been criticised from other perspectives, as we shall see below (section 2.4).

Box 2.3

Leavis and language

Individual human beings can meet in meaning in language – or let us say a language, meaning the English language (for there is no such thing as language in general) – it is for them in any present a living actuality that is organically at one with the 'human world' they, in growing up into it, have naturally taken for granted. There is in language a central core in which for generations individual speakers have met so that meeting takes place as something inevitable and immediate in relation to which it seems gratuitous to think of 'meeting' as being involved in meaning, or of conventions at all.

Leavis, 1962: 71, in Gervais, 1993: 152

2.2 | Signs and semiotics

As we have suggested above, much recent writing on the communication and representation of meaning has been influenced by **structuralism** (p. 24) and **semiotics** (or **semiology**) (p. 34). One important source of structuralism was the theories of the Swiss linguist Ferdinand de Saussure (1857–1913), whose ideas were developed in the 1960s by influential writers such as Althusser, **Barthes** (p. 52), Chomsky, **Foucault** (p. 28), Lacan and Lévi-Strauss. Keat and Urry (1975: 124–6) identify the main features of structuralism as follows:

1. Systems must be studied as a set of interrelated elements. Individual elements should not be seen in isolation. For example, in a set of traffic lights, green only means go because red means stop.

2. An attempt to discover the structure that lies behind or beneath what is directly knowable.

3. The suggestion that the structure behind the directly visible and the directly visible itself are both products of structural properties of the mind.

4. The methods of linguistics can be applied to other social and human sciences.

5. Culture can be analysed in terms of binary oppositions: for example, between good and bad.

6. The adoption of a distinction between synchronic (static) and diachronic (changing) analyses.

7. The attempt to identify similar structures in different aspects of social life.

2.2.1 | A semiotic analysis of a photograph

Semiotics (or semiology) is the systematic study of signs. To introduce some of the concepts and ideas associated with these approaches we can consider the photograph of two men reproduced here in Figure 2.1.

Certain features of this photograph can be identified immediately. It shows two men embracing; one is black and one white. On close inspection it is possible to suggest that these are two sportsmen and they look like they have finished some kind of sporting activity. In the language of semiotics, this is what the photograph *denotes*. We can understand, or *decode*, such meanings in a fairly straightforward manner, as they are relatively 'objective'.

However, the possession of other knowledge may facilitate more detailed *decoding* of the photograph. Thus, the running enthusiast may recognise that these were runners and the very knowledgeable fan that these were the first two finishers in the 1985 London to Brighton road race. Furthermore, he or she might know that these are both South African runners. Participation of black and white South Africans in major athletics events is now commonplace. However, in 1985 this was outlawed and the participation of these runners caused great controversy. The specifics of this controversy should not concern us here, as what is important are the further layers of meaning, or *connotations*, of this photograph which can be built up on the basis of this knowledge. It might be possible to argue that the reproduction of the photograph is suggesting that black and white can be brought together in sport in South Africa, or that the divisions between black and white have been overemphasised as these two runners look pleased to be in each other's company. Moreover, the implication may be that sport should be above politics and free from political interference.

Figure 2.1 ▪ Two runners.

2.2.2 | Roland Barthes: semiotics and myth

Key influence **2.1**

Roland Barthes (1915–80)

Roland Barthes was a French literary critic and cultural analyst. His development of **structuralist** and **poststructuralist** (p. 24) ideas in the context of writing on aspects of everyday life was particularly influential in the early development of cultural studies.

Barthes' early life was dogged by tuberculosis. He taught in French *lycées* and abroad before being appointed to the Ecole Pratique des Hautes Etudes in 1962. He was appointed to a Chair at the Collège de France (Paris) in 1976. He died after being knocked over by a truck outside the Collège.

Barthes' early work concerned the nature of language and representation from a **semiotic/structuralist** (p. 24) point of view. Examples of his general approach can be found in *Writing Degree Zero* (1953) and *Elements of Semiology* (1964). He worked on the formal properties of literary texts and carried out influential specific analyses such as *S/Z* (1970), which addresses the structure of a novella by Balzac. His identification of proairetic, hermeneutic, semic, symbolic and referential codes was innovative and consequential. Barthes was also concerned to apply the ideas of semiology to aspects of everyday life. He wrote a regular newspaper column in the 1950s which covered topics such as margarine, the brain of Einstein and wrestling from this point of view. These short analyses were collected in *Mythologies* (1957): a bestselling text which encapsulates some of the key aspects of decodings based in a cultural studies approach. Barthes sought to dig below the surface of the everyday for deeper meanings and to show how those meanings were implicated in relations of **power** (p. 94) and structures of domination. He mounted an attack on the role of such seemingly innocent representations and activities in the **ideological** (p. 84) dominance of the bourgeois class. He also examined fashion in *The Fashion System* (1967). The sometimes playful nature of Barthes' analyses became more prominent in his later work which, under the influence of **poststructuralism** (p. 24), is less concerned with the methodical mapping of codes and meanings and more with the interrogation of pleasure and the self. Examples of this can be found in *The Pleasure of the Text* (1973), *Camera Lucida* (1980) and *Roland Barthes on Roland Barthes* (1975).

Barthes' attention to everyday life and popular texts from an academic point of view was groundbreaking. It is likely that his later work would have developed further in parallel with the **postmodernist** (p. 400) emphases on **identity** (p. 224) and pleasure. He remains, however, one of the seminal figures of postwar French thought, who influenced a variety of disciplines in the humanities and the social sciences.

Further reading

Mythologies is a great place to start Barthes.

Sontag, S. (ed.) (1982) *A Barthes Reader*, London: Cape.
Barthes, R. (1976) *Mythologies*, St Albans: Paladin.
Culler, J. (1983) *Barthes*, London: Fontana.

One of the best-known examples of semiotic analysis can be found in Roland **Barthes**' (1915–80) analysis of a photograph from the magazine *Paris Match* (1976). This photograph was published at the time when France was embroiled in the conflict over the decolonisation of Algeria. As will be seen, this context of conflict over empire is very significant to the meaning and analysis of the photograph. Barthes says: 'I am at the barber's, and a copy of *Paris-Match* is offered to me' (1976: 116). He continues, 'On the cover, a young Negro in a French uniform is saluting, with his eyes uplifted, probably fixed on the fold of the tricolour. All this is the *meaning* of the picture.' Barthes has identified the denotative meaning of the photograph. Having done this, Barthes develops his analysis. He says:

> But, whether naively or not, I see very well what it signifies to me: that France is a great Empire, that all her sons, without any colour discrimination, faithfully serve under her flag, and that there is no better answer to the detractors of an alleged colonialism than the zeal shown by this Negro in serving his so-called oppressors. (1976: 116)

After identifying these connotations of the photograph, Barthes locates his discussion within the language of semiotics:

> I am therefore again faced with a greater semiological system: there is a signifier, itself already formed within a previous system (a black soldier is giving the French salute); there is a signified (it is here a purposeful mixture of Frenchness and militariness); and finally a presence of the signified through the signifier.

The discussion of these photographs has introduced several important points about semiotics which can be summarised as follows:

1. Any image or text can be said to contain different layers or levels of meaning. In particular there is a distinction between *denotative* and *connotative* levels.

2. The nature of such meanings will depend on the context in which they are contained, or the surrounding circumstances. Meaning is *relational*.

3. Some of the levels of meaning or *codes* are relatively neutral, or objective, whereas others will be saturated with social meanings or discourses.

4. The recognition and elucidation of these different meanings involves analysis or *decoding* which often depends on the nature of the knowledge and experience brought to the analysis.

Using the language of semiotics, the photographs considered here are acting as signs. The sign consists of two elements: the signifier and the signified. The signifier is a sound, printed word or image, and the signified is a mental concept. This structure is represented in Figure 2.2.

Signifier + Signified = Sign

Figure 2.2 ▥ The structure of the sign.

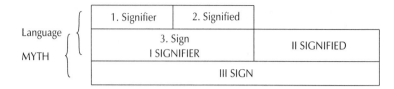

Figure 2.3 ▦ Language and myth. (Source: Barthes, 1976.)

The semiotic approach, which was developed from the study of language by de Saussure, has been applied widely. Thus, **Barthes** (p. 52) argues (1976: 113):

> take a black pebble: I can make it signify in several ways, it is a mere signifier; but if I weigh it with a definite signified (a death sentence, for instance, in an anonymous vote), it will become a sign.

Barthes shows how different levels of meaning are associated. This is shown in Figure 2.3.

This demonstrates the relationship between the denotative or connotative levels of meaning. Barthes also writes here about the distinction between language and myth. For Barthes, myths shore up existing structures of power, which favour the bourgeois class. Myths make what is historical or changeable appear to be natural and static and are thus ideological. Thus, the myth constructed in part by the photograph of the black soldier would seek to represent the Algerian conflict in such a way as to prevent change and decolonialisation.

2.3 | Advertising and representation

Signs are organised into systems which convey meaning; these systems are often called codes in structuralist and semiotic approaches (Fiske and Hartley, 1978: 59). One of the areas where such codes have been most studied is advertising (see, most importantly, Williamson, 1978), which forms the topic of this section.

2.3.1 | Different types of advertising

It is important to recognise the range of different types of advertising in contemporary societies. A useful categorisation of five different types has been suggested by G. Dyer (1982) who distinguishes between 'informational', 'simple', 'compound', 'complex' and 'sophisticated' advertisements.

Informational advertisements are like the classified advertisements found in newspapers. They are often brief and small, and may contain very little elaboration of the basic message. Simple advertisements are larger than informational advertisements, but they still contain relatively precise and clear information about a particular product or service. There is some degree of encouragement to buy the product. Many advertisements in the free local newpapers in Britain are of this type.

In compound advertisements there is more encouragement, which may be of a subtle kind. Pictures are more persuasive and facts may be contained in the copy that accompanies the advertisement. The picture is often 'glossy' and it is the intention of the advertiser that the reader will associate the product with the whole impression created by the picture. Advertisements in the magazines associated with newspapers are often of this kind. In complex advertisements the background takes over and the product merges into it. It is sometimes difficult to see precisely what is being sold. The whole image conveys a message of status, wealth and power. Sophisticated advertisements move beyond such complex advertisements and they often contain an attempt to draw upon hidden feelings through subtle associations. A deep-seated psychological appeal is often made.

2.3.2 │ A semiotic analysis of a sophisticated advertisement

A humorous semiotic analysis of a sophisticated advertisement (a contemporary advertisement for the cigarette Silk Cut) is contained in the extract from David Lodge's (1989) novel *Nice Work*. In this novel a university lecturer in English, Robyn Penrose, has been detailed to 'shadow' an industrialist, Vic Wilcox, with the aim of encouraging greater mutual understanding between academia and business. Much of the humour in the novel revolves around the interaction between the two main characters who represent very different worlds.

Box 2.4

A semiotic analysis of a Silk Cut advertisement

A typical instance of this was the furious argument they had about the Silk Cut advertisement. They were returning in his car from visiting a foundry in Derby that had been taken over by asset-strippers who were selling off an automatic core moulder Wilcox was interested in, though it had turned out to be too old-fashioned for his purpose. Every few miles, it seemed, they passed the same huge poster on roadside hoardings, a photographic depiction of a rippling expanse of purple silk in which there was a single slit, as if the material had been slashed with a razor. There were no words on the advertisement, except for the Government Health Warning about smoking. This ubiquitous image, flashing past at regular intervals, both irritated and intrigued Robyn, and she began to do her semiotic stuff on the deep structure hidden beneath its bland surface.

It was in the first instance a kind of riddle. That is to say, in order to decode it,

→

you had to know that there was a brand of cigarettes called Silk Cut. The poster was the iconic representation of a missing name, like a rebus. But the icon was also a metaphor. The shimmering silk, with its voluptuous curves and sensuous texture, obviously symbolized the female body, and the elliptical slit, fore-grounded by a lighter colour showing through, was still more obviously a vagina. The advert thus appealed to both sensual and sadistic impulses, the desire to mutilate as well as penetrate the female body.

Vic Wilcox spluttered with outraged derision as she expounded this inter-pretation. He smoked a different brand, himself, but it was as if he felt his whole philosophy of life was threatened by Robyn's analysis of the advert. 'You must have a twisted mind to see all that in a perfectly harmless bit of cloth,' he said.

'What's the point of it, then?' Robyn challenged him. 'Why use cloth to advertise cigarettes?'

'Well, that's the name of 'em, isn't it? Silk Cut. It's a picture of the name. Nothing more or less.'

'Suppose they'd used a picture of a roll of silk cut in half – would that do just as well?'

'I suppose so. Yes, why not?'

'Because it would look like a penis cut in half, that's why.'

He forced a laugh to cover his embarrassment. 'Why can't you people take things at their face value?'

'What people are you referring to?'

'Highbrows. Intellectuals. You're always trying to find hidden meanings in things. Why? A cigarette is a cigarette. A piece of silk is a piece of silk. Why not leave it at that?'

'When they're represented they acquire additional meanings,' said Robyn. 'Signs are never innocent. Semiotics teaches us that.'

'Semi-what?'

'Semiotics. The study of signs.'

'It teaches us to have dirty minds, if you ask me.'

'Why d'you think the wretched cigarettes were called Silk Cut in the first place?'

'I dunno. It's just a name, as good as any other.'

'"Cut" has something to do with the tobacco, doesn't it? The way the tobacco leaf is cut. Like "Player's Navy Cut" – my uncle Walter used to smoke them.'

'Well, what if he does?' Vic said warily.

'But silk has nothing to do with tobacco. It's a metaphor, a metaphor that means something like, "smooth as silk". Somebody in an advertising agency dreamt up the name "Silk Cut" to suggest a cigarette that wouldn't give you a sore throat or a hacking cough or lung cancer. But after a while the public got used to the name, the word "Silk" ceased to signify, so they decided to have an advertising

→

campaign to give the brand a high profile again. Some bright spark at the agency came up with the idea of rippling silk with a cut in it. The original metaphor is now represented literally. But new metaphorical connotations accrue – sexual ones. Whether they were consciously intended or not doesn't really matter. It's a good example of the perpetual sliding of the signified under the signifier, actually.'

Wilcox chewed on this for a while, then said, 'Why do women smoke them, then, eh?' His triumphant expression showed that he thought this was a knock-down argument. 'If smoking Silk Cut is a form of aggravated rape, as you try to make out, how come women smoke 'em too?'

'Many women are masochistic by temperament,' said Robyn. 'They've learned what's expected of them in a patriarchial society.'

'Ha!' Wilcox exclaimed, tossing back his head. 'I might have known you'd have some daft answer.'

'I don't know why you're so worked up,' said Robyn. 'It's not as if you smoke Silk Cut yourself.'

'No, I smoke Marlboros. Funnily enough, I smoke them because I like the taste.'

'They are the ones that have the lone cowboy ads, aren't they?'

'I suppose that makes me a repressed homosexual, does it?'

'No, it's a very straightforword metonymic message.'

'Metowhat?'

'Metonymic. One of the fundamental tools of semiotics is the distinction between metaphor and metonymy. D'you want me to explain it to you?'

'It'll pass the time,' he said.

'Metaphor is a figure of speech based on similarity, whereas metonymy is based on contiguity. In metaphor you substitute something *like* the thing you mean for the thing itself, whereas in metonymy you substitute some attribute or cause or effect of the thing for the thing itself.'

'I don't understand a word you're saying.'

'Well, take one of your moulds. The bottom bit is called the drag because it's dragged across the floor and the top bit is called the cope because it covers the bottom bit.'

'I told *you* that.'

'Yes, I know. What you didn't tell me was that "drag" is a metonymy and "cope" is a metaphor.'

Vic grunted. 'What difference does it make?'

'It's just a question of understanding how language works. I thought you were interested in how things work.'

'I don't see what it's got to do with cigarettes.'

'In the case of the Silk Cut poster, the picture signifies the female body metaphorically: the slit in the silk is *like* a vagina – '

→

Vic flinched at the word. 'So you say.'

'All holes, hollow spaces, fissures and folds represent the female genitals.'

'Prove it.'

'Freud proved it, by his successful analysis of dreams,' said Robyn. 'But the Marlboro ads don't use any metaphors. That's probably why you smoke them, actually.'

'What do you mean?' he said suspiciously.

'You don't have any sympathy with the metaphorical way of looking at things. A cigarette is a cigarette as far as you are concerned.'

'Right.'

'The Marlboro ad doesn't disturb that naïve faith in the stability of the signified. It establishes a metonymic connection – completely spurious of course, but realistically plausible – between smoking that brand and the healthy, heroic, outdoor life of the cowboy. Buy the cigarette and you buy the life-style, or the fantasy of living it.'

'Rubbish!' said Wilcox. 'I hate the country and the open air. I'm scared to go in a field with a cow in it.'

'Well then, maybe it's the solitariness of the cowboy in the ads that appeals to you. Self-reliant, independent, very macho.'

'I've never heard such a lot of balls in all my life,' said Vic Wilcox, which was strong language coming from him.

'Balls – now that's an interesting expression . . .' Robyn mused.

'Oh no!' he groaned.

'When you say a man "has balls", approvingly, it's a metonymy, whereas if you say something is a "lot of balls", or "a balls-up", it's a sort of metaphor. The metonymy attributes value to the testicles whereas the metaphor uses them to degrade something else.'

'I can't take any more of this,' said Vic. 'D'you mind if I smoke? Just a plain, ordinary cigarette?'

'If I can have Radio Three on,' said Robyn.

Lodge (1989)

In addition to conveying Robyn's attachment to the power of sustained rational analysis, this extract also introduces the important theme of gender.

2.3.3 | Advertising and gender

A number of writers have drawn attention to the way in which advertisements deploy particular representations of gender relations. Feminist writers have suggested that they often contain grossly caricatured or stereotyped representations of women.

An important theme, which is developed later in this chapter, concerns the way in which advertisements and other forms of representation construct the spectator to view them. A key idea here is that when we look at particular images they are placing us in particular positions from which to read them. This is important as this may be central to the process of operation of ideology, in that we are placed in certain restricted positions, which we do not reflect upon (see also sections 9.3.3 and 9.3.4). Thus the discussion of the advertisement in the extract below shows how particular representations of gender are deployed in such a way as to make an appeal to men.

In these approaches to gender and advertising, advertising represents or constructs particular images which contribute to the operation of power in contemporary

---

Box **2.5**

The invisible man

This woman is looking at a man (who may coincide with the reader: he is drawn in): her words are in reply to his 'what will you drink?' Her dress is unbuttoned provocatively, indicating beyond doubt that the invisible character *is* male; the final factor is the chess set visible behind her, implying a second person, an intimacy, yet defining her intellectual quality in relation to the man, as does her decided preference for a certain drink. The message is that she is at home in a man's world, yet is sexy; and not in a passive way, as is shown by her unbuttoning of her dress. Women (in media) are 'entirely constituted by the gaze of man'. This woman *is* alone, *is* decisive and intellectual: 'Femininity is pure, free, powerful; but man is everywhere around, he presses on all sides, he makes everything exist; he is in all eternity the creative absence....' The man in this picture is nowhere and everywhere, a pervasive presence defining and determining everything, and in whose terms the woman must define herself. She is doomed to see herself through *his* eyes, describe herself in his language.

Williamson (1978: 80)

societies. Further evidence of the gendering of advertisements can be found in the work of Goffman (1979) who uses these examples to examine the nature of gender display, rather than in a discussion of advertising *per se* (Smith, 1996). The implication of some of these such discussions is that a critique or unmasking of these gender representations will contribute to the fight against such gender inequality or oppression. Some aspects of contemporary cultural politics (see Chapter 6) were initially based around such premises. However, more recent approaches have tended to suggest that advertising has actually become very powerful in contemporary societies as a number of different institutions have adopted practices and forms of **representation** (p. 61) that were once the domain of advertising. Thus in the phrase of Andrew Wernick (1991), we increasingly live in a 'promotional culture'.

2.3.4 | Promotional culture

Wernick's (1991) argument is that very many contemporary institutions and practices have become rather like advertising. Thus, Wernick examines the promotional strategies of universities and in politics to draw out their similarities to advertising. For example, all universities now have logos, similar to multinational corporations. Furthermore, politics is now played out in terms of 'sound-bites' which are rather like advertising slogans (see further Chapter 6). It is not the detail of the case that matters but the snappy phrase that will attract attention. Prime Minister's question time in the British House of Commons is often devoted to the exchange of these remarks by the main participants. In this sense, advertising has become increasingly important, not just because of its increased prevalence, but because of the influence of the representation strategies it embodies on many different aspects of contemporary cultural and social life. We can now examine some of these issues of power in rather more detail.

2.4 | Language, representation, power and inequality

Representation and communication of cultural meaning takes place through language because of two sets of standardisations: the customary meanings attached to words and the customary ways of speaking in given social and cultural settings. In both instances membership of the language community may be tested or decided according to the familiarity of a language user with the conventions of use. In contrast to the sentiments of the quotation from Leavis (see Box 2.3 earlier), language use in this formulation is seen as *problematic* rather than automatic. This approach owes much to the development of social and cultural theorising which stresses the partial and contested nature of social life; such theorising is often labelled as **postmodern** (p. 400) but it also characterises much feminist analysis, as well as race, ethnic and class analyses.

These ideas, which criticise both the traditionalist emphasis of Leavis and the sometimes almost 'mechanical' structuralist and semiotic approaches, have been influential in much cultural studies. A key source for them is the work of the Russian

Defining concept **2.1**

Representation and realism

Raymond Williams (1983b: 296) points to two meanings of 'represent' that have developed through history. A representation, he suggests, can mean either 'a symbol or image, or the process of presenting to the eye or the mind'. The meaning of symbol or image is particularly important. A representation re-presents or stands for something else. As Williams explains, this meaning is complicated by the development of the idea of an 'accurate reproduction'. Hence, a photograph represents that which was arranged before the camera, but is also often thought to be an accurate reproduction of it. We are familiar with the common phrase 'the camera never lies'. However, we should also be aware that photographs may be cropped or doctored to produce a particular meaning.

Realism in art or culture seems to be simply captured in the idea that it attempts 'to show things as they really are' (Lovell, 1980). However, such simplicity is illusory and realism has been hotly debated. Berger (1972) points to the way in which realism in art develops at a particular historical moment. Likewise Watt (1963) illuminates the beginnings of the realist novel, which used real names for characters and was set in recognisable places and so on. Some versions of realism attempt to capture the details of everyday life in all its aspects. This approach was labelled naturalism in the nineteenth century. The novels of Zola are held to be an important example. Other forms of realism have worked through the practice of typicality. It does not matter, it may be suggested, that all life is not shown (indeed, how could it be?) as long as recognisable types are used for characters and events. However, some **Marxist** (p. 97) approaches to realism often criticise these ideas, as they suggest that there is some deeper truth or reality to be known which will not be captured by conventional realist depiction. Somewhat paradoxically, the attempt to capture this reality is often through avant-garde methods. Debates between the Marxist critics Lukács and Brecht pointed up some of these issues, as did the later work of MacCabe. The latter used a very wide definition of realism, which he then criticised as being unable to capture the real.

Despite the difficulties involved in defining realism, the term is much used in everyday discussions about fiction. Being authentic or real is often seen as praiseworthy and being melodramatic a criticism. However, such simplifications evade the difficulties surrounding the terms. For example, soap operas are often criticised for their inadequate representation of the real: too much happens, they do not contain enough ethnic minorities, whole rich families share one house and so on. They are not empirically or objectively real. However, as Ang (1985) in her discussion of viewers' reactions to the American soap *Dallas* shows, these representations may convey ideas and feelings that viewers feel to be subjectively real or important. They may be emotionally realist. Criticising or praising realism is not to be done lightly without a clear definition of the meaning of the term.

Further reading

Lovell, T. (1980) *Pictures of Reality: Aesthetics, Politics and Pleasure*, London: BFI.
Hill, J. (1986) *Sex, Class and Realism: British Cinema 1956–1963*, London: BFI.
Williams, R. (1983b) *Keywords: A Vocabulary of Culture and Society*, London: Fontana.

Marxist analyst of language V.N. Volosinov (1973) (see **Bakhtin**, p. 202). Volosinov argues that language has to be understood in social context and in social activity. It is this stress on social activity that is perhaps of central importance to subsequent developments. As **Raymond Williams** (p. 5) argues:

> We then find not a reified 'language' and 'society' but an active *social language*. Nor (to glance back at positivist and orthodox materialist theory) is this language a simple 'reflection' or 'expression' of 'material reality'. What we have, rather, is a grasping of this reality through language, which as practical consciousness is saturated by and saturates all social activity, including productive activity. And, since this grasping is social and continuous (as distinct from the abstract encounters of 'man' and 'his world', or 'consciousness' and 'reality', or 'language' and 'material existence'), it occurs within an active and changing society.   (Williams, 1977: 37)

Williams took these ideas very seriously in his own work – so much so that he devoted extensive sections of many of his own books to the consideration of the history and development in social context of important concepts. The zenith of this work came in his book *Keywords* (Williams, 1983b), which appears to be a dictionary, but is actually an investigation of the contested meaning and social import of some terms and concepts that Williams takes to be central in contemporary social and political struggles. As Eagleton (1983: 117) argues, concerning Volosinov but which could equally be applied to Williams, 'It was not simply a matter of asking "what the sign meant", but of investigating its varied history, as conflicting social groups, classes, individuals and discourses sought to appropriate it and imbue it with their own meanings.'

2.4.1 | Language and power

Cultural politics (see Chapter 6) introduces the dimension of inequalities in **power** (p. 94) and authority in cultural forms and the *contested* nature of cultural practice; it is these concerns that drive the analysis of language when it is linked with the domains of class, race or gender. Thus, as will be suggested below, language has become increasingly politicised and implicated in social struggles, especially in the arguments around 'political correctness'. Consequently, argument has moved from seeing language as a neutral instrument for objectively representing and communicating the views of a uniform grouping to seeing language as a politically and culturally charged medium over which groups wrestle for control.

Benedict Anderson (1991) drew attention to the role of print languages in enabling the rise and spread of nationalism. At present, it is sufficient to single out that thread of Anderson's argument that says that the invention of print language gave a 'new fixity' to language and created languages of power; particular forms of language became dominant. Spoken languages that were close in form and vocabulary to printed language were the most prestigious (Anderson, 1991: 44–5). In this way written language came to be viewed as more 'correct' than spoken language and oral communication was, and often still is, evaluated socially according to its degree of resemblance to written language (Street, 1993; Leech *et al.*, 1982). In this process of evaluation, ways of speaking such as dialect (local language), accent, choice of words and use of grammar were all assessed and ranked against the social conventions of language as typified in written language (Street, 1993; Labov, 1973). These rankings were extended to other areas of social experience and, through the overlaying of social action by cultural ways of speaking, became a symbolic representation of ways of life – a situation summed up by Pulgram in the following way:

> We can recognise a person by his speech quite apart from the intelligence or intelligibility of his utterance. The mere physical features of his speech, conditioned automatically and by habits, suffice for identification. If, in addition, what he says and how he says it, in other words his style, provide further clues all the better. The what and how are socially conditioned, however, by the speaker's education, surroundings, profession etc. Directors and actors of radio plays who cannot convey any part of the contents of the performance visually are very skilful in the art of voice characterisation. Even the psyche; the temperament of a person finds expression in his speech, to say nothing of his temporary moods and every hearer makes a certain value judgement of a speaker simply on the basis of 'what he talks like'.   (Pulgram, 1954, in Street, 1993)

A cultural studies approach reminds us that what is being described is not simply **difference** (p. 138) but hierarchies of prestige which are often also hierarchies of **power** (p. 94). Street (1993) alerts us to the resonances of words: he argues that the use of the word 'one' as in 'one knows' implies status; the use of the word 'we' can express solidarity but when used by a doctor, as in 'and how are we feeling today?', it can imply power and status (Street, 1993: 71).

The specialised lexicons and forms of speech that characterise certain social groupings serve to facilitate communication among those who belong to the group but exclude those who are outside and cannot speak the language. It is debatable whether specialised lexicons (semantic domains) can be ranked in terms of functional use – some being more useful than others (see sections 2.4.2, 2.4.3 and 2.4.4); but what is certain is that it is possible to rank the social groupings who use particular semantic domains, so, for example, the professional language of doctors and lawyers is more prestigious than that of youth groups (see below and Chapter 8). Language as a communicative form which represents, constructs and reproduces social and cultural inequality is the focus of the next sections.

2.4.2 | Language and class

The work of the sociologist Basil Bernstein (1924–) is an influential example of research linking social class, language and speech. Educational policies and practices in Britain and the United States in the 1960s were much affected in their design and implementation by his explanations of the educational failure of young people. In essence, Bernstein argued that his researches showed that lower-class members of English society spoke a language that was *restricted* in comparison with the *elaborated* code of the middle classes. This restricted code handicapped them in their quest for social and economic betterment because schools, which were seen by Bernstein as the chief agency for social mobility, required the use of elaborated codes. Elaborated codes were necessary for the intellectual activity of learning and for the social and political purposes of receiving favourable recognition from teachers. Restricted or public speech codes are characterised by the following:

1. Short, grammatically simple, often unfinished sentences with a poor syntactical form (stressing the active voice).
2. Simple and repetitive use of conjunctions (so, then, because).
3. Little use of subordinate clauses to break down the initial categories of the dominant subject.
4. Inability to hold a formal subject through a speech sequence: thus a dislocated informational content is facilitated.
5. Rigid and limited use of adjectives and adverbs.
6. Infrequent use of impersonal pronouns as subjects of conditional clauses.
7. Frequent use of statements where the reason and conclusion are confounded to produce a categoric statement.
8. A large number of statements/phrases that signal a requirement for the previous speech sequence to be reinforced: Wouldn't it? You see? You know? etc. This process is termed sympathetic circularity.
9. Individual selection from a group of idiomatic phrases or sequence will frequently occur.
10. The individual qualification is implicit in the sentence organisation: it is a language of implicit meaning.

Elaborated or formal speech codes are characterised by the following:

1. Accurate grammatical order and syntax regulate what is said.
2. Logical modifications and stress are mediated through a grammatically complex sentence construction, especially through the use of a range of conjunctions and subordinate clauses.
3. Frequent use of prepositions that indicate logical relationships as well as prepositions that indicate temporal and spatial contiguity.
4. Frequent use of the personal pronoun 'I'.
5. A discriminative selection from a range of adjectives and adverbs.
6. Individual qualification which is verbally mediated through the structure and relationships within and between sentences.
7. Expressive symbolism which discriminates between meanings within speech sequences rather than reinforcing dominant words or phrases, or accompanying the sequence in a diffuse, generalised manner.
8. Language use which points to the possibilities inherent in a conceptual hierarchy for the organising of experience. (Bernstein, 1961: 169f., in Dittmar, 1976)

Bernstein revised the characteristics of restricted and elaborated codes a number of times in the light of empirical and theoretical work and eventually abandoned them. It is important to note that the changing configurations reveal the difficulties of identifying a set of inherent characteristics of cultural forms, especially when, as in this case, they are linked in opposition to each other.

Bernstein's depiction of the relationship between language and class is reminiscent of the Sapir–Whorf hypothesis; indeed it is possible to recast Bernstein's analysis in terms of lower- and middle-class groups occupying different 'thought worlds'. Both hypotheses give weight to the effects of socialisation in establishing taken-for-granted ways of seeing the world that form the texture of thought for group members. And in both cases ways of thinking are a response to socioeconomic environments. Bernstein's work is distinctive in that it is looking at language use within an apparently homogeneous language group, whereas Sapir's and Whorf's studies relate to quite different and distinct language groups; the most startling difference for our purposes is Bernstein's linking of speech and language with the structured inequalities of the English class system. For Bernstein, class-based language is not simple variation but reflects the hierarchies of the English class system with the consequence that some languages are socially and culturally dominant. Success comes to those who speak the dominant language and use its skills. Bernstein argues that formal or elaborated language is better than public or restricted language because it is constituted through the operation of logic and abstract thought – qualities that are functionally necessary for learning. Lower-class language is more context bound and encourages the assertion of uniformity, not the appreciation of difference. In this sense lower-class language is a less competent form than middle-class language and its speakers and users are not able to benefit from education which requires discrimination and logic. Bernstein's analysis suggests that the class base of English society is perpetuated and made visible through language; language both **represents** (p. 61) and *constitutes* the class system.

New emphases in cultural and social theory, more empirical studies and changes in policy making and implementation have called into question many of the conclusions of Bernstein's work. Compensatory education was recommended for children who had allegedly suffered linguistic deprivation, a condition said to be rooted in the home life of the child and in particular in the mother–child relationship. Such policies have now been switched to working with schools to enable them to be more accommodating to all children, not just those with favoured cultural characteristics. This switch has been prompted by empirical and theoretical work which has shown that all languages are characterised by the capacity for logical argument and abstract thought; the privileging of one form of language against others is a *political* and not a linguistic act. Consequently the reasons that children fail must be sought in the realms of social and political economy. It is in these areas that the work of Bernstein remains influential, as his linking of social structure with language opened up a wider investigation into ideas of dominant cultures and their formation, transmission and maintenance. By drawing attention to the social and political dimensions of cultural forms Bernstein rebutted the contention that language is simply a technical device for the representation and communication of culture.

2.4.3 | Language, race and ethnicity

In 1966 Bereiter and Engelmann applied Bernstein's theories to the language of black children in the United States and concluded that 'the poor intellectual ability of Black lower class children is reflected in their inadequate speech' (Dittmar, 1976: 80) and the children showed 'a total lack of ability to use language as a device for acquiring and processing information. Language for them is unwieldy and not very useful' (Bereiter and Engelmann, 1966: 39, in Dittmar, 1976: 81). These conclusions were challenged by Labov (1972b) from the findings of a number of studies that he conducted on the use of non-standard English by black youths. His work demonstrated that the language of black youth (Black English Vernacular or BEV) was different from that of middle-class speech forms; however, to describe BEV as a poor language was simply middle-class ideology. Labov criticised the data collection methods of Bereiter and Engelmann's study on two counts: (a) the data did not describe natural black language use despite purporting to do so – in fact the material gathered was a set of responses to issues set by the researchers; (b) the interviewer in the study was a white adult – Labov contends that such a person would be seen by black youth as an authority figure, a representative of a dominant other culture, to whom they would not speak freely and openly. Although the criticism is a methodological one, it is another reminder that language and language use are political and that it is important to treat critically any claims that language speaks for everyone, everywhere, at all times.

The fabrication of language as a natural, politically neutral device which 'tells things as they are' is one of the means by which language and truth are associated. There is in English culture a widespread belief that nature and the natural are truthful and reliable since they are apparently outside the realm of human manipulation; language is, as we have seen, felt to be part of nature as it is so instinctive and taken for granted. It is a short step from these assumptions to see language as truth. This discourse about language offers the opportunity to know truth through language. In this reasoning language is extremely powerful for it both constitutes truth and guarantees truth. In this formula-tion, questions about language use and 'who speaks for whom?' are matters of great significance for whoever gives the account is able to pronounce the truth of things. Speakers and writers of non-standard language may suffer the fate of others claiming to speak for them or of their own accounts of their situation being declared untrue or unworthy of attention. Such practices have marked the discipline of literary criticism where, for example, writings from former colonial countries written in the metropolitan language have been declared not to be literature (Ashcroft *et al.*, 1989). This verdict is delivered on two counts: (a) local variants of the metropolitan language are not legit-imate for the writing of literature; (b) writing about colonial or postcolonial society from the experiences of native peoples is not a legitimate subject for literature. This example serves as another illustration of language as 'the medium through which a hierarchical structure of power is perpetuated and the medium through which conceptions of "truth", "order", and "reality" become established' (Ashcroft *et al.*, 1989).

In the face of the imperialising cultural power of metropolitan language the writers and speakers of local variations of the language are encouraged by their compatriots to

> *Box* **2.6**
>
> # Inglan is a bitch
>
> w'en mi jus' come to Landan toun
> mi use to work pan di andahgroun
> but workin' pan di andahgroun
> y'u don't get fi know your way aroun'
>
> Inglan is a bitch
> dere's no escapin' it
> Inglan is a bitch
> dere's no runnin' whey fram it
>
> Linton Kwesi Johnson

treat the language as if it was their own. They are urged to shrug off the metropolitan meanings and associations of the language and to appropriate it for their own use and by these actions 'make language "bear the burden" of one's own cultural experience' (Ashcroft *et al.*, 1989: 38) in order to '"convey in a language that is not one's own the spirit that is one's own"' (Rao, 1938: vii, in Ashcroft *et al.*, 1989: 39). An example of this can be seen in the extract from the poem 'Inglan is a Bitch' by the black British poet Linton Kwesi Johnson (see Box 2.6).

The work of Edward Said (1993) covers the same territory of cultural imperialism as cited above albeit with a perspective that illuminates how writers from metropolitan countries have, through their language, created an image of 'other societies' which is a product of language. His argument is that, alongside the devaluing of local culture and cultural products of 'other societies', a parallel process has taken place in which metropolitan versions of these societies have been configured. These versions are in accord with the imaginings of metropolitan society, not with the experienced realities of native social actors. The example serves as a further illustration of the power of language to constitute the object of regard and simultaneously affirm the truth of that regard.

The force of the comments about the political use of language moves the discussion away from language as a technical instrument communicating politically neutral information to one that stresses that language takes its meaning from the social settings in which it operates. When it is used by the powerful it may be a subtle instrument of oppression, the more so because of its apparently neutral and natural attributes. In these circumstances it is no surprise that aspirant national groups seek to recreate or revivify local languages to symbolise their identity and carry the weight of their political ambition. The revival of Hebrew in the creation of the nation-state of Israel is one example; language as a political issue in Canada, Spain, France and Wales are other examples. In all these cases the intent is to rid themselves of **identities** (p. 224) imposed by the language of others. Such processes have also been central to the debates about 'political correctness' and language in the 1990s. So there has been a concern to change language use to eliminate oppressive uses and implications. Some professional groups

Box **2.7**

BSA Guidelines

BRITISH SOCIOLOGICAL ASSOCIATION
GUIDELINES ON ANTI-SEXIST LANGUAGE

It is BSA policy that non-sexist language should be used in its journals, in conference papers and in the delivery of such papers at conferences and so on. These guidelines are intended to assist BSA members in avoiding sexist language by showing people some of the forms it takes and by suggesting anti-sexist alternatives. They will help readers to consider the extent to which and the ways in which we either challenge or reproduce inaccurate, sexist and heterosexist assumptions in our work. The guidelines will be relevant to teachers, students and authors in sociology.

'HE/MAN' LANGUAGE

Do not use *'man'* to mean humanity in general. There are alternatives:

SEXIST	ANTI-SEXIST
man/mankind	person, people, human beings
mankind	men and women, humanity, humankind

When reference to both sexes is intended, a large number of phrases use the word man or other masculine equivalents (e.g., *'father'*) and a large number of nouns use the suffix *'man'*, thereby excluding women from the picture we present of the world. These should be replaced by more precise non-sexist alternatives as listed below:

SEXIST	ANTI-SEXIST
the man in the street	people in general, people
layman	lay person, non expert
man-made	synthetic, artificial, manufactured
the rights of man	peoples'/citizens' rights; the rights of the individual
Chairman	Chair
foreman	supervisor
manpower	workforce, staff, labour power, employees
craftsman/men	craftsperson/people
manning	staffing, working, running

→

to a man	everyone, unanimously, without exception
manhours	workhours
the working man	worker, working people
models of man	models of the person
one man show	one person show
policeman/fireman	police officer/ fire-fighter
forefathers	ancestors
founding fathers	founders
old masters	classic art/artists
masterful	domineering; very skilful
master copy	top copy/original
Dear Sirs	Dear Sir/Madam
disseminate, broadcast	inform, publicise
seminal	classical, formative

The 'generic' 'man' is often accompanied by the 'generic' 'he'. The 'generic he' should be avoided. Both feminine and masculine pronouns can be used where appropriate: *he/she, s/he, his/her,* etc. Alternative strategies include (a) the use of the plural and (b) the omission of third person pronouns entirely:

(a) **SEXIST:**   Each respondent was asked whether **he** wished to participate in the survey.

   ANTI-SEXIST: Respondents were asked whether **they** wished to participate in the survey.

(b) **SEXIST:**   The child should be given ample time to familiarise **himself** with the test material.

   ANTI-SEXIST: Ample time should be allowed for the child to become familiar with the test material.

BSA Anti-Racist Language: Guidance for Good Practice

The following represents comments on the usage of terms by social scientists when referring to work based around ethnicity. It is by no means an exhaustive list, nor a definitive guide. As social scientists should be aware, language is not only powerful as it structures and reinforces beliefs and prejudices, but it is also dynamic. As such, it must be recognised that these and other terms will re-emerge, be revised or disappear at a faster rate than the guidelines may be published. In addition, these guidelines should act as an interchange within the social science community, so that comments will be taken into account and reviewed periodically. The BSA grants free rights to reproduce these Guidelines; we ask that the BSA is acknowledged. If you have any comments for amendments to these Guidelines, please contact the BSA Office at the address given at the end of these Guidelines.

→

African-Caribbean: This term is gradually replacing the term Afro-Caribbean to refer to Caribbean peoples and those of Caribbean origin who are of African descent. It should also be noted that there is now some evidence to suggest that the term should not be hyphenated and that indeed, the differences between such groups may mean the terms should be kept separate.

American: When referring to America, it is important to be aware of the fact that there is a North America and a South America – not just the USA. Consequently, when referring to the USA, it is best to be explicit about this.

Asian: Generally refers to people from the Asian sub-continent – namely, India, Pakistan, Bangladesh and Kashmir. However, under some circumstances there may be objections to bracketing together a wide variety of different cultural and ethnic groups often with very different positions within British society. Also, some members of particular ethnic groups may object to being referred to by their 'country of origin' when they have been living for several generations in Britain.

Black: Black is a concept that embraces people who experience structural and institutional discrimination because of their skin colour and is often used politically to refer to people of African, Caribbean and South Asian origin to imply solidarity against racism. The term originally took on political connotations with the rise of black activism in the USA in the 1960s when it was reclaimed as a source of pride and identity in opposition to the many negative connotations relating to the word 'black' in the English language (black leg, black list etc.). In the UK however, there is an on-going debate about the use of this term to define South Asian peoples because of the existence of diverse South Asian cultural identities. Some Asian groups in Britain object to the use of the word 'black' being applied to them and some would argue that it also confuses a number of ethnic groups which should be treated separately – Pakistanis, Bangladeshis, Indians and so on.

Whilst there are many differences between and within each of the groups, the inclusive term black refers to those who have a shared history of European colonialism, neo-colonialism, imperialism, ethnocentrism and racism. One solution to this is to refer to 'black peoples', 'black communities' etc., in the plural to imply that there is a variety of such groups. It is also important to be aware of the fact that in some contexts 'black' can also be used in a racist sense. The capitalisation of the letter 'B' in the term 'Black British', 'British Asian' are shifting ground and it should be stressed that social scientists need to be very clear that the use of these terms does not prioritise nor indeed conflate ethnicity and citizenship.

British: Many would argue that the one way to denote minority ethnic groups in

→

this country would be to describe them as 'British Asians', 'Chinese British' etc. One advantage is that by referring to two ethnicities it avoids any suggestion that a person has to choose between them for their identity. However, the idea of 'British' also implies a false sense of unity. Many Scots, Welsh and Irish resist being identified as British and the territory denoted by the term contains a wide variety of cultures, language and religions.

Civilised/Civilisation: This term can still carry racist overtones which derive from a colonialist perception of the world. It is often associated with social Darwinist thought and is full of implicit value judgements and ignorance of the history of the non-industrialised world. However, in some cases, such as the work of Norbert Elias, civilisation takes on a different meaning without racist overtones.

Coloured: This term is regarded as outdated in the UK and should be avoided as it is generally viewed as offensive to many black people. When applied to South Africa, the term reflects issues of ethnic divide and apartheid, and needs to be contextualised and used with specificity. In the United States of America, the term 'people of colour' is often used as a form self-reference for people who suffer from racism and discrimination on the basis of visible skin colour difference to the white anglo-saxon (WASP) political majority population.

BSA Anti-Racist Guidelines for Good Practice: March 1997

now offer clear guidance on these matters, as the extracts from the *British Sociological Association Guidelines* show (see Box 2.7).

2.4.4 | Language and gender

Elsewhere in this volume (Chapter 1) there is discussion of language as an expression of patriarchy. Just as postcolonial writers and speakers of non-standard language have protested that their voices are made inaudible or declared illegitimate by the power of dominant language, so women also assert that they are voiceless in language. As in the case of language and class discussed earlier in this chapter, the consideration of language and gender serves as a reminder that a language is not necessarily one's own even if one is a native speaker. The meaning and the power of language is determined by social practice; even a native speaker may be mute or dumb in certain settings. The suggestion is that this is the fate of women language users.

In this respect, Edwin Ardener (1974) suggested that 'women are often more "inarticulate" than men' by which he meant that the arenas of public discourse are typically dominated by men and the language of public discourse is 'encoded' with male meanings (Ardener, 1974: viii). The implication of this for women is that they must struggle to be heard and that they must learn male language.

Robin Lakoff (1975) is an influential early writer in the discussion of women and language; her book *Language and Women's Place*, which was based on the observation of her own and her friends' language use, set an agenda for the discussion of the topic, arguing that women's language is characteristically weak in form (not in content) and that this fits well with women's subordinate position *vis-à-vis* men. The characterisation of women's language as weak rests on Lakoff's assertion that women's speech has more 'tag' forms than men's speech. A typical example of a tag form is the statement 'It's a nice day, isn't it?'; in this example 'isn't it?' is the tag. The speaker is not seeking information but confirmation; there is the desire to achieve consensus with the hearer and the hearer is invited to participate in the statement and share the belief. Lakoff's contention is that women's speech is weaker than men's, less decisive and functionally less useful. Labov (1966), in his research on language and class, noted a gendered difference in language use which suggested that women were more deferential and less assertive than men. He found that lower middle-class women used fewer stigmatised forms than men of the same social class. The picture that emerges from this writing is one of highly gendered speech: men are said to use competitive, aggressive speech while women's speech is cooperative. Deborah Tannen (1990) argues that characteristics of the two forms of speech are so distinct that talk between men and women really represents a form of cross-cultural communication. In the language of the Sapir–Whorf hypothesis men and women inhabit different thought worlds. The characteristics of male and female talk (Tannen 1990) are as follows:

Male Talk	*Female Talk*
Hierarchies	Network
Independence	Intimacy
Information	Sharing
Attention	Symmetry
Big talk	Small talk
Superiority	Inferiority
Powerful	Powerless

The issue of cross-cultural communication between men and women is addressed in the cartoon by Jacky Fleming in Figure 2.4.

2.4.5 | Language as culture: language as power

Deborah Tannen's work introduces the consideration of an important issue in the study of language, communication and representation. The discussion of language using a sociolinguistic model has alerted us to how language is embedded in social practice and has drawn attention to the ways in which language is suffused with the significant structuring principles of society. We have examined language in relation to class, race, ethnicity and gender; arguably, there is also a case for looking at age. You may wish to consider this as a project as a way of putting into operation some of the ideas and analysis that you have been presented with in this chapter. The sociolinguistic analysis that has been employed in this chapter has linked language with hierarchies of power; the argument has been about the politics of language expressed metaphorically in

Figure 2.4 ▦ Communication between men and women. (Source: Fleming, 1992.)

terms of domination and subordination. Although Tannen's findings are broadly consistent with those of Ardener and Lakoff, her interpretation stresses cultural **difference** (p. 138) rather than super- and subordination. She does not see women's language as inferior to men's as, for her, the two languages are directed towards the creation of different **discourses** (p. 30) about the world. This difference does not imply that women's talk is trivial or less functionally useful than men's; indeed she would argue that women's talk has many positive virtues, stressing, as it does, inclusion rather than exclusion and cooperation rather than competition.

The possibility of interpreting gendered speech as **difference** rather than hierarchy reminds us that language is expressive and hence open to interpretation. Any discussion of language as a meaningful system must take account of the intentions of those who utter language and those who hear the utterances – in other words, how speech acts are transmitted and received. The ethnography of speaking is one technique that explores how meaning is generated and evaluated in speech acts.

2.4.6 | The ethnography of speaking

Ethnographic inquiry seeks to understand and account for social behaviour from the actors' points of view. The methods are observation and inquiry; data are interpreted in terms of a wide social field – the intention is to note the ways in which social behaviour is linked to events, ideas or institutions that are present in the field of inquiry, whether explicitly or implicitly. The ethnography of speaking examines speech acts, both naturally occurring and experimental (see also Labov, 1972b) in order to determine the principles that generate and shape speech in a given social situation. In undertaking the research, very detailed information is needed about the participants – their background, interests, social and personal characteristics, their interest in the speech encounter, etc. – and about the setting – the purposes and intent of the speech

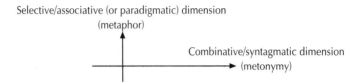

Figure 2.5 ▦ Syntagmatic and paradigmatic axes. (Source: Fiske and Hartley, 1978: 50.)

encounter, where it is taking place, the relationships between those who are participating, etc. One of the research methods of ethnographic investigations of language use is to examine the paradigmatic choices made by speakers in speech acts.

The model of paradigmatic and syntagmatic chains used in cultural analysis have been taken from work in structural linguistics. The model has been used extensively in many forms of **structuralist** (p. 24) inquiry (see section 2.2). The notion of the syntagmatic chain refers to the sequence of the encounter as it develops in time, one event after another; when expressed graphically the syntagmatic chain is the horizontal axis of the matrix – see Figure 2.5.

For every event on the syntagmatic axis there is a corresponding feature on the paradigmatic axis and the sequence of events unfolds as a product of the interplay between the two axes. At every point on the paradigmatic axis there is a range of possible choices available; in standardised encounters there are conventional expectations about the choice that is made. For example, if two acquaintances meet in the street in England a typical encounter might be as follows:

A: Good morning, how are you?
B: Very well, thank you, and you?
A: I'm fine. Lovely day, isn't it?
B: Yes it is, I'm looking forward to some good weather.

The conversation might continue in this vein for some time but for purposes of the analysis here it is sufficient to say that the sequence A:B:A:B represents the syntagmatic chain: the particular responses at each one of these particular points represents a choice in the paradigmatic axis. If different choices had been made then the encounter would have had a different content and perhaps a different form, for example:

A: Good morning, how are you?
B: Not very well and I don't want to talk about it.
A: Oh, I'm sorry.

In the second example the conversation is cut short by the paradigmatic choice made by B. In English culture this response, while not inappropriate, was probably not expected and so may have the effect of disconcerting the hearer and causing the encounter to end abruptly and incompletely, or at least to run a less than expected course.

A third version of this conversation shows another possibility:

A: Good morning, how are you?
B: A single return ticket, please.

In this case, although there is a response it is an inappropriate one in terms of the encounter as described (in the street between two acquaintances); for whatever reason, B replied with an unconventional paradigmatic choice. The intent may have been to disconcert A, to avoid further conversation, or because B is deaf and/or confused about the situation in which the encounter is taking place. While you, the reader, may guess which is the most likely explanation, the transmitter of the message (A) might be able to interpret the response more fully (and possibly more accurately) because s/he will have access to other information that is difficult to convey in written language. The response by B may have been shouted and accompanied by threatening gestures, or it may have been said quietly with a smile and the speaker A may know that this apparent miscue actually refers to a private joke between the two of them and so is entirely intelligible. The point at issue is that speech acts have immediate consequence for the transmitter of speech and the receiver; communicative competence requires that both interpret utterances in a satisfactory way.

The measurement of communicative competence and the extent to which it is achieved in speech acts is a technical and specialised branch of ethnographic inquiry and involves the painstaking counting of grammatical features in order to demonstrate speech patterns and the negotiation of meaning between transmitter and receiver of utterances. The search for theories of communication involves testing speech acts in a variety of different situations, sometimes face to face, as in the example above, and sometimes where people cannot see each other, as in the case of telephone conversations. Results from these experiments indicate that it is only very rarely that people in communicative acts speak absolutely according to the rules of grammar and the formal principles of language. The occasions when this does happen tend to be when only one communicative channel is available, for example when using the telephone. In such an instance speech tends to be formal and logical in an attempt to convey exact meaning. Recordings of naturally occurring speech are often unintelligible to hearers who were not present at the time of the recording but those who were there can make more sense because they are able to contextualise the recorded speech and remember events that gave meaning to particular statements. Written accounts of naturally occurring speech may be very misleading unless they provide indications of speech patterns, tone, volume and pitch and the general demeanour of the speaker(s), as the extract from an alleged incident in a murder trial shows (see Box 2.8).

Box 2.8

An alleged incident in a murder trial

PROSECUTOR: Mr X, the policeman's notes at the time of questioning report your answer to his statement to you that he believed that you murdered your wife as, 'I murdered her'. What is your response to that?

MR X: I never said that, what I said was 'I (incredulous gasp) murdered (disbelief) her (rising interrogative)?'

The process of giving accounts of the transmission and reception of meaning in the ethnography of speaking draws attention to the distinctive features of language in communicating information and representing ideas and thought. It is through the observation and analysis of language use that we understand how the instances of mutual interpretation which make up social life are possible (Jenkins, 1994).

2.4.7 | Language as communication and representation: a summary

There seems to be a paradox at the heart of language. On one hand it is effective as a means of communication and representation because its form and its associations are known, regular and conventional; on the other, the success of language seems to derive from its optional nature – it is arbitrary so speech communities can seemingly make of it anything that they choose. The argument here is that this apparent contradiction is the essence of language; language is *constituted through difference*. Language is flexible because it is simultaneously both regulated and creative. In any speech act either freedom or regulation may be stressed but the other is always there and its presence carries with it the potentiality of a failure of communication. Social life, which is made up of instances of mutual interpretation, is possible because language offers the possibility of the negotiation of meaning. The room for negotiation may differ according to the social situation and the semantic domain; we have seen earlier in the chapter that some semantic domains have very specialised and precise language – the language of the law is one such example. Yet even here there is negotiation, indeed most legal argument is about the meaning of language. This negotiable aspect of language is amplified by the *polysemic* character of language – words have many meanings. It is the act of communication that reveals the partial and the negotiated character of language, as Weiner (1991) says 'unspoken language is language taken for granted, spoken language is language problematized and therefore culture prob-lematized'. In our unspoken language we may establish clearly, linearly and logically the meaning and the sense of our thoughts. But in interaction we cannot guarantee an agreed outcome in meaning, not least because while language is linear thought is network-like (Bloch, 1991; Parkin, 1991).

The attempt to articulate a precise meaning may make a person speechless, habitual language is 'good enough' for routinised interaction and, as Bourdieu points out, much social activity is on the 'hitherside of language' – this is *mimesis* – action so habitual, so taken for granted that words are not needed because there is a practical mastery (Jenkins, 1994). Because language is specific, not general, then attempts to innovate, to be creative, have to take place within the metaphors of the specific language if meaning is to be communicated. There are forms and styles of language use which self-consciously seek to convey meaning through the indeterminacy of language: poetry is one example; humour, particularly the use of puns, is another. The creativity of language explores the opportunities to negotiate meaning in representation and communication. Those who are not poets buttress language with non-verbal gestures which convey meaning (see Chapter 7) and exploit the associations of volume and pitch in speech to convey meaning and, of course, silence may speak powerfully. The analysis of language will not provide a blueprint of the truth of things; indeed the flexibility and indeterminacy of language may mask meaning, often deliberately so. People may use language to lie; others may employ it to conceal the actuality of things, for example, quite deliberately unemotional language may be used to countenance brutal action – the language of war provides illustrations where soldiers going into action are told to 'deal with' the enemy.

Language seeks to encompass culture but does not define it. Language maps the social terrain of a speech community but never colonises it.

2.5 | Art and representation

So far in this chapter we have examined a range of different approaches to language and communication. We have been particularly concerned to identify different methods to the study of representation as they connect to the exercise and disposition of power. In developing this commentary, we can now focus on some more specific forms of representation. In this section we explore some aspects of art.

2.5.1 | John Berger: oil painting, realism and capitalism

In *Ways of Seeing* John Berger (1972) considers a number of different dimensions of the European tradition of oil painting. In particular he echoes the arguments of Walter Benjamin concerning the effects of the extended reproduction of paintings (see Chapter 9), discusses the representation and construction of gender, and locates the oil painting tradition in the development of Western capitalism. In this section we use Berger's arguments as a starting point for consideration of the connection of the representation of painting to patterns of class, capitalism, gender and sexuality.

Berger first of all locates oil painting historically. Despite the fact that the techniques involved in the production of oil paint have been known since ancient times, Berger (1972: 84) argues that the practice that is familiar as oil painting was not perfected until it was used to 'express a particular view of life'. According to Berger, this occurred in the sixteenth century. He further argues that, while it is not possible to date the end of the tradition of oil painting conclusively, it was 'undermined by Impressionism and overthrown by Cubism'. Therefore, 'the period of the traditional oil painting may be roughly set as between 1500 and 1900' (1972: 84).

In Berger's argument this tradition of oil painting involves realism. This does not mean that it simply captures the real, but rather that the oil allows the painter to create the 'illusion' that we are seeing the real. This connects to the way in which many of the paintings discussed by Berger depict objects as well as people, as is shown by Holbein's *Ambassadors* (see Figure 2.6).

In an important sense the tradition of oil painting depicts the possessions of those who were painted, or who commissioned the painting itself. This form of representation is concerned with possession in other ways as well. First, the paintings were themselves

Figure 2.6 ■ *The Ambassadors* (1533) by Holbein. (Source: reproduced by courtesy of the Trustees, The National Gallery, London.)

possessions which can now be exchanged on markets: they are commodities which often fetch extremely high prices. Second, the way of seeing that is constructed by the painting itself implies that things and people can be possessed. The gaze of the oil painting tradition is one of possession.

In Berger's argument these aspects of oil painting are intimately connected to the development of capitalism, which is a mode of production based on the production of goods to be bought and sold – to be possessed in such a way that they can be exchanged. The dominant class of such a mode of production is the capitalist or bourgeois class, which owns the property capable of producing the goods that are exchanged on the market. In Berger's view the period of the dominance of oil painting corresponds to the classical period of the dominance of this class. To simplify his argument somewhat, it can be suggested that the parallels between art and mode of production in this period are of the type depicted in Figure 2.7.

This relationship between a competitive capitalism based around the free competition of a large number of relatively small competing capitalists, where pictorial

Figure 2.7 ■ Realism and competitive capitalism.

representations are predominantly realist, began to break down in the latter part of the nineteenth century. This can be illustrated through the work of Clark (1985), who analyses the impressionist movement in art in the context of the changing nature of Paris in the second half of the nineteenth century.

2.5.2 | Impressionism and modernism

Clark's argument is complex, but to simplify, he argues that the re-development of the city of Paris in accord with the grand schemes of Baron Haussmann, where the boulevards were driven through previously densely populated working-class areas, was part of a process of struggle between social classes. Haussmann was partly concerned with facilitating the deployment of troops across the city to counter any working-class revolt, but the development of these roadways was also a way to rationalise the distribution of capitalist products to make them more easily available. In many other ways Paris was at the forefront of the development of modern social relations. New developments in shopping and other aspects of leisure took place here (see Chapter 9). For much of the nineteenth century Paris was a city in turmoil. Clark argues that impressionist art (and the art that immediately followed it) was a product of this context and in subtle ways addressed many of the issues that it raised. The paintings depict forms of city life and city space. Moreover, they often depict the outskirts of Paris and

Figure 2.8 ▪ *A Sunday on La Grande Jatte* (1884) by Georges Seurat. (Source: photograph © 1998, The Art Institute of Chicago. All Rights Reserved.)

Figure 2.9 ▦ Modernism and monopoly capitalism.

areas of *petit bourgeois* (middle-class) leisure, relating to the development of new leisure activities, new class relations and suburban life. These paintings also begin the break with the realist form, so described by Berger. A good example of this can be found in Seurat's *A Sunday on La Grande Jatte* (see Figure 2.8).

These developments represent the beginning of a new set of relations. Again to simplify somewhat, the new pattern is as represented in Figure 2.9.

It is possible then to suggest that these rather different forms of representation in art – **realism** (p. 61) and **modernism** (p. 400) – are connected to patterns of social changes and power relations, which they both represent and contribute to. So far, the power relations discussed have been ones of class; equally important are those of gender.

2.5.3 │ Art and gender

Berger (1972) shows how gender representations in painting are infused with power. Women are depicted to be looked at by men (see also section 9.3.4). The obvious case of this is the nude. Berger argues that the nude is a specifically Western art form, again partly constructed within the European oil painting tradition. He argues that the nude is a conventional form:

> We can now begin to see the difference between nakedness and nudity in the European tradition. In his book on *The Nude* Kenneth Clark maintains that to be naked is simply to be without clothes, whereas the nude is a form of art. According to him, a nude is not the starting point of a painting, but a way of seeing which the painting achieves. To some degree, this is true – although the way of seeing 'a nude' is not necessarily confined to art: there are also nude photographs, nude poses, nude gestures. What is true is that the nude is always conventionalized – and the authority for its conventions derives from a certain tradition of art. (1972: 53)

Following this, Berger argues that:

> In the average European oil painting of the nude the principal protagonist is never painted. He is the spectator in front of the picture and he is presumed to be a man. Everything is addressed to him. Everything must appear to be the result of his being there. It is for him that the figures have assumed their nudity. But he, by definition, is a stranger – with his clothes still on. (1972: 54)

The expressions of the nude, in Berger's argument, are inviting. They gaze out at the male spectator, inviting his look rather than challenging it (see also section 2.3). Women in these paintings are passive and powerless (Parker and Pollock, 1981: 116): they are the subject of the male gaze (Mulvey, 1981; see section 9.3.4). Thus, this conventional and familiar depiction is saturated with power and reproduces ideas of femininity and masculinity: women are available to be looked at, they are passive where men are active, they are vain in inviting the look of men, and so on.

As Berger suggests, these forms of representation are not confined to the high art tradition of oil painting. They are everywhere in contemporary popular culture, most notably in the pages of mass circulation tabloid newspapers and advertising. The traditions of these types of representation have not gone away, despite coming under attack from **feminists** (p. 120) and the development of **modernist** and **postmodernist** (p. 400) forms of **representation** (p. 61). However, Berger contends that the figure of the nude became much less important in modernist art, citing the case of Manet's painting *Olympia* which, he suggests, challenges many of the conventions of the nude (see also Clark, 1985). Feminist art strategies have also criticised and redefined the representation of the female body (Parker and Pollock, 1981; Parker and Pollock, 1987).

In this section we have related some particular forms of representation in art to relationships of **power** (p. 94). It can be suggested that in very broad terms dominant forms of representation such as realism (as in *The Ambassadors*) can be seen to develop in societies of a particular type. In this case, it is a society and a culture that increasingly emphasise the possession and material and symbolic centrality of possession of goods. As society and culture shift, so do forms of representation in a complex manner. It can be suggested that the shift from the dominance of **realist** (p. 61) forms to that of **modernism** in high culture connects to the different type of possession and representation of commodities that begins to develop in the late nineteenth century. Furthermore, it can be suggested that those forms known as **postmodern** are also related to different structures of **power**.

2.6 | Television and representation

Some of the most detailed work on representation has been carried out on television. In an obvious sense this stems from the central importance of television as the dominant form of contemporary representation and communication. A number of different dimensions of television have been subject to detailed analysis (see Abercrombie, 1996). Within cultural studies an important emphasis has been placed on the 'flow' of television programming (Williams, 1974) in that it is recognised that watching television is often an experience or activity in its own right. The contrast is with the idea that certain programmes are selected carefully to be watched (which of course may still happen) and to the idea that television is some kind of stimulus to particular forms of behaviour. It may be culture in the sense of a text, but it is also a central part of everyday life. However, despite this emphasis, there have been a number of important analyses of different parts of television programming. For example, examination of television news has demonstrated that it combines a number of different themes to produce a particular message. As a way of bringing together the twin foci of this chapter on specific representational techniques and the exercise of power, we wish to conclude with some consideration of these topics.

2.6.1 | The language of industrial disputes

One of the areas of television that has emphasised neutrality is news. Television news seeks to forward claims of objectivity and absence of bias. In a series of studies dating from the mid-1970s, the Glasgow University Media Group has sought to analyse and ultimately to contest these claims. Its work has ranged across the reporting of industrial disputes, the Falklands War, the peace movement of the 1980s, the British miners' strike of 1984 and AIDS. Some of the most detailed analysis examined the use of language and visuals in the reporting of 'industrial disputes' in the 1970s.

These disputes were reported in terms of a clash between two sides, using a relatively narrow set of words.

> In the detailed examination of the vocabulary used we have demonstrated that in disputes the traditional 'offers' of management are inevitably countered by the 'demands' of workers – to the point where nouns and verbs describing management actions are generally positive while the matching vocabulary for worker's actions is negative.   (Glasgow University Media Group, 1980: 401)

Management was seen to be making offers, a 'reasonable' action, whereas workers were unreasonable in making 'demands'. The suggestion is that the language of the news reports implies that workers are causing trouble for the management and the country. The conceptual organisation of industrial news is represented diagrammatically in the

---

Box 2.9

The conceptual organisation of industrial news

These deficiencies, absences and distortions may best be illustrated via a diagrammatic representation of the conceptual organisation of industrial news (Figure). The 'tree' or diagram is made up of the most frequently occurring terms in the bargaining, breakdown and resolution stages of the industrial relations process. It is arranged vertically since it represents a temporal as well as a logical sequence. The categories allow only the most simple distinctions to be made. The noun vocabulary does not provide a balanced set of descriptions of the so-called 'free collective bargaining' approach to industrial relations. If such a pluralistic approach were to operate there are a number of key terms which are absent which

→

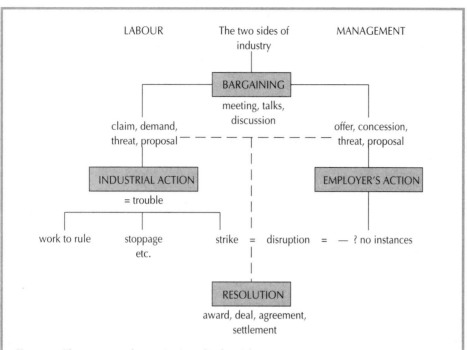

Figure ▦ The conceptual organisation of industrial news.

would have to be present. For example, labour would offer and make concessions and management would make claims and demands. Even less do they allow room for the expression of fundamental differences of values based on class opposition. The language implies a unitary frame of reference skewed towards management, who exercise control as of 'right'. The dominant value assumptions which are entailed by this view limit and qualify the use of causal and interpretative concepts (e.g. concepts which would explain behaviour in terms of 'class' or 'radical opposition' instead of 'militant', with its ambiguous, aggressive connotations). This deficiency is all the more serious because recent work by Moorhouse on political consciousness and beliefs about class in Britain reveals that in fact the mass perception of the class system is dichotomous. It is very close to the 'us' and 'them' view. When asked in a political context whether there is 'class struggle' in Britain most people seem to believe that there is. Gallup showed that in May 1974, 60 per cent of the respondents believed that there was class struggle, while 62 per cent of the *Daily Telegraph* poll in the same year also believed that there was a class struggle. But as the language of news reporting clearly reveals, this does not appear on our screens. It is lost in the process of mediation.

Glasgow University Media Group (1980: 186–7)

extract from the Glasgow University Media Group which is explained in the accompanying text in Box 2.9.

According to the Glasgow group, visuals in news bulletins are also used in a 'skewed' manner. In particular the status of the person will affect their visual representation. It is often noted that when they appear on television, academics are very often shown in front of a bookcase. This may be taken to signify (or denote) their learning, but also conveys (or connotes) some measure of authority. Interviewing an academic while he or she is engaged in some other aspect of their working life or daily round might upset some of these conceptions. Thus workers are often interviewed while leaving their place of work, academics never in the university car park. In the Glasgow University Media Group's analysis such distinctions even come out in the nature of the captions used to label different visual presentations. Equally importantly, there are great similarities

Defining concept 2.2

Ideology

Theories of ideology are an attempt to understand ideas in terms of **power** (p. 94). This has been most fully developed within **Marxist** (p. 97) theory (see Williams, 1977) and what follows is a consideration of that tradition and critiques of it. **Raymond Williams** (p. 5) (1977) stresses the various meanings that the term 'ideology' can have from explicitly acknowledged political ideologies to more subconscious 'common-sensical meanings' or 'taken-for-granted beliefs'. He identifies two components to Marxist understandings of ideology:

- Ideology as the ideas of a particular social group.
- Ideology as a system of illusory beliefs.

Ideologies as the ideas of a social group

This is the argument that social groups (and within Marxism the debate has revolved mainly around social classes) have particular beliefs associated with them. One source of this is **Karl Marx** (p. 97) and Fredrich Engels's *The German Ideology*. In this critique of idealism (a way of thinking that identifies ideas as the main properties of a society) they asserted that ideas were not independent. Instead ideologies come from social classes in their social relations with each other. Or, as Janet Wolff says, 'the ideas and beliefs people have are systematically related to their actual and material conditions of existence' (Wolff, 1981: 50).

Ideas, or ideologies, are seen to be rooted in the material conditions of the everyday life of classes (including their relations with other classes). Yet these classes are not equal; some ideas dominate because of the unequal material social relations of a class-based society. Marx sums this up in a famous phrase: 'The ideas of the ruling class are in every epoch the ruling ideas, i.e. the class which is the ruling *material* force

→

of society, is at the same time its ruling *intellectual* force' (Marx and Engels, 1968: 64). Indeed, these ideas are part of their rule. They serve to legitimate their domination (e.g. the Swedish ruling classes legitimating capitalist modernisation with ideologies of both progress and tradition – see section 4.2.3) and to reproduce the unequal social relations from which they benefit (there are a whole series of arguments about how education is part of the reproduction of class relations, e.g. Althusser, 1971, and Willis, 1977).

Generally, then, ideology (the realm of ideas) is seen to be shaped by something 'deeper' – the social (or class) relations within which people live their lives or even the economic organisation of society (or 'mode of production') which shapes those class relations. There is, however, a recognition that ideologies have real consequences. They operate as 'maps of meaning', used to interpret and define what is going on. That they work better for some groups than others is the second component of Marxist theories that Williams identifies.

Ideology as a system of illusory beliefs

This is the suggestion that, because of their origins as part of unequal social relations, ideologies are a distorted representation of the truth. This relies on the points set out above to argue that there are sets of ideas appropriate to each class, generated by their position within exploitative social relations, but that people may have adopted other ideas via education, the media, entertainment and so on. Since a true class consciousness with an objective material basis is being claimed here, then people who do not think that way are said to have 'false consciousness'. There is a sense that they have been hoodwinked. Their real interests are concealed from them and the real interests of the exploitative classes are also concealed (for example, nationalism which serves the political, military and economic interests of ruling classes might be said to be false consciousness for a working class that 'should' think of itself not as divided but as internationally united).

There are a series of problems with these ways of thinking. First, 'false consciousness' is always something that someone else has, not oneself. It has a tendency to define people as 'cultural dupes' who can be led out of their ignorance by a right-thinking vanguard or the visionary theorist who knows the 'Truth'. Second, can classes and ideas be matched as neatly as this way of thinking suggests? Can we allocate ideologies to social groups in this way? Third, can the world be understood in terms of class alone? If not, do the forms of analysis (often rooted in understanding economic relationships) set out above work for social groups defined in terms of gender, race, sexuality or age?

In response to these problems the 1970s and 1980s saw the development of more and more elaborate and difficult theoretical work on the relationships between ideas and power (see Althusser, 1971, and Thompson, 1984). The main path that this took was through understanding language, thinking about ideas not as something 'free-floating' but as existing as words spoken or written. It also meant a move away from only studying class.

→

This work has stressed that ideology is about the relationship between language and power. Instead of thinking about ideas being fixed to particular social groups or about them being untrue there is a sense that meanings are not fixed, that they arise in language, in communication and representation. This means thinking about many competing ideologies, not one dominant one, and about a whole range of social groups. The connection to power lies in the ways in which meanings present the world to the advantage or disadvantage of particular social groups, and the ways in which those groups can attempt to fix or challenge those meanings. For example, a set of widespread ideas about nature, motherhood and domesticity which served to legitimate women's dependence within the home benefited and were reproduced by men, but have in many ways been effectively challenged by women. As Thompson says: 'To study ideology, I propose, is to study the ways in which meaning (or signification) serves to sustain relations of domination' (Thompson, 1984: 4).

This way of thinking is very close to other theoretical concepts that look at the relations between meaning and power (e.g. **discourse** – p. 30) and has raised the question of whether we still need the concept of ideology. Those arguing against using it suggest that it still brings with it the problems of believing in something called 'the truth', and of being too rooted in economic class relations (Foucault, 1980). Those who want to retain it claim that it brings a necessary critical edge to making judgements about the power relations involved in statements (Eagleton, 1991; Purvis and Hunt, 1993).

Further reading

Eagleton, T. (1991) *Ideology: An Introduction*, London: Verso.

Thompson, J. (1984) *Studies in the Theory of Ideology*, Cambridge: Polity.

Williams, R. (1977) *Marxism and Literature*, Oxford: Oxford University Press.

between the different television channels in the sorts of pictures and graphics that they use. In these respects, then, news is routinised and conventional.

In addition to making these claims the Glasgow group suggest that the structure of the news allows it to function **ideologically** (see Defining Concept 2.2) in that it produces a version of reality that favours the dominant class. It does not do this by simply acting as a mouthpiece for the government or management, but through a set of representations which systematically skew stories in particular directions.

2.6.2 | Stuart Hall: encoding, decoding and ideology

Work on the media developed and operationalised some of the key debates on **ideology**. In particular the research carried out at the Birmingham **Centre for Contemporary Cultural Studies** (p. 327) was hugely influential. The cornerstone of this was the work of **Stuart Hall** (see Key Influence 2.2).

In 'Encoding/decoding', Hall (1980) argues that television programmes, and by implication all other forms of text, should be understood as 'meaningful **discourse**' (p. 30). In the language of **structuralism** (p. 24) and **semiotics** (p. 34) introduced earlier in this chapter, they consist of codes. To achieve this status they must be encoded by those involved in their production, and be capable of being decoded by the audiences who watch them. They are social phenomena subject to struggle and change. These relationships are summarised by Hall in the diagram reproduced in Figure 2.10.

Hall argues that the television text, or sign, is very complex; furthermore that it can be decoded in different ways by the audience. Hall identifies three positions 'from which decodings of a televisual discourse may be constructed' (1980: 136). These he calls the 'dominant-hegemonic', the 'negotiated' and the 'oppositional' (1980: 136–8). In the dominant-**hegemonic** position (p. 106) the logic of the television programme is gone along with.

> When the viewer takes the connoted meaning from, say, a television newscast or current affairs programme full and straight, and decodes the message in terms of the references code in which it has been encoded, we might say that the viewer is *operating inside the dominant code.*
> (Hall, 1980: 136)

Thus, it will be accepted that the management does make offers and workers do demand things. This is the dominant code of television news about industrial disputes, as articulated through the professional practices of television journalists. As such it also represents an influential form of 'common sense' in contemporary society.

The negotiated code may also operate within this framework, but will allow for disagreements within it. Thus, on the basis of experience, for example, there may be specific challenges to aspects of the dominant frame.

> Decoding within the *negotiated version* contains a mixture of adaptive and oppositional elements: it acknowledges the legitimacy of the hegemonic definitions to make grand significations (abstract), while, at a more restricted, situational (situated) level, it makes its own ground rules – it operates with exceptions to the rule.
> (Hall, 1980: 137)

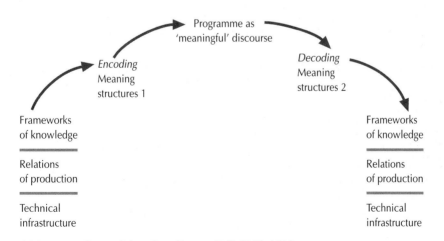

Figure 2.10 ▦ Encoding and decoding. (Source: Hall, 1980: 130.)

Key influence 2.2

Stuart Hall (1932–)

Stuart Hall is a Jamaican-born intellectual and political activist who can in many senses be seen as the crucial figure in the development of contemporary cultural studies through his own work, his stimulation of others and his continued attention to the interconnections between politics and the pursuit of knowledge.

Born into a middle-class family, Hall left Jamaica in 1951 to study at Oxford. He was active in left politics and became the first editor of *New Left Review* in 1960. In 1964 he was appointed as deputy director (to Richard Hoggart) of the newly created **Centre for Contemporary Cultural Studies** (p. 327). He subsequently became director, before taking the Chair of Sociology at the Open University in 1979.

Hall's early engagement with the New Left stimulated his interest in popular culture and he published an important text with Paddy Whannel, *The Popular Arts* (1964). This interest continued in a number of papers on diverse topics in the area of media and communication, including news photographs, the magazine *Picture Post*, and news and current affairs television. His ongoing concern with issues of race was combined with this emphasis in the influential (collectively authored) *Policing the Crisis* (1978). He wrote on subcultures specifically on hippies, but most importantly in the key collective text *Resistance through Rituals* (1976). His theoretical interests were developed in papers on ideology, which were influenced by both Althusser and **Gramsci** (p. 38). He was one of the first leftist analysts to confront Thatcherism and from 1979 on developed an analysis and critique based in a Gramscian approach. This resulted in the concept of 'authoritarian populism', *The Politics of Thatcherism* (1983) and *New Times* (1989), both edited with Martin Jacques. Confronting **postmodernism** (p. 400) led Hall to increased concern with issues around 'race' and **'identity'** (p. 224) in the 1990s, when he also continued to reflect on the development of 'cultural studies'.

The impact of Hall's own work, centred on the interconnections between **ideology** (p. 84), identity, culture and politics, on cultural studies cannot be overestimated. He remains at the cutting edge of developments, continuing to argue for the relevance of a sophisticated Marxism to the understanding of contemporary social formations, as well as a force for social change. Moreover, especially during his time at the Centre for Contemporary Cultural Studies in Birmingham, he influenced a generation of researchers who were themselves to become some of the leading writers in the field. His commitment to collective work is reflected in his joint authorship and editorship of many volumes.

Further reading

Morley, D. and Chen, K.-H. (eds) (1996) *Stuart Hall: Critical Dialogues in Cultural Studies*, London: Routledge.

Hall, S. and Jefferson, T. (eds) (1976) *Resistance through Rituals: Youth Subcultures in Post-war Britain*, London: Hutchinson.

Hall, S., Critcher, C., Jefferson, T., Clarke, J. and Roberts, B. (1978) *Policing the Crisis: Mugging, the State and Law and Order*, London: Macmillan.

In the oppositional position the dominant framework is directly resisted, in a '*globally contrary way*' (Hall, 1980: 137–8).

These potential positions were empirically considered by Morley (1980). Reiterating the influence of the sociologist Frank Parkin (1973) on his and Hall's position, Morley found evidence for the existence of the different positions among social groups to which he showed examples of the British current affairs magazine programme *Nationwide* (see further Abercrombie, 1996; Abercrombie and Longhurst, 1998).

2.6.3 | Television: ideology, discourse and power

Hall and Morley's argument represents a sophisticated account of the relationship between media messages and **ideology** (p. 84) and **power** (p. 94). Media messages are complex, but connect to the established patterns of the distribution of power and influence. They do not simply reflect this, but are ordered in such ways as to ultimately represent a particular view and construction of the world. These messages are normally dealt with in terms of the dominant or the negotiated code. They may be challenged in aspects of detail, but not in their entirety. There is, then, a hegemonic understanding and representation of the world, which benefits powerful groups and which is shared, as a form of common sense, by the majority of the population. This logic was worked out by Hall and his collaborators in *Policing the Crisis* (Hall *et al.*, 1978), where the moral panic (see Chapter 8) over 'mugging' generated by the media in the 1970s is connected to the shifting patterns of the reorganisation of state power in contemporary British society and to the 'common sense' of English racism (see further Barker, 1992).

In these arguments the media are seen to act **ideologically** (p. 84). They represent a partial view of the world, which operates in favour of the dominant groups. These are some of the most elaborated and complex developments of a Marxist account and theory of **representation** (p. 61). One of the key problems with them, however, has been the conceptualisation and account of ideology that they contain. In particular there is potentially too quick a movement from the analysis of the structure of the media text to its implication in the reproduction of common sense about industrial disputes or racism. More recent work has suggested that the text is rather more complex than these accounts allow and that its connection to audiences is even less straightforward. Thus it can be maintained that these sorts of Marxist account argue that there is a reality that is represented in the media, which ultimately misrepresents the true picture. While this text may be complex, a truth can be found, which is outside representation. Approaches that often have some of their roots in the work of Foucault oppose this view. Here the text is itself always discursively constructed and should not be understood within a frame of representation (as it does not *re*-present) but in the frame of construction. Texts are constructed within language. This sort of approach places emphasis on the category of discourse (which is often used in the more Marxist accounts as well – allowing some 'leakage' between them as much of the work in the 1980s and 1990s of writers like Morley (1992) and Hall (1996) indicates). However, it does suggest that the relationships between the production, structure and consumption of texts are much more contingent than even perhaps the most sophisticated Marxist account allows. The concept of discourse acts to facilitate such contingency. Thus, some of the codes in complex texts may well be ideological. However, others may not be or may be ideological in different ways. For example, a text may well construct a discourse of class that might be thought to be oppositional (or non-ideological) while constructing a discourse of race that is highly ideological. Thus, in the recent British television series *Our Friends in the North*, a series of political debates and struggles centred around class and inequality in Britain since the 1960s were dramatised, but other political issues (notably of race) were entirely absent. An interest in discourse is also a prevalent feature of some contemporary social psychological approaches, which criticise the Marxist approach.

This emphasis on discourse operates to move contemporary debate away from representation, whereby reality is represented in an adequate or inadequate fashion, towards an emphasis on the ways in which different texts construct discourses within them which are complexly related to the practices and discourse of those who produce and consume them. This allows a greater scope for the consideration of the wide ways in which texts are articulated with a plurality of aspects of power (see Chapter 6).

2.7 | Summary: reflecting and constructing

At the beginning of this chapter we introduced some issues raised by the concept of representation. The subsequent consideration of language and some specific forms and examples of representation has, we hope, pointed up some of these issues more starkly. Broadly we have sketched a movement from conceptions of language that imply that in some sense it represents or encodes the world, or in more Marxist accounts represents it partially, to one where representation is increasingly problematic. It has been argued by some postmodernist and poststructuralist writers that the world is actually made up of images and discourses. This is now the real. In many respects this is a radical version of the idea that language does not reflect or represent, but that it constructs. Communication and representation then assume crucial importance. The virulence and salience of contemporary disputes about language use and classification are not, then, some sideline to real debates: they are central. It should come as no surprise that the naming of groups and activities are of such significance. The real is not, in some sense, outside these representations/constructions. Rather than being jokes or side issues, matters of language use such as the title Ms and the reclaiming of terms like 'nigger' are at the very heart of social and political contestation (see further Chapter 6).

Re-cap

This chapter has considered:

- the significance of language and communication and their connection to issues of power;
- the semiotic approach to the study of signs and the application of this to advertising;
- the nature of artistic and television representations in relation to social change and the distribution of power.

Further reading

An excellent short introduction to issues of language and representation, especially as discussed in the structuralist and semiotic viewpoints, can be found in Terence Hawkes, *Structuralism and Semiotics* (1977). The classic study which applies these to advertising is Judith Williamson *Decoding Advertisements: Ideology and Meaning in Advertising* (1978), which might be used to prompt analyses of your own. Connections between representation and power (especially of class and gender) are economically and influentially dealt with by John Berger in *Ways of Seeing* (1972). John Fiske and John Hartley, *Reading Television* (1978) apply semiotics to television; Fiske's *Television Culture* (1987) develops the argument and approach.

chapter

Culture, power and inequality

3.0 | Introduction

The development and global expansion of a world capitalist system of production has generated increasing disparities of wealth, income and life chances within and between the populations of the world's nation-states. In 1996 the Organization for Economic Cooperation and Development (OECD) complimented the British government on its economic success in controlling inflation and reducing unemployment in the British economy but warned that there might be a high price to pay in terms of social disharmony and civil unrest because the policies of sound economics had produced a big gap in incomes and wealth in British society. Similar warnings have been given about the relationships between the industrially developed and economically advanced nations of the world and areas of the former communist world and countries of the so-called Third World. This is a political term which is used to describe poor countries in Africa, Latin America and Asia, many of which were former colonies of European states (see **colonialism and postcolonialism**, p. 189). In all cases the warning is that there are dangers to social cohesion and political stability as a result of the operation and continuing expansion of the capitalist system.

If we consider the global economic differences between societies, it is evident that the contrasts are very marked in scale and continuing to grow. Economists speak of these increasing differences in the wealth of First and Third World societies as the 'development gap'. One way of measuring the development gap is to compare the Gross National Product per head of the population (GNP per capita). This is the total value of goods and services produced annually in the society divided by its population. In 1995 the richest twenty-five societies in the world – which included the United States, Canada, Western Europe, Australasia and the Gulf states of the Middle East – made up only 16 per cent of the world's population yet had an average GNP per capita well over twenty times higher than the average for the rest of the world (see Figure 3.1).

Of course what these data overlook are the very considerable differences in income, wealth and associated life chances that individuals may experience *within* any given society. Even in a rich society such as the United States, the poor encounter real deprivation. Nevertheless, the differences between rich and poor societies in a global perspective are striking and remain an underlying source of tension and instability in the contemporary world.

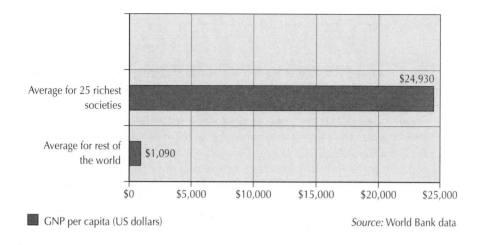

$24,930

Average for 25 richest
societies

Average for rest of
the world $1,090

$0 $5,000 $10,000 $15,000 $20,000 $25,000

 GNP per capita (US dollars)   *Source:* World Bank data

Figure 3.1 ▧ The development gap in 1995.

It seems that the pursuit of capitalist goals is inimical to social, economic and political egalitarianism; capitalism produces inequality. It is also becoming more and more apparent that the sources and manifestations of this inequality are not simply produced by the globalisation of market logics and mechanisms. The cultural dimension is increasingly significant. This chapter explores this idea: first, it examines theorising about the relationship of culture, **power** and inequality, looking at explanations of the origins of inequality in capitalist societies. Second, it considers how and why inequality is maintained in capitalist societies with particular reference to the role of culture. Third, it looks at systems of inequality that are commonly seen to be rooted and expressed in non-economic values, namely race, ethnicity, age and gender. This will allow us to examine the principal sources and characteristics of inequality (class, status and caste), the ways that inequality is made acceptable to people, that is how it comes to be seen as legitimate, and some of the leading cultural consequences of inequality. In the concluding section we shall examine the idea that different kinds of inequality interact to produce multiple disadvantages.

This chapter is designed to enable readers to:

▧ understand the main structural sources of social inequality;
▧ appreciate the various conceptions of the part played by culture in legitimating inequality;
▧ learn about the leading cultural manifestations of inequality;
▧ grasp some of the ways in which cultural power is displayed.

Defining concept 3.1

Power

Power has come to be one of the crucial concepts in cultural studies. Interpretations of culture that draw upon ideas of 'cultural politics' argue that everything is political and, as a result, that power is everywhere (see Chapter 6). For example, it is used in this book to understand relations of class, race, gender and age; to interpret the body and representations of people and places; and to make sense of our understandings of time and space. As **Michel Foucault** (p. 28), one of the theorists responsible for extending the use of ideas of power, put it: 'Power is everywhere; not because it embraces everything, but because it comes from everywhere.' To understand what he meant by this, and its implications, we need to look more closely at how power has been understood.

Steven Lukes (1974) argued that there are three views of power. The 'one-dimensional view' is that it means that person A can get person B to do something that they would not otherwise do. The 'two-dimensional view' is that group A has power to the extent that they can define not just the outcomes but the 'rules of the game' to their advantage. The 'three-dimensional view' is where the powerful have power to the extent that they can

> prevent people, to whatever degree, from having grievances by shaping their perceptions, cognitions and preferences in such a way that they accept their role in the existing order of things either because they can see or imagine no alternative to it, or because they see it as natural and unchangeable, or because they value it as divinely ordained and beneficial.   (Lukes, 1974: 24)

This third view has many similarities to that which is put forward in the notions of **ideology** (p. 84) and **hegemony** (p. 106), and it helps us to understand the importance of the ways in which the unequal distribution of power is made to seem appropriate – the way it is given legitimation.

The challenge that is offered to these views of power is that they are essentially *negative*. They all involve trying to understand how people are prevented from doing what they want, defining the 'rules of the game' as they want, or thinking their own thoughts. Instead of this Foucault suggests that power is *productive*. Power lies in the creation of **discourses** (p. 30), institutions, objects and **identities** (p. 224); power is all about making and remaking the world in a particular way. Thus, in his analysis, power produces classifications of knowledge which define our understanding of the relationship between people and nature; power produces bodies that can be made even more productive in factories and prisons; and power produces sexuality as the site that tells us most about ourselves. Power is not about saying 'no'; it is about producing things, identities and ideas.

Taking these views together, what we have are multiple forms of power. In each case, rather than trying to track down who finally holds 'power' and what that power is in the sort of abstract language that Lukes uses, we can try to understand how the relations of power work. There are plenty of examples in this book – such as analyses of orientalism,

→

monuments or the body – where we have tried to offer this sort of interpretation. What we find is that power works in many different ways because, as Foucault says, 'power comes from everywhere'; it is part of all relationships. Yet this is not a matter of reducing the world to a grey arena in which we are all totally dominated and controlled by capitalism or patriarchy or 'the system'. There are always **resistances** (p. 258) (which we need to think about not as qualitatively different from power but as forms of 'counter-power') which – together with the fact that the forces they oppose are often in conflict – produce a vibrant world of many contending people, institutions and discourses engaged in never-ending contests over resources, meanings, spaces, identities, positions and representations.

Further reading

Clegg, S.R. (1989) *Frameworks of Power*, London: Sage.
Lukes, S. (1974) *Power: A Radical View*, Basingstoke: Macmillan.
Lukes, S. (ed.) (1986) *Power*, Oxford: Blackwell.

3.1 | Theorising about culture, power and inequality

3.1.1 | Marx and Marxism

Much contemporary theorising about culture, power and inequality derives from **Marx's** theories (Marx and Engels, 1967; McLellan, 1977) and Marxian analyses and models of the social and economic processes of class formation in capitalist society. As Raymond Williams (1983a: 16) has noted, Marxism has made an influential contribution to modern cultural thought, even though Marx himself never developed a fully systematic theory of culture. The broad outlines of Marxian analysis delineate a historical progression from societies that Marx saw as exhibiting primitive communism through feudal society and into various forms of capitalist society, leading eventually to a revolution in which the agencies of the state would be overthrown and a socialist society emerge. There are a number of features of Marxian analyses that are significant for consideration of the connections between culture and inequality: the underlying economic structure of class inequality; Marx's emphasis on the opposed and antagonistic relationship between the classes; and the connection between power and culture.

It is economic relationships that underpin inequality for Marx; in all known societies (save the early state of primitive communism) there has always been the basic and fundamental contradiction that some members of society have owned and controlled the means of production, a characteristic that has given them power over the remaining members of society who, in order to make a livelihood, participate in production on terms and conditions set by these owners. For Marx, inequality in capitalist society hinges on whether one is an owner of the means of production or an owner of one's labour. As capitalism develops, the class structure simplifies around two main classes,

Key influence **3.1**

E.P. Thompson (1924–93)

Edward Palmer (E.P.) Thompson was a very influential English Marxist historian and political activist. His education at Cambridge was interrupted by war service in Italy, but he returned to finish his degree and then took up a position as extra-mural lecturer at Leeds University (1948–65). He was also a Reader at the Centre for the Study of Social History at the University of Warwick, where he influenced a whole generation of social historians. As well as writing on history and theory, he was an active campaigner for nuclear disarmament and a novelist.

E.P. Thompson's most influential work is probably *The Making of the English Working Class* (1968). This social and political history of the working class in the English industrial revolution attempted to present a 'history from below', one written from the perspective of an increasingly proletarianised and politicised working class. It sought, as he put it, 'to rescue the poor stockinger from the enormous condescension of posterity' and to present a history in which the working class were active in their own 'making'. In doing so he offered a challenge to Marxist interpretations of history which saw the history of capitalism as foretold by the inevitable movements of modes of production and social formations. This attention to agency – the power of people to shape history – was stated in opposition to the structuralist theories of Louis Althusser in Thompson's caustic attack entitled *The Poverty of Theory* (1978). It also offered an understanding of class and power which saw them not only as economic relationships but also as social and cultural ones. This led to studies of law and custom that considered class relations in eighteenth- and nineteenth-century Britain in terms of the ways in which classes defined themselves and were brought into conflict over questions of criminality and customary rights (see *Whigs and Hunters* (1975); *Albion's Fatal Tree* (1975) and *Customs in Common* (1991)).

Thompson has been criticised for failing to pay sufficient attention to issues of gender and race in the 'making of the English working class', and the role of agency and culture in the history of capitalism is still a matter of ongoing debate. However, his impact on cultural studies has been to stress the importance of theoretically informed histories, especially 'histories from below' (see **postcolonialism**, p. 189), and in attention to the active role of culture in the making of class relations.

Further reading

Kaye, H.J. and McClelland, K. (eds) (1990) *E.P. Thompson: Critical Perspectives*, Oxford: Polity Press.
Thompson, E.P. (1968) *The Making of the English Working Class*, Harmondsworth: Penguin (orig. 1963, Allan Lane).
Thompson, E.P. (1978) *The Poverty of Theory and Other Essays*, London: Merlin.

proletariat and bourgeoisie. The relationship between these classes is asymmetrical: there is an unequal distribution of power between them. In the context of the underlying economic relationship this asymmetrical relationship is an antagonistic one as the owners of the means of production increasingly seek to exploit the providers of labour. It is this antagonism and contradiction at the heart of society that acts as the dynamic that propels society on to new forms of exploitation. As it is inherent in capitalism to expand and to destroy all other forms of production, the relationship between the principal classes, the bourgeoisie (the owners of the means of production) and the proletariat (the owners of their labour), becomes ever sharper and more antagonistic until eventually the proletariat rise up in revolution and overthrow the bourgeoisie.

Key influence 3.2

Karl Marx (1818–83)

Marx's work has been widely influential in the social sciences, arts and humanities. He did not write much about culture itself, but Marxist cultural critics have developed his ideas and those of his collaborator, Friedrich Engels, on alienation, ideology, history and value.

Marx was born in Trier, Prussia, in 1818 to a Jewish family which later converted to Christianity. He studied law at Bonn and Berlin. In 1842 he became editor of the *Rheinische Zeitung*, and in this year he also met his lifelong collaborator Friedrich Engels. In the 1840s Marx began to study French utopian socialism. Combining socialist ideas and an interpretation of Hegel's philosophy, he developed a theory of consciousness as a product of human labour. In the writings later collected as the *Economic and Philosophical Manuscripts*, he argued that capitalism is the last in a series of modes of production that alienate workers from their labour. Earlier modes of production include primitive communism, the slave mode of production (employed in ancient Greece and Rome), and feudalism. In 1846 he published *The German Ideology* with Engels, in which they argued that: 'The ideas of the ruling class are, in every epoch, the ruling ideas.' *The Communist Manifesto* (1848) proposed that all history is the history of class struggle, and predicted the victory of the new industrial working class, the proletariat, over capitalist society. The demise of capitalism would lead to socialism and ultimately a higher form of communism, where alienation would be at an end. Marx's radical political views meant that he ran into trouble with first the Prussian, then the French and then the Belgian authorities. He and his family were eventually exiled to England. Here Marx worked on his most ambitious project, *Capital*, a detailed analysis of the development and workings of capitalist political economy. At the centre of the three volumes of *Capital* (only one of which was published before Marx's death) lies his account of the commodity. He noted a contradiction within capitalism between the market value (exchange value) of a particular product and its value as an item that somebody might actually use (use value). Capitalism holds the market value of goods and people to be worth more than the people themselves. In effect, both goods and people are commodified: they become no more than their exchange value. The capitalist allocation of goods by their market value leads to inequalities of wealth between rich and poor and large-scale wastage of resources.

In cultural studies it has been Western Marxism, and especially the work of Georg Lukács, the **Frankfurt School** (p. 109) and **Gramsci** (p. 38) that has had most influence. Marx's

→

theory of alienation has had a profound impact. Marxist cultural theorists view culture in relation to the mode of production, as a historical product of human labour rather than representing timeless human values. Marxist critics have understood art both as an expression of human alienation and as having the utopian potential to imagine an unalienated world. Marxist-informed theories of ideology have allowed critics to interpret cultural artifacts in relation to social structure. An understanding of cultural production in relation to political economy has been a vital part of studies of the culture industry and mass media.

Further reading

McLellan, D. (1975) *Marx*, London: Fontana.
Baxandall, L. and Morawski, S. (eds) (1973) *Marx and Engels on Literature and Art*, New York: International General.
Kamenka, E. (ed.) *The Portable Karl Marx*, Harmondsworth: Penguin.

For Marx, inequality in society is grounded in antagonistically related social classes. Marx addresses the question of how and why it is possible for the bourgeoisie to maintain their position of dominance for protracted periods, given the fact that they are a minority in society and given the level of oppression and hardship experienced by the masses, the proletariat. Part of the answer is that the bourgeoisie, through their economic power, also exercise political power and so shape and control the agencies of the state. Effective control of the state apparatus also gives them a monopoly on the use of force. Another aspect of their power to shape and control the state is the cultural control exercised by the bourgeoisie. Marx sees the bourgeoisie promulgating and implementing beliefs and values that sustain the unequal system of relationships by legitimising it through reference to non-economic domains of social experience. An example of this is the realm of spirituality and religious belief. Marx sees the particular beliefs of organised religion as buttresses for an unequal, unjust society. Religion, in his celebrated phrase, is the opiate of the masses. Thus Marx presents culture as ideology, as a partial, biased prop for the bourgeoisie, which is fashioned by them in their own interests. Culture as ideology blunts the understanding of the proletariat: it is the instrument of their deception, occluding their true interests. Culture in this sense stands as somehow opposed to the truth of things.

This is an important aspect of Marx's and Marxist thought and one that reverberates in wider discussions of culture, many of which are discussed in this book (see especially Chapters 1, 2, 6 and 8). The proposal is that culture is partial, often promoting a 'false consciousness' of the world and thereby acting as an instrument of oppression. Marx sees all the agencies of the state operating within cultural values that serve the interests of the bourgeoisie. The bourgeoisie have power, through their power they have knowledge and through their power and knowledge they create the dominant culture. Marxist thought draws attention to the connections between power, knowledge and

SUPERSTRUCTURE:

Family structures, religion and belief
systems, forms of political
organisation, systems of law and
education

MATERIAL BASE/
MODE OF PRODUCTION:

Relations of production
- social relations at the workplace
(worker–supervisor, contractual
agreements concerning terms of
employment, etc.)
- property relations: laws and
regulations about the ownership of property

Forces of production
- the land, raw materials, labour
power, plant, tools and technologies
needed to make things

Figure 3.2 ▪ Marx's base–superstructure model.

culture and proposes a systematic relationship in which cultural beliefs and practices are a cultural code for relationships of power.

Marx's favoured method for conceptualising these connections is the base–superstructure metaphor (see Figure 3.2). The formula that Marx proposes is that the economic (or material) base of a society determines the broad character of its superstructure. In other words, if we wish to understand the principal features of the superstructure (i.e. culture – including the legal institutions, political organisations and belief systems) of a society then we must carefully analyse the forces of production (productive technologies, institutionalised property relations) and the social relations of production consequent upon these productive forces. In a famous passage Marx and Engels (1968: 61) contend that 'the ideas of the ruling class are in every epoch the ruling ideas' (see Box 3.1).

When nineteenth-century capitalist England is analysed in these terms, it is no surprise to find that the state is the 'executive committee of the bourgeoisie' (Marx and Engels, 1967), that the laws and courts consistently favour the interests of capital as against those of organised labour, and that Christian doctrine as institutionalised in the established Church endorses the existing ordering of society and preaches the virtues of humility to the poor. Although Marx is sometimes equivocal about how strict a relation of determination obtains between base and superstructure, the broad thesis that he advances is that forms of consciousness crystallise into cultural forms and practices which are to be understood as originating socially. The social relationships that provide

---

Box **3.1**

Marx and Engels on 'ruling ideas'

The ideas of the ruling class are in every epoch the ruling ideas: i.e. the class which is the ruling *material* force in society is at the same time its ruling *intellectual* force. The class which has the means of material production at its disposal, has control at the same time over the means of mental production, so that thereby, generally speaking, the ideas of those who lack the means of mental production are subject to it. The ruling ideas are nothing more than the ideal expression of the dominant material relationships, the dominant material relationships grasped as ideas; hence of the relationships which make the one class the ruling one, therefore, the ideas of its dominance. The individuals composing the ruling class possess among other things consciousness, and therefore think. In so far, therefore, as they rule as a class and determine the extent and compass of an epoch, it is self-evident that they do this in its whole range, hence among other things rule also as thinkers, as producers of ideas, and regulate the production and distribution of the ideas of their age: thus their ideas are the ruling ideas of the epoch. For instance, in an age and in a country where royal power, aristocracy, and bourgeoisie are contending for mastery and where, therefore, mastery is shared, the doctrine of separation of powers proves to be the dominant idea and is expressed as an 'eternal law'.

Marx and Engels (1968)

---

the touchstone for understanding cultural forms and practices are those predicated on the mode of production.

At first sight this formulation seems to allocate a secondary role to culture as a mere reflection of the material base of a society. However, even Engels, whom many regard as a simplifier of Marx's ideas, baulks at the implications of this position. It is a view that gives culture no significant role in social change; for example, it denies the potentially revolutionary effects of art forms such as theatre and novels in transforming people's perception of the world and thus their action within it. The debate focuses around the determining power of the material base and the degree of autonomy to be given to the superstructure. Williams (1973b: 4) suggests that Marx 'uses the notion of determination and conditioning not in the narrow sense but in a much looser sense of setting limits, exerting pressure and closing off options'. He goes on to argue that Marx did not see either base or superstructure as fixed entities but as dynamic and shifting relationships, and this therefore precludes any simple formulaic conception of the relationship between the two. If determination is to be understood as setting limits, exerting pressure and closing off options, then what we have instead is an agenda for empirical inquiry. This is precisely the view taken by versions of cultural Marxism (e.g. Jameson, 1991), where the base–superstructure metaphor becomes simply a problem to guide inquiry, not a solution. Historically, the significant challenge to Marxian conceptions originates in the thought of **Max Weber** (1864–1920).

3.1.2 | Weber, status and inequality

Max Weber (1978) proposed a complex approach to inequality which expressly takes account of non-economic dimensions of ranking and inequality. Against Marx, Weber maintains that the operation of **power** (p. 94) in societies is yet more fundamental than their economic basis. Power is defined as the capacity of individuals or groups to realise their will, even in the face of the opposition of others. This yields three categories fundamental to the analysis of inequality: *class*, *status* and *party*. Inequality may be located in economically defined classes (here Weber emphasises market capacity in contrast to Marx's stress on property) but could also be founded in status groups (organised around notions of prestige and honour) and political parties and groupings. In this elaboration he sought to refine the measurement of inequality and to show the potential singularity of his criteria as well as their connectedness. For example, power is often linked to class-based wealth but it can be separated in situations where power is linked to knowledge. Status refers to style of life. It also refers to social esteem, the respect and admiration accorded a person according to his or her social position (see Box 3.2), and this can be local rather than structural and take account of interpersonal subjectivities. Marx's stress on structural relationships and on the duplicitous nature of culture tends to be replaced by a view of classes as ranked hierarchies of fixed groupings through which individuals may be mobile. While the categories are fixed and classes are bounded, individuals may, none the less, change their class position. Furthermore, Weber's discussion emphasises how both class and status distinctions can affect people's *life chances*, that is, the chances that an individual has to share in the economic and cultural goods of a society. Material and cultural goods are often asymmetrically distributed and class and status rankings will ensure that people will have differential access to these goods. These features of Weber's thought are important to bear in mind when considering non-class based systems of inequality.

The opening up of the relationship between inequality, meaning and manifestation allows for the consideration of systems of inequality other than class. There are ranked societies where there is unequal access to positions of status and prestige and these are not necessarily linked to economic wealth. An example is found in those traditional African societies where the chiefs did not live at a higher standard of living than their subjects and where economies were redistributive, that is the chief received tribute which he then gave back to his followers as a mark of his status and largesse. The position of many European noble families is a contemporary example of ranked society: access to claim a title is limited, usually to family members, and many of these titled families are no longer wealthy and have no power by virtue of their nobility in their societies. Within families there are usually ranked orders, sometimes of generations, sometimes of generation and gender. Once one starts to look and notice, it is clear that notions of rank and inequality are pervasive in English society. In England accent still serves as a telling sign of status. Other features of speech patterns also express status

Box 3.2

Weber on status

In modern 'democratic' society ... all explicitly regulated status privileges for individuals are done away with. [In some of the smaller Swiss cities] only families belonging to broadly similar taxation groups dance with each other ... But status is not necessarily connected with a 'class situation': normally it stands rather in glaring contradiction to the pretensions of naked property ownership ... The 'equality' of status of the American 'gentleman' finds expression in the fact that ... it would be considered the height of bad taste – wherever the old tradition prevails – for even the richest 'chief' to treat his 'clerk' as in any way at all of unequal rank, even in the evening in the club, over billiards or at the card table. It would be unacceptable to treat him with that kind of condescending affability which marks a difference in position, and which the German chief can never avoid entirely – one of the most important reasons why German club-life has never managed to seem so attractive there as the American club.

In content, social status is normally expressed above all in the imputation of a specifically regulated style of life to everyone who wishes to belong to the circle. This goes together with a restriction of 'social' intercourse – that is, intercourse that does not serve any economic, commercial or other 'practical' purposes – including especially normal intermarriage, to the circle of status equals ... [In the USA] one example of this is that only those who reside in a certain street ('The Street') are regarded as belonging to 'society' and as fit for social intercourse, and are accordingly visited and invited ... For the rest, social 'status' is usurped by certain families who have resided in a certain area for a long time (and who are, naturally, correspondingly well-to-do), such as the 'FFV' or 'first families of Virginia', or the descendants, real or alleged, of the 'Indian princess' Pocahontas or the Pilgrim Fathers, or the Knickerbockers, or the members of some extremely exclusive sect, or all kinds of circles of associates who mark themselves off by some criterion or other. In this case it is a matter of a purely conventional social differentiation based essentially on usurpation (although this is admittedly the normal origin of almost all social 'status'). But it is a short step from this to the legal validation of privilege (and lack of privilege), and this step is usually easy to take as soon as a certain arrangement of the social order has become effectively 'settled' and has acquired stability as a result of the stabilisation of economic power. Where the consequences are followed through to the limit, the status group develops into a closed *caste*. That is, distinction of status is guaranteed not only by convention and law, but also by ritual sanction to such an extent that all physical contact with a member of a caste regarded as 'inferior' is held to be ritually polluting for members of the superior caste, a stain which must be religiously expiated. The individual castes, indeed, in part develop quite separate cults and gods.

Weber (1978: 49–50)

rankings. Studies of who interrupts whom has found that parents interrupt children, men interrupt women, doctors are not to be interrupted by patients. All these are illustrations of the pervasive nature of hierarchy and status-based inequality in day-to-day living in which a socially adept member of society must be well versed.

3.1.3 | Caste societies

Comparisons are often drawn between caste and class societies. These comparisons sometimes draw attention to the apparent similarities of the structured system of groups and the fixed relationships between constituent groups. However, it is misleading to link the two systems in this way since to do so is to focus upon structure at the cost of overlooking culture. Class inequality is based on economic criteria and culturally it is open to an individual to achieve his or her own class position. Individual class mobility is possible in class systems, and indeed this is the ethos of most industrial class systems in the contemporary world. Caste systems are based on religious and ritual criteria. Castes cannot be understood in secular terms of inferiority and superiority for the principle that ranks the parts in the whole is religious (Dumont, 1970). In Hindu India there are four categories (varnas) which are distinguished from one another by degrees of **ritual** purity (p. 288) as established in the Sanskrit texts. These varnas are: Brahmins, who are the priests and scholars; Kshatriyas, who are the rulers, the warriors and the landowners; Vaisyas, who are the entrepreneurial middle classes; Sudras, who are the cultivators, workers and traders. The Harijans, or untouchables, perform the most menial tasks. In theory they lie outside the caste system because they are ritually impure. Although these broad varnas are associated with occupation, in practice within a village there will be a number of occupations associated with a particular varna, so although the system is clear and unambiguous in principle, empirically there may be variety and complexity.

A person's caste membership is ascribed; this ascription is given religiously and is dependent upon the individual's conduct in their past life. Reincarnation is a central doctrine of Hindu belief, and to lead a good life so that one may be given a favourable caste position one must live according to caste values and conventions. Being a good person means fulfilling caste expectations. If one fails to meet caste expectations then in reincarnation one will come back as a member of a lower caste or even in non-human form. The insistence upon living according to caste expectations places great value on maintaining caste boundaries, since contact with lower castes may be polluting and one may only carry out those tasks that are fit for one's own caste. The consequence of this is that there is a high degree of social segregation between castes but, of necessity, a high degree of economic interdependence as castes rely on others to perform tasks for them which they themselves are forbidden to carry out.

An important aspect of the maintenance of group boundaries is that marriage is endogamous, that is, individuals must marry within their own caste. This is an important difference from class societies where marriage is not formally circumscribed between classes. Although in practice people in class societies tend to marry within their social class, it is nevertheless permissible to marry into another social class and this is a known and socially acceptable means of achieving social mobility, especially for women.

The variety of occupational ranking and the diversity within villages means that in practice the significant groupings of caste in day-to-day relationships are the *jati*, endogamous groups of kin who are associated with certain occupations. These local subgroups of caste often compete with one another for ranking in the caste system and it is not unusual for a local *jati* to seek to improve their caste ranking by adopting the manner and practices of a higher-ranking group. It may take time for these aspirations to be met and their claims to be realised but movement is possible within the caste system and boundaries are more permeable than might at first seem possible. However it would be a mistake to assume that the possibility of mobility raises again the possibility of comparison with class systems. The mobility issue in the caste system is that the claim of the *jati*, the whole group, must be recognised, not just the claim of a single individual. Adrian Meyer (1960) observed that in one village in South India which he studied there were twenty-three castes which grouped themselves according to the use of the same smoking pipe, the provision of ordinary food for common meals and the provision of food for feasts. The higher castes in the village would share the pipe with almost all castes except four; between twelve and sixteen castes would smoke together, although in some cases a different cloth must be placed between the pipe and the lips of the smoker. Meyer writes that castes that enjoyed power in the village were not fussy about what they ate and with whom they ate. It was the middle range of castes who were very fussy so that if, for example, they were invited to a feast by a more powerful group, they would insist on having their food served raw and carrying it home to cook. The untouchables – the outcasts – are literally outside the caste system altogether. Caste discrimination is not allowed in modern India, but in practice the diversity of groupings and the complexity of relationships make such a ruling difficult to enforce.

There are other examples of religious ranking that you may wish to explore. Drid Williams (1975) notes that hierarchy is a defining characteristic of any Christian order and of many others too. She studied a group of nuns and remarked that, for the nuns, what mattered and what came first was the issue of nearness or distance from God. The hierarchies of the convent were hierarchies of spirituality, not power.

3.2 | Legitimating inequality

Whenever the topic of inequality is addressed, the question that sooner or later must be asked is: why do people allow such manifest inequalities, disadvantages and injustices to remain as an acceptable part of their lives? Weber's answer is that people believe in certain legitimate forms of authority – an ordering of the world which they accept as 'right', as justifiable and reasonable. Three bases of legitimate authority are identified: *traditional* ('accept this, because it is what our people have always done'), *charismatic* ('accept this, because of the leader or prophet's exceptional powers which can transform your life'), or *legal-rational* ('accept this, because this is what is specified in the laws and rules governing our society'). These forms of legitimacy show how cultural power is institutionalised and given moral grounding. They provide the bases on which people may tolerate inequality and subordination, if not actually embrace it. A somewhat different range of solutions to this problem gives more explicit attention to the cultural dimension. We consider next: Gramsci on hegemony; the Frankfurt School's development of the theory of ideology; and Bourdieu's theory of the habitus.

3.2.1 | Ideology as common sense: hegemony

One development of Marx's thinking about ideology which has proved influential and productive in cultural studies is the concept of **hegemony** (p. 106), advanced by the Italian Marxist Antonio **Gramsci** (1891–1937) (p. 38). He wanted to explain how, despite manifest evidence of inequality, capitalist ruling classes continue to rule. Only part of the explanation, Gramsci believed, was due to ruling-class control of the means of coercion in society (the military and police). At the back of repressive state power lay hegemony, 'a special kind of power – the power to frame alternatives and contain opportunities, *to win and shape consent*, so that the granting of legitimacy to the dominant classes appears not only "spontaneous" but natural and normal' (Clarke *et al.*, 1975: 38). Hegemony is about what passes as the common-sensical, unquestioned backdrop of reflection on the workings of society. Consequently, the terrain on which hegemony 'is won or lost is the terrain of superstructures'. The central institutions of capitalist society – its courts and schools, its churches and mass media – are immured in ideas and beliefs that promote ruling-class interests. The pervasiveness of hegemony is described by writers from the Birmingham School thus:

> A hegemonic cultural order tries to *frame* all competing definitions of the world within its *range*. It provides the horizon of thought and action within which conflicts are fought through, appropriated (i.e. experienced), obscured (i.e. concealed as 'national interest' which should unite all conflicting parties) or contained (i.e. settled to the profit of the ruling class). A hegemonic order prescribes, not the specific content of ideas, but the *limits* within which ideas and conflicts move and are resolved.
>
> (Clarke *et al.*, 1975: 39)

The notion of hegemony is related to the concept of ideology but can be distinguished from it:

> Hegemony works through ideology, but it does not consist of false ideas, perceptions, definitions. It works *primarily* by inserting the subordinate class into the key institutions and structures which support the power and social authority of the dominant order. It is, above all, in these structures and relations that a subordinate class *lives its subordination*.
>
> (Clarke *et al.*, 1975: 39)

Gramsci believed that capitalism could not be overcome until the working class developed its own counter-hegemony which successfully challenged the existing ruling-class cultural hegemony.

Existing power relations and inequalities are thus stabilised through cultural hegemony. The concept has been influential in cultural studies since the 1970s because it offered a more complex analysis of ruling-class domination than older models of ideological domination. The Birmingham School linked the concept of hegemony to

Defining concept 3.2

Hegemony

The concept of hegemony is used as a way of thinking through the relationships between culture and **power** (p. 94). It was developed within the work of the Italian activist and Marxist theorist **Antonio Gramsci** (p. 38). His concern was to understand how social groups organise their rule and, more pressingly for him, why there had been no proletarian revolution. His conclusion was that rule involves both domination (the coercive use or threat of force via the military and the police) and hegemony (the organisation of consent based upon establishing the legitimacy of leadership and developing shared ideas, values, beliefs and meanings – a shared culture). Rule for Gramsci was hegemony armoured with coercion (Gramsci, 1971; see also Williams, 1977, and Bennett *et al.*, 1981).

In his theoretical and political work Gramsci's aim was to show how this consent (hegemony) had two characteristics. First, that it was class based and class biased. He wanted to show that culture is saturated with class power. As 'hegemony', shared values, shared meanings and shared beliefs are seen to act in the interests of the dominant (or hegemonic) class. The examples that Gramsci uses are ideas like religion in Italy and Fordism in America which promote certain values and forms of conduct over others, e.g. the work ethic. He connects both with the economic and political development of class-divided societies. Second, hegemony does not just happen; it is something that has to be organised. This also carries the positive political message that the situation can be altered. In many way this goes beyond **Marxist** (p. 97) theories of **ideology** (p. 84). It rejects the notion that ideas are firmly rooted in class positions and sees them as 'material forces' which can organise groups, shape terrains of encounter and debate, and define positions to be attacked or defended. It also has a rather deeper notion of culture and meaning which sees them as basic to the formation of all social relations rather than as something 'added on', the icing on the economic cake. Here classes are defined as much culturally as economically.

There are several problems that must be noted. First, just as for ideology, Gramsci's concentration on class makes the concept of hegemony problematic. Any suggestion that people have singular **identities** (p. 224) and interests and that there is a singular political project is not useful when trying to deal with the multiplicity of interrelated identities and power relations within which we all live. These singular class identities also carry with them the unhelpful notion of 'false consciousness'. The question is whether we can extend the term to use it to talk about race, gender and sexuality. Second, the tendency to use the notion of 'hegemony' to imply the existence of one dominant, totalising culture of power must be avoided. Gramsci certainly did not mean the concept to be a rigid, static, uniform and abstract one. In part this means talking about counter-hegemonies and a whole series of competing alternative hegemonies. It also means recognising that hegemonies are constructed: they are forms of rule that social groups try to put together. We might think of them as ongoing 'projects' of legitimating leadership

→

and negotiating consent through a whole series of channels. Here is Gramsci on American Fordism:

> Recall here the experiments conducted by Ford and the economies made by his firm through direct management of transport and distribution of the product. These economies affected production costs and permitted higher wages and lower selling prices. Since these preliminary conditions existed, already rendered rational by historical evolution, it was relatively easy to rationalise production and labour by a skilful combination of force (destruction of working-class trade unionism on a territorial basis) and persuasion (high wages, various social benefits, extremely subtle ideological and political propaganda) and thus succeed in making the whole life of the nation revolve around production. Hegemony here is born in the factory and requires for its exercise only a minute quantity of professional political and ideological intermediaries.   (Gramsci, 1971: 285)

These 'projects' are about the organisation of ruling groups, the creation of alliances ('hegemonic blocs') and the forging of collective identities (perhaps via religion, politics or culture). They are also about the organisation of power-laden relations with others in order to create a managed consent. This is all to be understood as a continual process with a whole variety of different social groups involved. In order to understand this we can use another, related Gramscian term: 'war of manoeuvre'. This means seeing society as both a real and an ideological battlefield where everyone is trying to establish what side they are on, who are enemies, who are allies, what position they are in, what the terrain looks like, how the battle is progressing, and what weapons they should use. It is a constant ongoing struggle within which ideas, beliefs, values and meanings are among the weapons. However, what is important is not any innate characteristics of these weapons but whether they are effectively deployed. This sense of hegemony as a process of active organisation is a useful one which is not restricted to understanding class relations.

Further reading

Bennett, T., Martin, G., Mercer, C. and Woollacott, J. (eds) (1981) *Culture, Ideology and Social Process: A Reader*, Milton Keynes: Open University Press.

Gramsci, A. (1971) *Selections from the Prison Notebooks*, London: Lawrence & Wishart.

Williams, R. (1977) *Marxism and Literature*, Oxford: Oxford University Press.

Althusser's notion of ISAs (ideological state apparatuses – schools, churches, media, etc., which support state ideology) to present a more complex analysis of how class domination worked. Hegemony emphasises that the ruling class was itself composed of different fractions, that class rule also required the winning of the consent of the subordinate class, and that it facilitated the empirical exploration of the institutions through which cultural hegemony works such as youth subcultures (Hall and Jefferson, 1976), schools (Willis, 1978) and broadcast news (Glasgow University Media Group,

1976). Importantly, the notion of hegemony is amenable to historical analysis since it is not a 'given' of any particular class or organisation but is something that has to be worked for and sustained. So it can be argued, for example, that hegemonic cultural domination was a more significant source of working-class subordination in Britain in the 1950s than in the 1930s. That stabilisation was obtained in the 1930s by market effects (unemployment as an instrument of labour discipline), whereas in the prosperous 1950s working-class consent was obtained through the hegemonic domination of an ideology of affluence.

3.2.2 | Ideology as incorporation: the Frankfurt School

Members of the **Frankfurt School** (p. 109), in particular Theodor Adorno and Max Horkheimer (in *Dialectic of Enlightenment*, 1972) developed an analysis of the part played by the superstructure in accounting for the failure of the revolutionary social change that Marx had predicted. They focused on the role played by mass culture, or what they preferred to call the 'culture industry' (to distance themselves from the – erroneous – idea that mass culture is a spontaneously erupting popular culture) in securing the incorporation of the working class into capitalist society.

Through radio, TV, movies and forms of popular music like jazz, the expanding culture industries were disseminating ruling-class ideologies with greater effectiveness than Marx could have envisaged. The further development of consumer society in the twentieth century powerfully aided the process of working-class incorporation by promoting new myths of classlessness, and wedded the working class even more tightly to acquisitive and property-owning beliefs. Even oppositional and critical forms of culture can be marketed (consider Andy Warhol or the Sex Pistols). The development of the culture industries, one part of the superstructure, seemed destined to subvert the social changes that Marx saw as originating in society's material base. Other Frankfurt School theorists, notably Marcuse, condemned the 'one-dimensionality' of the society that the culture industries were shaping with increasing success. Unfortunately, the force of the Frankfurt School's critique was weakened by their apparently elitist dismissal of forms of popular culture.

The celebrated – some might say notorious – example of the Frankfurt School's dismissive approach to popular culture is Theodor Adorno's (1903–69) analysis of popular music. Writing in the late 1930s and early 1940s Adorno proposed that the industrialisation of musical production and the commercialisation of musical consumption had a baleful influence on musical form. Popular music had become standardised: 'all aspects of musical form – Adorno instances overall structure (the thirty-two-bar chorus), melodic range, song-types and harmonic progressions – depend upon preexisting formulae and norms, which have the status virtually of rules, are familiar to listeners and hence are entirely predictable' (Middleton, 1990: 45). Popular music has become standardised into particular types (country & western, heavy metal, etc.) and within each type particular formulas develop. Adorno contrasted popular with 'serious' music which was not standardised but distinctive and original. Beethoven's work was Adorno's exemplar of serious music. Not only were popular and serious music different

Key influence 3.3

The Frankfurt School

The Frankfurt School describes the social and cultural theorists who worked for, or were connected with, the Frankfurt Institute for Social Research. Their method, known as 'critical theory', has influenced the study of mass culture and elements of feminist, postmodernist and postcolonial theory.

The Institute was founded in 1923. At its inception, it was very much a product of the cultural freedom and political struggles of the German Weimar Republic (1918-33). Key members of the Institute were Max Horkheimer, Theodor Adorno and Herbert Marcuse. **Walter Benjamin** (p. 373) was an important associate. Along with **Gramsci's** (p. 38) writings, critical theory forms the main body of Western (as opposed to Soviet-influenced) **Marxism** (p. 97). Influenced by the ideas of **Marx** (p. 97) and Freud, it resists systematic, universal explanations of cultural and social phenomena. In 1933 the Nazis' rise to power forced the Institute into exile in Germany. Many of the members were Jewish and faced death if they stayed. Horkheimer, Adorno and Ernst Bloch all went to the United States. Post-Weimar, the School began its critiques of the Fascist system from which they fled and the new experience of North American mass culture: for example, Adorno's well-known critique of popular music. This culminated in Adorno and Horkheimer's best-known work, *The Dialectic of the Enlightenment* (1972, orig. 1944) which contains seminal chapters on the origins of **modernity** (p. 400), mass culture and anti-Semitism. After the war, the Institute returned to Germany. Adorno contributed works of philosophy, *Negative Dialectics* (1973) and *Aesthetic Theory* (1984). Hannah Arendt continued the critique of authoritarian regimes in *The Origins of Totalitarianism* (1958). Ernst Bloch and Herbert Marcuse explored the utopian dimension of critical theory in *The Principle of Hope* (1986, orig. 1959) and *Eros and Civilization* (1955). The political events of the 1960s led to a revival of interest in the School's work. Its recognised heir is Jürgen Habermas. True to its impulse, in his *The Philosophical Discourse of Modernity* (1987), he criticises both members of the School and poststructuralist thought.

The key to understanding critical theory is the recognition that it is not a unified body of thought. Rather, it defines itself 'negatively' against other theoretical systems. Each strand criticises and debates in a polemical style. Each thinker is best understood in his or her relation to other thinkers. For example, Adorno's apparent resistance to utopian solutions is best understood in relation to the more overt utopianism of Bloch and Benjamin. It is this tradition of critique and debate that is the School's most important legacy.

Further reading

Bloch, E., Lukács, G., Brecht, B., Benjamin, W. and Adorno, T.W. (1980) *Aesthetics and Politics: Debates between Bloch, Lukács, Brecht, Benjamin, Adorno*, London: Verso.

Jay, M. (1974) *The Dialectical Imagination: A History of the Frankfurt School and the Institute of Social Research 1923–1950*, London: Heinemann.

Held, D. (1980) *Introduction to Critical Theory*, London: Hutchinson.

in form, they encouraged different responses from listeners. Serious music made challenging demands on the listener while popular music made little – popular music had become just another stultifying element of mass culture. Adorno maintained that:

> Music for entertainment ... seems to complement the reduction of people to silence, the dying out of speech as expression, the inability to communicate at all. It inhabits the pockets of silence that develop between people moulded by anxiety, work and undemanding docility. ... It is perceived purely as background. If nobody can any longer speak, then certainly nobody can any longer listen. ... Today ... [the] power of the banal extends over the whole society.   (Adorno, quoted in Middleton, 1990: 34)

Adorno's searing critique of popular music places it alongside film, cheap holidays and comic books as a method of incorporating the working class. But it is an analysis that has a number of flaws (see Longhurst, 1995: 10–14 for a summary). The popular/serious distinction introduces a value judgement before the analysis has begun. The scope of Adorno's theory (all popular music under capitalism) seems far too broad and Adorno does not appear to appreciate how that scope might be constrained by his own social and historical location. Some types of music (jazz, blues) might have non-standard structures or might express resistance to dominant ideologies. The development of new musical technologies might also work against the tendencies that Adorno noted in popular music. Thus critics suggest that the claims of the theory exceed what can be reasonably sustained. As a critique of Tin Pan Alley in the 1930s and 1940s Adorno made some sense, but the application of his ideas to the proliferation of popular musical styles since then tells only a small part of the story.

The contribution of the Frankfurt School was to indicate the enormous expansion of the culture industries and their increasing influence in modern capitalism. Leo Lowenthal (1961) captured this change well in his study of the biographical articles appearing in popular US magazines between 1890 and 1940. He found that in the earlier period it was predominantly 'captains of industry and finance' who were profiled. This gave way in the later period to a preponderance of interviews with movie stars and singers. There had been a shift from the 'idols of production' to the 'idols of consumption' – the culture's heroes were now firmly located in superstructural occupations, not the material base. Unlike the economism of earlier Marxian traditions, the Frankfurt School attributes a significant role to the domain of culture in analysing relations of culture and power.

3.2.3 | Habitus

The work of Pierre Bourdieu (Robbins, 1991) stresses the learned, unquestioned, taken-for-granted aspect of cultural behaviour. He puts forward the notion of **habitus**, the cultural framework wherein and whereby the habitual aspects of everyday social thought and action operate. People's perceptions, thoughts, tastes and so forth are shaped by their habitus. These principles are symbolically mediated in action and are learned through experience. However, the power of the dominant classes ensures that their cultural habitus is preferred over others. Schooling is a process in which dominant class power works symbolically to legitimate the kinds of accomplishment that will count as knowledgeable and worthy and to relegate features of the habitus of working-class pupils as evidence of failure. In effect, one cultural system of **symbolism** (p. 288) and meaning is imposed on that of another social group – a process termed 'symbolic violence' (Bourdieu and Passeron, 1990).

Bourdieu is especially interested in the ways in which particular groups (classes) in society mark their identity, the symbolic ways in which they express values and seek to maintain boundaries between themselves and other groups. He describes this as the process of 'distinction' (Bourdieu, 1984). Again there is a stress that culture is deceptive. While novelty and creativity is acknowledged, the emphasis lies on the ways in which what is learned and practised is an affirmation of an existing set of hierarchically organised systems of relations. Bourdieu's position has been described thus:

> To a very large extent we do not choose our identity. We receive the cultural identity which has been handed down to us from previous generations. ... We adhere to groups, whether clubs or political or religious organizations, and we adopt the identifying images of social groups, whether in hair-style or clothing, so as to confirm our social identity. For the same reason, we take steps to distinguish ourselves from those who belong to different groups. Our tastes and our lifestyles have no intrinsic value but serve to maintain the coherence of the group to which we belong.
>
> (Robbins, 1991: 174)

Bourdieu's focus on distinctions between groups rather than on the whole system of which they are a constitutive part contrasts with the Marxian and the dominant ideology approach. Bourdieu sees cultural striving for individual expression as a sham but in many ways he has a more organic approach to the issue of inequality than Marx, Gramsci or the Frankfurt School. This difference is expressed in a sharper form between those theorists who see inequality as functional to the operation of society (Davis and Moore, 1945) and those who see it as conflictual (Marx). The issue of culture as ideology is neutral in these positions; ideologies that support the system, such as those based on religion (as, for example, the belief in the divine right of the sovereign in medieval Europe or the secular belief in deference in contemporary society) can be used to support either view of inequality.

These debates around hegemony, incorporation and habitus show how misleading it is to think of culture as a mere superstructural 'effect' determined by the material base. In the views of the theorists reviewed in this section, culture plays a part in legitimising and naturalising many forms of inequality. The extent to which dominant ideologies are themselves guarantors of social order has been questioned by some sociologists. Abercrombie *et al.* (1980) propose that the dominant ideology only brings coherence to the dominant class, not to the society as a whole. Subordinate classes are incorporated by political and economic control, not ideological dominance. A different approach is taken by other theorists who argue that the cultural dimension is a significant source of inequality. We next consider a selection of studies that examine this idea.

3.3 | Culture and the production and reproduction of inequality

In this section we explore the relevance of the explanations of inequality discussed above by means of a review of some cultural manifestations of inequality. We shall look at studies that focus on the key variables of class, ethnicity, gender and age as sources of cultural inequality.

3.3.1 | Class

The notion that cultural differences follow class lines has a long history. Weber's concept of status includes the notion of style of life and opens the way for considering overlaps and disparities between class and status. The early classics of cultural studies, notably Hoggart (1957) and Thompson (1968) were very much concerned with the shaping, characteristics and development of working-class culture. In more recent work on youth subcultures the notion of class cultures is also prominent (see Chapter 8). Cultural commentary has long addressed the lifestyles of the rich as well as the poor. Those living at the extremes of society, it is sometimes felt, are perhaps very different in their ways of life from the broad mass in the middle. In this section the issue of class, culture and inequality is approached by means of a survey of explanations of the lifestyles of the poor: we shall consider in turn the culture of poverty thesis, the cycle of deprivation theory and the putative emergence of an underclass.

The culture of poverty thesis was popularised in the 1950s and 1960s by the American anthropologist Oscar Lewis's studies of the poor in Mexico, Puerto Rica and the United States. He sought to understand how it was that poverty seemed to reproduce itself across generations: how poor people appeared to produce more poor people. His explanation concentrated on the distinctive cultural features shared by the so-called undeserving or disreputable poor. Lewis (1961, 1966) proposes that the poor have a distinctive subcultural lifestyle which, like any culture, is a design for living that provides a structure and rationale enabling the poor to go on with their lives. Controversially, he suggests that this way of life is passed down across the generations through the medium of the family. At the centre of this theory is the identification of about seventy traits said to characterise the culture of poverty. They include the following:

- The poor are not integrated into the major institutions of the society and remain fearful of them.
- There is a low level of community organisation or identification with place in slum neighbourhoods.
- Families display the following features:
    - absence of a lengthy childhood phase of the life-cycle
    - early initiation into sex
    - free unions or consensual marriages
    - high incidence of abandoned wives and children
    - female-centred households

the improvement in community services since the Second World War, deprivation and problems of maladjustment so conspicuously persist?' His reply was to posit a 'cycle of deprivation' (see Figure 3.3).

In Sir Keith's view, parents who were themselves deprived in one or more ways in childhood went on to become the parents of another generation of deprived children. This political initiative was recast in social scientific terms as an investigation of the intergenerational continuities in 'disadvantage', a more inclusive term than deprivation. It also conceded that factors other than family and culture might cause disadvantage, such as social group membership, ethnic discrimination or residence in a particular locality. The outcome of this research was to build a more comprehensive picture of the multiple disadvantages faced especially by members of the lowest social classes (see Rutter and Madge, 1976).

Blaming the poor for their circumstances is still a popular activity for cultural commentators. It sometimes surfaces in debates about the 'underclass'. Beginning with Marx's comments about the lumpenproletariat, class analysts have long recognised the existence of a class beneath the established working class. Attempts have been made to identify this class in structural terms, that is, in terms of the conditions of life encountered by people in particular circumstances. For example, in the United Kingdom the underclass is often felt to comprise groups such as the long-term unemployed, single-parent families and elderly pensioners. In the United States it is often associated with poor black residents of inner-city ghettos. Structural explanations of the underclass are usually advanced by academic sociologists who emphasise that these groups of people have most to lose from processes of continuous industrial restructuring

---

Box **3.3**

Poverty and ill health plague unskilled 'underclass'

More than 2 million people who left school with a poor grasp of reading have since sunk into poverty, ill health and depression, according to a study by the Basic Skills Agency.

Financial incentives were needed to get this potential underclass back into basic education and training, said Alan Wells, director of the agency. Those who became marginalised were not only more likely to be out of work or on low wages, but were less likely to vote or belong to community organisations. Women with very low literacy were five times as likely to be classified as depressed as those with good basic skills.

Educational prospects for their children, being brought up in 'stressful conditions', were bleak – parents were less likely to show a positive attitude to education or get involved with school. A third of the adults said they had difficulty

➡

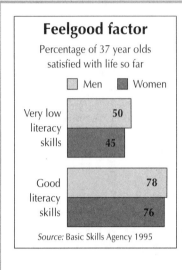

Feelgood factor

Percentage of 37 year olds
satisfied with life so far

☐ Men   ■ Women

Very low literacy skills: Men 50, Women 45

Good literacy skills: Men 78, Women 76

Source: Basic Skills Agency 1995

reading aloud from a child's book. Adult literacy and numeracy programmes must be expanded to prevent large numbers being excluded, the report said.

Mr Wells said the Government had made improving basic skills a priority in its Welfare to Work programme for young people. 'This report emphasises the dangers we face in developing an underclass of excluded people – out of jobs, not participating, increasingly depressed, and often labelled as failures.'

Using the National Child Development Survey of more than 17,000 people born in 1958, John Bynner and Samantha Parsons of City University interviewed a 10 per cent sample from England and Wales about their literacy and numeracy skills, jobs, health, and mental outlook.

One in five had low or very low literacy and numeracy problems, said the report, *It Doesn't Get Any Better.* This was almost certainly an underestimate, said Professor Bynner.

When these men and women left school in 1974 there were jobs available, but, without qualifications, their chances of employment have declined steadily. They started work younger, but from the age of 23 were more likely to be unemployed and by the age of 37 when they were interviewed had more 'lost years' of full-time work.

Among men, 46 per cent with very low literacy and 11 per cent with low literacy had no qualifications, compared with 4 per cent with good literacy. Figures for women followed this pattern.

They were more than four times as likely to live in a household where neither partner was working.

A standard psychological test revealed men and, especially, women with very low literacy were much more likely to show the symptoms of depression than those with average or good skills.

Guardian, 1 July 1997

and its impact on the patterning of work. But other commentators, notably the influential New Right theorist Charles Murray, have seen this phenomenon in primarily cultural (and by extension highly moralistic) terms. Murray focuses on the significance of illegitimacy, marital breakdown, inadequate patterns of childrearing and criminality among the poor (for a review of the debates about the underclass in the United States see Wilson, 1993; for the United Kingdom, see Lister, 1996). Correspondingly, the solutions advanced for the problems of the underclass differ. Structural explanations emphasise that underclass problems are rooted in the social and economic structures of societies. Culturalist accounts of the underclass seek changes to the moral fabric of individuals and their family circumstances. The debate between these two under-standings of the underclass reruns elements of a much older cultural distinction between the 'deserving' and 'undeserving poor'. An assertion of cultural difference is a response that is apparently only acceptable in the first case.

3.3.2 | 'Race' and ethnicity

The term 'race' is often placed in inverted commas in cultural studies to signal its historical dubiousness and its questionable status as an analytic concept. In the nineteenth century there were numerous attempts by European investigators to classify people according to racial groups ('white', 'yellow', 'black') and ascribe unchanging characteristics to them. These attempts to legitimate sets of stable racial differences scientifically are now widely regarded as spurious (Miles, 1989: 70). However, race is an everyday concept that people routinely employ to categorise themselves and others.

Irrespective of the scientific utility of the term, race is widely believed to serve as a potent marker of cultural difference. These differences, whether they are believed to be grounded in culture or biology, are often manifest in expressions of racism, the discrimination against others on the basis of their membership of a perceived 'racial' group. Racism, when it is practised by an individual towards another person, is often termed 'racial prejudice'. However, racism can also take institutional form, as when a political policy takes it for granted that immigration is a problem, or when schools systematically understate the contribution of ethnic minorities to the development of art and science and teach history that fosters a negative perception of Africa or Asia. Institutional racism may be more deeply taken for granted and thus harder to dislodge than a prejudicial attitude.

Sometimes the terms 'ethnicity' and 'ethnic groups' are employed in an attempt to put some distance between the historically racist implications of 'race' and to emphasise that it is cultural and not biological difference that is the key distinction. This move may not be sufficient to escape racist connotations of difference and inferiority, as we can see from some of the research carried out on language codes.

The marking of forms of language (language codes) as preferred or dispreferred in particular contexts is a common method of legitimising cultural inequalities. In the 1960s Basil Bernstein suggested that the speech of working-class children exhibited a 'restricted code' of simple sentence forms, incorrect grammatical structures and impoverished vocabulary. Middle-class speech displayed a grasp not only of the restricted code but also of an 'elaborated code', the standard English of public life and the mass media. In the United States these ideas were translated by social scientists into notions of 'cultural deprivation' or 'cultural deficit' (Bernstein quickly repudiated the association of his ideas with these theories; see Jenks, 1993: 164, 169). The tag became attached especially to predominantly black urban ghetto populations whose apparent 'verbal deprivation' disadvantaged this group, disenfranchising them from the mainstream institutions of society. The effects of this supposed deficit was claimed as the cause of the failure of black children to do well in school.

The idea that the language of black schoolchildren (Black English Vernacular – BEV) is nowhere near as flexible, as subtle and as detailed as standard middle-class forms is challenged by Labov (1972b) who, through a detailed analysis of actual instances of children's speech, presents a very different picture. He demonstrates the 'rich array of grammatical devices' (p. 212) through which the children display verbal dexterity and argues that many non-standard forms are no less adequate in conveying a reasoned argument than standard middle-class English and, further, that in some respects BEV expresses reasoned argument more directly and cogently than standard forms. (Standard English, Labov (1972b: 222) claims, can be 'simultaneously overparticular and vague', where 'the accumulating flow of words buries rather than strikes the target'.) By means of close examination of actual usage Labov shows how commentators have focused on surface differences between standard and non-standard forms and mistakenly concluded that BEV is an inferior method for conveying logical reasoning.

Labov and other sociolinguists established the logical and communicative adequacy of BEV in the 1970s. Since then the idea has emerged that black language is essentially different from standard English and that it should be taught in schools. Advocates of *Ebonics* suggest that language is a function of power and, in order to counter established distributions of power, it is necessary to institutionalise the teaching of BEV to give it legitimacy. In the Oakland School Board case of 1997 it was eventually agreed that black English should have the status of a second language, since to describe it as a primary language might imply a disposition towards its acquisition that could be negatively construed. The politics of multicultural education – that is, education that is organised to promote a recognition of cultural difference – are notoriously complex. Schooling takes place in the context of wider distributions of power and hegemony. And, as noted in Chapter 2, ways of talking unavoidably locate persons in networks of power and disadvantage.

Writers within cultural studies have tended to avoid the anodyne terminology of 'ethnicity' and headed straight for the freighted term 'race' in an attempt to grasp the real-world significances of this dimension of cultural difference and inequality. One early study in this tradition, by Stuart Hall *et al.* (1978), examined the moral panic surrounding the emergence of 'mugging' as a social problem. 'Mugging' was not a legal term ('robbery' and 'larceny from the person' being the English legal terms) but it quickly came into popular and media discourse from 1972. The category was imported from the United States and, translated into British society, it came to stand for a particular kind of perpetrator – a young, black male, usually acting with one or more accomplices. Hall *et al.* trace the development of a moral panic that bears some resemblances in form to the earlier moral panics surrounding 1960s youth subcultures (see the discussion of mods and rockers in Chapter 8). The myth of the black mugger condensed many exaggerated fears about youth, crime and personal safety, race and immigration. Hall *et al.* see mugging as an 'ideological conductor' of the 'crisis of hegemony of early 1970s Britain'. They show how the moral panic over mugging, a social constructed deviant behaviour, nevertheless articulated deeper concerns about British society. The exaggerated response to the 'problem' of mugging is indicative of a drift towards more authoritarian state interventions.

The theme of racial issues sparking a hegemonic crisis in Britain where established understandings about the ordering of ethnic groups come to be challenged is taken up in *The Empire Strikes Back* (Centre for Contemporary Cultural Studies, 1982). This is the work of seven members of the Birmingham centre who set out to analyse race and racism during the 1970s from a vantage committed to black resistance. They emphasise the need to locate racism not in individual psyches but in large-scale social processes. They draw particular attention to the change in Britain's international position since the end of the Second World War. They suggest that the prominence of 'race' as an issue in the 1970s is connected to the decline of Britain's position as a major trading nation. It is in the context of these changes that immigration policies, ethnic bases of competition in housing and labour markets, etc., must be set. In the crisis of hegemony facing British capitalism, the **Centre for Contemporary Cultural Studies** (CCCS) (p. 327) collective maintains, the British state is moving in authoritarian directions (which were shortly to become even more pronounced as Thatcherism became established). At the level of lived experience this issues forth in forms of popular authoritarianism of which racism is the most conspicuous example. Racism, then, cannot be understood as a simple ideological phenomenon. To appreciate its force requires a detailed and specific analysis of changes in the British state and Britain's dominant and working classes.

The Empire Strikes Back sparked a good deal of controversy when it appeared, not least because of its criticisms of the 'race relations industry' which they saw as just one more instrument of control over black working-class communities. They are especially critical of those studies that account for black disadvantage in terms of fractured nuclear families that fail to provide adequate material and emotional support to children. Such studies 'pathologise' black subcultures. The CCCS collective are hesitant about offering recommendations beyond a general endorsement of black **resistance** (p. 258). In the analysis of cultural forms, this emphasis on a complex Marxism in which close historical analysis of political and economic circumstances is combined with a commitment to black struggles has been taken forward most notably in the work of **Paul Gilroy** (p. 166).

Another part of the larger picture in which 'race' and racism is located is the history and consequences of **colonialism** (p. 189). Many influential conceptions of racial difference have their origin in the colonial encounters of European powers with the societies that they sought to dominate. Cultural analysts such as **Edward Said** (p. 168) and Gayatri Spivak have focused on colonial texts to consider what they tell us about oppressor and oppressed. Said's (1978) monumental study, *Orientalism* (see section 4.5) shows how European writing, from the nineteenth century onward, constructed a conception of the 'Orient' (the Middle East in particular) as exotic, glamorous and dangerous. This fictional, simplified framework nevertheless served to act as a potent cultural grid through which the cultures of the East were apprehended. Gayatri Spivak (1987) is more concerned with issues of power and representation. In a world dominated by Western discourses, how can the 'subaltern' status of Third World voices achieve parity in dialogue with those of the West? Said and Spivak deepen our understanding of racial difference by using the tools of literary and cultural analysis to problematise the representations of the 'other' contained in Western texts.

3.3.3 | Gender

Discussions about relationships between men and women mirror many of the arguments that have been discussed above. It is often remarked that, whatever the nature and type of relationships between men and women in whatever part of the world, there is inequality, men are the dominant sex and are regarded as superior to women. It is suggested that there is a natural hierarchy between men and women, a natural inequality. Support for this inequality is often drawn from historical evidence and from comparison with the animal world (the science of ethology, popularised by the works of Desmond Morris). It seems that it is impossible to think about gender without thinking about hierarchy (Moore, 1993). One suggestion about the seemingly inevitable connection between male superiority and female inferiority is that this thinking is congruent with other patterns of thought in Western society, namely the hierarchical relation between nature and culture. Moore (1993), Ortner (1974) and Strathern (1981) have all drawn attention to the association of female with nature and male with culture; female with the private and the domestic and male with the public and the collectivity. They argue that, in societies where culture is seen as preferable and superior to nature and where the public always encompasses the private, then it is inevitable that gender relations will be apprehended in hierarchical terms.

Defining concept 3.3

Feminism

Feminism describes both the broad movement that has campaigned against the political and social inequalities between men and women and the school of academic criticism that takes gender inequality as its object of study. Feminists all critique the subordination of women to men, but they differ widely in their strategies for empowering women. Feminist accounts of the role of culture in gender inequality have been central to the development of cultural studies.

A crude periodisation of feminism might identify three phases: first-wave, second-wave and postmodern feminism. First-wave feminism describes the women's movement of the late nineteenth and early twentieth century. While it contained many different political strands, first-wave feminists generally accepted a fundamental, natural difference between men and women, but argued for their political equality. The best-known campaign of first-wave feminism was for women's suffrage. Second-wave feminism describes the women's movement from the 1960s on. This period has seen an enormous growth in feminist scholarship, which has employed various forms of understanding inequality. An early concept used was patriarchy. This was originally an anthropological term which describes a social system in which older men are entitled to exercise socially sanctioned authority over other members of the household or kinship group, both women and younger men. However, this term has been criticised subsequently, because it does not discriminate

→

between the different forms of inequality manifested in different cultures. An alternative concept, proposed by Gayle Rubin, was the sex/gender system. This makes use of an important distinction between sex and gender where sex describes biological or natural differences, while gender describes the social roles of masculinity and femininity. Rubin argued that different societies assign different kinds of roles based on biological differences. The object of feminist inquiry should then be the kinds of cultural expectations that these roles presume. Research into gender identity has taken many different paths in the investigation of how gender is socially constructed. One influential strand has been post-structuralist, psychoanalytic feminism. This argues that gender identity is constructed through language. In Western culture, language is phallogocentric, or male centred. Because they are excluded from full access to language, women are refused entrance to a masculine symbolic order. However, psychoanalytic accounts have been criticised for universalising male dominance. More recently, postmodernist feminism has queried the sex/gender distinction. Judith Butler has suggested that it is a mistake to assume that there is a foundational, natural sex upon which gender identity is constructed. Instead, she argues that sex itself is socially constructed. To use a useful metaphor employed by Linda Nicholson, we use the body as a coat rack to hang our cultural assumptions about sexual differences. For example, women's bodies are soft, passive and yielding, men's are hard, active and forceful. Butler's argument usefully problematises the idea that sex comes first and that gender is somehow created from it. While no one argues that there are not physical differences between men and women, Butler directs the spotlight back onto the question of how culture interprets those differences. As white academic feminism has been challenged by the diverse strands of the women's movement worldwide, the question of cultural difference and the relationships between gender, 'race', sexuality and class have moved to centre-stage in feminist theory. However, there is a continuing and productive tension between this emphasis on difference and feminists' desire to assert a collective identity to combat the abiding social inequalities between men and women.

Further reading

Haraway, Donna (1991) 'Gender for Marxist dictionary', in D. Haraway, *Simians, Cyborgs and Women: The Reinvention of Nature*, London: Free Association Books.

Nicholson, L. (1995) 'Interpreting gender', in L. Nicholson and S. Seidman (eds) *Social Postmodernism*, Cambridge: Cambridge University Press.

The argument is similar to the discussion of caste and class above. It is necessary to understand that cultures may be organised differently and experienced differently from those in the West and that it is important not to fall into the trap of thinking 'that all societies struggle with the same givens of nature, so that all social formations appear equivalently and thus holistically organized to the same ends' (Strathern, 1988: 342–3). A general theme of women anthropologists writing about issues of gender and inequality (and some men, notably Ardener, 1974, and Errington and Gewertz, 1987) is that much of the writing on non-Western societies is formulated in terms of Western assumptions about persons and relationships; there is a Western folk model which sees social life in dichotomous terms and this is imposed onto the substance of other lives and other arrangements. In making this line of argument – namely that the dichotomies are a feature of anthropological discourse, not the social and symbolic systems of the societies studied by the anthropologist – the reasoning is similar to that made in discussions about writing culture (see Chapter 5). Errington and Gewertz (1987), who studied the Chambri people of Papua New Guinea (a people made famous by Margaret Mead and Reo Fortune as the Tchambuli), write that in her wish to explore variations in culture and personality, Mead, paradoxically, underestimated the extent to which cultures differ from one another. In a complex argument they contrast Western views of persons as distinct and competent individuals with private subjective selves and unique dispositions with the Chambri view that persons are constituted by social relationships. Individuals are not bounded entities who possess certain characteristics as they are said to be in the West (and note the value-laden term 'possess' – denoting a materialist view of persons) but persons who share and who are part of others through their relationships and are multiply constituted (see also Strathern, 1988). Errington and Gewertz (1987) argue that women among the Chambri are very different from women in the Western world and gender concepts have a different meaning.

The caution against assuming universal patterns of superiority and inferiority has a validity beyond that of the discussion of gender and has particular importance for discussions about the ways in which people are multiply constituted in Western society through race, ethnicity, class, age and gender. All these are attributes of personhood and the task for the analyst is to see how these different attributes constitute the person rather than assuming that these categories of difference simply attach to the person (Strathern, 1988). The reflexive process with regard to Western ideas of personhood and gender have been taken further by some to question the distinction between sex and gender (Collier and Yanagisako, 1987; see also Chapter 7). Collier and Yanagisako take from Foucault (1984b) the idea that sex is an effect rather than an origin; just as it has been argued above that gender is the product of discursive practices, so also is sex.

> The notion of 'sex' made it possible to group together, in an artificial unity, anatomical elements, biological functions, conducts, sensations, and pleasures and it enabled one to make use of this fictitious unity as a causal principle, an omnipresent meaning: sex was thus able to function as a unique signifier and as a universal signifier.
> (Foucault, 1984b: 154)

This does not mean that anatomical differences are not noted but these are not necessarily the basis of a binary sex classification (Moore, 1993). Notwithstanding the suggestion that perhaps sexual differences are culturally constructed, there seems to be general agreement among commentators about the cultural constructs of gender in Western society (Strathern, 1988; Moore, 1993; Butler, 1990; Tcherkezoff, 1993).

Taking up the issues of knowledge and the power to impose particular knowledge constructs on society as a whole, which were considered earlier in this chapter, feminists have developed the idea of patriarchy. The argument is that society is based on convention, a convention in which men are prominent – men have certain interests in the framing of cultural conventions which give them power and exclude women from power. Using the dichotomous model of Western thought, Strathern (1988) states that women experience a double arbitrariness: the Western dichotomous model creates opposed categories so women are what men are not, and since it is men who decide who men are, then women are doubly excluded. These feminist arguments rest on the cultural conventions about the nature of persons in Western society, the idea of duality and dichotomy and the connectedness of these ideas to the domains of the individual and society and to men and women/male and female in Western society. Strathern argues that there is in Western society a social contract view of society – culture is collective – held in common and so individuals willingly subordinate themselves to it (Strathern, 1988). This masks the reality that culture is 'authored' – 'it is patriarchy that produces cultures' (Strathern, 1988: 323).

These views have also been given voice in discussions about women's participation in science (Harding, 1991), where it is said that the idea of woman the 'knower' is a contradiction in terms. Harding points to the male domination in scientific fields. The production of scientific knowledge tends to be the province of those who have male characteristics and since it is predominantly men who have male characteristics so women are excluded (Harding, 1991: 48). Dale Spender (1982), writing about women in education, makes a similar cultural argument: that women cannot have a voice as producers of art and knowledge because they are not men. Spender cites the marginalisation of many women in the field of literature and women's rights, for example, Aphra Benn, Mary Wollstonecroft, Catherine Macauley (see also Chapter 6).

While feminism has served to refocus attention on the nature and sources of women's subordination it has also, obliquely, stimulated interest in the characteristics of masculinity and the sources of male domination. There is what is sometimes termed 'hegemonic masculinity' (Connell, 1987) (see also 7.4.3), the ideal form of being a man: a configuration of courage, physical strength and toughness that is endlessly paraded in the mass media (see also Chapter 7). One codification of the US version is offered by Brannon (1976):

- 'no sissy stuff' – the avoidance of all feminine behaviours and traits
- 'the big wheel' – the acquisition of success, status and breadwinning competence
- 'the sturdy oak' – strength, confidence and independence
- 'give 'em hell' – aggression, violence and daring

In recent times masculinity itself has, in some quarters at least, become another contested terrain. The pervasiveness of hegemonic masculinity has been empirically questioned and it is suggested that there are in fact multiple discourses of masculinity rather than a single ideal (Edley and Wetherall, 1996), a situation that has led some commentators to speak in the plural of 'masculinities' (Hearn, 1996). Masculinity or masculinities are undoubtedly real but whether the concept on its own has much efficacy in explaining the gendered basis of domination seems open to question.

3.3.4 | Age

Age and the ageing process are, like gender and the body (see Chapter 7), apparently natural processes. Yet it will come as no surprise that within this chapter, as in the book as a whole, the argument will be made that what seems straightforwardly natural is highly cultural and culturally specific, with the added twist that the cultural ordering locates age in the biological world. Culture naturalises age, as it also naturalises gender, race, ethnicity – all those aspects of human experience that seem to be rooted in biology. Age is a cultural construct symbolically located in a biological metaphor (Spencer, 1990). The apparently natural process of the person's passage from birth to death in chronological time is ordered, sometimes controlled, but always shaped by cultural ideas of what is appropriate and conventional behaviour at certain ages.

Age has different meanings among different peoples not only for the individual but for all those with whom the individual is associated; a change of status for an individual involves others in new roles and relationships. Also as with gender (see above), theorising about the significance of age must give regard to, and account for, the ways in which age is mediated by class, gender, race, ethnicity and all other culturally significant variables at particular moments and contexts. A small example to make the point is that most people who live in British society treat age as if it was a linear process in which one is born and one passes through measured time until one's death. However, there are those in British society who believe in reincarnation and so the ageing process is for them a circular and not a linear journey, and they look forward to a rebirth – equally for those who believe in the resurrection of the spirit and/or operate with a different sense of time than those who believe that death is the end of being.

In fact something that seems so taken for granted and unremarkable empirically turns out to be an important principle of social organisation and marker of social differentiation. It is arguable that age and gender are the most important shapers of social experience for individuals. It seems that in all societies people are treated differently on the basis of age. It is possible to speak of age roles, the clusters of expectations that accrue to certain chronological and structural age bands. Most societies have conventions about the age at which it is suitable for individuals to marry (this may be gendered), to engage in sexual relations, and in British society there are a set of age-determined laws regarding employment and retirement.

The significance of age is not just a matter for the individual; it is a relational matter touching on how one behaves to others. The ideas about the relationship are incorporated into social expectations, often into scientific, 'natural' ideas about how children should develop and how they should behave to others. The disciplines of child psychology and developmental psychology and the psychology of ageing rest on models of 'normal' (cultural) expectations. In the individual life course the experience and practice of age roles is common within the domestic life-cycle. Most people grow up in the company of others and learn the age-appropriate behaviour for their sex, class, race or ethnic group and according to scientific and medical knowledge.

Historical evidence shows that our ideas of age-appropriate behaviour have changed considerably in the recent past in Western society. Aries (1962) has written that the idea of childhood is a recent one, and Mayhew's (1968) survey of the London labouring classes in the middle of the nineteenth century showed clearly the class-based experience of childhood. Mayhew declared himself appalled by the lack of childhood for these children, noting how they looked older than their years and finding that children as young as 6 or 7 years old were making a living for themselves independently on the streets of London. Reports in the contemporary world often speak of the high incidence of child labour in Third World countries where children are seen as a resource to make a contribution to household economies. Caldwell (1982) points out that the flow of resources from parents to children in affluent Western societies is unidirectional, whereas in Third World countries resources flow both ways when children start to make a contribution to the household.

In some societies the transition to new status roles based upon age is highly ritualised. Such highly ritualised movements are named rites of passage. The seminal work on rites of passage was carried out by van Gennep (1960) who established a common threefold pattern in such rites: the phase of separation (when the initiate leaves old associations and relationships); the liminal (limbo) phase; and the phase of incorporation into the new status. It is possible to identify several rites of passage in modern society. Weddings and funerals are both loosely associated with age but not necessarily so. There are a few rites of passage that are tightly linked to age and to major shifts in life courses. The commonest example in Western society is that of the bar mitzvah for young Jewish boys (and bat mitzvah for girls) which takes place around the age of 13 when boys become ritually full adult members of the religious community. The best-known ceremonies of status change are to be found in African societies, for example among the Masai and the Hazda people. Young men, when they are initiated into the status of warriors, become the herders of cattle and serve in this role for several years until a new cohort of young men are initiated. Rites of passage often involve scarification or other forms of bodily mutilation so that there is a permanent, visible sign of changed status. Sociologists have taken these ideas further, advancing the idea that 'status passage' (Glaser and Strauss, 1971) is a very common feature of modern societies. For example, occupational life is increasingly frequently thought of in 'career' terms and the status passages associated with promotion, retirement and so forth are important ceremonial occasions in organisational cultures.

All this may yield the misleading impression that status passages are pre-programmed by the culture and unproblematically experienced by the passagee. Often there is considerable individual diversity of experience in negotiating status passages, even among persons in broadly similar situations. Consider the transition from school to work. Although it is becoming increasingly less common for this transition to be made at the age of 16, until the mid-1970s this was a standard trajectory for very many British schoolchildren (as late as 1976 only 25 per cent of pupils stayed on beyond their sixteenth year). Almost a quarter of school-leavers entered the labour market with no educational qualifications. Many end up in poorly paid occupations. Of course, the process is not random: this is an important moment of social and cultural reproduction. As Paul Willis pointedly puts it:

> The difficult thing to explain about how middle class kids get middle class jobs is why others let them. The difficult thing to explain about how working class kids get working class jobs is why they let themselves.   (Willis, 1977: 1)

The conventional sociological wisdom invokes a description of class culture that suggests that working-class children are enmeshed in cultural notions such as a lack of deferred gratification, weak or absent future orientations and the like. For Willis such explanations are doubly inadequate, for they fail to suggest where these attitudes originate (1977: 141) and they work with a notion of culture as something passively absorbed by the children rather than as at least in part actively constructed, a 'product of collective human praxis' (Willis, 1977: 4).

The core of Willis's explanation turns on his interpretation of the 'lads' counter-school culture. His ethnography of school-leavers in their final year at school distinguishes the 'lads' from the more conventional pupils (the 'ear 'oles'). The lad's culture is sexist and racist, as well as anti-school and anti-conventional morality. Most of the lads will end up with unskilled, heavy labouring jobs that pay reasonably well early on but which will soon take their toll on their health. Ironically, this is a future that the lads choose and willingly embrace.

Willis documents the features of the lads counter-school culture – drinking and smoking, sticking up for their mates, 'dossing, blagging and wagging', 'having a laff' and so on. He goes on to argue that the counter-school culture is both ideological in character and a rational response to the realities of their situation. The lads culture is ideological because it facilitates their smooth transition into dead-end work. As an ideology the culture masks the reality of the lads' situation and effectively dupes them into accepting the worst jobs going. But the counter-school culture is also a considered, rational response. The lads positively value manual work which they regard as masculine, an activity infused with machismo. Moreover they do not much care what work they do providing that it is a manual job (white-collar work they define as effeminate). In their indifference to occupational choice the lads effectively reaffirm their conviction that all jobs are essentially the same. And this, for Willis, represents a penetration of the real conditions of their existence as a class – it is a profound expression of the reality of their situation. As capitalism advances, labour becomes more abstract and thus it matters less and less what occupation you work in so long as you work. In this sense the lads counter-school culture is a rational assessment of the reality of their situation in the labour markets of advanced capitalism.

3.3.5 | Structural and local conceptions of power

To conclude this section we can make two general observations about the workings of culture, power and inequality. These concern power as a local phenomenon and the interrelations of systems of domination and disadvantage.

All the theories reviewed above tend to take an objectivist, structural view of power and inequality. They decode the cultural to reveal the true nature of the relationships involved and, as has been argued, much of that revelation has turned on power and its manifestations. Often that power seems to be encompassing in form, lodged in the class structure or ethnic hierarchy or institutionalised arrangements between men and women. But, as Foucault reminded us, power is also something diffused throughout the working of a society. So power is also local and can be understood contextually rather than structurally – a recommendation for a hermeneutic approach to understanding culture, power and inequality.

This can be illustrated by two studies of power and control in work organisations: Malcolm Young's study of the police (1991) and Sallie Westwood's study of Asian women garment workers (1984). In both cases control was in the hands of men, and in the case of the factory the control was experienced through the discipline of the operation of a capitalistic enterprise. The firm was, Westwood says, a reputable and paternalistic firm, which stressed good time-keeping and maximising output. There were separate canteens for management (all men) and workers (mainly women) and there were considerable differences in pay and conditions, with the management receiving company cars and allowances. Westwood describes how the women developed a 'shopfloor culture of resistance and celebration'. Elaborate rituals were engaged in to celebrate the events of the women's lives (weddings, engagements) and the women used company time and resources for their own affairs. The shopfloor culture was one that emphasised friendship and solidarity. The playful antics of the women can be regarded as rituals of resistance which served to emphasise 'sisterhood and strength against the patriarchy and gender inequalities of the company' (Westwood, 1984: 2).

The women police officers described by Young had scant opportunity to develop a counter-culture to the heavily masculine ethos of the police force. There were fewer women and they tended to be more isolated. Additionally they were not seen as legitimate members of the force by the policemen. Young describes (1991: 219, 242, 233) the ways in which the women were marginalised and denigrated by the men, given abusive and humiliating names, and repeatedly subject to sexual innuendo in an organisation that was dedicated to a traditional masculine ethos and imagery. Young remarks that the state of the institutional mind kept women in narrowly defined roles and subject to the formal and informal domination of men.

In this last illustration the power exercised was in terms of gender hierarchies, a reminder that modern societies are subject to many systems of domination, not simply that of class, which nevertheless tends to be the predominant typifying feature of modern industrialised society. Power also worked in a capillary fashion, in that it was evident in everyday acts and their implications and consequences. If there are different hierarchies through which power is 'exercised', or different forms of power through which domination works, how are these systems of domination interrelated?

This is sometimes formulated as: how do race, gender, age and class disadvantages relate to each other? Note that the very way that the question is formulated disposes us towards a structural rather than Foucauldian conception of power. Within the frame set by a structural approach there is, as we saw in considering the cycle of deprivation, substantial evidence that economic and cultural factors can overlap or interact to produce multiple disadvantage. Being a black woman can increase the likelihood of the person being found in an underclass location. A poor black woman is likely to face disadvantages that those situated higher up class, racial and gender hierarchies will not. These are well-supported facts. There is a risk, however, of running away with such geometrical metaphors of overlapping disadvantageous categories of class, race, gender and age. These factors certainly describe the broad patterning of disadvantage and the oppressions (racism, sexism, class oppression, etc.) that result. Whether they illuminate the particularities of people's ordinary cultural experience is more open to question, as in everyday life we are all gendered, raced, classed and aged and these categories may have variable relevance to how we are treated in particular instances in everyday life (see West and Fenstermaker, 1995). For instance, we may sometimes feel ourselves to be badly treated by a shop assistant. Is this because of our race or class or gender or age? In actual instances the answer can be very variable for any given person, so it can be very difficult to pin down which particular source of disadvantage is operating. This difficulty does not deny the reality and force of these disadvantages. But it does serve to further underline Foucault's fundamental point about the omnipresence of power and resistance: dominations of class or race or gender are never complete or total and can be challenged in the conduct of our everyday lives.

3.4 | Conclusion

News broadcasts daily provide us with information about the cultural differences between people. The inequalities premised on these differences are the basis of many social conflicts (witness, for example, the long-running conflicts in the Basque region, Northern Ireland and the former Yugoslavia). In this chapter we have reviewed explanations of the origin of inequality in capitalist societies and considered some of the leading theoretical ideas – hegemony, incorporation and habitus – which have been used to explain how inequality is justified and rendered acceptable. The chapter has also focused on the ways that these inequalities are made manifest through character-istic cultures of class, ethnicity, gender and age. The concepts, theories and studies reviewed above show some of the many ways in which all cultures are 'structured in dominance'. This work might also help to suggest ways in which strategies of resistance to systems of dominance might be organised.

Re-cap

This chapter has:

- reviewed the principal structural sources of inequality;
- surveyed explanations of the role of culture in legitimating forms of inequality;
- examined how class, race, gender and age inequalities are culturally produced and reproduced.

Further reading

A helpful survey of the base–superstructure debate and beyond can be found in Jorge Larrain's *The Concept of Ideology* (1979). Some of the ramifications of the dominant ideology debate are explored in Nicholas Abercrombie, Stephen Hill and Bryan S. Turner (eds) *Dominant Ideologies* (1990). Ruth Lister's collection *Charles Murray and the Underclass: The Developing Debate* (1996) contains short, lively contributions about the concept and reality of the underclass. On race and ethnicity, *The Empire Strikes Back* (1982), collectively authored by members of the (Birmingham) Centre for Contemporary Cultural Studies, is still an engaging read. There is a video of an illustrated lecture by Stuart Hall entitled 'Race as a floating signifier' available from Media Education Foundation, PO Box 570, Wembley, Middlesex HA0 2XN. Judith Butler's *Gender Trouble: Feminism and the Subversion of Identity* (1990) has been influential in shaping recent debates on gender. Many of the often overlooked cultural dimensions of ageing are discussed in Mike Hepworth and Mike Featherstone, *Surviving Middle Age* (1982).

Topographies of culture: geography, power and representation

4.0 | Introduction

Cultural studies is becoming increasingly aware of what we might call the geographies (or, indeed, topographies) of culture: the ways in which culture is, among other things, a matter of different spaces, places and landscapes. One sign of this is that the language of cultural studies is full of spatial metaphors. Chapter 1 of this book, for example, understands culture in terms of 'fields', 'maps' and 'boundaries'. Yet there is more to it than this since there is also a sense that culture – particularly when it is understood as something that is diverse, fragmented and contested – cannot be understood outside the spaces that it marks out (like national boundaries or gang territories), the places that it makes meaningful (perhaps the Statue of Liberty or your favourite coffee shop) and the landscapes that it creates (from 'England's green and pleasant land' to the postmodern shopping mall). What this chapter aims to do is to use a variety of examples, both historical and contemporary, to show the ways in which issues of culture, meaning and representation are geographical matters. It does this through discussions of issues such as place, territoriality, landscape, travel and **globalisation** (p. 159) which connect culture and geography at every scale from the local to the global. In addition, these examples also serve to introduce a range of theoretical issues central to cultural studies and to this book – issues of **power** (p. 94) and **representation** (p. 61) – to show that these are geographical too. What all this demonstrates is that there is a broad set of fascinating interdisciplinary issues that connect cultural studies and cultural geography, from the basic connections between **identity** (p. 224) and place, to more complex relationships which concentrate on flow, flux and change. If all this is new to you it is worth starting with a brief look at how geographers have understood culture.

Learning objectives

▪ To learn about the connections between 'cultural studies' and 'cultural geography'.

▪ To see how culture can be understood through its geographies: from the local to the global.

■   To understand the various ways in which spaces, places and landscapes (the subject matter of geography) can be interpreted in terms of cultural issues of meaning, representation and power.

4.1 | Cultural geography

4.1.1 | Cultural geography 'old' and 'new'

Perhaps it is unremarkable to suggest that cultures have geographies. We often think – as we watch TV or make travel plans – of different places having different cultures and in doing so we map out a more or less sophisticated cultural geography. Yet just as 'culture' is a contested concept, so is 'cultural geography'. We have to think carefully, and make serious choices, about how we understand these 'maps' of cultures and what their implications are for ourselves and others. Indeed, there are many ways of understanding 'cultural geography' and many ways of undertaking a study under this name. It is also clear that what people understand as cultural geography is different in different parts of the world and has changed dramatically over the last thirty years. What we want to do here is to concentrate on what has been called 'new cultural geography' – which is characterised by its strong links to other strands of cultural studies – and show how its practitioners understand culture's topographies. In order to do so it is useful to show how it developed in relation to another influential form of cultural geography which owes much to the work of Carl Sauer (1889–1975) who was professor of geography at the University of California at Berkeley from 1923 to 1954.

Sauer's cultural geography had particular characteristics. It was concerned with the relationships between humans (he would have said 'man') and nature within particular regions over long periods of time. One of his students has said of him that 'more than anything else, his appreciation of simple people living in close contact with inorganic nature and in symbiosis with plants and animals distinguishes Sauer's writing about man [sic] on the earth' (Leighly, 1963: 3–4). As a result, the regions he chose to study were generally rural ones which were only changing slowly. It also shaped how he thought it should be practised. Sauer was a strong advocate of active fieldwork. Even for past landscapes, it was seeing their traces for real that mattered. He also stressed the researcher's long-term immersion in a particular region in order to understand it, saying that:

> always there must be the base, the area for which the observer is making himself the expert. The human geographer cannot be a world tourist, moving from people to people and land to land, and knowing only casually and doubtfully related things about any of them.   (Leighly, 1963: 362)

Overall, his argument was that the material relationships between 'land' and 'life' were worked out differently in different places. In his view different cultures created, for example, different agricultural systems, different settlement systems and different transportation systems, all of which left their visible, material traces in the landscape as field systems, housing types or networks of tracks, paths and roads. Thus, distinct cultures created distinct landscapes as they shaped the natural environment slowly over time. It was the role of the cultural geographer to study those landscapes.

Figure 4.1 reproduces a diagram from Sauer's essay 'The morphology of landscape' (1925) in which he sets out his understanding of the relationship between the natural landscape and the cultural landscape. He shows a 'culture' operating over time on a 'natural landscape' to produce an amalgam of 'forms' (population, housing, production, communication) which can be summed up as a 'cultural landscape'. His model here is the ways in which physical processes – of erosion or vegetation – act over time to produce a natural landscape. This version of cultural geography can be summed up in his words: 'The cultural landscape is fashioned from a natural landscape by a culture group. Culture is the agent, the natural area is the medium, the cultural landscape the result.' This meant that it was cultural geography's role to study 'the impress of the works of man [sic] upon the area' or 'man's [sic] record upon the landscape' (quotations from Leighly, 1963: 343, 326 and 342). Moreover, the way in which that 'impress' or 'record' was to be studied or read was in terms of delimiting 'culture areas'. These were understood as regions of the world that had distinctive landscapes or unique ensembles of buildings, farming techniques and population patterns. For example, Sauer, in his essay on 'The personality of Mexico' (1941), described the Mexican cultural landscape as divided into two sets of cultures: 'the high cultures of the

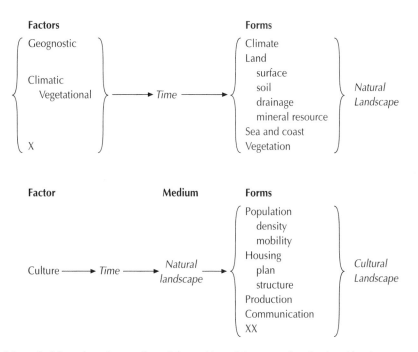

Figure 4.1 ▪ Carl Sauer's understanding of the making of the natural and cultural landscapes. (Source: Sauer, 1925: 337, 343.)

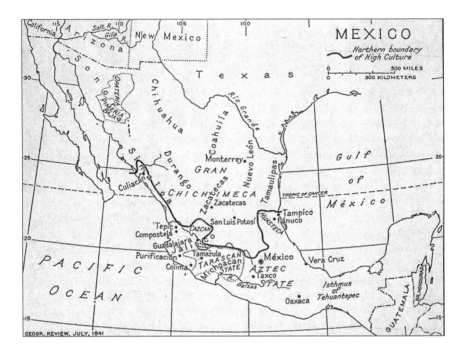

Figure 4.2 ▓ Carl Sauer's map of Mexico showing the boundary between the cultures of the South and the North. (Source: Sauer, 1941: 106.)

South and the ruder cultures of the North' (Leighly, 1963: 105) which could be mapped as two culture areas (see Figure 4.2). Thus Sauer's cultural geography created a 'map' of the world in which cultures occupied and shaped bounded and more or less homogenous areas. Cultural geographers might study the landscapes of those areas through material artefacts or the diffusion of cultural objects and traits – e.g. domesticated animals – between them. Indeed, much of what is taught and studied as 'cultural geography' – particularly in the United States where Sauer's influence was strongest – still retains this basic understanding of culture's geographies. Yet the connections between geography and other branches of cultural studies have, in various ways, fostered what has been called a 'new cultural geography' which questions many of Sauer's notions.

The first signs of change came from Britain where cultural geography was less well established. This did not, however, immediately entail a full-scale rejection of Sauer's ideas. Peter Jackson (1980) argued that geography could learn a lot from anthropology and that much common ground could be found in Sauer's humanism and his attention to the relations between nature and culture. Denis Cosgrove (1983) argued for a radical cultural geography which would align Marxist historical materialism and cultural geography. This was to be based upon an affinity between **Karl Marx** (p. 97) and Carl Sauer who, despite Sauer's lack of attention to class relations and the structures of social power, both began with the relationships between nature and culture and used that as a basis to understand material and cultural 'modes of life'.

Yet the direction in which cultural geography was moving was away from Sauer's vision. In 1987 Cosgrove and Jackson set out what they took to be the 'new directions in cultural geography'. It was to be:

- contemporary as well as historical (but always contextual and theoretical);

- concerned with space as well as landscape;

- urban as well as rural;

- concerned with relations of domination and **resistance** (p. 258);

- assertive of the centrality of culture to human life;

- concerned with 'representation' as much as 'reality'.

It was not going to be 'rural and antiquarian' and it would not be concerned with 'physical artefacts' or 'cultural areas'. The new cultural geography would be very different from what was seen as Sauer's conservative anti-modernism. In other writings the 'new' cultural geography was understood as a rejection of the 'old'. For example, in the first few chapters of Peter Jackson's (1989) *Maps of Meaning* he depicts Sauer's understandings of culture and cultural geography as 'badly outdated' and 'unnecessarily limited' (p. 9) and rejects them in favour of an analysis that owes much to the cultural politics of **Raymond Williams** (p. 5) and the work of the **Birmingham Centre for Contemporary Cultural Studies** (p. 327).

Although 'new' cultural geography has many different strands – and it is no longer quite so new – it can be argued that what characterises it is the way that it is concerned with issues central to cultural studies more generally (Shurmer-Smith and Hannam, 1994; McDowell, 1994; Carter *et al.*, 1993; Bird *et al.*, 1993). In turn, these interdisciplinary connections have meant that such issues are given a new twist by being considered in a geographical context, and that these geographical ideas – as we argued at the outset – are having a wider influence over the language and theory of cultural studies as a whole. The two key issues are:

1. Cultures of difference: meaning, power and resistance.

2. The poetics and politics of representation.

Cultures of difference: meaning, power and resistance

The main idea here is that culture is a contested domain. It is an arena of conflict between different social groups (defined by race, class, gender, age, sexuality and so on) which are trying to define and impose their ways of understanding – their systems of meaning – onto the world: 'It is a domain, no less than the political or the economic in which social relations of dominance and subordination are negotiated and resisted, where meanings are not just imposed but contested' (Jackson, 1989: ix). Here the cultural is political and cultures need to be understood as codes or 'maps of meaning' with which different social groups attempt to define themselves, others and their places in the world. Social, economic, political and personal relationships are defined through cultural meaning. There are many examples of this in what follows: battles between classes over the meaning and naming of urban places; gendered conflicts over the nature of nationalism; and the competing definitions of racial identities. In part this is about a celebration of **difference** (p. 138). It is about realising that there is a plurality of cultures and a multiplicity of geographies. However, unlike for Sauer, this is also a realisation that these groups are often making meanings in the same places and are bound to each other through relations of power and **resistance** (p. 258) rather than peacefully occupying separate 'culture areas'.

Defining concept 4.1

Essentialism and difference

Essentialism is the doctrine that ascribes a fixed property or 'essence' as universal to a particular category of people. To propose that women are good childcarers because they are women, that black people are good at sports because they are black, that Jews are good at arguing because they are Jews – all because 'they are like that' – is to engage in essentialist thinking. The basic principles of stereotyping any cultural grouping operates on essentialist lines.

In cultural studies there is a wariness of essentialist reasoning for at least four reasons: (I) positing supposedly 'essential' characteristics often simply involves the reproduction of the prejudices of one group about another – essentialist reasoning imposes a partial set of judgements grounded in the situation and interests of one social group upon another; (2) essentialist accounts of persons and activities as 'typical' usually involve enormous over-generalisation which ignores the differences between the members of a category (are *all* women really like that? *all* black people); (3) it follows that essentialist reasoning cannot explain why these differences within a category exist in the first place; (4) essentialist doctrines are especially pernicious when they postulate the presence of essential charac-teristics as a matter of biology and genetic inheritance. The alternative to essentialism is some form of social constructionist account. The prototypical view here is summed up in Simone de Beauvoir's statement: 'one is not born a woman; one becomes one'. Social constructionism emphasises the part played by social learning in the acquisition of supposedly 'essential' characteristics and can be regarded as a more realistic point of view which is better equipped to do justice to the diversity of experiences encountered by persons within a category. Constructionism does not have it all its own way, however. Some would maintain that we can speak of 'black music' or claim that only 'black' people can fully appreciate it on the basis of their shared origins and common experiences.

Cultural studies tends towards a valorisation of differences and a corresponding recognition of the plurality of identities to which persons can lay claim. Some of these identities arise from the increasing scale and complexity of modern societies (class, occupation, education, race, gender, regional and national identities). Others derive from

→

the emergence of new social movements (**feminism** (p. 120), gay rights, black struggles, the greens) and create the social basis for **identity** (p. 224) politics. The celebration of difference brings difficulties of its own. The relations between groups are power relations which mark off who is to be included and excluded and therefore entail valuations of relative worth made in the context of material interests. The policy of 'separate development' in apartheid South Africa was not simply about maintaining cultural differences. Also, the plurality of identities available can make for some strange alliances: for example, **bell hooks** (p. 223) (1991: 59) observes that 'sexism has always been a political stance mediating racial domination, enabling white men and black men to share a common sensibility about sex roles and the importance of male domination'. Rights to difference, it seems, can only be sustained within an agreed framework of rights and provision universal to all members of a society.

Further reading

Grossberg, L. (1996) 'Identity and cultural studies: is that all there is?', in S. Hall and P. du Gay (eds) *Questions of Cultural Identity*, London: Sage.

Sarup, M. (1996) *Identity, Culture and the Postmodern World*, Edinburgh: Edinburgh University Press.

The poetics and politics of representation

The key point here is that understanding cultures is not a question of understanding an objective 'reality' that can be found 'out there' in the world. The implication of what has just been said above is that there are many different realities; each collectivity has a view of the world which can claim to be 'real'. These views of the world are only made available through forms of **representation** (p. 61). They must be spoken as stories, written, painted, filmed or sung and played. We need to pay attention to the ways in which the world is portrayed (or re-presented) in all sorts of media (Duncan and Ley, 1993; Barnes and Duncan, 1992). This is very different from Sauer's belief that a culture is simply given to us in the landscape that we can see with our own eyes. We need to be attentive to a whole series of new questions about any representation: what is included? What is left out? What is the aim? What are the influences? What media have been used and why? What is the role of the audience? Again there will be many examples below. These questions all raise issues of what we can call 'poetics' – the way in which something is represented – and connect them to issues of 'politics' – the power-laden relationships between social groups and individuals. We shall see how they also involve spaces, places and landscapes.

All these new concerns with geography, power and representation mark substantial differences between the 'old' cultural geography and the 'new' cultural geography (Anderson and Gale, 1992). They have also been instrumental in the increasing importance of cultural geography and in the ways in which it has substantially influenced the discipline of geography as a whole as well as contributing a new angle to the conceptualisation of cultural studies (Matless, 1995a). Whether this continues into the future remains to be seen. What the rest of this chapter will do is to consider some of the ways in which these concerns with power and representation help us to understand culture's geographies.

So far we have used the crucial terms **space, place and landscape** (p. 141) without any reflection. However, they are very important to what follows and need some preliminary definition, although it must be remembered that these definitions are, like all representations, always contested in ways that will be explored throughout the chapter (see Johnston *et al.*, 1994). Using these terms we go on to explore cultural geographies at various scales from the local to the global, starting with the ways in which we can understand ideas of place – at a local level – in terms of cultural politics and ending with ways of thinking through our positioning within processes of **globalisation** (p. 159). This chapter also moves through different ways in which culture's geographies can be conceptualised; starting from the ideas of connections to place and representations of those places which make them meaningful and, by the end of the chapter, considering issues of **hybridity** (p. 159) and syncretism which mean that we all have to rethink notions of our place in the world. In between we consider the different meanings of the urban and the rural in terms of the power relations of class, gender and race that they reveal; the way that territories and landscapes are implicated in the making of national identities; and the power relations that are a crucial part of understanding how the West has represented the East. In each case – and we shall be introducing a variety of theoretical perspectives – there are different ways of thinking through the connections between geography, power and representation. However, each instance also reinforces our claim that cultural studies needs to think about culture's geographies because of the ways in which that can involve a rethinking of how we conceptualise culture.

4.2 | The power of place: locality, language and culture

While the brief definition of '**place**' (p. 141) is a start, it does not really capture the different ways in which this concept can be used to connect geography and cultural meaning. What this section aims to do is to consider some of the ways in which places (here understood at the local level although that is by no means the only scale at which place is important) are given meaning. What it shows is that understanding places in terms of **power** (p. 94), **resistance** (p. 258) and **representation** (p. 61) does much to illuminate how cultural worlds are constructed and contested. In order to understand this, however, it is necessary to begin with an approach to place that considers its meanings in a rather different way.

4.2.1 | Philosophies of place

Ideas of 'place', 'sense of place' and 'placelessness' were central to the work of early humanistic geographers like Yi-Fu Tuan and Edward Relph. They tried to think through

Defining concept 4.2

Space, place and landscape

Space

Considering space means considering the ways in which, in 'reality' or 'representation', the distribution of things and activities, the formation of boundaries and patterns of movements are both culturally produced and part of the construction of culture. The spaces that we inhabit, whether they are the sacred and profane spaces of an African village or of Wall Street, are intimately bound up with the ways in which we live out our lives.

Place

Considering place (see the more extensive discussion below) means considering the ways in which particular locations are important in the making of a cultural world. Our understandings of the world are tied closely to the ways in which we construct and contest the meanings of particular, often named, places. For example, the ways in which certain meanings of 'home' are used to support specific understandings of how families should work, or how understandings of 'London' capture the different political and economic relations of North and South.

Landscape

Considering landscape means considering how both an area and the look of that area are laden with meaning. 'Reality' and 'representation' are not easily separated here and the object of study can be a city skyline or a country scene in oils. What is at issue is the ways in which areas and representations of them are part of our cultural worlds. This means that the Los Angeles skyline can be read as an assertion of the power of big money and that depictions of certain sorts of rural landscapes have been made to represent a particular notion of Englishness.

---

people's relationships to the world by using philosophies that concentrated on how people know, understand and respond to their environments (philosophies such as existentialism and phenomenology). These were an antidote to the mathematical studies of human relationships to space then dominant within geography which largely ignored people's meaningful relationships in favour of a vision of them as wholly rational beings. For Tuan, place was to be understood in terms of meaning:

> Place ... has more substance than the word location suggests: it is a unique entity, a 'special ensemble'; it has a history and meaning. Place incarnates the experience and aspirations of a people. ... [I]t is ... a reality to be clarified and understood from the perspectives of the people who have given it meaning.   (Yi-Fu Tuan, 1974: 213)

These geographers sought a universal understanding of the characteristics of space and place, believing that they could make statements about meanings, feelings and emotional relationships to place that all individuals shared. At times this became rooted in biology:

> We need ... to be reminded of spatial perceptions and values that are grounded on common traits in human biology, and hence transcend the arbitrariness of culture. Although spatial concepts and behavioural patterns vary enormously, they are all rooted in the original pact between body and space.   (Yi-Fu Tuan, 1974: 219)

Instead of the differences of culture, there was attention to such 'basic' spatial relations as 'up/down', 'back/front' and 'centre/periphery'. Some of this can be seen in Table 4.1 where Tuan divides places into two sorts: public symbols and fields of care. Public symbols such as 'monuments, artworks, buildings and cities are places because they can organise space into centres of meaning ... centres of value and significance' (Tuan, 1974: 239). They are places that are consciously made, and their meanings are consciously manipulated. Fields of care are places that become meaningful as emotionally charged relationships between people find an anchorage at a particular site through repetition and familiarity. They are well-worn and well-loved 'corners' which become meaningful through the ways in which repeated use binds them into the relationships between people and builds up a storehouse of memories and associations. There is a definite moral message here. Being rooted in 'authentic' places is meaningful and good. 'Fields of care' are 'better' – more meaningful – than 'public symbols'. There is also a sense of the loss of places through the homogenising forces of the modern world and through travel, which has more than a few echoes of Carl Sauer (Tuan, 1974; Relph, 1976). For these thinkers, then, attachment to place (understood as a 'field of care') is thought of as universal, individualistic and a good thing. There are, however, other ways of thinking about place.

Table 4.1 ■ Place and meaning

Places as public symbols	Places as fields of care
(High imageability)	(Low imageability)
Sacred place	Park
Formal garden	Home, drugstore, tavern
Monument	Street corner,neighbourhood
Monumental architecture	Marketplace
Public square	Town
Ideal city	

Source: Tuan (1974: 237)

4.2.2 | Critical understandings of place

Towards the geographies of intersubjective lifeworlds

David Ley (1982) has argued that Yi-Fu Tuan's presentation of place is **essentialist** (p. 138). It attempts to define people–place relationships that hold for all people, all places and all times. What Ley suggests is that we need to understand how different people's relationships to place are different. Even if there are some 'essentials' in this relationship, then what the differences tell us is more interesting than sameness. These relationships can only be got at through grounded, contextual and specific studies of how places are part of what Ley calls (borrowing a term from humanistic philosophy) the 'lifeworlds' of different groups rather than by abstract theorising. This also means not just saying that places are meaningful but trying to get some handle on what those meanings are and trying to show how they are different for different social groups. Such studies show

> a genuine concern for the more 'everyday geographies' of the places in which we live and labour: for the houses, streets, factories, offices, schools, fields, parks, cinemas and so on where we spend most of our days, and about which we unavoidably develop a *sense of place* – a rudimentary understanding of how this place 'works' and a nagging feeling towards this place of liking, disliking, loving, hating, accepting, rejecting, or whatever. (Cloke *et al.*, 1991: 81)

What lies behind this is an idea that meanings are created 'intersubjectively' – between people (subjects) in 'local' places. It is social groups that make meanings and make places meaningful through social interaction. These rooted constellations of shared meanings are 'lifeworlds' (we could also call them cultures) and we can see that these are tied into particular places. In short, we can begin to talk about 'local cultures' bound up with particular places. The problem then becomes one of understanding these meanings, these 'local cultures', if we are not part of that culture. One solution, borrowed from the American anthropologist Clifford Geertz (who uses the term 'local knowledges') is to think about them as texts or languages that can be interpreted as long as we realise that we are all part of 'local knowledges' and that working between them is a matter of *interpretation* not *translation* (Geertz, 1983a). Thinking through 'lifeworlds' means, therefore, thinking about place, language and culture in terms of how places are collectively made meaningful. It does not, however, mean thinking about power.

Power and place: the constitution of society

A series of more sociological understandings of place began to introduce notions of power relations into our ways of understanding localities. In part this continued the earlier humanists' interest in how places are constructed through the intersection of people's routine movements and activities (the ways in which repetition makes 'fields of care') and also their implied interest in how the powerful make places through making public symbols. However, a new and explicit interest in understanding the world in terms of the power relations between social groups found the early humanists' analysis wanting (e.g. Rose, 1993). In turn this was coupled with a recognition that the world was not becoming more homogenous but that the differences between places and the interconnectedness of places was crucial to the ways in which social, political and economic structures and social relations operated (the classic example is Massey, 1984).

This way of understanding places in terms of both their individuality and their interdependence can be seen in John Agnew's (1987) *Place and Politics*. Here he understood place as having three dimensions: locale (place as the setting for action, e.g. Parliament or a city); location (the locale as set within wider social relations, e.g. the position of the city with respect to national politics or global economic development); and sense of place (the subjective dimensions of place). All these were to be understood as bound together, and all social, economic, political and cultural relations were understood as made within particular places, and made of power relations. The details of this are not important. It is, however, vital to note that the language he uses and his way of understanding place involve 'practices', 'projects', 'routine social interaction', 'constraints', 'structures', 'time-space paths', 'nodes' and so on. It is a sociological language (see Agnew and Duncan, 1989) and is not primarily concerned with the interpretation of cultures. For example, for one of these authors culture is to be understood as 'a complex sedimentation of the structuration process' (Pred, 1984: 284).

What we want to argue is that the deficiencies and strengths of the 'lifeworld' way of understanding place and the 'social constitution or structuration' way of understanding place are complementary. In the former there is a clear and 'thick' notion of culture but a very weakly developed sense of power relations. In the latter there is a strong sense that places are made within webs of power relations, but this is coupled with a very 'thin' notion of culture. What can be seen in discussions of place now is that the basic building blocks of these two sorts of thinking about place are being put together in different ways by different people in order to understand culture in terms of power and power in terms of culture. We will give one example here.

4.2.3 | Culture, power and place: Stockholm 1880–1900

In several different contexts Allan Pred has written about how places are implicated in the transformations of power relations and lifeworlds, and about how people's languages and day-to-day practices of life, love and labour are woven in and through those places. The example that we want to take is from his work on late nineteenth-century Stockholm which seeks to recover meaningful words and cultural worlds lost in that city's *fin-de-siècle* modernisation (Pred, 1990a and 1992b). In order to understand why Pred works to recover the lost names for things, people, places and practices we need to look at the theoretical framework within which he understands place.

Figure 4.3 shows the architecture of Pred's way of thinking. He is concerned with 'the locally spoken word' (1989: 230) – an intimate connection between place and language which means that every place has a different language. In each place you can

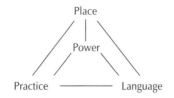

Figure 4.3 ■ Pred on place. (Source: adapted from Pred, 1989 and 1990b.)

find different words, phrases, sayings, names and meanings which set that place apart. The reason for this connects place and language to practice. In every place there are different meanings (a different language) because each place involves different material practices which generate those meanings. The history of a place is the history of its practices – of work, of home, of play – whose combinations are unique to that place and give it meaning. It should be noted that, for Pred, language pretty much stands in for culture, and words pretty much stand in for language. As he puts it, experimenting with language himself:

> Words spoken in place,
> Meanings made in place,
> Words and meanings here, but not there.
> (Pred, 1989: 211)

Yet, to see why words are 'here but not there' each of the points of the triangle needs to be understood in terms of power. The practices that make places are forged within social relations of class, race and gender which extend way beyond the boundaries of any particular place. Meanwhile, the specific relationships between capital and labour, men and women, black and white, shape the places within which these relationships are lived out. Finally, these relationships of power also structure the languages that are spoken, differentiating them between more or less powerful social groups and establishing their words and meanings as vital parts of the negotiations and conflicts between them.

This is, however, rather abstract and it is easier to see how it works through looking at what he makes of the lost words of nineteenth-century Stockholm. Broadly, it means that in his work recovering these lost words – and therefore lost practices and lost connections between people's lives and the places in which they lived – is also the recovery of lost lives. There are, as he says, lost worlds as well as lost words and what survives or is forgotten is a matter of power. This is perhaps most vividly seen in his discussion of place names.

Box 4.1 reproduces some of the street and place names that Pred discusses. They all come from a Stockholm (1880–1900) that was undergoing capitalist modernisation – an enormous transformation of its economic, political and social relations and its geographies. As the city's spaces and places and the ways of life within them were thrown into turmoil, so was the language of getting around that city. People needed ways of orienting themselves in space, they needed to be able to direct themselves and

Box **4.1**
Changing Stockholm place names

Folk geography

Pubs and cafes named after their operators:

Fosbergs or Karlbergskan – Karlberg's wife

or their geographic origins:

Ryskan – the Russian woman
Skånskan – the woman from Skåne

or their real or imagined characteristics:

Vackra frun – the beautiful wife
Halta Lotta's – Lame Lottas
Glaskalles – Glass Karlssons (a reference to his dependence on a glass tube for urinating)

or the characteristics of the place:

Futten – the shabby place
Konstgödingen – the Artificial Fertilizer
Döden i grytan – Death in the pot
Brakskiten – The Loud Fart

These uses of humour or irony also extended to the names for other parts of the city:

Military housing – *Korvkasern* – sausage barracks
Police station – *Torpet* – the croft
Workhouse – *Träffen* – the meeting place
An obelisk to King Oscar II – *Kungens tandpetare* – the King's toothpick
Fyllbacken – Booze Hill
Svältholmen – Starvation Islet – for a very poor part of the city
Snobbrännen – the Snobgutter – for promenade in the Royal Gardens
Mahognyvillorna – Mahogany Villas – for a poor area of wooden houses

Official geography

From 1885 the categories for street names were:

Patriotic and historical names
Nordic mythology
Famous places near the city
The southern provinces
The northern provinces

→

Two were added later:

Famous Swedish authors
Prominent men within technology and engineering

Think about the differences between these two lists of street and place names.

■ How are the names decided in each case?

■ What role does humour play in each case?

■ How have class and gender played a part in shaping these names?

Source: Pred (1990a and 1992a)

others and to arrange meeting places. Thus Pred traces a burgeoning 'folk' or 'popular geography', a language of what he calls 'footing it around the city' (tying together words, places and practices). This language has certain characteristics. It is 'local' and practice based. Names refer to meanings specific to places and what goes on within them. This means that the language is distinctly gendered. The folk geography that Pred studies is a predominantly masculine one, given the places and practices he has chosen to concentrate on. It is also rude and anti-authority in its ironic and boisterous humour. The names often concentrate on bodily functions distasteful to respectable middle-class Swedes. This is important, given the comparison that Pred makes with the official street names that were increasingly being enforced across the city from 1885 as part of a set of strategies of policing, cleaning, lighting, regulating and surveillance intended to order the spaces of the new city. In contrast to the 'folk geography', these names are laden with middle-class ideas and values of progress, tradition, national integration, civilisation and high culture. What is important is that these two 'cultural geographies', these two ways of giving meaning to space and of making places, are in competition for the same city. In short, imposing the official place names through the state apparatus meant erasing the folk geography.

Allan Pred's interpretation of these place names is that they were weapons in a cultural class war being fought out in a rapidly changing city. These representations of places are part of battles for power being waged by competing social groups. Using rude and ironic names for places was a form of symbolic resistance guaranteed to shock the middle classes. Calling a phallic monument – the obelisk to King Oscar II – *Kungens tandpetare* (the King's toothpick) 'was a verbal act combining politically laden irreverence with at least subconscious obscenity' (Pred, 1992b: 135). Resisting the language of the powerful was also to resist their practices, their places and their power. The attempted imposition of a new geography of respectability, on the other hand, was a conscious effort to dismantle a vibrant oppositional culture and the oppositional politics that went with it.

This brief example has shown one way in which a concern for culture and a concern for power can be combined in an understanding of place. (See also Azaryahu, 1996, and

Yeoh, 1992. For a different sort of example see Rose, 1988, and Morgan, 1993b.) Here this is at the level of the locality and we might note Pred's own explanation of what he is interested in:

> place-specific cultural (re)form(ation)s,
> in localised meaning-centred everyday struggles
> that are at once political and cultural.
> (Pred, 1992a: 107)

Indeed, before moving on to think about contested meanings at other scales it is worth comparing versions of 'place' to see more clearly how the 'new cultural geography' works. If you compare Table 4.1 with Box 4.1 you can see that the distinctions being made are very similar – both make the same binary distinctions:

- official/unofficial;

- imposed/organic;

- bad/good.

Their interpretations, however, are very different. Tuan thinks in terms of the human universals that are bound up in the notion of place. Pred thinks in terms of specific class struggles and the relations of power and meaning that are tied together in places. We can see this as a mark of the changes in the understanding of place which new perspectives on culture bring. These are extended in the next section by looking at representations of the country and the city in terms of power.

4.3 | The country and the city

As well as using Pred's work to talk about place it is important to realise its limitations and to look at other ways of connecting ideas of culture, power and geography. Two limitations that we want to stress now are the way in which language gets reduced to single words (see the box on **discourse**, p. 30) and the lack of attention that is paid to issues of representation. What we want to do in this section is to think less about particular places and more about types of places – the rural and the urban – and to see how representations of these generic places are bound up in many relations of dominance and **resistance** (p. 258) involving social groups defined by class, race and gender.

Thinking about the poetics and politics of representation means acknowledging that in order for us to interpret their meanings we must understand that all representations are made from particular positions within the structure of social relations; they all come out of particular contexts that shape both their form and their content. In understanding how cultural products are part of power relations it may be useful to use two related concepts: **ideology** (p. 84) and **hegemony** (p. 106). In using these we do not want to apply them rigidly but to think about how they might be useful in understanding geography, power and representation. Ideology attempts to relate ideas to notions of power, while hegemony attempts to understand power in cultural terms.

4.3.1 | Representing the country and the city

What images do we have of the countryside and the city? What representations of them do we find most powerful? What representations of them do we make for others? The answers will be very different for different people. The countryside and the city, the urban and the rural, have no fixed images, meanings or representations. They mean different things in different contexts. The countryside can be the beautiful rural idyll of an eighteenth-century English oil painting or the exciting wilderness of a tourist brochure. Both can be positive images. On the other hand, the country can be portrayed as dull and backwards, what **Karl Marx** (p. 97) once called 'the idiocy of rural life'. In turn, the city can be the site of excitement and pleasure, or of sin and danger – both positive and negative at the same time. These are all representations of the country and the city that might be said to be one or a mixture of the following: pro-rural, anti-rural, pro-urban, anti-urban. They might also be said to be ideological or part of hegemonic projects as different groups are advantaged or disadvantaged by different meanings. What we want to do here is to look at some examples of how images of the country and the city are connected to issues of power (Williams, 1973a).

4.3.2 | Cultural images of the rural

John Constable: class and the representation of rural life

Within a particular English cultural tradition John Constable's famous painting *The Hay-Wain* (1820–1) presents an undeniably positive view of the countryside (see Figure 4.4). Here the rural is represented in terms of harmony, beauty, stability, tradition, peace, innocence and virtue. Why are these meanings being attached to the countryside in this and many other similar paintings? John Barrell (1980) has set himself the task of exposing the ideologies at work within eighteenth- and nineteenth-century English landscape painting (works produced for the rich) by interpreting them within the context of the coming of capitalist agriculture and the class struggles that that involved. As he says:

> For the most part the art of rural life offers us the image of a stable, unified, almost egalitarian society, so that my concern ... is to suggest that it is possible to look beneath the surface of the painting, and to discover there evidence of the very conflict it seems to deny. (1980: 5)

What he is particularly interested in is how people, particularly labourers and the rural poor, are depicted in these landscapes. He argues that representing these people presents great difficulties within the highly charged class relations of the time (are they to be given prominence, should they be shown happy or sad, at work or at play?) and that the figures in these paintings are a crucial part of determining the meanings that these representations attribute to rural life. What Barrell very effectively shows is that different painters at different times deal with these issues very differently.

In the case of Constable, Barrell argues that he paints 'productive landscapes'. He aims to produce 'the image of a productive and well-organised landscape, as it relates to

Figure 4.4 ■ *The Hay-Wain* (1820–1) by John Constable. (Source: reproduced by courtesy of the Trustees, The National Gallery, London.)

the idea of a well-organised society' (1980: 133). The **ideology** (p. 84) at work is seen to be an old-style Tory politics which presents agriculture as the root of wealth, but denies the labourer's part in it: 'No painter offers us a more civilised landscape than Constable, but the existence of the men who have civilised it has for the most part to be inferred from the image of what their effort has achieved' (1980: 133). *The Hay-Wain* fits neatly into this analysis. The painting is organised so that we see the landscape and not the figures. Our eyes are drawn to river, trees and sky. The haymakers in the distance are just blobs of white paint, hard to make out even though they are the brightest things on the canvas. In the foreground the wagon driver has his back to us and the angler is half hidden by vegetation: 'The landscape is still, an image of stability, of permanence; the stability of English agriculture seems to partake of the permanence of nature in this image of luxuriant meadowland' (1980: 149). The working figures support this idea of stability and order. They are workers and no more, 'tokens of a calm, endless and anonymous industry' (1980: 149) which is their natural state. Represented in this way they cease to be individuals and become 'general figures', 'symbols and tokens of humanity', 'objects of colour'. Indeed they have to be represented in this way. Any fuller depiction, any bringing them further under the gaze of the viewer, would not be able to sustain this ideological portrayal of contented work in a time of class conflict. Barrell refers to it as

> Constable's contrary attempt to present his peopled landscape as an image of the harmony between man and nature, at a time when ... the rich knew only too well how ragged and how over-worked were the rural poor, even those in regular employment.
> (1980: 133)

It is ideological not because it is in some way 'false' but because Constable is able 'at once to depict and conceal the actuality of rural life' (1980: 156).

This positive view of the countryside is still very much with us, even though the social relations of rural life have changed somewhat since the early nineteenth century. Other examples, this time more contemporary ones, show how such representations are about gender and politics as well as class.

Gender, nature and the rural

A series of advertisements were run in American *Good Housekeeping* magazine in the early 1990s in order to attract advertising. One depicts a white, middle-class woman content to be 'at home' in the country with her family (see Figure 4.5). This image was accompanied by text which reinforced its messages: 'She started a revolution with some not very revolutionary ideals. She was searching for something to believe in and look what she found. Her husband, her children, herself' (quoted in Leslie, 1993). D.A. Leslie (1993) argues that, in part, these images need to be interpreted in terms of class and she situates them within the arguments about how 'the new service class' has tried to appropriate the connected cultures of the countryside and of heritage and tradition in both Britain and America in order to create a viable **hegemony** (p. 106) (to define themselves as leaders, to create alliances, and to mediate economic change). Yet these images cannot be understood without interpreting them in terms of gender (and it must also be said that Barrell's reading of *The Hay-Wain* should consider the masculinity of the workers depicted as the 'tokens of industry').

Leslie argues that what we are seeing is an attempt to reassociate women and domesticity through the deployment of the positive meanings associated with nature and rurality. This is seen to be part of a reconfining of women to the home as part of the creation of a flexible female labour force. This means making new identities for women which are based in home and family:

> In all of these advertisements, nature is not very far away. Fall leaves, large windows looking outdoors, flowers, forest views, apples, hay, and farmhouses signify the ties between nature and femininity. The houses shown are old or decorated in a traditional style. ... The return to tradition, an anti-urban sentiment, clearly associates women with nature and rurality.
> (Leslie, 1993: 702)

Yet none of these meanings are fixed. As we turn our critical attention to these images we have to recognise the role of the 'spectator' or 'reader' and our ability to create different interpretations, alternative ideologies or counter-hegemonies. Different viewers or readers who are differently positioned will provide different interpretations of such images combining different mixtures of scorn, scepticism, nostalgia, envy and other responses.

Figure 4.5 ■ Gender and rurality: the new traditionalist. (Source: © *Good Housekeeping*, The Hearst Corporation.)

Challenging the rural idyll

This ability to create alternative responses – to challenge ideologies with other ideas and to construct alternative hegemonies – means also looking at images of the countryside that present other versions of it. There are a whole series of 'alternative' versions of the countryside which are associated with the 'alternative' lifestyles of travellers, tepee-dwellers and environmental protesters, among others. That these come into conflict with more conventional depictions of 'the rural idyll' is indicated in responses like that given by MP Judith Chaplin in Parliament in 1993 during a debate on the Caravan Sites (Amendment) Bill:

> People are worried, because larger numbers are arriving, settling for longer periods and doing immense damage. The beautiful Hungerford common ... has been the scene of great difficulties. ... Three years ago, a large convoy of travellers stopped on the common and caused great distress to the inhabitants of the town. They then went into the town, many of them strangely dressed, and into shops, where they offended the local people.   (quoted in Halfacree, 1996: 63–4)

Such defences of a particular version of the countryside leave the so-called 'New Age travellers' somewhat 'out of place'. There are, however, different versions of the rural which seek to be more inclusive. For example, the 'The Land is Ours' campaign in Britain – conducted through use of the media and the Internet – combines environmental politics with notions of social inclusion and community ownership to suggest a different future for the countryside based around social housing, organic small-holdings and rights of access to uncultivated land. Indeed, this challenging of the English 'rural idyll' on the basis of the inclusions and exclusions that it sets out while representing the countryside as an arena of harmony and tranquillity has also been a feature of the work of artists interested in the cultural politics of race in Britain. For example, the photographer Ingrid Pollard aims to challenge directly ideologies of rurality, nature and Englishness which unproblematically define them as white. She seeks to make representations that will disrupt any easy assumptions that the country-side and its 'traditions' are only part of white Englishness. This is about developing an awareness of how ideas of rurality and nature, of England's green and pleasant land, cannot be separated from the exclusionary and violent practices of present racism and past slavery. Her representations offer a direct political challenge to the ideological assumptions that lie beneath the surface of hegemonic representations of the English countryside (see Kinsman, 1995, and Gilroy, 1993a).

4.3.3 | The country and the city

Yet images of the countryside cannot be considered alone. It is important to understand that they are given meaning not only by other images of the countryside (and there are negative ones which we have not really dealt with here; see Williams, 1973a), but by images of the city. We need to think about them together. Constable's rural landscapes were being produced at the same time as worries were being expressed over the new industrial and commercial cities, and Leslie notes that the rurality of neo-traditionalism is also an anti-urbanism. Equally, the positive understanding of the city (as excitement, change, anonymity and progress) depend upon negative images of the country (as staid, boring, hidebound, deferential and backward). In turn, the images of any one city are equally complex and contradictory and can be seen to underpin meanings that can be interpreted in terms of power. The example that we want to explore here is Los Angeles.

4.3.4 | Cultural images of the urban: imagining Los Angeles

The city, as has been said above, can be seen as positive or negative. Moreover, both happen *at the same time* as different people interpret in different ways the social structures and cultural changes indicated by the shifting urban scene. Indeed, at certain times certain cities become the places people go to look at what the future might be like. Unsurprisingly, although they are looking in the same place, they find quite different things. What was true of Manchester in the 1840s, Chicago in the 1920s and New York in 1940s has been true of Los Angeles in the 1990s. As its foremost cultural commentator says, 'the ultimate world-historical significance – and oddity – of Los Angeles is that it has come to play the double role of utopia *and* dystopia for advanced capitalism' (Davis, 1990: 18).

Davis (1990) thinks about this in terms of competing understandings of Los Angeles: 'Sunshine' and 'Noir'. The first is a combination of boosterist dreams of urban economic growth and the LA myth of sun, sex and success. This is the American Dream of eternal prosperity and all its trappings. We can see this in key boosterist documents such as the *LA 2000* report which proclaims that 'Los Angeles will be THE city of the 21st Century'. We can see it in the optimism of the middle-class, white Angelenos that David Rieff meets on his travels round LA (Rieff, 1992). We can see it in LA's cultural products on film and TV: in *Baywatch* and *Beverley Hills 90210*. We can see it in the new-built environment of Downtown's glass skyscrapers and unbelievably richly endowed museums and galleries. It should also be clear that this vision of the future is class, race and gender specific in many ways, relying as it does on wealthy, white, male definitions of success.

'Noir' (named after a style of bleak LA-produced films and novels) paints a rather different picture of the same scene. The hunt for wealth becomes a shallow, parasitic enterprise for the politically and morally corrupt and LA becomes an 'automotive wasteland ..., a smog-smeared, lobotomised universe of fast food, endless car trips, and airheads of both genders ...' (Rieff, 1992: 16). The American Dream becomes a nightmare and Los Angeles is the place where American society is spectacularly falling apart along its class and race divides. This is the landscape of cultural products such as the novel *Less Than Zero*, the film *Grand Canyon* and NWA's album *Straight Outta Compton*. It is also the landscape represented in the video of the LAPD beating Rodney King and the media coverage of the ensuing riots. Again it is a vision shaped by race, class and gender in complex ways.

It is important to stress that these contradictions are not just a matter of representations. Davis brilliantly shows how the same city offers very different experiences and life chances for those living within it. For example, he shows that the processes of the production of public space within LA by private enterprises (often huge transnational corporations) are leading to very different outcomes. On the one hand, there is the production of malls and plazas devoted to conspicuous consumption and overt displays of the power of capital. On the other hand, this 'privatisation' of public space has meant that certain activities in and inhabitants of these spaces – like LA's vast homeless population, for example – are restricted access to and even 'designed out' of these spaces. The contradictions of 'Sunshine' and 'Noir' are there in material geographies of the city and the lives that are lived within them.

It is also important to stress that this means that it is not the case that we can somehow pick which is the 'correct' view of Los Angeles (and, some might say, the future of other cities). Instead we must realise that these are both visions of the same city which can tell us about the future from different angles. People will be living on the streets and lying on the beach. Indeed, some commentators have used the multiple and contradictory worlds present in Los Angeles and its representations (and the two are by no means easy to disconnect) to suggest that LA is the ultimate 'postmodern city'. **David Harvey** (1990), in his influential analysis of the cultural and economic relationships of **postmodernism** (p. 400), provides an interpretation of the film *Blade Runner* which represents the Los Angeles of 2019. He reads it as a vision of today's urban forms extrapolated into the future. At street level the city is 'a decrepit landscape of deindustrialisation and post-industrial decay' (1990: 310). It is a mish-mash of languages, cultures, and high-tech and low-tech on a dripping, dirty streetscape where 'the chaos of signs, of competing significations and messages, suggests a condition of fragmentation and uncertainty' (1990: 311). However, there is another world within the city too because

> above the scenes of street-level and interior chaos and decay, there soars a high-tech world of zooming transporters, of advertising …, of familiar images of corporate power (Pan Am, surprisingly still in business in 2019), Coca-Cola, Budweiser, etc., and the massive pyramidal building of the Tyrell Corporation that dominates one part of the city.   (1990: 310)

Harvey reads the two cityscapes together as a representation of the contradictions of postmodernism and his reading has many similarities with Edward Soja's inter-pretations of the LA cityscape which suggest that completely new geographies – Soja calls them postmodern too – are being formed in Los Angeles. Soja's analysis is a complicated one, but it relies upon showing both the ways in which 'image' and 'reality' collapse in Los Angeles and the multiplicity of contradictory 'worlds' that exist in that city (Soja, 1996). Concentrating on the city's economy he notes that:

> One can find in Los Angeles not only the high technology industrial complexes of the Silicon Valley and the erratic sunbelt economy of Houston, but also the far-reaching industrial decline and bankrupt urban neighbourhoods of rust-belted Detroit or Cleveland. There is a Boston in Los Angeles, a Lower Manhattan and a South Bronx, a São Paulo and a Singapore.   (Soja, 1989: 193)

This city – where, as Soja argues, 'it all comes together' – is impossible to represent as either 'Sunshine' or 'Noir'. It always brings with it the contradictions of the city and of postmodernism. However, it is always possible to ask questions about each representa-tion and to understand the ways in which they present the city in a particular light.

Key influence 4.1

David Harvey (1935–)

David Harvey is a **Marxist** (p. 97) geographer who has, in various ways, written studies of the historical geography of capitalism. He has worked in universities in Britain and the United States of America. From 1987 to 1993 he was Halford Mackinder Professor of Geography at Oxford University; he is now Professor of Geography at Johns Hopkins University in Baltimore.

Harvey's early training was in historical geography. He then wrote a major work on spatial science, *Explanation in Geography* (1969). However, his ideas underwent a dramatic shift with *Social Justice and the City* (1973) which claimed that problems of urban inequality could only be understood and solved with the tools of Marxist historical materialism. This commitment to understanding the social and spatial inequalities produced by capitalism – what is called 'uneven development' – at all scales from the ghetto to the global inequalities of 'First' and 'Third' worlds led Harvey into an attempt to rethink the theoretical framework that **Karl Marx** (p. 97) had set out so that it could deal with these questions of geography. This was published as *The Limits to Capital* (1982). Many of the ideas that were set out in this book in rather abstract terms were further explored in relation to nineteenth-century Paris in *The Urbanisation of Capital* (1985) and *Consciousness and the Urban Experience* (1985). This combined studies of the political economy of urbanisation with discussions of culture, consciousness and politics. He argued that they could be connected together through the experience of the new forms of space and time which capitalist urbanisation brought, particularly the continual transformation – or 'creative destruction' – of the city as capital sought to realise profit through cycles of investment in the built environment. The same 'logic' underpins Harvey's best-known work, *The Condition of Postmodernity* (1990). Here he argues that the cultural experience of **postmodernity** (p. 400) is a result of new forms of economic organisation, for which he uses the term 'postfordism'. The increasing speed of change, flow and circulation – particularly of images and cultural goods – which has been labelled postmodernism is, he argues, the result of new ways of realising increased profits within capitalism. His latest work has returned explicitly to questions of social justice, this time in relation to nature and the environment.

David Harvey had been criticised for presenting a version of cultural change which argues that it is determined by economic change. However, in doing so he has provided an influential Marxist interpretation of postmodernism which counters 'postmodern' claims for the primacy of the cultural. He has also brought attention to questions of space and the city within cultural studies.

Further reading

Harvey, D. (1982) *The Limits to Capital*, Oxford: Basil Blackwell.
Harvey, D. (1988) *The Urban Experience*, Oxford: Basil Blackwell.
Harvey, D. (1990) *The Condition of Postmodernity*, Oxford: Basil Blackwell.

Interestingly, Mike Davis argues that Soja's representations of the city themselves remain within the conventions of representing LA as endlessly fascinating and appalling, and especially as the city where the future can be seen.

4.3.5 | Conclusions

While this section has not been an exhaustive survey of the usefulness of notions of **ideology** (p. 84) and **hegemony** (p. 106) to understanding the country and the city in terms of geography, representation and power, we can draw some conclusions. It seems clear that any uses of ideology and hegemony that attempt to limit them to the power relations of class will not understand the range of contested meanings that are involved in representing the world. The examples here have shown that 'classed' meanings of country and city cannot be separated from those tied to race and gender. This has three implications. The first is that we always need to think about multiple identities and the ways in which they are related. There are an infinite number of positions from which representations can be made. We need to think about ideologies in the plural instead of trying to judge them as 'true' or 'false'. We also need to think about the complexities that this introduces into attempts at establishing hegemonic meanings. We need to remember that there will always be alternatives that are being articulated. The second implication is that this means that there are multiple meanings for entities like the country and the city (and for particular places). We must understand how ideologies shift and change and not assume that they are fixed. We also need to understand how they are being deployed within and between hegemonic blocs. Finally, these meanings are contested. We must think about ideologies and hegemonies as engaged in a constant 'war of manoeuvre' where the outcome is never certain.

Thus, taking up these ideas of geography, representation and power through the notions of ideology and hegemony has led to a complex understanding of the contestation of the meanings of the country and the city. It has also raised the question of the relationship between the meanings attached to places, spaces and landscapes and issues of **identity** (p. 224) (see also Urry, 1995, and Matless, 1995b). These themes are continued in the next section which considers these connections more closely.

4.4 | Culture and national identity

4.4.1 | Nations, national identity and territoriality

One of the key concerns of cultural studies is the notion of **identity** (p. 224). How do people understand who they are and how do they differentiate themselves from others? This is also a matter of the ways in which people identify with places or are identified with them by others. This might involve a few streets, a region, England, 'the West', or Africa. One of the crucial dimensions of identity is national identity. How and why do people identify themselves as members of distinct national collectivities and what are the implications of this? In nationalism what we can see is the cultural relationship between the individual and the collectivity as it is understood through territoriality. We see that it is a portion of the earth's surface or a specific landscape that is divided off and given particular meanings with which people identify.

Nationalism is a relatively modern thing. Although nations claim very long histories stretching back into mythological pasts, national identity in its modern form is a product of the eighteenth and nineteenth centuries. There is a lively debate over the origins of the nation and the nation-state (its political form) and indeed there are probably differences between their formation in different places (see Cooke, 1989). Instead of rehearsing these debates, we want to give a very general explanation of the rise of nationalism which understands it in terms of geography and cultural identity. This is to argue that 'premodern' identifications with locality, tribe, family or religion are shattered in a modern world whose new social and cultural relations (capitalism, state formation, global communication) disrupt both the stable, local relations and the global identifications of religion. Nationalism is about finding an alternative that is in tune with the modern world in various ways. It is about providing a collectivity that has some effectiveness in the new situation and which offers something around which people can build their identities and those of others. A key way of understanding this is through Benedict Anderson's (1991) notion of nations as 'imagined communities'.

4.4.2 | Nations as 'imagined communities'

Anderson (1991) sets out to understand the intense and deep personal attachments that nations generate. Why is it that so many people have been willing not only to kill but to die for their countries? This, he argues, is especially hard to believe, given that the philosophical bases of the nationalist arguments for which people go to war are so shallow. In part, his answer is about the ways in which nations offer a sense of identity and security in the modern world by replacing wider and 'vertically' ordered religious and dynastic forms of social organisation with a new sense of time (a linear 'history' rather than a cyclical sense of time) and a new sense of space (the world divided into well-demarcated 'territories') which shore up some of the insecurities of **modernity** (p. 400).

These collectivities, and the ways of identifying with them, should, Anderson argues, be understood as 'imagined communities'. They are *imagined* 'because the members of even the smallest nation will never know most of their fellow-members, meet them, or even hear of them, yet in the minds of each lives the image of their communion' (1991: 6). It is only in the imagination that collectivities at this scale can exist. Moreover, in order to imagine this number of people as a collectivity sharing those characteristics that are most fundamental to their identities means that a lot has to be forgotten about internal social divisions. In short, they are imagined as *communities*, 'because regardless of the actual inequality and exploitation that may prevail in each, the nation is always conceived as a deep, horizontal comradeship' (1991: 7). This in turn means that these communities are imagined as *limited* 'because even the largest of them ... has finite, if elastic, boundaries, beyond which lie other nations. No nation imagines itself coterminous with mankind' (1991: 7). There are two points here. First, this means that nations are identified with particular territories, parts of the world that are meaningful to them as the historical home of their nation. Second, this means that nationalisms and national identities are always built as much on the exclusion of people who do not fit and the drawing of boundaries as on the imagining of a community and the territory where they can live together.

The imagining of this community is a collective (or intersubjective) cultural process. It is about creating the nation through its representation to both members and outsiders through writing fictions and histories, painting landscapes and portraits, and choreographing parades and ceremonies. It is about trying to establish the existence of the collectivity by defining what makes it a community: isolating national characteristics, defining crucial historical moments or significant places (for Englishness we might think of 'the Bulldog breed' or 'England expects every man to do his duty' or 'this green and pleasant land'). None of this implies that these meanings can be fixed (it might be useful to think of nations as 'projects' which are never fully achieved). There are always alternative accounts which are being given, and alternative interpretations being made from different positions. We shall see some of these below. It does mean, however, that the community is a cultural one. Culture is not something 'added on' later; it defines nations, national identities and territories.

The geographies of this process of constructing the 'imagined community' of a nation through a 'national culture' can be looked at in two ways: first, the practicalities of creating a 'national culture' across the space of a nation-state; second, the role of landscape in forging and contesting national identity.

Defining concept 4.3

Globalisation–hybridity

Globalisation describes the process of gradually intermeshing world economies, politics and cultures into a global system. While some commentators argue that a world trade system has been in operation since ancient times, the contemporary world is marked by a greater and faster flow of goods, images and communications than ever before. The trade routes that have linked Africa, Asia and Europe for hundreds, if not thousands of years, cannot compare with the present volume and speed of interactions and flows.

The growth of a world system is usually associated with the rise of capitalism in the fifteenth and sixteenth centuries. The capitalist mode of production spread with the expansion of European powers into the Americas and later Asia and Africa. Capitalism undercut earlier forms of economic relations, for example, the non-money economies of North and South America. However, while the European empires linked far-flung parts of the globe, their economies were characterised by the import of raw materials from the colonies by the European power and the export of manufactured goods in the opposite direction. Thus, the European empires marked the beginnings rather than the establishment of a world system. Two periods of what **David Harvey** (p. 156) has called 'time–space compression' (see Chapter 5) saw an acceleration of this process. The first occurred at the turn of the twentieth century. New technologies like telegraph, telephone, rail and steam ships permitted speedier flows of goods and faster communications. The volume

→

of world trade grew rapidly until it was stalled by the First World War. The inter-war period was one of protectionism, but since 1945, world trade has increased to the point where the concept of a global system seems plausible.

The debate about globalisation in the late twentieth century has fallen into two camps: proponents of hyperglobalisation and the globalisation sceptics (Perraton *et al.*, 1997). The proponents of hyperglobalisation maintain that a world system now operates and that national and regional economies are both subject to the global economy. Such is the **hegemony** (p. 106) of the world system that there is little that national governments or regional bodies (like the European Union) can do to protect themselves from the ups and downs of international financial markets and trade cycles. Globalisation sceptics argue that the volume of world trade is, in fact, not much greater at the end of the twentieth century than it was in 1913 (Glyn and Sutcliffe, 1992). Perraton criticises both these positions as too simplistic, because they posit an idealised version of a perfect global market. Instead, Perraton argues that globalisation is a process. It is not that nation-states or regional trade blocs have no power, but that their power is now dependent on their place in a developing, but unequal global system.

Globalisation affects culture as well as trade. In fact, rather than one global system there are different processes of globalisation occurring at the same time. The world system has facilitated the global distribution of Hollywood's films and North American television. Chinese, Indian, American and European cooking is available in most of the world's large cities. International communications are now more widely available. A three-minute telephone call between London and New York cost $244.65 in 1930 (1990 cost equivalent); in 1996 it was possible to ring London from the United States for 30 cents a minute. While it is possible to point to large-scale population movements in the past – for example, the voluntary (migration) and enforced (the slave trade) movement of people to the Americas, low-cost air travel has meant that contacts between distant cultures have increased in frequency. Cities like Los Angeles are made up of a patchwork of different cultures from around the world.

The speed and frequency of international contact have led to a phenomenon which has been called, variously, *mestizo* culture or hybridity. *Mestizo* culture referred originally to the mixture of cultures, African, Native American and European, found in South America. It has been used by Gloria Anzaldúa and Cherie Moraga to describe the permeable and shifting identities that come into being in the human and cultural border traffic between the United States (particularly the state of California) and Mexico. Anzaldúa writes of 'the new *mestiza*' (literally 'mixed woman') as on the border between two cultures. The new *mestiza* is not defined by an essentialist **identity** (p. 224), but by *una lucha de fronteras* (a struggle of borders). This mapping of boundaries has much in common with comparable **postcolonial** (p. 189) projects, fictional and theoretical, which have attempted to engage with the intensifying pace of global interactions. Salman Rushdie's *The Satanic Verses* (see Chapter 6), for example, charts the metamorphoses that occur in the process of migration from the Indian subcontinent to the former imperial centre, a process that creates, in the words of the postcolonial critic, Homi Bhabha, a kind of third space of cultural hybridity.

→

for me the importance of hybridity is not to be able to trace two original moments from which the third emerges, rather hybridity to me is the 'third space' which enables other positions to emerge. This third space displaces the histories that constitute it, and sets up new structures of authority, new political initiatives, which are inadequately understood through received wisdom.

(Bhabha, 1990: 211)

Paul Gilroy's concept of the 'Black Atlantic' (see 4.6.2) constitutes a similar attempt to think outside the fixed and misleading boundary lines of nation-states and to create a space in which a double consciousness that is both inside and outside modernity can be thought. The point here is not, of course, to say that the new *mestiza*, Bhabha's hybridity, or Gilroy's development of du Bois's double consciousness delineate the same space. It is rather to suggest that current conditions create the same kinds of problems for meaningful narratives in different parts of the globe. Gloria Anzaldúa, between Mexico and California, tackles similar kinds of dislocation as (albeit in a very different way) Salman Rushdie between Bombay and London. They all give examples of new identities which, although created by the new global capitalism, are resistant to its logic.

Further reading

Harvey, D. (1990) *The Condition of Postmodernity*, Oxford: Blackwell.

Featherstone, M. (1996) *Undoing Culture: Globalization, Postmodernism and Identity*, London: Sage.

4.4.3 Making the nation

Philip Corrigan and Derek Sayer (1985) have argued that nation-states need to be understood as both political and cultural entities. For them, the state is a cultural entity which is actively involved in regulating cultural forms (see Chapter 6 below). In order to understand this we need to think about how the state promotes certain ways of life and discourages others across its whole territory. In large part this is a matter of creating or making the nation as a cultural entity (Gruffudd, 1995). In the British case we might think about the ways in which different languages have been supported or marginalised by the state-regulated educational system. There is much truth in the joke that a language is simply a dialect with a police force. In the French or Israeli cases we might think about how mass military service has been used to forge a national consciousness among, in the first case, men with disparate regional identities and, in the second case, men and women from a whole range of other parts of the world (Weber, 1976). Finally, in all cases we might think about how states carefully construct both ceremonies and administrative systems that work at the national level and seek to produce a coherent national arena and experience even as they represent and order it. In large part the nation is made by the state, it is a 'project' of trying to create a homogenous culture across a given territory.

4.4.4 | Imaging the nation

We must also understand the ways in which nations claim a deep affinity with a national territory made meaningful to them through a sense of community and history connected to particular symbolic places and landscapes within that territory. Moreover, it is less these territories, places and landscapes themselves that are important than the representations that are made of them. Just as the members of the nation cannot all know each other, neither can they know intimately all the spaces, places and landscapes of that nation. They can, however, experience them through representations which are mass-reproduced in all sorts of forms and circulated widely within the imagined community.

This connection has been explored in detail by Stephen Daniels (1993) in his discussions of what he calls the 'symbolic landscapes of national identity' in England and the United States. Daniels understands national identities as being given shape and content by legends and landscapes, as being formed by stories of golden ages, traditions, heroic deeds and dramatic destinies located in ancient or promised homelands, with hallowed sites and scenery. Connecting these ideas with Anderson's, he says that the making of these histories and geographies 'gives shape to the imagined community of the nation' and that 'Landscapes ... picture the nation' (Daniels, 1993: 5; and Schama, 1995). One example among many that he gives is the work of John Constable and we can return to *The Hay-Wain* to read it in these terms.

What Daniels does is to show how Constable's work can be seen as 'harnessing the twin virtues of nature and nation' (1993: 200). This, he argues, is more a matter of the changing ways in which the paintings and the painter have been understood than any fixed interpretation of Constable's art. Daniels shows how Constable's Englishness was constructed through nineteenth-century biographies and how, with its presentation to the National Gallery (and extensive cheap reproduction) in 1886, *The Hay-Wain* began to become a national icon understood to represent a typically English natural and cultural landscape. This symbolic power meant that it has been used and reused over the last century to bring various forms of patriotism to bear in contests over change which have also been contests over Englishness. It was used in battles for modernist planning between the wars. It was enlisted against Nazi Germany and post-war planning. It was recruited in arguments over class politics in the 1970s and nuclear disarmament in the 1980s. In the 1990s it is playing its part in debates over Europe.

What it is necessary to stress is that these representations of the nation are always produced from particular positions – they have a politics as well as a poetics. In this we see two things: first, the problematic relationship between the imagined community and the social divisions that it is trying to contain; second, the ways in which nationalism is based upon a series of exclusions which are made real in the ways in which the community is imagined. This is clear, for example, in late nineteenth-century Canadian nationalism (Osborne, 1988, and Shields, 1991). The crucial symbolic landscape was the far North. This was understood as an icy and unpeopled wilderness which defined

Box 4.2
Men of the Northern Zone

O, we are the men of the Northern Zone;
Shall a bit be placed in our mouth?
If a Northman ever lost his throne
Did the conqueror come from the South?
Nay, nay – and the answer blent
In a chorus is southward sent:
'Since when has a Southerner placed his heel
On the men of the Northern zone?'

R.K. Kernighan, 1896, quoted in Shields (1991)

Canada as fundamentally different from France, Britain and the United States (all of which challenged its national sovereignty in various ways) and acted as a place of salvation, redemption and moral regeneration. This nationalism was defined as white (excluding indigenous peoples and other non-white Canadians). It was also defined as masculine. For example, R.K. Kernighan's poem 'Men of the northern zone' (Box 4.2) shows how this regionalism and nationalism are gendered. Another example which demonstrates the relationships between landscape, nationalism and gender and shows the implications for women and men is early twentieth-century Irish nationalism (Nash, 1993 and Nash, 1996).

4.4.5 | Nationalism, landscape and women

The question of women and nationalism raises two connected issues. The first issue is the role of women as national symbols: think of France embodied as 'Marianne' and Britain as 'Britannia', as well as the uses of allegorical figures of women on national monuments (Warner, 1985). The second issue is the understanding of women as the mothers of the nation and the mainstays of its families. Nation-builders often value women for their roles as wives and mothers and often see the nation as both built upon strong 'family values' for which women are held responsible and as a family itself. This begins to define particular roles for women within the 'imagined community'.

Catherine Nash (1993) discusses these issues in relation to the construction and representation of the Irish nation in the early twentieth century. One of the artists that she considers is the painter Paul Henry. He was a modernist and nationalist who was seeking spirituality, stability and authenticity on the Celtic fringe. He was looking for a certain version of Irishness and looking for it in the West of Ireland. In turn he was among those who created images of that area 'as an Irish cultural region, whose physical landscapes provided the greatest contrast to the landscape of Englishness' (1993: 44–5) (for example, his paintings *The Potato Diggers* (1912) and *Connemara Cottages*). A crucial part of the creation of this symbolic landscape of national identity was the representation of women (see Figure 4.6). As Nash argues, 'the women in Henry's painting became part of the visual iconography of the West and acted as emblems of an idea of femininity based on a supposedly natural identification with nature and the landscape' (1993: 45). This natural identification depicted motherhood, health and rural family values as the building blocks of the nation and challenged more active political roles for women. Their place in the nation was captured in the image of the cottage (see Figure 4.7):

> Thus the isolated rural cottage represented the realisation, both in the physical fabric of the landscape and in the moral and spiritual domain, of the ideal form of Irish society. ... Representation of landscape in early twentieth-century Ireland was coded with meaning in terms of both national and gender identity. (1993: 49)

In these visions of the gendering of the nation, women were tied to certain identities; they were limited in their roles. Their place in the new nation was to be at the centre of the family rather than at the centre of politics. In turn, masculinities were also reimagined through particular understandings of nation and nature (Nash, 1996). There were, of course, challenges to these ideas yet in all of them we see how nations as 'imagined communities' are imagined as gendered in various ways (Morris, 1996), and how these are always part of the inclusions and exclusions of the making of national identities.

Figure 4.6 ▪ *The Potato Diggers* (1912) by Paul Henry. (Source: courtesy of the National Gallery of Ireland.)

Figure 4.7 ■ *Connemara Cottages* by Paul Henry. (Source: courtesy of the National Gallery of Ireland.)

4.4.6 | Nationalism: inclusions/exclusions

Their geographies show us that nations are very often built upon a 'project' of the creation of cultural homogeneity and the prioritisation of certain ways of imagining the community. This is a matter of both inclusion and exclusion. Identities of all kinds are formed as much through statements about what one is not as through statements of what one is. The process of making group and individual identities is about identifying differences and making them meaningful. So it is the perceived differences between nations that are vital to nationalism. For example, Linda Colley has argued that Britain was forged into a nation during the eighteenth century by its francophobia as much as anything else (Colley, 1992). Another set of exclusions are those based on defining gender identities within the nation, so that certain forms of masculinity and femininity do not fit (see above). This is also possible in terms of class. Those who took part in the miners' strike of 1984 were defined as 'the enemy within', enemies of the nation rather than the government or the economically powerful. Their exclusion from the nation allowed the use of force against them by the police. The final exclusions that we want to discuss are those based upon race.

There are clearly connections between nationalism and racism which are evidenced in the most obvious exclusions: through immigration policies, through racist violence and through the programmes of racist political parties. Yet these connections can also take more subtle forms. In thinking through the implications of the **discourses** (p. 30) of 'race' and 'nation' in his book *There Ain't No Black in the Union Jack*, **Paul Gilroy** was concerned with the ways in which understandings of race that deal with it in terms of culture and identity have led to a 'new' racism which is in danger of producing a situation in which 'Blackness' and 'Englishness' are understood as mutually exclusive. This is directly tied to nationalist or 'ethnic absolutist' understandings of culture which, instead of seeing it as fluid and ever changing, divide it up into solid national blocks and try to fix identities once and for all. Within such a way of thinking, complex cultural processes are reduced to metaphors of the dilution or destruction of the 'traditional' or 'host' culture. What is happening here is that definitions of Englishness are being created by constructing the black presence within Britain as a problem or threat – as the 'Other' against which identity is constructed. Gilroy sees this happening in political campaigns, in history writing of various sorts, and in responses to Frank Bruno and

Key influence 4.2

Paul Gilroy (1956–)

Paul Gilroy is a black British cultural analyst. The main focus of his work has been on the cultural politics of 'race'.

Gilroy studied as a postgraduate at the **Centre for Contemporary Cultural Studies** (CCCS) (p. 327) at the University of Birmingham. He is currently Professor of Sociology at Goldsmith's College, University of London.

Gilroy's early work on race and culture appeared in contributions to the edited collection from CCCS, *The Empire Strikes Back* (1982). In *There Ain't No Black in the Union Jack* (1987) he carried out a multilayered analysis which emphasised the complexity and centrality of inter-actions and struggles around race, class and nation in contemporary Britain. He was critical of cultural studies' general lack of consideration of 'race' but more importantly suggested that concern with this arena would have to transform cultural studies itself. He paid particular attention to the nature and importance of 'black expressive culture', especially in music, which, while appealing to many whites, articulated core concerns of the black diaspora, especially in some anti-capitalist themes. If this work is contextualised by capitalism, in his more recent work Gilroy has taken on conceptions of **modernity** (p. 400). In *The Black Atlantic* (1993b) he argued for the integration of the experience of black people into conceptualisa-tions of modernity, but perhaps more significantly emphasised the **hybridity** (p. 159) of cultures as they interact and develop to form new connections and patterns. This emphasis on

→

new connections and the re-thinking of the work of major black writers led Gilroy to what he called a position of 'anti-anti-essentialism'. For example, in discussions of 'black music' it has been maintained that such categories should be rejected as there is no 'essence' to black music in either racial or musical terms. Gilroy accepts this critique of essentialism but argues that it is possible to trace the interconnections in 'black identity' in social and cultural terms. As with his earlier works, many of the examples discussed come from the area of music.

Gilroy's influence has been in re-thinking aspects of cultural studies from within. His arguments tend towards suggestions for the transformation of the approach to take account of ever more complex connections of **identity** (p. 224) formation in **modernity** (p. 400). This is in many respects a working out of the implications of **poststructuralist** (p. 24) critiques of fixed identities and characterisations.

Further reading

Gilroy, P. (1987) *'There Ain't No Black in the Union Jack: The Cultural Politics of Race and Nation'*, London: Hutchinson.

Gilroy, P. (1993b) *The Black Atlantic: Modernity and Double Consciousness*, London: Verso.

Gilroy, P. (1993a) *Small Acts: Thoughts on the Politics of Black Cultures*, London: Serpent's Tail.

Salman Rushdie. He also sees it being challenged in black British culture and politics, in, for example, the music of *Soul II Soul* and the photography of Ingrid Pollard and David A. Bailey (see Gilroy, 1987, 1992 and 1993a).

4.4.7 | Conclusions

This section has been concerned with understanding how culture is crucial to the making of national identity. While demonstrating the ways in which nations as 'imagined communities' and people's identifications with them are culturally constructed, it also deals with other aspects of the connections between culture, geography and identity. First, we can see again that identities are multiple. National identity is not something separate from other forms of cultural identity. They are entwined in various ways. Second, the ways in which they are connected is fundamentally geographical. The making of national identity is a process of inclusion, of defining what 'we' are by identifying with various geographies. This may be the space of the national territory made meaningful on maps and banners. This may be the nation as 'place'. Think, for example, of the complex relations between nation and gender written into the terms 'motherland' and 'fatherland'. Finally, this may be the nation as landscape, visions that symbolise the characteristics of place and people upon which identities are based. Yet this making is also often a problematic process of exclusion. It is about defining 'us' by defining 'them' and, in turn, disallowing 'them' real or symbolic access to the nation's geographies. These processes, as we shall see in the next section, are present in other ways of constructing identities.

4.5 | Orientalism: discourses of the East

The idea that **identity** (p. 224) is built upon the characterisation of others as different from oneself is a useful one. It ties into how we might think about the cultural geographies of the differences between people and places in terms of power relations, and allows us to think about the city and the country as well as nationalism and national identity. We can also see it at work elsewhere. One of the key uses of this idea is in **Edward Said**'s (1978) notion of Orientalism which addresses how representations of the East made by those from the West have been involved in the identification of cultural differences and the making of a set of unequal power relations. In doing this he makes use of theories of **discourse** (p. 30) to think about how power and knowledge are connected in the representation of places. What we want to do here is to think through what Said tells us about geography, representation and power, as well as look at some of the criticisms of his work.

Key influence 4.3

Edward W. Said (1935–)

Edward Said was born in Jerusalem in 1935 and educated in Cairo. Like millions of other Palestinians his family became part of the Palestinian diaspora after the foundation of the State of Israel in 1948. He completed his education in the United States of America, at Princeton and Harvard universities. As Professor of Comparative Literature at Columbia University he has published on nineteenth- and twentieth-century literature and music, and on the politics and culture of the Palestinians. He has also been an outspoken critic of both Israeli and Palestinian political leaders.

Said's book *Orientalism* (1978) has had an enormous impact on cultural studies (and on many of the disciplines that contribute to it). It offered a way of understanding the 'politics of **representation**' (p. 61) in texts and images which connected their words and pictures to issues of **power** (p. 94) and domination. Drawing on the work of **Michel Foucault** (p. 28), and combining it with close attention to a range of texts, Said offered a reading of 'The West's' representations of 'The East' – in novels, poems, scientific texts and academic monographs – which implicated the written word in the practices of imperialism. He argued that the version of the East which was created within this **discourse** (p. 30) was one that was created for the West. It was both a romanticised view of what the West lacked – spirituality, exoticism – and an image that justified the West's imperial domination of the East by portraying it as weak and degenerate. This pioneering work has been followed by a range of similar studies – on other sorts of texts and other places – and has been an important part of the development of a body of **postcolonial** (p. 189) theory and of other studies which connect language and power. Much of this has also involved criticisms of Said for the ways in which he dealt with power, agency and gender (see section 4.5.3).

→

Said's other work has attempted to publicise and analyse the plight of the Palestinians. This has been done through historical and political writings (some of which use ideas of 'Orientalism' to understand the history of Palestine); through attempts to show how they have been misrepresented in a range of texts and images; and through the production of alternative images which offer another view. For example, Said's *After the Last Sky* (1986), which combines his text with photographs by Jean Mohr, is an attempt to evoke and represent the experience of a people who have been displaced and dispossessed. As such it offers an attempt to avoid the discourses that Said set out in *Orientalism* and a corrective to their more recent counterparts.

Further reading

Said, E.W. (1978) *Orientalism*, Harmondsworth: Penguin.
Said, E.W. (1995) *The Politics of Dispossession*, London: Vintage.
Sprinker, M. (ed.) (1992) *Edward Said: A Critical Reader*, Cambridge, MA: Blackwell.

4.5.1 | Orientalism

Said's *Orientalism* is a study of 'the West's' representations of 'the East' and, in particular, how they underpinned imperialist political ambitions and administrations. There are, however, some limitations on this. It is primarily a study of the Arabic or Islamic world rather than other 'Orients'; it deals almost exclusively with textual sources (for painting, see Nochlin, 1991a, and Heffernan, 1991; and for photography, see Schwartz, 1996); and it is concerned mainly with English, French and North American representations in the nineteenth and early twentieth centuries. What Said is challenging is the way in which these representations divide up the globe, assuming that there is some real meaning in the notions of 'West' and 'East' (or 'Occident' and 'Orient'). As he says: 'the notion that there are geographical spaces with indigenous, radically "different" inhabitants who can be defined on the basis of some religion, culture or racial essence proper to that geographical space is ... a highly debatable idea' (Said, 1978: 322). What he is questioning is what we can call 'geographical **essentialism**' (p. 138): the absolute fixing of a singular set of meanings to a portion of the globe and its people. This objection is not just a theoretical one but an ethical and political one too. He asks us to consider what the consequences for 'humanity' are of these forms of division and representation.

Said's argument is that the 'Orient' is a Western invention: 'a place of romance, exotic beings, haunting memories and landscapes, remarkable experiences' (1978: 1). This imaginary quality distinguishes it from the more prosaic 'East'. It is, he argues, produced within the discourse he calls 'Orientalism', a way of talking about the world that has operated in a great variety of ways over a substantial period. Orientalism is a way of thinking about, talking about and representing the world that makes sense of it, and makes statements about it, based on a division of it into two parts: West and East. So we can say that Orientalism *dichotomises*. Second, there is an assumption that one can speak about these parts in general terms. As Said notes, 'One could speak in Europe of an Oriental personality, an Oriental atmosphere, an Oriental tale, Oriental despotism, or an Oriental mode of production, and be understood' (1978: 32). This allows statements such as that made by Lord Cromer ('Egypt's master' (1978: 38) under British imperial rule) in 1908 to be acceptable: 'Want of accuracy, which easily degenerates into untruthfulness, is in fact the main characteristic of the Oriental mind' (quoted in Said, 1978: 38). Humanity is stripped down to 'ruthless cultural and racial essences' (1978: 36). So we can say that Orientalism *essentialises*. Finally, there is in all of this a strong sense that East and West are to be compared, with the East eventually coming off worse, even though this may be tinged with nostalgia. As Lord Cromer continued: 'The European is a close reasoner; his statements of fact are devoid of any ambiguity...' (quoted in Said, 1978: 38). So we can say that Orientalism *creates hierarchies*. These, then, are the 'rules' according to which this discourse works.

Box 4.3 shows some of the characteristics of Orient and Occident produced within this discourse. It is important to note that as it dichotomises, essentialises and creates hierarchies, Orientalism is talking about the West as much as about the East. It is creating the East as the West's 'Other': the place that it uses to distinguish its own identity. The pairs of words show how the East is produced as both something dangerous and something desirable. In turn the West is both powerful and unexciting (this parallels the ambiguous meanings of the country and the city above). You should also note the way in which the discourse works through gendered categories, making the binary divide meaningful by associating the East with women and the West with men (Kabbani, 1986). Delacroix's painting *The Death of Sardanapalus* (1827) dramatises and develops many of these issues (see Figure 4.8). Based upon a theme from Byron, it represents Sardanapalus lying on a magnificent bed on top of a funeral pyre. He is commanding his eunuchs and officers to cut the throats of his wives, his attendants, his horses and his dogs so that they will not survive him. It represents the East as a place of sex, death and power and you might think about how this painting (now in the Louvre in Paris) represents issues of political power through ideas of 'Oriental despotism', issues of gender through ideas of 'Oriental eroticism', and issues of history through a mythical 'Oriental past'. You might also think about how such an image would have been seen by a nineteenth-century French audience as both pleasurable and as a justification for European imperial expansion.

Yet this is not simply a matter of words: it is also about power. Orientalism is not just a way of describing the East: it is 'an institution' which has three parts. First, it is the style of thought as set out above. Second, it is an academic discipline. Academics associated with institutions such as the Royal Asiatic Society identified themselves as 'Orientalists' and set out to produce knowledge about the Orient. Indeed, the sorts of knowledges that they produced were prioritised. The West's intellectuals spoke for the East. Finally, it is what Said calls 'a corporate institution for dealing with the Orient' (1978: 3). This certainly involved words and knowledge since a large part of dealing with the Orient was about 'making statements about it, authorising views of it, describing it', yet this was also connected to a set of other institutions and material practices of education and

Box 4.3
Some characteristics of 'East' and 'West' within Orientalism

East	*West*
Splendour	Utility
Despotism	Democracy
Cruelty	Fair treatment
Sensuality	Self-control
No self-government	Self-government
Artistic	Practical
Mystical	Sensible
Irrational	Rational
Illogical	Logical
Intrigue	Straightforwardness
Cunning	Trust
Lethargy	Activity
Depraved	Virtuous
Childlike	Mature
Exotic	Unexotic
Fatalist/passive	Active
Mysterious	Obvious
Silent	Articulate
Weak	Strong
Dark	Light

Do you think that these differentiations establish the West as 'normal' and the East as 'different' in the discourse of Orientalism? Do these categories define the Orient as feminine and the Occident as masculine?

Adapted from Said (1978)

imperialism. The Orient was to be dealt with by 'teaching it, settling it, ruling over it' (1978: 3). Using **Michel Foucault**'s (p. 28) ideas of discourse to understand Orientalism has important implications. It means that Said is not treating the statements made about the Orient as lies that can be disproved; instead he is arguing that Orientalism as a discourse *creates* the Orient. It only really exists for the West within those statements about it and the actions that flow from them. That, however, does not make the consequences of imperialism any less real. The representations of the East that Orientalism makes are part of a relationship of power between East and West which sets severe limitations on the autonomy and freedom of those being represented.

Figure 4.8 ■ *The Death of Sardanapalus* (1827) by Eugène Delacroix. (Source: by permission of The Louvre, Paris.)

4.5.2 | Power and geographical representation

Representation is a crucial part of the ways in which the making of identities is a matter of the power of some groups over others. In this context Said (1978) talks about what is involved in the creation of what he calls 'imaginative geographies'. This process of making geographical distinctions between places, of drawing boundaries and of naming places is part of the making of identities through oppositions between 'us' and 'them'. As he says, 'There is no doubt that imaginative geography and history help the mind to intensify its own sense of itself by dramatising the distance and difference between what is close to it and what is far away' (1978: 55). As such, Orientalism is not simply a process of description, but a relation of power and domination whereby one group gets to define identities for all by defining the 'Orient' and 'Orientals' in certain ways.

Yet the sorts of knowledge produced within these representations are connected to the power of the West over the East in a much more direct sense. We need to understand the ways in which knowledge of the Orient was the basis of imperial domination. It provided a set of ideas that were vital to the process of conquering, settling and governing the East. For example, Said (1993) writes of the *Description de l'Egypte*. This was a 24-volume product of Napoleon's 1798 expedition to conquer Egypt which legitimised French conquest with an account of Egyptian history, derogated contemporary Egyptian culture by obsessive attention to a 'glorious past' and provided the grounding for administration, settlement and exploitation in its exhaustive survey of land and resources. The French had to know Egypt in order to possess it and to this end they marched on Egypt with an army of Orientalists as well as a regular army (Godlewska, 1995). In this and many other instances the connections between Orientalism and imperial power are clearly made (Driver, 1992).

4.5.3 | Critiques of Said's *Orientalism*

However, Said's work has not escaped criticism. The following section outlines some of the difficulties with it and looks at the ways forward that others have found.

The problem of agency

This is, in part, a matter of how Said deals with the Orientalists. Although he claims to be trying to hear the different voices of different people within the discourse of Orientalism, his critics have said that he fails. They argue that there is not enough attention to how there were many strands to Orientalism (including a self-consciousness on the part of Orientalists about how they were creating the Orient), how there were conflicts within it, and how national traditions and change over time meant that Orientalism spoke with many voices rather than the single voice that we hear in Said's book. It is also a matter of how he deals with those being described as 'Orientals'. Here he gives them no room to reply or to shape the forms that the discursive and real relations between East and West took. Their voices need to be heard too in making descriptions of themselves and descriptions of the West (Mitchell, 1989). Indeed, the important place of Said's work in the development of **postcolonial** (p. 189) criticism and subaltern studies (colonial histories written 'from below'), as well as his own political activism, suggest that these voices are forceful ones.

The problem of humanism

Said's book raises a series of difficult questions about how we can speak about and know about other cultures. His general claim is that we should expose the consequences of discourses like Orientalism in the name of a liberal humanism that seeks less oppressive visions of others. However, he does this by undermining the key liberal humanist idea: our power to know the truth. His critics have said that he cannot have it both ways and have criticised the humanism that underlies what he does (Clifford, 1988).

The problem of gender

Gender is largely ignored by Said. Although we have considered it above, he does not pay attention to how the relationship between **power** (p. 94), **identity** (p. 224) and

geographical representation within Orientalism operated through gendered categories which defined the West's relationships to the East in terms of a power-laden
dichotomy between male and female. He also pays no attention to whether there are
gendered differences between the sorts of knowledges and representations of the East
produced by male and female Orientalists (for example, Lewis, 1996, and Gregory,
1995).

These criticisms do not necessarily imply that Said's general framework, or his use of
discourse, are to be abandoned (Said, 1993). They do, however, call for a much more
nuanced account of how different forms of power and different forms of knowledge
work within the varied and changing discourses of 'Orientalism' (Driver, 1992). This
more varied perspective will enable us to better understand the variety of connections
that there are between space, power and knowledge.

4.5.4 | Conclusions

This section has tried to show how theories of **discourse** (p. 30) might be useful in
connecting ideas of power and identity to geographical representation. Said shows us
that the making of 'imaginary geographies' is part of a power-laden process of
defining 'us' and 'them' which has very real consequences. Overall, Said's work,
coupled with that of his critics, allows us to begin to see the ever-changing
complexities of these relationships between language, power, identity and geography.
Indeed, we need to be aware of how the languages and practices of Orientalism are
still very much a part of the discourses of politics and economics in the contemporary
world. This becomes apparent if you think about hostile American responses to
Japanese economic power (which might be read through films like *Black Rain* or *Rising
Sun*) or the discussions of politics in the Middle East which are conducted through
notions of terrorism, despotism and fundamentalism (for example, in the TV coverage
of the Gulf War and in a film like *Jewel of the Nile*) which replay older notions of the
Orient (Said, 1981). However, the situation is not simply the same now as the one that
Said described for the nineteenth century. In some ways the tables are turned,
particularly in relation to the increased power of Japanese corporations (Morley and
Robins, 1992). In addition, we may also be witnessing less dichotomised cultural
transactions between 'East' and 'West' as Japanese video games or Indian foods,
fashions and musics are globalised and incorporated into 'Western' cultural practices
(Turner, 1994; Shurmer-Smith and Hannam, 1994). This realisation, however, should
not be confined to the present. Thinking about the ways in which there have always
been exchanges and transactions between 'East' and 'West' – in the past as well as the
present – means thinking critically about the borders and boundaries that are set up
between these entities (see Sidaway, 1997). Once we start to do this, new versions of
the relationship between culture and geography come into view which challenge many
deeply held assumptions.

4.6 | Travelling cultures, diasporic cultures and global cultures

So far this discussion of culture's geographies has been a matter of thinking about how spaces, places and landscapes are given meaning by being set apart from other spaces, places or landscapes as special or different. Meanings are given to them by drawing boundaries around them. In part this has meant asking certain sorts of questions: what is the culture of any particular place? How is the city understood? Why are national cultures gendered in certain ways? How is the Orient represented? Yet at times we have also had to be attentive to the connections *between* places: in thinking about how ideas of the countryside cannot be separated from ideas of the city, and about how different national identities and ideas of East and West are dependent upon sets of oppositions that people use to define their identities. In this section we want to take this further to argue that there are ways in which we can understand the geographies of culture which pay much more attention to the relationships between places and spaces. To do this we want to talk about the work of three people: James Clifford, **Paul Gilroy** (p. 166) and Doreen Massey. These authors suggest that we need to understand cultures in terms of **hybridity** (p. 159). They argue that no cultures are formed in isolation; they are all the product of a complex history of interrelation and connection. They also suggest that we need to think of cultural products in terms of syncretism. This suggests that cultural objects are formed at the intersection between cultures rather than at the 'heartland' of any one. For example, James Walvin (1997: ix) starts his history of eighteenth-century British taste by asking 'What could be more British than a cup of sweet tea?' before going on to show that this icon of Britishness is the hybrid and syncretic product of long histories of imperial relations with India and the Caribbean. The aim of this section is to show that histories and geographies of cultural connection such as this one involve considerations of travel, diasporas and **globalisation** (p. 159).

4.6.1 | James Clifford's 'Travelling cultures'

Clifford's (1992) work has grown out of a sense that anthropologists and others who study culture have missed some of the most interesting things that are going on because of their belief that cultures can be neatly pigeonholed and tied down to particular places. He suggests that, instead of studying people staying at home, we should study travel. He wants 'dwelling' to be thought of not as normal but as something that needs explanation within an understanding of culture that sees it as the relationships between dwelling and travel. This, he suggests, would give us access to 'the wider world of intercultural import–export' (1992: 100) to which we *all* belong. Quoting Appadurai as saying that 'natives, people confined to and by the places to which they belong, groups unsullied by contact with a larger world have probably never existed' (1992: 100), he presents the world of culture as a hybrid, cosmopolitan experience.

   The sorts of analysis that he suggests are of forms of travel (of travel patterns and travel practices) and he has in mind some very different sorts: the leisured travel of the Western bourgeois male; the forced displacement of refugees; the travel-as-work of eighteenth-century Atlantic sailors; pilgrimages and ways of travelling in the mind. The differences between these lead him to question using the term 'travel' to cover all these ways of moving. Indeed, others have suggested that certain ways of understanding travel are specifically masculine and should not be promoted to a central place in cultural studies (Wolff, 1993). (On women travellers see Blunt, 1994; Blunt and Rose, 1994; McEwan, 1996.) However, he retains the term because of the ways in which talking of 'travelling cultures' can avoid thinking of culture in terms of 'us' and 'them' and instead understands it in terms of a whole load of connections. A good example is what he calls 'the Squanto effect':

> Squanto was, of course, the Indian who greeted the pilgrims in 1620 in Plymouth, Massachusetts, who helped them through a hard winter and who spoke good English. To imagine the full effect, you have to remember what the 'New World' was like in 1620; you could smell the pines fifty miles out to sea. Think of coming into a new place like that and having the uncanny experience of running into a Patuxet just back from Europe.
> (Clifford, 1992: 97)

This means that the New World encounter can be understood not as a singular 'culture contact', or even a 'culture clash', but as the mingling of hybrid and syncretic forms of travel and dwelling across the Atlantic. Indeed, it is the ways in which studies of those who have criss-crossed the ocean between Africa, Europe, the Caribbean and North America change how we think about the 'location' of culture that have been developed in the work of **Paul Gilroy** (p. 166).

4.6.2 | Paul Gilroy's *Black Atlantic*

In a series of books and articles Paul Gilroy (1987, 1992, 1993a, 1993b) has tried to understand issues of the politics and culture of race and racism in Britain (see 4.4.6). In doing so he has argued that in British political life (and also in African–American black nationalism) there is a danger of thinking of culture only in terms of internally homogenous and nationally bounded units: the sort of presentation of culture as defined within the nation that drives many of the territorially based forms of nation- alism and national identity discussed in a previous section. This, he argues, is both racist and fails to understand black culture and experience fully because it is operating with a limited geographical focus. As he puts it: 'I want to support the idea that cultural historians should take the Atlantic as a unit of analysis in their discussions of the modern world to produce an explicitly transnational perspective' (Gilroy, 1992: 192). His aim is to study transatlantic interconnections. This follows the ways that Peter Linebaugh (1982) and Marcus Rediker (1987) have tried to write histories of eight- eenth-century Atlantic crossings and international connections: of the Atlantic working class; of the ships and sailing routes that bound them together; of the commodities that were traded; and of the political struggles that flowed back and forth across the ocean (see also Linebaugh and Rediker, 1990). But Gilroy also has his own particular perspective.

What he does is to consider the *Black Atlantic* (1993b), or the African diaspora (the global spread of black people which has resulted from a series of forced and voluntary migrations), which binds together the black people of Africa, the Americas, the Caribbean and Europe in a long history of intercultural connection. This has worked through the flows of people, ideas, money, objects and music back and forth across the Atlantic. This not only includes the slave trade but also free political agitators travelling in the other direction. His argument is that no one part of the Black Atlantic can be understood without considering its connections to the other parts. Thus, within the diaspora all cultures are hybrid and all their products are syncretic. Gilroy shows this many times in his writings on the music of the black diaspora (Gilroy, 1995). He details how musicians from Britain and producers from Jamaica can come together in New York to make a record which will be played in a Caribbean club in Manchester. The final product is a product of the diaspora. He gives the example of rap:

> Rap is a hybrid form rooted in the syncretic social relations of the South Bronx where Jamaican sound-system culture, transplanted during the 1970s, put down new roots and in conjunction with specific technological innovations, set in train a process that was to transform black America's sense of itself and a large proportion of the popular music industry as well.
> (Gilroy, 1993a: 125)

We might also think about what has happened to this syncretic music now that these connections involve Californians (Cypress Hill), Southern blacks (Snoop Doggy Dogg; Arrested Development), Haitians in New York (The Fugees), Irish Americans (House of Pain) and British Asians (Apache Indian). In the latter cases we need to begin to think what the interconnection of diasporas means and the ways in which Britain is located in relation to these hybrid connections (Back, 1996). It certainly means that any 'ethnically absolutist' notions of British or European culture have to be radically revised:

> [T]he complex pluralism of Britain's inner urban streets demonstrates that, among the poor, elaborate syncretic procedures are underway. This is not simple integration, but a complex non-linear phenomenon. Each contributory element is itself transformed in their coming together. The kaleidoscopic formations of 'trans-racial' cultural syncretism are growing daily more detailed and more beautiful.
> (Gilroy, 1993a: 101)

These complex relationships – producing new hybrid forms as each element is transformed as they connect – are understood and experienced very differently by different people and different social groups. We need to think about how people differ in terms of their locations (or positions) with respect to these global-scale cultural flows and connections because of race, class, gender, sexuality, age and ethnicity. This will mean thinking about diasporas, the intersections between different diasporic cultures, and the way in which we all – whether we have migrated or not – live in a 'diasporic space' whose social and cultural relations are shaped by these processes (Brah, 1996). One person who has considered this issue of 'locations' within globalisation in relation to how it changes our understandings of culture, space and place is Doreen Massey.

4.6.3 | Doreen Massey's 'Global sense of place'

There are a variety of different ways in which we can think about culture and the global scale. We can look at how the globe itself has been represented in different contexts (Cosgrove, 1994) or we can argue about whether global communications are producing something we could call a global culture. What we want to do here is to look at the work of those who have argued that what we need to understand are a series of global cultures (in the plural) and a set of processes of **globalisation** (p. 159). They argue that the world is not becoming more homogenous (as the prophets of modernisation and Americanisation argued in the 1950s) but that these interconnections are making it more differentiated. While this is not a new phenomenon (Wallerstein (1974) dates the development of a capitalist world system to the fifteenth century, and Abu-Lughod (1989) traces one that existed before that), it may be working through different processes. We can certainly see that the situation has changed since the last century. We are not now experiencing processes of globalisation driven by the claims of powerful nation-states. In fact the situation is quite the contrary, in that we are seeing the breakdown of many of the close relationships between cultural identity and the nation-state. A new international division of labour, new forms of cultural production (via CNN, MTV and satellite broadcasting), new political forms (e.g. the European Union) and new understandings of ecological interdependence have challenged the power of the nation-state and created a cultural geography that does not match its borders (Hall, 1991, and Featherstone, 1990). In response, in many parts of the world, those who feel threatened by these changes have met them with a resurgence of nationalism (Johnson, 1995).

To understand what is going on we need to understand the flows and interconnections of money, people, images and commodities. As I write this I am wearing a watch made in the Soviet Union when it still was the Soviet Union, shoes made in the United States, a shirt made in the United Kingdom, trousers from Singapore and underwear from Hong Kong. And that is only what the labels tell me. Where the materials, the workers and the capital came from, I do not know. We need to ask ourselves James Clifford's question: who and what is travelling and how? We also need to be attentive to how 'different social groups, and different individuals are placed in very distinct ways in relation to these flows and interconnections' (Massey, 1991: 25). There is a great difference between international business people and refugees and how they 'experience' and 'imagine' the global and these globalising processes. It is also by understanding these positionings that we can begin to understand places in a much richer sense. We can begin to see how the uniqueness of any place and its location within much wider processes are connected in an understanding of that place not as a bounded entity but as an intersection of these flows. Doreen Massey (1991) uses the example of Kilburn High Street in London to demonstrate the hybridity and syncretism of this everyday locality – formed out of the 'coming together' of a variety of cultures – and to show how this 'global sense of place' is a progressive sense of place which avoids defensive and exclusionary definitions of place and culture because they cannot be sustained in a world where understanding a place means understanding its connection to other places (for another view, see May, 1996).

4.6.4 | Conclusions

This brief discussion of a few authors who are trying to think through notions of connection, flow, hybridity and syncretism begins to open up a series of new ways of thinking. They are all insistent on allowing the complexity of the world's geographies and the complexities of culture to show through rather than stilling them with the imposition of artificial boundaries. Their insistence that all cultures are hybrid and all cultural products are syncretic means that we have to be much more attentive to the geographies of interconnection than we have been up until now. The geography of culture is not simply about 'locating' cultures, but about understanding the connections between people and places which transcend the borders and boundaries that so often define our 'maps' of culture.

4.7 | Conclusion: separation and connection

In some ways there are vast differences between where this chapter started and where it ends. Recalling Carl Sauer's declaration that 'the human geographer cannot be a world tourist' means realising that in many ways that is exactly what she or he has to become in order to understand culture's geographies (although we might also ask some interesting questions about the discourses and ideologies of tourism). Yet, in other ways we have come full circle. Massey's discussions of globalisation help us to understand spaces, places and landscapes in ways that are sensitive to the lives lived within them, and this was something that Sauer also aimed to do. What this chapter has tried to show is some of the ways in which we can pay attention to how geography and culture are interwoven in shaping people's lives. This might be through investigations of power and meaning through the naming of streets or the painting of landscapes; considerations of identity and representation in the making of nations and empires; or tracing the transoceanic flows and connections within which new cultural products are formed. In general, therefore, we might talk about culture's geographies as being about both separation and connection. This involves understanding the ways in which meanings are made, identities are created and power-laden relationships are forged through the dual processes of separation – the setting apart of places, spaces and landscapes as somehow special or different – and connection – the ways in which meanings, places and identities are always tied up with one another.

Doing this promises a rethinking of how we understand culture and cultural studies which would make it a fully interdisciplinary exercise. Understanding culture through its geographies suggests, as we pointed out at the beginning of this chapter, that we might best conceptualise the differences and contestations that make up the stuff of cultural studies in terms of spatial metaphors of terrains, borders, flows, positions and locations. These terms – which have to be seen as ways of theorising culture – allow us to think through and represent the differences and fragmentations of culture more adequately, and also the differential power relations that it involves. It changes the way in which we think about culture and cultural studies. Yet, this chapter has also shown that this is not simply a matter of spatial metaphors. It is also a matter of investigating spaces, places and landscapes – real and imagined – for what they can tell us about the different ways in which meanings and power are tied together in different situations. It is up to you, however, whether you are more convinced by, for example, explanations that work through theories of **ideology** (p. 84) or those that deploy notions of **discourse** (p. 30). Indeed, there is much work still to be done in tracing the ways in which geographical representations and imaginative geographies are made and shaped in different power-laden contexts. This chapter has tried to set out some of the tools with which that can be done. There are also other questions which are beginning to be addressed. The future directions of cultural geography seem to lie in thinking through the relationships between the symbolic and the material. This means moving away from struggles that are conceived as being only over representation and the politics of image or language to the ways in which material objects and material social relations are also matters for cultural studies (for example, Matless, 1996, and Mitchell, 1995). This has involved careful consideration of, for example, the ways in which what had previously been questions of economics (e.g. consumption or corporate organisation) are now seen to be cultural questions. It also involves a radical rethinking of the ways in which the symbolic and the material come together in our relationships to nature and technology (Livingstone, 1995; Haraway, 1989; Latour, 1993). Again, these questions are being considered in ways that connect the local and the global and suggest that how we understand culture's geographies alters the ways in which we think about the world and our position in it.

Re-cap

- Cultural geography is an important part of cultural studies.
- Questions of culture help us to understand the ways in which spaces, places and landscapes (and their representations) are laden with meaning within varied relationships of power and resistance.
- Questions of geography help us to understand the ways in which culture is differentiated, fragmented and contested through processes of both separation and connection.

Further reading

Different sorts of introductions to the new cultural geography are provided by Peter Jackson in *Maps of Meaning: An Introduction to Cultural Geography* (1989) – who draws on cultural materialism – and Pam Shurmer-Smith and Kevin Hannam in *Worlds of Desire, Realms of Power: A Cultural Geography* (1994) – who provide a more poststructuralist interpretation. Kay Anderson and Fay Gale's edited collection *Inventing Places: Studies in Cultural Geography* (1992) and James Duncan and David Ley's *Place/Culture/Representation* (1993) are selections of essays that use a variety of perspectives to address a wide range of geographical subject matter. For a general discussion of changes in cultural geography, see Linda McDowell's essay 'The transformation of cultural geography' (1994).

5

Culture, time and history

5.0 | Introduction

In this chapter we discuss time and history as cultural formations. By this we mean that our temporal and historical perceptions are constructed through culture. This is an idea that challenges two common-sense assumptions: (a) history as a linear progression of events; and (b) time as objective, mechanical clock time. Both assumptions are relatively recent, dating from the period known as **modernity** (p. 400), which covers approximately the last 400 years. Both simplify temporal experience which, on closer examination, is not unified but various. For example, time is perceived differently under different circumstances. It will go quickly when we are enjoying ourselves, drag when we are bored. In a different but related sense, history is experienced differently by different social groups. The victor's history is not the same as the history of the defeated. There is not one history, but many histories, just as there is not one time but many times. Both a temporal sense and a historical sense are achieved through culture. Our perception of time comes with the culture in which we live. A history cannot be detached from the culture in which it is produced and received. As we shall see below, it is only in the last 250 years that there has been a clear distinction between tales or stories and history as a distinct form of narrative that attempts to represent the truth of past events. As cultural formations, time and history are subject to the issues of relativism, meaning, value, power and conflict discussed in Chapter 1. Time is experienced differently by different cultures. It is given different values and meanings in different places and at different historical periods. The ability to control our own time or that of other people is a matter of power and conflicts over time occur at home, in the workplace and in the wider political arena.

In this chapter, we have split the discussion of time and history into three sections, 'Now', 'Then' and 'If/when', each of which corresponds to one of the tripartite divisions of time into the present, the past and the future. Beginning with some common preconceptions about time and history we move towards a more complex argument about time and difference and history and difference.

Learning objectives

▨ To learn about the relationships between time and culture and history and culture.

▨ To learn about conflicts over time as they are mediated through culture.

▨ To learn about history as a cultural formation.

▨ To learn about issues of conflict and difference in cultural history.

5.1 | Now: modernity and the present

In this section we look at our sense of the present. We suggest that the concept of the present is a relatively recent invention. It is a product of modernity, a concept that we look at below. The modern sense of time has unique characteristics which differentiate it from premodern perceptions of time. However, the modern sense of time is not uniform: it contains a diversity of different perceptions. Not only do some premodern senses of time persist, but different social groups have different understandings of the time of modernity.

First, however, we must recognise that it is difficult to think ourselves out of our own culture of time. Success with this manoeuvre brings a sense of defamiliarisation akin to that gained by reading a fictional account of time travel. We feel, like William Morris's time traveller in his novel *News from Nowhere* (first published in 1891) 'stripped bare of every habitual thought and way of acting' (Morris, 1986: 286–7). The easiest method is through a comparison with another culture's sense of time; but such is our investment in our own temporal sense that the contrast can be deceptive. There is an overwhelming desire to impose our own view of time onto the other culture, so that the other temporal sense is distorted. Different temporal senses are sources of cultural conflict. The power to make others conform to your time is a vital part of any form of social control. In the modern world the hegemonic or dominant time is mechanical clock time. Every part of our lives is divided into hours, minutes and seconds. Time is envisaged as a taskmaster. We have to keep up with it. We would like more of it; but we ration it to make sure there is enough to go round. The hegemony of mechanical clock time means that it is difficult to imagine other kinds of time; but mechanical clock time is a relatively recent development. It dates from the carefully ordered routine of monastic life in the Middle Ages, where each part of the day had a different task allotted to it. Mechanical clocks were first used consistently to order life in monasteries, making for a strange combination of sacred and mechanical time (Zerubavel, 1982). An objective, scientific sense of time became the norm in the period known as modernity. Such is the complexity of modern, industrial societies that mechanical clock time is necessary for the coordination of the large numbers of different tasks that have to be done. Large, powerful organisations like hospitals, businesses and governments could not operate without it (Zerubavel, 1979). The historical period in which this perception of time has come to dominate is known as modernity.

5.1.1 | Modernity

The historical period described as modern is usually defined as beginning at the end of the Middle Ages, and is variously dated from the Reformation, the Italian Renaissance or the rise of capitalism in the place of feudalism. At least six points can be made about modernity and its sense of time:

1. While premodern perceptions of time are often characterised (not always correctly) as circular, the modern sense is linear, with a past, a present and a future.
2. In the modern period the hegemonic culture of time has been mechanical clock time.
3. The modern sense of time is characterised by a heightened sense of the present, which Walter Benjamin called 'now-time', so that our sense of time becomes more open-ended, a time of possibility.
4. The modern sense of time is global in its impact.
5. It is powerful, undercutting premodern cultures of time.
6. Despite its hegemony, the modern sense of time is not all-powerful. Premodern conceptions of time persist in modernity. Different social groups experience different temporal senses within modernity

In the following sections we look at the development of the modern sense of time. We examine the homogenising effect of industrial time and mechanical clock time: how they attempt to erase earlier various senses of time. We then look at the paradox of modern time: the way in which, despite the homogenising effect of industrial time, new and different perspectives emerge.

5.1.2 | Task-based time and industrial time

In his essay 'Time, work-discipline and industrial capitalism' (in Thompson, 1991), the historian **E.P. Thompson** (p. 96) describes the changes in temporal understanding that occurred in the modern period. He begins by using comparisons with other cultures, starting with the famous account by the anthropologist E.E. Evans-Pritchard of the culture of the Nuer, a pastoral people living in Sudan (see section 2.1.1). The Nuer divided the day into units measured by the work pattern imposed by tending cattle:

> [T]he daily time-piece is the cattle-clock ... taking of the cattle from byre to kraal, milking, display of youths with their oxen, driving of the adult herd to pasturage, milking of the goats and sheep, driving of the flocks and calves to pasture, churning, cleaning of byre and kraal, drying of dung fuel, herding in the pastures, bringing home of the flocks and calves, return of the adult herd.   (Evans-Pritchard, 1939: 207)

The modern industrial culture of time discipline is different in important respects to that of the pre-industrial period. Whereas previously work had been task orientated, that is judged by the length of time it took to do a particular task, the modern period saw work become systematised into disciplined units measured by weeks, days, hours, minutes and seconds. Thompson gives other examples of time measurements like the time it takes to cook rice, used in Madagascar, and timing an egg by reciting an 'Ave Maria' in seventeenth-century Chile (Thompson, 1991: 353). These examples demonstrate the relative novelty of clock time, which only gradually asserted its hegemony in Europe from the fourteenth century onwards. This dominance was facilitated by technological innovations in clock making and the gradual increase in the ownership of personal clocks and watches; but the change was as much cultural as technological. The possession of a clock or watch was a symbol of a disciplined attitude to work. Thus the gift of a watch from a firm to a worker on retirement represents not just time served (or, more macabrely, time left before death) but his or her service to the culture of time imposed by the firm.

5.1.3 | Industrial time

The industrial revolution spread the modern sense of time, incorporating the Puritan time ethic: time had to be used well and not wasted, in order to build up 'profit' for the future, a word that originally meant all-round benefits as well as its more specific monetary sense of today. The timetables of schools and railways and the shift patterns of factories conditioned a more disciplined and systematised culture of time in the modern period. Railways in particular standardised time between different parts of the country, where differences of minutes had not mattered for slower methods of transport. A passage (see Box 5.1) in Charles Dickens's novel *Dombey and Son* (1848) describes how the railways transformed areas of London from isolated, run-down districts into part of a national system. Note that he includes a sly dig at the Puritan ethic in the first sentence, and in the last sentence contrasts 'railway time' with the more traditional, rural use of the sun to mark the beginning and the end of the day. In *Dombey and Son*, the ubiquity of railway time signifies the pressure to discipline and systematise the culture of time that is one of the defining characteristics of modernity. E.P. Thompson speculates that the notorious Victorian obsession with death and mourning was perhaps a response to the heightened sense of time passing in the period. However, Thompson is careful to make clear that while the new time discipline of industrial capitalism is hegemonic, it is not all-powerful. In fact, a closer examination of modernity's culture of time shows two things: (a) that earlier time senses are still with us; and (b) that although modernity is characterised by a single, normative culture of time, different social groups experience that culture in different ways. The latter point is a matter of power and consequently a source of social conflict. In a study of an Intensive Care Unit the sociologist Joel Leon Telles (1986) demonstrated that those of higher rank were given greater control over how they used their time, while those lower down in the hospital hierarchy had to arrange their time according to the convenience of their superiors. Such differences can lead to conflict. The battle for first a ten-hour and subsequently an eight-hour day was a struggle by workers conducted within the definitions of mechanical clock time to wrest more control over their lives.

Box **5.1**

Charles Dickens, *Dombey and Son*

As to the neighbourhood which had hesitated to acknowledge the railroad in its straggling days, that had grown wise and penitent, as any Christian might in such a case, and now boasted of its powerful relation. There were railway patterns in its draper's shops and railway journals in the windows of its newsmen. There were railway hotels, office-houses, lodging houses, boarding-houses; railway plans, maps, views, wrappers, bottles, sandwich-boxes, and time-tables; railway hackney-coach and cab-stands; railway omnibuses, railway streets and buildings, railway hangers on and parasites, and flatterers out of all calculation. There was even railway time observed in clocks, as if the sun itself had given in.

Dickens (1970: 289–90)

5.1.4 | Time and difference

However, the dominance of mechanical clock time is not total. Despite 24-hour work schedules and communication across time zones, all cultures recognise the difference between day and night, times governed by the rotation of the planet. Weeks, on the other hand, vary between cultures. In pre-industrial cultures, weeks can be found that are as short as three days (the Muysca in Bogota) and as long as ten (the Incas). In these societies, the week's end is almost always related to a periodic market and thus to a social rather than an astronomical function (Sorokin and Merton, 1937: 624–5). The modern seven-day week (which, as a quarter of the lunar cycle, also corresponds to astronomic time) dates from the Hebrew week, with the sabbath punctuating secular toil with rest and worship. Christianity and Islam adopted the seven-day week, but changed the sabbath (to Sunday for Christianity and to Friday for Islam) in order to mark their difference from Judaism. This change demonstrates the importance of a different temporal sense in the establishment of a new cultural order. The seven-day week, with its division of sacred time and non-sacred time, has proved extraordinarily durable in the modern world, resisting attempts to change it after the French Revolution to ten days and then after the Russian Revolution to five (Zerubavel, 1982). Religious festivals like Christmas, Passover and Ramadan are important moments in the calendar even where religious observance has been largely replaced by secular society. Thus, earlier senses of time related to the natural world and religion coexist in the time of modernity. Conflicts over the preservation of a sacred day like that conducted by the British campaign 'Keep Sunday Special' resist the penetration of a time structured by the demands of a modern consumer economy.

5.1.5 | The paradox of modern time

It is one of the great paradoxes of the time of modernity that, on the one hand, time is organised according to an objective, scientific model, and, on the other, everyday life fragments into multiple cultures of time. This is perhaps explained by the revolutionary nature of modernity which sweeps away old orders in the name of the new, but which is constantly creating new forms of culture which contest a single, normative standard. The conflicts that emerge are demonstrated by campaigns for particular days to be marked out in the calendar, like Martin Luther King Day in the United States, which assert distinctive cultures against the hegemony of a uniform national culture. Certain days, like May Day, are fought over by traditionalists who want to preserve customs like maypoles and Morris dancing, the labour movement which celebrates it as a workers' day and conservatives who wish to ignore it in favour of other patriotic festivals. The paradox of modern time is demonstrated most clearly in 'modernist' art and literature. The French poet, Charles Baudelaire, described modernity's sense of time as 'the transient, the fleeting, the contingent' (Habermas, 1987: 8). The cultural historian Stephen Kern has described how the time of modernity was represented in modernist artistic movements of the period 1880–1920 (Kern, 1983). Kern argues that the new technologies of speed, steam, the telegraph and the telephone, created a sense of simultaneous time and space. The geographer, **David Harvey** (p. 156) describes this process in terms of periods of 'time-space compression', which were not just techno-logical but economic. He cites the railway boom described by Dickens above as one early example: 'Even though, for example, excessive speculation in railroad construc-

Figure 5.1 ■ *The Eiffel Tower* by Delauney. (Source: The Museum of Modern Art, New York.)

tion triggered the first European crisis of overaccumulation, the resolution of the crisis after 1850 rested heavily upon further exploration of temporal and spatial displacement' (Harvey, 1990: 264). In a later period of time–space compression, the modernist prose of Marcel Proust and James Joyce and the Cubist paintings of artists like Picasso represent a new sense of the contemporary. Kern gives the example of Delauney's painting of the Eiffel Tower (see Figure 5.1), itself a powerful symbol of modern culture, where the painting represents the tower as if it was being viewed from several angles simultaneously. The result is to fragment the steady 'realist' gaze of earlier painting (see Chapters 2 and 9). Instead, the viewer is presented with a new reality where the culture of time is the simultaneity of the present.

This simultaneity was termed *Jetztzeit* or 'nowtime' by the German cultural critic **Walter Benjamin** (p. 373) (Benjamin, 1970). A passage (see Box 5.2) from Virginia Woolf's *Mrs Dalloway* (1925) gives an example of how it is represented in modernist prose. It describes a moment in London when a car passes, containing an unknown dignitary. Note that the moment is contrasted to a mathematical, quantitative value system: 'no mathematical instrument … could register the vibration'. In the passage, the paradox of modernity is expressed by the contradiction between the car, which represents a powerful, homogenising, cultural force that radiates out through society and beyond England to the British Empire, and the fragmented perspective which, like Delauney's painting, depicts several different views of same event: for example, the opposition to Empire expressed by the 'Colonial'. Thoughts of 'the dead' refer to the novel's setting in England after the First World War, but memories of those

---

Box **5.2**

Virginia Woolf, *Mrs Dalloway*

The car had gone, but it had left a slight ripple which flowed through glove shops and hat shops and tailors' shops on both sides of Bond Street. For thirty seconds all heads were inclined the same way – to the window. Choosing a pair of gloves – should they be to the elbow or above it, lemon or pale grey? – ladies stopped; when the sentence was finished something had happened. Something so trifling in single instances that no mathematical instrument, though capable of transmitting shocks in China, could register the vibration; yet in its fullness rather formidable and in its common appeal emotional; for in all the hat shops and tailors' shops strangers looked at each other and thought of the dead; of the flag; of Empire. In a public house in a back street a Colonial insulted the House of Windsor, which led to words, broken beer glasses, and a general shindy, which echoed strangely across the way in the ears of girls buying white underlinen threaded with pure white ribbon for their weddings. For the surface agitation of the passing car as it sunk grazed something very profound.

Woolf (1964: 20–1)

who have died could be seen to relate to an older perception of time beyond life, of eternity. Thus, the global dimensions of modernity coexist with a multiplicity of different cultures of time. These manifest themselves above all in the modern city (see Chapter 10).

5.1.6 | Women and time

One of the perspectives highlighted in Woolf's novel is the different perspective on time experienced by women in modernity. Much of the text is from the point of view of Mrs Dalloway, who experiences the capital of the British Empire from an oblique angle. This equates with the French feminist, **Julia Kristeva**'s (p. 232) argument that women's relationship to time is 'diagonal':

> While it is obvious that 'young people' or 'women' in Europe have their own particularity, it is nonetheless just as obvious that what defines them as 'young people' or as 'women' places them in a diagonal relationship to their European 'origin' and links them to similar categories in North America or in China, among others.
>
> (Kristeva, 1986: 190)

While she accepts that the adjective 'diagonal' is spatial rather than temporal, Kristeva argues that women are more usually defined in terms of space than of time: they occupy a different position to that of men. Women are outside the time of modernity. They represent eternity or repetition rather than historical progress (Kristeva, 1986: 191). Kristeva draws on Freudian **psychoanalysis** (p. 8) to understand this as related to the way in which femininity is 'reproduced' in society. Women occupy a symbolic position as 'castrated', which for Kristeva means they are denied a full participation in culture. If we apply Kristeva's ideas to the excerpt from *Mrs Dalloway* then not only Clarissa Dalloway's position but the position of most of the bystanders, the women shopping, the occupants of the pub and the 'Colonial' in the above passage might be described as 'diagonal' to the symbolic power signified by the car.

Kristeva goes on to argue that **feminism** (p. 120) has produced differentiated times within modernity. The response of the first generation of feminists (at the end of the nineteenth century) was to try to claim a place for themselves in 'linear time as the time of project and history' (Kristeva, 1986: 193). They did this by demanding the vote, equal pay and equal rights. This might be described as a 'modernist' project in a different sense to **modernism** (p. 400) in art and literature. Feminists sought to make women's emancipation one of the grand political projects of modernity. The second phase of feminism described by Kristeva occurred after 1968. Then women refused the linear temporality of modern historical narrative and the power politics that it implied. An increased understanding of women's position in culture meant that 'second-genera-tion' feminists attempted to create a language that went beyond the hope of participating in culture as it exists, and promised to change and expand culture to include women's experience. Instead of just demanding a political identity, women demanded a recognition of their **difference** (p. 138), which may have no (masculine) equal in culture as it currently exists: 'exploded, plural, fluid, in a certain way non-identical, this feminism situates itself outside the linear time of identities' (Kristeva, 1986: 194). Much feminist criticism has argued that while modernity is characterised by systematisation and homogenisation, women's experience of those processes has always been different. Rita Felski points to the confusing number of social and cultural practices to which the term 'modern' refers, and argues that:

> For every account of the modern era which emphasizes the domination of masculine qualities of rationalization, productivity and repression, one can find another text which points ... to the feminization of Western society, as evidenced in the passive, hedonistic, and decentred nature of modern subjectivity.   (Felski, 1995: 4)

Defining concept **5.1**   # Colonialism and postcolonialism

There are a bewildering number of terms that refer to the history of colonialism. These include: imperialism, colonialism, neocolonialism and postcolonialism. Of these, imperialism is the broadest. It describes the domination of one society by another. Thus, we can talk of French or American imperialism in terms of the sphere of control that each country exercises over other parts of the world. Colonialism describes more direct control by settlement and military subjugation. Examples are the Spanish colonisation of South America or the British colonisation of India. In practice, however, the terms 'imperialism' and 'colonialism' are often used interchangeably.

Neocolonialism and postcolonialism refer to the period after decolonisation and the end of formal colonial rule. Most North and South American states gained independence in the nineteenth century. In the decades after the Second World War, nations in Africa and Asia assumed control over their affairs. Neocolonialism refers to the continuing control of such countries (sometimes referred to as the 'Third World') by imperial powers through military, political and economic means, despite their formal independence. Neocolonialism is characterised by domination of former colonies' economies by large transnational corporations and their dependence on the export of natural resources and the import of manufactured goods.

Postcolonial theory, by contrast, is a catch-all term for the theories that have analysed at least four distinct areas: (1) imperial cultures; (2) the cultures of resistance that opposed imperialism; (3) the cultures of decolonised states; (4) the relationship between First World metropolitan and Third World (sometimes called peripheral) cultures. Postcolonial theory now finds its origins in those intellectuals who were the champions of the national liberation movements that fought for independence, for example: Frantz Fanon, **C.L.R. James** (p. 191) and Amil Cabral. However, the first example of what is now called postcolonial criticism was **Edward Said**'s (p. 168) *Orientalism* (1978). Said used a combination of **Gramscian Marxism** (p. 38) and **Foucauldian discourse** (p. 28) theory to identify a colonial discourse, orientalism that denied and misrepresented Eastern and particularly Arabic culture. Subsequent theorists have also used poststructuralism and

→

psychoanalysis to analyse imperial cultures. However, equal emphasis is now given to the problems of understanding colonised cultures. Gayatri Spivak has questioned the ability of finding the voice of the 'subaltern' when, of necessity, that voice is heard through the academic discourses of Western metropolitan culture (Spivak, 1994). Homi Bhabha has attempted to understand the stereotyping that occurs in colonial discourse, for example 'racial' stereotyping, in relation to psychoanalytic theory. He argues that the need to repeat a 'racial' insult indicates an unconscious ambivalence in the mind of the coloniser. Repetition demonstrates the need to continually remake the relationship of dominance between the coloniser and the colonised (Bhabha, 1994). Postcolonial literature describes writing that has emerged in the aftermath of decolonisation. It reflects on the colonial period, as in the Nigerian novelist Chinua Achebe's *Things Fall Apart*; it criticises the impact of neocolonialism, as in the novels of the Kenyan writer Ngugi wa'Thiongo; or, as in novels like Salman Rushdie's *The Satanic Verses* (see Chapter 6), it explores the increasingly interrelated cultures of the First and Third Worlds, in this case between India and Britain. These kinds of relationships mean that there are strong theoretical commonalities between postcolonial theory and some strands of postmodern theory.

Further reading

Chrisman, L. and Williams, P. (eds) (1993) *Colonial Discourse and Post-colonial Theory*, Hemel Hempstead: Harvester Wheatsheaf.
Barker, F., Hulme, P. and Iverson, M. (1994) *Colonial Discourse/Postcolonial Theory*, Manchester: Manchester University Press.

5.1.7 | Modern time versus traditional time

A related argument has been made about the uses of the term 'modernity' to represent non-European societies. Such societies are often designated 'primitive' or 'traditional' in comparison with 'modern', 'developed' nation-states. In a notorious statement, the German philosopher G.W.F. Hegel described Africa as without history (Snead, 1984: 62–4). This misconception is based on a comparison between the forms of time used in non-literate agricultural societies and the times of modernity. The oral histories of such societies do not extend back beyond three or four generations and the future is often described in terms of what has always been done. However, it would be wrong to mistake this conception of time as a lack of history or development. In fact, one anthropologist has claimed that 'Nothing is less traditional than a primitive society ... to impute tradition to such societies is merely to push them into the background and leave them aside from our own society.' The lack of a written culture means that new developments are not compared with the ancient past, 'they are not subject to bureaucratic centralised states which capitalise on the written word and serve as both guarantor and witness to social changes' (Amselle, 1992: 50). Thus, changes in the pattern of life are not recorded as 'progress' but are simply fitted in with current practice.

In such cases, the idea of tradition is, paradoxically, an invention of European modernity, which needed cultures that it could designate as static in order to define itself as progressive. Non-European societies then suffered by comparison and from the forced imposition of a European model of development. This perspective can be seen

Key influence **5.1**

C.L.R. James (1901–89)

C.L.R. James was a historian, political activist, literary critic and avid cricket fan. He excelled in all these areas but, as with many figures who have influenced cultural studies, it was the way he combined his diverse interests that made him an original thinker.

As a historian, James is best known for his pioneering work *The Black Jacobins* (1938). It charts the history of the Haitian revolution against French colonial rule at the end of the eighteenth century. Its contemporary political relevance was that it saw the Haitian slaves as modern political agents rather than as victims of imperialism. As a history of resistance it looked forward to the national liberation movements that ended Europe's empires after the Second World War. In the 1930s and 1940s James was associated with Trotskyist groups in Britain and the United States. It was during this time that he developed his theories of black political organisation. He gradually moved away from Trotskyism towards an independent **Marxism** (p. 97) which anticipated many of the ideas of the 1960s. His views on black political autonomy and self-determination have remained particularly influential. In 1952 he was interned on Ellis Island, prior to being expelled from the United States for his political activities. While imprisoned he wrote *Mariners, Renegades and Castaways* (1953), a powerful reading of Herman Melville's novel *Moby Dick* (1851) as an allegory of modern capitalist society. He was himself a novelist and an advocate of black writing. He was one of the first people to recognise the importance of writers like Alice Walker and Toni Morrison and was responsible for bringing them to the attention of a British audience. In the 1950s and 1960s, James became the leading intellectual in the struggles for independence in Africa and the West Indies. Perhaps his best-known work is *Beyond a Boundary* (1963), a cultural study of cricket. It brings together James's historical, political and cultural concerns. He treats cricket as a cultural form that is the product of centuries of political struggle in Britain, its colonies and ex-colonies. *Beyond a Boundary* also expresses James's lifelong enthusiasm for the game.

James's impact in cultural studies reflects his wide range of interests. His persistent exploration of the relationship between culture and politics was exemplary. His development of an independent strain of Marxist cultural analysis is perhaps more studied now than in his lifetime. His contribution to decolonisation and his criticisms of post-independence politics have meant that he is an important figure in **postcolonial** (p. 189) theory.

Further reading

A useful introduction is Anna Grimshaw (ed.) (1992) *The C.L.R. James Reader,* Oxford: Blackwell. James's *Selected Writings* are collected in three volumes published by Allison & Busby (London: 1977, 1980, 1984).

in two of the cultural critics already discussed. E.P. Thompson describes how he thinks the transition from a traditional to a modern culture of time will be repeated in the 'developing nations' (Thompson, 1991: 399). Julia Kristeva universalises women's time to include not just Europe and the United States but also China. However, the idea that the Third World is 'behind' Europe and needs to catch up has been criticised by **postcolonial** (p. 189) critics. In a work we discuss below, *The Black Jacobins* which was first published in 1938, a history of the Haitian revolution in the 1790s, **C.L.R. James** (p. 191) argues that the slaves who worked on the plantations of Haiti were subject to the forces of modernity and lived a modern life. Consequently, although Haiti is now one of the poorest countries in the world and would be classified by economists as 'developing', its history is a very modern one. Similarly Hazel Carby, in her essay, makes the case that colonialism brought colonised people directly into a global economic system, and it is therefore incorrect to understand colonised cultures as premodern (Carby, 1982). Frantz Fanon criticises the idea that postcolonial African culture represents a stage on the road towards a European model (Fanon, 1968). There is no one path of development in modernity. Different cultures will develop in different ways. Both

---

Box 5.3
Alejo Carpentier, *The Kingdom of This World*

What did the whites know of Negro matters? In his cycle of metamorphoses, Macandal had often entered the mysterious world of the insects, making up for the lack of his human arm with the possession of several feet, four wings, or long antennae. He had been fly, centipede, moth, ant, tarantula, ladybug, even a glow-worm with phosphorescent green lights. When the moment came, the bonds of the Mandingue, no longer possessing a body to bind, would trace the shape of a man in the air for a second before they slipped down the post. And Macandal, transformed into a buzzing mosquito, would light on the very tricorne of the commander of the troops to laugh at the dismay of the whites.

... That afternoon the slaves returned to their plantations laughing all the way. Macandal had kept his word, remaining in the Kingdom of This World. Once more the whites had been outwitted by the Mighty Powers of the Other Shore. And while M. Lenormand de Mézy in his nightcap commented to his devout wife on the Negroes' lack of feeling at the torture of one of their own – drawing therefrom a number of philosophical considerations on the inequality of the human races which he planned to develop in a speech larded with Latin quotations – Ti Noël got one of the kitchen wenches with twins, taking her three times in a manger of the stables.

Carpentier (1990: 34–7)

Thompson and Kristeva universalise a temporal sense that is in fact particular to an aspect of their own culture.

Alejo Carpentier's novel about the Haitian revolution, *The Kingdom of This World* (1949), explores the different kinds of cultural perspectives that arise from these kinds of conflicts. It describes how an early rebel leader, Macandal, is burned at the stake by the French colonists in order to impress upon the African slaves the irresistible nature of their power. The demonstration is unsuccessful because the slaves interpret the event in terms of a magical world-view, where Macandal does not die, but metamorphoses and escapes. In common with much Latin American 'magical realism', the passage given (see Box 5.3) juxtaposes two world-views, corresponding to two different temporal senses: one a sense of temporal progression, the other a cycle of death and rebirth.

Latin American magical realism can be described as a later form of modernism, which explores the contradictions of modernity from outside Europe. It is, in the words of Gerald Martin (1989: 127), 'a juxtaposition and fusion, on equal terms, of the literate and preliterate worlds, future and past, modern and traditional, the city and the country'. In these passages, M. Lenormand de Mézy fits the events into his preconceived cultural sense of progress, his 'philosophical considerations', which justify a racist theory of development. Conversely, Ti Noël, one of the slaves, fits it into a temporal sense of death and rebirth. Macandal's reincarnation is celebrated with a joyful act of sex, which is humorously contrasted with de Mézy's quotation of Latin to his wife at bedtime. In the novel Carpentier shows how the slaves' temporal sense provides one of the cultural resources that allows the successful overthrow of the colonial regime, whose own rigid sense of history permits no room for the slaves' culture of 'the Other [African] Shore' or for the shock of revolution.

5.1.8 | Conclusion

We conclude this section with a summary of the three aspects of modernity that complicate the hegemony of mechanical clock time and the culture of its disciplined observance.

1. *The persistence of earlier senses of time.* The hegemony of modern time is not total. Earlier senses of time persist and coexist with industrial time and mechanical clock time. These different senses of time means that a modern sense of time may develop differently in different places and at different historical periods.

2. *The different experiences of modernity by different social groups.* These different temporal senses lead to conflicts within the modern sense of time. Such conflicts occur over marking particular days or holidays, in the workplace (where control over schedules and timetables is a key indicator of power) and at the borders between different cultures where religion, politics and economics structure time.

3. *The emergence in modernity of new, revolutionary forms of consciousness, which fragment a sense of homogenised objective time.* We might point to the attempts after the French and Russian revolutions to change the length of the week, to arguments by feminists that

women experience time differently, or to the reassertion of an oppressed culture's sense of time in uprisings against European rule during the age of imperialism.

5.2 | Then: history and the past

In this section, we consider the past and the different ways of understanding history. We look at the difference between the idea of an objective history, of external events that happen to people, and of subjective histories, how history is perceived by those who take part. Different theories of history are discussed: for example, history as facts, Marxist history, history as narrative and Foucauldian history. The different historical narratives that emerge through the exploration of class, gender, 'race' and sexuality are described. Finally, we look at the example of one cultural historian, Judith Walkowitz, who combines some of these different approaches in her work.

It is only in the last 250 years that there has been a clear distinction between tales or stories and history as a distinct form of narrative that attempts to represent the truth of past events. Thus, the idea of an objective history which exists outside culture is relatively new. In the 1830s, the historian Leopold von Ranke (1795–1886) talked of writing history 'as it actually happened'. This modern historical sense was made possible by modernity's paradoxical culture of time. On the one hand, an objective sense of time allowed an understanding of history as an objective, progressive movement. In the words of the anthropologist Lévi-Strauss, history is 'continuous, homogenous and linear'. On the other, modernity's heightened consciousness of the present permitted an understanding of history as something that is constantly in the process of becoming. Modern historical narrative emerges from this consciousness. Some of the grand historical narratives of the modern age, including nationalism, imperialism, communism and fascism, emerge out of the modern temporal sense. However, the multiplicity of viewpoints opened up by the time of modernity has meant that even where an objective history is believed possible, it is not easily accessible. Just as different experiences of time are a source of social conflict, so history is fought over by different social groups. In the words of Walter Benjamin, 'there is no document of civilization which is not at the same time a document of barbarism'. With Benjamin, cultural studies is interested to examine both sides of history: 'to brush history against the grain' (Benjamin, 1970: 256–7). Because the relationship between objective and subjective ideas of history is complex, it is a good idea to separate them out before going any further.

An objective history assumes that history is about real events that happen in objective time. It consigns culture to the medium through which history is perceived and understood. Words that are used to describe this understanding of history are 'materialist', 'real', 'absolute' or 'objective'. Subjective histories give more weight to the cultural context in which histories are made and told. Words that are used to describe this understanding of history are 'idealist', 'fictions', 'relativist' or 'subjective'. In fact, very few historians write history in a way that assumes that either culture or an objective history are straightforwardly pre-eminent. Instead, they are more likely to argue that there is a complex relationship between the two.

'Materialist' historians will contend that the reality of history is so complicated and contradictory that no single version could possibly represent the truth; consequently different interpretations are inevitable. One of the best-known introductions to historical study, which takes as its title the question 'What is history?', is a series of lectures by E.H. Carr. Carr begins his discussion of the topic by looking at how history is written, taking his examples from the way that historians of the nineteenth and twentieth centuries research and write historical accounts. His argument is that it is impossible to know 'what actually happened'; instead, the historian must make do with the evidence that has been left from former times. This evidence does not represent the truth, but everything from the opinions of those who were powerful enough to get them recorded to the accidental leftovers that survived wars and natural catastrophes (Carr, 1964: 7–30). However, this is not to say that Carr believes that objective history does not exist; rather our idea or 'philosophy of history' will be formed only through the incomplete evidence available. It also contains a warning, in that if the evidence is fragmented and contradictory then it will always be possible, and indeed tempting, to impose an interpretation on it that conforms to a prejudged view of 'what actually happened'.

Historians accused of 'idealism' by materialist historians may not actually deny a real history, but will argue that real history is only accessible through the documents that represent it, documents that can include everything from the Doomsday book to paintings, sculpture and the literature of a particular period. Consequently, there is no point in speaking of a reality outside those documents. Despite the fact that these two forms of historical understanding coexist, it is worth keeping them in mind, because they act as a starting point from which we can begin to understand the complexity of that relationship. In the meantime, however, it is worth considering how cultural studies approaches a familiar and still common account of what history is: history as facts.

5.2.1 | History as facts

The best-known and most criticised version of objective history is history as facts: for example, history as a succession of dates of kings and queens. The acquisition of facts as a substitute for a fuller knowledge of the world was famously parodied by Charles Dickens (1812–70) in his novel *Hard Times* (1854), when the character Mr Gradgrind says: 'Facts alone are wanted in life' (see Box 5.4). Dickens's parody has been a favourite of historians like E.H. Carr and E.P. Thompson. Carr wrote that the 'belief in a hard core of historical facts existing objectively and independently of the interpretation of the historian is a preposterous fallacy, but one which is hard to eradicate' (Carr, 1964: 12). The assumption behind Mr Gradgrind's philosophy is that facts provide positive and unquestionable knowledge of the world. This knowledge is described as 'positivist' or 'empiricist', meaning that the facts gained are provable by experience. However, it is difficult to establish proof for historical facts. While some facts may seem indisputable, there is always room for another account. For example, the historical fact that Queen

---

Box 5.4
Charles Dickens, *Hard Times*

Now what I want is, Facts. Teach these boys and girls nothing but Facts. Facts alone are wanted in life. Plant nothing else, and root out everything else. You can only found the minds of reasoning animals upon Facts: nothing else will ever be of any service to them. This is the principle on which I bring up my own children, this is the principle on which I bring up these children. Stick to Facts, sir!

Dickens (1969: 47)

Victoria died in 1901 appears to be straightforward. The importance of the queen in British life at the historical period in which she died means that there are plenty of documents that can provide this evidence, and the accounts provided by the documents are unlikely to conflict. But such accuracy is unlikely in the case of someone who is less central to the way that society is organised or who lived at a time for which there is less documentation. For example, there is no contemporary written evidence to tell us about 'Lindow Man', a man whose well-preserved body was found in a peat bog near Wilmslow in the North of England and is now in the British Museum. Historians have to rely on different kinds of evidence that are less accurate and that may conflict with one another. This evidence includes the age of the peat in which he was found, the clothes he was wearing and even the undigested food that was found in his stomach. From these facts historians and archaeologists have attempted to piece together a picture of who the man was and how he died, but, understandably, much of what they suggest is speculation. As a consequence, what sense is made of these facts is a matter of dispute. It depends upon the already existing theories about Lindow Man's society and religion, and the lack of evidence means that these theories are not fixed nor do they necessarily agree with one another.

Mr Gradgrind might argue that this does not invalidate his claim that all we need to know is facts. It is simply that for some periods and people we know more facts and for others we know less. History, then, is still the process of acquiring facts about the past. But if we return to the death of Queen Victoria in the light of the work of making sense done by historians and archaeologists, it is possible to see that the Gradgrindian approach assumes that his facts make sense in themselves. Two assumptions that make sense of the death of Queen Victoria are, first, that we know of which country she was queen, and second, we know the role of the monarch in British nineteenth-century politics and society. These assumptions are cultural in two ways: the fact of Victoria's death had a cultural meaning and the facts make sense only if they signify something within a known cultural context. Cultural meaning is always a matter of interpretation; and the interpretation of facts, even when they are known and agreed upon, is a matter for dispute among historians.

E.P. Thompson (p. 96) argued that facts cannot simply be received by the historian as unquestionable evidence (see Box 5.5). Instead, the historian is better understood as being in dialogue with facts, fitting them into theoretical frameworks in which they make sense and then perhaps changing the 'framework' because the facts invalidate some of its assumptions. Thompson used the word framework as a way of resolving the problem for materialist history that facts never provide positive evidence. Thompson's framework is comparable to E.H. Carr's 'philosophy of history'. A changing framework or philosophy allows the historian to get as close as possible to an objective history, using the evidence at hand. Both Carr and Thompson worked within the Marxist historical tradition. A Marxist understanding of history has had an important influence in contemporary cultural studies.

5.2.2 | Marxism and history

As a materialist philosophy, one of the central principles of Marxism is that there is a real history, and that culture exists as part of that real history. However, in order to understand the long-lasting influence that Marxism has had on historical study and on cultural studies it is important to understand how historical materialism, the name that Friedrich Engels gave to his and Marx's philosophy, differs from an idea of history 'as it actually happened'. While crude or 'vulgar' Marxism maintains that culture is part of the superstructure which is determined by the economic base, the range and complexity of Marx's work suggests that there is a two-way relationship between culture and economics (Williams, 1977: 75–82).

E.P. Thompson has described the relationship between the material and the cultural as analogous to the relationship between a block of wood and what the joiner does with that wood (see Box 5.6). First, whatever material is available, human agency is essential, but the human presence is not enough on its own. The materials do not determine the

---

Box **5.5**
E.P. Thompson, 'The Poverty of Theory'

That dead, inert text of ... evidence is by no means 'inaudible'; it has a deafening vitality of its own; voices clamour from the past, asserting their own meanings, appearing to disclose their own self-knowledge as knowledge. If we offer a commonplace 'fact' – 'King Zed died in 1100 A.D.' – we are already offered a concept of kingship: the relations of domination and subordination, the functions and roles of the office, the charisma and magical endowments attaching to that role ... this evidence is received by the historian within a theoretical framework (the discipline of history, which itself has a history and a disputed present) which has refined the concept of kingship ... very different from the immediacy ... of those who actually watched King Zed die.

Thompson (1978: 18–19)

Box **5.6**

E.P. Thompson, 'The Poverty of Theory'

No piece of timber has ever been known to make itself into a table: no joiner has ever been known to make a table out of air, or sawdust. The joiner appropriates that timber, and, in working it up into a table, he is governed both by his skill (theoretical practice, itself arising from a *history*, or 'experience', of making tables, as well as a history of the evolution of the appropriate tools) and by the qualities (size, grain, seasoning, etc.) of the timber itself.

Thompson (1978: 17–18)

---

product absolutely, 'the wood cannot determine *what* is made', but it can limit the product: 'it can certainly determine what can *not* be made, the limits (size, strength, etc.) of what is made, and the skills and tools appropriate to the making' (Thompson, 1978: 18). Thus, while the type of product may be formed within a wide and diverse cultural sphere, in the final instance the material qualities of the block of wood will define the conditions within which that culture can exist. In Marx's thought it is the relations of production that condition the culture of a particular time. Marx wrote that history is about the growth of human productive power; thus, within that context, human culture too will grow and expand in a dialectical relationship with the relations of production. In his most famous pronouncement on the relationship between human beings and history, he wrote: 'Men make their own history, but are born into conditions not of their own making.'

The Marxist literary critic and cultural theorist Fredric Jameson argues that history is real, but is 'fundamentally non-narrative and non-representational' (Jameson, 1981: 82):

> history is *not* a text, not a narrative, master or otherwise, but ... as an absent cause, it is inaccessible to us except in textual form, and ... our approach to it and to the Real itself necessarily passes through its prior textualisation, its narrativisation ...
>
> (Jameson, 1981: 35)

Jameson uses the word 'text' in its **poststructuralist** (p. 24) sense to mean any historical document or artifact which can be 'read' for signs that tell us about the past. However, this formulation of real, material history might well be criticised for its vagueness. How, it might be asked, do we know that there is a real history behind all the texts? To answer this, Jameson uses the concept of necessity to describe the conditions that limit culture, just as the block of wood (above) limited the carpenter. For Marx, history is about the struggle between freedom and necessity, where freedom is won through the uses of human productive power. History is felt through the limits imposed by necessity. 'History', writes Jameson, 'is what hurts, it is what refuses desire and sets inexorable limits to individual as well as collective praxis, which its "ruses" turn into grisly and ironic reversals of their overt intention' (1981: 102). Thus, it can be seen that the kind of Marxism practised by Jameson sees no obvious relationship or causation between real history and the representation of history. It is impossible to represent history 'as it actually happened' even though it did happen. Because of this difficulty one concern of cultural studies has been to analyse history as narrative.

5.2.3 │ History as narrative

One of the original meanings of the word 'history' was a narrative account of events, and a simplified version of the idea of subjective history is that history is no more than a collection of narratives. Clearly all histories are structured as narratives in so far as they give an account of past events, but even if this version of subjective history is accepted, it hardly simplifies the problem. Narratives can be of many types, from the simplest sentence – 'The storming of the Bastille took place on 14 July 1789' – to the rhetorical complexity of Thomas Carlyle's history of the French Revolution (1837) (see Box 5.7).

  Narratives are one of the forms through which a culture understands itself and its past. They provide origins or beginnings which explain subsequent events. For example, many cultures have what are known as founding myths, which provide a story that gives a sense of pride and identity. The Roman poet Virgil wrote *The Aeneid* (19

Box **5.7**

Thomas Carlyle, The Storming of the Bastille from *The French Revolution*

On, then, all Frenchmen, that have hearts in your bodies! Roar with all your throats, or cartilage and metal, ye Sons of Liberty; stir spasmodically whatsoever of utmost faculty is in you, soul, body, or spirit; for it is the hour! Smite, thou Louis Tournay, cartwright of Marais, old-soldier of the Regiment Dauphiné; smite at that Outer Drawbridge chain, though the fiery hail whistles round thee! Never, over nave or felloe, did thy axe strike such a stroke. Down with it, man; down with it to Orcus: let the whole accursed Edifice sink thither, and Tyranny be swallowed up forever! Mounted, some say, on the roof of the guard-room, some 'on bayonets stuck into joints of the wall,' Louis Tournay smites, brave Aubin Bonnemère (also an old soldier) seconding him: the chain yields, breaks; the huge Drawbridge slams down, thundering (*avec fracas*). Glorious: and yet, alas, it is still but the outworks. The Eight grim Towers, with their Invalide musketry, their paving stones and cannon-mouths, still soar aloft intact; – Ditch yawning impassable, stone-faced; the inner Drawbridge with its *back* towards us: the Bastille still to take!

Carlyle (1971: 122)

BC), an epic poem based on the Greek epic poems of Homer, which tells how Aeneas escaped from Troy when it was destroyed by the Greeks and, after a series of heroic adventures, founded the city of Rome. The poem gave legitimacy to Roman culture by connecting it to an earlier heroic period, the Trojan War, and to an earlier, admired culture. While there is little in *The Aeneid* that tells the historian about the 'facts' of the origins of Rome, the poem tells us much about the Roman culture of Virgil's time.

In the modern world, nation-states have constructed narratives that emphasise moments of collective achievement which perform similar functions to *The Aeneid* (Anderson, 1991) (see Chapter 4). For example, in the aftermath of European imperialism, European historical narratives were more likely to emphasise the benefits felt to have been brought by a European nation to its colonies and to represent independence as something granted by the colonisers to the colonised. The newly independent states, on the other hand, were more likely to emphasise **resistance** (p. 258) against the imperial power and represent independence as the victory of a liberation struggle.

The modern narratives that constitute history (including histories of the nation-state) created a new, more precise distinction that had not previously existed between narratives as fiction and historical narratives as what actually occurred. This occurs within the modern understanding of time as something that is progressive, moving forward. While the research methods of modern historians might claim to be more scientific (and this itself is a term that means different things in different contexts) than earlier narratives of the past, the writing of history is still considered by C.L.R. James to be an art. Modern history has to take its forms from already existing narratives. In an analysis of nineteenth-century philosophers of history, Hayden White has described how writers like Hegel, Marx and Burkhardt use the narrative forms of romance, comedy, tragedy and satire, singly or in combination, to express their view of how history works. Different kinds of narrative form can express not just history as it happened but elements of desire and **transgression** (p. 258).

5.2.4 | Mikhail Mikhailovich Bakhtin

A sophisticated approach to the way that narratives represent ideas of time and space is provided by the Russian critic **Mikhail Mikhailovich Bakhtin** (p. 202) (see Chapter 1). Bakhtin's work is important because it incorporates two ideas that are not usually included in an abstract history of facts: desire and the carnivalesque. Bakhtin uses the concept of the 'chronotope', from two Greek words *khronos* (time) and *topos* (space), to describe how earlier forms of narrative convey different senses of time and history to those of the modern period. For example, the epic form of writers like Homer and Virgil represents an absolute past, a past of beginnings and peak times in the national history (Bakhtin, 1981: 13). What is known as 'epic distance' separates the heroic world of the epic from the present absolutely. The epic mode represents an understanding of time and history which is still used in the modern world, but which has lost the authority it had in the culture of the original epic poems, that of ancient Greece. The novel, on the other hand, represents the time of modernity: 'it is extraordinarily sensitive to time in language, the past and the future' (1981: 67).

Two other key examples in Bakhtin's essay 'Forms of time and chronotope in the novel' (in Bakhtin, 1981) are 'adventure time' and what he calls 'everyday time'. Adventure time is the time of desire and is found in the romances of ancient Greece. In adventure time nothing matters except the passion of the two lovers and the desire to satisfy it. In the typical Greek romance the lovers meet but are then separated and the entire novel is concerned with the time that elapses before they are finally reunited. In this time the lovers encounter numerous adventures, may visit four or five countries and may discourse on numerous topics, but in adventure time nothing actually changes – both the lovers remain totally in love, both remain chaste and faithful to one another and there is no development of their individual characters. In everyday time this would not be possible because events would occur during the adventures and journeys that would change the lovers' relationship. The chronotope for everyday life is the road, which forms the essential metaphor for life in many kinds of narrative from the folk tale to the novel. The road or 'path of life' represents the episodes in a character's life and gives each turning or intersection a meaning. Bakhtin writes: 'Space becomes more concrete and saturated with a time that is more substantial: space is filled with real, living meaning, and forms a crucial relationship with the hero and his fate' (1981: 120). He gives a modern romance, Voltaire's *Candide,* as an example of a modern text where everyday time intrudes upon adventure time. The two lovers, Candide and Cunde-gonde, are finally reunited, but they are so old that all their youthful beauty is long gone and the romance is lost.

Clearly modern histories have much more in common with the metaphor of the road than they do with the fantastical and passionate elements of adventure time. However, to represent history simply as the everyday or as a steady progress from one place to another would be to miss out people's hopes and desires; it would be to ignore people's fantasy lives and their experience of time which cannot be measured in terms of biography. Yet, these experiences of time and history are as much part of cultural experience as what is traditionally understood as historical narrative. Perhaps Bakhtin's most important term is the 'carnivalesque' which describes how laughter has the ability to dissolve all powerful and authoritative versions of temporal understanding in the physicality of obscenity and transgression that marks festivity. Carnival revels in the topsy-turvy, in reversal, the back-to-front, and inversion, the upside down. In the carnivalesque, high becomes low, the spiritual becomes the bodily, the refined, vulgar. Conventional identities are transgressed, the masculine is feminised, the feminine masculinised and desire breaks free from its 'correct' object. Bakhtin claimed that the truly modern form of narrative is the novel because the novel contains all previous understandings of time but does not prioritise any of them, incorporating a form of the carnivalesque within itself. The novel represents the culture of modernity from within which the modern histories of the nineteenth and twentieth centuries have been written. It opened up a 'new zone ... for structuring literary images, namely, the zone of maximal contact with the present (with contemporary reality) in all its openendedness' (1981: 11). Just as the novels of the nineteenth century broadened out from the metaphor of the road to encompass the European city, so traditional forms of temporal and historical understanding were transformed by plurality and transgressions of urban

Key influence 5.2

Mikhail Mikhailovich Bakhtin
(1895–1975)

Although Bakhtin's main ideas were formulated in the 1920s and 1930s, they did not reach the West until the 1960s. Since then, his theories of the novel and the carnivalesque have influenced studies of the cultural politics of **transgression** (p. 258).

Bakhtin was born in Orel, Russia. There is now some dispute about his university career, but there is no doubt that he was influenced by the debates about literary form and avant-garde art that took place in St Petersburg, immediately before and after the 1917 revolution. The 'Bakhtin Circle' first formed in the years 1918–20 in Nevel, West Russia. It included Lev Pumpianskij, V.N. Volosinov, M.V. Judina, I.I. Sollertinskij, B.M. Zubakin, and Matvej Isaic Kagan. In 1929 Bakhtin published an early version of his theory of the novel as a modern, transgressive form in *Problems of Dostoevsky's Poetics*. Several works of disputed authorship, but in which Bakhtin probably had a part, emerged from the circle in the late 1920s, including *Freudianism* (1927), *Marxism and the Philosophy of Language* (1929) published under the name of V.N. Volosinov, and *The Formal Method in Literary Scholarship* (1928) published under the name of P.N. Medvedev. Bakhtin's work then became submerged in the Stalinist purges of the 1930s. He was sent to Kustanaj in Kazakhstan. One manuscript of his book on the eighteenth-century German novel was lost and Bakhtin used the other to roll cigarettes during the Second World War. He was refused a doctorate for his dissertation on Rabelais. It was not until 1965, after he had retired because of ill health, that *Rabelais and Folk Culture in the Middle Ages and Renaissance* was published. It was this book more than any other that established his international reputation. In it he described the important influence of a transgressive popular culture, particularly carnival, on Rabelais's (1494–c.1553) early novel, *Gargantua and Pantagruel* (1532–64). Bakhtin points to Rabelais's use of the 'grotesque body' as a collective popular form that persists in opposition to the 'classical body' of high culture. As a study *Rabelais* has inspired critics to research the cultural politics of transgression in high and low culture. The publication of *The Dialogic Imagination* in 1981, a translation of four of Bakhtin's essays on the novel from before the war has changed the way that the history of the novel is understood. While before it was commonly understood as a middle-class form, Bakhtin's history of its relationship with a multiplicity of different popular discourses has caused cultural critics to reassess the relationship between literature and popular culture.

Bakhtin's influence on cultural studies has reached into literary, social and historical research. Perhaps the most influential piece of work using his methods is Peter Stallybrass and Allon White's *The Politics and Poetics of Transgression* (1986), a study of the emergence of middle-class, individualist subjectivity in opposition to popular culture and collective conceptions of the grotesque body.

Further reading

The Dialogic Imagination, Austin: University of Texas Press (1981).

Problems of Dostoevsky's Poetics, Manchester: Manchester University Press (1984).

Bakhtin School Papers, ed. Ann Shukman, Oxford: Russian Poetics in Translation (1988).

experience. Narrative analysis demonstrates that linear histories are not the only model for recording the past. Bakhtin's account of the multiple representations of time in the novel show that history need not only look at causation and continuity; it can also highlight discontinuities and transgression. One of the most influential theorists in this area has been Michel Foucault. Foucault argued that the proper task of the historian is history 'in the form of a concerted carnival' (Foucault, 1984a: 94).

5.2.5 | Michel Foucault

The work of Michel Foucault has been enormously important in recent years in new understandings of the relationship between culture and history. While Foucault would probably not have gone as far as to say that objective history does not exist, he considered the question essentially irrelevant. Foucault's work is concerned with the understanding of history as culture, and takes as its object of study the way what he calls the 'human sciences' create systems of knowledge. Grasping how Foucault uses two of his key terms – 'archaeology' and 'genealogy' – is essential in getting to grips with his understanding of history. In the first of the definitions in the extract (see Box 5.8), truth is understood as an archaeology, in the second as a genealogy (Davidson, 1986: 221). With the first definition, Foucault proposes an 'archaeology of knowledge', a history of how **discourse** (p. 30) has been ordered at particular times of history into ways of knowing or *epistemes*, which unexpectedly link apparently separate areas of knowledge in the same period. History for Foucault, then, is not a linear narrative, where one event follows another, but may be discontinuous. One order of discourses can break down and give way to a new order of things. New ideas do not emerge in isolation, but in the context of changes in whole systems of knowledge production. Foucault uses the concept of genealogy, from the German philosopher Nietzsche, to widen the terms of an archaeological analysis (Davidson, 1986: 227). In his essay 'Nietzsche, genealogy, history' (Foucault, 1984b) he argues that, in order to present themselves as valid and truthful, most histories root themselves in an idea of origins. Ideas of cause and effect in history and of history as an absent cause (see above) rely on determinist or reductionist concepts. Marxism, for example, believes in a real history that determines and Freudian

---

Box **5.8**

Michel Foucault on 'truth'

'Truth' is to be understood as system of ordered procedures for the production, regulation, distribution, circulation and operation of statements.

'Truth' is linked in a circular relation with systems of **power** which produce and sustain it, and to effects of **power** which it induces and which extends it. A 'regime' of truth.

Foucault (1984a: 74)

psychoanalysis depends on the idea of repression, so that any cultural phenomenon can be interpreted as really about, say, sexuality. These ideas of origins enable most histories to appear truthful. However, Foucault argues that:

> What is found at the historical beginning of things is not the inviolable identity of their origin; it is the dissension of other things. It is their disparity.
>
> ... the origin makes possible a field of knowledge whose function is to recover it, but always in a false recognition due to the excesses of its own speech. The origin lies at a place of inevitable loss, the point where the truth of things corresponded to a truthful discourse, the site of a fleeting articulation that discourse has obscured and finally lost. (Foucault, 1984a: 79)

For the historian to subscribe to any particular account of origins is to subscribe to the power that has made that account appear truthful, or what Foucault calls a 'regime of truth'. The work of the Foucauldian historian is not to seek origins, but to trace the ways in which 'dissension' develops into a regime of truth. As with other **post-structuralists** (p. 24), Foucault's genealogies are dependent on an analysis of discourses. Histories are discursively constructed, and Foucault is primarily interested in how they are discursively constructed rather than achieving an empirical account of what actually occurred, which, for Foucault, would be a discursive construction in itself. Thus a genealogy will not look for an ordered narrative, but at the carnivalesque of 'accidents, chance, passion, petty malices, surprises, feverish agitation, unsteady victories and power' (Davidson, 1986: 224). The last of this list, **power** (p. 94), is a key factor in defining the 'truth regime'. When Foucault talks about power he is not just talking about something outside discourse, which imposes order upon it (anyway, in Foucault's theory it would be impossible to talk about power without talking about the discourse through which it manifests itself); he is talking about how discourses are organised in relation to each other, how they are ordered to achieve 'their internal regime of power' (Foucault, 1984a: 55). Through this kind of analysis it becomes possible to analyse the workings of power not as one thing on another, for example the ruling class on the working class, but dispersed, working throughout the realm of discourse.

Foucault's ideas get round many of the traditional problems associated with the practice of historians. His method avoids simplistic accounts of what is real history or the truth: 'the political question, to sum up, is not error, illusion, alienated consciousness, or ideology; it is truth itself'. However, the Foucauldian historical method brings new problems of its own. It can be argued that Foucault does not really confront the problem of historical change, which takes place over time, but steps back and looks at how history is discursively constructed at any one time. He cannot really account for the 'events' that create changes in the episteme. As one of his critics, Jürgen Habermas, puts it, the relationship between discourses and practices is unexplained (Habermas, 1987: 247). His idea of power is nebulous and ahistorical, so difficult to incorporate into an account of how human history is made. Here Marxist accounts of human agency are more useful.

5.2.6 | History and difference

Against this, one of the reasons that Foucault's historical method has been so influential in recent years is that he provides a way of understanding how new subjectivities are produced in history. Foucault does not assume a human subject 'man', who makes history; rather he sees subjects being constructed discursively, produced within the *episteme* of a particular time. Thus, in *The Order of Things* (1970), Foucault argues that 'man' is a relatively recent invention, and will soon disappear again. By this he means that the idea of the self-conscious human subject that emerges in modernity is historical. It did not exist, for example, in the medieval world, where human beings were part of a large divine plan. This account of the subject has been used by feminists and historians of sexuality to show that new gendered and sexual identities emerge, for example the male homosexual at the end of the nineteenth century, and that the systems of knowledge that are associated with these identities permit new and potentially subversive histories. Current historical work being done in cultural studies usually borrows from both Marxist and Foucauldian influences. The following sections look at the kinds of history that are produced by historians interested in brushing history against the grain to examine the cultural history of class, gendered histories, histories of 'race' and nation and histories of sexuality.

The books of two pioneering writers in cultural studies exemplify this kind of historical work. **E.P. Thompson**'s (p. 96) historical study *The Making of the English Working Class* (1963) changed the understanding of the role of class in history by arguing that culture was a key element in its formation. People make class consciousness through culture. Thompson paid particular attention to the culture of Protestant dissent and its relationship to radical political activity. He reassessed the Luddites, arguing that they were not just machine breakers, but were conducting their campaigns as part of a campaign of political resistance. In *Culture and Society 1780–1950* (1963) and *The Long Revolution* (1965), **Raymond Williams** (p. 5) reinterpreted Victorian and twentieth-century culture so that culture was understood not as something that was owned by the middle and upper classes and aspired to by the working class, but as 'a way of life' in which all classes participated. Both Thompson and Williams used methods taken from literary criticism to look at written culture, including poetry, novels, drama and the writings of cultural critics and journalism. They reinterpreted the values contained within these texts in relation to the values and conflicts that ran through the whole of society in the periods they studied. They differed in that Williams paid more attention to values and what he called 'structures of feeling', while Thompson criticised *The Long Revolution* for being insufficiently concerned with culture in history as not so much a 'way of life' as a 'way of conflict' (Thompson, 1961: 39). Both, however, were essentially agreed on the need for the historian to extend the range of evidence beyond what had hitherto been considered proper 'historical' documents. Neither was as concerned as more recent practitioners of cultural studies with the question of the individual historian's relationship to his or her material, what is sometimes called the 'subjectivity' of the historian or cultural critic. This issue relates to the question of identity raised in Chapter 1. The lack of interest in questions of identity other than class identity has led to Williams and Thompson being criticised for their apparent disinterest in questions of gender, 'race' and sexuality.

Contemporary feminist history has been consistently critical of the idea of history as homogenous, linear and causal. Feminist historians have pointed out that women's lives have been neglected in almost all historical records and are 'hidden from history'. However, feminist historians have argued that simply to include women in traditional historical narratives is not enough, as those narratives have been written from a masculine perspective: 'adding women to history is not the same as adding women's history' (Fox-Genovese, 1982: 6). As Maïté Albistur has argued, women's history is as complex as men's history, but following a similar argument to Kristeva in 'Women's time' (Kristeva, 1986), Albistur writes 'we may assume that time as lived by the female part of humanity does not pass according to the same rhythms and that it is not perceived in the same way as that of men' (Bock, 1989: 7). Feminist history calls for a 'gendered analysis', that is an understanding of what a masculine or a feminine perspective might mean in any one historical period. Joan Scott describes the task as

> to understand the significance of the *sexes* of gender groups in the historical past. Our goal is to discover the range in sex roles and in sexual symbolism in different societies and periods, to find out what meaning they had and how they functioned to maintain social order or to promote change.   (Scott, 1986: 1054)

Historians of gender relations have argued with Scott that the relationship between men and women is not fixed – it is 'problematic rather than known' – and the task of the historian to investigate it has been 'contextually defined, repeatedly constructed' (Scott, 1986: 1074).

As important for the development of cultural studies has been the work of the historian C.L.R. James. His best-known history *The Black Jacobins* (1980), mentioned in 5.1.7, was written twenty years before *The Making of the English Working Class* or *Culture and Society*, but it was a work that looked forward to the decolonisation of Africa and has been most influential on postcolonial and anti-racist cultural critics like **Edward Said** (p. 168) and **Paul Gilroy** (p. 166). James's book was originally published in the same year as *The People's History of England* by A.L. Morton (1965), another work that pioneered the movement for history 'from below'. However, while Morton's text was radical for its time and deeply influential on later English Marxist historians like E.P. Thompson, Christopher Hill and Eric Hobsbawm, it was relatively narrow in its geographical and political focus. *The Black Jacobins*, by contrast, explored the relationship between European history and colonial history. James showed how the Haitian revolution drew on both African culture and the Enlightenment ideas that inspired the French Revolution. Most importantly, he portrayed African slaves as agents, active in making their own history and in changing European perceptions. From the political and 'partisan' perspective of the national liberation struggles against **colonialism** (p. 189), James explored issues of 'race' and class in history and showed how these categories defined one another both in Europe and in the Caribbean. He demonstrated that the ideals of freedom and citizenship developed in Europe were formed in relation to an oppressive imperial policy. By writing from a position that was critical of the political culture from within which most European history had been written, he was able both to shed new light on European history and to provide a historical framework for understanding the historical and cultural processes of decolonisation after the Second

World War. *The Black Jacobins* legitimated struggles for Third World independence, because it showed that those struggles had their roots within a historical relationship between European modernity and the history of European imperialism. In cultural studies, work by James and other historians has influenced postcolonial studies – work that has addressed, for example, how colonised cultures were represented in the West and forms of cultural resistance to colonial cultures (Chrisman and Williams, 1993).

One of the most recent areas of historical research has been the history of sexuality. The lesbian and gay movement in the postwar period inspired attempts to trace the history of same-sex relationships. In its early form this meant the documenting of famous figures who were 'homosexual' – for example, Shakespeare, Michelangelo and Julius Caesar – as a way of legitimating a gay identity in the present. Later research started to examine how sexual relations influence forms of cultural organisation and power. Anthropological research has shown the wide varieties of sexual relations found in human societies (Chauncey *et al.*, 1991: 10–11). Research into these different forms has led historians of sexuality to argue that sexuality is not about fixed or **essentialist** (p. 138) identities; rather it is 'constructed'. Social constructionist versions of sexuality argue that particular forms emerge within particular kinds of society. Again the inspiration for much of this research has been lesbian and gay history. Historians have argued that contemporary lesbian and gay identities have only emerged relatively recently. Some historians date their appearance to the urban subcultures of eighteenth-century European cities, others to the late nineteenth century or, in the case of lesbian identities, early twentieth century. Below we look at how the historian Judith Walkowitz represents the cultural conflicts that led to legislation on sexuality in England in the late nineteenth century. Work on the social construction of homosexuality has opened up research into the social construction of heterosexuality. Historians have shown that the modern, absolute divide between heterosexual and same-sex relations is not true of all societies or all periods. Ideas of acceptable masculine or feminine behaviour vary widely and sexual practice is often much more varied than the dominant codes of acceptable behaviour would suggest. Work by cultural critics like Eve Kosofsky Sedgwick (1985), who is part of the critical movement known as 'queer theory', has shown that the codes of behaviour that signified upper-class masculinity in nineteenth-century England were governed by what she calls 'male homosocial desire'. Upper-class men socialised in all-male institutions like public schools, Parliament, the army and the Church. Strong bonds were established between men to the exclusion of women and men deemed less than masculine. Yet the nature of these bonds was contradictory. Despite their overt heterosexuality, a covert homoeroticism characterised the men's relationships with one another. Social power along class and gendered lines was reinforced by male homo-social desire. Sedgwick's thesis demonstrates how a particular social form of organis-ation can derive some of its power through sexual relations, even when sexuality is not seen by the actors themselves as an important determinant of their behaviour (Sedgwick, 1985). In an essay on schoolgirl crushes, Martha Vicinus examines same-sex attraction between young women and finds that many of them lacked a language of sexuality into which to put their feelings. Instead, they expressed their sentiments through a sense of duty or through religious fervour (Vicinus, 1991). Nonetheless, sexuality was as important in the socialisation of young women as it was among young men in single-sex schools in Britain and the United States.

In the twentieth century, political and cultural movements have identified more strongly with particular sexual identities. Jonathan Dollimore has described how lesbians and gay men have deployed both essentialist and non-essentialist strategies to legitimate what he calls 'dissident' sexualities. A writer like the French novelist André Gide argued that his homosexuality was as natural and normal as heterosexuality. The English playwright Oscar Wilde, on the other hand, deliberately subverted the idea of naturalness itself in his writing. He practised what he called paradox in art and perversity in life. For Wilde, 'life imitates art'; in other words, there is no essential or natural way of being, all identities are performances, in which we act out roles that our culture has already written for us. This idea has been pursued by queer theorists like Judith Butler, who argues that identity is always a product of the powerful discourses that try to constrain it (see Chapter 6). The most common example given in the history of sexuality is the response of many men to the trial of Oscar Wilde in 1895, when he was sentenced to two years' hard labour for acts of 'gross indecency' with another man. The Wilde trial and the publicity that surrounded it confirmed for many men that their desires for other men constituted a 'Wildean' identity and resistance to the repressive legislation against male homosexuality provided the impetus for the early campaigns for homosexual rights. Over the twentieth century, movements emerged that represented sexual identities in different ways. In the 1960s, gay liberation argued for a gay identity to be recognised for an end to discrimination. Lesbian movements emerged and differentiated themselves from gay liberation, which was primarily a movement of men. In the 1990s, groups like Queer Nation in the United States have tried to move away from fixed identities altogether and argue for a spectrum of sexual behaviours and performances. To recognise this, in 1996 the annual demonstrations for Gay Pride in San Francisco, the gay capital of the world, welcomed lesbian, gay, bisexual, transgendered and 'questioning'. In cultural studies this new pluralism has effectively changed critics' assumptions about the nature of sexuality. However, despite the liberating nature of ideas like 'performativity', historians of sexuality need to keep in mind the particular cultural circumstances that permit different kinds of sexual identities.

One solution is offered by Dollimore's *Sexual Dissidence* (1991). Dollimore has been one of the foremost practitioners of 'cultural materialism'. This historical method of criticism, originated by Raymond Williams, attempts to bring an activist politics to the politics of texts. It allows Dollimore to approach **essentialist** (p. 138) theories of sexuality as part of larger political debates, leading him to argue for the need to 'disentangle a radical essentialism from its conservative counterparts'. Dollimore suggests what he calls the 'paradoxical perverse' and the 'perverse dynamic' as methodologies that allow for an account of sexual dissidence. He argues (see Box 5.9) for a four-part methodology for historical enquiry in relation to the sexual.

5.2.7 | Example: 'A maiden tribute to modern Babylon'

An example of recent historical writing that exemplifies some of these new approaches

---

Box 5.9
Jonathan Dollimore, *Sexual Dissidence*

In attempting to recover *what* is repressed and disavowed – the unacceptable histories of perversion – I have been led beyond formal definitions to a conceptual development which in turn has facilitated historical recovery.

This fourfold procedure – (1) attention to formal definitions, provoking (2) a historical enquiry which in turn leads to (3) a conceptual development facilitating (4) a further historical recovery – I see as a materialist project.

Dollimore (1991: 228)

---

is Judith Walkowitz's (1992) book, *City of Dreadful Delight: Narratives of Sexual Danger in Late-Victorian London*. Walkowitz uses feminist, Marxist and poststructuralist approaches to complicate the idea of what history is. In the introduction she writes that she has resisted a narrative of 'change over time', that is the kind of narrative we would expect from modern histories. Instead, she emphasises the different 'cultural and social perspectives' involved in a historical period and how they work in relation to one another. She chooses the city, nineteenth-century London, as an example of modernity, but in order to explore the different perspectives within modernity rather than history and time as a uni-linear progress.

Her work, published as two consecutive chapters in the book, on the impact of articles in the *Pall Mall Gazette* in 1885 has provoked a debate around not just feminist history but many of the issues raised in the chapter, including history and **modernity** (p. 400), history as fact and history as narrative. The facts, which have been discussed from a variety of perspectives by a number of historians, are as follows. In July 1885, the editor of the *Pall Mall Gazette*, W.T. Stead, published a series of articles under the title 'A maiden tribute to modern Babylon', claiming to have exposed the sale of young working-class girls for the purposes of prostitution. The articles caused a furore. A month later, on 10 August 1885, the Criminal Law Amendment Act was passed in Parliament, raising the age of consent for girls from 13 to 16, giving police new powers to prosecute prostitutes and brothel-keepers and making illegal indecent acts between consenting male adults. On 22 August a crowd estimated at 250,000 people demonstrated in Hyde park for the enforcement of the legislation to protect young girls. Vigilance committees were set up and attacked music halls and theatres. As a consequence the police cracked down on prostitution and homosexual men. In the short term, the circulation of the *Pall Mall Gazette* increased, but W.T. Stead was prosecuted for 'purchasing' a young girl as part of his investigations into the trade and spent three months in Holloway prison.

The truthfulness of Stead's account was questioned at the time and has been questioned subsequently by historians (Gorham, 1978; Weeks, 1981). Judith Walkowitz, however, approaches the article not in terms of how truthful it was, but as a narrative.

This kind of approach has been pioneered by the school of historical criticism known as 'new historicism'. The inventor of this term, Stephen Greenblatt, defines the conceptual origins of new historicism as a reaction to the inadequate treatment of history by both **Marxism** (p. 97) and **poststructuralism** (p. 24). Neither, he argues, can cope with the complexity of modern culture. Greenblatt criticises Fredric Jameson's Marxism for arguing that alienation creates artificial divisions, while Lyotard's poststructuralism argues that capitalism makes everything seem the same (Greenblatt, 1989). In order to show how a properly historical approach can resolve this dilemma, Greenblatt tells a series of stories or anecdotes. Narrating stories is a characteristic of the new historicist school and it is something that Greenblatt does with great wit and skill. New historicist writers, in effect, return to the older form of history as narrative as a way of resisting grand narratives of modern(ist) history. Their interest is directed towards the ways in which history is represented as narrative and how different narratives relate to one another.

Using the language of Foucault, whose theory has been very influential on new historicism, Walkowitz's interest is directed towards how Stead's article imposed a 'certain narrative logic on the story of prostitution' and how this narrative 'ordered people's experience and helped construct a sexual subjectivity for men and women' (Walkowitz, 1992: 83). Interestingly, Walkowitz also quotes Fredric Jameson's work on narrative and history, where he says that the narrative can 'lead us back to the concrete historical situation of the text itself'. In other words, she draws on both Marxist and Foucauldian theory, but, as a feminist historian, she is critical of both for giving little or no space to the question of women's place in history. Among the narrative forms she finds in Stead's article are those of melodrama, late Victorian pornography and fantasy and the Gothic fairy tale; but melodrama provides the primary structure through which the tale of the seduction of 'poor girls by vicious aristocrats' is told. Walkowitz argues that, as the most important theatrical and literary form of the nineteenth century, melodrama appealed to a popular audience. It incorporated both a class and a sexual narrative, the most common scenario including an upper-class male villain, a working-class hero or grieving father and the heroine. Class exploitation and working-class victimisation were represented through a narrative of sexual exploitation. This narrative of the rapacious aristocrat was used by both radical, working-class organisations and by feminists in the nineteenth century as part of arguments for socialism and women's emancipation. Thus, Stead's narrative had both popular and political resonances for its audience. However, Walkowitz's point is to show that not only was the narrative of 'A maiden tribute' both popular and political, but that its reception and the cultural consequences of that reception were contradictory, with implications for the history of class, gender, 'race' and sexuality.

In relation to class, at first the article appeared to have a unifying effect, bringing together a wide constituency of middle-class and working-class women, male trade unionists and Christians in a campaign against upper-class 'vice'. The Criminal Law Amendment Act was the most tangible result of the popular mobilisation, causing Parliament to pass legislation that had been stalled for years. As events unravelled, however, the consequences were uneven and inconsistent. Walkowitz points out that the political positions that melodrama creates are themselves contradictory. Women and working-class men were represented as victims of class and sexual exploitation and this gave them a rallying point for protest. On the other hand, the subjectivities created by the construction of their victimhood were passive and thus the political discourse limited the possibilities for their self-construction as political agents.

This construction of subjectivity had a specifically gendered dimension. The heroine is constructed as the weakest character in the narrative and is denied any expression of her own desires. Desire, in fact, is entirely the property of the villainous aristocrat, so that there is no room for sexual expression that is not an expression of vice. This meant that the debate was conducted in terms that refused a recognition of women's desires. The political and cultural consequences were similarly contradictory. While the protests were against the exploitation of working-class women, increased police activity meant that unaccompanied women, especially working-class women, were subject to restrictions on their movement in public places. Walkowitz writes that the movement for social purity 'imposed a disciplinary regime on working-class women' but it caused middle-class women to 'explore their own sexual subjectivity', leading to experiments in non-marital relationships and a reconsideration of the role of birth control.

Issues of cultural difference might seem remote from the political events. In fact, London's position as capital of an international empire meant that upheaval there had reverberations around the world. For example, the consequences of a change in the law spread throughout the British Empire. European constructions of femininity were exported unproblematically to the colonies where they combined with racist practices. Attempts to suppress prostitution in England were transformed into legal measures to stop relationships between whites and colonised peoples. Walkowitz records that, in some cases, the attempt to suppress prostitution meant the imposition of 'official prohibitions against liaisons with "native' women". Thus, a law enacted in the imperial metropolis had far-reaching effects in the definition of 'racial' and sexual identities in British colonies.

One important offshoot of the Act was the creation of a new crime relating to homosexual men, and it was under this law that Oscar Wilde was sentenced to two years' hard labour ten years later (see above). Thus, rather than providing equality between men and women, the law and the vigilance committees acted together to restrict all expressions of desire. History has to chart the unpredictable results of modernising plans which, far from providing an unproblematic movement forward, have consequences that require a complex narrative strategy on the part of the historian.

5.2.8 | Past and present

Walkowitz's account of the aftermath of the publication of one, albeit highly significant, article shows how complicated the relationship between culture and history actually is. What in a linear, causal history could be seen as one legal act of progress is seen to create subjectivities along divisions of gender and class (ideas of passive, victimised, working-class femininity and active, predatory, upper-class masculinity), of sexuality (new legal definitions of male homosexuality) and of 'race' (the redefinition of the relationship between European men and the women of colonised countries). Walkowitz's point is that these cultural consequences cannot be understood as part of one historical narrative. They are, in fact, produced by the narratives through which people understood their own time, and the business of history is to analyse those narratives.

This account of Walkowitz's historical method leaves out one important aspect, that is how the present deals with the narratives left to it by the past. The conclusion to *City of Dreadful Delight* makes it clear that the concerns that guided the book's form and content were provoked by the politics of the women's movement and in particular the debates about sexual violence that occurred within British feminism during the 1980s. Walkowitz reads the late nineteenth century through the political concerns of the present, which 'incited the cultural and historical inquiry resulting in *City of Dreadful Delight*'. She describes the book's project as an attempt to return to 'a formative moment in the production of feminist politics and of popular narratives of sexual danger' (1992: 243). In this sense the cultural politics of the present can inform our understanding of the past. In this case, a feminist perspective illuminates certain aspects of nineteenth-century history. However, Walkowitz is careful to point out that contemporary feminist debates about sexual danger, for example that over the case of Peter Sutcliffe who murdered thirteen women between 1975 and 1981, are also framed within narratives and that writing history is about relating the narratives of the present to those of the past in such a way that they do not show it to be about single causes and effects (1992: 244–5). Where new historicism has used Foucault and narrative analysis to re-examine history, the importance of contemporary politics in Walkowitz's work takes her closer to Dollimore's cultural materialism. For cultural studies the contemporary political uses of cultural history remain an important factor in all historical work.

5.2.9 | Conclusion

We can conclude this section by outlining five key areas of interest to historical work in cultural studies:

1. The form and content of a particular historical text. For example, its narrative structure, literary techniques and relationship to other texts in the period.

2. The values and conflicts contained within the text. For example, its ideology, discourses, how the text takes sides, mediates conflicts or attempts resolutions.

3. The way that the historical research has been conducted: how the evidence was selected and used. For example, has it used historical documents or archeological evidence or both? What philosophy of history or historical framework is the historian using?

4. Histories need to be placed in their broader cultural context, seen as of their time and place. We need to know about the culture within which the history was researched and written, its values and conflicts.

5. We also need to know the place of the individual historian within that culture and her or his relationship to its values and conflict; for example, his or her political beliefs, the academic school to which she or he belongs.

The kind of historical work done within cultural studies is concerned to foreground these issues so that culture is not seen as a sub-branch of the discipline of history where cultural history is bracketed along with military history, scientific history and so on, but rather that all forms of history work within a context where cultural values and meanings act so as to create understandings and disputes.

5.3 | If/when: the future

In this section, we look at the concept of the future. Of necessity this means that this section is shorter than the previous two. The future does not yet exist. It acts, rather, as a border or horizon beyond which we cannot go, but onto which we can project our hopes and fears. Below we look at the future orientation of modernity, its preoccupation with the new and its belief in the prospect of change rather than stasis. We consider the concept of utopia and the importance of utopianism and dystopianism in our perceptions of future time. The science fiction genre of 'cyberpunk' is discussed as an example of narratives of the future. We suggest that it is the uncertainty of the future in modernity that spurs our interest in history. We wish to learn to predict possible outcomes from the experience of the past. Finally we suggest that Walter Benjamin's concept of the constellation is the best way to understand the non-linear relationship between past, present and future.

It would be wrong to say that the future is a modern invention. The concepts of past, present and future exist in different forms in most cultures. However, it is true to say that modernity has been unusually orientated towards the future. Antony Giddens talks of modernity's 'colonisation of the future', its projection forward into time in an attempt to control and organise the outcome of current events (Giddens, 1991: 111). The modern idea of an objective linear history assumes a certain past and a future that can be planned for. Institutions, businesses, governments and individuals prepare for what is to come by considering what has happened before. Fredric Jameson argues that in the mid-nineteenth century a new historical sense in the novel gives way to a sense of the future. The emergence of science fiction in the second half of the nineteenth century led to a shift in 'our relationship to historical time' (Jameson, 1982: 149). Novels of the future succeed the historical novels of the early nineteenth century: 'SF as a form ... now registers some nascent sense of the future, and does so in the space on which a sense of the past had once been inscribed' (1982: 150). For Jameson science fiction is about the difficulty of coming to terms with the present. It dramatises our 'incapacity to imagine the future', and as such is 'a contemplation of our own absolute limits' (1982: 153). Interestingly, modern science fiction emerges at the same time as modernism in art and literature. Its appearance in the second half of the nineteenth century corresponds to the emergence of modernist fiction and poetry in France: the novels of Gustave Flaubert (1821–80) and the poetry of Charles Baudelaire (1821–67). Jules Verne (1828–1905) published *Voyage to the Centre of the Earth* in 1864. In England, modernist traits do not become fully present until the 1890s, among aesthetes like

Oscar Wilde and novelists like Joseph Conrad. The 1890s was the decade when H.G. Wells published his first novels: *The Time Machine* (1895) and *The War of the Worlds* (1898).

5.3.1 | Utopia and dystopia

The future orientation of modernity affects the way we think about both time and history. The future acts as a kind of horizon, which, in the words of Niklas Luhmann, can never begin (see Box 5.10). We project best and worst outcomes onto the future horizon: utopias and dystopias. The word 'utopia' is a neologism invented by Thomas More, combining the Greek *eutopia* (a happy place) and *outopia* (no place). This combination neatly defines the distinction between a utopia and utopianism. A utopia is a blueprint of a better society – a happy place – but has the disadvantage of closing down other possible ways of imagining improvement. Utopianism, by contrast, is less specific; it offers no place in particular. Instead, it defines a sense of lack which stimulates a 'desire for a better way of being' (Levitas, 1990: 8). The difference between the representation of a utopia and utopianism might be described as the difference between determinate and conditional futures. Determinate futures extrapolate from present tendencies and may portend dystopias as well as utopias. Conditional futures explore the contradictions of the present, pursuing their complexity, and offer futures that are possible rather than predetermined outcomes. Narratives of conditional futures resist technological determination and concentrate more on the complex interaction of social relations and technological change.

5.3.2 | Narratives of the future

The time of modernity incorporates a kind of yearning for a better place that we might be able to achieve in the future. Consequently, we arrange our conception of the past and the present in relation to our desires for the future. Some narrative forms are able to represent this better than others. Romance is perhaps the most effective, because it

---

Box **5.10**

Niklas Luhmann, on the future

Future itself, and this means past futures as well as the present future must be conceived as possibly quite different from the past. It can no longer be characterized as approaching a turning point where it returns into the past or where the order of this world or even time itself is changed. It may contain, as a functional equivalent for the end of time, emergent properties and not-yet-realized possibilities. It becomes an open future.

Luhmann (1976: 131)

> *Box* **5.11**
> ## Donna Haraway, 'A cyborg manifesto'
>
> From one perspective, a cyborg world is about the final imposition of a grid of control on the planet, about the final abdication embodied in the Star Wars apocalypse waged in the name of defense, about the final appropriation of women's bodies in a masculinist orgy of war. From another perspective, a cyborg world might be about lived social and bodily realities in which people are not afraid of their joint kinship with animals and machines, not afraid of permanently partial identities and contradictory standpoints.
>
> Haraway (1991: 154)

incorporates desire into its structure. The utopianism of romance lies not in its construction of a particular utopian blueprint, but in its expression of a sense of lack, so that we feel that what we have is inadequate, but that satisfaction may be attained some time in the future. Whatever our certainty about the past or the present, the future always involves a sense of uncertainty which unsettles our temporal sense. The end of the twentieth century has been a particularly uncertain period of modernity, to the extent that it is sometimes characterised as postmodern. **Postmodernity** (p. 400) describes a number of different social changes: the 'globalisation' of the world's economy, the growth in population movements and the speed and quantity of information exchanges – all of which have changed our visions of the future. In her essay, 'A cyborg manifesto' (Haraway, 1991), Donna Haraway outlines these developments as paving the way for two possible futures: a terrifying vision of social control or new, emancipatory possibilities (see Box 5.11 and refer to section 7.5). This opposition operates a dialectic between determinate and conditional futures. Where a determinate future promises fixed and controlled identities, an alternative, and perhaps equally frightening, prospect is the lack of any unified identity at all. Postmodern 'cyborg fictions' explore the kinds of identities needed to live in the new world (McCracken, 1997). They attempt to think through the problem of the self in a context where the cultural boundaries are constantly shifting. The new pluralism suggested by postmodernism is often difficult to reconcile with the twentieth century's tendency towards globalisation and standardisation. Some of the contradictions of the new constellation are explored in a science fiction movement which emerged in the 1980s: cyberpunk. Cyberpunk has been described by Fredric Jameson as 'a new type of science fiction ... which is fully as much an expression of transnational corporate realities as it is of global paranoia itself' (Jameson, 1991: 3). The movement is true to its name in its skilful self-promotion. It extrapolates from the cut-throat consumer society of the 1980s and that decade's increasing divide between rich and poor. The fictional world of the best-known proponent of cyberpunk, William Gibson, describes a recognisable geo-political system, characterised by weak nation-states and dominant transnationals. Its inequalities reflect the long-term tendencies of the global economy predicted by David Harvey: 'heightened international and inter-regional competition, with the least advantaged countries and regions suffering the severest consequences' (Harvey, 1990: 183). But, though inspired by the development of new technologies like virtual reality, personal computers and the Internet, Gibson's narratives focus as much on the social contradictions thrown up by technology as the machinery itself. On the one hand, cyberpunk is resolutely posthumanist. It delights in the transformation of what is meant by being human: Gibson's characters employ genetic engineering, drugs and advanced forms of surgery to transform themselves. On the other hand, the cyberworld is peopled with the descendants of postwar counter-cultures who represent a persistent romanticism.

Gibson's style is influenced by hard-boiled detective fiction. A consequence is that the most marked aspect of his world is a sense of lack or unfulfilled potential. His novels and short stories explore the forms of hybrid, 'cyber' consciousness that arise from the employment of new technologies as a means of domination. His most famous contribution to the genre is the idea of 'jacking in'. Using a jack into their central nervous system, his characters are able to plug themselves directly into the 'matrix' (an enhanced form of the Internet) and explore a virtual world of information, described as 'A graphic representation of data abstracted from the banks of every computer in the human system. Unthinkable complexity. Lines of light ranged in the nonspace of the mind, clusters and constellations of data. Like city lights, receding' (Gibson, 1986: 67). The matrix acts as a metaphor for the kinds of cultural collisions and re-inventions of the self made possible by new technologies.

Gibson's science fiction alternates between the transcendent utopian freedom of the matrix and the banal ordinariness of everyday life. One criticism that has been made of cyberpunk is that it is literature for boys (Nixon, 1992) and certainly Gibson's fictions are often structured as a kind of masculine romance. However, this is not intrinsic to the form. The feminist writer Marge Piercy sets her novel, *Body of Glass* (1992), in a cyberpunk world, but the shifting boundaries of that world are used to explore, among other cultural borders, the limits and definitions of gender.

In her acknowledgements, Piercy recognises the influence of Donna Haraway's essay, 'A cyborg manifesto'. Haraway argues that the boundaries between human and animal and human and machine were always and will always be fictional because our interaction with technology will always change what it means to be human. Central to Haraway's argument is the Marxist idea that what is important about machines is the way they fit into social organisation. It is not the technology itself, but the way that the machines relate to and recreate relations between people. This is one of the themes of *Body of Glass*.

The novel alternates two narratives, one historical and one of the future; both are concerned with boundaries. A historical narrative about seventeenth-century Prague tells the story of the Golem, a giant made out of clay by the Rabbi Judah Loew to protect the inhabitants of the Jewish ghetto. The parallel story of the twenty-first century also concerns a ghetto, Tikva. Tikva exists at a time when transnational corporations rule most of the globe, leaving the parts that they do not need to administer to violence, poverty and anarchy. In Gibson's stories these areas are called the 'sprawl'. Piercy calls them the 'glop'. The stories of the Prague ghetto and Tikva tell of the boundaries that define a particular culture against the threatening world beyond. The ghetto has only its wall and the ingenuity of its Rabbi. Tikva survives as an independent 'free town' by selling its innovative high-tech products to the corporations and protecting itself from the pollution and radiation that exist beyond its limits. Both Tikva and the ghetto are prisons as well as protected zones. The protection that they afford is a reminder of the limits put on the lives of their inhabitants. Those limits are defined by the dominant power outside the ghetto: in Prague the Christian state, for Tikva the hegemony of the transnationals. However, while in the seventeenth century the boundaries are fairly fixed, in the twenty-first they have become more fluid, defined by the shifting space of the glop and the possibility of jacking in and moving through cyberspace. In each case, the ghetto is a metaphor for the vulnerability as well as the creativity of minority cultures which allow the possibility of different kinds of *self*-determination.

When the borders of Tikva are threatened, a modern-day Golem, Yod, is created by the scientist Avram. Yod is part machine, part genetically engineered cyborg and a strange hybrid of masculine and feminine attributes. His predecessors, starting with Alef (the first letter of the Hebrew alphabet; Yod is the tenth), all turned violent and had to be destroyed. Yod has been half-programmed by a woman, and has a more balanced personality. He is a constructed hybrid self, created, like the Golem, to police boundaries, but is not himself of the place he protects or the place that threatens. As a cyborg he has no essential identity. He is the border. Haraway writes of the relationship between bodies and machines as a 'border war' (Haraway, 1991: 150). Science fiction, speculative fiction and fantasy are useful modes in this context because their subject is the point at which the boundaries between what is 'real' and what is possible are drawn (1991: 201). Cyborg fictions are ways of theorising and narrating these boundaries. The consequence is monster stories: 'Monsters have always defined the limits of community in Western imaginations' (1991: 180). Cyborgs are the monsters that populate the margins of discourse: 'These boundary creatures are, literally, monsters, a word that shares more than its root with the word to *demonstrate*. Monsters signify' (1991: 2). At this point, analysis of the narrative, of the fiction, becomes as important as the discovery of the facts, which have themselves been constituted as a story. Science, as the 'most respectable legitimator of new realities' (1991: 78), can provide the narratives that society needs to resolve 'the contradiction between, or the gap between, human reality and human possibility in history' (1991: 42). But Haraway is not content to let those narratives be authoritative. They are always fictions, mediating social reality.

Body of Glass describes a process whereby machines are becoming more human and humans more like machines. As Yod says: 'I'm a fusion of machine and lab-created biological components – much as humans frequently are fusions of flesh and machine' (Piercy, 1992: 96). Yod's counterpart is a human, Nili, who has been genetically enhanced to give her superhuman powers. This corresponds to Haraway's new world of 'partial identities and contradictory standpoints'. Yod combines aspects of human and machine, masculinity and femininity in a way that is genuinely utopian in its transgression of old boundaries and the creation of something new: 'Creation is always perilous, for it gives true life to what has been inchoate and voice to what has been dumb. It

---

Box 5.12

Marge Piercy, *Body of Glass*

Her deep and almost violent sexual pleasure not only disturbed but confused her. She had imagined that it was her love for Gadi, that early emotional bonding, that had made the sex with him much more satisfying and engaging than anything in her life since. But what she was responding to in Yod was simply technique. He had been programmed to satisfy, and he satisfied. She had to admit she was perhaps a little disappointed in herself that she could indeed be pleased by what was programmed to do just that.

Piercy (1992: 241)

---

makes known what has been unknown, that perhaps we were more comfortable with not knowing. The new is necessarily dangerous' (1992: 91).

Like Gibson's fictions, *Body of Glass* is a romance, but this time the traditional gender relationships in Gibson's tales are reversed and questioned. The two narratives are told not from man to man, but through two feminine voices, Shira and her grandmother, Malkah, who tells Yod the story of the Golem. Inverting the structure of Gibson's prose, it is Yod who becomes the object of Shira's desire. Yod offers the fantasy of creating a being who is perfectly suited to one *self*. But because he has been manufactured, Shira's relationship with him is unnerving. She can never be sure whether what she experiences with him is genuine or pre-programmed (see Box 5.12). Sleeping with Yod confuses Shira's sense of self, which she had believed was based on experiences that were particular to certain relationships, times and places. The utopian promise of perfect satisfaction is again compromised by the uncanny sense that what she is experiencing is an inhuman, mechanical repetition. The image conveys a sense of alternative futures, one desirable, one unsettling. In science fiction the shock of alien encounter produces two contradictory possibilities: one of a better place, the other of our worst nightmare. The cyberpunk narratives of Gibson and Piercy negotiate the dialectic between new pleasures and the 'grid of control' directs how we experience them.

5.3.3 | History and the future

The uncertainty of the future is one of the most effective spurs to historical research. It inspires us to continually re-evaluate the past in the context of a constantly evolving present. This process has been described most effectively by Benjamin (see Box 5.13). Benjamin attempted to reconcile the paradox of modernity with its twin sense of history: on the one hand a sense of an objective, linear history, on the other a sense of the present as open-ended and characterised by modernity's sense of time, by 'the transient, the fleeting, the contingent'. He calls the former historicism; and he contrasts it with what he calls 'Messianic time', a sense of the future in which the potential of the

---

Box 5.13

Walter Benjamin, 'Theses on the Philosophy of History'

Historicism contents itself with establishing a causal connection between various moments in history. But no fact that is a cause is for that reason historical. It becomes historical posthumously, as it were, through events that may be separated from it by thousands of years. A historian who takes this as his point of departure stops telling the sequence of events like the beads of a rosary. Instead he grasps the constellation which his own era has formed with a definite earlier one. Thus he establishes a conception of the present as the 'time of now' which is shot through with Messianic time.

Benjamin (1970: 263)

---

past will be brought to fruition. The constellation is perhaps the most useful metaphor for how cultural studies approaches the problems of history and time. Rather than a linear history, which Benjamin describes as like 'the beads of a rosary' where events come one after the other, it recognises the complexity of both the present and the past. As with Walkowitz's account of the multiple consequences of a series of newspaper articles, we need to look at a historical moment in terms of all the social relations involved and then relate those relations to the complexity and open-endedness of our own present. This is easier said than done; but it is the difficulty of the task that interests cultural studies.

5.4 | Conclusion

In this chapter we have considered both time and history as cultural formations. Starting with basic concepts like modern and premodern time, we have moved towards a conception that introduces difference and complexity into our understanding. Premodern time has often been characterised as static, but we have seen how this is a modern assumption, imposed on the premodern in order to emphasise the dynamism of modernity. In fact, cultural studies show a diversity of conceptions of time in different cultures. Within modernity itself, we find a comparable diversity which challenges the uniformity of mechanical clock or industrial time. The revolutionary nature of modernity means that it is constantly creating new forms of culture which contest a single, normative standard. Consequently, different social groups experience modernity in different ways. While history as a linear, progressive narrative is a product of modernity, different social groups have constructed different historical narratives to explain their modern identities. These narratives complicate any sense of one 'grand' narrative of history or a simple causal relationship between past and present. Relating the past to the present thus becomes a task that involves relating a whole constellation of different positions. One aspect of modernity, its orientation to the future, also means that, whether we believe in an objective history or not, our sense of history, sometimes described as our philosophy of history or the framework within which we work, is constantly changing as we incorporate not just new events, but our hopes, desires and fears of what is to come.

Re-cap

- Time and history can be understood as cultural formations.
- Conflicts exist both within cultures of time and between cultures of time.
- History is characterised by different, conflicting accounts or narratives which complicate any sense of 'what actually happened'.

Further reading

A good introduction to the cultures of time is Eviatur Zerubavel, *Hidden Rhythms: Schedules and Calendars in Social Life* (1982). David Harvey's *The Condition of Postmodernity* (1990) is a compelling account of modernity's culture of time. The best way to approach questions of time in history is to read the key historical studies, for example: Stephen Kern, *The Culture of Time and Space: 1880–1918* (1983); or E.P. Thompson's famous essay 'Time, work-discipline and industrial capitalism' in *Customs in Common* (1991). Judith Walkowitz's *City of Dreadful Delight: Narratives of Sexual Danger in Late-Victorian London* (1992) is an excellent example of a critical narrative approach to history. William Gibson's collection of short stories, *Burning Chrome* (1993), provides some terrifying visions of the future.

Politics and culture

6.0 | Introduction

One of the ways in which cultural studies has been influential is in its transformations of the ideas of what is 'political'. Indeed, many of those who want to use the term 'cultural politics' for their work on culture would argue that 'everything is political'. By this they mean that everything is a matter of contested power relations (see, for example, Jordan and Weedon, 1994). **bell hooks** (p. 223) argues that 'Vigilant insistence that cultural studies be linked to a progressive radical cultural politics will ensure that it is a location that enables critical intervention' (hooks, 1991: 9). This means a move away from more conventional notions of what is 'political' – the realm of parliaments, political parties, international relations, state institutions, bureaucracies, trade unions and so on – and broadens out the field of study to include the politics of art and literature, the politics of gender and race, and the politics of everyday life.

Much of the rest of this book might be seen as a product of this expanded notion of 'politics' as 'cultural politics', but in this chapter we focus specifically on the relationship between politics and culture. We acknowledge that it is still important to retain something of the conventional sense of politics as a particular set of arenas in which certain strong claims to legitimacy and power are made. What we want to do is to understand formal politics through the lens provided by the expanded notion of politics we provide, that which includes what is sometimes called 'informal politics' (Painter, 1995). This focus offers a sense of the particularity and peculiarity of formal politics as a set of arenas of power relations, and as a set of arenas that operate in terms of some quite particular cultural practices and products. In the end we hope that this serves not to maintain it as a privileged arena of power but to show how it claims that privilege. Thus, this chapter looks at the way that the arena of formal politics is made through culture and, more generally, at the politics of culture.

Learning objectives

■ To learn about the role of culture in the formal politics of states, parties and bureaucracies as well as in the arena of informal politics.

- To understand the importance of symbols and representation in establishing political legitimacy.
- To learn about the ideas of performativity and transgression as cultural practices that can challenge formal political power.

6.1 | Cultural politics and political culture

6.1.1 | From politics to cultural politics

The success of cultural studies since the 1970s and the transformation of older disciplines such as geography, sociology and English literature in the same period have been based upon an understanding of politics that goes way beyond the confines of the conventional delimitation of it in terms of legislative bodies, states and diplomacy. Politics now is as much about textual politics or sexual politics as it is about elections and party activism. This change is based on a set of understandings of the world, many of which owe a lot to the work of **Michel Foucault** (p. 28) and other broadly **poststructuralist** (p. 24) authors, who think about it in terms of 'power' and 'power relations'. While an interest in power relations is also shared by some **Marxist** (p. 97) theorists, **Marx**'s (p. 97) understanding of power as class power, where one class rules another or as the power of capitalism to transform lives and landscapes, has been modified and rendered more complex by Marxist and poststructuralist political theorists confronted with the social transformations of the twentieth century. Now, for example, thinking in a broadly poststructuralist vein, authors like Glenn Jordan and Chris Weedon can say things like the following:

> In this book we make a scandalous claim: *everything* in social and cultural life is fundamentally to do with *power*. Power is at the centre of cultural politics. It is integral to culture. *All signifying practices – that is, all practices that have meaning – involve relations of power.*   (Jordan and Weedon, 1994: 11, emphasis in original)

Power (p. 94) has become a (if not *the*) key term in cultural studies and is used in the interpretation of the whole range of cultural practices and products. So, if we take 'politics' as the realm of power relations in general, then 'politics' has expanded its definition to cover all social and cultural relations, not just those of class. We now hear, among other things, of the politics of masculinity, queer politics, the politics of vision and the politics of identity (Sinfield, 1994; Nochlin, 1991b; Keith and Pile, 1993).

Understanding the controversial issue of **identity** (p. 224) politics and its importance at the end of the twentieth century means thinking about the context in which French poststructuralists and European Marxists have developed their theories. It means thinking about why this new definition of power might have made sense to people working to understand their social and cultural worlds both inside and outside academia. While this is clearly a complicated question, and not one to which we should expect to find a single answer, we would argue that it is bound up with a whole series of 'new social movements', most prominently the women's liberation movements,

Key influence **6.1**

bell hooks

bell hooks's work explores the cultural politics of race and gender. In a series of books she has written on racism, television, literature, feminism and postmodernism. Her work considers topics such as black subjectivity, whiteness, community and utopian longing.

hooks was born in Kentucky and teaches in New York. In 1981 she published *Ain't I a Woman: Black Women and Feminism*, a major contribution to feminist debates. She has published *Black Looks* (1992) and *Art on My Mind* (1995) on visual representation. She has also written on education in *Teaching to Transgress* (1994). Her work is an example of a move in the 1980s and 1990s towards the study of our subjective understandings of culture and politics. Readers of her books will notice that the copyright is in the name of Gloria Watkins, not bell hooks. Although she uses autobiographical experiences to insert her own subjectivity into essays on culture and politics, bell hooks is a pseudonym. Thus, in essays like 'The chitlin circuit: on black community' she writes about her own childhood in another persona. At the end of *Yearning: Race. Gender, and Cultural Politics* (1991), in a piece subtitled, 'no not talking back, just talking to myself', Gloria Watkins interviews bell hooks about her work. Watkins asks her why she chose to do the interview and she replies:

> for me these are two parts of a whole self that is composed of many parts. And as you know in many parts of my life I am such a serious person. To be contemplative in these times is to be seriously serious and I have to take a break now and then to balance things. So I indulge the playful in me. That me that in a very childlike way loves play, drama and spectacle. Of course there is a way that play is very serious for me. It is a form of ritual.

(hooks, 1991: 221)

Through her double persona, hooks is able to show the gap between how **identities** (p. 224) are defined, for example by categories like gender and race, and how they are performed. She demonstrates the difference between representing one's experience and analysing it as part of cultural studies. Her interest in the fragmented self has much in common with postmodern culture, but at the same time she is critical of **postmodernism** (p. 400) for absorbing many of the insights of African–American cultural politics, but still not recognising the importance of black culture. Her work demonstrates that concepts like postmodernism are contested. There is, in other words, a politics of postmodernism.

bell hooks's work is an example of the importance of critical writing on the cultural politics of race and gender to cultural studies.

Further reading

hooks, bell (1982) *Ain't I a Woman*, London: Pluto.
hooks, bell (1991) *Yearning: Race, Gender and Cultural Politics*, London: Turnaround.

anti-racist movements, lesbian and gay liberation movements, and peace and green movements. All of these, in various ways, began to bring into the realm of 'politics' issues that were not previously considered as political. One key example is the feminist slogan 'the personal is political' which sought to put a whole range of questions about personal identity, personal lives and personal conduct onto an explicitly political agenda. In turn, these new political movements have been responded to in various ways by new political ideologies – of the 'New Left' and the 'New Right' – which have also challenged conventional definitions of politics, though in quite different ways. We would also want to argue that the context for these changes in the definitions of politics is a massive shift in geopolitical organisation which involves both the **globalisation** (p. 159) of the world's economy and transitions from 'industrial' to 'postindustrial', from 'socialist' to 'postsocialist', from 'colonial' to 'postcolonial'. These changes have entailed the transformation of lives, formal politics and broader power relations for most of the world's population.

Defining concept 6.1

Identity

Identity is about how we define who we are. Literally, both identity and the self mean 'the same as'. In cultural theory identity is used to describe the consciousness of self found in the modern individual. The modern self is understood to be autonomous and self-critical. The German philosopher G.W.F. Hegel saw individualism, the right to criticism and autonomy of action as the three main characteristics of modern subjectivity. This self-reflexive aspect of identity means that, in the modern age, identity is understood to be a project. It is not fixed. The autobiographical thinking that characterises modern identity creates a coherent sense of a past identity, but that identity has to be sustained in the present and remade in the future. The constant remaking of identity reveals that the sense of self is to some extent an illusion, because the making of the self requires a constant interaction with the not-self or non-identity: the external world.

In modern Western societies, certain identities have been privileged over others. Men have been privileged over women. White Europeans have been privileged over non-whites. Certain modes of sexual behaviour have defined normal against deviant sexual identities. 'Identity politics' is the term used to describe the emergence into the political arena of identities other than those of white, European, heterosexual men. The assertion of alternative identities has followed a number of different strategies which Jonathan Dollimore (1991) divides into four types of 'reverse discourses': (1) the assertion of a positive identity as normal and natural as the dominant 'norm'; (2) the assertion of a negative identity, which is abnormal, but can be explained and assimilated by recourse to legitimating (for example, medical or scientific) discourses; (3) the assertion of a different identity as more natural and normal than the dominant norm; (4) the strategy of transgression, where the very categories that define what is normal and abnormal are

→

subverted. The first of these four can be described as essentialist strategies. They assert oppositional identity as essentially unchangeable. An example would be the cultural movement known as 'negritude' which emerged at the end of the French Empire. One of its leading proponents, Leopold Senghor (1993: 30) argued that African culture is 'more sensitive to the external world, to the material aspect of beings and things'. However, the result of such strategies is often anti-essentialist. An assertive African culture will in fact change the nature of both African and European identities. The fourth reverse discourse is explicitly anti-essentialist. **Identity** (p. 224) is understood to be performative, not based on any essential characteristics, but rather is a performance based on cultural expectations. Dollimore's example of an anti-essentialist identity is Oscar Wilde, who famously argued for the primacy of culture in his statement that 'life imitates art'.

One of the most interesting developments in identity politics emerging from this insight has been queer politics. This has developed from lesbian and gay politics; but queer politics resists the division of sexuality into a binary opposition of essentialist homosexual or heterosexual identities. Instead, Judith Butler (1993) argues that identities are the products of the **discourses** (p. 30) that define sexuality. We perform masculinity or femininity, homosexuality or heterosexuality according to a script already written as the cultural conventions of our society. In this view, identities are cultural constructions rather than pre-set.

The concept of identity politics has been subject to criticism from a number of different perspectives. Some Marxists have argued that a focus on identity gives a fragmented perspective and detracts from the need for a universal message of emancipation (Hobsbawm, 1996). Critics of queer politics have argued that the idea that we can perform identity downplays the powerful social forces that make us who we are and over which we have little control. While the performative element in sexuality makes it particularly appropriate to this approach, it is less apt for identities constructed by class, 'race' or disability.

Further reading

Hall, S. and du Gay, P. (eds) (1996) *Questions of Cultural Identity*, London: Sage.
Dollimore, J. (1991) *Sexual Dissidence: Augustine to Wilde, Freud to Foucault*, Oxford: Oxford University Press.

It is important to stress therefore that, alongside a broadening of many political agendas (academic and non-academic) towards what we might call 'cultural politics', there has also been a series of transformations in formal politics. In part these are a matter of what is happening 'on the ground'. It is also a matter of how these changes are being interpreted by researchers. In considering changes 'on the ground' we need to take seriously a whole series of fundamental political reorganisations at a connected series of scales. For the historian Eric Hobsbawm, for example, 'The history of the twenty years after 1973 is that of a world which has lost its bearings and slid into instability and crisis' (Hobsbawm, 1994: 403). One key arena of formal politics that has been thrown into confusion is the nation-state:

> As the transnational economy established its grip on the world, it undermined a major, and since 1945, virtually universal, institution: the territorial nation-state, since such a state could no longer control more than a diminishing part of its affairs. Organizations whose field of action was effectively bounded by the frontiers of their territory, like trade unions, parliaments and national public broadcasting systems, therefore lost, as organizations not so bounded, like transnational firms, the international currency market and the globalized media and communications of the satellite era, gained.
>
> (Hobsbawm, 1994: 424)

Other commentators have also noted these changes, arguing that 'Politically . . . things are falling apart' (Ó Tuathail and Luke, 1994: 384). They point to: the collapse of the Soviet Union; the unpredictable outcomes of German reunification; the difficulties experienced by the new European Union; the end of nation-states like Czechoslovakia and the creation of new ones like Macedonia; the end of the Warsaw Pact, but the expansion of its adversary, NATO; the corruption brought to light in the governments of established industrialised democracies like Japan, Italy and France; the contradiction between the United States' attempts to maintain security across the globe and the anarchy in its inner cities (Ó Tuathail and Luke, 1994: 381–4).

The changing nature and declining power of the nation-state has inaugurated a period in which attention has shifted both to the global and to the local scale. Global concerns such as environmental issues are now commonly politicised alongside, and often in relation to, more local concerns (like motorway building). New political alliances have developed as arguments over sovereignty in the new Europe are worked out. New political forces have emerged as local grievances over resources boil over into racial tension. New state forms are being made as health and welfare services are privatised and we learn to live with the chaotic fragmentation of 'community care'. A new politics of identity has been crucial to these developments. In the late twentieth century, as Hobsbawm points out, the discourse of nationalism has moved from the state to 'identity groups':

> human ensembles to which a person could 'belong', unequivocally and beyond uncertainty. . . . Most of these for obvious reasons, appealed to a common 'ethnicity', although other groups of people seeking collective separatism used the same national-ist language (as when homosexual activists spoke of 'the queer nation').
>
> (Hobsbawm, 1994: 428)

These related processes of political fragmentation and universalisation that form the combination of the local and the global have been increasingly conducted through the expanding realm of the international media. Politics is now as much a matter of opinion polls, sound bites and spin doctors as party organisation, activists and militants. The amount of information that people have is massively increased and previously separated places are brought crashing together by new communications technologies (see section 6.3.2).

In response to these issues, people who study 'politics' are having to change too. In the most general sense there is a broadening of political analysis which is evident in the development and use of terms such as 'governance' which seek to expand what might be included in the remit of formal politics to include all forms of regulation, control and guidance. A more specific example would be what is happening in the debates over developing a 'new critical geopolitics'. Its practitioners and promoters have tried to shake off the old association of geopolitics with analyses of comparative state power which sought to help states win trade wars and real wars with each other. Instead they seek a 'cultural turn' towards a very broad notion of geopolitical power and, along with it, a critical stance. This has involved taking just that expanded notion of power developed within cultural studies – as textual, as gendered, as visual – and applying it to an arena of traditional political debate:

> Critical geopolitics opens up spaces for long-overdue dialogues between geography or international relations and social theory, feminism, psychoanalysis, deconstruction and social movement theory. Among the themes emerging from this conversation are the importance of constructing theoretically informed critiques of the spatializing practices of power; undertaking critical investigations of the power of orthodox geopolitical writing; investigating how geographical reasoning in foreign policy in-sights (enframes in a geography of images), in-cites (enmeshes in a geography of texts), and, therefore, in-sites (stabilizes, positions, locates) places in global politics, and examining how this reasoning can be challenged, subverted, and resisted.
>
> (Ó Tuathail and Dalby, 1994: 513)

Thus, in the new critical geopolitics, questions of formal and informal politics are being brought together in fruitful ways which enable, among other things, an understanding of the complex cultural, political and economic phenomena of globalisation. In these analyses questions of writing, visual representation and identity are as much a part of the analysis of global political arrangements as warfare, international relations and uneven economic development, and, more importantly, they alter the ways in which we understand these issues. In many ways it is this agenda that we want to address here. Our concern with culture and politics (or cultural politics) is, therefore, not just the understanding of culture as political. Those themes are addressed elsewhere in the book as they are the very stuff of cultural studies (for an analysis of art and literature that presents them as part of the political contestations between powerful and less powerful groups, see Jordan and Weedon, 1994). We mainly want to address how formal politics – the world of political parties, parliaments, bureaucracies, state formation, protest movements and the rest (although we leave you to find your way through the new geopolitics literature on your own; see Ó Tuathail, 1996) – are cultural: how they are arenas of contested meaning rather than places of privileged sanctity and power. To do all this we first need to introduce some of the concepts that are most useful in the discussion of cultural politics.

6.1.2 | Legitimation, representation and performance

The rest of this chapter will look at examples of cultural politics that are concerned with legitimation, **representation** (p. 61) and performance. By legitimation we mean the way in which individuals and groups present themselves as the authentic and lawful holders of power. All but the most brutal forms of government rule through a mixture of coercion (rule by force and violence) and consent (rule by voluntary agreement – see **hegemony**, p. 106). In order to rule with some measure of consent, the government of a constitutional state must establish its legitimacy in the eyes of the ruled. Culture is a key factor in securing the legitimacy of governments. Historically, the original legitimating claim to the right to rule in many societies is the claim to divine right. According to this claim, the ruler is appointed by divine power (God or the gods) to represent the interests of the people. Religion furnishes the authority by which rulers secure the consent of the ruled. Government is legitimated by using the religious culture of the society. Later in this chapter we shall see how culture is used to legitimate various forms of rule through literature, dress and architecture.

Representation (p. 61) can mean two different things in relation to politics and culture respectively. Political representation refers to the way in which rulers claim to represent the people over whom they rule. Political representation may be democratic, where political representatives seek a mandate from their electorate to represent them in an assembly (like the British Parliament or the American Congress), or undemocratic. However, representation has a different but connected meaning in the context of culture, where it means 'a symbol or image, or the process of presenting to the eye or mind' (Williams, 1988: 269). These two meanings come together in the context of cultural politics. A political representative (whether democratic or authoritarian) must represent themselves and their principles, convictions and opinions as the image of those whom they claim to represent. Thus, to continue the example of divine right given above, this kind of government involved the appropriation of religious imagery in order to represent the ruler as symbolising divine authority. The Queen of England, for example, is also head of the Church of England and has the title *Fidei Defensor* (Defender of the Faith). 'F.D.' is imprinted on all British coins. The government of a state which claims to rule by divine right is represented through symbolism and imagery as the proper and lawful servants of divine power.

Often politics is conducted through and against symbolism and imagery, rather than through rational debate or physical conflict. This is as true for those who resist as for those who uphold power. In a state where rule was legitimated by divine power, intervention by or against the rulers normally also took its authority from religion. In this kind of a conflict, each side needed to legitimate itself as the proper, lawful defender of religion and the conflict was often cultural as well as openly violent. During the Civil War in England (1642–7) both sides claimed to represent the same religion. Radical Protestants accused Catholics of idolatry – the worship of false idols. Members of the Parliamentary forces destroyed figures and paintings in churches because they had associations with the Roman Catholic Church. Another example is the native Amerindians who were forcibly converted to Christianity by the Spanish conquerors of South America. However, when they were permitted to decorate the insides of churches they combined Christian and native imagery in their paintings, in a way that transformed both their own culture and the nature of Roman Catholicism in Latin America. Many religious festivals in the continent which claim Christian legitimacy can be traced back to earlier pre-Conquest religious rites (Martin, 1989). Political interventions are thus made through culture and by culture.

We would argue that, in all these cases, claims to legitimacy and battles over representation are a matter of performance. Politics is always a performance because however much each side claims to represent the truth, in the debate each participant must perform a role through which they enact their position. The concept of performance or performativity is a useful one in the study of cultural politics, because it emphasises the ways in which particular political positions, whether positions of power or resistance, have to be continually made and remade. The idea that politics must be performed inevitably questions any claim to permanent legitimacy. Legitimacy has to be made through a performance that accrues to itself the trappings of power. That performance will often disguise the fact that the positions held are as much the products of debate and conflict as those that oppose them. Broadly speaking, legitimacy is secured by disguising the performative element of politics. Oppositional political movements may seek to establish an alternative form of legitimacy; but, even if this is the ultimate goal, they must first reveal the extent to which power is a performance. Not surprisingly, one of the best theorists of politics as performativity (although he did not use the word himself) was a dramatist, Bertolt Brecht (1898–1956). In his plays he used what he called a distancing or alienation effect. By means of the staging, lighting and the behaviour of the actors, he never let the audience forget that they were in a theatre. By this means he hoped to promote a critical attitude, which would in turn instil a sense of political power. The alienation effect created the conditions in which the legitimacy of the social order could be questioned: 'The new alienations are only designed to free socially-conditioned phenomena from that stamp of familiarity which protects them against our grasp today' (Willet, 1978: 192).

In the rest of the chapter we discuss both conventional and unconventional forms of political activity as performances. First, however, we examine some of the political theories that form a background to this approach. We begin with the work of Niccolo Machiavelli (1469–1527), who was one of the first people to question the idea that political legitimacy is performed and not granted by divine sanction. He suggested that politics can be detached from religion and should be thought of as an 'autonomous science' (Gramsci, 1971: 136). In *The Prince* (1513) he argued that religion might be used by a ruler for political ends. He suggested that it could be a way of gaining legitimacy and of making rulers 'representative'. Machiavelli's ideas were both useful and threatening to forms of government that legitimated themselves through religion. The idea that religion could be used politically undermines its claims to absolute authority and opens up a much wider space for a politics of culture. It is through Machiavelli that politics starts to get a bad name as trickery or hypocrisy.

This broadening of politics was taken further by **Antonio Gramsci** (p. 38) – an important figure in the development of cultural studies. He was a great admirer of Machiavelli's interventionist stance but argued for an understanding of politics that would take into account the whole culture and philosophy of a period (Gramsci, 1971: 140). This meant moving away from just thinking about the rulers and the ruled (which Gramsci described as a 'war of manoeuvre' characterised by an attempt to defend the state or overthrow it). Instead he understood politics as a 'war of position', a much more general conflict in which politics is fought out in all the institutions of civil society – religion, the media, entertainment. He argued that culture can act to fortify the state, and later on we will look at some of the cultural formations that perform this function: the culture of the British Parliament, of bureaucracy and of imperial and military monuments. Those influenced by Gramsci have also stressed how political opposition, or resistance, is also a matter of cultural politics. For example, **E.P. Thompson** (p. 96) has stressed the role of culture in making classes. As he says, 'class-consciousness is the way in which … experiences are handled in cultural terms: embodied in traditions, value-systems, ideas and institutional forms' (Thompson, 1980: 9). He has shown how what were often crude and brutal customs, like the sale of wives and the tradition of 'rough music' (the use of loud raucous music to punish those who were felt to have transgressed the rules of a community), can be understood as examples of ways in which ordinary people could take back through the performance of rituals some of the power denied to them by society. Thus, the wife sale could be a form of divorce, as well as an act of misogynist male power, while rough music could be 'a property of a society in which justice is not wholly delegated or bureau-criticised, but is enacted by and within the community' (Thompson, 1991: 530).

By picking up on these issues of power, identity and performance we might broaden the analysis still further. **Michel Foucault** (p. 280) helps us argue that politics is a matter of **power** (p. 94) relations and that 'power is everywhere … because it comes from everywhere' (Foucault, 1984b: 93). Such insights, taken up by gender politics, lesbian and gay politics, queer politics and the politics of cultural, ethnic or religious identity, have produced creative forms of political protest (some of these tactics will be described later in the chapter) which play upon the idea of performance to throw both the legitimacy of governments and the legitimacy of identity into doubt. For example, queer politics has developed from within the lesbian and gay movement. It refuses **essentialist** (p. 138) hetero- or same-sex identities, which exclude, for example, bisexual men and women. The movement Queer Nation had no patience with exclusions of this kind. Embracing many communities of sexual dissidents, it promoted a discursive strategy to create an innovative paradigm for thinking about sexuality (Bristow, 1997: 217). The 'queer theorist' **Judith Butler** (p. 231) has argued that questions of identity are governed by legitimating and 'juridical' discourses. Here juridical means not just relating to the law, but to processes of 'limitation, prohibition, regulation, control and even "protection" of individuals' (Butler, 1990: 2). Her critique argues that there is no such thing as a legitimate gender identity, that what we understand to be masculinity and femininity are, in fact, performances conditioned by society: 'there is no gender identity behind the expressions of gender; that identity is performatively constituted by the very "expressions" that are said to be its results' (Butler, 1990: 25). Just as Brecht prompted his audience to think about the possibility of changing their society through his performances, so queer politics, by performing transgressive sexual identities (which can range from drag queens to two lesbian mothers bringing up their children together), can challenge the naturalness of heterosexuality. So, performance is the thing – it makes new transgressive political

Key influence **6.2**

Judith Butler

In the 1990s Judith Butler has become one of the most influential writers in feminism and lesbian and gay studies. Her work combines cultural criticism, philosophy and political ideas. She is one of the leading proponents of queer theory.

Judith Butler is Professor of Rhetoric and Comparative Literature at the University of California at Berkeley. Her book *Gender Trouble: Feminism and the Subversion of Identity* (1990) proposed a radical critique of many of the assumptions of second-wave **feminism** (p. 120). Butler challenged the distinction between sex and gender that formed the basis for many earlier analyses of women's subordination. She argued that the idea of sex is culturally constructed. There are no pre-existing biological characteristics which we do not already come to with a set of cultural expectations: 'sex will be shown to have been gender all along' (1990: 8). Instead, Butler develops what she calls a performative theory of identity. Against the normative stigmatisation of gay and lesbian identities as unnatural, she argues that heterosexuality is as much a performance of cultural conventions as homosexuality. In her influential essay 'Imitation and gender insubordination' (1992) she uses the example of the male drag artist. His (or her) performance is enabled by the conventional nature of heterosexual femininity, which is itself a performance of certain expectations of what is natural. The theory of performativity argues that there is no original sexual identity, only a constantly repeated imitation of an idea of an original. Butler develops these ideas further and responds to some of her critics in *Bodies that Matter: On the Discursive Limits of 'Sex'* (1993). Her most recent book, *Excitable Speech: A Politics of the Performative*, she tackles the question of censorship and 'hate-speech'. Her recent work has led her to apply some of her ideas to political questions like the status of gays in the American military and racism.

Butler's work is an example of the growing importance of feminist and lesbian and gay perspectives in cultural studies over the last two decades.

Further reading

Abelove, H., Barale, M.A. and Halperin, D.M. (eds) (1993) *The Lesbian and Gay Studies Reader*, London: Routledge (contains Judith Butler, 'Imitation and gender insubordination', as well as many other useful essays).

Diamond, E. (ed.) (1996) *Performance and Cultural Politics*, London: Routledge.

identities and in doing so it unmakes and unmasks identities that were pretending not to be performances.

The concept of transgression is an important one here. It involves an overturning of the 'proper' order of things. This is described by **Mikhail Bakhtin** (p. 202) as the 'carnivalesque', referring to the brief period of anarchy that occurs during carnivals: 'a world of excess where all is mixed, hybrid, ritually degraded and defiled' (Stallybrass and White, 1986: 8). It turns the world upside down. At carnival, kings become fools and fools become kings. What lies behind carnival is not just disorder, but a conception of an alternative order. The French feminist Julia Kristeva writes that **transgression** (p. 258) of 'linguistic, logical and social codes within the carnivalesque only exists and succeeds ... because it accepts *another law*' (Kristeva, 1986: 41). In this sense, transgressive performances oppose or challenge the legitimacy and representativeness of the

Key influence 6.3

Julia Kristeva (1941–)

Julia Kristeva is a Bulgarian critic and philosopher who has lived in France since 1966. Her work explores the relationship between language, literature and psychoanalysis.

In England and the United States, Kristeva is usually identified with French feminism, which includes theorists such as Hélène Cixous, Luce Irigaray and Monique Wittig. Educated in Marxist and formalist theory in Bulgaria, Kristeva was instrumental in introducing the work of **Mikhail Bakhtin** (p. 202) to the West. Her writings on transgression (see the collection *Desire in Language*, 1980) are strongly influenced by his work. In Paris she worked closely with the French **structuralist** (p. 24) critic **Roland Barthes** (p. 52). Like Barthes, she became critical of structuralism. In 1970 she joined the editorial board of the influential **post-structuralist** (p. 24) journal *Tel Quel*. With other French intellectuals of the time, she was much effected by the uprising of May 1968, the fall-out from which led to a disillusionment with orthodox Marxism and a search for new forms of political organisation. In 1974 she published *Revolution in Poetic Language* (1984), a book that combined linguistic and psychoanalytic theory with an analysis of literary texts. In it Kristeva argues for a micropolitics of identity, to be effected through a psychoanalytic understanding of the subject rather than conventional political struggle. In the same year she also published *About Chinese Women* (1977), a book that reflects the influence of Maoism on the Left in the 1970s and the search for an alternative model to the Soviet Union. Her exploration of the constructions of femininity continued in her study of the Virgin Mary, 'Stabat mater' (1986) and in her influential essay 'Women's time' (1981). Her research into the construction of subjectivity has continued in books like *Powers of Horror: An Essay on Abjection* (1982). She has also written about the representation of time in the works of Marcel Proust.

Kristeva's work has had most impact in feminist and literary theory, but her work on transgression has also been influential in cultural politics. In particular, her interest in psychoanalysis has been important in relation to identity politics. Her work in the area of linguistics and on the construction of the subject has important implications for cultural history.

Further reading

The best introduction to Kristeva's work up until 1982 is Toril Moi (ed.) (1986) *The Kristeva Reader*, Oxford: Blackwell.
Kristeva, J. (1982) *Powers of Horror: An Essay on Abjection*, New York: Columbia UP.

ruling law, suggesting that another set of values is possible. We will look further at the concept of transgression (and some of its limits) in sections 6.2.2 and 6.3.1.

We have now identified some of the ways in which both the culture of politics and the politics of culture might be analysed. The next section will take up some of these themes to look at some of the ways in which political structures can be understood as cultural through notions of representation, performance and identity. The examples include: the use of cultural representations to make political interventions (discussing Benjamin Disraeli's novel, *Sybil*); the performance of Parliamentary identities in late twentieth-century Britain; the cultural politics of bureaucratic performances, identities and ethics; and monuments as political statements that transform space and meaning. The final section of this chapter will look in more detail at cultures of resistance and the limits of the concept of transgression.

6.2 | Cultures of political power

6.2.1 | The cultural politics of democracy in nineteenth-century Britain

Any period of political change will inevitably also be a time of cultural change. Cultural studies is interested in such periods and an interest in cultural politics means an interest in the ways that cultural change is characterised by conflict and struggle. The politics of nineteenth-century Britain were characterised by the demand for suffrage by the majority of the population who did not have the vote. Two major Acts of Parliament extended the vote. The Reform Bill of 1832 increased the electorate from 220,000 to 670,000 men in a population of 14 million. The Reform Bill of 1867 extended the franchise to all male householders in the boroughs, leaving voteless lodgers and workers outside the Parliamentary boroughs. Women were denied the vote until 1920.

The struggle for democratisation produced major shifts in cultural politics. The debate was characterised by two contrasting forms of legitimacy: on the one hand, the old symbols of authority – the monarchy, the Church and the aristocracy; on the other, the democratic principle that only the votes of the people can legitimate a government. According to the critic Catherine Gallagher, the struggle over legitimacy was not just about the 'politics of representation': who represented whom. It also included a cultural conflict about 'the representation of politics' (Gallagher, 1985: 188). One of the arenas of conflict was the novel – in particular, the 'industrial' or 'condition of England' novels of Charles Dickens, Elizabeth Gaskell, Benjamin Disraeli and George Eliot.

One of these novelists, Benjamin Disraeli, was himself a member of Parliament who later, as prime minister (and in response to extreme pressure from extra-Parliamentary agitation), introduced the second Reform Bill in 1867. One of the reasons that Disraeli chose to write political novels when, as a politician, he had access to far more conventional outlets for his opinions, demonstrates an understanding of politics in modern societies that comes closer to Gramsci's war of position than to simplistic notions of rulers and ruled. Disraeli's novels can be seen as a form of complex intervention, designed not just to make a particular political point, but to negotiate the process of cultural change in such a way that elements of his beliefs and principles (which were fundamentally anti-democratic) could be maintained.

As many critics have pointed out, much of the pleasure of Disraeli's novel *Sybil*, what **Raymond Williams** (p. 5) calls his 'likeable panache' (Williams, 1963: 108) is in the way in which Disraeli appears to undermine his own case, exposing the illegitimacy of the aristocrats he advocates as political representatives (see Box 6.1). English lords are revealed to be from families that have bought their right to titles and in numerous passages are shown to be no more discriminating of cultural value than the working-class Disraeli thinks they should represent. The attitude of both classes to drinking is shown to be remarkably similar. First, in high society: '"I rather like bad wine,'' said Mrs Mountchesney; "one gets so bored with good wine''' (Disraeli, 1845: 3); and later during a riot, when the ironically titled 'Bishop' and his followers break in the cellars of Mowbray Castle:

Box *6.1*

Sybil, or The Two Nations by Benjamin Disraeli

Sybil is the second book of a trilogy of three novels: *Coningsby*, *Sybil* and *Trancred*. Charles Egremont, an aristocrat and Member of Parliament, meets and falls in love with Sybil Gerard in the ruins of Marney Abbey. Sybil is the daughter of the Chartist leader Walter Gerard and through her Egremont discovers the difference between England's two nations, the rich and the poor. It is revealed that the estate belonging to Egremont's elder brother, Lord Marney, was taken from Sybil's family during the reign of Henry VIII. Thus, the novel represents the current demands for political reform in terms of the cause of a disenfranchised aristocracy. It describes Chartist political agitation and Egremont's attempts to secure reform through Parliament. The political activities of the Chartists end in riots which leave Sybil's father, Lord Marney, and Egremont's rival for Sybil's hand, Stephen Morley, dead. The way is then open for Sybil, the rightful heir to the Marney estate, to marry its new owner, Egremont, and in that marriage to make one nation out of two. The term 'one-nation Tories' is still used to describe the left wing of the British Conservative Party.

According to Raymond Williams, other 'Condition of England' (or 'Industrial') novels are:

- *Mary Barton* (1848) and *North and South* (1855) by Elizabeth Gaskell
- *Hard Times* (1854) by Charles Dickens
- *Alton Locke* (1850) by Charles Kingsley
- *Felix Holt* (1866) by George Eliot

> [T]he Bishop himself, seated on the ground and leaning against an arch, the long perspective of the cellars full of rapacious figures brandishing bottles and torches, alternately quaffed some old Port and some Madeira of many voyages, and was making up his mind to their relative merits.
> (Disraeli, 1845: 411)

By criticising both sides equally, Disraeli successfully represents a society in which all cultural values have become illegitimate. Under these circumstances, his solution is not a democratic one, but a symbolic one in which he unites both upper and working classes in the figure of the novel's heroine, Sybil. Sybil is at once a working-class activist and, it turns out, from a family descended from the original Anglo-Saxon aristocracy. In addition, as a Roman Catholic she represents the older form of Christianity in England and as a woman can be taken to stand for the monarchy in the shape of the young Queen Victoria. Having represented Victorian England as without values, the character of Sybil brings together those marginalised by that society (the industrialised working class, Roman Catholics and, when represented as a 'Hebrew Maiden' by her association with the Virgin Mary, Jews (Gallagher, 1985: 213)) with a legitimate ruling class, Church and state. She thus performs the symbolic work of uniting a fragmented political culture which has lost its legitimacy. Catherine Gallagher argues that this results in the 'exclusion of politics from the novel, even in the work of a writer who was above all a political man and who believed that politics, like literature, provided the best hope for reconciling facts and values' (Gallagher, 1985: 217–18). However, this can only be accounted an exclusion of politics if politics only involves the narrow definition of the politics of political institutions. In terms of the wider definition of cultural politics, *Sybil* counts as an important intervention because, in the context of a conflict over political rights, the novel intervened in the way that politics was represented, creating new symbols of political legitimacy out of that conflict. In the nineteenth century 'the politics of culture' were:

> one very significant component within a larger ideological battle between the gentry, with its allies in the intelligentsia, and the industrial middle-class, a battle that was handily won by the gentry. Their ideological victory, it seems, contributed to the decline of the England as an industrial power.
> (Gallagher, 1985: 267)

In fact, it is very difficult to judge the success or failure of an intervention in cultural politics, because the relationships between a particular debate and such material factors as economic growth or decline are very difficult to measure. What can be said is that the conflicts and disputes that characterise cultural politics are a crucial part of cultural studies, while their outcomes become debates in competing accounts of cultural history (see Chapter 5). What can also be said is that such cultural interventions are a matter of the representation and performance of political identities.

6.2.2 | Performing identities in conventional politics

Conventional politics, that is the politics of governments and political parties, appears at first to be least open to a discussion of cultural politics. Closer examination, however, reveals that conventional politics are constructed by and through culture. For example, one important way that conventional politics establishes its cultural legitimacy is through the impression of continuity. The rituals and traditions of the British Parliament give an impression of stability and longevity that contributes to the sense that it is a legitimate institution. The often-made claim that this Parliament is the 'mother of all Parliaments' is an example of how legitimacy is established through the representation of the British Parliament as the origin of Parliamentary democracy. Such commonly known facts about the debating chamber as that the distance between the two sides is the length of two swords – so that no one may be harmed for speaking their opinions – signify a tradition of free debate that stretches back into distant history.

Our analysis of the cultural politics of the British Parliament, however, is interested in how the representation of tradition is sustained and performed – in other words, how tradition has to be made and remade. One example that demonstrates the cultural politics of what we have been calling formal politics would be the way that politicians dress. Politicians' dress codes can be seen as evidence that the role of Parliamentary politician is not something to which individuals are born, but something they have to *perform*. The advantages of the theory of performativity here are that it allows an understanding of conventional and non-conventional political activity that relates the question of **identity** (p. 224) to political practice. In the case of conventional identities it allows what appears to be normal and natural to be seen as culturally constructed.

Male members of the Conservative Party, for example, commonly wear pin-stripe suits when they are in London, but are often filmed wearing tweed jackets when they give interviews in their constituencies at the weekends. These two 'uniforms' allow the politician to perform a particular role which signifies something about the kind of politics they represent. The pin-striped suit is commonly worn by men who work in the City of London and might be seen to signify a knowledge and control of financial matters. The tweed jacket, on the other hand, has associations of a more leisured, rural, upper-class life. The two dress codes indicate the different aspects of the MP's life. During the week he is an efficient worker in London; at the weekend he leads a more leisured existence in his rural constituency (though not one that precludes television interviews if the matter is important enough – see Figure 6.1). At the same time the codes bring together two perhaps contradictory elements of Conservative political philosophy: a belief in finance capitalism and in the traditions of rural England.

It is easy for such codes to become naturalised as the normal dress for politicians, so that they go unquestioned. The fact that the performance of being a politician is enacted through dress codes only becomes apparent when they are transgressed in a public way. One example of transgression in the sphere of conventional Parliamentary politics occurred in November 1981 when the leader of the Labour Party, Michael Foot, attended the ceremony at the Cenotaph in London to commemorate those who died in the two world wars (see Figure 6.2). The formal dress expected on such an occasion was described by the *Daily Express* as that worn by the Prime Minister, Margaret Thatcher, the leader of the Liberal Party, David Steel, and Princess Diana:

> Mrs Thatcher wore a smart tailored black topcoat with matching hat, handbag and shoes. David Steel was in black morning suit. The Princess of Wales wore a smart black coat with a white lace collar and a black hat with a plume feather.
>
> (*Daily Express*, 9 November 1981)

Figure 6.1 ▦ The cultural politics of tweed. (Source: PA News Ltd.)

By contrast, Michael Foot is claimed by the *Express* to have 'angered millions of television viewers yesterday. He turned up for the solemn Cenotaph Remembrance Day ceremony in a donkey jacket, plaid tie and dirty shoes'. The multiple nature of Mr Foot's transgression is indicated by the readers who, the *Daily Express* claims, phoned in to complain:

> Reader Mrs Margaret Tully of Bettesford, Nottinghamshire said: 'Foot looked like he had come out of Steptoe's yard'.
>
> RAF veteran Robert Brookes of Brockham, Surrey said: 'Foot came as though he had just been dragged through a hedge. His dress, manner and behaviour was a direct insult to our war dead'.
>
> Mrs Linda Caine, of Toton, Notts, said: 'I expected him to be carrying a Right to Work placard. I blame his wife. No self-respecting wife would let her husband go out like that. I just can't get over it. Even his shoes were mucky'.

The objections chosen for the article indicate certain expectations of the leader of Her Majesty's Opposition. Mrs Tully's reference to 'Steptoe's yard' alludes to a popular television situation comedy about a scrap dealer and his son. Her contribution suggests that, at least during formal, ritualised public appearances, Foot should dress according to the dress codes of the upper, not the working class. Robert Brookes' complaint refers to the fact that Foot did not appear to bow when he placed his wreath or join in the hymns. This articulates an expectation that he will pay tribute to the religious elements and patriotic elements of Remembrance Sunday. Mrs Caine asks that his appearance should reflect a family background where the traditional gender roles of husband and wife are sustained. If Mr Foot and his wife did occupy these roles, it is suggested by Mrs Caine, the transgression would never have occurred.

The *Daily Express* is not usually sympathetic to the Labour Party, and its criticisms are in turn criticised as 'petty' by left-leaning papers like the *Daily Mirror* and the *Guardian*. However, even the more sympathetic papers emphasise the importance of appearance for a politician. There is a recognition on all sides that performativity is an important part of the way in which politics is conducted. On 10 November, the *Daily Express* asked the consultant who 'groomed Ronald Reagan' (then President of the United States and a former Hollywood film star) how he would advise Mr Foot and produced a mocked-up photograph of the result. Nor should Foot be seen to be an innocent player in the politics of performance. He is criticised in the *Times* for looking as if he had just returned from walking his dog on Hampstead Heath; but Hampstead, where Foot lives, is a part of London with a reputation for bohemianism and middle-class radicalism. His dress and actions, while described by the *Daily Telegraph* as having 'all the reverent dignity of a tramp bending down to inspect a cigarette end', could be seen as signifying Julia Kristeva's definition of the carnivalesque as the acceptance of 'another law' (see section 6.1.2 above), which creates the dialogue or debate of cultural politics. Here, the other law is the radical political tradition in which Foot usually wishes to place himself, signified by a more informal mode of dress that recalls protest demonstrations (Foot was renowned for his involvement in the Campaign for Nuclear Disarmament). This comes into conflict with the rituals of Remembrance Sunday, which often recalls national pride in military victories as well as commemoration of the dead.

One aspect of Foot's transgression that is interesting for the student of culture is the way in which it does not matter exactly what Mr Foot was wearing. The versions of his dress change from paper to paper. The 'donkey jacket' becomes a 'green donkey jacket' in the *Daily Telegraph*, a 'duffel coat' in the *Mirror*, and in the *Times* the shoes become 'sneakers', while the 'plaid' (*Express*) or 'check' (*Mirror*) tie becomes 'Paisley'. What is important are not the details themselves, but that his dress places him outside the codes that stabilise the significance of his position as representative of authority (the dress codes of class), loyalty (religion and patriotism) and masculinity (the gendered roles of husband and wife). We can see from these examples that conventional political identities are performed within sharply defined cultural boundaries and that these boundaries are shaped by the broader contexts of political debate. Cultural expectations are a key determinant of political identities and thus culture itself is an enormously powerful factor in limiting the terrain on which traditional politics is conducted.

These limitations become more obvious when social groups enter Parliament that, for reasons of culture and background, cannot lay claim to the traditions of formal politics. When the first four black MPs entered Parliament in 1987, newspaper coverage paid great attention to putative differences between the culture of Parliamentary

Figure 6.2 ■ Michael Foot at the
Cenotaph. (Source: PA News Ltd.)

tradition and that of the new representatives. Many papers commented on the fact that
the first black woman MP, Diane Abbot (see Figure 6.3), sat in the seat formerly
occupied by Enoch Powell, who had made inflammatory speeches advocating the
repatriation of non-whites:

> Where he sat, cadaverous and grimly mocking, sits now dusky Diane Abbot (Lab.
> Hackney N.). As if to emphasise that times have changed, she took out a make up case
> and sensuously painted her lips. For the rest she and her coloured colleagues listened
> decorously, no doubt amazed by the ceremonious mysteries and ancestral mumbo-
> jumbo of what they have invaded and challenged.   (*Daily Mail*, 26 June 1987)

The satirical tone that is commonly used in Parliamentary sketches here employs the
language of 'racial' stereotypes ('mysteries', 'mumbo-jumbo') to describe the traditions
of Parliament. This upset or inversion, however, maintains the idea of cultural conflict
in the words 'invaded and challenged', which reproduce some of the discourse of
Enoch Powell's anti-immigration speeches. The limits of the concept of performativity
to understand political identities are also glimpsed here. While the concept works well
to deconstruct codes that legitimate power, in the case of social groups that have
historically been labelled as illegitimate it is not enough to argue that they can perform
an oppositional identity. For those who have to compete with the way they are identified

by restrictive definitions of 'race' and 'gender', the room to 'perform' can be severely circumscribed.

It is in this context that it is interesting that three newspapers chose to emphasise Abbot's make-up, which was mentioned by the *Guardian* and the *Express* as well as the *Mail* in their reporting of the Queen's Speech. The limited room allowed Abbot is shown by the way that three journalists concentrate on not just her appearance but the way in which she herself makes up that appearance. In the context of her symbolic position as the first black woman MP, the way that she constructs her self, her identity – in other words, the mechanics of Abbot's performance in terms of her gender and 'race' – becomes the focus of discussion. The racist overtones of this focus are most clear in the quotation from the *Mail* above, but the implication underlies all the reports that, because she is black and a woman, she will not be able to perform the role of MP as naturally as a white woman or man. The examples of Michael Foot and Diane Abbot demonstrate how transgression can both be empowering in its challenge to legitimacy and how 'another law' can be quickly marginalised as frivolous or disrespectful.

We have shown, therefore, that political identities must be performed, and that different sorts of performances carry different meanings. Yet, so far this has all been conducted in terms of the most visible political 'actors' – Parliamentary politicians. The

Figure 6.3 ■ Diane Abbott and Bernie Grant, who also transgressed convention by not wearing the traditional jacket and tie. (Source: PA News Ltd.)

next section looks at a different site of political power, one that is, as we say, 'behind the scenes'. This is the world of the bureaucrats. The aim here is to show that the apparently dehumanising, routine and supposedly invisible forms of social organisation which characterise bureaucracy also involve cultural meaning and performance in the structuring and legitimating of power relations.

6.2.3 | Bureaucracy as culture

Introducing bureaucracy

Most discussions of bureaucracy begin with the work of the sociologist **Max Weber** (p. 243) (see Weber, 1967). He argued that what he called the 'characteristics of bureaucracy', or 'modern officialdom', could be set apart from the ways in which other forms of rule operated. For example, they are different from older monarchical states where the administration was an extension of the king's household run by patronage and tradition. In this sense Weber is one of those thinkers discussed above in section 6.1.2, who are interested in analysing the complexities of the relationship between rulers and ruled. By separating out these characteristics Weber hoped to understand bureaucracy (see Box 6.2).

Box **6.2**
Max Weber's bureaucratic ideal type

1. 'There is a principle of fixed and official jurisdictional areas, which are generally ordered by rules, that is, by laws or administrative regulations ... Permanent and public office authority, with fixed jurisdiction, is not the historical rule but rather the exception.'
2. 'The principles of office hierarchy and levels of graded authority mean a firmly ordered system of super- and subordination in which there is a supervision of the lower offices by the higher ones.'
3. 'The management of the modern office is based upon written documents ("the files"), which are preserved in their original or draught form ... In principle, the modern organisation of the civil service separates the bureau from the private domicile of the official, and, in general bureaucracy segregates official activity as something distinct from the sphere of public life.'
4. 'Office management ... usually presupposes thorough and expert training.'
5. '[O]fficial activity demands the full working capacity of the official ...'
6. 'The management of the office follows general rules, which are more or less stable, more or less exhaustive, and which can be learned. Knowledge of these rules represents a special technical learning which the officials possess.'

Weber (1967: 196–8)

What Weber presents us with is a bureaucratic system in which full-time, salaried, trained, qualified, appointed and finely graded staff, with job security, career prospects and pension rights, operate according to sets of written and rational rules to make administrative decisions within specific areas of official competence which are carefully demarcated to separate them from each other, from their home lives and from the public. It is a rationally organised and objective system whose calculable rules operate 'without regard for persons' rather than on the basis of doling out personal favours or on the basis of tradition. Weber suggests that the reasons for its success (as measured by its dramatic historical development and geographical spread alongside capitalist economic relations; see Lefort, 1986) can be understood as the same as the reasons for the success of machines in arenas where things had previously been produced without them. As he said:

> The decisive reason for the advance of bureaucratic organisation has always been its purely technical superiority over any other form of organisation. ... Precision, speed, unambiguity, knowledge of the files, continuity, discretion, unity, strict subordination, redirection of friction and of material and personal costs – these are raised to the optimum point in the strictly bureaucratic administration.   (Weber, 1967: 214)

What all this suggests is that bureaucracy is somehow outside the sphere of culture. It operates in a world of cold, hard economic and political realities which do not admit the claims of meaning, feeling and intersubjective interpretation that come within the reach of what we call the cultural. Weber's analysis suggests that older forms of rule – operating according to ancient religious traditions or the whims of despotic emperors – were 'cultural' (see the discussion of divine right above). He notes that they were coupled with educational systems designed to produce 'the cultivated man' whose criteria for acceptability for governing was 'the possession of "more" cultural quality' (Weber, 1967: 243). Rationalised bureaucracy is very different:

> Its specific nature ... develops the more perfectly the more the bureaucracy is 'dehumanised', the more completely it succeeds in eliminating from official business love, hatred, and all purely personal, irrational, and emotional elements which escape calculation. This is the specific nature of bureaucracy and it is appraised as its special virtue.   (Weber, 1967: 243)

Instead of seeking those with 'cultural quality' (whatever that may mean), bureaucracy is tied to educational systems that produce technical experts or 'the "specialist type of man"' (Weber, 1967: 243). Thus, as bureaucratic forms develop, there also develops a series of conflicts between these specialists and those who had previously ruled on a different – 'cultural' – basis: 'This fight is determined by the irresistibly expanding bureaucratisation of all public and private relations of authority and by the ever-increasing importance of expert and specialised knowledge. This fight intrudes into all intimate cultural questions' (Weber, 1967: 243).

We can see that bureaucracy, for Weber, has crucial implications for 'cultural questions', but is not presented as being 'cultural' itself. It is this last assumption that we want to question here and the reason for setting out Weber's thinking on bureaucracy in so much detail is to show that many of the issues we want to develop can be found lurking in Weber's own texts. The first is that for bureaucracy to be successful is not merely a technical administrative matter – like Parliamentary identities it must be *performed*. The various 'eliminations' and 'separations' that Weber refers to must be performed for the publics that legitimate its authority. That issue will be taken up below by considering how bureaucratic office buildings perform bureaucracy in different ways. This performance is, however, also a matter for the bureaucrats themselves and here it connects to issues of identity and power which will be investigated by considering how the bureaucratic persona is gendered. Weber was aware of the 'production' of different sorts of ruling men but he did not follow up the implications of that. Finally, we briefly consider how the bureaucratic structures and the bureaucratic personas constructed within them are ethically problematic. Again this is something that Weber was aware of in his discussion of the difficulties of dismantling a bureaucracy but which he did not take further. So, bring on the performing bureaucrats.

Key influence **6.4**

Max Weber (1864–1920)

Born in Erfurt, Central Germany, the son of a lawyer and National Liberal politician, Weber was schooled in Berlin before studying law and history at the universities of Heidelberg, Berlin and Gottingen. Following spells of military training and work in criminal law courts, he returned to university to specialise in economic history. He obtained a doctorate in 1888 and completed his postdoctoral habilitation thesis in 1891 which allowed him to pursue an academic career. He married Marianne Schnitger in 1893. Marianne became an influential figure in the German feminist movement. In 1896 Weber was appointed Professor of Economics at Heidelberg University, where he settled for the rest of his life. However, his father's death in 1897 provoked the onset of a depressive illness which led to lengthy sick-leaves from his post.

In 1902 Weber resumed academic work and his 1904 visit to the United States influenced his famed *The Protestant Ethic and the Spirit of Capitalism* (1904–5). Around this time he began to reorient his intellectual interests in the direction of sociology and the 'cultural sciences'. He emphasised the centrality of the meanings that people attach to objects and activities, defining **culture** (p. 355) as the 'finite segment of the infinity of the world process, a segment on which *human beings* confer meaning and significance'.

According to Weber, rationalisation was the master trend accounting for the broad development of Western societies. More and more spheres of life were being wrested from the influence of the incalculable, the whimsical, the magical and the non-standardised, and brought under rational control. The application of instrumental rationality was facilitated by the emergence of modern science, systematic forms of accountancy and law, but above all by bureaucracy as the dominant form of social organisation. Weber viewed rationalisation as a relentless process. He saw the future in bleak terms as an 'iron cage' in which human individuality would be increasingly circumscribed:

→

No one knows who will live in this cage in the future, or whether at the end of this tremendous development entirely new prophets will arise, or there will be a great rebirth of old ideas and ideals, or, if neither, mechanized petrification, embellished with a sort of convulsive self-importance. For of this last stage of cultural development, it might truly be said: 'Specialists without spirit, sensualists without heart; this nullity imagines it has attained a level of civilization never before achieved.'

(Weber, 1930:182)

Weber held that facts and values occupied radically different domains, and that science and politics were distinct spheres of activity. But he was not afraid to become involved in practical action and political activity (for example, at the outbreak of the First World War he took up the post of Director of Army Hospitals, Heidelberg; later, he became a critic of Germany's war policies and was a delegate to the Versailles peace conference).

Weber's analysis of the impact of rationality on the cultural features of modern societies has been enormously influential on subsequent theorists. His methodological writings, which deal with questions about how cultures and societies can be investigated in a principled manner, have a contemporary relevance in light of their stress on the unavoidably partial and fragmentary character of cultural and scientific knowledge.

Further reading

Parkin, F. (1982) *Max Weber*, Chichester: Ellis Horwood.
Runciman, W.G. (ed.) (1978) *Weber: Selections in Translation*, Cambridge: Cambridge University Press.

Bureaucracy and the performance of power

The French social theorist Henri Lefebvre understood modern societies as shaped by a process of 'bureaucratisation through space' which subjected social life to increasing regulation and surveillance (Gregory, 1994: 401; see also Foucault, 1977; Dandeker, 1990; and Giddens, 1985). This is coupled with a heightened 'bureaucratisation of space' whereby each administrative system 'maps out its own territory, stakes it out and signposts it' (Lefebvre, 1991: 387). While these ideas are useful for understanding how states administer societies, they can also be turned towards understanding bureaucracy itself. One of the implications of Weber's work is that bureaucracies involve tight internal surveillance, and that the putting into place of these forms of surveillance means a careful attention to organising space within bureaucratic offices (Giddens, 1984). This, then, is a matter of how best to regulate the flows of people, papers and ideas within an office to get the job done: 'bureaucratisation through space' in the bureaucratic office. Where should departments be located? Which offices should be open plan, which private? What are the 'correct channels' for people and files to go through? More interesting perhaps is the 'bureaucratisation of space' within bureaucracy. While the mapping and staking out of territory and the erection of signposts is a useful metaphor for the division of administrative responsibilities between ministries or departments – separating education and employment, home and foreign, agriculture and industry – it is also inscribed onto bureaucratic space. These signposts exist in the form of the offices that the bureaucracy inhabits.

There are several points that can be made about the sorts of buildings that bureaucrats occupy in terms of how they are part of a culture of bureaucracy. First, simply as separate buildings they make statements about the nature of bureaucracy. Their separation from each other, from the homes of the bureaucrats, from Parliament or other centres of power is not merely a question of efficiency but is a demonstration – a performance – of the autonomy of the bureaucrats and bureaucratic processes housed within them from 'political' influences which might question whether they really function 'without regard for persons'. Second, the architecture is important in this performance too. The way the buildings look makes statements about what goes on inside. Some of this is about various representations of the functions of the ministries – e.g. bulls' heads on the Ministry of Agriculture Food and Fisheries – and these small signs help to make these more than just anonymous office blocks. However, the primary role is to 'perform' the legitimate authority of bureaucracy, and this is not so easily done with such specific symbols. The solid, geometrical, well-built, large, clean buildings with their imposing entrances and uniform, regularly spaced windows speak of the importance, solidity, rationality and efficient impersonality of bureaucracy. These are all the characteristics that give it legitimacy as a way of ruling. The buildings themselves demonstrate the 'precision, speed, unambiguity, knowledge of the files, continuity, discretion, unity, strict subordination [and] efficiency' that Weber saw as characteristic of bureaucracy. What we want to add is that this is a matter of cultural politics in that it is *performed*: not only must it be done, it must be seen to be done.

It might, however, be argued that, just as state forms are changing in the late twentieth century, then so are forms of bureaucracy and the ways in which their presence is performed. Some of these issues are raised in relation to MI6 (see Box 6.3) and a tentative answer to these questions might note the changing nature of geopolitics, outlined in the introduction above. Previously, the British security services were part of a national bureaucracy at the centre of a world-wide empire. As a secret organisation, MI6 saw itself as playing a discreet role – no one was supposed to know where its headquarters were – and was happy for its public image to be represented by fictional agents, like James Bond, who was a heroic but human figure, carrying out Britain's purpose in a hostile world. The new building fits in with the new **postmodern** (p. 400) architecture of the City of London (which, as a centre of finance capital, is one of Britain's last claims to international leadership), announcing itself as part of the new transnational world. It represents the new business of intelligence, which involves high-tech surveillance techniques like satellites (James Bond specialised in small, pocket-sized gadgets) and Britain's new role within international organisations like NATO and the United Nations, and the more complex interaction of diplomacy, military might and economic aid that structures interventions in the new multipolar world described above. Thus, looking at this building in relation to the geopolitical situation within which it operates shows how questions of representation and **symbolism** (p. 288) are inseparable from those of political power and the ways in which it is always changing.

Box *6.3*

MI6 and the architectural performance of power

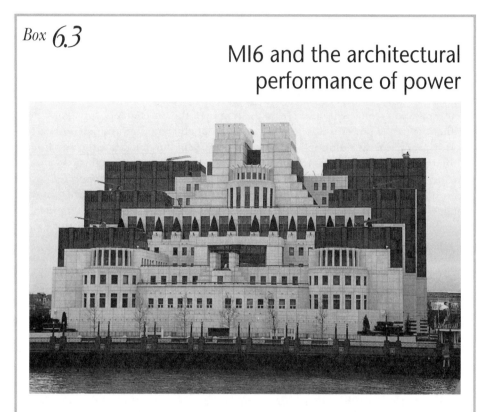

None of these interpretations of bureaucratic buildings can be static. The forms that they take are always changing. The question is whether these changes are significant ones and how we might interpret them. For example, this new building on the south bank of the River Thames at Vauxhall, into which MI6 (part of the British government's secret service) recently moved, raises some interesting questions

How does it differ from the traditional architecture of bureaucracy? Is this part of a shift from 'modernism' to 'postmodernism'?

What does it say about a government department that it is housed in something reminiscent of a postmodern version of a Babylonian temple? What relations of authority are being performed here?

Bureaucracies, however, are not simply a matter of offices; they are also about bureaucrats. These issues of performance can be widened in order to understand the culture of bureaucracy in similar terms to those we have used for Parliamentary identities, addressing them in terms of issues of identity and, particularly, gendered identity.

Bureaucracy and identity

In part, questions of **identity** (p. 224) within bureaucracy can be understood in the terms used above. The mapping and signposting of territories goes on as much within offices as it does between them. The signalling of hierarchies with more and more elaborate and graded office spaces, office furniture, and the rituals and ceremonies of super- and subordination are very much part of our common currency of jokes about what bureaucrats are like. Yet these issues of identity run much deeper than which sort of wastepaper bin a Grade 5 civil servant has. As Claude Lefort (1986) has argued, 'Bureaucracy loves bureaucrats just as much as bureaucrats love bureaucracy' (1986: 108) and one reason for this situation is that bureaucratic society forms 'a concrete milieu from which each individual derives his own identity' (1986: 113). Indeed, as in all workplaces there is a complex process by which the organisational culture shapes the identities that are available to workers. As Paul du Gay (1996) has shown for the retailing sector, changes in organisational forms (often away from 'bureaucratic' or 'authoritarian' modes towards ones associated with 'flexibility' and 'enterprise') mean that new identities arise which are adopted, resisted and negotiated by workers and managers. We need to understand organisations and identities at the same time. That Lefort does so in terms of class means that he has not investigated the arena in which this has been most dramatically demonstrated: gender.

Anne Witz and Mike Savage (1992) have challenged the idea that what Weber presents is the general form of bureaucratic organisation. Instead, they argue that it is just one 'historically and spatially specific form of organising' (1992: 3) among many. Moreover, their argument is that each of these organisational forms can be seen to 'rest upon particular gendered foundations' (1992: 3) and, as a result, the gender relations upon which Weber's model depends can be uncovered. Instead of being a matter of technical efficiency, bureaucracy is seen to be a matter of social relations and power relations. They show how hierarchies within bureaucracies have been gendered: how the employment of women within subordinate, often clerical, offices was essential to guaranteeing meritocratic career structures for male bureaucrats. Moreover, they show how these careers were also dependent on having a wife at home to do all the work necessary to send the bureaucrat back to the office, day after day, clean, fed, rested and ready for work. This all means that Weber's notions of the bureaucratic career need to be understood as gendered. It also means that we have to think carefully about what this gendering of bureaucracy means for Weber's sense of the objectivity and rationality of such organisational forms.

Let us go back to what Weber calls bureaucracy's 'specific nature' and 'special virtue', the elimination 'from official business [of] love, hatred, and all purely personal, irrational, and emotional elements which escape calculation' (Weber, 1967: 243). What Weber refers to as a process whereby bureaucracy becomes 'dehumanised' has been seen by those interested in gender as the construction of a particular form of masculinity which is built upon its exclusion of the personal, the sexual and the feminine. Rational administration can only exist if those characteristics constructed as 'masculine' and mental – distance, objectivity and reason – are given precedence over those characteristics constructed as feminine and bodily – closeness, compassion and emotion. The imagined bureaucrat is the dark-suited man with the tightly rolled umbrella and the briefcase. However, this cannot be a simple separation of the 'masculine' and the 'feminine'. First, the 'male' sphere of rational, objective reason and action can only exist if a space is made for it by a whole load of other work being done. This work is gendered feminine. As Savage and Witz argue, women are 'housekeeping' in the office as well as at home. 'They are facilitating, cleaning, tidying, bolstering, soothing, smoothing over, sustaining ... relieving men of having to bother with the messy, untidy, unpredictable bodily mode of existence' (Savage and Witz, 1992: 23). Gender is there right at the root of bureaucracy. Second, men cannot so easily escape the body and sexuality. As we have already seen in relation to Parliamentary identities, the supposedly asexual and unbodily identity is one that has to be performed constantly using suits, ties, postures and briefcases. Here is Malcolm Young talking about policemen's bodies:

> To walk into a pub function room as I have often done during the ten years I was collecting fieldnotes and to see two or three hundred detectives in their 'uniform' of modern suit and tie, neat haircut, and the fashionable moustache of the times, is to be visibly reminded that there is a narrow symbolic range of bodily correctness within which all policemen can properly operate. (Young, 1991: 83)

As with Parliament, entry into organisations like the police is restricted by cultural factors which are built into bureaucratic forms of organisation. Indeed, even when perfectly performed it is not actually an asexual identity but a particular mode of sexuality that is constantly used to gain and maintain power within the organisational setting. Michael Roper (1994), discussing businessmen, has argued that the bureaucratic life is a vividly emotional one where bonds and divisions between men – young and old – animate working lives via a struggle to maintain a sufficiently masculine identity: an identity that, it must be noted, is assertively heterosexual (men who desire women) while operating through homosocial (men who work with men and exclude women from the world of work) relationships.

In thinking about why all this is the case, we clearly need to situate it within the cultural struggles for power which are the stuff of cultural politics. There are gendered power struggles in the office within which identities are a weapon. As much as in the sphere of formal politics, this involves bids for legitimacy to civil society (or the public) within which the connected performances of masculinity and objectivity are crucial. However, legitimation is not simply a one-way street. Thomas Osbourne (1994) stresses that those involved in bureaucracy also have to convince themselves that they are fit to rule. He suggests that the question that we need to ask is: 'What do those who rule have to do to *themselves* in order to be able to rule?' In answering this question in terms of the development of a civil service in Britain through the Northcote–Trevelyan Report of 1854, he shows how competitive examinations were used for the first time to legitimate the authority of the bureaucracy by developing a sense of vocational unity, an attachment to a wider public (who could take the exams if they wanted, and might even pass if they had a classical education) and a particular mode of masculinity (which

Osbourne calls 'muscular liberalism') which made them feel fit to govern. As Lord Ashley put it in 1844: 'we must have nobler, deeper, sterner stuff; less of refinement and more of truth; more of the inward and less of the outward gentleman; a rigid sense of duty and not a delicate sense of honour' (quoted in Osbourne, 1994: 306). That the rooting of this in the classics bound it to a particular class and that the examination system had been first developed in British India as part of a racialised bureaucratic system stresses that class, race and gender are again bound together in these issues of bureaucratic identity.

What are the costs of this masculinisation of bureaucratic identity? Certainly for women it presents a crucial problem in terms of the ways that they can operate within such organisations. As Savage and Witz say, they have to perform a particularly problematic identity, one that is gendered but not sexualised: they 'must behave like men but not be men and behave unlike women and yet be women' (Savage and Witz, 1992: 53). There are also what we might think of as costs to men (although we must also bear in mind the benefits they stand to gain as men from the process) through the circumscribed forms of life that are connected to bureaucratic success. Finally, we need to think about the ethical costs of masculinised bureaucratic systems which emphasise objectivity, rationality and efficiency above all else.

Bureaucracy and ethics

In his investigations of the Holocaust the sociologist Zygmunt Bauman (1989) has begun to question the ethics of bureaucracy and to stress the ways in which it is able to silence morality. Again, his argument runs against Weber's since for Bauman bureaucracy is not neutral, it is positively dangerous. He argues that the meticulous functional division of labour and the replacement of moral responsibility by a purely technical responsibility (getting the job done efficiently) distances bureaucrats from the final products of the bureaucratic processes of which they are a part. They become concerned only to carry out the orders that come from above, believing that this absolves them of moral responsibility for their actions. This means that they only pay attention to how smoothly their part of the process operates rather than considering the final outcomes and their responsibility for them. They become insulated from the results of their actions via the structure of bureaucracy and, as a result, they can operate in a language of rational and technical efficiency which only concerns itself with seemingly neutral measures of efficiency and with rational input–output equations. What is being dealt with – and in the case that Bauman is concerned to investigate it is people being transported to death camps and then killed on a huge scale – becomes less important than that the process operates efficiently and cost-effectively. Bauman's argument is, therefore, that these processes bring with them a 'dehumanisation of the objects of bureaucratic action' (Bauman, 1989: 102). In the bureaucrats' forms, ledgers, graphs and accounts, people become units to be processed, no different from pig iron or potatoes, and not 'potential subjects of moral demands' (Bauman, 1989: 103). For Bauman, bureaucracy, in its pursuit of rationality and efficiency, silences morality. As a result he can point to the bureaucrats whose actions moved millions of Jews through the railway system to their deaths in Germany and Poland and argue that 'bureaucracy made the Holocaust. And it made it in its own image' (Bauman, 1989: 105). He also enables us to ask difficult ethical questions about seemingly neutral rational and technical processes.

It should now be clear that bureaucracy needs to be understood as cultural, as part of the world of cultural politics. It involves questions of performance, identity and ethics which cannot simply be understood as matters of technical rationality. That this is also true of other arenas of state activity, particularly warfare, now needs to be explored.

6.2.4 | Performing state power

Having explored the question of the performance of power in relation to Parliamentary politics and bureaucratic administration, we want to argue that it is useful in understanding how states (political entities which claim rights to violence, taxation and administration over specific territories) display their power in order to claim authority and legitimacy. In particular it will be concerned with the ways in which the culture of politics is crucial to understanding how states manage to legitimate their extensive use of violence. This will also mean showing how partial these performances are, particularly in terms of gender, and how restrictive they are in terms of the identities that they offer and the moralities that they suggest (see also section 4.4). Finally, it will mean thinking about how these cultural claims to power are challenged.

One excellent starting point for a discussion of what we might call the connections between 'state formation' (the making of state power) and 'cultural politics' is the work of Peter Corrigan and Derek Sayer:

> States, if the pun be forgiven, *state*; the arcane rituals of a court of law, the formulae of royal assent to an Act of Parliament, visits of school inspectors, are all statements. They define, in great detail, acceptable forms and images of social activity and individual and collective identity; they regulate ... much – very much, by the twentieth century – of social life. Indeed, in this sense 'the State' never stops talking.
>
> (Corrigan and Sayer, 1985: 3)

In other words, states have to assert their legitimacy, and one place where the state keeps on and on at us about this is in the city streets. Its insistent voice can be 'heard', or rather its statements can be seen, in the monuments that it erects and maintains (including the bureaucratic buildings discussed above). These monuments give meaning to certain, and carefully selected, groups, institutions, people, places and events. In the process they also *make* those groups, institutions, people and so on by marking them as important and defining them in certain ways. So, 'the State' states by making and marking space with monuments, but what is it saying?

Monuments and the marking of centres

Political power, as we keep stressing in this chapter, must be performed. In order for it to be sustained this must be a credible performance (Scott, 1990). This is partly achieved by the various props that can be used in the performance. As the anthropologist Clifford Geertz has it, elites 'justify their existence and order their actions in terms of a collection of stories, ceremonies, insignia, formalities, and appurtenances that they have either inherited or, in more revolutionary situations, invented' (Geertz, 1983b: 124). All these trappings of rule serve to mark where these elites are as the centre, symbolising it as the place where the power lies and symbolising the people there as the powerful. Even despotic monarchs, including those who claim divine authority, had to perform that authority. Geertz works through several examples of royal progresses (journeys made by monarchs around the territories that they claim) – Queen Elizabeth I in sixteenth-century England, Hayam Wuruk in fourteenth-century Java and Mulay Hasan in nineteenh-century Morocco – to show how they all try to perform political power by presenting themselves as symbolically central. This is also the way in which many monuments work. The Victoria monument – erected between 1908 and 1911 as a memorial to the Queen – stands in front of Buckingham Palace, at the end of the Mall and at a point where several major roads meet (see Figure 6.4). Along with the Palace it is part of the marking of the symbolic centre of the nation through the monarchy (at least since the nineteenth century), showing in its grandeur and mass of symbolic figures the importance and moral virtues that the state associates with its symbolic head. The ways in which this symbolism is gendered is crucial. The figure on the side of monument

Figure 6.4 ■ The Victoria Monument, London.

facing Buckingham Palace (balancing the statue of Victoria on the other side) is a woman suckling an infant. Victoria is the 'mother' of the nation. It also marks this place as the centre of Empire. Each of the gates through which we must pass to approach the monument has its gateposts inscribed with the name of an imperial dominion: South Africa, West Africa, Australia, Canada, the Malay States and so on. Thus, the nation and the empire are seen to have the same centre. This is not Parliament, the war office or the colonial office, but the monarchy and, more specifically, Queen (and Empress) Victoria. This symbolic marking is a statement about **power** (p. 94), monarchy, nation and empire which presents a particular version of how they are related.

Monuments as partial performances

In interpreting monuments, as with all cultural artifacts, we need to be aware of the partiality of the statements that they make (see also the discussion of buildings in section 9.8). They are constructed by certain groups, people or institutions for certain purposes and, like all symbol – or meaning-laden objects, they present particular views of how things are. Thus, the Victoria monument tried to legitimate Britain's imperial power. Indeed, if we can reveal the partiality of these statements we can diffuse some of the power that rests in making a partial world-view seem like the way that the world *really* is. There are plenty of examples of readings of monuments that seek to reveal their partiality by uncovering the ways in which their symbolism is shaped by class, race, gender and sexuality: for example, David Harvey's reading of the Sacré Coeur in Paris as an anti-revolutionary symbol of conservative Catholic Monarchism (Harvey, 1985a), or Marina Warner's understanding of New York's Statue of Liberty as the taming of a powerful female symbol of revolutionary change into a staid and matronly figure (Warner, 1985). Two brief examples will suffice here. They both concern the ways in which gender was used by the early twentieth-century British state to discuss warfare.

Admiralty Arch, built in 1910, stands at the other end of the Mall from the Victoria monument and is the entrance to it from Trafalgar Square. The concave (Mall) side has two allegorical statues on either end. One represents 'gunnery', the other 'navigation'. The statue shown in Figure 6.5 is 'gunnery'. As you can see, the practice of firing missiles from or at ships at sea is represented by a woman. More importantly, the destructive power of the British Navy is represented by a maternal figure: a mother who cradles a cannon in her arms as if it were a baby. By presenting gunnery as a mother, the statue makes a statement about warfare as a natural action, and of the navy as a protecting force rather than an aggressive institution built upon violence. It also makes statements about women's roles within the nation-state which reinforce the partial role given to them as carers for and mothers of the nation rather than the other political roles they might adopt. Women, who are supposedly unlucky aboard ship, are excellent material for partial statements about what those warships do.

A monument erected to Edith Cavell (1865–1915) stands near Trafalgar Square in London. It is one of the few statues to a woman in the city. Edith Cavell was a nurse who trained in England and moved to Belgium in 1906 to help establish a training school for nurses. When war broke out in 1914 her school became a Red Cross hospital treating

Figure 6.5 ▪ Statue of Gunnery on Admiralty Arch, London.

both Allied and German prisoners. As the British and French forces were pushed back late that year, it became a place where Allied soldiers trying to escape sought refuge. Edith Cavell helped them. For this she was arrested, held in solitary confinement, tried by a German court martial on the basis of her written confession, and sentenced to death. She was shot at 2 a.m. on 12 October 1915. She rapidly became a martyr. She also became a symbol of the inhumanity of the enemy. They were presented as people who would not only execute a woman but a woman for whom, as the *Dictionary of National Biography* puts it, 'Charity and the desire to aid the distressed were the mainsprings of her life.' The monument (see Figure 6.6) presents her in a particular way, which again connects warfare, gender and the nation-state.

Edith Cavell is presented as a particular sort of woman, a figure that Klaus Theweleit (talking about the cultural politics of German masculine militarism in the early twentieth century) has called the 'white nurse'. This is a male image of the perfect woman: so perfect that no woman can ever live up to it. These are 'sisters' and 'disinfected sweethearts' who are, for these soldiers, 'the essential embodiment of their recoiling from all erotic, threatening sexuality' (Theweleit, 1987: 125–6) and whose purity is symbolised by the white uniform. They share with mothers 'a loving, caring side [that] is posed in opposition to a cold, distantly heroic side' (Theweleit, 1987: 104). This image was used by both the British and the Germans in the First World War (and before and since) to spur soldiers on and to justify the punishing (and killing) of women whose political and military actions made them 'impure'. It is within this

Figure 6.6 ▪ Monument to Edith Cavell.

gendered cultural politics of warfare that Edith Cavell has to be understood. For the Germans she was a spy, an evil woman whose position as a nurse made her crime all the worse. She had to be shot. For the British her death meant that she could be presented as a martyred 'white nurse' and her image used to demonise the German enemy for their inhumanity. Propaganda pictures showed a nurse in white uniform lying dead while a black-cloaked skeleton played the piano behind her. The legend read: 'The murder of Miss Cavell inspires German "*Kultur*".'

The monument, designed by Sir George Frampton, participates in this form of representation. Her pose captures the two sides that Theweleit talks about: she is presented as both caring and distantly heroic. The monument carries the words 'Humanity', 'Devotion', 'Sacrifice' and 'Fortitude' and the inscription 'Faithful unto Death' which repeat this dualistic message. Most importantly, the whiteness of the stone chosen for her statue works to make her into a 'white nurse'. It performs this gendered identity. The statue's whiteness is set off by the grey granite background much more dramatically than it would be by the sky. She is memorialised here as a 'white nurse'. It is, however, worth pointing out that, as with the example of Michael Foot's clothes above, what is important is not so much what she actually wore, but how she was represented. In fact, most photographs of her show her in the dark suit that she wore as director of the training school rather than in a nurse's uniform.

This, then, is a monument not so much to a real woman as to an image of the 'white nurse'. It is also a monument that stresses how Edith Cavell is less important than the values and moralities that she might inspire in the nation. Instead of topping a pedestal, she is backed and overshadowed by a grey stone block bearing the words 'For King and Country' and the pronouncement 'Patriotism is not enough I must have no hatred or bitterness for anyone', a statement that claims the moral high ground for a moralised British patriotism by opposing it to the supposedly 'blind' patriotism of the Germans. Finally, the monument is capped by an allegorical woman and baby. The baby is protected by the maternal figure while she also gazes into the distance.

We want to read this monument as a public statement about the connection of the 'white nurse' and mother to the nation. The memorial to Edith Cavell operates as a connected set of symbols which work to justify patriotism and the wars fought in its name through the presentation of certain sorts of female figures (nurses and mothers, both real and allegorical) and the virtues that they, and therefore the nation, are said to stand for. It presents a very partial view of what warfare might mean and, like the statue of gunnery, this statement by the state severely circumscribes the political positions that women can adopt in relation to the nation, the state and warfare.

Challenging monuments

We have argued that states are continually performing their power in attempts to claim authority and legitimacy. Yet this does not go unchallenged. Monuments are also the sites of **resistance** (p. 258) to the meanings that they try to fix, and this resistance may come from various quarters, conservative and radical. Indeed, it is the power of monuments as symbols that sets them up as sites where challenges to authority can strike at what the powerful hold most dear. A brief example will suffice before we move onto more general questions of the cultural politics of resistance.

In 1871 the column erected in the Place Vendôme as a monument to the European and imperial victories of Napoléon's Grand Army was pulled to the ground and its destroyers danced among the rubble (see Figure 6.7). The context was the Paris Commune and its revolt against hierarchy. In the aftermath of the disastrous French defeat in the Franco-Prussian war, many Parisians revolted and took over the city. In part this was a workers' revolt, many of them women; in part it was a massive 'rent strike'; in part it was a revolt of the city against the provinces; in part it was a battle over who had the right to define what sort of city Paris should be. Since 1850 Paris had been transformed by the state and capital into a place for the display of state power and into a playground for financial speculators (Harvey, 1985b). It would now be transformed some more. The largely leaderless protesters declared Paris an autonomous commune. This political transformation only lasted seventy-three days and ended in much bloodshed, but as an opposing army massed at Versailles the communards set about transforming the social organisation of the city. Part of this was an attack on the **symbolism** (p. 288) of the prior regime, on its monumental statements. As one Commune decree stated:

Figure 6.7 ■ *The Toppling of the Vendôme Column* (1871) by unknown artist. (Source: reproduced by permission of the Musée Carnavalet, Paris.)

The Commune of Paris:
    Considering that the imperial column at the Place Vendôme is a monument to barbarism, a symbol of brute force and glory, an affirmation of militarism, a negation of international law, a permanent insult to the vanquished by the victors, a perpetual assault on one of the three great principles of the French Republic, Fraternity, it is thereby decreed:
    Article One: The column at the Place Vendôme will be abolished.
                                                            (quoted in Ross, 1988: 5)

This 'refusal of the dominant organisation of social space and the supposed neutrality of monuments' (Ross, 1988: 39) was understood by both the communards and the anti-communards as a blow to the heart of the powerful. The poet Catulle Mendès, an observer and opponent of the Commune, wrote:

the Vendôme column is France, yes, the France of yesteryear, the France that we no longer are, alas! It's really about Napoléon, all this, it's about our victories, superb fathers moving across the world, planting the tricoloured flag whose staff is made of a branch of the tree of liberty.   (quoted in Ross, 1988: 5–6)

It may have been a symbolic gesture of resistance but its target was evidently a good one.
    Indeed, it is in exactly this way (if rather less dramatic) that contemporary protesters choose to protest by occupying symbolic spaces in the city. In Britain they may try to get through the police cordon and iron gates into Downing Street, where the Prime

Minister occupies Number 10, or they may try to climb onto the roof of or even invade the Houses of Parliament (see below). In countries of the former Soviet bloc, protestors were quick to pull down statues of Marx and Lenin after the 'revolutions' of 1989. In either place people are challenging the partial versions that such spaces or monuments present, and they are seeking to use some of the symbolic power of these monuments – the way that they mark a centre – to promote their cause. It is to a fuller consideration of these cultures of resistance that we now turn.

6.3 | Cultures of resistance

6.3.1 | Performing identities in unconventional politics

The idea of cultures of **resistance** (p. 258) brings us back to the concept of **transgression**. Julia Kristeva's view of the carnivalesque suggests that its transgressions actually equalise the **power** (p. 94) relations between the official law and that which challenges it:

> Carnivalesque discourse breaks through the laws of a language censored by grammar and semantics and at the same time, is a social and political protest. There is no equivalence, but rather identity between challenging official linguistic codes and challenging official law.   (quoted in Stallybrass and White, 1986: 201)

But this optimism is modified by Peter Stallybrass and Allon White: 'Only a challenge to the hierarchy of *sites* of discourse, which usually comes from groups and classes "situated" by the dominant in low or marginal positions, carries the promise of politically transformative power' (1986: 201). This section gives some examples of political protest, which are also performances, that challenge political power in an attempt to transform it.

During periods of military dictatorship, women activists in Argentina and Chile used various types of symbolism as part of their protests in an attempt 'not just to get women to participate more in traditional politics but to find new ways of engaging in politics' (Waylen, 1992: 311). According to Georgina Waylen, this invokes a particular form of the carnivalesque: 'carrying photographs of their children and cut-out images of missing people, covering their hair with kerchiefs embroidered with their names and using silence' involves the 'concept of the spectacle ... expressing the oppositional culture of the oppressed'. This oppositional culture invokes Kristeva's 'another law', so that two political positions then enter into dialogue with one another. Kristeva describes this 'dialogism' as not 'the freedom to say anything', but as a kind of 'dramatic banter' (Kristeva, 1986: 41). One example of *dramatic* banter was seen in protests against the new consumerism in Chile, from which many women were excluded:

> On Saturday afternoons (the busiest time), women would abandon full trolleys, blocking the supermarket checkouts, with a note on each one saying: 'It's a pity we can't afford to buy because we don't have any money.' These protests were carefully organized to receive the maximum amount of coverage from the opposition media

Defining concept 6.2

Resistance and transgression

One of **Foucault**'s (p. 28) fundamental messages was that power always brings forth opposition and resistance to its effects. **Power** (p. 94) will seek to contain and control such resistances, often by incorporation through the working of **hegemony** (p. 106). Resistance is a kind of 'counter-power' always likely to surface in response to power's expression. Resistance takes many forms ranging from micropolitical gestures of contempt and alienation in the classroom to full-scale social and political revolutions.

Transgression involves exceeding the 'acceptable' boundaries set by established customs, hierarchies and rules. Cultural studies first appropriated the notion from **Bakhtin**'s (p. 202) (1984) writings on carnival – predominantly pre-industrial events such as fairs, popular feasts and wakes, processions and the like. The 'world upside down' (WUD) (Stallybrass and White, 1986) created in carnival links the inversion of hierarchy (kings become paupers, criminals make laws, men dress as women) with a 'grotesque realism' towards the human body which is depicted as bulky, protuberant, its orifices open and its lower regions (belly, buttocks, genitals, feet) ruling its upper parts (head, reason). The significance of carnival, according to Bakhtin, is that it is a **ritual** (p. 288) occasion where transgressive desires can be temporarily voiced and vented, established hierarchies momentarily inverted and forbidden pleasures briefly indulged. For Bakhtin the notion of carnival refers not only to a ritual occasion but also to a 'mode of understanding ... a cultural analytic' which draws attention to the cultural significance of symbolic inversions and transgressions (Stallybrass and White, 1986: 6, 183ff).

Cultural studies has used the pioneering ideas of Bakhtin and Foucault to explore the organised ways that subordinate and marginalised groups resist the imposition of dominant meanings (expressed via the dominant **ideology** – p. 84). Oppositional tendencies can make for cultural creativity. Youth subcultures are sometimes seen as structured environments for the expression of beliefs and attitudes that run counter to the adult world's. Often the opposition runs no deeper than the adoption of particular clothing styles and musical tastes and thus the resolutions they represent to the 'contradictions' that young people encounter are only 'magical' or 'imaginary' resolutions – giving rise to the notion of 'resistance through rituals' (Hall and Jefferson, 1976). But within the space opened by youth subcultures such symbolic resistances also afford real opportunities for personal expression that close down again once young people make the transition to the demands of work, marriage and family.

Cultures are not just creative; they are also 'contested terrains', sites of struggle. The dominant ideology does not simply and inevitably reproduce itself. **Stuart Hall**'s (p. 88) (1980) important essay 'Encoding/decoding' suggested that the encodings of TV programme makers might not go on to be straightforwardly decoded by the television audience. The variable social situations of the audience need to be taken into account. The encoded text may bear the dominant ideology and this would be the 'preferred reading' of it, but viewing that text is a 'negotiation' between it and the viewer, and other

→

('against the grain') readings could emerge. Hall's theory was empirically tested by Morley's (1980) study of the audience for the *Nationwide* television news programme. Morley found that some groups made a dominant decoding of the programme (managers, apprentices). Others presented a negotiated decoding, inflecting the programme makers' message with elements drawn from their own social position (university students, trade union officials). Two groups (shop stewards, black further education students) offered an oppositional decoding which directly contested many of the programme's encoded claims and assumptions. This group simply refused to accept the dominant ideology as it worked through the programme. Hall and Morley show that it is necessary to adopt a more active and differentiated conception of the audience, who draw on their own cultural experience when viewing television, to understand fully the dynamics of reception.

In cultural studies the notions of **transgression** (p. 258) and resistance serve to underline the embodied and agentic characteristics of persons and the creative and contested dimensions of culture.

Further reading

Bakhtin, M. (1984) *Rabelais and His World*, Bloomington, IN: Indiana University Press (orig. 1968).
Morley, D. (1980) *The 'Nationwide' Audience*, London: BFI.
Stallybrass, P. and White, A. (1986) *The Politics and Poetics of Transgression*, London: Methuen.

and were seen as a symbolic act sabotaging consumption, and challenging and subverting ... a dominant image of the Pinochet government ... its success in promoting wealth and economic prosperity.   (Waylen, 1992: 312)

An even starker example of the use of culture to make a political statement was the use of the Chilean national dance, the Cueca, by Chilean women whose relatives had disappeared. The Cueca is usually performed by a man and a woman. Wives of political prisoners who 'disappeared' during the Pinochet dictatorship (1973–89) danced the Cueca alone (the Cueca Sola), in public, to make the point about how the regime's repression had destroyed the families and the national culture it was claiming to preserve. The protest was publicised world-wide through *arpilleras*, stitched pictures of the dance (see Figure 6.8) and by the popular musician Sting in his song 'They danced alone'.

The Cueca was also appropriated as a form of protest by gay men in Chile, who danced together to protest against the regime's family policy which denied the legitimacy of gay relationships. The political group Outrage has organised similar forms of public protest in London. Kiss-ins and public marriage ceremonies between lesbians and gay men have been used by Outrage to attract maximum press attention to laws that discriminate against same-sex relationships. The carnivalesque has been used to great effect by lesbian and gay movements internationally. In San Francisco in the United States and in Sydney, Australia, gay and lesbian carnivals have appropriated the traditional forms of cross-dressing, satirical floats and parodic styles as a way of asserting

Figure 6.8 ■ An *arpillera* made to publicise the fate of the 'disappeared' in Chile.

the diversity of lifestyles that exist in those cities. These 'performances' are political and cultural both in their subversion of the expected norms of public behaviour and in their skilful use of the media to announce the presence of lesbian and gay men on the political scene.

Some of the limitations of using **identity** (p. 224) as a form of protest are exemplified in the case of *Las Madres* (the Mothers) of the Plaza de Mayo in Argentina. They were a group of women whose relatives had 'disappeared' during the 'dirty war' conducted by the military regime against those who opposed it. The women protested silently in the main square, the Plaza de Mayo, in Buenos Aires. The protest can be interpreted in two ways. First, staying within the military regime's version of gender relations, they were protesting as mothers, because mothers are naturally concerned about the family. A second view, however, which takes into account notions of performativity, suggest that the women's use of motherhood was *strategic*. They used the fact that the military government believed that women's place was in the home to protest in a way that the military found difficult to suppress: as mothers who cared about their families. This strategy was successful even after the end of the dictatorship, because it allowed them to 'act as a political conscience, resisting the tendencies to reconstruct periods of military rule as times of stability or economic growth' (Jaquette, 1994: 224).

If we return to the debate about **transgression** (p. 258) which introduced this section, we can understand the Mothers' challenge to the military regime as introducing the kind of dialogue described by Kristeva. However, as Stallybrass and White suggest, the two sides of the dialogue are not equal: the women's roles as mothers were imposed by the official culture, and this limited the part that they were able to play in public politics. None the less, and despite the fact that the women did not entirely reject a traditional view of motherhood, they were able to use that conventional role and to politicise it: 'the politicization of motherhood breaks down the rigid boundary of public and private' (Jaquette, 1994: 224). While the protest cannot be said to have transformed political power, it created a space in which a dialogue about justice and events that the military government wanted to suppress could take place. Stallybrass and White suggest that it makes little sense to argue about the 'intrinsic' radicalism or conservatism of the carnivalesque: 'The most that can be said ... is that ... given the presence of sharpened political antagonism, it may often act as *catalyst* and *site of actual and symbolic struggle*' (Stallybrass and White, 1986: 14).

Cultures of **resistance** (p. 258) are, thus, most effective when they involve the symbolic performance of some kind of cultural conflict. An example that brought together (and into conflict) conventional and unconventional identities in politics was the protest organised in the House of Lords by a group of women on 2 February 1988 against Clause 28 of the Local Government Act 1988. Clause 28 was a wide-ranging and ill-defined clause introduced to prevent the 'promotion of homosexuality' by local councils. When the vote for the clause was announced, three women abseiled down into the chamber, supported by shouts from the public gallery. This transgression intro-duced 'another law' by subverting a passive version of femininity. In press coverage, the act was described as 'SAS-style' (*Daily Mail*, 3 February 1988), 'commando-style' (*Daily Telegraph*, 3 February 1988) and a 'Tarzan raid' (*Daily Mirror*, 3 February 1988). The women's unconventional behaviour was contrasted with the 'legitimate' conventions of the House of Lords. Peers were described as 'startled' (*Telegraph*) and as 'watching in disbelief' (*Mail*). The women temporarily created a carnivalesque atmosphere, upset-ting the authority of the chamber. Unruly scenes followed: 'They descended into the chamber, and were met by three House of Lords ushers – all retired naval warrant officers' (*Guardian*), 'Parliament's most distinguished official, Black Rod, grabbed one of the women' (*Mirror*). The carnivalesque unleashes laughter, so that the conflicts appear to border on the farcical. One Tory MP, Dame Elaine Kellet-Bowman, commented: 'One chap almost lost his trousers in the melee' (*Mirror*). The actual conflict, which the *Telegraph* reported as quite violent, is represented in the press as a symbolic battle between the forces of order and disorder.

The debate or dialogue that emerges out of the protest revolved around the sense of exclusion from the formal political process felt by the women. This was articulated by one of the women, Stella Blair, as follows: 'I think they probably have never seen anything like it before. We planned it in the morning. We felt it was time we had our say. It is all right for them to have a say about us but we should have a right to answer these things' (*Guardian*). The protest was successful in so far as it reveals the conventions of the House of Lords to be as far removed from any version of what is 'normal' as the lifestyles of the women. However, the transgressive or carnivalesque situation that the protest brought about only achieved the stated aim of 'answering' the conventional legislative process in so far as the women's points of view as well as their actions were articulated. The protest, like the supermarket protests of Chilean feminists, was timed for maximum press coverage; but this meant that it was dependent on how the press represented it. While the *Guardian* printed the fullest justification of the women's position, less sympathetic papers gave more attention to the protestors' shouted 'abuse', representing them as rude and inarticulate. As we shall see in the final section, there are always limits to transgression.

6.3.2 | The limits of transgression: *The Satanic Verses*

In 1981, as well as his prize-winning novel, *Midnight's Children*, Salman Rushdie published a short story in the *London Review of Books*, 'The Prophet's hair'. The story describes an event which also occurs in the novel, the theft of a holy relic, a hair of the Prophet Mohammed, from the shrine at Hazratbal in Kashmir. The disappearance of the hair sets off a series of events which, seven years later, was to move from the world of fiction into real life: processions through the streets of 'endless, ululating crocodiles of lamentation ... riots ... political ramifications and ... men whose entire careers hung upon this single lost hair'. The effect of the hair on the rich moneylender who finds it is equally familiar. He abandons his liberal Western values and imposes a new tyrannical regime on his family. All books in the house are burnt except the Koran. Prayers five times a day become mandatory and his daughter and wife are forced into purdah. In a manner that is characteristic of all Rushdie's prose, the tale combines elements of the contemporary short story with elements of the fairy tale or parable. It contains a thief who could have come from the *Arabian Nights*, yet whose sons are modern Islamic fundamentalists, denied a pilgrimage to Mecca because their father has smashed their legs at birth to give them an income as beggars. To use a term introduced earlier, it is 'carnivalesque'. Indeed, **Bakhtin** (p. 202) originally introduced his concept of the carnivalesque in relation to literature (Bakhtin, 1981). The narrative of 'The Prophet's hair' deliberately transgresses cultural conventions: the magic and the modern, the secular and the sacred, the political and the traditional clash and reinterpret one another.

On 26 September 1988, Rushdie's carnivalesque novel *The Satanic Verses* was published. Its transgressive qualities had rapid consequences. On 5 October it was banned in India. On 14 January 1989 the book was burned during demonstrations in Bradford, England. In February seven people were killed in rioting in Pakistan and

India; and on 14 February, the head of state of Iran, Ayatollah Khomeini, proclaimed a *fatwa* on Rushdie. Shortly afterwards, a price of £1.5 million was put on his life (Appignanesi and Maitland, 1989). 'The Prophet's hair' demonstrates that the issues that caused this storm of protest were not new to Rushdie's work. What, then, was the relationship between the transgressive cultural artifact, the novel, and the politics in which it became embroiled?

Rushdie's two most successful novels before *The Satanic Verses* were deliberately transgressive in their criticism of the post-independence governments of India and Pakistan. He has also been consistently critical of racism in England, where he has lived since he was 14. His use of the novel form to parody claims to political legitimacy is continued in *The Satanic Verses*, but the novel goes further in an attempt to represent international cultural conflict. Its subject matter is the effects of **globalisation** (p. 159), where different cultures are brought into contact with one another through migration and the increasingly powerful international culture industries (see section 6.1.1). The central idea of the novel is the way in which things that are considered sacred in one culture are treated irreverently when they come into contact with another culture. In Rushdie's words, it is about 'migration, metamorphosis, divided selves, love, death, London and Bombay' (Appignanesi and Maitland, 1989: 44). It suggests that transgression, sacrilege and blasphemy are part and parcel of the **postmodern** (p. 400) world.

One example of this is the novel's use of language. The narrator makes a case for the reuse of insults by those who have been insulted. He cites the term 'black', which was reappropriated by the Civil Rights Movement in the United States as a proud self-definition (another example would be the use of the terms 'gay' or 'queer', which have been reappropriated by the lesbian and gay movements). In *The Satanic Verses*, the name 'Mahound', an insulting reference to the Prophet Mohammed, is given to one of the characters. The narrator's argument is that it is possible to reappropriate this name, as part of a reinterpretation of myth in the context of the modern world. The novel, then, should act as a free space where different and conflicting positions are in dialogue. In an interview, Rushdie wrote 'in writing *The Satanic Verses*, I wrote from the assumption that I was, and am a free man' (*Independent on Sunday*, 4 February 1990).

As is now well known, the fate of the novel and its author have not exemplified freedom. The Ayatollah's *fatwa* has forced Rushdie into hiding. *The Satanic Verses*, far from being a free space, has become a political football, representing for some the epitome of liberal values and the rights of the individual to free speech, and for others a gross insult to the Islamic faith. Despite the text's attempt to reflect on the how cultures represent themselves, Rushdie has even been accused of racism in his representation of African characters (Mazrui, 1989).

The case of *The Satanic Verses* demonstrates an aspect of cultural politics that has already been touched on in this chapter: the importance of not just representation and performance, but also of reception. While the novel is transgressive and is about transgression, that transgression is limited by how it has been received. The novel was originally banned in India as a result of protests by a Muslim MP, Syed Shahabuddin. The Congress Party, then in power, became worried about the Muslim vote at the next election. Despite the fact that Shahabuddin proclaimed that he had not read the book, the novel started to signify a crisis between state and religion (Spivak, 1990: 50). When the Ayatollah Khomeini pronounced the *fatwa* in the context of the Iranian revolution, the meaning of that crisis widened to include the relationship between the 'West' and the Islamic world. This does not mean that the transgressions that the text is interested in are irrelevant. Despite not having read it, Shahabuddin shows a good understanding of the subject matter: 'your book only serves to define what has gone wrong with the Western civilization – it has lost all sense of distinction between the sacred and the profane' (Appignanesi and Maitland, 1989: 47). Rather, it is an example of how the relationship between a text and its audience, whether they had read it or simply heard about it within a religious, national or other political discourse, is, as Gayatri Spivak describes it, 'transactional' (Spivak, 1990: 50).

In this context, the intentions of the author become irrelevant to how the text is understood, but in so far as the author is seen to be responsible for the text, Rushdie has become implicated in the crisis. The consequences have been as ironic as any novel. Rushdie is now protected by the security forces of the British state, which he has long criticised. He continues his support for the reform and modernisation of Britain's political structures and traditions, but he is forced to speak only through the establishment media, the BBC and major newspapers. Where he once spoke in solidarity with the British Asian community, he is now seen by many (but by no means all) to speak against it.

In the tragi-comic finale of 'The Prophet's hair', all but one member of the moneylender's family are dead, and she has gone mad, while the fairy-tale thief's religious sons have been miraculously cured of their disabilities. It appears to be the perfect ending of an Islamic morality tale, where the virtuous are rewarded and the wicked get their just deserts. It is comparable with a thriller filmed in Pakistan which ended with a fictional Rushdie being struck down by Allah. But the tale can also be read in another way. The violent ending seems extreme and unnecessary and it is notable that the sons, rather than welcoming the restoration of their limbs and the opportunity of making a pilgrimage to Mecca, complain instead that their earnings have been reduced by 75 per cent. The tale and the case of *The Satanic Verses* illustrate that although transgression creates another law, it rarely replaces the ruling law. Instead it creates dialogue, debate and an arena in which conflict can be represented. If this arena is described as the carnivalesque, then, as we have already seen, the transgressions that take place are not always revolutionary or subversive. If the carnivalesque is

> Refreshingly iconoclastic, this nevertheless resolves none of the problems raised so far concerning the politics of carnival: its nostalgia; its uncritical populism (carnival often violently abuses and demonizes *weaker*, not stronger, social groups – women, ethnic and religious minorities, those who 'don't belong' – in a process of *displaced abjection*); its failure to do away with the official dominant culture, its licensed complicity.
>
> (Stallybrass and White, 1986: 19)

The Satanic Verses affair illustrates many of these problems, not least the difficulty of defining what is the official or ruling law and what can be counted as oppositional culture. These problems are, however, the very meat and drink of cultural politics.

6.4 | Conclusion

An expanded notion of politics has led to an increasing interest in the role of culture in a world where conventional political boundaries are breaking down. This chapter has shown the importance of culture in the politics of identity, social organisation, architecture and literary texts as well as in formal politics. The politics of nations, states and governments are conducted on a terrain that is created and circumscribed through culture. Apparently small things like dress, language and the organisation of an office can be the site of meaning where important battles are fought out. One instance that we have emphasised as an example of the politics of identity is that of gender. In conventional politics, bureaucracy, struggles over issues of consumption (in the case of women's protests in supermarkets in Chile) and battles over the right of the silenced to be heard (in the case of *Las Madres* in Argentina), gender plays a vital role. The danger with such an approach is that it is used to argue that everything is politics, or, following the introduction, that everything is about power. We hope that the examples in this chapter show that cultural politics is not just about expanding the notion of politics to include culture, but about making that notion more sophisticated, and showing that formal politics also has an important cultural dimension. While this is sometimes a case of demonstrating that areas like the personal are indeed political, it is also about showing that dialogues, debates, disputes and outright conflict cannot be easily categorised in terms of two rational positions. The case of *The Satanic Verses* shows that one political 'message' can be transformed and made illegitimate when it is taken out of its cultural context. Representation and performance are very much of the moment. What in one time and place is a subversive (even revolutionary) politics can, when used in a new context, become precisely the opposite. An efficient and productive form of social organisation in one sphere can become a means of mass destruction in another. Buildings that were designed to turn slums into an urban utopia can come to signify the worst aspects of social decay and deprivation. Symbols that announce peace in one society can mean hatred and war in another. This is why notions of resistance and transgression, while essential to our understanding of the relationship between culture and power, are slippery at best. During the carnival you do not know who is wearing what mask.

Re-cap

- Both formal and informal politics are conducted to some extent through culture.
- An important site of contestation in cultural politics is around questions of identity.
- Cultural politics describes a shifting, transient arena in which meanings are constantly in dispute.

Further reading

For a general discussion of the field of cultural politics which deals with class, race and gender, see Glenn Jordan and Chris Weedon, *Cultural Politics: Class, Gender, Race and the Postmodern World* (1994). The specific themes of performance and identity politics in relation to race, gender and sexuality are taken further in bell hooks, *Yearning: Race, Gender and Cultural Politics* (1991) and Alan Sinfield, *Cultural Politics, Queer Reading* (1994). For the culture of bureaucracies a good starting point is Mike Savage and Anne Witz, *Gender and Bureaucracy* (1992) and the cultural politics of monuments are introduced in terms of gender, and with lots of good examples, in Marina Warner, *Monuments and Maidens: The Allegory of the Female Form* (1985). The debates over transgression and resistance are well covered by Peter Stallybrass and Allon White, *The Politics and Poetics of Transgression* (1986).

Cultured bodies

chapter

7

7.0 | Introduction

Cultural studies takes seriously the notion that the human body is a cultural object. Initially, this may strike us as absurd. After all, our bodies are most decidedly a part of nature, subject to natural processes such as growth and decay, hunger and illness and so forth, all of which daily remind us of our connection to a realm outside culture and society. This chapter will examine the idea that while the human body consists of an indisputable natural substratum, its appearance, condition and activity are culturally shaped. We do not have to look far for illustration of this fundamental theme.

In the film *Big* (dir. Penny Marshall, 1988) Tom Hanks plays the part of a 13-year-old boy who is granted his wish to become – overnight – an adult. Much of the humour of the film turns around the amusing consequences of a 'grown man' behaving like an 'adolescent'. Although he has the body of an adult, he still has many childish expressions, interests and attitudes. When he brings a girlfriend back to his apartment, instead of the expected seduction scene he coaxes her into joining him in treating beds as trampolines. His tastes and desires, his ways of moving and talking, his concerns and skills, his thoughts and feelings are all incongruous with the grown man's body he now inhabits. (And ironically it is because this grown-up has such a childish imagination that he is able to find well-paid work as an adviser to a toy manufacturing company.) The film clearly shows the close tie of our notions of personhood with our bodies. Who and what we are taken to be is very much bound up with the appearance and movements of our body. In possessing a body of a given age and gender we are culturally expected to be a certain kind of person, and it can be a source of considerable surprise, annoyance or amusement when these expectations are breached.

Just as the human body has become a compelling focus of popular concern in contemporary Western societies – as is witnessed by the mass media's preoccupations with sex, sport, stars and diet – so too have cultural studies come to take increasing interest in the body as a key site for the playing out of social and cultural difference. As nicely summed up by Arthur Frank, 'bodies are in, in academia as well as popular culture' (1990: 131). Among the reasons for this upsurge of academic interest in the body have been the influence of the work of Michel Foucault, the enormous impact

267

of feminism on a range of academic disciplines, and the growth of consumer culture especially since the end of the Second World War. Foucault drew attention to the practices, discourses and technologies through which power is imprinted or 'inscribed' on the human body. A variety of feminisms have suggested that the starting point for analysis and test of theoretical adequacy is to be located in the specificity of women's embodied experiences. Finally consumer culture has accelerated the commodification of the human body, creating ever more finely graded status hierarchies based around the costuming and display of embodied **difference** (p. 138).

Six broad aspects of the cultural shaping of human bodies are charted in this chapter. It begins with a consideration of the *social construction* of human corporeality which is followed by a review of a notion fundamental to a fully cultural understanding of the body, Mauss's concept of *body techniques*. Next, the chapter examines the cultural *regulation* of the human body, with particular reference to the works of Elias and Foucault to show how cultural values are 'inscribed' onto the body. The chapter then reviews some issues of *representation*, considering how embodied states are depicted with particular reference to fashion, femininity and masculinity. The following section considers some aspects of the body as *a medium of expression and transgression* – a vehicle for the realisation of personal preferences, some of which may run against widely held cultural standards. The last section of the chapter examines developments in technoculture around the *figure of the cyborg* which is widely believed to presage the end of the human body as we know it.

Learning objectives

▦ To appreciate the respects in which the human body is socially constructed.

▦ To understand the cultural shaping of body techniques.

▦ To learn how forms of power are 'inscribed' on the human body and how the body is 'civilised' by cultural codes.

▦ To understand the place of the body in the construction of femininity and masculinity.

▦ To grasp the varying ways in which the body is a medium of cultural expression and a key site for transgressing cultural beliefs.

▦ To perceive the potential of new technologies to challenge conventional beliefs about the coherence of the human body.

7.1 | The social construction of corporeality

The most general feature of the studies examined in this chapter is that they adopt a *constructionist* approach to the human body, that is they identify a range of social and cultural influences that shape its appearance and activity. A constructionist approach, as we shall see, can take many forms but what each of these varieties have in common is an opposition to simplified **essentialist** (p. 138) explanations, i.e. explanations of bodily appearance and activity that assign sole or major significance to biological factors (such as the gender or ethnic categorisation of the person).

Discussions of the human body in cultural studies often also refer to the related terms 'mind' and 'self'. What are the differences and relations between these notions? A place to begin is the material human body as evolutionary biology might consider it. It is now widely accepted that *homo sapiens* emerged from a long process of evolution. The precise point when recognisably modern humans appeared is still a matter of dispute among specialists, although it does seem that they were present in Europe by 35,000 years ago. At least five specific features of the bodies of humans can be identified that distinguish the species and frame the range and kinds of activity in which humans can engage:

1. *The capacity for binocular vision.* Certain aspects of how we interact with the world arise from humans' capacity for vision. Most social encounters begin with an assessment, however fleeting, of the appearance of the other. Consequently blind persons experience very obvious handicaps in their interaction with others. Most generally vision serves as the coordinator of the senses: an awareness of our body in its own right is crucially tied to vision, to our capacity to scan and thus monitor many areas of our own bodies.

2. *The audio-vocal system.* The throat, mouth and ears are coordinated with the brain and the central nervous system to enable us to speak. The use of language is our fundamental symbolic capacity (see Chapter 2).

3. *Bipedalism.* We walk upright. Even in the West's automobile-dominated culture, walking remains the basic way of moving around in our world. Bipedalism also enhances the way that our vision works.

4. *Hands.* The fingers and opposing thumb of the human hand permit the manipulation of objects in a precise and careful way. Tool use involves complex bodily coordination focused around the skilled use of the hands. The physical environment is more malleable to the will of humans, as tool-using creatures. This capacity is thought to have contributed to the development of sociality by providing a basis for cooperation arising from the need to coordinate tool-using activities.

5. *Expressive capacity.* Humans have a capacity for greater gestural complexity than other primates. The faces of humans, for example, can express a wide range of emotions and some embodied gestures, notably laughter, appear to be unique to humans.

These species-specific capacities can be mobilised by all healthy adult humans, irrespective of time or place. The distinctive take of cultural studies is to approach the body as an acculturated state that varies across cultures and through history. Thus, cultural studies emphasises that the body is not merely a material entity, biological datum or physiological fact but is, in a real and significant sense, a social construction.

Mind is the capacity for reasoned thought and reflection, carried out by the brain but not reducible to it. At least since Descartes' famous dictum 'I think therefore I am', a radical split between body and mind has been widely accepted. The mind is regarded as dwelling in a human body but remains somehow distinct from it. Direct access to the mind is believed to be only possible from within, via introspection. A number of further contrasts are predicated around this fundamental dualism:

mind	body
private	public
inner	outer
culture	nature
reason	passion

This schema gives prominence to mind in defining the person. The body is seen, at best, as the mind's vehicle and, at worst, as driven by desires and appetites which need the mind's restraining influence, guidance and command. However, dualism of this kind generates difficulties. Chief among these is the classic philosophical problem of how it is possible to know other minds (e.g. how can we defensibly know that, for example, 'Susan seemed bored by the whole occasion'?). Plainly, we readily do have knowledge of other people's states of mind in everyday life, so there must be something misleading about the dualist account. Body and mind are better conceived as interdependent, not separate. Jeff Coulter (1979) has noted that 'transparency of mind' (i.e. our ordinary ability to figure out mental states, such as Susan's boredom) is closely dependent upon people's mundane social competence in making sense of talk and human expressions. These are embodied and deeply cultural capacities.

If mind is the rational faculty, the capacity for thought and reflection, then *self* (or self-identity) refers to who and what the person is in social terms. According to the philosopher and social psychologist George Herbert Mead (1934), the distinctive quality of the self is that it can be an object to itself: as selves, we can reflect upon what we have done, contemplate alternative scenarios and choose between alternative lines of action. According to Mead:

> We can distinguish very definitely between the self and the body. The self has the characteristic that it can be an object to itself, and that characteristic distinguishes it from other objects and from the body. It is perfectly true that the eye can see the foot, but it does not see the body as a whole. We cannot see our backs; we can feel certain portions of them, if we are agile, but we cannot get an experience of our whole body.
>
> (Mead, 1934: 136)

Sociologists like Goffman have proposed that any person has a 'multiplicity of selves', some relatively enduring, like those premised on occupational roles (e.g. a shop assistant self), while others may be fleeting, as when we tease a friend about her dress sense (e.g. a teasing self).

For constructionism, it is important to understand that the human body straddles the realms of nature and culture. The functioning of the material body is governed by natural processes but its activity in the world is inescapably framed by social and cultural factors. Consider the pervasive significance of age and gender in the treatment of human bodies (already touched upon above in the filmic example of *Big*). Except for transsexuals, the assignment of 'male' or 'female' is a categorisation that is exhaustive of the population and lifelong in duration. The engendering of bodies – the attribution of culturally conventional correlates of sex to produce the qualities recognised as 'masculinity' and 'femininity' – begins almost immediately as what arrives in the world as a dimorphically classifiable organism is rapidly transformed into such eminently social constructions as a 'little boy' or 'little girl'. Age is, in many societies, no less significant. At every conventionally recognised stage of the life course there are expected forms of behaviour and culturally defined and approved experiences. Shakespeare gave canonical form to this idea with his notion of the 'seven ages of man' (Jacques' speech in *As You Like It*, II. vii. 135ff.). Gender, usually in tandem with age, provide two of the deepest determinants of the cultural shaping of the human body.

The example of the film *Big* also helps to illustrate a fundamental duality about the human body: we *have* bodies and we also *are* bodies (cf. Berger and Luckmann, 1966). We 'have' bodies whose material 'needs' (for food and drink, rest and shelter) must be met. The health of our bodies is a frequent source of concern to us as, too, is their shape and appearance. But we also 'are' bodies in the sense that our bodies are vehicles of our existence as individuals. Our being in the world, our agency as humans is grounded in our embodied state and we know that our eventual fate is to age and die.

A parallel distinction is between the body as an object and as a subject. Depending upon the point of view from which it is approached, my body is an object that others can categorise and which I can own or possess (according to Simmel (1950: 322), the body is my 'first "property"'), or it can be seen as a subject, the physical embodiment of a self or seat of subjectivity (the 'I' writing these words is the embodied human with very modest keyboard skills in his hands and an aching neck sitting in front of a PC). In cultural studies this contrast has led some theorists to argue for a distinction between 'the body' and 'embodiment' – between the objectified bodies we have and the embodied beings we are (Hayles, 1992; Turner, 1992). In this chapter some studies (e.g. Foucault, Elias) tend to emphasise external constraints on the body, while others (e.g. Theweleit, Wacquant) tend to stress the experiential dimensions of embodiment (although, as we shall see, there are often intricate relations between the two).

7.2 | Techniques of the body: embodied instrumentalities

Very obviously, the body is the means or instrument for carrying out all the practical actions through which persons engage the world. Accordingly, the notion of body techniques (or 'techniques of the body') is a pivotal concept.

7.2.1 | Mauss on body techniques

In a 1934 lecture the French anthropologist Marcel Mauss (1872–1950) devised the concept of 'body techniques' to describe 'the ways in which from society to society men [sic] know how to use their bodies' (Mauss, 1979: 97). There is no 'natural' form to bodily actions, no pan-human, precultural, universal or inherent shape to actions such as walking, swimming, spitting, digging, marching, even staring or giving birth (see Box 7.1). Rather, bodily actions are historically and culturally variable, acquired attributes that speak to culturally specific memberships. According to Mauss, the human body is our 'first and most natural instrument ... [our] first and most natural ... technical

Box **7.1**

Checklist: Mauss's budget of body techniques

1. *Techniques of birth and obstetrics*
   (a) positions for giving birth
   (b) care of the mother and infant
2. *Techniques of infancy*
   (a) rearing and feeding the child
   (b) weaning
   (c) the weaned child
3. *Techniques of adolescence*
   (a) initiation rituals
4. *Techniques of adult life*
   (a) techniques of sleep
   (b) waking: techniques of rest
   (c) techniques of activity, of movement:
       (i)   walking
       (ii)   running
       (iii) dancing
       (iv)   jumping
       (v)   climbing
       (vi)   descent
       (vii) swimming
       (viii) pushing, pulling, lifting
   (d) techniques of care of the body:
       (i)   rubbing, washing, soaping
       (ii)   care of the mouth
       (iii) hygiene in the needs of nature
   (e) consumption techniques:
       (i)   eating
       (ii)   drinking
   (f) sexual techniques

Based on Mauss's 'biographical list of body techniques' (1979)

means'. When we engage the material world, for example when we drink, we employ 'a series of assembled actions, [which are] assembled for the individual not by himself alone but by all his education, by the whole society to which he belongs, in the place he occupies in it' (Mauss, 1979: 104, 105). Sometimes the individual's society may not provide the relevant technique. Mauss tells how he taught a little girl with bronchial problems in a remote part of France how to spit. At four *sous* per spit, she proved to be an adept learner!

Having established the cultural shaping of body techniques, Mauss then goes on to identify topics worth further investigation. Among these are gender and age differences, the effects of training, and the transmission and acquisition of these techniques. Body techniques vary quite conspicuously according to gender and age. For example, women deliver weak punches (at least they tended to in the France of Mauss's day!) in part because they usually clasp their thumbs inside their fingers; women throw differently from men (see Young, 1980, below); children can squat with ease while most adult Westerners cannot. Body techniques can also be more efficiently executed as a result of training or cultivation: dexterity as a trained accomplishment is a key notion here. Finally Mauss argues for close observation of socialisation practices in order to learn more about how these techniques are acquired. For example, we cannot understand why the pious Muslim will only eat food using the right hand by referring to physiology or the psychology of motor asymmetry. Close study of how such techniques are transmitted to children is required (in many if not most cases, Mauss surmises, oral instruction will be involved).

7.2.2 | Feminine motility: 'Throwing like a girl'

The notion of body techniques is designed to bring some order to a large collection of Mauss's miscellaneous observations about human actions and has thus helped to legitimate an area of inquiry. However, Mauss himself never went beyond his personal observations as anthropologist, sportsman and soldier. What, more concretely, might a more systematic analysis of techniques of the body include? As an illustration of what is involved, we can consider Iris Marion Young's 1980 paper 'Throwing like a girl' (see also Crossley, 1995). Though not explicitly mentioned (the theoretical basis of Young's study is the phenomenology of Merleau-Ponty and the feminism of de Beauvoir), her analysis usefully illuminates Mauss's thinking about body techniques. Young is interested in those gender differences in bodily existence and movement described in the vernacular as throwing like a girl (the selection of the term 'girl' is intendedly ironic), running like a girl, climbing like a girl, hitting like a girl and so forth. She focuses on ordinary purposive action and deliberately excludes expressly sexual uses of the body and also non-task-oriented activity, such as dance. Young picks out features of feminine existence that she sees as produced by the structures and conditions that women face in a particular society, not some mysterious quality assigned to all biological females everywhere. Consequently, there will be exceptions to the patterns that she identifies. This does not invalidate her analysis; rather, it is to be expected that some women will manage to escape or transcend the typical conditions that women face in any society.

Young identifies differences in Western industrial societies in how women 'hold' themselves (comportment), their manner of moving (motility) and their relation to space (spatiality) which are more limited and circumscribed than the corresponding behaviours of men. Beginning with how girls throw differently from boys, she writes:

> ... girls do not bring their whole bodies into the motion as much as the boys. They do not reach back, twist, move backward, step and lean forward. Rather the girls tend to remain relatively immobile except for their arms, and even the arm is not extended as far as it could be.   (Young, 1980: 142)

Feminine comportment and movement is characteristically marked by a failure to use the body's full potential range of motion. Some examples:

> Women are generally not as open with their bodies as men in their gait and stride. Typically, the masculine stride is longer proportional to a man's body than is the feminine stride to a woman's. The man typically swings his arms in a more open and loose fashion than does a woman and typically has more up and down rhythm in his step. Though we now wear pants more than we used to, and consequently do not have to restrict our sitting postures because of dress, women still tend to sit with their legs relatively close together and their arms across their bodies. When simply standing or leaning, men tend to keep their feet further apart than do women, and we also tend more to keep our hands and arms touching or shielding our bodies. A final indicative difference is the way each carries books or parcels; girls and women most often carry books embraced to their chests, while boys and men swing them along their sides.
> (Young, 1980: 142)

Many of the differences between men and women in the performance of tasks such as lifting and carrying heavy things are not due to simple strength variations. Women often lack ready technique and easeful engagement with such physical tasks which comes quite readily to many men. Women will often lift things using their arms and shoulders rather than also bringing the power of their legs to the task. Young portrays these limits on feminine motility as an 'inhibited intentionality' (1980: 145) and draws on the ideas of the phenomenologist Maurice Merleau-Ponty, who maintains that the primary locus of human being in the world is not mind or consciousness but rather the body orienting itself to its surroundings. Through approaching, grasping and appropriating these surroundings the body realises its intentions. But currently dominant forms of feminine motility serve to restrict and inhibit the realisation of women's intentionality.

The origins of these characteristic features of feminine comportment and movement are not innate; they flow from women's situation in a sexist, patriarchal society. In such a society women are 'physically handicapped', according to Young: 'as lived bodies we are not open and unambiguous transcendences which move out to master a world that belongs to us, a world constituted by our own intentions and projections' (1980: 152). This embodied dimension of women's subordination is rooted in the way in which women live and experience their bodies as not simply subjects, vehicles of their own intentionality, but also as an object to be gazed on simply as a mere body, the object of an objectifying regard that is appraised only in terms of its appearance. What Young's study brings to light is taken-for-granted aspects of the engendering of body techniques in modern societies. Does it matter that women cannot throw? Young says yes. A lack of confidence about bodily capacities may infuse other areas of women's lives, becoming manifest, for example, as doubts about intellectual or managerial capability. But if feminine comportment and movement are culturally shaped, then they are also open to cultural transformation: there is nothing ingrained in the 'nature' of women that decrees that they must always throw like girls.

7.2.3 | Body idiom and body gloss

In emphasising the cultural basis of embodied action, Mauss's notion of body techniques tends to look to the biographical and historical origins of these techniques. Indirectly Young extends Mauss's concept (she does not expressly refer to it) in showing some important gender differences in the lived experience of how men and women carry themselves and move. But how are body techniques enacted in the actual situations of everyday life? Here the sociology of Erving Goffman (1922–82) can help us to appreciate how body techniques feature in ordinary interaction (see Crossley, 1995).

Goffman proposes that a special set of cultural understandings obtains whenever people are in the physical presence of each other. In situations of co-presence (social encounters), such as when we are engaged in a conversation with a friend or are travelling on public transport, we have a pressing practical need to acquire information about others, about their status and identity, mood and orientation towards us and so forth. Some of this information is given verbally by what people say to us, but other information is 'given off' or exuded by non-verbal conduct: their facial expressions, the stance they adopt, the disposition of their limbs, the tone of their speech. The cultural meanings associated with these gestures is not so much a language (the popular phrase 'non-verbal language' is at best a metaphorical usage) as an idiom: a standardised mode of expression. Hence the concept 'body idiom', which describes 'dress, bearing, movements and position, sound level, physical gestures such as waving or saluting, facial gestures and broad emotional expressions' (Goffman, 1963a: 33). There is no time out from body idiom in any social encounter, for although 'an individual can stop talking, he cannot stop communicating through body idiom; he must say either the right thing or the wrong thing. He cannot say nothing' (Goffman, 1963a: 35). Some elements of body idiom can be employed by the person to provide a gloss or explanation or critical comment on an untoward feature of the immediate social situation. Waiting on a street to meet someone, the person may scan the surrounds or glance ostentatiously at a wristwatch in order to graphically display an innocent intent to passers-by. A pedestrian on a crossing may shake a head or wag a finger at a motorist who has only just managed to stop. These acts of 'body gloss' (Goffman, 1971: 125) are identified as gestures that broadcast to anyone who cares to witness them our attitude towards some real or potentially threatening act. In another influential study Goffman (1963b) investigated the vicissitudes facing those who have some physical attribute or handicap (anything from a nervous tic to paraplegia to a visible ethnic identity) which acts as a 'stigma', that is, which disqualifies persons from full social acceptance in their encounters with others. Our gender is also marked in face-to-face conduct. Goffman (1979) analysed features of 'gender displays', the culturally conventional expressions of sex-class membership that are ordinarily available to us 'at a glance'. Gender displays are the taken-for-granted ways of conducting ourselves in the presence of others; 'sitting' in a feminine way or 'taking charge' in a manner that bespeaks of 'masculinity'. These gender displays are social constructions, i.e. not innate but rather the product of the acquisition of cultural knowledge and skills. In Goffman's perspective, then, the human body is the prime instrument of face-to-face interaction, an expressive entity capable of complex and nuanced communicative activity. Although the body was never a major analytic focus of Goffman's inquiries, his studies have proved a rich resource for constructionist analyses of embodiment.

As an illustration of this potential, consider how Goffman's focus on the specifics of interaction can serve to develop Mauss's notion of body techniques (Crossley, 1995). Take the example of walking. Mauss (1979: 100, 102) recognises that different groups acculturate a characteristic gait and posture in their members. He mentions the loose-jointed, hip-rolling *onioi* gait of Maori women, notes how as a small boy he was schooled to walk with his hands closed not open, and offers some plausible speculations about the impact of American cinema on French women's style of walking in the early 1930s. Goffman takes this constructionist stance as his starting point for investigating how walking figures in face-to-face situations, such as making one's way down a busy city street (see Box 7.2) or shopping mall. He shows how walking involves a range of cultural understandings about types of persons who may have to be managed or avoided (beggars, market researchers, pamphleteers), those to whom special care must be exercised (the frail, persons with white canes or guide dogs, toddlers), those who can be turned to for reliable directions (traffic wardens, police), those who want us to stop and listen and watch (buskers, mime artists), those who look likely to threaten our persons and property. In walking down a street we must constantly monitor our own bodies and those of others in order to avoid collisions – less complicated when we are a 'single' (i.e. a solitary walker) than if we are a 'with' (accompanied by others with whom we must coordinate our progress). This involves scanning upcoming pedestrians but doing so in an unobtrusive and non-threatening way (Goffman calls this the norm of 'civil inattention' (see section 9.7.2), the cardinal rule making for orderliness in public places). These skilled, embodied actions (and many others detailed in Goffman, 1963a and 1971) are body techniques at the micro level of everyday social interaction.

Goffman's conceptual apparatus thus provides the basis for an analysis of the *exercise* or *performance* of body techniques. In addition, it shows how a rigid mind–body dualism cannot be sustained since mind (e.g. the mundane practical intelligence required to get down the street without mishap) is implicated in interactional conduct that is unavoidably mediated through the human body. In examining the exercise of body techniques we can come to see that mind and self are not ghosts in the machine of the body, resident in the upper portion of the skull, which somehow lie 'behind' action. Rather, mind and self are better understood as encoded in the ordinary enactment of body techniques.

7.3 | Culture as control: the regulation and restraint of human bodies

One of the simplest ways to conceive of culture's impact on the body is to consider the early socialisation of infants and small children. In the West a primary concern of adult

Box 7.2
Marshall Berman: the modern city and the embodied experience of the pedestrian

In the middle of the nineteenth century Baron Haussmann's reconstruction of the centre of Paris created new wide boulevards which attracted a big increase in pedestrian and vehicular traffic. Berman draws on the observations of the poet Charles Baudelaire to describe the change in the pace of life that ensued:

> the life of the boulevards, more radiant and exciting than urban life had ever been, was also more risky and frightening for the multitudes of men and women who moved on foot.
>
> This, then, was the setting for Baudelaire's primal modern scene: 'I was crossing the boulevard, in a great hurry, in the midst of a moving chaos, with death galloping at me from every side.' The archetypal modern man, as we see him here, is a pedestrian thrown into the maelstrom of modern city traffic, a man alone contending against an agglomeration of mass and energy that is heavy, fast and lethal. The burgeoning street and boulevard traffic knows no spatial or temporal bounds, spills over into every urban space, imposes its tempo on everybody's time, transforms the whole modern environment into a 'moving chaos'. The chaos here lies not in the movers themselves – the individual walkers or drivers, each of whom may be pursuing the most efficient route for himself – but in their interaction, in the totality of their movements in a common space. This makes the boulevard a perfect symbol of capitalism's inner contradictions: rationality in each individual capitalist unit, leading to anarchic irrationality in the social system that brings all these units together.
>
> The man in the modern street, thrown into this maelstrom, is driven back to his own resources – often on resources he never knew he had – and forced to stretch them desperately in order to survive. In order to cross the moving chaos, he must attune and adapt himself to its moves, must learn to not merely keep up with it but to stay at least one step ahead. He must become adept at *soubresauts* [jolting movements] and *mouvements brusques* [sudden moves], at sudden, abrupt, jagged twists and shifts – and not only with his legs and his body, but with his mind and his sensibility as well.
>
> Baudelaire shows how modern city life forces these new moves on everyone; but he shows, too, how in doing this it also paradoxically enforces new modes of freedom. A man who knows how to move in and around and through the traffic can go anywhere, down any of the endless urban corridors where traffic itself is free to go. This mobility opens up a great wealth of new experiences and activities for the urban masses.

Berman (1983: 159–60)

carers is instilling such basic skills as the bodily management of eating, elimination and the expression of the emotions. But beyond childhood socialisation there continue to be a wide range of regulations and restraints on the bodies of persons, some set in law, others in custom and convention. Two of the most important analysts of culture's supervisory impact on the human body are **Michel Foucault** (1926–84) (p. 28) and Norbert Elias (1897–1990). Foucault shows how bodies are disciplined by power operating through discourses which are institutionalised (in modern society by bureaucratic organisations – hospitals, prisons, asylums – but also by more diffusely located forms, e.g. discourses about sexuality). Elias identifies a 'civilising process', a long historical transformation which is marked by significant changes in manners, in how people regard their own and others' embodied actions. This section will review their contributions to the understanding of the body and, with reference to the topic of diet, consider their utility.

7.3.1 | Power, discourse and the body: Foucault

Michel Foucault's singular intellectual project explores the shifting and contested relations between power, knowledge and the human body. Most generally Foucault attempts to produce historically grounded analyses ('genealogies') of the discourses that organise social arrangements and practices. By 'discourse' Foucault intended not simply a specialist language that described the world. He stressed that **discourse** (p. 30) was itself part of the broader phenomenon of **power** (p. 94) and thus deeply implicated in how social arrangements were formed as such. His most influential studies were of the discourses of punishment, madness, medicine and sexuality (Foucault 1973, 1975, 1977, 1984b).

Foucault (1977) draws a contrast between the *sovereign power* that rulers exercised over their subjects in medieval times and its gradual replacement in the modern period by *disciplinary power*. In a study of the development of the modern prison system, Foucault shows how those who contravened the monarch's law and wishes were often publicly punished by methods that directly assaulted the body of the wrongdoer (whipping, branding, the pillory, torture, dismemberment and execution). Foucault's *Discipline and Punish* opens with a gruesome account of the 1757 execution in Paris of Damiens the regicide, which graphically details the difficulties the executioner faces in exercising his craft. Before his life is extinguished, Damiens is burnt, dismembered, drawn and quartered. The spectacle of public punishment, Foucault argues, awesomely dramatises and reinforces the sovereign's authority and right to rule.

Since the eighteenth century this 'gloomy festival of punishment' (Foucault, 1977: 8) has given way to forms of imprisonment as the major method of punishing offenders. Foucault follows the description of the execution of Damiens with an extract from the rules governing inmate conduct in a Paris prison for young offenders. The rules tell how prisoners are expected to rise at a specified hour early in the morning and work nine hours each day. The rules specify that prisoners must rise, dress and make their beds between the first and second drum-roll every morning. They state how long religious instruction will take, when and where they may wash and receive their first ration of bread, how they will assemble before being allowed to eat dinner and so forth. What these illustrations portray are two very different penal styles. The body of the wrongdoer remains central, only that body is now incarcerated rather than mutilated and the 'souls' of 'docile bodies' become the focus of reform. The objective of punishment changes from displaying the dreadful consequences of contravening the sovereign's will to instilling discipline in the offender, ensuring that bodies and souls function in a

---

Box 7.3

Foucault: the body of the condemned

The disappearance of public execution marks therefore the decline of the spectacle; but it also marks a slackening of the hold on the body. In 1787, in an address to the Society for Promoting Political Enquiries, Benjamin Rush remarked: 'I can only hope that the time is not far away when gallows, pillory, scaffold, flogging and wheel will, in the history of punishment, be regarded as the marks of the barbarity of centuries and of countries and as proofs of the feeble influence of reason and religion over the human mind'. Indeed, sixty years later, Van Meenen, opening the second penitentiary congress, in Brussels, recalled the time of his childhood as of a past age: 'I have seen the ground strewn with wheels, gibbets, gallows, pillories; I have seen hideously stretched skeletons on wheels' (*Annales de la Charité*, 329, 30). Branding had been abolished in England (1834) and in France (1832); in 1820, England no longer dared to apply the full punishment reserved for traitors (Thistlewood was not quartered). Only flogging still remained in a number of penal systems (Russia, England, Prussia). But, generally speaking, punitive practices had become more reticent. One no longer touched the body, or at least as little as possible, and then only to reach something other than the body itself. It might be objected that imprisonment, confinement, forced labour, penal servitude, prohibition from entering certain areas, deportation – which have occupied so important a place in modern penal systems – are 'physical' penalties: unlike fines, for example, they directly affect the body. But the punishment–body relation is not the same as it was in the torture during public executions. The body now serves as an instrument or intermediary: if one intervenes upon it to prison it, or to make it work, it is in order to deprive the individuals of a liberty that is regarded both as a right and as property. The body, according to this penalty, is caught up in a system of constraints and privations, obligations and prohibitions. Physical pain, the pain of the body itself, is no longer the constituent element of the penalty. From being an art of unbearable sensations punishment has become an economy of suspended rights. If it is still necessary for the law to reach and manipulate the body of the convict, it will be at a distance, in the property way, according to strict rules, and with a much

→

'higher' aim. As a result of this new restraint, a whole army of technicians took over from the executioner, the immediate anatomist of pain: warder, doctors, chaplains, psychiatrists, psychologists, educationalists; by their very presence near the prisoner, they sing the praises that the law needs: they reassure it that the body and pain are not the ultimate objects of its punitive action. Today a doctor must watch over those condemned to death, right up to the last moment – thus juxtaposing himself as the agent to welfare, as the alleviator of pain, with the official whose task it is to end life. This is worth thinking about. When the moment of execution approaches, the patients are injected with tranquillizers. A utopia of judicial reticence: take away life, but prevent the patient from feeling it; deprive the prisoner of all rights, but do not inflict pain; impose penalties free of all pain. Recourse to psychopharmacology and to various physiological 'disconnectors', even if it is temporary, is a logical consequence of this 'non-corporal' penality.

The modern rituals of execution attest to this double process: the disappearance of the spectacle and the elimination of pain. The same movement has affected the various European legal systems, each at its own rate: the same death for all – the execution no longer bears the specific mark of the crime or the crime or the social status of the criminal; a death that lasts only a moment – no torture must be added to it in advance, no further actions performed upon the corpse; an execution that affects life rather than the body. There are no longer any of those long processes in which death was both retarded by calculated interruptions and multiplied by a series of successive attacks. There are no longer any of those combinations of tortures that were organized for the killing of regicides, or of the kind advocated, at the beginning of the eighteenth century, by the anonymous author of *Hanging not Punishment Enough* (1701), by which the condemned man would be broken on the wheel, then flogged until he fainted, then hung up with chains, then finally left to die slowly of hunger. There are no longer any of those executions in which the condemned man was dragged along on a hurdle (to prevent his head smashing against the cobble-stones), in which his belly was opened up, his entrails quickly ripped out, so that he had time to see them, with his own eyes, being thrown on the fire; in which he was finally decapitated and his body quartered. The reduction of these 'thousand deaths' to strict capital punishment defines a whole new morality concerning the act of punishing.

Foucault (1977: 9–11)

uniform and regular way in the interests of the smooth functioning of the prison. Thus the modern prison regulates its inmates by a regimen that precisely stipulates when eating and sleeping, work and instruction may take place. In this way standardised and uniform inmate conduct can be secured.

Foucault strongly opposed any simple theories of historical progress and emphasised instead the discontinuity, complexity and fragility of many historical changes. Thus he recognised that these developments in the treatment of offenders often proceeded unevenly in actual societies as struggles occurred around the attempt to supplant one form of domination with another. For example, the removal from public view of execution and other forms of punishment between 1760 and 1840 was not a single event in several European societies but is better understood, Foucault suggests, as a series of advances and retreats as governments reintroduced more punitive measures in times of social unrest. Moreover the treatment of offenders was also influenced by changes occurring outside the juridical system. Foucault emphasises the part played in this process by the emergence of the new sciences of criminology, modern medicine and psychiatry which sought to understand and control the human body by making it an object of knowledge. *Disciplinary power* had its basis in the knowledges and technologies produced by these new sciences. The modern prison and the juridical system it serves uses disciplinary power exercised through prison governors, probation officers, psychiatrists and the like.

The work of these officials involves examining and assessing people. They interview and observe, analyse and classify, write and file reports, all in the name of designing the most appropriate regimen of punishment and reform of the offender. At the back of such exercises of disciplinary power is the process of *normalisation*. The aim of examination and assessment is to determine the nature and extent of the offender's deviation from the norm and to devise the most efficacious means of remedying their criminal behaviour and restoring them to normal, conforming conduct. A further extension of disciplinary power is found in the new methods of *surveillance* incorporated in the design of prison buildings. The 'panopticon', a building designed by Jeremy Bentham, the nineteenth-century utilitarian philosopher, epitomised this new trend for Foucault (see Figure 7.2). The panopticon was a circular building constructed around a central axis that allowed the guards to observe prisoners while themselves remaining unobserved. The point of this design was to induce in inmates the belief that they were under constant surveillance, irrespective of whether this was always actually the case (see also section 9.4). The panopticon design influenced the construction of prisons built in Britain from the early nineteenth century but Foucault goes on to suggest that these processes can be generalised beyond the precincts of the prison.

Thus, the panopticon comes to stand as a metaphor for many leading features of modern society. Other bureaucratic organisations are also in the business of surveillance. The police and security companies patrol public places and oversee private property. Schools and colleges monitor the education and accreditation of the population. Public health authorities and social service agencies keep extensive records on citizens' uptake of services. Government revenue offices check whether we have paid our taxes. All these forms of surveillance have been powerfully aided by advances in computing and video technology. These technological advances have enlarged the opportunities for overseeing and controlling the conduct of individuals and extended the range, scope and ease with which personal information can be acquired.

Foucault's early work considers the relation of body to power and knowledge and focuses on techniques of domination. Thus in his study of the development of modern

PANOPTICON;

OR,

THE INSPECTION-HOUSE:

CONTAINING THE

IDEA OF A NEW PRINCIPLE OF CONSTRUCTION

APPLICABLE TO

ANY SORT OF ESTABLISHMENT, IN WHICH PERSONS OF ANY
DESCRIPTION ARE TO BE KEPT UNDER INSPECTION;

AND IN PARTICULAR TO

PENITENTIARY-HOUSES,

PRISONS,   POOR-HOUSES,   LAZARETTOS,
HOUSES OF INDUSTRY, MANUFACTORIES,   HOSPITALS,
WORK-HOUSES,   MAD-HOUSES,   AND SCHOOLS:

WITH

A PLAN OF MANAGEMENT

ADAPTED TO THE PRINCIPLE:

IN A SERIES OF LETTERS,

WRITTEN IN THE YEAR 1787, FROM CRECHEFF IN WHITE RUSSIA,
TO A FRIEND IN ENGLAND.

BY JEREMY BENTHAM,

OF LINCOLN'S INN, ESQUIRE.

DUBLIN, PRINTED: LONDON, REPRINTED; AND SOLD BY T. PAYNE,
AT THE MEWS GATE, 1791.

Figure 7.1 ■ Title page of Jeremy Bentham's *Panopticon* (1791).

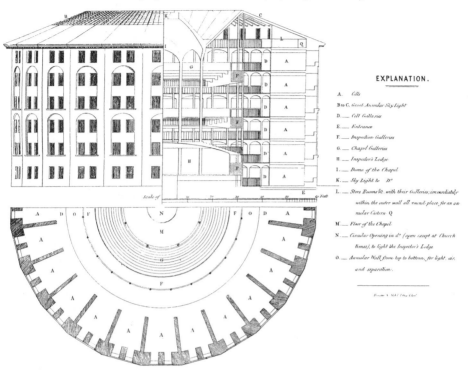

A General Idea of a PENITENTIARY PANOPTICON in an Improved, but as yet (Jan 23d 1791), Unfinished State.
See Postscript References to Plan, Elevation, & Section (being Plate referred to as N° 2).

Figure 7.2   Plan of the Panopticon. (Source: *The Works of Jeremy Bentham*, ed. Bowring, Vol. IV, 1843: 172–3.)

medicine Foucault (1973) showed how changes in medical technologies (the stethoscope, the microscope, laboratory testing) and in medical practices (the physical examination, the post-mortem), together with the development of disciplines such as anatomy, radiology and surgery and the institutionalisation of the hospital and the consulting room, served to subject the patient's body to unprecedented medical power. In this process the consultation with a physician came to resemble not so much a puzzle-solving encounter as a confessional in which the secrets of the body are revealed (Armstrong, 1983). In his later work on sexuality (Foucault, 1984b) there is a shift towards *techniques of the self* as Foucault became interested in how subjectivity is constituted through discourse. Techniques of the self are the ways that individuals can form and transform themselves by monitoring their bodies, souls, thoughts and conduct. This should not be seen as a piece of southern Californian lifestyle exported to the rest of the world! Foucault shows that a 'culture of self', an intense preoccupation of self with self, was a feature of a number of societies beginning with the early Greek states.

According to Foucault, **power** (p. 94) (or power/knowledge, as he sometimes terms it, to emphasise how each conditions and transforms the other) is not to be understood in conventional political senses as something to be 'held' by special groups, 'won' or 'exercised' over others – power is not simply about securing one's own will over that of others. Rather, power is dispersed in a society and works in capillary fashion through discourses. Wherever there is power there will be **resistance** (p. 258) to that power, often based in local or disqualified discourses. Further, Foucault argues that power should not be simply seen as essentially repressive in character. It can also be 'productive'.

A good example of the positive and productive conception of power is Foucault's discussion of 'bio-power'. This refers to disciplinary power over life as it affects both individual bodies and social bodies (entire populations). Sexual discourses are prime concerns for understanding the operation of bio-power for they connect both to conceptions of individuality and pleasure and to the management of populations (in the shape of birth statistics, contraceptive practices, sexually transmitted disease, longevity, and the community's general level of health). Unlike the Victorians, in the late twentieth century we are 'free' to talk about sex – more, compelled to talk about sex almost incessantly. Discourses about sexuality are produced by newspapers, magazines, film, health workers and so forth. In this way sexual discourses extend the hold of their power over our selves and bodies. Sexual discourses, internalised by the self, are no less effective than the more repressive orders and regimes that formerly imposed their demands on the self. When power is seen as dispersed through a multiplicity of discourses it becomes difficult to narrowly identify the operation of power with sectional interests. So sexual freedom cannot be identified with sexual indulgence – that would be to fall under the sway of a sexual discourse that recommends repression. For Foucault the self must come to see such discourses for what they are (often devices that extract guilt, confession, renunciation from the self and result in a loss of self) and attempt to reach an informed decision that strikes a balance between continence (encratics) and pleasure.

7.3.2 | Civilising the body: Elias

In *The Civilizing Process* (Elias, 1978) the German sociologist Norbert Elias analyses a long historical process through which people acquired the capacity to control the expression of their emotions and other embodied acts along increasingly circumscribed lines. What is now taken as 'proper' and 'civilised' behaviour is the outcome of a wide range of social processes which resulted in the redefinition of standards of propriety and repugnance (in the direction of greater refinement and polish). Accompanying these changes was a reconceptualisation of the nature of human nature, of what human beings were expected to be – especially as this was manifest in their embodied actions.

Drawing principally on books of manners such as the 1530 volume by Erasmus of Rotterdam, *On Civility in Children*, but also taking into account the evidence of literature, paintings and drawings, Elias constructs a history of the manners of the medieval upper classes in Europe. In a discussion rich in vivid historical illustration Elias charts the characteristics of acceptable conduct. Table manners involved eating with one's fingers or perhaps a spoon; forks did not appear in daily use until the sixteenth century. People served themselves from a common pot and used the tablecloth to wipe their greasy fingers (though not their noses!). The 'natural functions' were often carried out in the public company of others and spoken of without shame or embarrassment; Erasmus advises that 'It is impolite to greet someone who is urinating or defecating' (Elias, 1978: 130). It is only in later centuries that these become private matters sequestered from public view and incurring shame and repugnance. In medieval times people used their fingers to blow their noses. Handkerchiefs were only adopted in the seventeenth century by the upper classes. The habit of spitting was commonplace and the convention was to tread on the sputum. The spittoon came later (and persisted in many public places in Europe until the twentieth century).

Sharing beds in inns with persons of the same sex was commonplace. People were advised to be modest when undressing, to bow to their social superiors in the choice of the side of the bed to be slept in and when to go to bed, and to lie straight and still. It was common for people to sleep naked, but the bedroom did not then have the modern connotation of privacy and intimacy. The sight of naked humans, in bed or at public bath-houses, was an everyday occurrence. Correspondingly, Elias (1978: 177–8, 214) suggests that sexuality was marked by an absence of modern notions of shame and obscenity in the Middle Ages. One illustration of this is the custom (varying between classes and countries) of wedding guests undressing the bride and groom so that they could be 'laid together' on the marital bed (Elias also acknowledges that there was a good deal of sexual violence within marriage). Furthermore, medieval society was itself marked by much aggressiveness and cruelty to both humans and animals: 'Rapine, battle, hunting of men and animals ... for the mighty and strong these formed part of the pleasures of life' (Elias, 1978: 193). Medieval people were more volatile and fiercer when roused than is found to be acceptable in the twentieth century.

From the fifteenth century on, changes took place that brought manners increasingly in line with modern standards. Elias emphasises that he is not in the business of endorsing modern standards against the 'inadequate' customs of the past; indeed, the civilising process is a process with no beginning. How did the transformation come about? Not for material reasons: for example, the rich had special cutlery for Lent that was simply considered unnecessary at other times of the year. Nor did it come about because of greater concern for health and hygiene or respect for one's fellows and social superiors – these reasons, Elias demonstrates, were very much retrospective justifications for changes after they had occurred (see Mennell, 1989: 45–7). The key factor, for Elias, arises from changes in the composition of the upper class occurring in the late Middle Ages. A fundamentally warrior class became transformed into a court society. The new aristocracy came from diverse social backgrounds and were politically organised around the court. Thus the new upper-class courtiers found themselves in the close company of others in the court, others upon whom they were dependent for patronage, favour, advancement, etc. Living closely with such significant others made for 'stricter control of impulses and emotions ... first imposed by those of high social rank on their social inferiors or, at most, their social equals' (Elias, 1978: 137). But court society was highly competitive, so what was first imposed (e.g. Brunswick Court

Regulations of 1589 stated: 'Let no-one, whoever he may be ... foul the staircases, corridors, or closets with urine or other filth, but go to suitable, prescibed places for such relief' (Elias, 1978: 131)) soon became a matter of self-restraint. Over time there was an internal dynamic built around the *interdependencies* of court society that made for increasingly refined standards. These standards in turn spread downwards through the social structure as the socially striving bourgeoisie sought to emulate their superiors.

Elias (1982) went on to further situate these changes in a long process of state formation centring on a monopoly mechanism in which territorial expansion was linked to the concentration in single hands of the means of administration, taxation and violence. Elias offered a complex account of 'the historical development of human bodies' (Shilling, 1993: see esp. ch. 6) that for some commentators (e.g. Mennell, 1989) is more historically nuanced than Foucault's view. Some of these differences can be further illuminated through the comparison of two influential studies of eating, Turner's (1991) Foucauldian examination of the discourses that have arisen around the notion of a healthy diet and Mennell's (1991) Eliasian investigation of the civilising of the appetite for food and drink.

7.3.3 | Eating: a disciplined or a civilised cultural practice?

Eating and drinking are plainly learnt, culturally shaped activities, as observation of small children at mealtimes readily attests. The consumption of food and drink is also a generic cultural practice: 'Of everything which people have in common, the most common is that they must eat and drink' (Simmel, 1994). What we eat, how and how often are influenced more by cultural than biological factors. The contributions of a Foucauldian and an Eliasian approach to this cultural practice can be appreciated by comparing the studies of Turner (1991) and Mennell (1991) respectively.

The inscription of power on the body can be seen in the dietary advice directed at particular populations of a society. Foucault (1973, 1977) recognised the disciplining function of institutional diets in prisons, workhouses, armies and asylums. Popular literature on dietary advice has a long history. Around the early eighteenth century, advice on 'diaetetick management' became fashionable among the professional and upper classes in Britain seeking to sustain good health. A key figure in the promotion of this discourse was George Cheyne, a Scottish physician who wrote several books recommending the psychological and physical benefits of regular sleep, moderate exercise, temperance and a diet high in milk and vegetables. Cheyne conceived the human body in mechanistic terms as a fluid-filled hydraulic system and combined his medically based advice with Christian principles in sufficiently forthright a manner as to attract the endorsement of the influential founder of Methodism, John Wesley. For Cheyne, according to Turner:

> Lack of exercise, a surplus of food, intoxicating drinks and urban life-styles were particularly threatening to the health standards of the upper classes, especially among 'the Rich, the Lazy, the Luxurious, and the Unactive' [Cheyne 1733]. The availability and abundance of strong drinks among the elite enraged their passions to 'Quarrels, Murder, and Blasphemy' [Cheyne 1724]. Changes in eating habits and fashions in

cuisine stimulated the appetites of the upper classes in ways which were contrary to nature and which interfered with the natural process of digestion. ... Cheyne [1733] lamented that 'When Mankind was simple, plain, honest and frugal, there were few or no diseases. Temperance, Exercise, Hunting, Labour and Industry kept the Juices Sweet and the Solids brac'd.'   (Turner 1991: 162)

This discourse was not relevant to the working classes who in the eighteenth century still encountered starvation periodically. Only with the establishment of capitalism in the nineteenth century did a distinct dietary discourse targeted at the labouring classes emerge. This was a discourse founded on scientific principles of modern dietetics. It sought to establish the minimum amount of protein and calories necessary to sustain the physical efficiency of the working body, which was essential for the productivity of capitalist enterprises. Thus, thermodynamic images of the human body replace the earlier hydraulic portraits. Unlike the eighteenth-century discourse it was bereft of religious justifications. However, moral connotations still figured in the new discourse. Rowntree in his famous survey of York in 1899 found that the working class was underfed and that the artisan class could only manage to meet his minimum nutritional standards provided there was no 'wasteful expenditure on drink'. So sobriety was justified not in divine terms but by the demands of the prudent housekeeping needed to sustain physical efficiency. In the late twentieth century dietetic discourses have become secularised. But moral elements have not disappeared, as is evidenced by the endorsement of very particular conceptions of the body's shape and appearance in discourses surrounding contemporary fitness enthusiasms (step classes, fitness videos, running, bodysculpture and the like (see section 7.5.4 below)).

Medical and scientific discourses on diet, however, represent but one set of constraints on the appetite. According to Mennell medical discourses 'are only small parts of the complex history of appetite and its control in European society' (1991: 127). To begin with, appetite is not quite the same as hunger. Hunger is physiological, a bodily grounded drive, while appetite is psychological, an inclination and desire to eat that is itself culturally shaped. Accepted present-day standards of eating – what we eat, how quickly food is consumed, when we eat – involve a considerable degree of self-control. In medieval Europe rather different patterns of eating obtained. The popular conception of the banquet was a predominantly upper-class phenomenon but variants were to be found throughout society. Even among the aristocracy, however, such indulgent events were interspersed by significant spells of frugal living. In the Middle Ages an oscillating pattern of fasting and feasting was widespread. This pattern parallels Elias's description of medieval people as emotionally more volatile than moderns, as more likely to fluctuate between extremes in the expression of their feelings. Changes in eating patterns thus reflect the civilising process writ small.

The fasting/feasting pattern arose from pervasive uncertainties about food supply. Famines were regular occurrences in the Middle Ages, as were fires, epidemics, wars and vagrancy, and the interacting effects of these led to recurrent 'steeples' of mortality which often cut across social class differences. Food scarcity was a real threat until well into the eighteenth century. The perception of the threat of food scarcity, especially by the lower levels of society, persisted through to the nineteenth century. Fasting was required of the medieval good Catholic by the Church on at least three days a week and, although it did not involve total abstinence, it was expected that people would eat only a small simple meal, usually in the evening. Sumptuary laws, which specified what could be eaten by particular categories of person as well as what they could wear, were promulgated in the late Middle Ages, partly in order to restrict conspicuous consumption. Medical opinion, which tended to recommend moderation in eating, was another source of external constraint on people's desires to indulge their appetites.

The fasting/feasting pattern eventually gave way to a modern self-controlled pattern from the eighteenth century on. 'The civilizing of appetite' says Mennell (1991: 141) was linked to 'the increasing security, regularity, reliability and variety of food supplies' that accompanied the commercialisation and industrialisation of European society. The extension of trade, the growth of the economy, divisions of labour and processes of state formation all contributed to the abolition of endemic food scarcity in Europe. Feasting involving the conspicuous consumption of large quantities of food became less of a status symbol and in its place the qualitative possibilities opened by the developing gastronomic arts helped to instil a new spirit of moderation. The old distinctions between foodstuffs consumed at banquets and those suitable for everyday eating disappeared; and the fare of the wealthy increasingly resembled the food eaten by ordinary members of society. The growing interdependence characteristic of modern societies has contributed to a levelling out of the kinds of foods eaten by the different classes and thus to an extension of the self-controls over appetite. In addition, Mennell argues that obesity and anorexia nervosa are best understood as disturbances in the normal patterns of self-control over appetite expected in prosperous Western societies (anorexia in particular seems to be largely confined to modern societies where the supply of foodstuffs is not at issue). The historical shaping and constraint of the appetite

Defining concept **7.1**

Ritual and symbolism

We live, in Victor Turner's (1967) celebrated phrase, in 'a forest of symbols'. Objects in our environment – things, people, activities – make sense to us in terms of their meanings. We act toward objects on the basis of the meanings that these objects have for us. These meanings are conventional, learned as part of socialisation (the process of acquiring cultural knowledge and competence) and, importantly, these meanings are shared. In some versions of semiotics, the favoured method in cultural studies for interpreting meanings, it is suggested that a distinction can be made between signs and symbols. The relationship of a sign to what it signifies is that of a part to a whole (i.e. is *metonymic*) as the word 'apple' is to a certain kind of fruit. The relationship of a symbol to what it stands for is an arbitrary similarity (i.e. is *metaphoric*), as the apple proffered by Eve in the Garden of Eden symbolises 'worldly knowledge'.

The sharing of symbols (wearing your team's colours on the way to a match) breeds

→

social solidarity – a sense of belonging to a group, and confirms social identity – a sense of who and what you are (a Blackburn Rovers supporter). **Symbolism** (p. 288) has been examined in cultural studies in a variety of ways, perhaps most memorably with respect to youth subcultures. Since the 1950s a succession of youth subcultures have used diverse symbols – long hair, cropped hair, quiffed hair, spiky hair, beads, safety pins, all kinds of thoroughly distinctive clothing styles – to convey their distance from conventional society and thereby to challenge its **hegemony** (p. 106) (Hebdige, 1979). Often the symbolism involves *bricoleur* logic: something intelligible in one context is recontextualised in another, as in the Ted's appropriation of the Edwardian gentleman's jacket ('drapes'). Sometimes homological relation can be discerned between different elements of a subculture's chosen symbols. Willis (1978) suggests a homology between motorbike boys' fascination for the speed and hardness of the motorcycle and their liking for late 1950s rock 'n' roll.

Rituals involve a standardised sequence of acts and utterances 'of a symbolic character which draws the attention of participants to objects of thought and feeling which they hold to be of special significance' (Lukes, 1975). The form of the sequence is more or less invariant and the acts must be enacted – the fundamental rule being no performance, no ritual. Religious ritual involves acts and attitudes of respect and reverence toward some sacred object (something that is placed beyond the everyday profane world and regarded with awe) but all rituals direct people towards things symbolically significant to them. Political rituals, such as Cenotaph ceremonies, May Day parades or street demonstrations, are believed to build social solidarity among participants and reaffirm shared values. To the extent that the contemporary world is witnessing a decline in organised religion and a corresponding rise in the importance of individualistic ideologies, the individual person is coming to be regarded as a minor deity (Goffman, 1967), normally to be accorded obeisances in the shape of polite acts and other interaction rituals.

Further reading

Hebdige, D. (1979) *Subculture: The Meaning of Style*, London: Methuen.
Leach, E. (1976) *Culture and Communication*, Cambridge: Cambridge University Press.
Lukes, S. (1975) 'Political ritual and social integration', *Sociology* 9(2), May, 289-308.

is thus a complex affair best understood, Mennell suggests, as 'one more example of a long-term civilizing process' (1991: 152).

The dietic discourses sketched by Turner have certainly been influential in shaping patterns of eating. A Foucauldian perspective highlights how human bodies are constituted by power mediated through particular kinds of discourse. Mennell's Eliasian perspective, however, provides a method for exploring in more detail the links between discourse and cultural practice, demonstrating how the cultural patterning of the appetite is shaped by a range of social interdependencies. An Eliasian perspective thus shows us how particular discourses are established in relation to shifting sets of social interdependencies.

7.4 | Representations of embodiment: culture's depictions

This section addresses how the human body is represented in everyday life, popular culture and the mass media. Beginning with an examination of the phenomenon of fashion, it then reviews studies of the representation of femininity and masculinity and concludes with a consideration of some of the debates around pornography in order to illustrate the issue of the effects of bodily representations and the limits of representation.

7.4.1 | Fashion

The adornment of the human body by a variety of methods (clothing, make-up, jewelry, accessories, tattooing, scarification, etc.) expresses fundamental dimensions of cultural identification and social participation – of who and what we consider ourselves to be. Stylistic changes and preferences in adornment are often described as fashion, but it is hard to define the term precisely and generally. To begin with, it is best thought of in relation to its opposite, the outmoded. The basic pattern involves cultural forms which enjoy a 'temporary acceptance and respectability only to be replaced by others more abreast of the times' (Blumer, 1968). Thus fashion can be distinguished from custom which is established and fixed forms of belief and conduct. In traditional societies where customs are slow to change, fashion is an alien notion. Yet fashion itself has a customary basis. It exemplifies a dual tension, as Georg Simmel (1957) recognised long ago, between differentiation and affiliation. On the one hand, the fashionable individual wants to stand out from the crowd and appear special. On the other hand, by dressing in a certain style the individual is displaying a kinship with other similarly fashionable persons. The anthropologist Edward Sapir nicely refined this idea in stating that 'fashion is custom in the guise of departure from custom' (1931: 140).

Since fashion is always responsive to what is considered 'up to the minute', it is a sharp indicator of the so-called 'spirit of the times', a telling reflection of contemporaneity. Fashion, of course, is not a phenomenon confined to adornment. It occurs in a wide variety of fields including architecture, drama, household furnishing, literature and the theories and methods of the natural and social sciences. Sometimes a fashion can be responsive to changes in other spheres of life, as in the link between young people's clothes and pop music. Since this chapter is concerned with the cultural bases of the body, our concern will be restricted to its adornment.

A celebrated theory of the purpose of clothing was advanced in a number of works by the historian of costume James Laver (see, for example, 1946, 1950). Clothing, he suggested, is motivated by three basic principles: utility, hierarchy and attraction (or seduction). Very simply, clothes can serve a useful purpose (a sunhat to protect the head, a macintosh to keep the wearer dry in the rain), or they can distinguish us in social status terms (suits and ties rather than jeans and t-shirts), or they are designed for purposes of sexual attraction. Laver's own assumption about the prevalence of these principles (that modern clothing is little concerned with utility, that men's clothing turns on the hierarchical principle while women's is based on the seduction principle) looks somewhat absurd nowadays and probably was never meant to be taken too literally. But it is easy to see how close these principles stand to the much more seriously advanced contentions of functionalist sociologists (Barber and Lobel, 1952) who argue that clothes have a *utilitarian function* (all clothes may be more or less useful), a *symbolic function* (all clothes may be more or less indicative of the wearer's social status) and an *aesthetic function* (all clothes may be more or less attractive).

A key feature of fashion is a 'rapid and continual changing of styles' (Wilson, 1985). Fashion is intimately connected to **modernity** (p. 400). In particular, it reflects and is made possible by two characteristic aspects of modernity: (a) the sense of perpetual change generated, especially by advertising and the mass media; (b) the wide range of choice of consumer goods which gives people alternatives and control over their self-presentation. The point can be made conversely. Fashion is exclusively a significant feature of societies with a more or less open class system where the elite can mark itself off from neighbouring classes by wearing costume and insignia that are not institution-alised signifiers of rank but which are seen as stylish and distinctive. The fashions of the elite, so the theory goes (Simmel, 1957; Veblen, 1934), will trickle down to the other classes. When other classes copy these fashions, the elite will adopt a new one. This theory explains why fashion is a recurring process and also explains why it is absent in caste and other traditional societies because social position is rigidly enforced (so in classical China the mandarins were required to wear ankle-length gowns; in pre-revolutionary France only the aristocracy were allowed to wear silk).

Trickle-down theory may have validly explained fashion in nineteenth-century urban industrial societies but is not adequate to explain the complexities of the fashion process in the twentieth century. Fashion increasingly seems to work as a bottom-up rather than a top-down process. Lower groups actively construct their own styles (e.g. youth subcultures) or seek out the styles of higher classes rather than passively absorb what comes down from above. Alternatively, this can be regarded as a 'trickle-across' process that works from minority group to mainstream consumption. Some writers have argued that it is more profitable to regard fashion as a sign system like language (Barthes, 1985) or that it *is* a language (Lurie, 1992) with its own grammar and syntax. Attempts to specify in detail the language of clothing have not been conspicuously successful and the idea seems at best metaphorical: after all, clothing cannot commu-nicate anything like the complexity of ideas that spoken or written language can, nor does it permit the complex combinations of ideas that can be conveyed by sentences.

Another view is that not just fashions but *fashion* itself is changing in late modern or **postmodern** (p. 400) society. Commentators such as Fred Davis (1992) argue that the weakening of the formerly tight tie of status and occupation to clothing suggests that the signifier–signified link in contemporary clothing is becoming increasingly loose or under-coded. With the growing diversity of subcultural and retro styles, fashions can now not merely be followed but actively played with by the wearer. Knowledge of the identity and mood of the wearer and the context in which clothes are worn become pivotal to an adequate understanding of their meaning. The plasticity and productivity of these meanings cannot be underestimated:

> The systems of meaning within which … practices of looking [at clothes], buying and even just day-dreaming take place are constantly regenerating themselves. What we buy and consequently wear or display in some public fashion in turn creates new images, new, sometimes unintended constellations of meaning. In a sense we become media forms ourselves, the physical body is transformed into a compact portable 'walkman'.
>   (McRobbie, 1989: xi)

Clothing and fashion are nowadays better regarded as aesthetic than as communicative codes, i.e. codes that express ideas and feelings that are often difficult to directly express rather than straightforward indicators of social standing and moral worth. This leads Davis (1992) to propose that modern fashions are fuelled by *identity ambivalence*. Our identities are not cut and dried but subject to all kinds of dislocations, pressures and contradictions, which we express through the clothes we wear. Among the **identity** (p. 224) ambivalences expressed through clothing are the following:

youth	vs	age
masculinity	vs	femininity
work	vs	play
revelation	vs	concealment
licence	vs	constraint
conformity	vs	rebellion

Items of clothing can encode these tensions, highlighting one or other pole. Post-modern theorists go one step further than Davis and suggest that the relaxation of vestimentary norms, the variability of styles and the stress on individual diversity in the clothing that people now wear ultimately signify nothing (socially). Whether such a dramatic cultural shift in fashion has actually been accomplished is, however, an open question and some commentators (e.g. Tseëlon, 1995) are sceptical.

But alongside such developments has been the revival of some of the earliest forms of adornment: body painting, ornaments, scarring, tattooing, and the like, which are associated with very distinct personal and social meanings. Among some cultures the marking of the body has long held established ritual significance, often marking the

Figure 7.3 ■ Body piercing and Celtic tattoos (the subject is Irish, hence the tattoos show membership of a Celtic group).

transition from one state to another. In many traditional African societies, for example, scarification of the cheeks or forehead symbolises the passage to adult malehood. Circumcision is a religiously justified form of body modification long practised by Jews and other groups. Men in military occupations often bear tattoos which proclaim their membership of a regiment, ship, etc. Pierced ears have become a mainstream form now widely accepted for both sexes in Europe and America and other styles, such as pierced nostrils, are ceasing to have the shock value that punks could once count upon. Other forms of 'non-mainstream body modification' such as branding, cutting and scarring the skin and genital piercing (Myers, 1992) are becoming more commonplace. The motives for engaging in non-mainstream body modification are varied, including sexual enhancement, displaying trust and loyalty towards a significant other, aesthetic value, group affiliation and sheer shock value. Underlying these diverse motives is a more general function of body modification and ornamentation. These practices serve to 'socialise' the body, bringing certain biological aspects of the person into the social realm, converting a raw and mute body into an active communicator of symbolic significance. This function is present even in these minority pursuits:

> As surely as the Suya highlight the importance of hearing by wearing large wooden discs in their earlobes, so the genital piercers in contemporary American society celebrate their sexual potency by sporting a Prince Albert in the head of the penis or a silver heart on a labia piercing. (Myers, 1992: 299)

These forms of adornment, along with clothing more generally, serve to link biological body to social being and underscore the point that the body is considerably more than a biological entity. They also raise questions about where the body ends. With our skin or with our clothes, jewelry, make-up? What is the status of our bodily products and emissions? We can 'donate' our blood, eggs and sperm which medical technology can preserve for long periods of time. The boundaries of the human body are not unambiguous. These questions become all the more pressing in light of developments in bio-engineering and computing technologies which promise to take the figure of the cyborg out of science fiction and into lived cultures (see section 7.6 below).

7.4.2 | Gender difference and representations of femininity

Gender is often regarded as a cultural overlay to the anatomically founded differences between the sexes. Sex refers to biological differences between males and females while gender refers to the culturally specific ways of thinking, acting and feeling. Femininity and masculinity are thus gender terms, referring to the ways of thinking, acting and feeling considered appropriate in a society for females or males. Sometimes the relation between biology and culture is thought of in additive terms (Connell, 1987) – culture rounds out and amplifies the dimorphism that nature provides so that, for example, a propensity towards care of infants is linked to the biological capacity to breastfeed.

Such an essentialist view is difficult to sustain. To begin with, there seems to be no reliable way of apportioning accurate values to the biological and the cultural. Second, they seem to be predicated on assumptions implicit in the natural attitude of Western societies towards sexual difference, namely that there are two and only two sexes, that male or female are the only possible categories to which individuals can be assigned, that this determination is made on the basis of possession of a penis or vagina, that assignment to either male or female categories is lifelong and cannot be retrospectively altered after the person's death (Garfinkel, 1967: 122–6). A further reason for questioning the additive conception of the relation of biology and culture is that there seems to be considerable variability in acceptable forms of femininity and masculinity. For example, the North American Indian practice of *berdache*, which allows anatomical males to engage in 'women's work', dress like women and move in women's circles, gainsays any doctrine of a natural dimorphism of the sexes. Rather, it seems that cultural definition actually plays a major part in the constitution of gendered bodies, as the discussion of 'throwing like a girl' (see section 7.2.2) above suggests. Gender difference is so closely bound up with the workings of cultural definitions and interactional practices (Connell, 1987; Goffman, 1977, 1979) that essentialist views positing some biological feature that is shared by all men or all women and which can account for how people think, act or believe seems absurd.

In large-scale societies it is inevitable that there will be a range of femininities and masculinities to be found. However, some will be preferred over others – an idea that Connell (1987: 183–8) captures with his concepts of 'hegemonic masculinity' and 'emphasized femininity'. These notions articulate the culturally dominant gender codes that movies, advertising and so on both draw upon and help to construct. Also, it is important to distinguish between the versions of femininity and masculinity presented in dominant discourses and people's actual lived experiences, which may well be significantly at variance with these. In contemporary Western culture, femininity – or at least emphasised femininity – seems to be very much more a representational and self-presentational matter than is masculinity. It is said that men act, while women appear (Berger, 1972) – women trade on their 'looks', men on their 'presence'. Contemporary discourses of femininity are not seamless ideological webs but rather contain ambiguities and contradictions within them. Tseëlon's (1995) examination of how heterosexual women present themselves in everyday life explores five paradoxes through which culturally dominant beliefs and expectations about women's personal appearance can be understood:

- *The modesty paradox* – women are constructed as seduction, ever to be punished for it.

- *The duplicity paradox* – women are constructed as artifice, then marginalised for lacking essence and authenticity.

- *The visibility paradox* – women are constructed as a spectacle, yet are culturally invisible.

- *The beauty paradox* – women embody ugliness while signifying beauty.

- *The death paradox* – women signify death as well as the defence against it.

Contemporary femininity is constructed; it is in Tseëlon's term a kind of 'masque', in which women reach a *modus vivendi* in relation to these paradoxes. Consider just one example from this list, the beauty paradox. The looks of the human body are very much more important for women than for men: attractiveness matters much more to how women are regarded and regard themselves. While men also express concerns about their appearance, it is much less consequential for them (indeed, men who pay too much attention to their looks are likely to be dubbed 'effeminate'). Female beauty, it is felt, is an ideal state that can be attained by only a few and then for only a short period of the lifespan. So many women work hard to stave off the threat of ugliness by means of cosmetics, diet regimes, plastic surgery, implants, liposuction and the like. But attractiveness itself can become a kind of stigma, a discrediting attribute, since female beauty is a temporary state to be transgressed by even the most beautiful woman. Furthermore, it implies that her bare and uncontrolled body is unacceptable, something requiring intervention and disguise. The cultural valorisation of youthful beauty means that the ageing process urgently brings women up against what may be seen as 'ugliness'. If women attempt to contest ageing too vigorously they encourage unkind comments about their refusal to 'gracefully' yield to the years. Such reasoning is very much a cultural, not natural logic and the standards thereby invoked are not universal but culturally specific. Very different logics and standards seem to apply to men.

7.4.3 | Representations of masculinity

One element of hegemonic masculinity involves bodily displays of aggression and violence. This is often regarded as facilitated, if not actually caused, by male musculature and chromosomal heritage. Studies of the cultural and social dimensions of violent behaviour suggest that these biological endowments are, at best, enabling devices and that there is a complex cultural context mediating aggressive acts from the interpersonal (e.g. assault) to the institutionalised (e.g. wars). But since actual displays of interpersonal violence are often frowned upon, it is the potential for aggressive action that is critical – a potential that is often translated into the stance, posture and muscle tensions of the male body. Among teenage working-class boys, for example, a certain amount of pushing and punching, playfully framed, can function as a signifier of friendship.

Sometimes this aggressive behaviour can be institutionalised, for example in fascist ideologies. Klaus Theweleit's (1989) extraordinary study of the inner experience of German fascism explores the doctrine's appeal to many different kinds of men. The study is premised on the assumption that fascism itself was a distinct culture created by and for its adherents and which cannot be properly understood as a culture if it is reduced to other factors (e.g. class interest, character structure). Theweleit draws mainly on the novels and memoirs of the Freikorps, a right-wing militia which flourished in 1920s Germany. The Freikorps was a proto-fascist organisation whose ideology and activities foreshadowed the later ascendancy of the Nazis. Although his ultimate aims are psychoanalytic, Theweleit portrays some significant cultural features of the Freikorps and links them to the organisation's conceptions of masculinity. The military culture of the Freikorps exalted war and maintained that only through battle could men's wholeness be fully attained. These beliefs about masculinity are well captured in the words of a popular Freikorps writer:

These are the figures of steel whose eagle eyes dart between whirling propellers to pierce the cloud; who dare the hellish crossing through fields of roaring craters, gripped in the chaos of tank engines; who squat for days behind blazing machine-guns, who crouched against banks ranged high with corpses, surrounded, half-parched, only one step ahead of certain death. These are the best of the modern battlefield, men relentlessly saturated with the spirit of battle, men whose urgent wanting discharges itself in a single concentrated and determined release of energy. ... Tomorrow, the phenomenon now manifesting itself in battle will be the axis around which life whirls ever faster. A thousand sweeping deeds will arch across their great cities as they stride down asphalt streets, supple predators straining with energy. They will be the architects building on the ruined foundations of the world.   (quoted in Theweleit, 1989: 160–2)

This warrior mentality sharply polarises bodily characteristics along gender lines. Women are regarded as soft, fluid, a subversive source of pleasure or pain who must be contained, a negative 'other' to be hived off from authentic masculine existence. Men therefore need to police the boundaries of their bodies carefully, and through drills and exercises develop a machine-like, organised and hard body that can resist merger or fusion with others, that is reliably autonomous and subservient only to the correct political leader. In this belief system the rapture of combat is extolled and killing comes to be seen as a means of affirming a man's wholeness, a way of asserting the coherence of his body and self by invading the bodily boundaries of the other. Whilst Theweleit presents an extreme case, many twentieth-century military cultures have incorporated elements of this world-view.

The movie industry, now just a century old, has proved to be a potent source of representations of masculinity. Arguably, there is a greater range of masculinities on offer in popular film than femininities – that the models of masculinity represented by the roles played by James Dean, Sean Connery and James Stewart, for example, are more diverse than those acted by comparable cinematic icons of femininity such as Marilyn Monroe and Madonna (but note Burchill's (1986) survey). One very influential role model and mythic resource for dominant conceptions of masculinity is *film noir*. A genre of Hollywood film whose classics originally appeared between 1940 and 1955, *film noir* was popularised by Humphrey Bogart's detective roles taken from Raymond Chandler's and Dashiell Hammett's novels. Its conventions include a compromised protagonist and a *femme fatale* with whom he becomes involved. The action takes place in predominantly urban locations with many night-time settings. *Film noir* often used the techniques of the voice-over and the flashback and can be identified by its distinct visual style which includes the use of chiascuro effects, low-key lighting, high or low camera angles, skewed framing and strongly contained, claustrophobic close-ups.

The 'tough' hero of *film noir* is usually a flawed character, often neurotic, alienated and shabby, but with a number of redeeming qualities which become evident as the plot unfolds. Many commentators suggest that he is an attractive, but certainly not a sterling model of masculinity. The standard representation of the tough hero was described by one commentator in 1947 as follows:

He is unattached, uncared-for and irregularly shaven. His dress is slovenly. His home is a hall bedroom, and his place of business is a hole in the wall in a rundown office building. He makes a meagre living doing perilous and unpleasant work which condemns him to a solitary life. The love of women and the companionship of men are denied him. He has no discernible ideal to sustain him – neither ambition, nor loyalty, nor even a lust for wealth. His aim in life, the goal to which he moves and the hope which sustains him, is the unravelling of obscure crimes, the final solution of which affords him little or no satisfaction. ... His missions carry him into situations of extreme danger. He is subject to terrible physical outrages, which he suffers with a dreary fortitude. He holds human life cheap, including his own. ... In all history I doubt there has been a hero whose life was so unenviable and whose aspirations had so low a ceiling. (John Houseman, cited in Krutnik, 1991: 89)

How is such a difficult and discordant conception of masculinity to be interpreted? From a psychoanalytic point of view this can be seen as a form of turning in on oneself, an inversion or narcissism. That such characteristics could be glamorised and achieve wide popularity first in the 1940s and now in the 1980s and 1990s with the *noir* renaissance and the growing intertextual significance of the genre, could suggest 'some kind of crisis of confidence within the contemporary regimentation of male-dominated culture' (Krutnik, 1991: 91).

Military combat and the work of the private detective (or at least its fictionalised version) may seem to be two fairly extreme sites of the exercise of male bodily power. Two caveats must be entered. First, these representations personify certain cultural idealisations of exemplary masculinity that few can hope to even approximate in everyday life. Nevertheless, these idealisations provide exemplary forms towards which ordinary conduct gestures. Second, it needs to be emphasised that male bodily power is evident in many, very much more mundane settings, such as angling on a river or canal bank. Anglers are overwhelmingly male, which is testimony to the unequal rights that men and women have to occupy public space; it involves embodied skills (control, patience, sensitivity to the elements); and it involves moments of excitement – 'action' – which are themselves strongly gendered (Morgan, 1993). Since male power is so highly pervasive a cultural feature it is easy to overlook more mundane features of its representation.

7.4.4 | Effects of bodily representations and the limits of representation

The representation of the human body, in particular by the modern representational technologies of photography and film, have stimulated a range of debates about the limits of acceptable images of the human body. While it is possible to use these technologies to picture all manner of pleasures experienced and pains and degradations endured by human bodies, convention circumscribes the free availability of such images. Much debate has centred on violent and sexual imagery. Here we focus on some of the issues raised by sexual representations, and in particular pictorial representations of human sexuality.

At the outset it is important to offer some definitions and draw some distinctions, however provisional they may seem. First, there is the distinction between *erotica* and *pornography*. Erotica has its roots in the Greek word for love and generally connotes a diffuse source of sexual stimulation. Rodin's statue 'The kiss' would be considered to be erotic by many people. Pornography, however, pushes sexual explicitness to the extreme. It is a form of representation that graphically depicts sexuality for the express aim of stimulating its consumer. Pornographic magazines and videos have long excited controversy because they are seen, variously, as offensive or harmful. Thus it is also necessary to distinguish between *offence* and *harm*. What persons and groups find offensive varies and is a matter of taste and moral conviction: you may well find offensive the cartoons that children watch on TV. But it is a different matter entirely to hold that these cartoons are harmful. When we claim that some object or arrangement is harmful we are maintaining that it has measurable deleterious effects on people's attitudes and behaviour. Manifestly, there are many sexualised images that give offence to individuals or groups. But to claim that pornography is harmful is to propose that negative, anti-social consequences (e.g. increases in sexual offences towards women and children) can be proven to follow from its existence and consumption.

Three kinds of evidence have been drawn upon to investigate the harmful effects of pornography on its predominantly male consumers. *Anecdotal* evidence draws on connections deemed to exist between an individual's consumption of pornography and the commission of a sexual offence. An offender charged by a court may seek to mitigate the offence by blaming his predilection for pornography. However, this evidence proves nothing beyond the individual case; it cannot be used to support generalisations of a stable relation between pornography and sexual violence. In order to do this it is necessary to employ much larger samples than N = 1. One such source of large-scale data is found in *criminal statistics*. Criminologists have attempted to find patterns in the availability of pornography in a society and changes in the commission of sexual offences by examining cross-cultural evidence. Thus far the evidence has been ambiguous or contradictory and no clear patterns have emerged. An apparently more promising line of research has involved testing people in psychological laboratories to measure changes in their personality as a consequence of exposure to large amounts of pornographic imagery (see Linz and Malamuth, 1993, for a summary review). A number of experimental studies have found that significant shifts in men's personalities in the direction of greater tolerance of violence towards women have been detected. However, there remain doubts about extending the findings of this research beyond the psychological laboratory to the everyday sexual cultures in which pornography figures.

A range of feminist positions have been drawn upon all three kinds of evidence about pornography's harmful effects. Anti-porn feminists have used the experimental research in particular to provide scientific legitimation for attempts to change the law (e.g. the Minneapolis ordinance promoted by Catherine MacKinnon and Andrea Dworkin) to eliminate some of the prevalent forms of pornography. Dworkin (1983) has taken the debate about anti-social effects one step further by proposing that, by its very nature, pornography *is* violence towards women in an insidious form. In contrast, anti-censorship feminists (e.g. Assiter and Carol, 1993) have emphasised the ambiguity of the research and pointed to the historical connection of the repression of porno-graphy and the disvaluing of women's rights. They suggest that societies that allow pornography to flourish seem to offer the conditions in which the collective interests of women are best preserved in law and custom.

Cross-cutting both these positions are feminist critiques of pornography as a representational genre. Feminists have proposed that the form and content of much current pornographic imagery is founded upon overwhelmingly phallocentric premises. In much pornography the male gaze (see section 9.3.4) rules: women are portrayed as sex objects designed only to satisfy male sexual desire. Questions about gender relations inevitably arise since pornography can be regarded as a mirror of wider power relations in society. This has led to a debate about the possibility of a 'feminist erotica' (Myers, 1982) or an 'erotica for women' (Semple, 1988). More is involved than simply replacing naked female models with males (attempts to do this have not been very successful commercially and seem to attract a large unintended audience of gay males). Erotica for women tends to adopt a different form and content than pornography aimed at heterosexual men. Among the candidates for inclusion are popular romantic fiction (Radway, 1987) and the production of lesbian pornography by lesbians themselves. One of the themes that has emerged from these debates is the issue of pleasure, and women's sexual pleasure in particular (Kaplan, 1983). Pornography is an avowedly transgressive genre which is a potent source of fantasy. This dimension of the debate is advanced by some feminist and gay theories which endeavour to reclaim at least a part of sexuality for the private sphere. In this view the pleasures of the body are considered to reside in a non-public realm. Further, it is suggested that the enticements of the forbidden, the danger and excitement associated with certain kinds of sexual practice, are civil liberties not to be given up lightly. From this point of view, legal attempts to circumscribe transgressive sexual practices, such as the Spanner trial of 1990–1 where gay men were prosecuted under the law of assault for engaging in mutually consenting sado-masochistic activities, stand as an important incursion into personal freedom and the rights of the citizen.

This last position is often linked to arguments about the vagaries of interpreting sexually explicit material. There may be a personal aspect to these interpretive matters (whatever turns you on). But there is also a pervasive social dimension: Clark Gable's cinematic kisses are seen as only 'staged' kisses, whereas it is difficult to extend the fictional frame fully to hard-core pornography – the sex itself seems always to be 'real' sex, not an imaginary, theatrical version. It appears that hard-core trades on certain documentary conventions which could never enter the minds of the audience for *Gone With the Wind*. What this underlines is that the distinguishing features of pornography do not merely concern graphicness of depiction of sexual organs and activities (if that were true, gynaecology and urinary–genital medicine textbooks could be categorised as pornographic). Rather, pornography has to be understood as a 'regime of representation', a genre assembled out of certain combinations of camera angles and lighting, bodily postures, apparel, footwear and the like (see Kaite, 1995, for a semiotic analysis). Mainstream pornography is a genre that turns sex into a spectacle in which the male gaze predominates. It is a discourse where male desire has triumphed over representational form (Williams, 1990). Pornographic images in themselves do not cause sexual violence but they do powerfully shape the sexual basis of gender relations.

7.5 | The body as a medium of expression and transgression: culture's idioms

In the logocentric world, language occupies a privileged place as our most distinctively human capacity. The remaining expressive and communicative capacities of the body often assume secondary status. This section picks up some of the themes of the earlier discussion in section 7.2 to consider some of the key respects in which the body is a medium of expression, its techniques serving as a vehicle for our being-in-the-world. A closely related theme is how the body can also serve as a medium of **transgression** (p. 258). This section explores the themes of bodily expression and transgression under five headings: the emotional body, the sporting body, body arts, the fit body and the symbolism of body building.

7.5.1 | The emotional body

The cultural shaping of the body's emotions is built into their expression. Arlie Hochschild (1983) speaks of the 'feeling rules' specific to cultures and subcultures which specify the kind and level of emotional expression appropriate to any situation. We feel happy at parties and sad at funerals in part because we are meant to – we are conforming to the locally relevant feeling rule. From this it follows that persons are capable of 'managing' their emotions, and this emotion management, this control over the expression of embodied feelings, is a key part of what it is to be regarded as a competent adult. Among the Inuit of northern Canada, for example, any show of strong emotion by adults is frowned upon; only very small children are allowed to behave in that way. So when an anthropological fieldworker vigorously remonstrated visiting Western fishermen who were taking advantage of the Inuit's generosity, she found herself shunned by the very people she was attempting to defend (Briggs, 1970). The Inuit could neither comprehend nor accept what they saw as her 'childish' outburst.

Emotion management is part of our daily lives. Some emotions such as shame or embarrassment are eminently social in character: they are elicited by the real or imagined responses of others. Embarrassment minimally seems to involve the projection of one's self as a given kind of person (a competent driver, a reliable colleague, a trustworthy friend) which the facts of a situation then come to contradict (we dent the car's bumper while parking, we make a foolish mistake in our work, we disclose personal information to the 'wrong' person). Some categories of person are required to be particularly skilful in the management of emotions. Hochschild (1983) examines the training and working techniques of flight attendants for a big US airline. Part of their working personality involves being continually courteous and smiling in their dealings with passengers, no matter how they are actually feeling. Flight attendants receive schooling in these techniques by the company, techniques that are then refined on the job, e.g. in coping with difficult or demanding passengers – attendants call them 'irates' ('a noun born of experience', as Hochschild observes). The control of one's own emotions in this manner often paves the way to the successful management of the feelings of others.

7.5.2 | The sporting body

In increasingly sedentary contemporary societies, sporting activities, whether undertaken professionally or recreationally, are a major form of physical engagement in the world, especially for men. The 'disciplining' that practice and training in a sport involves can be regarded in Foucauldian terms as producing 'docile bodies' (Hargreaves, 1986) but the element of choice even in professional sports makes the comparison less than perfect and suggests that other analytic frameworks may shed some useful light. In this section we consider a study of the culture of professional boxing based on its author's four years of participant observation in a gym in Chicago (Wacquant, 1995). This study takes up a key Bourdieu concept, **cultural capital** (p. 355) (see Chapters 1 and 3) but divests it of its rationalistic, logocentric connotations in devising the notion of 'bodily capital'.

Boxers, like dancers, strongly identify with their bodies: they *are* their bodies, and they clearly see their skill at using their bodies for pugilistic purposes as an asset that can be translated into worldly success. Boxers thus own a certain 'bodily capital' that they seek through training practices to convert into 'pugilistic capital, that is ... a set of abilities and tendencies liable to produce value [i.e. recognition, titles, financial rewards] in the field of professional boxing' (Wacquant, 1995: 66–7). Bodily capital is thus closely interrelated with the bodily labours undertaken in the gym and the regimens that extend beyond the gym to the boxer's entire way of life.

Bodily labour is undertaken by a fighter who, as an untrained novice, has a certain height and weight, deportment and motility, facial shape and skin tone, all of which are noticed by the trainer in assessing the novice's potential as a boxer. These characteristics define but do not determine the likely future of the novice. The gym is a kind of factory for retooling, refurbishing and restructuring the novice's body into a fighting machine. A trainer is quoted as saying 'I like creatin' a monster, jus' to see what you can create ... like the master Frankenstein: I created a monster, I got a fighter, I created a good fighter, same difference' (quoted in Wacquant, 1995: 70). The specific work of bodily labour is much the same the world over: running, skipping, punch-bag work, callisthenics, sparring and shadow boxing. The result of such repeated and intense training is to change the boxer's physique but also to change his 'body sense', his awareness of his own body and how it stands to the world. The development of this physique and body sense comes about also by what the boxer does *not* do, the pleasures deliberately forgone. Wacquant speaks of the 'trinity of pugilistic sacrifice': food, sociability and sex (in that order). Boxers need to pay close attention to their diet in order that they can make the weight of the class in which they plan to compete. The training is physically demanding, often requiring an exacting routine of early morning runs and strenuous workouts which make a social life difficult. Near a fight, trainers will insist that their charges abstain from sexual activity in the belief that if they do not, they will lose their edge, their sharpness. One fighter says of these sacrifices: 'You're in jail when you're trainin', it's like doin' time, you know' (quoted in Wacquant, 1995: 82). Body and self become so immersed in the sport of boxing that the risks – which most commonly involve not brain damage or broken noses but chronic pain from deformations of the hands – are minimised by the boxer as the desire to fight grows.

7.5.3 | Body arts

> It is not to the physical object that the body may be compared, but rather the work of art.   (Maurice Merleau-Ponty, quoted in Benthall, 1975: 5)

Embodied capacities, particularly those located in the hands and eyes, are central to the production of artistic objects such as paintings and music. These skills are often the product of long periods of patient cultivation. In this section we briefly review some of the cultural significances of dance, an activity where the artistic product is quite literally inscribed on the body, where the movements of the body serve as expressive and aesthetic vehicles.

There is an initial distinction to be drawn between *performance dance* (a ballet performance, Ginger Rogers and Fred Astaire musicals, the 'Come Dancing' television programme) and *social dance* (in clubs, dance-halls and, since rave, even open fields). The distinction echoes but does not exactly reflect the earlier discussion of culture in the sense of elevated artistic standards and culture as a whole way of life, the means through which a sense of 'we-ness' is assembled. Performance dance is usually approached as a source of artistic contemplation and enjoyment while social dance is regarded as part of the lived experience of members of a group. Performance dance itself has 'high' and 'popular' forms (consider the very different appeals of Ballet Rambert and Riverdance). Ballet, for example, attracts a predominantly female audience from professional and semi-professional backgrounds (Novack, 1993; Sherlock, 1993). Feminists have argued that classical forms of ballet employ costume, movements and narrative structures that reproduce nineteenth-century dimorphic gender stereotypes of female passivity and male dominance.

Cultural studies has tended to focus on social dance and to consider its subcultural location and functions. Thus dance in black popular culture is seen as a form of resistance to cultural hegemony; for many non-white and white young people, dance is a form of escapism, instrumental in the construction of fantasy (Ward, 1993). Willis (1978) argues that bikers' dance is 'homological', directly extending other themes and attitudes in the subculture, while Hebdige (1979) sees pogoing as another element of punk 'bricolage'. Dance is certainly linked to sexual pursuit in many youth subcultures but that is only part of its significance for members, males no less than females, who often consider competence in a particular dance style as a key subcultural emblem (e.g. Teds and jiving). According to **Angela McRobbie** (p. 343), dance's subcultural significance has to be seen in relation to other subcultural elements such as music, fashion, graphic design and drugs. Writing of rave, she observes:

> What image of femininity, for example, is being pursued as female ravers strip down and sweat out? Dance is where girls were always found in subcultures. It was their only

entitlement. Now in rave it becomes the motivating force for the entire subculture. This gives girls a new found confidence and a prominence. Bra tops, leggings and trainers provide a basic (aerobic) wardrobe. In rave (and in the club culture with which it often overlaps) girls are highly sexual in their dress and appearance, with sixties TV stars like Emma Peel as their style models. The tension in rave for girls comes, it seems, from remaining in control, and at the same time losing themselves in dance and music. Abandon in dance must now, post-AIDS, be balanced by caution and the exercise of control in sex. One solution might lie in cultivating a hyper-sexual appearance which is, however, symbolically sealed or 'closed off' through the dummy, the whistle, or the ice lolly. . . . The communality of the massive rave crowd is balanced by the singularity of the person. Subcultural style is in this instance a metaphor for sexual protection.   (McRobbie, 1993: 419–20)

But dance styles themselves are not irrevocably tied to given subcultures. Frith (1983) shows how disco started in black clubs in Detroit and New York, and was then taken up by young people more widely in Europe and North America before finally being appropriated by urban gay populations. Dance, then, is a **hybrid** (p. 159) activity carrying a variety of subcultural significances which may change over time.

7.5.4 | Discoursing the fit body

While the body has probably always been as a major focus of care and concern, that attention has intensified since the 1970s in Europe and North America mainly due to the big upsurge of interest in physical fitness. The marathon boom has peaked and declined but runners are now an established feature of the urban landscape. There has been a rapid expansion in the numbers of gyms, often lavishly reconfigured as health clubs which epitomise not so much a hobby or pastime as a lifestyle choice. 'Working out' is no longer the province of a minority of sports enthusiasts but embraces a significant proportion of the population. Movie stars market their own fitness videos and exercise programmes. The wealthy hire personal trainers who will, for a fee, design a customised exercise and diet programme and supervise the anticipated physical metamorphosis of their charges. At the back of this is a scientific rhetoric based on research studies that trumpet the merits of regular exercise in reducing cardiovascular disease, cancer and a host of other ailments to which flesh is heir. Only exercise, goes the constant refrain, and you will live longer and live better. It is as if the body has become a work of art, an object of special cultivation, a project in its own right. Of course it is only in affluent Western societies, which have significant sections of the population who enjoy high levels of health and longevity and ample discretionary time, that such body projects can flourish.

Fitness concerns chime in with Lasch's (1980) thesis about the emergence of the narcissist personality type which is highly self-conscious, constantly monitoring the body for signs of decay, perpetually afraid of the advancing years and the certain prospect of death, who wants to be liked but who is unable to sustain friendships and who treats the self as a marketable commodity. This broad line of theorising is taken further by Featherstone (1991) in his writing on consumer culture. Consumer culture fully emerges in the early twentieth century as production is dramatically increased in Western economies and as advertising comes to assume a prominent place in securing a market for the proliferation of consumer goods. Traditional values are eroded as advertising in particular advances consumer culture values:

> Certain themes, infinitely revisable, infinitely combinable, recur within advertising and consumer culture imagery: youth, beauty, energy, fitness, movement, freedom, romance, exotica, luxury, enjoyment, fun. Yet whatever the promise in the imagery, consumer culture demands from its recipients a wide-awake, energetic, calculating, maximising approach to life – it has no place for the settled, the habitual or the humdrum.   (Featherstone, 1991: 174)

The preponderance of visual images in consumer culture heightens the significance of the body's appearance. The 'look' of the body, its demeanour, clothing and adornment came to assume an importance that it did not have in the nineteenth century when the idols of production (Lowenthal, 1961) held sway, or in earlier times when Christianity vilified the human body by subjecting it to ascetic regimes in order to cultivate the soul. The massive impact of Hollywood cinema throughout most of the twentieth century reinforced the importance of 'looking good'. Fitness and slimness became linked to attractiveness and worthiness as a person.

These changes are crystallised by Featherstone (1991) in the notion of 'the performing self' which emphasises the current importance of display and impression management. Nineteenth-century conceptions of 'character' involved ideas of duty, work, honour, reputation and integrity, to be achieved through industry, thrift and sobriety. These beliefs come to look outmoded by the middle of the twentieth century with the ascendance of the notion of the 'personality' that is judged by its charm, fascination and its ability to be found attractive and likeable by others. This in turn could be achieved by a proper balance of good conversation and flawless manners, appropriate clothing, energy and poise. The need to produce a consistent performance every time calls for a disciplining and rationalising of the spirit of the kind epitomised by the flight attendants studied by Hochschild (1983) (see section 7.5.1 above). Gone is the older recognition of the possibility of a discrepancy between inner self and outward appearance and conduct, and between self and body. For the performing self, impression management is all and the body comes to be taken as emblematic of the soul.

The enormous explosion of interest in diet and exercise programmes, epitomised by developments such as the increase in health clubs and gymnasia, the ubiquity of runners on city streets and mountain bikers in the countryside, the growth of health food shops and the commercial success of companies such as Nike, point to the emergence of a concern for health as a good to be obtained through individual achievement rather than acquiescence to medical regimes. This amounts to a contemporary 'cult of the perfect body' (Edgley and Brissett, 1990), a quest for an ideal that is now firmly entrenched in popular culture. The perfect body

> is slender, fit and glowing. It does not smoke. If it drinks, it does so in moderation. It carefully regulates its diet in terms of calories, carbohydrates, fats, salts and sugars. It

exercises regularly and intensely. It showers (not bathes) frequently. It engages only in safe sex. It sleeps regular hours. It has the correct amount of body fat. ... It has flexibility. ... It has proper muscle strength. ... It has appropriate aerobic capacity. ... In short the perfect body is one that is biochemically, physiologically and autonomically balanced. Moreover, it is one that does not allow toxic substances and activities to disturb its inner harmony. It is wrapped in a protective membrane around itself. It is, in a word, 'healthy'.   (Edgley and Brissett, 1990: 261–2)

Often, however, the quest for the perfect body is accompanied by an intolerance towards those who are sedentary, who eat the 'wrong' foods and drink to excess, who smoke and who engage in other unhealthy habits. This zealous underside to healthist ideologies has been termed a perspective of 'health fascism' and its exponents 'health nazis'. Health nazis are critical of the lifestyle of what they derisively label 'couch potatoes' whom they regard as 'an inferior class of people, certainly unfit, undependable, inefficient and probably unclean in mind as well as body' (Edgley and Brissett, 1990: 263). These attitudes no longer obtain only in the private spheres of home and leisure but increasingly come to figure in the public domains. Consider the growing restrictions on smoking in public and work places. In some corporate cultures there is evidence that smoking is seen as a real handicap to career advancement. 'Passive smoking' has emerged as a health problem trumpeted on cigarette packet labels but also figuring as a basis for litigation. There is a similarity between the new health fascism and Puritan ethics: just as suffering, self-sacrifice and denial paved the way to a proper relationship with God in the Protestant ethic, so too there is a conviction among health nazis that physical deprivation and forsaking the easy pleasures will ennoble the spirit. The 'me generation' of the 1960s and 1970s which sought salvation through reforming the self (consciousness-raising, therapy) has given way in the 1980s and 1990s to a 'no generation' obsessed with improving the body. Of course, these beliefs are not distributed equally through societies; in the West they are first the province of the professional middle classes (though by no means exclusive to them). The rise of these ideologies and the evidence of the increasing fashionability of running, aerobics and working out in the gym seems to be linked to the emergence of **postmodern** (p. 400) culture.

According to Barry Glassner (1990), current fitness enthusiasms are best understood as a quest for postmodern selfhood. Modernist discourse from the nineteenth century through to the 1950s proposed that exercise and sound diet could help combat the ills of affluence and thereby build a better society. Fitness was thus positively implicated in progressivist convictions concerning national regeneration and social improvement. Contemporary fitness concerns have a different character. They can be seen as responses of persons who seek regeneration in the face of the assaults of an increasingly technological, affluent society. Risks to health and personal wellbeing, it is contended, can best be managed by exercise and diet which will produce stronger, healthier people better able to cope with the daily stresses of life. Thus 'fitness' now connotes not merely an exercise regime but a whole range of lifestyle choices bearing on the physical and mental wellbeing of the individual. At the heart of current fitness concerns lies the individual – notions of the consequential improvement of the collectivity have dwindled into insignificance.

Furthermore fitness, this health-conscious complex of exercise and diet, is most appropriately regarded as a postmodern activity. It comprises a 'pastiche, a borrowing from diverse imagery, styles, and traditions, including both "high" and "low", mundane and special, and past, present and future, wherever these seem usable; a form of contentless quotation' (Glassner, 1990: 217). Step classes will be anathema to those who dislike contemporary pop music, even though workouts may be occasionally accompanied by the nostalgic references of 1950s rock 'n' roll numbers like 'Blue suede shoes'. There are tie-ins between exercise programmes and diets (Shredded Wheat giving its consumers a special offer on a Cher workout video). Fitness imagery and equipment have the properties of *simulacra*, representations that are more copies of other images than they are reproductions of real-world originals. The models who appear in fitness videos are themselves simulacra, unobtainable ideals carefully constructed through make-up, pose and lighting. The shifting ideal of the fit body is in keeping with postmodernism's borrowings and adaptations. The androgenous figures of the 1970s have been replaced by the more substantial and transparently gendered figures of the 1980s and 1990s. Voluptuous female body shapes once again became fashionable, as did muscles for men (and increasingly for women). (In this process the role of media imagery such as provided by *Baywatch* or the *Terminator* movies should not be underestimated). A similar process is at work in the development of exercise equipment: exercise bicycles were once modelled after their road counterparts (for

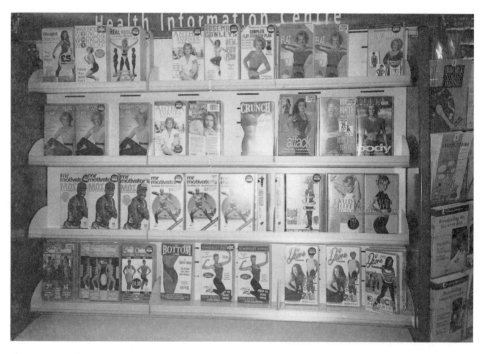

Figure 7.4 ■ Training videos for the postmodern self?

which they were mere substitutes); now their appearance owes much to motorcycle design and many of their riders would never dream of pedalling on a road.

What makes contemporary fitness discourses decidedly postmodern, according to Glassner, is that they propose to undo some longstanding dualities:

- *Male and female.* Fitness as an avenue of female empowerment has been – contentiously – advocated by Jane Fonda and others. The new fitness movements differ from their predecessors in that their recommendations apply equally to women as to men: women are urged to undertake the same forms and intensity of exercise as men and to follow the same dietary recommendations.

- *Inside and outside.* The (outer) appearance of health has come to be seen as no less important than the (inner) actuality – so much so that the decision to have plastic surgery can be justified in terms of a concern for health and fitness. Once clearly distinguishable notions of 'health' and 'vanity' become interchangeable.

- *Work and leisure.* Modernism brought us labour-saving machines, the postmodern health club labour-*making* devices. Leisure becomes something to be worked at, while many work organisations offer fitness programmes and on-site gymnasia to their employees. Keeping the employee in shape is not so far removed from keeping the business in shape. The modernist divide between work and leisure has clearly narrowed.

- *Mortality and immortality.* Postmodern fitness discourses obviously cannot promise immortality, but they do point a way to a postponement of mortality. Through exercise and the right diet, it is claimed, a longer life and a more active life can be obtained.

Whatever other uncertainties and contradictions it faces, the postmodern self finds a compelling sense of security in its well-conditioned body.

7.5.5 | Bodybuilding: comic-book masculinity and transgressive femininity?

Contemporary fitness discourses have also served to redefine conceptions of masculinity and femininity, and in particular the desirable looks of the human body. One currently popular set of images of masculinity and femininity is provided by the youthful, shapely bodies of the professional actors in the TV series *Baywatch*. These images are, of course, subject to modification and change, perhaps more so in respect of desirable female than male body shapes. In recent years there have been some contradictory shifts. On the one hand, top fashion magazines like *Vogue* have increasingly featured anorexic-like female figures. On the other hand, a more solid and muscular build has been popularised by the likes of Madonna and Linda Hamilton (in *Terminator 2*). In this latter trend the sport of bodybuilding has begun to impact on circles outside its own subculture. It is therefore worth examining the conceptions of masculinity and femininity found in bodybuilding since this is an activity that exemplifies an extreme preoccupation with gender issues and the appearance of the body.

The statuary of ancient Greece and Rome provide evidence of some long-term stabilities in Western standards of the desirable appearance of the male body. It seems that men have long desired muscles and have regarded a visibly developed musculature as emblematic of masculinity. A muscular physique in many societies is indicative of warrior competence or employment in a physical occupation (and may therefore also carry the stigma of low class position), although nowadays it is more likely to evidence involvement in fitness pursuits. Muscles come to be seen as an accomplishment, not natural endowments but cultured products. They are achievements, the outcome of time and effort put into their cultivation (Dyer, 1989: 205). The sport of bodybuilding emerged in Europe and North America in the 1930s and 1940s as men used weight training and dietary techniques to increase the size and definition of their muscles and achieve desirable physical proportions. In appearance male bodybuilders seem to portray a magnified version of the idealised male body. A key element of the culture of top bodybuilders has been described as 'comic-book masculinity' (Klein, 1994). This can be seen in the chronically hyperbolic discourses of bodybuilding which employ mechanistic terms to describe the techniques of body sculpting. Klein suggests that bodybuilding culture plays with fascistic imagery, exhibits homophobic and misogynist tendencies and embraces a view of masculinity closely resembling that of comic-book superheroes, and incomplete superheroes at that – Superman without his feminine, Clark Kent side. For Klein the hypermasculinity of bodybuilding subculture represents a triumph of form over function since it is only the appearance of masculinity that is sought, not its enactment. And this appearance can itself be a tenuous accomplishment, a costly body project. Bodybuilders get sore backsides and acne from the steroid injections, drugs and diet; they have calloused hands; they ache all the time from training; and they drastically restrict their diet prior to a competition. As one bodybuilder put it (quoted in Fussell, 1991: 153), 'this is about *looking* good, not feeling good'.

Box 7.4

Kathy Acker: building a body

I am in the gym. I am beginning to work out. I either say the name 'bench press', then walk over to it, or simply walk over to it. Then, I might picture the number of my first weight; I probably, since I usually begin with the same warm-up weight, just place the appropriate weights on the bar. Lifting this bar off its rests, then down to my lower chest, I count '1'. I am visualizing this bar, making sure it touches my chest at the right spot, placing it back on its rests. '2'. I repeat the same exact motions. '3' . . . After twelve repetitions, I count off thirty seconds while increasing my weights. '1' . . . The identical process begins again only this time I finish at '10' . . . All these repetitions end only when I finish my work-out.

On counting: Each number equals one inhalation and one exhalation. If I stop

→

my counting or in any other way lose focus, I risk dropping or otherwise mishandling a weight and so damaging my body.

In this world of the continual repetition of a minimal number of elements, in this aural labyrinth, it is easy to lose one's way. When all is repetition rather than the production of meaning, every path resembles every other path.

Every day, in the gym, I repeat the same controlled gestures with the same weights, the same reps ... The same breath patterns. But now and then, wandering within the labyrinths of my body, I come upon something. Something I can know because knowledge depends on difference. An unexpected event. For though I am only repeating certain gestures during certain time spans, my body, being material, is never the same; my body is controlled by change and by chance.

For instance, yesterday, I worked chest. Usually I easily bench press the bar plus sixty pounds for six reps. Yesterday, unexpectedly, I barely managed to lift this weight at the sixth rep. I looked for a reason. Sleep? Diet? Both were usual. Emotional or work stress? No more than usual. The weather? Not good enough. My unexpected failure at the sixth rep was allowing me to see, as if through a window, not to any outside, but inside my own body, to its workings. I was being permitted to glimpse the laws that control my body, those of change or chance, laws that are barely, if at all, knowable.

By trying to control, to shape, my body through the calculated tools and methods of bodybuilding, and time and again, in following these methods, failing to do so, I am able to meet that which cannot be finally controlled and known: the body.

In this meeting lies the fascination, if not the purpose, of bodybuilding. To come face to face with chaos, with my own failure or a form of death.

Canetti describes the architecture of a typical house in the geographical labyrinth of Marrakesh. The house's insides are cool, dark. Few, if any, windows look out into the street. For the entire construction of this house, windows, etc., is directed inward, to the central courtyard where only openness to the sun exists.

Such an architecture is a mirror of the body: When I reduce verbal language to minimal meaning, to repetition, I close the body's outer windows. Meaning approaches breath as I bodybuild, as I begin to move through the body's labyrinths, to meet, if only for a second, that which my consciousness ordinarily cannot see. Heidegger: 'The being-there of historical man means: to be posited as the breach into which the preponderant power of being bursts in its appearing, in order that this breach itself should shatter against being'.

In our culture, we simultaneously fetishize and disdain the athlete, a worker in the body. For we still live under the sign of Descartes. This sign is also the sign of patriarchy. As long as we continue to regard the body, that which is subject to change, chance, and death, as disgusting and inimical, so long shall we continue to regard our own selves as dangerous others.

Other interpretations of bodybuilding are less judgemental of the culture. They depart from 'emic' concerns with the experience of the lived body – with embodiment rather than with Klein's 'etic' discourse-oriented focus on the objective body. Monaghan (1997) has argued that bodybuilders themselves develop a complex understanding of the symbolism and aesthetics of excessive muscularity. Bodybuilders' own standards of appreciation involve an inversion of the wider society's generally hostile attitudes and appraisals. In Monaghan's 'ethnophysiology thesis', bodybuilders identify different types of excessive muscularity, each of which can be understood as aesthetically pleasing in its own terms. Bodybuilders themselves do not seem to conceive their body symbolism in Klein's terms and instead invoke their own transgressive aesthetics of the muscular body.

Bodybuilding competitions for women have an even more recent – and controversial – history, dating from the late 1970s. The sight of elite female bodybuilders strikes many people as even more shocking than their male colleagues. The author of an anthology of photographs of these women writes:

> The images on these pages are as powerful as the women they depict, and many will find both to be threatening. No wonder. The association of women and muscles developed to this degree is unprecedented in history. These images press hard against every notion of femininity with which we are familiar. Here is the female form remade and reconsidered.
>
> The idea of men with muscles is easily accepted. It requires no new concept or category to do so. ... The muscular female physique is something else; it doesn't fit with most people's idea of the norm. Muscular women are a contradiction to, even an attack on, our sense of reality.   (Dobbins, 1994)

Just as the comic-book masculinity of male bodybuilding culture represents an exaggerated stereotype of conventional conceptions, so too female bodybuilding seems to occupy a clearly transgressive position, challenging conventional discourses of the female body in an overt way.

For some commentators (e.g. Bartky, 1988) the Amazon femininity encoded in the appearance of female bodybuilders clearly establishes the body as a site of cultural resistance. Others are less sanguine about the sport's potential for resistance. Bordo (1988) concentrates on the experiences rather than the appearance of female bodybuilders and argues that, with their emphasis on diet and exercise as techniques to achieve bodily perfection, they can be grouped with anorexics and bulimics. Like anorexics they perceive their body as an alien object constantly at risk of running out of control and therefore needing to be disciplined. Like anorexics they get a kick out of being completely in charge of their bodies. But female bodybuilders do not seem to have escaped patriarchal standards of beauty. In comparison to anorexics the standards by which they judge themselves are different (wanting to be muscular rather than thin) but the means (diet, exercise) are the same, as are their motivations (again, variable conceptions of what it is to look good, particularly as framed by 'the male gaze' – see section 9.3.4). There are clearly a number of ironies and contradictions in the current practice of bodybuilding by women. The clearly coded messages of masculinity connoted by muscularity are mollified by the use of hairstyles and make-up that are hyper-feminine, by plastic surgery techniques such as breast implants, and by posing styles that are linked to the graceful movements of dance and so forth. In this way female bodybuilding is 'made safe' for participants and onlookers (Mansfield and McGinn, 1993). Female bodybuilders are playing the beauty game by different rules but it is still a beauty game. Until the subculture develops an alternative 'care-of-the-self ethic' – and there are some real possibilities here – it is argued that it will remain an insurrectionary rather than truly transformational practice (Guthrie and Castelnuovo, 1992).

7.6 | Cyborgism, fragmentation and the end of the body?

As the studies considered in sections 7.4 and 7.5 indicate, the human body is increasingly coming to be treated not as a unitary whole but as a differentiated entity requiring specialised treatment. Consumer culture fragments the body into a series of body parts to be maintained through diet, cosmetics, exercise, vitamins. Fashion, advertising and pornography all give testimony to the ever more fragmented ways in which the body is conceptualised and treated. There are a wide range of cosmetics to be applied to the many different parts of the body: mouth, hair, skin, eyes, lips, teeth, legs, feet – and products and applications continue to diversify. Health care is provided by medical specialisms which divide the body up into regions and functions. For many health-care purposes the person is not an ailing body but a set of symptoms to be assessed in terms of what is signified by the evidence of X-rays, blood pressures, blood tests, scans and invasive techniques. The fragmentation of the human body into a collection of body parts can be regarded as implicated in the larger process of fragmentation in the contemporary world which postmodern theory in particular addresses.

The concept of the cybernetic organism or 'cyborg' is another challenge to conventional essentialist understandings of the human body. The term was coined in 1960 by two American astrophysicists, Manfred Clynes and Nathan Kline, to describe the 'artifact organism' that could meet the very different environments that would be encountered in space travel. The cyborg was conceived as a neurophysiologically modified human body that could withstand the demands of space journeys. Science fiction movies such as *Blade Runner* (dir. Ridley Scott, 1982), *Robocop* (dir. Paul Verhoeven, 1985) and *The Terminator* (dir. James Cameron, 1985) have popularised the cyborg concept but its reality is not as remote as might seem. The cyborg combination of the mechanical with the human is already with us, evident in the extensive use of simple prosthetic devices such as spectacles but also apparent in the wide acceptance of cosmetic surgery, biotechnological devices like pacemakers, the use of vaccination to programme the immune system to destroy viruses and advances in genetic engineering (Featherstone and Burrows, 1995). These developments give rise to questions about where the human ends and the machine begins and serve to relativise our conventional understandings about the embodied basis of human identity.

Such conjectures sit easily with some postmodern theses postulating the disappearance of the natural body (Kroker and Kroker, 1988). Postmodern culture 'invades' the body. This 'panic body' is so fully inscribed by cultural rhetorics of postmodernity, so completely interpellated by its ideologies that no 'natural' residue can be discerned. For Arthur and MariLouise Kroker:

> *Semiotically*, the body is tattooed, a floating sign processed through the double imperatives of the cultural politics of advanced capitalism: the *exteriorization* of all the body organs as the key telemetry of a system that depends on the *outering* of the body's functions (computers as the externalization of memory; *in vitro* fertilization as the ablation of the womb; Sony Walkmans as ablated ears; computer-generated imagery as *virtual perspective* of the hypermodern kind; body scanners as the intensive care unit of the exteriorization of the central nervous system); and the *interiorization* of ersatz subjectivity as a prepackaged ideological receptor for the pulsations of the desiring-machine of the fashion scene.   (Kroker and Kroker, 1988)

For the Krokers, it is consistent with the conditions of postmodernity that the body is disappearing into a kaleidoscope of changing signs.

Some of these questions have been explored in science fiction. For example, *Blade Runner* thematises the role of memory in guaranteeing the individual's biographical continuity by giving 'replicants' a 'memory implant' (Landsberg, 1995). The genre of cyberpunk (see also section 5.3.2) has posed questions about the integrity of the human body in an especially pointed form. Cyberpunk suggests that the invasive nature of cyborgism combined with the expansive aspects of cyberspace thoroughly relativise conventional conceptions of the body. Case, the protagonist of William Gibson's *Neuromancer* (1986), views his body as 'meat' and talks of 'escaping the prison of his own flesh' through 'jacking in' to cyberspace. Elsewhere in Gibson and the works of cyberpunk there is consideration of the nature of immortality (Wintermute in *Neuromancer*), the implications of various prosthetic and bionic aids (e.g. Case's internal organs have been surgically adjusted to modify his drug-taking habits) and the blurring of categories produced by **hybrid** (p. 159) species such as dogpeople. Our ordinary notions of the body and embodiment are thoroughly problematicised in cyberpunk. The 'meat' component (or 'wetware') is often regarded as something to be transcended through drugs, surgery, genetic manipulation and cruising cyberspace. Yet the human – or perhaps 'posthuman' – body is always there in some shape to fix subjectivity and **identity** (p. 224) (Bukatman, 1993).

The productivity of the cyborg notion has also been appropriated by feminist writers who see it as a route out of dimorphic gender relations towards new possibilities of human being (McCracken, 1997). The germinal text for cyberfeminism is Donna Haraway's 1985 essay 'A manifesto for cyborgs' (reprinted as 'The cyborg manifesto' in Haraway, 1991). The hybrid status of the cyborg, part machine and part organism, presents an effective metaphor for exploring the diverse relationships between humans and technologies: she sees the cyborg as 'an imaginative resource suggesting some very fruitful couplings' (Haraway, 1991: 150). The importance of the cyborg figure emerges from the leakiness and potential imminent breakdown of two once robust distinctions: between humans and animals (language, tool use, social behaviour can all be possessed

Key influence **7.1**

Donna J. Haraway

'Once upon a time,' writes Donna Haraway in the introduction to *Simians, Cyborgs and Women* (1991), 'the author was a proper, US socialist-feminist, white, female hominid biologist, who became a historian of science to write about modern Western accounts of monkeys, apes, and women.' In the following decade her work broadened to explore the potential opened by 'cyborg feminism', a notion first introduced in her celebrated 1985 essay, 'A Manifesto for Cyborgs'. Haraway's essay established her place as a leading theorist of 'technoculture', of the complex interdependencies between humans and technologies. Her career has crossed several disciplinary boundaries. She studied English, biology and philosophy as an undergraduate at Colorado College and went on to complete a Yale doctorate that spanned philosophy, history of science and biology. Now a professor in the History of Consciousness Board at the University of California, Santa Cruz, she is internationally renowned for her distinctive and critical analyses of the relations between culture, nature and technoscience.

Haraway's cyborg manifesto is an intricately woven text which is premised on the belief that the cyborg, 'a hybrid of machine and organism', is now 'a creature of social reality as well as a creature of fiction'. Scientific and technological developments are making the old distinctions between humans and machines and humans and animals increasingly untenable. Haraway therefore has some sympathy for postmodern theorists who likewise suggest that established dualisms are breaking down. But she is also enough of a materialist to stress the importance of the ways in which technologies are used. It is imperative, therefore, for feminism and cultural studies to reject anti-science metaphysics. New technologies offer the potential to transcend the old determininations of class and gender.

Haraway endorses the advocacy by feminists of partial, situated knowledges as against the usual canons of scientific objectivity. Such situated knowledges can enable the enquirer to escape the 'god-tricks' of totalising objectivity on the one hand and thoroughgoing relativism on the other. In acknowledging the socially constructed character of scientific knowledge she shows how science studies needs cultural studies. But she insists also on recognising the obduracy of nature, which she sometimes depicts with a coyote metaphor: nature as a trickster with a constant capacity to surprise humankind.

Haraway's writing is intendedly lively, ironic and playful. In form and content it seeks to disrupt the reader's deeply taken-for-granted assumptions about the boundaries marking off such fundamental categories as 'nature', 'culture' and 'humans'. The stylistics of Haraway's texts thus match her characterisation of her work as 'an argument for *pleasure* in the confusion of boundaries and for *responsibility* in their construction'.

Further reading

Haraway, D. (1991) *Simians, Cyborgs and Women: The Reinvention of Nature*, London: Free Association Books.

in some measure by other primates) and between machines and humans (bio-engineering, computerised expert systems). As the boundaries of the different parts of the world become more permeable, the established dualisms (mind/body, culture/nature, truth/illusion, civilised/primitive, active/passive, etc.) cease to hold the relevance they once did. Humans are immersed in the world, producing their humanness in relationships with each other and with objects. We exercise in the gym, play sports in specialist shoes and contact people by telephone. These routine interactions with machines and technologies draw us into increasingly international technocultural networks. Haraway argues that humans might be better thought of as nodes, as intersections of a multiplicity of networks rather than independent monads. There is an important sense in which, Haraway claims, we are all cyborgs now (later acknowledging that the precise constituency of 'we' in a world riven with inequalities is an open question).

For Haraway the cyborg notion refers not to Frankenstein figures or swimmers or runners built on steroids and hormones but to the hybrid networks that arise from the incorporation of humans into technologies designed to facilitate human projects. The enormous impact of technoscience ('the informatics of domination') on the home, the market, the workplace, the school and the hospital offers the potential to occlude the old determinations of class, race and gender and establish new modes of human being. In the postmodern world, identities, relationships and categories are up for grabs. Transformation and reconstruction increasingly centre on the emergent social relations of science and technology. Haraway suggests that the fluidity and openness presented by cyborg imagery is a helpful guide for understanding the immense implications of these changes. She sees the cyborg as a significant oppositional figure which transgresses boundaries and which is capable of suggesting new modes of gendered being and new forms of politics. Haraway urges us to embrace the new technologies rather than turn away from them in the manner of some New Age ideologies – hence her declamation 'I would rather be a cyborg than a goddess' (1991: 181).

Haraway's work, continued most recently in the engagingly entitled *Modest_Witness-@Second_Millenium.FemaleMan©_Meets_Oncomouse™* (Haraway, 1997), is hugely controversial. For example, there is some scepticism that gender can be readily dissolved or constructed anew by technological developments when many bio-technologies continue to construct women in essentialist terms (as 'reproductive', 'womb', 'maternal', etc.), thereby perpetuating conventional gender associations (Balsamo, 1995; Hayles, 1992). Cyborg imagery may effect a thorough dislocation of our easy notions that closely tie the body and the natural; dislodging the body from established cultural discourses may prove more difficult.

7.7 | Conclusion

This chapter has reviewed some contributions to cultural studies of the body. The chapter has sought to examine some of the diverse ways in which human corporeality is best understood in non-essentialist, cultural terms. The constructionist stance employed does not deny the biological dimensions of the material body but does serve to underline the limitations of such explanations in accounting for the enormous variety of corporeal beliefs and practices. Essentialising explanations cannot do justice to the cross-cultural variety of body techniques or their historical evolution through transformations in forms of power or developments in the civilising process. Likewise, consideration of issues of the body's representation, its expressive modalities and the impact of technoculture cannot be easily accommodated within explanations couched only in biological terms. Cultural studies of the body is a large field to work. Bodies are likely to be 'in' in cultural studies for some time to come.

Re-cap

This chapter has:

- introduced the fundamental concepts and theories in constructionist accounts of the body – techniques of the body, forms of power/knowledge, the civilising process;

- considered aspects of the debates around the representation of the human body and its use as an instrument of expression and transgression;

- examined the impact of modernity, postmodernity and technoculture on conceptions of human embodiment.

Further reading

The principal works of Michel Foucault on the body – *The Birth of the Clinic* (1975), *Discipline and Punish* (1977) and the three-volume series on *The History of Sexuality*, *The Use of Pleasure* (1986) and *The Care of the Self* (1990), are challenging reading. In sociology the seminal text, Bryan S. Turner's *The Body and Society* (1984)) blends the analytic concerns of Parsons and Weber with those of Foucault. Anthropological interest is much older; see the very useful collection edited by Ted Polhemus, *Social Aspects of the Human Body* (1978). In addition, Horace Miner's satirical analysis of the body ritual of one very well known tribe, 'Body ritual among the Nacirema' (1956 and widely reprinted) is still an illuminating read. Michel Feher *et al.*'s 1,600-page, three-volume *Fragments for a History of the Human Body* (1989) is an important resource. Postmodern interests in the body are well represented by contributions to Arthur and MariLouise Kroker's edited collection, *Body Invaders: Sexuality and the Postmodern Condition* (1988). A historically wide-ranging photographic compendium of images of the human body is William A. Ewing's *The Body: Photoworks of the Human Form* (1994). There is much to debate concerning both the material accomplishment and representation of the female body in Bill Dobbins' *The Women: Photographs of the Top Female Bodybuilders* (1994). Chris Hables Gray (with the assistance of Heidi J. Figueroa-Sarriera and Steven Mentor) has edited a useful collection on many aspects of cyborgism: *The Cyborg Handbook* (1995). This might be read alongside Judith Halberstam and Ira Livingston's edited collection *Posthuman Bodies* (1995).

chapter 8

Subcultures: reading, resistance and social divisions

8.0 | Introduction

In this chapter we are concerned with subcultures, which in broad terms are often defined as subgroups of a wider culture. A significant proportion of the chapter is devoted to the exegesis of the way in which the idea of subculture was developed and used in research at the Birmingham Centre for Contemporary Cultural Studies during the 1970s which, despite the numerous criticisms that have been made of this body of work, remains very influential. This literature concentrates overwhelmingly on young people so that what is normally being examined is youth subcultures. While this particular emphasis is followed in much of the chapter (especially in sections 8.4 to 8.8), we also explore the relevance of the idea to subcultures less tied to age. This is done in a later part of the chapter through discussions of fans (section 8.11), which also points to the significance of identity and performance in everyday life.

The learning objectives of this chapter are to:

- familiarise readers with the main contours of the approach to the study of youth subcultures developed at the Birmingham Centre for Contemporary Cultural Studies;
- examine the critique of the Birmingham approach;
- point to developing alternative studies of youth and fan cultures.

8.1 | Subcultures: power, divisions and interpretation

In the course of this chapter we shall consider three important themes. First, subcultures, we shall suggest, are intimately connected to issues of **power** (p. 94) and struggle. Thus, one of the most important approaches to subcultures, developed at the **Centre for Contemporary Cultural Studies** (p. 327) at the University of Birmingham during the 1970s, conceptualises and analyses youth subcultures in terms of opposition to, and incorporation in, dominant culture. Each youth subculture seeks to mark itself off from the dominant culture while simultaneously also accommodating to certain aspects of it.

Second, as the concept of subculture divides wider forms of culture into smaller units, which may exist in relationships of opposition to wider cultures, the concept potentially allows consideration of the division of culture. One of the most important criticisms made of the idea of culture is that it tends to lead to the bringing together of disparate components to produce an over-simplified description of a phenomenon that is actually very complex. For example, familiar formulations like the 'American way of life' or 'European culture' seem to obliterate some important distinctions. In Chapter 1 we examined the way in which cultures are actually built up out of forms of cultural struggle and argued that they should never be taken at face value, as cultures are actually divided. Many different writers have utilised the concept of subculture in attempts to overcome such problems. Thus, we can examine how American culture can contain subcultures based on hot-rod car enthusiasm (Moorhouse, 1991), *Star Trek* fans (Bacon-Smith, 1992; Jenkins, 1992; Tulloch and Jenkins, 1995; Penley, 1992) and soap opera fans (Harrington and Bielby, 1995), in addition to the more often considered youth subcultural groups. Moreover, as well as facilitating examination of cultural divisions, the concept of subculture also aids analysis of how culture is fragmenting. Are there more and more subcultures and does this mean that it is now impossible to separate subcultures from the 'mainstream'?

The third theme running through the chapter concerns interpretation. Chapter 1 examined some of the general issues, but a discussion of subcultures concretises some of the dilemmas involved. For instance, influential accounts of subcultures, such as that produced by Hebdige (1979), read or decode subcultures using the tools of **semiotics** (p. 34). As we shall see, Hebdige's interpretation of punk is controversial. However, the general point is that different interpretations can be offered of the meaning of any subculture. Moreover, such readings or interpretations tend to neglect the meaning of the subculture for its participants (Widdicombe and Wooffitt, 1995; Muggleton, 1997). This difficulty is compounded by the fact that youth and other subcultures are often highly visible in the mass media, where they are often stereotyped, as folk devils who provoke moral panic (Cohen, 1973). However, there are other forms of representation that require interrogation. For example, we all 'know' that *Star Trek* fans are 'nerdish' men who are 'personally inadequate'. It is therefore surprising to read studies (for example, Bacon-Smith, 1992; Jenkins, 1992) that point to the importance of this series in the lives of 'normal' women.

At this point it may be illuminating to pause and reflect on your own enthusiasms and activities: do you belong to a group that you think of as a subculture? Would you class yourself as a fan of any form of culture (music, television, sport and so on), and how important are these activities in your everyday life? Do you collect things? Do you discuss your interests with others? Do you get depressed when your team loses? It might be useful to use the material discussed in this chapter to analyse these experiences but also, perhaps more importantly, to evaluate that material in the light of your own experience.

The influential literature on subculture developed at the Birmingham Centre for

Contemporary Cultural Studies had some of its roots in American work that attempted to explain the behaviour of young, male 'deviant' (especially criminal) groups. It is important to examine this literature briefly, as the assumption that subcultural adherents are in some sense 'deviants' from the mainstream culture, or different from the 'rest of us', has run though a great deal of subsequent work. However, as will become clear, there is some distance to travel from the 'violent' gangs of inner-city Los Angeles to the analysis of British punk subcultures. A connecting thread can be found in the notion that in different ways such groups are a problem for society (see Hebdige, 1988). The chapter therefore begins with a brief discussion of the literature on gangs and 'deviants' to provide some of this context.

8.2 | Deviants and gangs

There is a wide range of theory and empirical work in a variety of disciplines which attempts to explain and characterise the nature of 'deviant' behaviour. One distinctive sociological and criminological strand explains deviance through the concept of subculture.

8.2.1 | Deviance and subculture

The American writer Albert Cohen (1955) argued that deviance arises at those points in society where structure and culture come into conflict. For example, working-class boys, deprived through the structural forces of society, would commit 'deviant' acts which rejected the values of middle-class culture. 'Pressure' develops at such points and distinctive subcultures arise, which exhibit values and activities that oppose those of dominant or 'respectable' culture. This approach, which focused on the activities of gangs or deviant subcultures, their core ideas and values and so on, was developed and refined in subsequent American research (e.g. Cloward and Ohlin, 1960).

Such accounts, which make a causal connection between subcultural values and beliefs and deviant behaviour, were criticised by David Matza (1964). Matza argues that deviance is much more intermittent than these theories suggest and that it is associated with a period of 'drift'. Delinquency or deviance is only one possible result. Subcultural values may explain some aspects and forms of delinquency. For example, the stealing of fast cars by young men might be explained by particular subcultural beliefs that value speed as a form of masculinity, but they do not explain all aspects of deviance in a tight and general fashion. Matza's ideas resonate with later, more general, considerations of youth subcultures, which are not criminal to the extent or degree of the gangs examined by this American literature. For instance, it might be argued that subcultures develop at points where social controls are relatively weaker, or where individuals are between life stages. For example, they may occur in the stage of 'adolescence'.

Other American work (for example, Miller, 1958) emphasised the way in which forms of deviance may be seen as expressions of 'lower-class' culture. Thus, rather than involving the frustrated pursuit of dominant goals (or opposition to them), a subculture represents the development of values associated with groups at the bottom of the social structure. The focal concerns of such groups are detailed below:

- trouble
- toughness
- smartness
- excitement
- fate
- autonomy (derived from Miller, 1958).

While Miller's approach is not able to explain why some members of the working class become deviant while others do not, it does seem to capture some characteristics of 'deviant subcultures', especially among young working-class men, where there may be a particular emphasis on more aggressive aspects of masculinity. Some contemporary attempts to explain the criminal behaviour of young men on council estates in contemporary Britain have used a similar approach. Here, actions are interpreted as the assertion of a particular kind of working-class masculinity, where unemployed young men do not exist in 'stable relationships' but drift from home to home where they are looked after by women (Campbell, 1993).

Such forms of masculinity have often been seen as expressed in the values and activities of criminal *gangs*, which are a particularly clearly bounded and coherent form of 'deviant subculture'. Most of the research on this topic has been conducted in the United States and it is not clear that it is applicable straightforwardly to other countries. Thus, while there has been research conducted in Britain that suggests that there were such gangs (for example, Patrick, 1973; Parker, 1974), the dominant trend argues that social bonds are rather looser than would be associated with a gang, and that consequently subcultures cannot be equated with gangs (Downes, 1966). Despite this, recent work by writers such as Mike Davis (1990), continues to emphasise the prevalence of gang groups in some cities in the United States. It is worth considering this in some detail as it raises some important general themes.

8.2.2 | Mike Davis: gangs in Los Angeles

Davis (1990) argues that black gangs in Los Angeles emerged in the 1940s in response to white violence against the black community. The most important divide between these black gangs was the geographical one between the east and west in the black community. The gangs were often centred in school-related territories. During the 1950s the position of the gangs was strengthened by a number of factors. The police adopted the view that the ghetto contained a large number of hard-core criminals (a view that took on the status of a self-fulfilling prophecy). The period also saw a worsening of economic and job prospects for blacks in Los Angeles.

In Davis's view, during the mid- and late 1960s, the black gangs were politicised under the influence of civil rights and black power campaigns. The Black Panther party was particularly influential, leading to a decline in conventional criminal activity by the gangs. However, during the late 1960s and early 1970s the Black Panthers came under attack from the police who decimated the leadership of this radical organisation in various parts of the United States. The new street gangs that developed from this point stepped into the place of the Panthers but did not share their political programme of black power and community self-help.

The 'Crips', as they are called, developed in the ghetto between 1970 and 1972. These gangs were particularly centred in areas dislocated by the building of new roads and redevelopment. This is a process that parallels the conditions promoting the emergence of youth subcultures in postwar London (see section 8.3). The development of the Crips, thought to be so named 'from the 107 Hoovers' distinctively "crippled" style of walking' (Davis, 1990: 299) although Davis also says that the name may have been derived from the slogan 'continuous revolution in progress', led to further gang reorganisation. The diagram (Figure 8.1) from Davis (1990)

> shows a quiltwork of blue-ragged Crips, both Eastside and Westside, as well as miscellany of other gangs, some descended from the pre-Watts generation. Under incessant Crip pressure, these independent gangs – the Brims, Bounty Hunters, Denver Lanes, Athens Park Gang, the Bishops, and, especially, the powerful Pirus – federated as the red-handkerchiefed Bloods. Particularly strong in Black communities peripheral to the Southcentral core, like Compton, Pacoima, Pasadena and Pomona,

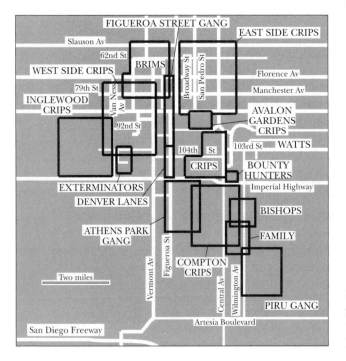

Figure 8.1 ■ Gang territories in Los Angeles in 1972. (Source: Davis, 1990: 301.)

the Bloods have been primarily a defensive reaction-formation to the aggressive emergence of the Crips.   (Davis, 1990: 299)

Davis argues that the Crips spread through the ghetto during the 1970s as a 'hybrid of teen cult and proto-Mafia' (1990: 300). This was facilitated by a number of social changes. There was a social polarisation taking place in employment within the black community, with the development of upward mobility for some black workers, especially in state and federal bureaucracies, but otherwise economic depression and lack of jobs for others (see also section 8.3). Furthermore, many of the employers that provided jobs for earlier generations of blacks were relocated to the suburbs. Job opportunities were (and continue to be) few and far between for young blacks in the city.

Such unemployment is correlated with the 'juvenation of poverty' (Davis, 1990: 306) where the poor are increasingly the young. The Los Angeles school system is also in a state of crisis, blocking off educational opportunities. The outcome of these social factors is that

Southcentral L.A. has been betrayed by virtually every level of government. In particular, the deafening public silence about youth unemployment and the juvenation of poverty has left many thousands of young street people with little alternative but to enlist in the crypto-Keynesian youth employment program operated by the cocaine cartels.   (Davis, 1990: 309)

Davis argues that, while gangs are very important in the crack business, they are not 'crime corporations', as they operate at low levels of the drug hierarchy. Latino gangs are also involved in the crack business on the street level and territory tends to be shared out in accord with potential and actual drug sales. Gang subculture is becoming increasingly prevalent in the depressed and dislocated areas of Los Angeles. Thus, according to Davis (1990: 316):

Aside from the 230 Black and Latino gangs which the LAPD have identified in the Los Angeles area, there are also 81 Asian gangs, and their numbers are rapidly growing. In Long Beach gangs of wild, parentless Cambodian boatchildren terrorize their elders and steal their hoarded gold. While the Filipino Santanas favor Chicano gang styles, the role model of the Viet Crips (supposedly robbery specialists) is obvious.

Davis's account of gangs in Los Angeles is significant for a number of reasons. First, it identifies the historically changing nature of the gangs, their relations with other social groups such as white people and the police and their location in particular territories. Second, the way in which the gang is a response to the problems caused by social position of its members is clearly stated in the way in which Davis discusses black unemployment, the relocation of jobs to the suburbs where whites form the majority, the increased poverty of young blacks and the problems of the school system – developments that take place within a city that is extensively 'zoned' along class and ethnic lines. Third, the 'option' or 'solution' of acting illegally to solve the 'problem' of making a living through the crack trade is clearly explicated. These themes of change, response and solution are prominent in writing on youth subcultures (see section 8.3). One of the weaknesses of Davis's analysis is that he pays little attention to other dimensions of what has been happening in the cultural life of black American ghettos. For example, he neglects political expression in contemporary rap music and hip-hop culture (Cross, 1993). While there is a great deal of debate about the politics of rap (for example, Cross, 1993; Rose, 1994), its neglect renders invisible the development of a different kind of cultural politics in the 1980s and 1990s from that which dominated in the 1960s and early 1970s (see Chapter 6). These earlier times operate as a kind of golden age in Davis's otherwise extremely pessimistic diagnosis and prognosis. More optimistically perhaps, as some commentators have suggested, the increased popularity of rap can build inter-racial communication (Stephens, 1992) as part of a process of the generation of new alliances and relationships between groups.

Davis (1993a, 1993b) elaborated upon his account of gangs, although the above criticism still applies. In particular, in the context of an analysis that demonstrates the continued, and indeed worsening, exploitation of black and Latino groups in Los Angeles in both political and economic terms, where promises of aid and new jobs after the riots/uprising of 1992 have been broken, Davis argues that the gangs have increasingly been demonised as the latest threat to white suburban Americans, replacing the now extinct communist menace.

In such demonising **discourse** (p. 30), the gangs are presented as the cause of the riots of 1992, which followed the first Rodney King trial where members of the Los Angeles Police Department were acquitted. It has been suggested that the way forward is increased police action against these groups. Thus one of the architects of the truce between the gangs, which was agreed before the verdict in the Rodney King trial, was subsequently arrested and imprisoned on a relatively small-scale offence. Davis's argument is that, in effect, this allows the appearance that 'something is being done' when in fact such police action will only make the problems of Los Angeles worse. In this sort of analysis the gangs have become the contemporary folk devils of the United States; a moral panic has been generated around them which has led to the expansion of the culture of social control. These are concepts, while not used directly in Davis's discussion, that were first developed by Stanley Cohen in the early 1970s (see section 8.3).

This section discussing deviance, subcultures and gangs has pointed up a number of issues that resonate through more general work on youth subcultures. Thus, it has been argued that youth subcultures arise at specific points of stress between social structure and culture and that they may oppose or resist dominant or mainstream values and culture. More specifically, subcultures can arise at points of economic dislocation or in the context of social dislocation caused by redevelopment and so on. A different emphasis can be found in the idea that these activities result from 'drift' at particular points in the life-course, and yet another in the idea that the culture of the subculture relates to the class context in which it is found. Finally, there is the attention paid to the role of masculinity within the subculture. These are all themes that appear in the work in Britain of the Birmingham Centre for Contemporary Cultural Studies. However, before this can be discussed it is necessary to consider a rather different form of attention to subculture, as this points to the role of the media in generating images of youth.

8.3 | Folk devils, moral panics and subcultures

Stanley Cohen's *Folk Devils and Moral Panics* (1973) acted as one important bridge between the emphasis on deviance in the American literature on subcultures and the emerging British approach. This section examines this work in some detail, before considering some more recent discussions of the nature of moral panic.

8.3.1 | Stanley Cohen: *Folk Devils and Moral Panics*

Stanley Cohen developed and expanded upon the work of American writers such as Howard Becker (1963), who emphasised the way in which deviants and deviance are created by the way in which they are labelled as such by powerful agencies of social control. Cohen moved away from a focus on the nature and values of deviant subcultures and the explanation of their deviance. Instead, he emphasised the *reaction* of various official bodies and the media (especially the press) to relatively small-scale disturbances that took place at English seaside towns between 1964 and 1966, which created a moral panic in society around the folk devils of mods and rockers. This moral panic is a central aspect in the development of a control culture. The specific moral panics examined by Cohen and the folk devils around which they centred are now part of history. However, his ideas and approach have continued to be highly influential and used in analysis of present-day issues (see, for example, Taylor, 1991).

Cohen spends little time describing what actually occurred in the towns. Indeed most of the description that he does provide comes towards the end of his book rather than at the beginning. Rather, he begins with what he calls 'The Inventory', which emphasises the media reporting of the clashes of mods and rockers (see Box 8.2 for photographs of these early 1960s subcultures). Cohen argues that the media reporting systematically exaggerated and distorted the events, maintained that they would inevitably happen again therefore predicting future occurrences of the same type, and used mods and rockers in a symbolic way. According to Cohen, there are 'three processes in such symbolization: a word (Mod) becomes symbolic of a certain status (delinquent or deviant); objects (hairstyle, clothing) symbolize the word; the objects themselves become symbolic of the status (and the emotions attached to the status)' (Cohen, 1973: 40).

Cohen develops his analysis through a detailed examination of the reaction to the seaside events. He first discusses what was thought about the mods and rockers and follows this with a consideration of what was proposed should be done about them. He argues that there were three themes running through the first dimension of reaction (Cohen, 1973: 51):

- 'Orientation': 'the emotional and intellectual standpoint from which the deviance is evaluated'.
- 'Images': 'opinions about that nature of the deviants and their behaviour'.
- 'Causation': 'opinions about the causes of the behaviour'.

There were two main themes running through orientation. First, there were those whose spoke as if what had occurred was akin to a natural disaster. For example, there was talk of towns being 'wrecked'. Second, many statements saw what had occurred as presaging worse developments. They were prophecies of doom. Likewise, two recurring themes ran through the images: that young people were affluent and bored. In terms of causation, mods and rockers were seen as indicators of social decline. 'The aspects of the social malaise most commonly mentioned were: the decline in religious beliefs, the absence of a sense of purpose, the influence of the do-gooders' approach and the coddling by the welfare state' (Cohen, 1973: 62). The behaviour of the young people was often seen as a kind of disease. Through these processes from, in Cohen's view, relatively trivial occurrences, a moral panic was generated.

The generation of a moral panic in turn produces opinions and actions to do 'something about it'. Cohen (1973: 77) discusses these responses through three further categories: '(i) Sensitisation; (ii) the Societal Control Culture; (iii) Exploitation'. He argues that the process of sensitisation involves far more attention being taken of acts of 'hooliganism', the description of such acts in terms of mods and rockers when previously they may have been described as acts of other young people, and the expansion of the symbolisation process described above.

The reaction of the 'Societal Control Culture' is a particularly important part of Cohen's analysis. He examines three main agents of social control – the police, the courts and local 'action groups' – suggesting that three common elements were of particular importance in the actions of these institutions: diffusion, escalation and innovation. Reaction diffused away from the original point of occurrence to other institutions. Thus, for example:

> in response to the Mods and Rockers, involvement diffused (not, of course, in a straight line) from the local police force, to collaboration with neighbouring forces, to regional collaboration, to co-ordination activity at Scotland Yard and the Home Office and to the involvement of Parliament and the legislature. (1973: 86)

Furthermore, this process involved escalation of the perceived seriousness of the problem. Innovation involved the introduction, or ideas for introduction, of new methods of social control to deal with the perceived problem. Cohen discusses the actions of the different components of the control culture in some detail, before considering the exploitation of the phenomenon much more briefly. For example, consumer goods such as sunglasses were advertised using mod imagery. Cohen sees a 'flow' taking place of the kind shown here:

(i)   *Initial deviance* leading to:

(ii) the *inventory* and (iii) *sensitization* which feed back on each other so as to produce:

(iv) an *over-estimation* of the deviance which leads to:

(v)   an *escalation* of the control culture. (Cohen, 1973: 143)

In the final chapter of his book, Cohen considers the development of the subcultures of the mods and rockers although, as he subsequently recognised (1987: ii–iii), his

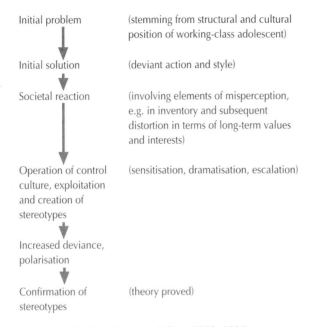

Figure 8.2 ▨ Deviance amplification. (Source: Cohen, 1973: 199.)

analysis here was not particularly innovative, owing a lot to the earlier work of Downes (1966) who, drawing on the American ideas discussed in section 8.2, had argued that 'The English "corner boy" successfully traverses the humiliations of school and job allocation by his re-affirmation of traditional working-class values' (1966: 258). As Cohen says, 'It is quite true that the book was more a study of moral panics than of folk devils. Influenced by labelling theory, I wanted to study reaction; the actors themselves just flitted across the screen' (1987: iii). The discussion of the generation and nature of subcultures was taken forward in the work carried out at the Birmingham Centre for Contemporary Cultural Studies (sections 8.4–8.8).

The sort of approach that he elaborated, which is represented in the diagram from Cohen in Figure 8.2 has been hugely influential.

8.3.2 | Moral panic today

The idea of a moral panic has passed into everyday speech and examples of the process described by Cohen seem to occur at regular intervals. All sorts of groups from football hooligans and striking workers to single mothers seem to be labelled as folk devils and to generate moral panics. You may wish to think of some examples of your own to consider. In accord with the rather pessimistic tone of Cohen's work, these panics are seen by some commentators as strategies on the part of those in power to create diversions from 'real issues'. Thus, the idea of blaming single mothers for delinquency and for taking up council housing is used to divert attention from more important causes of rule-breaking such as unemployment or the under-funding of public services. However, one problem with this point of view is that it is not clear that the wider public actually agrees with the definitions of these groups that are contained in the tabloid press. Indeed, Cohen himself found that significant proportions of the public were much less concerned about mods and rockers than the press hysteria would have led the commentator to believe. Thus these representations may be more important to members of the control culture than to the wider public, which does not mean that they are any less effective or consequential.

Furthermore, it can be suggested that various groups have become more sophisticated in their understanding and use of the idea of a moral panic since Cohen's original analysis. For example, in discussion of the development and reaction to rave culture in Britain, Sarah Thornton (1994, 1995) argues that, in part due to the way that he focused his attention on national and local newspapers, Cohen misses the way in which moral panic is both a marketing strategy and something sought by potential 'folk devils' (see also Angela McRobbie, 1994). Thus many such groups would actually welcome negative tabloid coverage as it can promote the group and music more widely. As Thornton argues:

> Although negative reporting is disparaged, it is subject to anticipation, even aspiration. Affirmative tabloid coverage, on the other hand, is the kiss of death. Cultural studies and sociologies of moral panic have tended to position youth cultures as innocent victims of negative stigmatization. But mass media understanding is often a goal, not just an effect of youth's cultural pursuits. Moral panic is therefore a form of routinized hype orchestrated by the culture industries that target the market. Moralizing denunciations are, to quote one music monthly, a 'priceless PR campaign'. They render a subculture attractively subversive as no other promotional ploy can.
>
> (Thornton, 1994: 184)

Subcultures are as much generated by music magazines and the music press (which are themselves parts of multinational companies) as they are by subcultural adherents themselves (Thornton, 1994, 1995). They do not exist in some pure state ready to be exploited and demonised. Furthermore, most fanzines tended to appear after the tabloid moral panic rather than before it (1994: 185). They were thus heavily nostalgic for the supposed pure rave scene which had existed prior to tabloid exploitation!

The points made by Thornton should alert the student of moral panics to the complexity of the relation between subcultures, the media and societal or control culture reaction. While the idea of moral panic remains a useful tool, it should perhaps be used carefully in the context of thorough analysis.

Having considered some of the early material which looked at the way in which subcultures are developed and the values that they express, as well as the importance of media reaction to them, it is now possible to consider the way in which the influential discussion of subculture at the **Birmingham Centre for Contemporary Cultural Studies** inflected these ideas in particular, distinctive and influential ways.

8.4 | Youth subcultures in British cultural studies

Much research on subculture, which has focused on youth subcultures, draws on the two most important meanings of culture outlined in Chapter 1: first, that which uses culture to refer to the works and practices of artistic and intellectual activity. In this sense, music or a painting is a form of culture, where schoolwork, for example, is not. At times, this definition of culture involves a judgement of value. Thus, certain forms of writing, such as by Dickens or Shakespeare, are held to be proper 'culture' and works by writers such as Jackie Collins or Harold Robbins to be trash. As we have shown, the second sense of culture is rather different, referring to the idea of culture as a 'way of life'. This more inclusive definition can be found in problematic expressions such as 'the American way of life' or 'British culture'. Both of these definitions fed into the development of what has increasingly become known as British Cultural Studies (Turner, 1990) in the **Centre for Contemporary Cultural Studies** (CCCS) at the University of Birmingham and it is from within this approach that many of the most important studies of youth subcultures have been carried out.

Key influence **8.1**

The Centre for Contemporary Cultural Studies (CCCS)

Also known as the Birmingham Centre for Contemporary Cultural Studies or the 'Birmingham School', the Centre was the key site for the development of cultural studies. Birmingham is now less influential as cultural studies has expanded to become an international activity.

The Centre was founded by Richard Hoggart in 1964 initially within the English Department. Hoggart was the first director, with Stuart Hall as his deputy. Hall became director in 1968 when Hoggart left to work at UNESCO. Hall led the Centre through its most productive period before leaving in 1979. He was succeeded by his own deputy, Richard Johnson. In the wake of upheavals in the Social Sciences and Arts at the University of Birmingham, the Centre became the Department of Cultural Studies.

Founded in many ways to develop the approach formulated by Hoggart in *The Uses of Literacy* (1957), the Centre rapidly made its mark through its Stencilled Occasional Papers Series which included papers on topics as diverse as women domestic servants, the Kray twins and the theory of Karl Marx. It also produced its own journal, *Working Papers in Cultural Studies*. These were the sites for the first publication of many of the Centre's best-known writers whose ideas later appeared in book form. By the 1970s, the Centre's activities were contextualised by a **Gramscian** (p. 38) Marxist emphasis on the role of culture in **resistance** (p. 258) and **hegemonic** (p. 106) domination. This informed the analyses in collective texts such as *Resistance through Rituals* (1976), *Policing the Crisis* (1978), *On Ideology* (1977) and

→

Working-Class Culture (1979). The Marxist emphasis on class was contested by feminists at the Centre in *Women take Issue* (1978) and its relative inattention to 'race' in *The Empire Strikes Back* (1982). The work of Richard Johnson led to a more historical approach in *Making Histories* (1982). Writers associated with the Centre through this period include Stuart Hall, Paul Willis, Dick Hebdige, Angela McRobbie, Iain Chambers and Paul Gilroy. There are many others. The upheavals of the 1980s and the expansion of cultural studies made Birmingham less important, although it continues to publish a journal, *Cultural Studies from Birmingham*, and books.

The Centre's attention to youth culture, news, ideology, race, cultural politics and gender in ways that took popular culture seriously from within an academic Marxist approach was the key moment in the formation of the cultural studies approach. Authors once associated with the Centre continue to fill some of the most senior and influential positions in academic cultural studies. However, the points of view developed at Birmingham (the over-unified idea of a 'school' is very misleading) are now only a part of the much wider activity of cultural studies.

Further reading

Hall, S. and Jefferson, T. (eds) (1976) *Resistance through Rituals: Youth Subcultures in Post-war Britain*, London: Hutchinson.

Hall, S., Critcher , C., Jefferson, T., Clarke, J. and Roberts, B. (1978) *Policing the Crisis: Mugging, the State and Law and Order*, London: Macmillan

Hall, S., Hobson, D., Lowe, A. and Willis, P. (eds) (1980) *Culture, Media, Language*, London: Hutchinson.

8.4.1 | *Resistance through Rituals*: the general approach

The cornerstone paper which outlines many of the concepts and themes pursued in the work from Birmingham is 'Subcultures, cultures and class' (Clarke *et al.*, 1976) in the collection *Resistance through Rituals* (Hall and Jefferson, 1976). Some key definitions are set out in this paper. A particularly important passage is reproduced in Box 8.1.

There are *seven* concepts introduced in this passage which need to be considered in some detail: culture, **hegemony** (p. 106), dominant culture, dominant ideology, class culture, subculture and parent culture. All of these are used extensively in CCCS work and in much of the subsequent literature on subcultures.

The definition of culture produced within this tradition (Clarke *et al.*, 1976: 10) explains that:

> we understand the word culture to refer to that level at which social groups develop distinct patterns of life, and give *expressive form* to their social and material life experience. Culture is the way, the forms, in which groups 'handle' the raw material of their social and material existence.

Box 8.1

Some definitions

We begin with some minimal definitions. The term, 'Youth Culture', directs us to the 'cultural' aspects of youth. We understand the word 'culture' to refer to that level at which social groups develop distinct patterns of life, and give *expressive form* to their social and material life-experience. Culture is the way, the forms, in which groups 'handle' the raw material of their social and material existence. 'We must suppose the raw material of life experience to be at one pole, and all the infinitely complex human disciplines and systems, articulate and inarticulate, formalised in institutions or dispersed in the least formal ways, which "handle", transmit or distort this raw material, to be at the other' (Thompson, 1960). 'Culture' is the *practice* which realises or *objectivates* group-life in meaningful shape and form. 'As individuals express their life, so they are. What they are, therefore, coincides with their production, both in *what* they produce and with *how* they produce' (Marx, 1970: 42). The 'culture' of a group or class is the peculiar and distinctive 'way of life' of the group or class, the meanings, values and ideas embodied in institutions, in social relations, in systems of beliefs, in *mores* and customs, in the uses of objects and material life. Culture is the distinctive shapes in which this material and social organisation of life expresses itself. A culture includes the 'maps of meaning' which make things intelligible to its members. These 'maps of meaning' are not simply carried around in the head: they are objectivated in the patterns of social organisation and relationship through which the individual becomes a 'social individual'. Culture is the way the social relations of a group are structured and shaped: but it is also the way those shapes are experienced, understood and interpreted.

A social individual, born into a particular set of institutions and relations, is at the same moment born into a peculiar configuration of meanings, which give her access to and locate her within 'a culture'. The 'law of society' and the 'law of culture' (the symbolic ordering of social life) are one and the same. These structures – of social relationship and of meaning – shape the on-going collective existence of groups. But they also limit, modify and *constrain* how groups live and reproduce their social existence. Men and women are, thus, formed, and form themselves through society, culture and history. So the existing cultural patterns form a sort of historical reservoir – a pre-constituted 'field of the possibles' – which groups take up, transform, develop. Each group makes something of its starting conditions – and through this 'making', through this practice, culture is reproduced and transmitted. But this practice only takes place within the given field of possibilities and constraints (see, Sartre, 1963). 'Men make their own history, but they do not make it just as they please; they do not make it under circumstances chosen by themselves, but under circumstances directly

→

encountered, given and transmitted from the past' (Marx, 1951: 225). Culture, then, embodies the trajectory of group life through history: always under conditions and with 'raw materials' which cannot wholly be of its own making.

Groups which exist within the same society and share some of the same material and historical conditions no doubt also understand, and to a certain extent share each other's 'culture'. But just as different groups and classes are unequally ranked in relation to one another, in terms of their productive relations, wealth and power, so *cultures* are differently ranked, and stand in opposition to one another, in relations of domination and subordination, along the scale of 'cultural power'. The definitions of the world, 'the maps of meaning', which express the life situation of those groups which hold the monopoly of power in society, command the greatest weight and influence, secrete the greatest legitimacy. The world tends to be classified out and ordered in terms and through structures which most directly express the power, the position, the *hegemony*, of the powerful interest in that society. Thus,

> The class which has the means of material production at its disposal, has control, at the same time, over the means of mental production, so that, thereby, generally speaking, the ideas of those who lack the means of mental production are subject to it ... Insofar as they rule as a class and determine the extent and compass of an epoch ... they do this in its whole range, hence, among other things rule also as thinkers, as producers of ideas, and regulate the production and distribution of the ideas of their age: thus their ideas are the ruling ideas of the epoch.
>
> Marx (1970: 64)

This does not mean that there is only *one* set of ideas or cultural forms in a society. There will be more than one tendency at work within the dominant ideas of a society. Groups or classes which do not stand at the apex of power, nevertheless find ways of expressing and realising in their culture their subordinate position and experiences. In so far as there is more than one fundamental class in a society (and capitalism is essentially the bringing together, around production, of two fundamentally *different* classes – capital and labour) there will be more than one major cultural configuration in play at a particular historical moment. But the structures and meanings which most adequately reflect the position and interests of the most powerful class – however complex it is internally – will stand, in relation to all the others, as a *dominant* social-cultural order. The dominant culture represents itself as *the* culture. It tries to define and contain all other cultures within its inclusive range. *Its* views of the world, unless challenged, will stand as the most natural, all-embracing, universal culture. Other cultural configurations will not only be subordinate to this dominant order: they will enter into struggle with it, seek to modify, negotiate, resist or even overthrow its reign – its *hegemony*. The struggle between classes over material and social life thus always

→

assumes the forms of a continuous struggle over the distribution of 'cultural power'. We might want, here, to make a distinction between 'culture' and 'ideology'. Dominant and subordinate classes will each have distinct cultures. But when one culture gains ascendancy over the other, and when the subordinate culture *experiences* itself in terms prescribed by the dominant culture, then the dominant culture has also become the basis of a dominant ideology.

The dominant culture of a complex society is never a homogeneous structure. It is layered, reflecting different interests within the dominant class (e.g. an aristocratic versus a bourgeois outlook), containing different traces from the past (e.g. religious ideas within a largely secular culture), as well as emergent elements in the present. Subordinate cultures will not always be in open conflict with it. They may, for long periods, coexist with it, negotiate the spaces and gaps in it, make inroads into it, 'warrenning it from within' (Thompson, 1965). However, though the nature of this struggle over culture can never be reduced to a simple opposition, it is crucial to replace the notion of 'culture' with the more concrete, historical concept of 'cultures': a redefinition which brings out more clearly the fact that cultures always stand in relations of domination – and subordination – to one another, are always, in some sense, in struggle with one another. The singular term, 'culture', can only indicate, in the most general and abstract way, the large cultural configurations at play in a society at any historical moment. We must move at once to the determining relationships of domination and subordination in which these configurations stand; to the processes of incorporation and resistance which define the cultural dialectic between them; and to the institutions which transmit and reproduce 'the culture' (i.e. the dominant culture) in its dominant or 'hegemonic' form.

In modern societies, the most fundamental groups are the social classes, and the major cultural configurations will be, in a fundamental though often mediated way, 'class cultures'. Relative to these cultural-class configurations, *sub-*cultures are sub-sets – smaller, more localised and differentiated structures, within one or other of the larger cultural networks. We must, first, see sub-cultures in terms of their relation to the wider class-cultural networks of which they form a distinctive part. When we examine this relationship between a sub-culture and the 'culture' of which it is a part, we call the latter the 'parent' culture. This must not be confused with the particular relationship between 'youth' and their 'parents', of which much will be said below. What we mean is that a sub-culture, though differing in important ways – in its 'focal concerns', its peculiar shapes and activities – from the culture from which it derives, will also share some things in common with that 'parent' culture. The bohemian sub-culture of the *avant-garde* which has arisen from time to time in the modern city, is both distinct from its 'parent' culture (the urban culture of the middle class intelligentsia) and yet also a part of it (sharing with it a modernising outlook, standards of education, a

→

privileged position vis-à-vis productive labour, and so on). In the same way, the 'search for pleasure and excitement' which some analysts have noted as a marked feature of the 'delinquent sub-culture of the gang' in the working class, also shares something basic and fundamental with it. Sub-cultures, then, must first be related to the 'parent cultures' of which they are a sub-set. But, sub-cultures must *also* be analysed in terms of their relation to the dominant culture – the overall disposition of cultural power in the society as a whole. Thus we may distinguish respectable, 'rough', delinquent and the criminal sub-cultures *within* working-class culture: but we may also say that, though they differ amongst themselves, they *all* derive in the first instance from a 'working-class parent culture': hence, they are all subordinate sub-cultures, in relation to the dominant middle-class or bourgeois culture. (We believe this goes some way towards meeting Graham Murdock's call for a more 'symmetrical' analysis of sub-cultures . . .

Sub-cultures must exhibit a distinctive enough shape and structure to make them identifiably different from their 'parent' culture. They must be focussed around certain activities, values, certain uses of material artefacts, territorial spaces etc. which significantly differentiate them from the wider culture. But, since they are sub-sets, there must also be significant things which bind and articulate them with the 'parent' culture. The famous Kray twins, for example, belonged both to a highly differentiated 'criminal sub-culture' in East London and to the 'normal' life and culture of the East End working class (of which indeed, the 'criminal sub-culture' has always been a clearly identifiable part). The behaviour of the Krays in terms of the criminal fraternity marks the differentiating axis of that sub-culture: the relation of the Krays to their mother, family, home and local pub is the binding, the articulating axis (Pearson, 1973; Hebdige, 1974).

Sub-cultures, therefore, take shape around the distinctive activities and 'focal concerns' of groups. They can be loosely or tightly bounded. Some sub-cultures are merely loosely-defined strands or 'milieux' within the parent culture: they possess no distinctive 'world' of their own. Others develop a clear, coherent identity and structure. Generally, we deal in this volume *only* with 'sub-cultures' (whether drawn from a middle- or working-class 'parent culture') which have reasonably tight boundaries, distinctive shapes, which have cohered around particular activities, focal concerns and territorial spaces. When these tightly-defined groups are also distinguished by age and generation, we call them 'youth sub-cultures'.

'Youth sub-cultures' form up on the terrain of social and cultural life. Some youth sub-cultures are regular and persistent features of the 'parent' class-culture: the ill-famed 'culture of delinquency' of the working-class adolescent male, for example. But some sub-cultures appear only at particular historical moments: they become visible, are identified and labelled (either by themselves or others): they

→

command the stage of public attention for a time: then they fade, disappear or are so widely diffused that they lose their distinctiveness. It is the *latter* kind of sub-culture formation which primarily concerns us here. The peculiar dress, style, focal concerns, milieux, etc. of the Teddy Boy, the Mod, the Rocker or the Skinhead set them off, as distinctive groupings, both from the broad patterns of working-class culture as a whole, and also from the more diffused patterns exhibited by 'ordinary' working-class boys (and, to a more limited extent, girls). Yet, despite these differences, it is important to stress that, as sub-cultures, they continue to exist within, and coexist with, the more inclusive culture of the class from which they spring. Members of a sub-culture may walk, talk, act, look 'different' from their parents and from some of their peers: but they belong to the same families, go to the same schools, work at much the same jobs, live down the same 'mean streets' as their peers and parents. In certain crucial respects, they share the same position (vis-à-vis the dominant culture), the same fundamental and determining life-experiences, as the 'parent' culture from which they derive. Through dress, activities, leisure pursuits and life-style, they may project a different cultural response or 'solution' to the problems posed for them by their material and social class position and experience. But the membership of a sub-culture cannot protect them from the determining matrix of experiences and conditions which shape the life of their class as a whole. They experience and respond to the *same basic problematic* as other members of their class who are not so differentiated and distinctive in a 'sub-cultural' sense. Especially in relation to the *dominant* culture, their sub-culture remains like other elements in their class culture – subordinate and subordinated.

Clarke *et al.* (1976: 10–15)

There are three aspects of social life identified in this definition: social experience, social groups and patterns of life. In their view, social groups develop distinct patterns of life, based on their own social experiences, in relation to other social groups and forms of experience. Culture is both a level or area of society (distinct from the economic or political) and the forms in which the raw material of social experience is handled.

We shall explore the particular way in which **hegemony** (p. 106) is subsequently used in this essay below. Clarke *et al.* further argue that there is a dominant culture which connects to the dominant class. However, they do not actually identify the content of this dominant culture, nor likewise do they explicate the specific content of the dominant **ideology** (p. 84), nor provide much detail on the conceptualisation of this concept, which is further discussed in Chapter 3.

The argument of Clarke *et al.* rests on Marxist premises, which is reflected in their assertion that classes are 'the most fundamental social groups'. This generates the further assumption that cultures are fundamentally class cultures. Subcultures are 'sub-sets – smaller, more localised and differentiated structures, within one or other of the larger cultural networks' (p. 13). Subcultures in this approach have to be seen in a class context. Finally, the paper elucidated the concept of parent culture. Thus, there was a working-class parent culture which generated other distinguishable subcultures, as the discussion of the East End working class in Box 8.1 shows.

The analysis in the paper and, despite some differences of emphasis, in the CCCS tradition, is based around the study of the 'double articulation of youth subcultures' (p. 15). Youth subcultures are connected, first, to their parent culture; in the case of working-class youth subcultures, this is to working-class culture; and second, to the dominant culture.

After outlining their general approach and some of their key concepts, Clarke *et al.* examine some of the different dimensions of the debate on youth and youth culture that had emerged since the Second World War. In what was a common mode of exposition in work from CCCS, the discussion seeks to outline and then recontextualise everyday debates and common sense. They begin by identifying the factors that had been thought in earlier literature to be responsible for the generation of the new youth culture. These included: first, affluence in that society in general, and young people in particular had more money to spend; second, the spread of mass communication, especially television; third, social dislocation brought on by the Second World War; fourth, educational changes which produced more extensive participation; and finally, the emergence of new styles and fashions.

These factors in themselves were to be understood in the wider context of debate about social change since the war. There were three key terms in this debate: affluence, consensus and embourgeoisement. The new affluence, apparent agreement on politics and the decline of political dispute were, in the eyes of many commentators, leading the working class to adopt middle-class values and practices. Class was thought to be becoming less important in society. Clarke *et al.* recognise that there was evidence for the existence of some aspects of this idea. There had been a rise in living standards, although the established pattern of social inequality remained, and party politics did seem to be based on substantial agreement, with the two main parties between them gathering a very high proportion of the total votes cast in elections. The actual evidence for embourgeoisement was much less convincing, although there did appear to be some shifts in the values of more affluent workers. Despite this, class and social inequalities had not disappeared.

Clarke *et al.* are critical of the American deviance literature summarised in section 8.2 for its relative neglect of class. They also suggest that the beginnings of a more satisfactory approach to the study of youth subcultures had begun to be developed in Britain by Mike Brake and Graham Murdock, who had taken class seriously. The fault of these approaches was that, in attempting to see subcultures as engaged in collective 'problem-solving', these authors had accepted the idea of a problem 'too unpro-blematically' (p. 29). They did not accord sufficient weight to aspects of class culture and class socialisation. The most sophisticated precursor to the *Resistance through Rituals* approach, which greatly influenced Clarke *et al.*, was a paper by Phil Cohen (1980, first published in 1972 in the CCCS journal *Working Papers in Cultural Studies*) which examined the nature of youth subcultures in the East End of London in the 1960s.

8.4.2 | Phil Cohen: working-class youth subcultures in East London

Phil Cohen (1980) argued that, after the Second World War from the 1950s onwards, the East End working-class community was disrupted by three factors: first, migration out of the area to new towns such as Harlow, Stevenage and Basildon; second, the redevelopment of housing involving the building of new tower blocks which were patterned on a middle-class nuclear family model that destroyed the communal spaces and the patterns of female support characteristic of the East End; third, a series of economic changes, which led to a 'polarization of the labour force' (Cohen, 1980: 80) between specialised, 'high tech', well-paid jobs and dead-end, unskilled labour.

One outcome of this process of dislocation was the development of youth sub-cultures, like teds, mods and skinheads, which opposed the working-class parent culture. In Cohen's (1980: 82) view, 'the internal conflicts of the parent culture came to be worked out in terms of generational conflict'. Furthermore Cohen argued that youth subcultures 'express and resolve, albeit "magically", the contradictions which remain hidden or unresolved in the parent culture' (1980: 82). Subcultures are ways of dealing

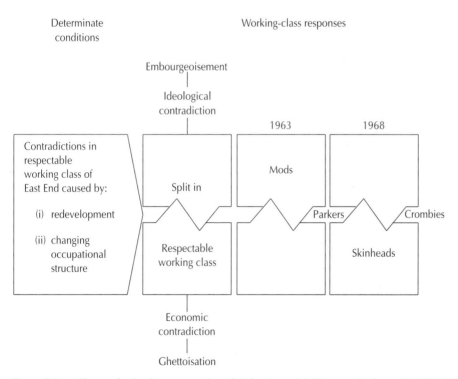

Figure 8.3 ▪ Class and subcultures: a version of Cohen's model. (Source: Clarke et al., 1976: 34.)

with the difficulties that structural transformations in society have produced in the parent culture to which they belong. Following the pattern of the polarisation of the workforce between an upward or downward option, Cohen argues that youth sub-cultures can express such routes in a variety of different ways. Hence:

> [M]ods, parkas, skinheads, crombies are a succession of subcultures which all correspond to the same parent culture and which attempt to work out, through a system of transformations, the basic problematic or contradiction which is inserted in the subculture by the parent culture.   (Cohen 1980: 83)

This sort of approach was represented diagrammatically by Clarke *et al.* (1976), as shown in Figure 8.3. Cohen argued that there were upward (for example, mod) and downward (for example, skinhead) responses to these conditions which attempted to resolve structural problems in an ideological fashion.

Box **8.2**

Some readings and pictures of subcultures

A young Teddy Boy, 1955. (Source: Getty Images.)

Thus the 'Teddy Boy' expropriation of an upper class style of dress 'covers' the gap between largely manual, unskilled, near-lumpen real careers and life-chances, and the 'all-dressed-up-and-nowhere-to-go' experience of Saturday evening. Thus, in the expropriation and fetishisation of consumption and style itself, the 'Mods' cover for the gap between the never-ending-weekend and Monday's resumption of boring, dead-end work. Thus, in the resurrection of an archetypal and 'symbolic' (but, in fact, anachronistic) form of working-class dress, in the displaced focussing on the football match and the 'occupation' of the football 'ends', Skinheads reassert, but 'imaginarily', the values of a class, the essence of a style, a kind of 'fan-ship' to which few working-class adults any longer sub-scribe: they 're-present' a sense of territory and locality which the planners and speculators are rapidly destroying: they 'declare' as alive and well a game which is being commercialised, profes-sionalised and spectacularised. 'Skins Rule, OK'.

Clarke *et al.* (1976: 48)

8.4.3 | Ideology and hegemony

Clarke *et al.* (1976) identified a number of problems with Cohen's article, including the historical specificity of the analysis, the precise way in which the structural conditions affected the subcultural adherents, the causes of the upward and downward solutions and so on. However, they were concerned to build upon Cohen's approach which was therefore a crucial influence on their arguments. In particular they wanted to emphasise the idea that subcultures represented an ideological or, in a phrase influenced by the work on **ideology** (p. 84) of the French Marxist Louis Althusser (1971), an 'imaginary relation' to their real conditions of life.

Clarke *et al.* explore in some detail structural and class changes and the relations between dominant and parent cultures which produce subcultures. The working class had been affected by changes in employment patterns and housing which affected the

top left: A 'ton-up' woman on her bike, *c.* 1960. (Source: Getty Images.)

top right: A Skinhead, 1980. (Source: Getty Images.)

bottom: A Mod on his scooter, 1964. (Source: Getty Images.)

nature of the working-class family and the way in which it could act to protect the working class from the power of the dominant class. The generation of subcultures was also located in the changing patterns of **hegemony** (p. 106).

We have discussed this concept in other places (Chapter 3); however, it is important to pay attention to the specific way in which this concept is used in this approach. Clarke *et al.* (1976: 38) argue that:

> Gramsci used the term 'hegemony' to refer to the moment when a ruling class is able, not only to coerce a subordinate class to conform to its interests, but to exert a 'hegemony' or 'total social authority' over subordinate classes. This involves the exercise of a special kind of power – the power to frame alternatives and contain opportunities, to win and shape consent, so that the granting of legitimacy to the dominant classes appears not only 'spontaneous' but natural and normal.

Furthermore, such hegemony 'works through ideology, but it does not consist of false ideas, perceptions, or definitions. It works primarily by inserting the subordinate class into the key institutions and structures which support the power and social authority of the dominant order' (Clarke *et al.*, 1976: 39). Hegemony is not consistent in that at some points the dominant class is dominant without the aid of hegemony. Hence, at times 'economic crisis' and 'unemployment' do the job just as well. Furthermore, at other points the dominant class will be overthrown and by definition hegemony does not exist. In sum, 'the idea of "permanent class hegemony" or of "permanent incorporation" must be ditched' (1976: 41).

Within the context of such patterns of domination the working class had won space for themselves, where they often developed their own forms and ways of life. Subcultures do the same sort of thing, winning space for young working-class people. 'They "solve", but in an imaginary way, problems which at the concrete material level remain unresolved' (Clarke *et al.*, 1976: 47–8).

Clarke *et al.* apply this idea to three subcultures in the passage reproduced in Box 8.2, where you will also find visual representations of these three subcultures, among others. Furthermore, 'In organising their response to these experiences, working-class youth sub-cultures take some things principally from the located "parent" culture: but they apply and transform them to the situations and experiences characteristic of their distinctive group-life and generational experience' (1976: 53).

8.4.4 | Structures, cultures and biographies

Three key terms are used by the authors of this article to summarise their approach: *structures*, *cultures* and *biographies*. The definitions given by Clarke *et al.* (1976: 57) of these are detailed in Box 8.3.

These can be used as keywords to remember the theory and approach developed in *Resistance through Rituals*. The essay by Clarke *et al.* concludes with a rather dated section on the counter-culture and a discussion of the reaction to youth which considers the idea of moral panic introduced above. The book also contains a number of discussions of specific subcultures: teds, mods and skinheads and elaborations of some of the key

Box 8.3

Structures, cultures and biographies

Structures are the set of socially-organised positions and experiences of the class in relation to the major institutions and structures. These positions generate a set of common relations and experiences from which meaningful actions – individual and collective – are constructed.

Cultures are the range of socially-organised and patterned responses to these basic material and social conditions. Though cultures form, for each group, a set of traditions – lines of action inherited from the past – they must always be collectively constructed anew in each generation.

Biographies are the 'careers' of particular individuals through these structures and cultures – the means by which individual identities and life-histories are constructed out of collective experiences. Biographies recognise the element of individuation in the paths which individual lives take through collective structures and cultures, but they must not be conceived as either wholly individual or free-floating.

Clarke *et al.* (1976: 57)

concepts such as style. It also includes some significant criticisms of the approach. However, before these difficulties are discussed it is important to consider some of the other most important work that emanated from CCCS in this period.

8.5 | Three studies from the Birmingham Centre for Contemporary Cultural Studies

In this section we examine three studies which have been taken as very influential exemplars of the CCCS approach: *Learning to Labour* (Willis, 1977), *Profane Culture* (Willis, 1978) and *Subculture: The Meaning of Style* (Hebdige, 1979).

8.5.1 | Paul Willis: *Learning to Labour*

Learning to Labour has achieved the status of a classic text. Its title and subtitle – *How Working Class Kids Get Working Class Jobs* – summarise its content clearly. Working in the context of a discussion of how school prepares young people for different slots in the labour market and therefore ensures the continued reproduction of a division of labour in contemporary capitalist society, Willis demonstrates the continuities between the culture of a group of secondary school working-class rebels and the culture of their subsequent employment.

Willis's study mainly focuses on a group of twelve boys in a school that he calls Hammertown Boys. He identifies the different components of the culture of the boys whom he terms 'lads'. The lads oppose the authority of the school and they reject the conformist attitudes of those boys who follow the accepted ethic of the school who they call 'ear 'oles' or 'lobes', defining themselves as a group with an oppositional stance. One of the greatest sins that one of the 'lads' can commit is to 'grass' to the school authorities. The 'lads' attempt to get out of as much work as possible and to miss school if they can. At school they are concerned to 'have a laff', enjoying their own culture in the context of the school. This can involve goading teachers, bending the rules to see how far they can go and so on. They try to bring excitement into what in other ways may be boring lives and this can occur through expressions of 'hard' masculinity and in fighting. On one hand, women are treated as sex objects, and the lads will attempt to see 'how far they can go'; on the other, a steady girlfriend will be looked upon as a future wife to service domestic needs. In the often reported and continuing double standard of sexual behaviour, women who are sexually active will be derided. The 'lads' were also racist in behaviour and beliefs, expressing hatred of Pakistanis and Jamaicans, and reporting being involved in 'paki bashing'.

Willis argues that the main contours of this culture, despite bringing the 'lads' into conflict with the school authorities, actually prepared them for incorporation in forms of repetitive, heavy industrial work on the shopfloor. This was also based around forms of masculinity, practical joking, getting away with what you can, sexual bragging and so on. So in adopting what in some ways can be seen as an oppositional culture (to the school), or in ways opposing the dominant culture of their experience, by drawing on the resources of their working-class (male) parent culture the 'lads' were actually preparing themselves for the world of manual labour. In lots of ways this aids the reproduction of established patterns of exploitation. The culture of opposition actually suited the dominant culture.

8.5.2 | Paul Willis: *Profane Culture*

In *Profane Culture*, which reports on work carried out before that discussed in *Learning to Labour*, Willis (1978) examined various dimensions of the lives of two youth subcultural groups in the late 1960s: the motorbike boys and hippies. While these examples are rather dated, it is the nature of the link that Willis makes between different aspects of the lifestyle of these groups that resonated through work on subcultures. Thus, for example, Willis argued that the musical preferences of these groups were intimately connected to the nature of their lives. The motorbike boys' preference for early rock'n'roll in a 45 rpm single format and the hippies' like of album-based progressive rock was no accident. Rock'n'roll music matched the restlessness and mobility of the motorbike boys' lives:

> the suppression of structured time in the music, its ability to stop, start and be faded, matches the motor-bike boys' restless concrete life style. As we have seen, it is no accident that the boys preferred singles, nor is it an accident that the rock 'n' roll form

is the most suited to singles and its modern technology (fading, etc.). Both the music and its 'singles' form are supremely relevant to the style of the bike culture.

(Willis, 1978: 77)

Willis mounts a similar sort of argument about the homologous relationships between different aspects of a youth subculture for the hippies (see especially Willis, 1978: 168–9). In Hebdige's words (1979: 113) this expresses: 'the symbolic fit between the values and life-styles of a group, its subjective experience and the musical forms it uses to express or reinforce its focal concerns'. This means that subcultures are structured in that different aspects of the lifestyle of the subculture fit together to form a whole. So there is a homology between an 'alternative value system', 'hallucinogenic drugs' and progressive rock for the hippie subculture. Subcultures express a response to a set of conditions and the different aspects of the subculture are tied together into structured, relatively coherent wholes. The introduction of this concept, which was also used by Clarke *et al.*, was a very significant innovation on Willis's part.

8.5.3 | Dick Hebdige: *Subculture: The Meaning of Style*

Hebdige (1979) developed the reading of the styles of subcultural groups using the tools of the **structuralist** (p. 24) and **semiotic** (p. 34) approaches discussed in Chapter 2. In particular, he focused on the different dimensions of the style of subcultural groups. Using the general definition of culture proposed by Clarke *et al.* (1976), Hebdige argued that the styles expressed by different subcultures are a response to social conditions and experiences. Furthermore, according to Hebdige, such styles often encode an opposition to the dominant or **hegemonic** (p. 106) forms of culture associated with dominant groups. Such challenges are often indirect and can involve the utilisation and transformation of forms of culture that were previously the property of dominant groups. In engaging in such practices, subcultural members act as *bricoleurs* engaging in a process of *bricolage*, responding to the world around them by improvising in a structured fashion, creating meanings that are different from those of the dominant culture or dominant groups. As Hebdige (1979: 104) says about the teddy boy's style:

In this way the teddy boy's theft and transformation of the Edwardian style revived in the early 1950s by Saville Row for wealthy young men about town can be construed as an act of bricolage.

Hebdige argues that subcultures often **resist** (p. 258) the dominant social order, though indirectly and in symbolic ways. However, he also argues that forms of subcultural expression are often incorporated into the dominant social order through two main routes. First, there is the commodity form which involves 'the conversion of subcultural signs (dress, music, etc.) into mass-produced objects'. Second is 'the "labelling" and re-definition of deviant behaviour by dominant groups – the police, the media, the judiciary' (Hebdige, 1979: 94) in a process of ideological incorporation.

This sort of account of the ways in which subcultural groups produce new and resistant meanings which are then bought off or incorporated by the capitalist system is now relatively familiar. It entails the notion that there is some kind of sphere where 'authentic' meanings are produced which are then corrupted. However, Thornton (1994, 1995), as discussed in section 8.2, problematises this aspect of Hebdige's work, showing how media images are involved in subcultures from their inception.

8.6 | Youth subcultures and gender

One of the most important problems with the literature discussed in this chapter so far is its almost exclusive focus on boys or men. This myopia was first challenged from within the CCCS approach by **Angela McRobbie** (p. 343) and Jenny Garber (1976: 211) who asked four main questions:

> (1) Are girls really absent from the main post-war sub-cultures? Or are they present but invisible? (2) Where present and visible, were their roles the same, but more marginal, than boys; or were they different? (3) Whether marginal or different, is the position of girls specific to the sub-cultural option; or do their roles reflect the more general social-subordination of women in the central areas of mainstream culture – home, work, school, leisure? (4) If sub-cultural options are not readily available to girls, what are the different but complementary ways in which girls organise their cultural life? And are these, in their own terms, subcultural in form?

In response to (1) they argued that, at least partly because of the male bias of previous investigations, it was difficult to answer the question they had set. As the men who had studied subcultures had not looked at the possible participation of girls in them, girls' invisibility tended to be a self-fulfilling prophecy. In pursuing questions (2) and (3) they looked in more detail at the parts that women have played in three subcultures. First, in the rocker, greaser or motorbike subculture as described by Willis, women were subordinate. They were passengers on the motorbikes – they did not control them. Second, they considered the mod girls of the early 1960s, whom they see as prominent within the mod subculture. Third, they examined hippie culture, identifying two particular confining roles for women: the earth mother and the pre-Raphaelite fragile lady.

McRobbie and Garber argued that the places for women in the subcultures so far described were related to their wider social roles. They also suggested that girls tended to organise their cultural life differently to boys, forming a more home-based, romantic or 'teenybop' culture. This point and others made by McRobbie were developed in a subsequent critique of the male-dominated nature of research on subcultures (McRobbie, 1980) which argued that there are two main approaches that can be taken to previous male-dominated writing on subcultures. First, such accounts can be dismissed, or accepted as applicable only to boys, and attention placed on the different nature of girls' culture. Second, previous accounts, such as those by Willis (1977) and Hebdige (1979), can be read 'against the grain' to see what they can offer for the analysis of masculinity, both in the nature of the subcultures and the writing on them.

Key influence 8.2
Angela McRobbie (1951–)

Angela McRobbie is a British cultural analyst. She combines the study of different dimensions of youth culture with commentary on developments in cultural theory and politics.

McRobbie studied as a postgraduate at the **Centre for Contemporary Cultural Studies** (CCCS) (p. 327) at the University of Birmingham. She lectured in London before moving to Loughborough University. She is currently Professor of Communications at Goldsmith's College, University of London.

McRobbie's most well-known work centres on the analysis of gender in youth culture. She was critical of the 'malestream' nature of work carried out at CCCS on youth subcultures, emphasising the need to critique work by such as Paul Willis and Dick Hebdige for its lack of attention to gender, and the partial nature of its consideration of women. Moreover, she argued for the need to analyse the nature of the cultural life of young women, to see if this is structured in different ways to that of boys. This approach resulted in papers on the culture of femininity, romance, pop music and teenybop culture, the teenage magazine *Jackie* and so on. These earlier researches can be found collected in *Feminism and Youth Culture* (1991). McRobbie developed this approach and the entailed research and argument through the 1980s. She wrote influentially on the importance of dance in female youth culture and pointed to the developing informal economy of second-hand markets in a paper in her own edited collection *Zoot Suits and Second-hand Dresses* (1989). Cultural change in gender roles (as well as her own position as a parent) led to reconsideration of some of her earlier arguments. She has analysed rave culture and the opportunity that it provides for new roles for young women as well as discussing the shift to the centrality of pop in magazines for young girls such as *Just Seventeen*. These concerns were connected to the influence and evaluation of debates about **postmodernism** (p. 400) in theory and culture which are to be found in *Postmodernism and Popular Culture* (1994). She has also commented on debates in left cultural politics, especially around the concept of 'New Times'.

McRobbie's essays have had a large impact of the consideration of youth culture. She has been at the forefront of arguments emphasising the importance of taking gender into account and for the need to examine the works of male writers for the versions of masculinity they contain.

Further reading

McRobbie's work has appeared in essay form. Excellent collections now exist:

McRobbie, A. (1991) *Feminism and Youth Culture*, Basingstoke: Macmillan.
McRobbie, A. (1994) *Postmodernism and Popular Culture*, London; Routledge.
McRobbie, A. (ed.) (1989) *Zoot Suits and Second-hand Dresses*, Basingstoke: Macmillan.

In developing her points about the different nature of girls' culture, McRobbie argues that the street is a potentially dangerous place for girls:

younger girls tend to stay indoors or to congregate in youth clubs; those with literally nowhere else to go but the street frequently become pregnant within a year and disappear back into the home to be absorbed by childcare and domestic labour.

(McRobbie, 1980: 47)

McRobbie argued that the use of drink and drugs can induce the same sort of perils: 'it is clear from my recent research, for example, that girls are reluctant to drink precisely because of the sexual dangers of drunkenness' (1980: 47).

8.6.1 | The teenybop culture of romance

McRobbie suggested that the working-class girls she studied tended to form a teenybop culture based around romance. These girls spent more time in the home, at least partly because of the dangerous nature of public places, like the street. Frith (1983) added three other aspects to this when he argued: that girls are more subject to parental control and discipline than boys are; that girls are often expected to carry out work in the home, in a way that boys are not, a point that was illustrated graphically by McRobbie (1978) where she pointed out that girls were expected to perform large amounts of work in the home for very little financial recompense; and, finally, that girls spend more time at home getting ready to go out than boys do.

This form of girls' subculture identified in the 1970s consisted of the following features:

1. The centrality of the home and often of the bedroom. Girls tended to get together with other girls and listen to records by their favourite artists in each other's bedrooms.

2. Girls formed a *teenybop* culture, where there was a romantic attachment to one star or group. There is a history of different stars and groups that have filled such a role.

3. When girls did go out, it was most likely to be a youth club.

4. Dance was important to girls in ways that it was not for boys. McRobbie (1984, 1993) has continued to stress the importance of dance to girls.

5. For the girls in McRobbie's study, the relationship with a *best friend* was very important and they valued this more than their relationships with boys.

6. The idea of romance was very important. Many of the girls, despite at times showing a 'realistic' appreciation of some aspects of marriage, place great stress on the idea of romance and the romantic attachment to one boy. This can be related to the continued existence of a sexual double standard, where girls could easily become known as 'slags' if they went out with several boys (see the discussion of *Learning to Labour*, Willis 1977, in section 8.5.1).

7. McRobbie argued that the girls she studied stressed some dominant ideas of femininity in an exaggerated fashion. This may form part of a culture that opposed the perceived school ethic of responsibility, hard work and seriousness. The girls spent much time talking about boys and wanted to bend the school rules about dress and make-up in as fashionable a direction as possible. McRobbie argued that this culture,

while it may oppose official culture in some ways, reinforces the culture of romance and the idea of femininity which is a part of this. This parallels the argument advanced by Willis (1977) concerning the way in which the exaggeration of masculinity among working-class boys, in opposition to school norms, suited them for manual labour.

Various writers have identified some problems with this idea of the teenybop culture of romance. First, McRobbie may have underestimated the participation and seriousness of the commitment of some girls to 'deviant' subcultural groups (for example, Smith, 1978). Second, Cowie and Lees (1981) found that girls had a more realistic appraisal of the potential problems in marriage than McRobbie found in her group. Cowie and Lees found far more emphasis on having a good time before marriage. Third, Cowie and Lees (1981) suggested that McRobbie's work tended to isolate a discrete female youth subculture, over-integrating and separating it off from the relations between men and women which existed in society more widely. Relatedly, they argued that too much emphasis is placed on the **resistance** (p. 258) entailed in the culture of femininity. Fourth, McRobbie's work concentrated mainly on white working-class girls, and more evidence is needed about black and middle-class girls for comparison. Furthermore, it might be that some of this work is now rather dated. This point can be considered through an examination of McRobbie's more recent work.

8.6.2 | Pop music, rave culture and gender

In her earlier work, McRobbie had drawn attention to the role of magazines like *Jackie* in the culture of romance. In reconsidering this argument, McRobbie (1991) demonstrated the difference between contemporary magazines like *Just Seventeen* and *Jackie*. Romance has drastically declined in importance and pop and fashion are central, leading to a greater emphasis on image and the pop star. McRobbie argues that 'It is pop rather than romance which now operates as a kind of conceptual umbrella giving a sense of identity to these productions' (1991: 168). In such girls' magazines:

> there is an overwhelming interest in personal information. The magazines increasingly play the role of publicist for the various bands who fall into the teenybopper camp. In return their pages are filled with glossy pictures and they can claim to have a direct line to the stars. This makes for cheap and easy copy. Three pages can be covered in a flash with the help of a transatlantic telephone call, a tape-recorder and a selection of publicity shots often provided by the record company.   (McRobbie, 1991: 169)

In McRobbie's view, pop music is more important to girls now than it was in the 1970s. However, girls are not only involved with pop music of the teenybop type, and McRobbie has also drawn attention to their participation in rave culture. She argues that such culture can be connected to drastic changes in femininity over recent years in Britain, which have opened up the possibility of new roles for women, suggesting that 'girls both black and white have been "unhinged" from their traditional gender position while the gender and class destiny of their male counterparts has remained more stable' (McRobbie, 1993: 408). McRobbie suggests that white middle-class women are increasing their participation in traditional professions like medicine and that black working-class girls are more likely to go into higher and further education than their male peers. Moreover, McRobbie reiterates some of the points already made about the changing nature of girls' magazines, but develops her arguments about dance. She points to the continuity of rave culture with earlier cultures in that 'dance is where girls were always found in subcultures. It was their only entitlement.' However, 'in rave it becomes the motivating force for the entire subculture' (McRobbie, 1993: 419). The centrality of dance allows a far more important place for girls within such contemporary subcultures. However, in continuity with earlier work, McRobbie still sees the danger of these occasions for girls, even if at this later date it is as a parent rather than as a sociological observer.

8.7 | Youth subcultures and race

The most significant consideration of 'race' from within the **Centre for Contemporary Cultural Studies** (p. 327) had come in the collectively authored *Policing the Crisis* (Hall *et al.*, 1978). This considered media construction of 'mugging' in the context of the re-patterning of hegemony in Britain. More specifically in the context of consideration of subcultures, Hebdige (1979) had stressed the centrality of black culture and the black presence in Britain in the generation of the style of white subcultures. Hebdige's interest was in the effects of black culture on white youth. 'Race' was reconsidered in *The Empire Strikes Back* (Centre for Contemporary Cultural Studies, 1982). This collection of articles examined the place of race in the political problems of British capitalism in the 1970s; explored and criticised representations, theories and investigations of race in mainstream sociology; examined representations of black criminality; and considered the challenge presented to white feminism by black women and the political experience of Asian women in Britain. The predominant tone of the volume was a critique of what had gone before and the **ideological** (p. 84) or 'common-sensical' images of race that had informed so-called scientific research.

Some of these themes were further developed by **Paul Gilroy** (p. 166) (1987) which built upon the discussions of the earlier collective CCCS volume. Again, this book criticised a great deal of established work, and sought to explore the relations between race and class in contemporary Britain. It examines a number of different dimensions of black expressive culture and includes extensive discussions of black music (see also Hebdige, 1987). In more recent work, Gilroy (e.g. 1993) has continued to emphasise the nature of black culture in the contemporary world, in developing an alternative account of the nature of **modernity** (p. 400) (see further, Chapter 4).

For present purposes, it is important to note that there was relatively little discussion of subculture in this predominantly critical and reframing literature. There had been studies, from outside the CCCS tradition, of black subcultures in Bristol in the work of Ken Pryce (1979), but one of the important studies influenced by this critique re-examined the idea of racial identity in contemporary Birmingham, although his primary emphasis was on white youth.

8.7.1 | Simon Jones's *Black Culture, White Youth*: new identities in multiracial cities

Simon Jones's (1988) book on *Black Culture, White Youth* falls into two relatively discrete parts. In the first he presents an overview of the development of reggae and its connection to forms of culture in Britain and Jamaica. However, it is the second half of the book, which contains an ethnography of black and white youth in Birmingham, that is of greater interest. Jones discusses the formation of identity in a multiracial area of the city of Birmingham in the English Midlands. Thus many white boys had adopted forms of culture that would in more conventional analyses be seen as black. In particular, 'Black' language was used to express opposition to authority on the part of white children (1988: 149).

Reggae was adopted by the young white people growing up in this environment, and Jones shows how different themes from Jamaican music were adapted by young white men and women (see also Jeater, 1992). Thus, he maintains that:

> Black music generally and Jamaican music in particular have functioned as transmitters of oppositional values and liberating pleasures to different generations of whites for nearly three decades. They have consistently supplied white youth with the raw material for their own distinctive forms of cultural expression. Through the political discourses of Rastafari, reggae has provided young whites with a collective language and symbolism of rebellion that has proved resonant to their own predicaments and to their experiences of distinct, but related, forms of oppression.
>
> (Jones, 1988: 231)

However, Jones recognises contradictions that existed around these modes of appropriation. Thus, 'powerful feelings of attraction to black culture could easily coexist with perceptions of that culture as threatening and with resentment and fear of black people' (Jones, 1988: 216).

Jones suggests that new forms of 'racial' identity are being formed in parts of Birmingham and other inner-city metropolitan areas. He ends his book with a quotation from one of the people he studied which captures this. He says:

> [in Jo-Jo's] eloquent conclusion is captured both the reality of the new 'England' that is already emerging, as well as the hope that such an England might itself not be 'recognisable as the same nation it has been', or perhaps, one day, 'as a nation at all':

> > Its like, I love this place ... there's no place like home ... Balsall Heath is the centre of the melting-pot, man, 'cos all I ever see when I go out is half-Arab, half-Pakistani, half-Jamaican, half-Scottish, half-Irish, I know 'cos I am [half-Scottish-Irish] ... Who am I? ... Tell me? Who do I belong to? They criticise me, the good old England. Alright then, where do I belong? ... you know, I was brought up with blacks, Pakistanis, Africans, Asians, everything, you name it ... Who do I belong to? I'm just a broad person. The earth is mine. You know, 'we was not born in England, we was not born in Jamaica' ... we was born **here** man! It's our right! That's the way I see it ... That's the way I deal with it.   (Jones, 1988: 239–40)

Jones's discussion resonates with those **postmodernist** (p. 400) arguments, outlined at other points in this book, that suggest that there has been a 'decentring' of our **identities** (p. 224) in contemporary culture. For example, it has been suggested by a number of writers that we no longer have the same attachments to place as earlier generations. This might be the result of living in a society where, in some respects, it is easier to see what is happening on the other side of the world through television coverage than it is to observe events at the other end of the street.

In an introductory discussion of the idea, Hall (1992) distinguishes three concepts of identity: 'Enlightenment', 'sociological' and 'post-modern'. The 'Enlightenment' concept rested on the idea of the existence of an essential core to identity which was born with the individual and unfolded through his or her life. The sociological concept argued that a coherent identity is formed in relations with others and thus develops and changes over time. The postmodern subject is thought to have no fixed or essential identity. In postmodern societies identities have become 'dislocated'. The emphasis on identity shifts the focus on the CCCS approach (see sections 8.11 and 8.12) from class to more diffuse sources of social belonging.

8.8 | The Birmingham Centre for Contemporary Cultural Studies and youth subcultures: a general critique

At this point it is necessary to consider some of the main points made against the CCCS approach to youth subcultures. In a very useful overall critique, Gary Clarke (1990) makes a number of specific criticisms of work from CCCS:

1. Much of this writing is imprecise on the nature of the 'structural location' of subcultures and the nature of the problem solving involved in the subculture.

2. There is relatively little explanation of where the different subcultural styles actually come from. For example, why does one working-class subculture adopt the foppish sartorial style of the Edwardian era, while another caricatures the boots and braces dress of the factory worker?

3. There is a rigidity in the analysis, as the subcultures that are identified tend to be 'essentialist and non-contradictory', meaning that there is little attention paid to variations of style and commitment within different subcultures. In part this is a consequence of the tendency for these analyses to start from subcultures and work backwards to class situations and contradictions. This leads to a kind of 'freezing' of distinct subcultures.

4. There is a lack of attention to the way in which individuals move in and out of subcultures. Thus, Clarke (1990: 82–3) argues that Phil Cohen 'classifies Crombies and parkas as distinct subcultures, but surely the only "problem" which distinguished them from skins and mods respectively was the need to keep warm'.

5. There is a dichotomy between subcultures and the rest of young people, who are in the mainstream.

Clarke identifies *three* important consequences that stem from these criticisms. First, there is the lack of consideration of 'subcultural flux and dynamic nature of styles' (1990: 84). Second, there is the separation of subcultures from the rest of society which is incorporated into a 'consensus' or dominant social relations. Third, a 'vague concept of style' is elevated 'to the status of an objective category' (Clarke, 1990: 84).

Stanley Cohen (1987) used the introduction to a new edition of *Folk Devils and Moral Panics* to develop a critique of the CCCS approach, which had become influential since his book was originally published. Cohen organised his critique with respect to the Birmingham keywords of structure, culture and biography.

With respect to structure, Cohen argues that in much recent work on subculture there is an 'over-facile drift to historicism' (1987: viii). By this phrase Cohen suggests that there is too much contextualisation and overemphasis on historical development within the Birmingham work, which often involves the particular emphasis of one historical variable at the expense of a variety of others. He argues that often 'a single and one-dimensional historical trend is picked out – commercialization, repression, bourgeoisification, destruction of community, erosion of leisure values – and then projected on to a present (often by the same sociologist's own admission) which is much more complicated, contradictory or ambiguous' (1987: viii–ix).

Moving on to consider the area of culture, Cohen (1987: x) characterises the Birmingham approach to style in terms of two dominant themes, which should come as no surprise by this stage:

1. Style 'is essentially a type of **resistance** (p. 258) to subordination'.
2. '[T]he form taken by this resistance is somehow symbolic or magical, in the sense of not being an actual, successful solution to whatever is the problem.'

Cohen makes a number of points against this approach. First, he maintains that it is over-simplistic to decode styles only in terms of resistance and opposition. In his view, styles may be both reactionary and indeed inconsistent. Thus, some aspects may be oppositional and others reactionary. Second, he suggests that the development of style is often seen as somehow internal to a group. Commercialisation comes later. In fact, as we have seen, there are much more intimate relations between the development of subcultures and commercial activities. Third, Cohen argues that too often the activities of subcultural adherents are understood or interpreted in the context of traditions of English working-class resistance to dominance. Thus, Cohen (1987: xiii) maintains that 'where we are really being directed is towards the "profound line of historical continuity" between today's delinquents and their "equivalents" in the past'. This leads to the fourth issue of whether subcultural members are 'aware' of what they are doing, whether they are doing it intentionally, or would see it in the same terms as the analyst. Cohen's point is that these theories, especially Hebdige (1979), play down the meaning of style and subcultures to those who are a part of it. He contends that 'it is hard to say which is the more sociologically incredible: a theory which postulates cultural dummies who give homologous meaning to all artifacts surrounding them or a theory which suggests that individual meanings do not matter at all' (Cohen, 1987: xv). Finally, Cohen raises a number of issues concerning the methods and results of the readings performed by the likes of Hebdige (1979). He poses the question of why we should believe the interpretations offered of these subcultures and to what extent there is any rigour in the way in which they have been arrived at. A graphic example of this point can be seen in the extract from Cohen in Box 8.4 which criticises Hebdige's reading of the symbolism of the swastika.

Box **8.4**

Stanley Cohen's critique of Hebdige's reading of the symbolism of the swastika

Let me conclude this section by giving an example of the dangers of searching the forest of symbols without such a method – or indeed any method. This is the example often used by Hebdige and other theorists of punk: the wearing of the swastika emblem. Time and time again, we are assured that although this symbol is 'on one level' intended to outrage and shock, it is *really* being employed in a meta-language: the wearers are ironically distancing themselves from the very message that the symbol is usually intended to convey. Displaying a swastika (or singing lyrics like 'Belsen was a gas') shows how symbols are stripped from their natural context, exploited for empty effect, displayed through mockery, distancing, irony, parody, inversion.

But how are we to know this? We are never told much about the 'thing': when, how, where, by whom or in what context it is worn. We do not know what, if any, difference exists between indigenous and sociological explanations. We are given no clue about how these particular actors manage the complicated business of distancing and irony. In the end, there is no basis whatsoever for choosing between this particular sort of interpretation and any others: say, that for many or most of the kids walking around with swastikas on their jackets, the dominant context is simply conformity, blind ignorance or knee-jerk racism.

Something more of an answer is needed to such questions than simply quoting Genet or Breton. Nor does it help much to have Hebdige's admission (about a similar equation) that such interpretations are not open to being tested by standard sociological procedures: 'Though it is undeniably there is the social structure, it is there as an immanence, as a submerged possibility, as an existential option; and one cannot verify an existential option scientifically – you either see it or you don't.'

Well, in the swastika example, I don't. And, moreover, when Hebdige does defend this particular interpretation of punk, he does it not by any existential leap but by a good old-fashioned positivist appeal to evidence: punks, we are told, 'were not generally sympathetic to the parties of the extreme right' and showed 'widespread support for the anti-Fascist movement'. These statements certainly constitute evidence, not immanence – though not particularly good evidence and going right against widespread findings about the racism and support for

→

restrictive immigration policies among substantial sections of working-class youth.

I do not want to judge one reading against the other nor to detract from the considerable interest and value of this new decoding work. We need to be more sceptical though of the exquisite aesthetics which tell us about things being fictional and real, absent and present, caricatures and re-assertions. This language might indeed help by framing a meaning to the otherwise meaningless; but this help seems limited when we are drawn to saying about skinhead attacks on Pakistani immigrants: 'Every time the boot went in, a contradiction was concealed, glossed over or made to disappear'. It seems to me – to borrow from the language of contradictions – that both a lot more and a lot less was going on. Time indeed to leave the forest of symbols; and ' ... shudder back thankfully into the light of the social day'.

Cohen (1987: xvii–xviii)

Cohen also examines the issue of biography. He suggests that the Birmingham approach tends to focus too much on the spectacular and not enough on everyday deviance or 'ordinary' working-class activities. Furthermore, the boundaries around subcultures are often drawn in far too tight a manner. Cohen maintains that they are actually much looser and that people drift in and out of them over time and indeed at one point in time. Moreover, can the theory explain why one individual becomes involved in a subculture and others do not?

In this vein, Clarke argues that there is a need to study what all categories of youth are doing, rather than just subcultures:

> It is true that most youths do not enter into subcultures in the elite form described in the literature, but large numbers do draw on particular elements of subcultural style and create their own meanings and uses of them.   (Clarke, 1990: 92)

Furthermore, he suggests that there are important differences in the early 1980s from the situation described in the 1960s and 1970s by the classic writers from Birmingham. Thus, there was the combination of styles involved in movements like punk and two-tone, and the argument that 'new wave' broke the 'distinction between "teenyboppers" and youth' based around the distinction between LPs and singles. Thus, Clarke's (1990: 95) general conclusion is that:

> what is required is an analysis of the activities of all youths to locate continuities and discontinuities in culture and social relations and to discover the meaning these activities have for the youths themselves.

Some recent literature which has attempted to take up this challenge is analysed in the next section.

8.9 | Aspects of contemporary youth culture

8.9.1 | Symbolic creativity

Willis *et al.* (1990) argue that as human beings we are symbolically creative, saying that 'we argue for symbolic creativity as an integral ("ordinary") part of the human condition, not as the inanimate peaks (popular or remote) rising above the mists' (Willis *et al.*, 1990: 6). Being symbolically creative involves work of a **symbolic** (p. 288) kind, which is:

> the application of human capacities to and through, on and with symbolic resources and raw materials (collections of signs and symbols – for instance, the language as we inherit it as well as texts, songs, films, images and artifacts of all kinds) to produce meanings. (Willis *et al.*, 1990: 10)

The basic elements of symbolic work include language and the active body, and symbolic creativity involves the 'production of *new* ... meanings intrinsically attached to feelings, to energy, to excitement and psychic movement' (Willis *et al.*, 1990: 11). A number of different products are produced through symbolic work and symbolic creativity. These include our own individual identities, the location of those identities in a wider social context and the notion that we have the capacity to change things in some respect. Thus, in a general sense, Willis *et al.* (1990: 16) argue that:

> In a way the spectacular sub-cultures of the 1950s and 60s prefigured some of the general shifts we are claiming for the contemporary situation. They defined themselves very early and gained their very spectacle from seeking visible identities and styles outside or against work and working respectabilities. Now the idea of a spectacular sub-culture is strictly impossible because all style and taste cultures, to some degree or another, express something of a general trend to find and make identity outside the realm of work.

However, it does seem to be the case that some subcultures are rather more spectacular than others. Examples of the more spectacular to be found in early 1990s Manchester can be found in Figure 8.4.

Willis's book explores the symbolic creativity of young people across a number of different dimensions, including television, VCR and microcomputer use, relationships to film, advertising, and magazines and engagements with fashion, pub culture, street culture, sport and romance. Perhaps for current purposes one of its most important points is the attempt to break down the barriers between subcultures and other young people. The idea that people are in general more creative has been linked to the development of new forms of consumer expression and the idea of a postmodern society.

8.9.2 | Postmodernism and youth culture

Some themes concerning postmodernism and the study of youth culture have been addressed by Redhead (1990; see also Redhead, 1993, 1995, 1997, and Redhead *et al.*,

Figure 8.4 ■ Youth subcultural styles in Manchester in 1992. (Source: courtesy of Julie Weir.)

1997) who places a particular emphasis on the examination of the relationships between music and subcultures. Redhead criticises the idea of a neat fit between different elements of youth subculture, which are entailed in the concept of homology used by Willis (1978) and Hebdige (1979). He also suggests that it is problematic to see music as the straightforward expression of a subcultural community. For example, it is often difficult to specify what the community is of which music is an expression. Furthermore, the subcultures and communities from which music is often held to issue or which put it to use, do not simply exist, but have to be examined within language and communication. They are, in important senses, constructed within writing about them or in other terms, discursively constructed.

Redhead considers whether there was a clear fit between music and subcultural use in the way identified by the Birmingham writers, or whether there has been a change in the articulation of music with subcultures in the period since punk rock in the late 1970s. In some accounts **postmodernism** (p. 400) in pop has developed through the 1980s, leading to the break-up of the forms of association identified by earlier writers.

However, Redhead argues that in many respects pop music has always possessed some of those features that are characteristic of postmodernism. For example, he maintains that pop music has broken barriers between high and popular culture at different points. In common with theories of postmodernism, he argues that the best way to understand contemporary pop music is not through some of the conventional 'oppositions' which have often been used to study it, like those between 'rock and pop', 'authentic and synthetic', 'true and false' and 'high and low', but through the distinction and relationship between the local and the **global** (p. 159). Thus 'world musics' are affecting local music making in a number of complex and diverse ways.

8.9.3 | Rave and dance culture

More recent work has considered different dimensions of contemporary music and youth. For example, Rietveld (1993) examines a number of different dimensions of rave culture in the north of England in the late 1980s. The account given of this form of culture is not dissimilar from that of the CCCS writers. For example, Rietveld (1993: 53) argues with respect to rave culture that:

> Not only the lack of finance, but also the intensive dancing and the use of the drug Ecstasy determined the style. It makes a person sweat, so baggy cotton clothing is the most comfortable to wear. Make up is useless in those circumstances, because it would simply 'wash' off in a short time. The euphoria caused by the excitement of the rave events, the excessive body movement and drug use all interfere with a person's sense of balance: high heels are therefore definitely 'out of order' from a raver's point of view.

This is very close to the sort of homology argument used by Hebdige and Willis which continues therefore to be influential. However, other recent work on rave culture has been more critical of the Birmingham approach. We have already considered the work of Thornton (1994, 1995) in relation to moral panic and the role of media in the creation of youth subcultures, but she also, in direct criticism and the working out of her own analysis, makes an important contribution to the analysis of more contemporary youth culture. Thornton argues that what she calls 'club cultures' are 'taste cultures' (1995: 3). This is significant as it means that she is concerned to examine the role of distinction in club cultures. Conflicts and hierarchies are of central significance, both within the culture and in analysis. Thornton considers three important 'distinctions': 'the authentic versus the phoney, the "hip" versus the "mainstream", and the "underground" versus "the media"' (1995: 3–4). In developing this approach, Thornton moves away from the emphasis within the CCCS approach on the difference between the subcultural and the mainstream or the mass, as she suggests this tends to reproduce a core aspect of subcultural ideology itself. Hence, her argument and analysis 'is not about dominant ideologies and subversive subcultures, but about subcultural ideologies' (1995: 10). Her arguments are influenced by, and developed from, the French sociologist Pierre Bourdieu. She argues that subcultures trade in what she calls 'subcultural capital', the currency of which is 'hipness'. The circulation of subcultural capital is 'governed' by media. Thornton's approach draws attention to the complexity, fluidity and rapidity of change in contemporary youth culture. Furthermore, in her view, it is important to consider the relations within cultures, rather than any simple opposition between the dominant and the subcultural. If the work of Hebdige (1979), Willis (1977, 1978) and McRobbie (1978) can be seen as concerned with the dynamic between incorporation in the mainstream and resistance, or opposition, to it, then Thornton is addressing far more complex and intricate relations between **power** (p. 94) and culture. This is not simply a process that is confined to the study of subcultures, but can also be traced in the studies of media audiences as well (see further Abercrombie and Longhurst, 1998). Thornton's analysis represents an important corrective to some of the classic formulations of the CCCS approach. However, it does tend to retain an emphasis on some of the more spectacular dimensions of contemporary youth culture. There still tends to be relatively little investigation of the 'ordinary'. For Hollands (1995) the idea and practice of 'going out' can be seen as an important aspect of contemporary youth activity across a wide spectrum.

Defining concept 8.1   Cultural capital and habitus

The concepts of cultural capital and habitus, developed by the French sociologist Pierre Bourdieu, have become increasingly influential in cultural studies.

Initially best known in Britain and the English-speaking world through his work on education, Bourdieu's book *Distinction* (1984, orig. 1979) represented an important potential bridge between those in the social sciences concerned with class inequality and domination, and the developing emphasis on culture in a number of disciplines, including cultural studies.

Bourdieu's central innovation was to coin the concept of cultural capital, which he used in tandem with the more familiar idea of economic capital. Thus, in discussing the ways in which classes seek distinction from each other, Bourdieu pointed out that some groups, while high in economic capital, are low in cultural capital. Hence businesspeople may be well paid and own shares in their company but they may not be able to appreciate or understand fine art or classical literature. On the other hand, there are some groups that are high in cultural capital but relatively low in economic capital, university lecturers for instance. Cultural capital, like economic capital, is a resource to be drawn upon in the pursuit of power. Cultural capital is not secondary to economic capital in general, as each may be important in different contexts. *Distinction* used survey data to map some of the complexities of the relations between different sectors of the French middle class. This has inspired theoretical refinement of the concept as well as further empirical work in a number of countries. Increased attention to the cultural significance of consumption has been influenced by Bourdieu. One clear implication of Bourdieu's work is that distinctions between a variety of groups may be based

→

on differences in capitals. For example, Thornton (1995) argues that subcultural groups mobilise subcultural capital, through the notion of 'hipness', to create their own distinction. It is important to possess or have knowledge of the hip dance record and to be wearing the right clothes.

Bourdieu, in addition to a range of other conceptual innovations, developed the concept of habitus to refer to the way in which different social groups classify the world and view it. Rather than arguing that a particular class position carries with it a specific ideology, Bourdieu points to the way in which groups have habituated ways of seeing or a disposition to classify the world. Groups inhabit a particular cultural space. Again, this emphasis on classification has been influential especially as it echoes and connects to the centrality of such ideas in social anthropology, which itself has been important to some variants of cultural studies.

Bourdieu's reliance on survey data, and his inattention to the aspects of culture shared across social classes and groups, may be criticised, but his concepts and approach are likely to become more influential in the future as more empirical work is done.

Further reading

Jenkins, R. (1994) *Pierre Bourdieu*, London: Routledge.
Bourdieu, P. (1990) *In Other Words: Essays towards a reflexive sociology*, Cambridge: Polity.
Thornton, S. (1995) *Club Cultures: Music, Media and Subcultural Capital*, Cambridge: Polity.

8.9.4 | Going out and extending youth

Hollands suggests that there has been a shift in youth culture in the sense that 'going out', especially on a Friday or Saturday night, to the centre of a large city (in his analysis, Newcastle-upon-Tyne in the north-east of England) has become a central aspect of culture for young people between 16 and 30. In response to economic change which means that young people are less likely to be employed, get married and start families, going out often in a group has become less of a 'rite of passage' from childhood to adulthood, which is then curtailed, but more an ongoing part of the everyday. The meeting of friends (often in mixed groups for more middle-class young people) is an important part of this process. Going out, in Hollands' words, is 'a permanent fraternisation ritual' (1995: 41).

The work examined in this section on more contemporary youth culture has demonstrated some of the ways in which analysis has moved beyond the Birmingham approach. It can be argued that there is less concern with the spectacular. Moreover, there is a break with some of the more simple oppositions between the subcultural and the mainstream in a way that reduces the influence of Marxist theories of power and opposition to hegemony. Furthermore, there is an increased concern with the empirical investigation of subcultures and less with the 'decoding' of their inner meanings. Finally, there is a move away from the examination of youth to a more expanded notion of what is happening in people's cultural lives more widely. One way forward from this sort of work is to reconsider a rather different approach to the study of subculture.

8.10 | Rethinking subcultures: interactions and networks

The American interactionist authors Gary Fine and Sherryl Kleinman (1979) argue that the concept of subculture needs to be rethought within a framework derived from sociological approaches that emphasise interaction. In the main, by implication their approach is critical of the sort of work associated with the CCCS which placed emphasis on the structural aspects of society, like class. They argue that the concept of subculture had previously been used in a confused and unclear fashion. They identify four conceptual problems with this literature, which concern: first, subculture and sub-society; second, the referent; third, subculture as a homogeneous and static system; and finally, the value orientation in subcultural research.

With respect to the first point, they argue that because of the way in which subcultures have been structurally defined 'as aggregate of persons' they have often been treated as a subdivision of society, as what they call a subsociety. However, in contemporary societies which allow movement between different groups and which have a number of different belief systems, it is difficult to see subsociety and subculture as the same thing. As Fine and Kleinman (1979: 3) explain:

> Thus, all members of the age category 13–21 might, according to a 'structural' conceptualization, be considered part of the youth subculture. However, it is clear that many of the persons within that age cohort do not share common cultural values and behaviors.

On this basis Fine and Kleinman argue that it is important to distinguish between subsocieties and subcultures.

Concerning the second issue, they argue that the concept of subculture is often used without a referent – 'a clearly defined population which shares cultural knowledge' (1979: 4). Thus, as they explain:

> Although researchers identify the subculture to which the group 'belongs' (such as the delinquent subculture), they have no way of knowing the extent to which the cultures of the gangs overlap, the extent to which the particular gang examined is representa- tive of all gangs in the population segment, and the degree of interrelatedness among the cultures of the gangs under study (1979: 4).

The third point is more familiar in that Fine and Kleinman argue that the study of subcultures tends to treat them as if they were both homogeneous – more or less as if all members of the group were the same and all shared exactly the same beliefs and practices – and unchanging. In fact what should be kept in view is the *fluidity* of subcultures. Finally, they argue that through the *selectivity* of the way in which the subculture is discussed or *read*, the representation of it often becomes little more than a caricature. There is a tendency to focus on the central themes of the subculture at the expense of the complex interplay of different cultural aspects which may be a part of the subculture.

Fine and Kleinman argue that there is a better way to understand subcultures, proposing that 'the conceptualization of the subculture construct within an interactionist framework will provide a more adequate account of subcultural variation, cultural change, and the diffusion of cultural elements' (1979: 8). They argue that subculture should be used to refer to an interacting group. On first sight this would seem to produce rather small subcultures. However, Fine and Kleinman argue that subcultures exist beyond immediate groups because of the way in which cultural patterns are diffused in contemporary societies. The network that results from the diffusion of cultural elements is then the referent which did not exist in most earlier writing. Subcultures start from group cultures:

> Cultural forms are created through the individual or collective manipulation of symbols. From its point of creation, the cultural form is communicated to others, and diffused outward from the individual's own interaction partners. The transmission of culture is therefore a product of interaction. The diffusion may remain quite limited unless the information reaches wider audiences via the mass media.
>
> (Fine and Kleinman, 1979: 9)

Fine and Kleinman identify four mechanisms by which communication can occur. First, individuals may be members of a number of different groups; second, there may be other interconnections which do not involve group membership as such but which are based on 'weak ties', casual conversations with acquaintances and so on; third, some individuals or groups perform what Fine and Kleinman refer to as structural roles, in linking groups that may not otherwise be in contact and providing cultural information (drug dealers, for example); and fourth, there may be media diffusion as when certain films or television programmes influence cultures in the wider sense.

This approach also emphasises the need for analysis to concern itself with what they call the 'affective' dimension of subcultures (Fine and Kleinman, 1979: 12). People need to be seen as involved in choices about culture and the extent of the identification with the culture needs to be considered and researched. These are important points, which need to be recognised in contemporary work on subcultures. Indeed, they have been echoed, if in an indirect way, in work that has begun to explore the subcultures or groupings of television and pop music fans (for example, Lewis, 1992; Aizlewood, 1994; Roberts, 1994) and enthusiasts and hobbyists (for example, Hoggett and Bishop, 1986; Moorhouse, 1991). It can be suggested that attention to contemporary cultural life has to pay greater attention to actual processes of interaction, the role of the media in the construction of the network (as Thornton's (1995) study maintains in relation to club cultures), and the importance of 'affect' (Grossberg, 1992) or pleasure. Recent studies of fans can be taken as examples of this developing approach.

8.11 | Fans: stereotypes, *Star Trek* and opposition

We all probably have common-sensical images of the fan in our minds and they would perhaps be linked by the idea of some kind of excess of admiration of an activity or star. Moreover, there has been a clear tendency for much writing on fans to suggest that there is something wrong with being a fan. Fans are seen as fanatics (from the origin of the term) and deranged (Jenson, 1992: 9). Jenson maintains that the literature on fans has produced two models of the 'pathological fan'. First, there is the 'obsessed loner', 'who (under the influence of the media) has entered into an intense fantasy relationship with a celebrity figure. These individuals achieve public notoriety by stalking or threatening or killing the celebrity' (Jenson, 1992: 11). Second, there is the 'frenzied or hysterical member of a crowd' (1992: 11), shouting at a rock star or misbehaving at a sports match.

Jenson contests this idea that there is something wrong with the fan by contrasting the traits of the fan with those of the high culture or academic 'aficionado'. She argues that many academics form attachments to their favourite writers or theorists which are just as obsessive as those the fan may feel for the pop star. However, the division of the world between fans and non-fans allows those who define themselves as non-fans to suggest that others are abnormal and thus to constitute themselves as the normal or the safe. For Jenson (1992: 24):

> Defining fandom as a deviant activity allows (individually) a reassuring, self-aggrandizing stance to be adopted. It also supports the celebration of particular values – the rational over the emotional, the educated over the uneducated, the subdued over the passionate, the elite over the popular, the mainstream over the margin, the status quo over the alternative.

Characterising fans as 'other' in this way blocks analysis and proper understanding of how people actually interact with the media in contemporary society. Further, writers like Fiske (1992) have suggested that fan activities are actually more like those of 'ordinary' people. Two studies of fans have been particularly influential.

8.11.1 | Fans of *Star Trek*

Camille Bacon-Smith (1992) considers the appropriation and reusing of television texts like *Star Trek*, *Blake's 7* and *The Professionals* as the basis on which to develop new cultural forms. So the women in Bacon-Smith's study do things with such texts. They go to conventions on them, dress up as characters from the shows, write and perform 'filksongs' about them, paint pictures of the characters, and produce music videos about them.

Bacon-Smith devotes much discussion to the types of written text that are produced, utilising the characters and situations from the different series, although again her main focus is on *Star Trek*. Characters and situations from the series are placed in new situations and different 'universes'. New characters are introduced or ones who had only relatively minor roles are developed at much greater length and depth. She examines four main genres of *Star Trek* writing. The first of these is the 'Mary Sue' which entails the introduction of a young woman into the crew of the Enterprise who manages to save the ship and its crew from disaster, but who perishes due to her efforts. This is often the first sort of story written by the developing *Star Trek* fan, and has become a relatively disliked form. The term 'Mary Sue' is often used in a negative sense, the phrase 'it's a bit of a Mary Sue' indicating disapproval.

The second type of writing is the 'lay Spock' (or someone else from the crew). This involves producing a story which entails placing Spock in a heterosexual relationship, for example with Nurse Chapel, who is thought to be attracted to him. The third type of writing is the 'K/S' or 'slash' (see also Penley, 1992) which places Kirk and Spock in a homosexual relationship. This form of writing seems particularly 'transgressive' of the accepted meanings of *Star Trek*. It is suggested that female fans have taken up an affective core of *Star Trek* (the friendship of Kirk and Spock) and inflected it in a rather surprising direction.

The final type is 'Hurt/Comfort' which again often places two of the central characters into a close relationship. One of the characters suffers pain through a terrible injury and the other character is involved in caring and comforting the injured friend. This genre is explained by Bacon-Smith to be particularly controversial among fans due, for example, to the distressing effects that the reading about the severe pain inflicted on a much liked character can have on them.

These texts are often produced in a collective manner. One individual may be primarily responsible for the initial development of an alternative *Star Trek* universe, but this is then opened up for expansion by others who can fill in gaps and open up new possibilities in the story. In an important sense, the authorship of these stories is shared and is a part of a network in the sense identified by Fine and Kleinman. Their production goes against the stereotype of the lone author at work in creating for an industrialised book market.

This subculture is also involved in a form of **resistance** (p. 258), like that described in the CCCS approach. Bacon-Smith describes the way in which the women in her study carve out a 'female-terrorist space' for their activities. One of the things which is significant about Bacon-Smith's book is her characterisation of the women as opposing the dominant male controllers of the more official forms of science fiction fandom. The established male science fiction (SF) conventions are both organised and often disapproving of the activities of the female fans. There is also some insightful material of the intimidation of women in the role-playing sections of the SF conferences. These, on Bacon-Smith's account, are virtually completely male-dominated. Dominant forms which are opposed by the female forms tend to be both individualistic and masculine, although when they are engaged in struggle or are under attack they tend toward associative modes of organisation. This can be seen as a network of interaction which forms a subculture on the basis of which mass-circulated stories and characters are re-worked and developed in a way that opposes the control of the wider science fiction culture by men. Henry Jenkins (1992), in another study of *Star Trek*, reinforces these points.

Jenkins emphasises the creativity of fans. He shows how they are involved in the writing of different stories based on the characters from familiar television programmes and, like Bacon-Smith, discusses some of the different genres of these stories. In addition fans indulge in video making, painting, singing and so on. Like a great deal of the writing on fans, Jenkins argues against the ideas that fans are somehow figures of fun, deranged, or isolated (sad and lonely) individuals. They are seen as active and involved in extensive communicative networks forming a subculture that is open to outside influences. The members also engage in a full range of 'normal' activities. Jenkins also shows how technologies like computer networks are facilitating new forms of interaction, adding significant new dimensions of the communication possibilities that were detailed in Fine and Kleinman's earlier article. In sympathy with much other writing on subculture, these fans are seen as engaged in reframing the meanings of a dominant culture; they are not so far away from Hebdige's (1979) youth subcultural *bricoleurs*. However, one of the significant issues that this literature raises is the extent to which all television viewers are becoming as skilled and active in their understanding of television programmes as the fans described by Bacon-Smith and Jenkins. This refers back to the point made by Willis *et al.* (1990) about the essential creativity involved in everyday cultural life. However, as Jenkins (1992) shows through his discussion of the failure of fans to convince the producers of particular programmes to keep them running or not to develop a particular storyline, the fans tend to be in relatively weak positions in a wider sense. Moreover, some more recent work on the fans of daytime television programmes in the United States has taken a rather different view of fandom.

8.11.2 | Fans of daytime soap opera

Harrington and Bielby (1995) examine a different type of fan from that considered by Bacon-Smith (1992), Jenkins (1992) and Penley (1992) in that these are not people who engage in the productive generation of new texts in the concrete sense on the basis of their fan attachments; rather, they suggest that fan feelings and identifications are central in the productive construction of identity. Their approach is 'to question not just what fans *do* but who they *are*' (Harrington and Bielby, 1995: 7). In important respects this lack of 'concrete' production is related to the pleasure that fans find in the already existing texts. As Harrington and Bielby (1995: 21) explain, 'It is *because* female consumers of women's texts – including soaps – find it easier to identify with and find pleasure in the primary narrative that they rarely produce derivative texts.' However, partly because of the derision to which soaps and their fans are subjected, involvement tends to take place within a supportive environment. The increasing identification with the soap and the **identity** (p. 224) of a soap fan is difficult.

As has been argued by Grossberg (1992; see further Longhurst 1995: 233–5), the fan forms an affective link to the object of attachment. This is critical to Harrington and Bielby's examination of soap fans, where pleasure in the product is central. This may be an essentially private pleasure, or it may become more public through participation in fan lunches, correspondence, computer bulletin boards and so on. Harrington and Bielby emphasise the pleasure that is involved in these affective connections and suggest that this should be considered in its own sense as a form of love attachment rather than being explained in other terms as a form of struggle and opposition. This does not mean that they ignore struggle and opposition but, as we have argued in general terms, they relocate these ideas in a different framework with an emphasis on spectacle and performativity (see Chapter 6 for discussion of performativity in contemporary politics). They argue:

> Unlike most media theorists who posit a barrier between subject and object, we believe that soap watching (like reading or fantasy gaming) is simultaneously a spectator and participant activity. It is participatory in that the story and the alternative world do not exist until we consciously and actively engage the text . . .; it is a spectator activity in that we necessarily adopt a bordered position to the fictional world.
>
> (Harrington and Bielby, 1995: 132)

For Harrington and Bielby (1995: 178–9), 'soap fans' practices are guided by a sense of agency – an awareness of their ability as socially embedded individuals to initiate and control behaviour. Soap fans' viewing choices and practices emerge for a myriad of reasons, including pleasure and experience of emotion. The concept of agency more adequately captures the general process of intentionality that is obscured by a focus on hegemonic resistance'. What fans are or what they do are extensions of their integration and participation in viewing and everyday life. In the conclusion to this chapter we shall build on this important point.

8.12 | Conclusion: from resistance to identity and performance

At the outset of this chapter we suggested that attention to subcultures was important through the consideration of three issues: resistance/incorporation; social divisions and fragmentation; and interpretation/representation. The core of the chapter (sections 8.4–8.8) examined the approach developed at the **Centre for Contemporary Cultural Studies** (p. 327) at the University of Birmingham which focused on the way in which the distinctive patterns of life associated with subcultures could be read or interpreted within the frame of their **resistance** (p. 258) or incorporation within dominant culture and their relation to parent culture. This approach was sophisticated and influential. However, the discussion in the subsequent sections suggests that it now seems inadequate as a way of understanding the complexity of contemporary culture.

More recent studies of youth and fans can be read to suggest that what is important is not so much the reading of subcultures for resistance and opposition, but the understanding and gathering of evidence about the activities of a diverse range of groups which point to the meanings of the activities, especially in terms of pleasure, to the people that engage in them. Further, it may be suggested that these activities concern the performance of self (see Chapter 6).

Postmodernist (p. 400) arguments have suggested that society has become both more fragmented and more media saturated. Moreover, **identities** (p. 224) have become more complex. The burden of much of the literature considered in the later sections of this chapter is to support such ideas, despite the framing of some of the fan studies in terms of opposition and resistance. It can be suggested that our sense of self is often constructed in relation to our enthusiasms as well as in the context of family and occupation. Youth subcultures seemed to be a place for resistance and opposition at a particular stage in the life course, where movement from one set of relations in the family was managed in the process of transition to a new set. However, contemporary society offers fewer jobs for life and involves more divorce, family break-up and reconstitution. In such a context, the concern with youth subcultures may have been a starting point, but such study now needs to be reconsidered within the development of the life course, in fragmented and complex ways. Some people may be members of reasonably tight subcultures, but perhaps a better way to look at the complexities of everyday cultural interaction is through networks oiled by media, where complex identities are reconstructed in the performances of everyday life (an argument developed further in Abercrombie and Longhurst, 1998).

Re-cap

This chapter has considered:

- a range of conceptual issues introduced by the concept of subculture;
- literature on deviance and gangs and the concept of moral panic;
- the nature and the critique of the approach to the study of youth subcultures developed at the Birmingham Centre for Contemporary Cultural Studies;
- the nature of fans and enthusiasts and the developing importance of the concept of identity in this field.

Further reading

Ken Gelder and Sarah Thornton's *The Subcultures Reader* (1997) contains an excellent selection of papers and extracts on subcultures. Stuart Hall and Tony Jefferson's *Resistance through Rituals* (1976) is the classic collection from the Centre for Contemporary Cultural Studies. Many of the subsequently influential Birmingham writers such Dick Hebdige (*Subculture*, 1979), Angela McRobbie (*Feminism and Youth Culture: From 'Jackie' to 'Just Seventeen'*, 1991; *Postmodernism and Popular Culture*, 1994) and Paul Willis (*Learning to Labour*, 1977; *Profane Culture*, 1978; Willis *et al.*, *Common Culture: Symbolic Work at Play in the Everyday Cultures of the Young*, 1990) can be found in shorter form in these books. For fans, Lisa Lewis's *The Adoring Audience* (1992) is a good collection. Less academic but equally enlightening are the works of Nick Hornby (*Fever Pitch*, 1994; *High Fidelity*, 1995).

chapter

Visual culture

9.0 | Introduction

In this chapter, three main themes are used to organise our consideration of visual culture. First, there is a historical theme. In accord with other chapters in the book we have organised material here in terms of a shift from **modernity** to **postmodernity** or late **modernity** (p. 400). We shall suggest that forms of visual culture are intimately connected to changes in society – moreover, that such shifts are themselves part of the re-ordering of **power** (p. 94) relations, especially in respect of their gendered dimensions. Second, in the context of this historical change we introduce the theme of the alternative ways in which different aspects of visual culture can be studied, in both textual and practical senses. Third, we shall place particular attention on the city in this context. This is partly because some more general forms of representation and visual culture, such as painting and television, have already been raised in other parts of the book (see Chapter 2), but more importantly it also allows specific focus to fall on a key site of social transformation. In 1975 some 39 per cent of the world's population lived in cities. By 2000 it is estimated that this figure will have risen to 50 per cent and by 2025 over 63 per cent of the world will live in urban environments (Giddens, 1993: 556). Cities, which have always been significant centres of science and culture, are now accommodating an increasing proportion of the population, a trend that can only accentuate the significance of the social and cultural developments concentrated therein.

After a consideration of the ideas of visual culture and visual representation (section 9.1), these three general themes are addressed in this chapter through the examination of a range of aspects of the visual culture of cities, beginning with the ideas advanced in the earlier part of the twentieth century by the work of Simmel and Benjamin (section 9.2). We then consider photography and film as modern representational practices which are widely regarded as outstanding methods for 'capturing' elements of that visual culture (section 9.3). In the next section (9.4) we consider the important work of **Michel Foucault** (p. 28) on surveillance and the gaze. Work on a different type of gaze is considered in a section on tourism which also examines the application of the concept of postmodernism to this activity (section 9.5). This is followed by an examination of the differences between the glimpse, the gaze, the scan and the glance

364

(section 9.6). The visual culture of cities, especially behaviour in public places and the built environment itself, forms the topic of the next two sections (9.7–9.8). Finally, some of the ideas first introduced in the earlier sections are reconsidered in the light of suggestions that visual culture is assuming the increasingly simulated forms characteristic of postmodernism (section 9.9). However, in order to appreciate the purchase of these studies, it is essential to give attention to the concept of visual culture.

The learning objectives for this chapter are:

- to understand changes in visual culture as connected to the re-ordering of power relations;
- to appreciate different ways of studying visual culture;
- to identify the key importance of the changing visual culture of the city.

9.1 | Visual culture and visual representation

Of all of the senses that humans possess, sight is the most developed. The structure of human eyes and their placement at the front of the head gives human vision some important capabilities. The eyes of humans can detect and resolve fine detail; they are capable of distinguishing a wide range of colours of the spectrum; and their broad area of binocular overlap permits ready appreciation of the depth of visual fields (Passingham, 1982: 36–48). These capabilities are part of the universal biological features assigned to *Homo sapiens* in the evolutionary sequence, distinguishing us from other species. Together they form the biological basis for the primacy accorded to sight among human senses. 'Seeing comes before words', says John Berger (1972: 7), 'the child looks and recognises before it can speak.' The primacy of vision is evident in many everyday sayings such as: 'seeing is believing', 'I wouldn't have believed if I hadn't seen it with my own eyes', 'if looks could kill', 'it's staring you in the face' (readers might like to furnish further examples of their own). Seeing provides a certainty that no other sense seems capable of affording. It is therefore unsurprising that scientific discourse is replete with visual imagery. Science is based on true 'observations' of the world and endeavours to develop objective, 'clear-sighted', unbiased 'views' of the phenomena that it investigates.

Although vision is a naturally endowed sense, our ways of looking at things and seeing the world are thoroughly cultured. The biology of vision cannot explain the way that we actually interpret the appearances of the world. Seeing is always cultured seeing. Anthropologists report instances of uncomprehending responses when certain non-Western peoples, unfamiliar with modern photographic technology, are shown photographs of ordinary objects. These peoples lack the appropriate cultural literacy to grasp what the photographs represent. As cultural beings we are able to 'see' two people walking down the street as 'a mother going shopping with her child' or to 'see' the persons embracing at a railway station as 'lovers saying their farewells'. Objects, types of person and relationships are regularly rendered intelligible to us by looking. This quite ordinary and easily exercised skill is not innate but is acquired through social learning. What we see is always conditioned by what we know – the cultural categories we employ, the common-sense knowledge we possess – and what we know is the product of long periods of socialisation. The world that we experience is full of appearances, the looks of things which make sense to us, at least as adult members of a culture. Yet we have all encountered situations where the looks of things are not always transparent; our knowledge may be deficient to grasp what is actually going on, or we may sense that something is not quite right, out of place, and infer that a puzzling or untoward event is happening. (Sociologists of everyday life, notably Erving Goffman – see section 9.6 below – have shown the importance of vision in encounters between unacquainted persons in public places.) For the most part, however, our ordinary knowledge of the world is adequate for us to understand its appearances. That knowledge and those appearances are subject to constant revision since, as Berger (1972) reminds us, what we know and what we see never stand in a finally settled relation – words and images are complexly intertwined.

This leads us to the influential notion of *visual culture*. Like any influential idea it defies straightforward characterisation but we can make a beginning by proposing that visual culture encompasses all those socially standardised ways of thinking, acting and feeling towards the appearances of the world. More specifically, we wish to reiterate the idea pursued through earlier chapters of the book that culture can be usefully understood and analysed in general terms as a text and as a way of life. As *text*, the concept of visual culture draws attention to those objects (drawings, paintings, photographs, film, fashion and adornment, etc.) conventionally regarded as the acceptable target of sustained looking, and the technologies (pencils, crayons, 35 mm cameras, VCRs, ear-piercing equipment, etc.) involved to produce these objects. As *way of life*, visual culture points to one dimension of the 'design for living' held by any group of people. Every culture provides its members with an ordinary capacity to decode the appearances of things, persons, relationships and so forth that are encountered every day. As adults walking down a city street we will be careful to give that blind person escorted by a guide dog plenty of room to pass; if we are female, we may avoid the importunate behaviours of male workers on a building site by taking another route to our destination. We are able to figure these things out, as we say, 'just by looking'. What such simple acts do not disclose is the considerable social learning lying at the back of these lines of conduct, learning that (as children) may have included being forcibly pulled out of the path of a blind person or that (as adolescent girls) may have involved an embarrassing episode of running the gauntlet of building workers' catcalls.

As way of life, visual culture suffuses our everyday experience but it also takes more institutionalised forms. Svetlana Alpers (1983) shows how seventeenth-century Holland had a richly developed visual culture which was most obviously marked by the work of the great landscape painters of the era (visual culture as text) but which itself was embedded in wider arrangements including the development of many optical instruments (camera obscura, telescope, microscope) and mapping devices. These permitted the accurate charting of space and built up a discriminating vocabulary for interpreting visual representations that was shared by many ordinary Dutch people. The advent of modernity (p. 400) has heightened the significance of the visual. Although the verbal, in both spoken and written forms, is the primary means of communication, Western culture's pervasive concern with the appearance of objects makes it decidedly ocular-centric. There is a privileging of seeing as a sensorial mode, a 'hegemony of the visual' (Tyler, 1984) embodied in the language and thought of Europeans and North Americans.

A **hegemony** (p. 106) of the visual can only arise in a culture where visual – or more specifically pictorial – representations saturate everyday life. As was argued in Chapter 2, the term **representation** (p. 61) most generally means one thing standing for another. How a picture can resemble the object to which it refers is a matter of debate among philosophers and psychologists. Some argue that a picture *resembles* that to which it refers (e.g. the painting entitled the Mona Lisa bears a resemblance to a real woman). Others suggest that a picture is a functional *substitute* or surrogate that elicits from viewers the same response that they would have if they encountered the represented scene or figure face to face (e.g. curiosity about the motives for Mona Lisa's smile). Still others maintain that a picture merely *denotes* its object and that this relationship is as arbitrary as any relationship between a sign and its referent, and thus does not necessarily entail either elements of resemblance or substitution (thus, for example, the Mona Lisa as the embodiment of a historically specific conception of womanly virtue) (Cohen, 1989). Photographs can be regarded as just another type of visual representation which can be understood in each of these three senses, or they can be regarded as a special type of representation on account of their causal relationship to what they refer. This 'photographic causality' view emphasises the necessary tie between the photographic image and objects in the world that results from the photograph's production through the action of light exposed to photographic film. This feature of photographs, as we shall see in section 9.2 below, is strongly accentuated in documentary photography.

9.2 | Modernity and visual culture: classic writers and key themes

In this section we shall consider the influential ideas of two early twentieth-century German theorists, Georg Simmel and Walter Benjamin. Their ideas have provided a benchmark for subsequent analyses of the visual culture of modern cities. In particular, they have done much to rekindle interest in the figure of the *flâneur*, a key metaphor in the appreciation of the visual dimensions of city life.

9.2.1 | Georg Simmel: metropolitan culture and visual interaction

Georg Simmel (1858–1918) is now best known as one of the earliest exponents of sociology in late nineteenth-century Germany. He was originally trained as a philosopher and his interests ranged well beyond the narrow confines of a single discipline. Simmel's contribution to our understanding of visual culture and modernity principally stems from his thinking on visual interaction and the distinctive features of metropolitan culture. These analyses in turn have to be located in the context of Simmel's broader theory of **modernity** (p. 400) articulated most fully in *The Philosophy of Money* (1978).

Key influence **9.1**

Georg Simmel (1858–1918)

Georg Simmel was born on 1 March 1858 in the centre of Berlin, a cosmopolitan city in which he spent all but the last four years of his life. His parents had converted from Judaism to Protestantism, a faith Simmel also embraced, albeit weakly. However, others defined him as a Jew and for much of his career Simmel fell victim to the pervasive anti-Semitism in the German university system of the time. He was denied a full-time appointment commensurate with the growing recognition of his intellectual stature. When he did finally obtain a salaried post, it was at the university of the border city of Strasbourg, in 1914 – just in time to see the cessation of normal academic activity by the outbreak of the First World War. For most of his life Simmel was dependent upon the per capita fees paid by students who enrolled in his classes and the legacy he was left by the friend of the family who had brought him up after death of his parents.

Anti-Semitism is only part of the story. Throughout his life Simmel was no stranger to controversy. He was widely regarded as a brilliant philosopher and sociologist, but also recognised as a maverick intellectual, the possessor of a mind that delved into a range of topics and areas that was perhaps too wide for his own scholarly good. After initial studies at Berlin University in the fields of history and folk psychology, he settled on philosophy, the discipline that provided an enduring identity for his intellectual interests. In 1881 he was awarded a doctorate by Berlin University. His first thesis (on the psychological and ethnological origins of music) was rejected as unsatisfactory but an earlier, prize-winning essay was allowed to stand in its place. In 1885 he was finally awarded the Habilitation (a higher doctorate which is a prerequisite for university teaching). At the oral defence of his thesis Simmel responded to one of his examiners in a manner that was construed as offhand and sarcastic, and he was sent home for six months 'to ponder how one behaves toward worthy older scholars'. Throughout his subsequent career Simmel attracted a reputation for the dangerousness of his thinking.

Working for fees only, Simmel quickly established a reputation as a gifted lecturer at Berlin. His classes became attractions for the cultural elite of the city, as well as large numbers of foreign and women students, a following that did not endear Simmel to the state's educational authorities. Simmel's forte was as an essayist. His writings reveal a sharp eye for the universal elements ('forms') underlying the manifestations of cultural phenomena. He was not interested in building a system or inventing a method. Rather, he sought to find 'in each of life's details the totality of its meaning'. His essay on fashion shows how clothing styles can articulate apparently contradictory wishes for difference (e.g. use of clothing to set

→

oneself apart from others) and similarity (e.g. belonging to a group of fashionably costumed persons). His enormously influential essay on cities, 'The metropolis and mental life' (1903), emphasises the emergence of shared cognitive dispositions among modern city-dwellers, a distinctive mental set of reserve and calculation. Fashion flourishes in the city because people there often experience themselves as undistinguished and diminutive and see others as a source of unanticipated demands. Fashion, because it is encoded in people's clothing, is compatible with a cool, detached metropolitan outlook but it can also serve as a device whereby people can exaggerate their singularity and thus protect themselves from being overwhelmed or submerged by the demands of city living.

Although Simmel was most at home in the essay format and published regularly in newspapers and periodicals, he also wrote some large 'academic' books, most notably for students of cultural studies *The Philosophy of Money* (1900; the English translation did not appear until 1978). This, Simmel's major treatise on **modernity** (p. 400) traces the diverse impacts that money economies make on social and cultural life. Simmel also addressed the massive expansion in the scale and availability of culture in modern life which enormously increased the scope for cultural deformation and domination – 'the tragedy of culture'.

Simmel's impact was felt originally in sociology, where he conceived a distinctive focus for the discipline (investigating the forms of human association) and in philosophy, where he influenced the thinking of **Benjamin** (p. 373) and Lukács. In the English-speaking world a 'Simmel renaissance' has taken place over the past two decades as more of his writings have been translated into English. His contemporary relevance for cultural studies lies in his original understanding of the bases of modernity, constructed out of a plethora of close studies of cultural minutiae.

Further reading

Featherstone, M. (ed.) (1991) A special issue on Georg Simmel, *Theory, Culture and Society* 8(3), August.

Frisby, D. (1984) *Georg Simmel,* London and Chichester: Tavistock/Ellis Horwood.

Weinstein, D. and Weinstein, M. (1993) *Postmodern(ized) Simmel,* London: Routledge.

Simmel's work does not sit easily within disciplinary boundaries as ultimately he was concerned with analysing the essential features of modernity, a task that lay outside the purview of any academic discipline. For Simmel, modernity involved 'the modes of experiencing what is "new" in "modern" society' (Frisby, 1985: 1). Many of Simmel's observations were sparked off by his knowledge and experience of the city of Berlin, a cosmopolitan urban centre in which he spent nearly all his life. Simmel sought to penetrate the 'inner nature' or 'soul' of modernity by contemplating the conditions of existence of its products. What resulted was a form of analysis that was as much aesthetic in character as scientific. Simmel held out the prospect 'of finding in each of life's details the totality of its meaning' (1978: 55); he sought to extract the most general principles from the inspection of cultural minutiae, for example elucidating features of the instrumentality bred by the money economy by reference to the practice of prostitution or the contrasting attitudes of the miser and the spendthrift.

For Simmel, modernity was not to be understood as simply the culture of capitalism or industrial society. Its roots lay further back in history. Modernity's origins are to be found in the advent of a fully monetarised economy rather than in variants of the traditional society/industrial capitalism distinction. For Simmel it is the replacement of seigniorial dues and other forms of barter by money as the principal medium of economic exchange that has far-reaching consequences for the contours taken by modernity. In a detailed and complexly argued analysis Simmel shows how money is a highly flexible form of exchange which can be divided in any number of ways and which can be put to an infinity of purposes. Money, then, is pure instrumentality, completely subservient to the ends to which it is put. In this respect it breeds the calculative outlook so typical of modern societies. The processes of rationalisation so well explicated by Weber (see Chapters 1 and 6) have their origins in monetary exchange which becomes almost synonymous with calculation.

In his classic essay of 1903, 'The metropolis and mental life', Simmel (1971) elucidates some social psychological features of the culture of modern cities. In the modern city many anonymous persons come into fleeting contact with one another, for example travelling on public transport or purchasing goods in a department store. Individuals are removed from the emotional ties and social bonds that link people together in smaller communities. Simmel describes a social psychological configuration which seems characteristic of those who live in large urban centres. The urban dweller's mental life is predominantly *intellectualistic* in character. People respond to situations in a rational rather than an emotional manner. The broad orientation of urban dwellers tends to be *calculative*; the daily life of people is filled 'with weighing, calculating, enumerating' which reduces 'qualitative values to quantitative terms' (1971: 328). A common stance of urban dwellers is thus the *blasé outlook*, a renunciation of responsiveness, an indifference towards the values that distinguish things. The world of the blasé person is flat, grey and homogenous. Often accompanying this outlook is to be found an attitude of *reserve*. A reserved attitude acts as a protective shield for the urban dweller behind which candid views and heartfelt sentiments can be preserved from scrutiny.

Simmel's influential paper has often been mistakenly construed by commentators as turning around an analysis of the contrast between urban and rural ways of life. But this is by no means the case (see Savage and Warde, 1993: 110–14). Very often what Simmel is seeking to contrast are the differences between the *traditional* village or small town and the modern city. Moreover, Simmel maintains that within modern societies it is not easy to sustain a distinction between rural and urban ways of life because the city's influence ramifies throughout the entirety of the society. Further, Simmel does not see the features he describes as simply originating from the ecology and organisation of the modern city. Instead he regards the city as the prime 'seat of the money economy' through which are refracted features (calculativeness, the blasé attitude) that ultimately derive from the advent of fully monetarised systems of exchange.

The features of modern urban culture delineated by Simmel point to the predominance of the visual sense. In public places, for example, it is essential that the calculative, blasé, reserved urban dweller is able to scan the immediate environment for all kinds of practical purposes – finding one's way about, avoiding colliding with others on a busy street, being watchful for potential sources of danger. These everyday interactions were considered by Simmel be the basic material of society. Although it is commonplace to think about society in terms of institutionalised social structures such as political and economic organisations, social classes and the like, these large-scale structures are themselves crystallisations of multitudes of everyday interactions between people (buying tickets, asking the way, dining together, standing in a queue and so forth). Simmel considered a fundamental task for sociology to be the description and analysis of the characteristic features of these forms of interaction (or 'sociation' in Simmel's term) and he eventually consolidated these inquiries in a substantial volume, *Sociology: Investigations of the Forms of Sociation*, published in German in 1908 and not yet translated in its entirety into English.

In a brief section of this pathbreaking book entitled 'Sociology of the senses', Simmel gave particular attention to sight, for of all of humanity's senses 'the eye has a uniquely sociological function' (Simmel, 1969: 358). Consider first the mutual glance, when two persons look at ('into') each other's eyes, as distinct from the simple observation of one person by another. In the mutual glance, says Simmel, we find 'the most direct and purest reciprocity that exists anywhere'. Each person gives equally to the encounter. 'The eye cannot take unless at the same time it gives. ... In the same act in which the observer seeks to know the observed, he surrenders himself to be understood by the observed' (1969: 358). Naturally enough, glances are transitory phenomena, gone in the moment they occur. But social interaction as we know it would not be possible if humans did not have the capacity for the mutual glance, since the glance serves as a vehicle for conveying recognition, acknowledgement, understanding, intimacy, shame and so forth.

Simmel draws out further aspects of the sociological significance of the eye. When humans interact the face tends to be the primary focus of visual attention because it is a crucial indicator of mood and intent; people are first known by their countenance, not their acts. Indeed, the human face serves no practical purpose except to tell us about the state of mind of its possessor.

It follows from these observations about glances and faces that the attitude of the blind characteristically differs from that of the deaf. 'For the blind, the other person is actually present only in the alternating periods of his utterance' (1969: 359). This gives the blind, Simmel suggests, 'a peaceful and calm existence' in contrast to the often 'more perplexed, puzzled and worried' (1969: 360) attitude of the deaf. Moreover the visual mode assumes a greater significance in the large city because the person is likely to encounter many people in a relationship of anonymity, a relationship in which all that is available to the person is the appearance of the other. Cities present a range of situations (cinemas, theatres, restaurants, buses and trains) in which the individual is placed in the company of anonymous others who are only known to the individual through what can be inferred about their appearance. The increased role of 'mere visual impression' (1969: 360) is characteristic of modern, large-scale society. People living in such a society, Simmel concludes, suffer from some of the same perplexity that afflicts the deaf: the increased role of 'mere visual impression' contributes to a widespread sense of estrangement.

'A visionary of the real world' (Sennett, 1969: 10; note the metaphor!), Simmel's thinking about metropolitan culture and visual interaction indicates the ways in which modernity impacts on visual culture. His frequently diffuse, elliptical yet persuasive writings have influenced further studies of the visual dimensions of ordinary city life, including those of Walter Benjamin.

9.2.2 | Walter Benjamin: mechanical reproduction, aura and the Paris arcades

As with Simmel, **Walter Benjamin**'s (p. 373) (1892–1940) writings are wide ranging and challenging, resisting disciplinary classification. He studied a diverse set of topics in an often literary and philosophical style reflecting the influence of progressive artistic movements and the German philosophical tradition. We want to highlight his contribution to debates on **modernity** (p. 400) and visual culture in two main areas. First, Benjamin pointed to the significant transformations effected by the development of new technology (specifically photography and film) for representing visual culture. Second, he considered particular aspects of everyday life in the changing cities (particularly Paris) of the nineteenth century.

In his most famous essay, 'The work of art in the age of mechanical reproduction' which was first published in 1936, Benjamin (1970) asks the question of how art is changed or affected in an era when it can easily be reproduced by mechanical means. For film and photography allow a large number of copies to be made of an art work that originally had a single unique existence. He suggests that this process leads to a decline in what he calls the *aura* of the work. Benjamin argues that in previous periods in history the work of art was specifically located in time, space and tradition (churches and chapels, religious ritual, aristocratic patronage and so forth). Such traditions were not unchanging but they did give the work of art a specific and original meaning. Contemporary reproduction techniques (photography, film, audio recordings on records, tapes and CDs) lift works of art out of tradition and lead to a decline in what he called the aura or unique meaning of the work.

Tradition is particularly important in Benjamin's argument. Tradition mobilises rituals and cultic meanings. Thus, paintings and objects would have possessed a secure meaning arising from their clear anchorage in the religious and cultic practices of particular social groups. In a sense this generates a sense of reverence or power around the object. Within the Christian tradition, for example, art objects located in churches such as the paintings on the walls of the Sistine Chapel in Rome possess an aura in the tangible sense that they create a space around them. The work of art was then located in tradition and had power due to its presence in that tradition creating aura. The text was an original in the sense that it existed in a specific physical location and could only be seen and appreciated by visiting that location. The development of mechanical reproduction (photography and film principally) transforms this situation. As Benjamin explains: 'for the first time in world history mechanical reproduction emancipates the work of art from its parasitical dependence on ritual. To an ever greater degree the

Key influence 9.2
Walter Benjamin 1892–1940

Walter Benjamin's work combined a creative **Marxism** (p. 97) with elements of Judaic Messianic theology. He was a close associate of members of the **Frankfurt School** (p. 109). He wrote about modernity, the city, baroque and nineteenth- and twentieth-century literature.

Benjamin was born in Berlin and studied philosophy and literature in Berlin, Freiburg, Munich and Bern. His first and only published book-length study, *The Origin of German Tragic Drama* (1928), failed to secure him an academic job. After the First World War he worked as a freelance critic and translator. In the late 1920s he met Bertolt Brecht whose work he defended and championed. With Brecht he took a more optimistic view of mass culture than members of the Frankfurt School like Theodor Adorno. He argued that the 'mechanical reproduction' of art and culture could be used in a progressive politics as well as be the tool of Fascist propaganda. In the 1930s, Benjamin moved to Paris to escape the Nazis and there worked on his most ambitious undertaking, the 'Arcades Project', which attempted to read the work of the poet Charles Baudelaire in the context of nineteenth-century capitalism. The unfinished work has proved a rich resource for sociologists and cultural critics writing about the modern city. After the German invasion of France, Benjamin escaped to the Franco–Spanish border, where he committed suicide rather than be handed over to the Nazis. As a consequence, most of his work was published posthumously. Theodor Adorno and Gershon Scholem helped to revive interest in his work after the Second World War and collections of his essays began to appear.

Benjamin's influence in cultural studies has been diffuse. His work on Brecht and Kafka has been important to the understanding of the relationship between modernist art, politics and mass culture. His essays have sparked debates within feminism, postcolonial theory and historical studies. One of his best-known essays is 'Theses on the philosophy of history', which criticised the idea of a linear, causal history. Instead, Benjamin proposed the spatial metaphor of the constellation as the way in which the cultural historian should relate the present to the past.

Further reading

The best introduction to Benjamin's work are the collections of his essays:

Illuminations, London: Fontana (1970).
Charles Baudelaire: A Lyric Poet in the Era of High Capitalism, London: Verso (1983).
Understanding Brecht, London: New Left Books (1977).

work of art reproduced becomes the work of art designed for reproducibility' (1970: 226).

Benjamin argues that this lifting out, or 'disembedding' (Giddens, 1990), of art from tradition leads to a politicisation of art. Since techniques of mechanical reproduction make knowledge of the art work so much more widely available, it can become the subject of contested meaning and implicated in a much more developed sense in wider attempts to justify the exercise of power. Thus, it can be suggested that familiarity with certain films and photographs can provide the basis for attempts to influence the public in particular directions, but that the audience can in fact often find different meanings within those forms. It also leads to the increased importance of what Benjamin calls 'exhibition value' which he traces in the development of photography and film. We will concentrate on the themes introduced by Benjamin on film at this point, as this illustrates some important aspects of Benjamin's theses on aura.

Benjamin argues that the performance of an actor in a play has auratic elements. It is (and remains) a unique performance in the sense that it is socially located in one place – the actor performed his or her part in the particular performance of the play, in *that* place, on *that* night. With the development of film, clear changes occur. The audience might watch the same performance in a number of places (the same film can be watched by audiences in the United States or in France at the same time). Importantly, the notion of performance also changes. The performance of the actor in the film is actually made up of a number of segments edited together long after the actors have finished their work. This suggests a decline in the originality of the work and the authenticity and originality of the performance.

The decline in the aura of the performance, Benjamin maintains, is compensated by the rise of the phenomenon of 'personality' and 'stardom', where actors and performers are stars who generate audience appeal by their special personal qualities. The production of films to be sold on a market, that is as commodities, is facilitated by the fact that a secure demand for them can be generated by the use of stars. One consequence of this arrangement is that the decision by a star as to whether he or she wants to act in a particular film can determine whether that film is made or not. Stars can generate a form of brand loyalty (Lury, 1993) from the public.

In some respects Benjamin viewed such developments rather more positively than several other writers associated with the **Frankfurt School** (p. 109). He recognised that the wider availability of works of art made possible by processes of mechanical reproduction could lead to a greater democratisation of art. Thus, culture could become part of a progressive political practice in the ways that it was used, by Brecht for example (see Chapter 6). But Benjamin was also very critical of aspects of these developments. He saw that they could lead to the commodification of art and also to the use of movies and personalities to prop up exploitative and repressive political regimes through propaganda. As he says:

> The cult of the movie star, fostered by the money of the film industry, preserves not the unique aura of the person but the 'spell of the personality', the phoney spell of a commodity. So long as the movie-makers' capital sets the fashion, as a rule no other revolutionary merit can be accredited to today's film than the promotion of a revolutionary criticism of traditional concepts of art. (1970: 233)

To summarise, Benjamin sees a decline in the aura of art as it becomes reproduced. This reproduction lifts art out of specific and traditional contexts and allows it to be relocated more widely. The work of art loses originality and uniqueness in this process.

Table 9.1 ■ Auratic and non-auratic art

Auratic art	Non-auratic art
Original	Copy
Tradition	Modern
Ritual	Entertainment
Religion	Secular
Use	Exchange
Distance	Immediacy
Whole	Fragmented

Furthermore, mass or commodified art tends towards the superficial and the phoney. Surface appeals are made and the public is manipulated by the cult of personality and stars. Some of the key differences between auratic and non-auratic art are indicated in Table 9.1.

In addition to these important and influential ideas concerning aura and reproduction, in 'The work of art in the age of mechanical reproduction' Benjamin also offers some significant comments on architecture and the ways in which buildings are appropriated by members of the public. In this discussion he emphasises the role of touch, in that buildings are *used* by people, and sight, in that people perceive images of buildings and the city. However, it is in various of his other writings and in particular in his work on Paris in the nineteenth century that Benjamin explores the visual and everyday culture of the city at greater length (Buck-Morss, 1989).

In this work Benjamin explores the relationship between the city as text and as experienced by the people who live, work and play in it. However, Benjamin was not so much interested in the conscious ways in which people use cities as in the ways that they experience them unconsciously, almost without cognition in a straightforward sense. There is in Benjamin's view a sense in which cities may be experienced almost as a dream (Savage and Warde, 1993). There is, then, a relationship between the meanings that are stored up in the city and the associations that they possess and the experience of those meanings for the inhabitant and the visitor. We shall return to these issues in the later sections of this chapter. First, we consider an important form of analysis of the experience of the city, issuing from the idea of the *flâneur*.

9.2.3 | The figure of the *flâneur*

A number of convergent themes concerning **modernity** (p. 400), visual culture and the city in the thought of Simmel and Benjamin are captured by the figure of the *flâneur*. Simmel's broad analytic stance, it has been suggested, is that of a *flâneur* (Frisby, 1981; but see Weinstein and Weinstein, 1993), the gentleman stroller of the city streets who, in the nineteenth-century French poet and writer Charles Baudelaire's expression, goes 'botanising on the asphalt' (Benjamin, 1973: 36) as he observes the urban spectacle.

This interpretation of Simmel itself has its origins in Benjamin's interest in the way in which cities are experienced by people in the course of ordinary work and leisure activities. In essays written in the mid-1930s Benjamin (1973) was led to examine the work of Baudelaire who had earlier popularised the concept of the *flâneur*, drawing attention to this figure who takes an almost voyeuristic pleasure in detachedly watching the doings of fellow city-dwellers.

The recent efflorescence of interest in the figure of the *flâneur* has several dimensions. First of all it seems that the *flâneur* was a type of person with a real historical existence, as this anonymous description from Paris (1906) shows (adapted from Wilson, 1992: 94–5):

- A 'gentleman' who spends most of the day roaming the streets observing the urban spectacle – the fashions in dress and adornment, the buildings, the shops, the books, the novelties and attractions. A kind of voyeur with an endless curiosity for witnessing the ordinary scenes of city life.

- His means of support are invisible; there is the suggestion of private wealth (he is possibly a *rentier*) but an apparent absence of family, business or landowning responsibilities.

- His interests are primarily aesthetic and he frequents cafés and restaurants where actors, journalists, writers and artists gather.

- For the *flâneur* a significant part of the urban spectacle is provided by the behaviour of the lower orders (workers, soldiers, street vendors and street people).

- He is a marginal figure, tending to be portrayed as isolated from those he observes, a solitary figure in crowds.

No one knows just how widespread this social type was in Paris and other cities of nineteenth-century Europe. In many respects the significance of the figure of the *flâneur* lies not so much in the historical phenomenon as it does in the observational stance that it denotes. The *flâneur* is an intellectual figure speaking to the new conditions of modernity. *Flânerie* – a leisurely amalgam of strolling, loitering and, importantly, gazing at the urban spectacle – only becomes possible in the social conditions provided by the big cities of industrialising Europe. Thus, the *flâneur* can be considered to typify the experience of modernity's public places.

The *flâneur*, strolling through the city streets and preserving his incognito in the anonymity of the crowd, witnesses a variety of situations which are seen at a safe and detached distance. Watching the world go by lies at the heart of the *flâneur*'s stance: simple observation, not prescription or remedy. Vision is paramount: 'the *flâneur* moves through space and among the people with a viscosity that both enables and privileges vision' (Jenks, 1995: 146). For the *flâneur* the city is not a home but a showplace. The labyrinthine images of metropolitan culture provide an endless source of fascination tinged with mystery. 'This inconspicuous passer-by', says Benjamin, has 'the dignity of the priest and the sense for clues of a detective' (cited in Frisby, 1985: 229–30). In varying degrees *flânerie* is evident in the novels of Charles Dickens (Benjamin specifically identifies *Sketches by Boz*), the documentary reports of the Victorian 'social explorers' like Booth and Mayhew, the 'man in the crowd' of Edgar Allen Poe and the sociology of **Georg Simmel** (p. 368), as well as Benjamin's own reflections on Paris (the Arcades Project).

Feminists have highlighted the taken-for-granted male associations implicit in the *flâneur* figure. From one point of view the non-existence of the role of *flâneuse* symbolises women's restricted participation in public places as well as the malestream bias of some of the classical literature on modernity (Wolff, 1985). The invisibility of the *flâneuse* underscores how the freedom to roam was very much a male freedom: the *flâneur*'s licence to watch the city sights can be regarded as the walking embodiment of the 'male gaze' (see below). Other feminists have argued that there is a risk of over-generalising this argument. They point out that women's experiences of urban life, even in the nineteenth century, varied from city to city and from class to class. Thus Elizabeth Wilson (1992) has suggested that it is misleading to claim that women were comprehensively excluded from public spaces in late nineteenth-century England. She maintains that the growth of department stores, tea rooms, railway station buffets, ladies-only dining rooms, public conveniences with female attendants and so forth, made it possible for middle- and lower middle-class women to experience public places and thus afforded at least some women the opportunity for *flânerie*. These issues connect to more contemporary empirical investigations of behaviour in public places (see also section 9.7 below).

9.3 | Technologies of realism: photography and film

As Benjamin's discussion of aura implies, photography and film are each nineteenth-century technical innovations that have made a major impact on the development and apprehension of the visual cultures of **modernity** (p. 400) and late modernity. In this section we consider how photography and film have promoted a concern with the **realistic** (p. 61) representation of the world, a claim that needs to be approached cautiously and treated critically.

9.3.1 | The development of photography and film

Cameras existed long before photographs did. The camera obscura was in widespread use as a drawing aid by the sixteenth century, although the principle on which it was based (light entering a small room or box through an aperture or lens throws an inverted image against the back wall) was known to the ancients. Photography is a modernist technology. The world's first genuine photograph was taken by the French inventor Joseph Niepce in 1826. Early photographs were one-of-a-kind images produced by the action of light on specially treated plates. Through the 1830s the search was on to refine the technique. One of the most influential techniques was daguerreotypy, devised by a colleague of Niepce, Louis Daguerre, who sold his invention to the French government in 1839. The daguerreotype quickly became popular throughout Europe and America but its big drawback was that it could only produce single images. In England the scientist, traveller, linguist and MP William Henry Fox Talbot finally perfected the calotype in 1841. The calotype only required an exposure time of a couple of seconds and it was the first system to print multiple copies of positives off a single negative. Indeed, the word 'photography' and the terms 'positive' and 'negative' originated from Talbot's friend, the scientist Sir John Herschel. The commercial possibilities of photography were quickly exploited and soon photographic studios were to be found in every town and city, first in Europe and North America, then quickly elsewhere.

For most of the nineteenth century, photography remained largely in the hands of small numbers of technically knowledgeable practitioners. Its popularisation as an everyday practice requiring no special skills came about with the American Max Eastman's marketing of the Kodak box camera in 1888 under the famous slogan, 'You press the button, we do the rest'. The camera was equipped with a roll of film that took 100 pictures. Once the whole film was used, the camera was returned to the factory where the old film was developed and a new one installed. This marked the beginning of the major revolution in the history of photography which was advanced by the introduction of the Brownie box camera at the turn of the century. A simple and cheap camera, unlike the expensive Kodak and its successors, this really put photography into the hands of large sections of society. This 'democratisation' of photography has been advanced by a number of important technical developments this century including the invention of the 35 mm camera (the Leica, 1925), the Polaroid instant camera (by the American Henry Land, 1947), the cartridge Instamatic (1963) and the widespread availability of colour photography from the late 1960s on. Today the act of taking pictures is an accepted part of weddings, christenings, holidays and other occasions of ceremonial significance. We take photos of our families, our friends, our pets, our heroes. We use the pictures we take to construct our biography (see Spence and Holland, 1991). Photography is a 'middle-brow art' (Bourdieu *et al.*, 1990). Yet as a mass vernacular practice photography is only a century old.

Film – motion photography – has an even briefer history than still photography. The cinematograph was invented by the brothers Louis and Auguste Lumière who opened the world's first cinema in Paris in 1895. Unlike other prototypical movie cameras the cinematograph was portable and this, combined with the energetic entrepreneurial activity of the Lumières, ensured that their invention was installed in every major city of the world by the century's end. Nowadays, of course, the movie business is the leading entertainment industry on the planet and its impact is felt everywhere. We need to remember that both motion and still photography can serve diverse purposes – as scientific instruments, as entertainment, as forms of art, as methods of surveillance, for example. As we shall see in our consideration of the documentary photography of city life, these purposes are often complexly interwoven.

9.3.2 | The documentary tradition

The documentary tradition of photography and film emerged in the late nineteenth century in Europe and America as a socially conscious endeavour to depict graphically the actualities of the world. Documentary has a rich and varied history. In the United States a significant early contributor was Jacob Riis whose New York pictures of Lower East Side poverty in *How the Other Half Lives* (1890) had a major impact on public opinion. In the early decades of the twentieth century Lewis Hines' photographs of industrial working conditions influenced US reform movements and legislation. A generation later, a large collection of pictures was assembled by photographers working for the Farm Security Administration. Disseminated through the popular press, especially the new mass-circulation picture magazines like *Life* which employed photo-essay formats, they brought home to wider publics the misery faced by small farmers in the 1930s and the troubles they encountered when migrating to the towns and cities of the west as droughts turned agricultural land into dustbowls. Perhaps the most famous book to describe these dislocations was *Let Us Now Praise Famous Men* (1941) by James Agee and Walker Evans. In Europe, the pictures of Parisian street scenes and café life made by Henri Cartier-Bresson and Brassai reached wide audiences (see Westerbeck and Meyerowitz's (1994) excellent history of street photography). At a time when television was still in its infancy, documentarists found a mass outlet for their work through the new and influential occupation of photojournalism. That documentary found such a ready audience in the 1930s, in both Europe and America, has to be understood as part of wider social currents which showed a new sensitivity to the description of the experiences of the ordinary person and which found expression through such diverse forms as Mass Observation, community studies, phenomenology, folk art, public art, newsreel cinema, photojournalism magazines and soap operas.

One of the first motion pictures ever produced showed workers leaving the Lumières' factory. The Lumières used their new invention to cast new light on many aspects of daily life both at home and abroad. Indeed, they coined the term *documentaires* to describe their short travel films. Although film was quickly exploited by Hollywood for entertainment purposes, its capacity to document ways of life was not neglected. One milestone was Robert Flaherty's account of Eskimo life in *Nanook of the North* (1922). In the Soviet Union aspects of the new society being forged were captured by *Kinopravda* (Film Truth) cinematographers. The ideological potential of documentary was also recognised in Nazi Germany where Leni Riefenstahl's epic documentary *Triumph of the Will*, of the 1934 Nazi Party national rally, lent new dimensions to the propaganda function of film.

It is customary to distinguish documentary from fictional work. Documentary is about reporting, not inventing, whatever is in the world. According to Michael Renov (1986; cited in Winston 1995: 6), 'every documentary issues a "truth claim" of a sort, positing a relationship to history which exceeds the analogical status of its fictional counterpart'. The realist impulse is paramount: documentary pictures and film aim to exhibit the facts of a situation.

> [Documentary] imposes its meaning. It confronts, us, the audience, with empirical evidence of such nature as to render dispute impossible and interpretation super-fluous. All emphasis is on the evidence; the facts themselves speak . . . since just the fact matters, it can be transmitted in any plausible medium. . . . The heart of documentary is not form or style or medium, but always content.
>
> (Stott, 1973)

But documentary is also designed to encourage viewers to come to a particular conclusion about how the world is and the way it works. Often what is depicted is the everyday activities and pleasures of ordinary people or the experiences of the suffering and oppressed, who are portrayed in a way that enables the viewer to empathise with their situations. Documentary starts off by avowing merely descriptive concerns, 'telling it like it is'. As one distinguished exponent, Dorothea Lange, put it, 'documentary photography records the social scene of out time. It mirrors the present and documents for the future' (quoted in Ohrn, 1980: 37). Routinely, however, these realist concerns of documentary are linked to persuasive ones, enjoining the viewer to take a particular attitude to what is depicted. For example, John Grierson, the Scottish filmmaker of the 1930s and 1940s who is widely regarded as a pivotal figure in the development of British and North American traditions of documentary film, expressly considered the cinema to be a pulpit and explained that his philosophy was to exploit the observational potential of film in order to construct a picture of reality and thereby to realise cinema's destiny as a social commentator and source of inspiration for social change (see Barnouw, 1974).

Documentary thus capitalises upon photography's immense descriptive potential. Photographs provide a precise record of material reality, what is indubitably there in the world. Photography has been described as 'a benchmark of "pictorial fact"' (Snyder and Allen, 1982: 66) arising from the automatism of the process through which photographs are produced (by the machine-generated exposure of light to chemically treated paper) which is said to remove human agency and yield a representation possessing an authenticity and objectivity that easel painting can never obtain. In John Berger's (1989: 96) summary, 'Photographs do not translate from appearances. They quote them.' The camera is, in the famous slogan, 'a mirror with a memory'. These are all powerful claims on behalf of photographic **realism** (p. 61). But they do not support the more exaggerated affirmation that artifice is foreign to photography, nor do they support a hard and fast contrast between documentary (or scientific) and art photography. Art photography emerges around the recognition that photographs are not simply documents but are also aesthetic objects. As Susan Sontag (1979: 85) put it: 'Nobody ever discovered ugliness through photographs. But many, through photographs, have discovered beauty.' Some of the issues at stake are summarised in Table 9.2.

What Table 9.2 sets out are not two distinct types of photograph but rather two dimensions for appraising photographic images. Indeed, the most credible view to take is that documentary is defined by its use; documentary pictures are those that are used in documentary ways (Snyder, 1984). This also allows aesthetic considerations a place in documentary photography: a powerful image is often the most effective way of driving home the facts of some situation. The persuasiveness of documentary is achieved through the artful fusion of descriptive and aesthetic concerns: production decisions about pose, light, composition, lenses, types of film and focus, as well as editing judgements such as cropping and the like, are guided by the photographer's sense of what makes an effective image.

The realism of documentary is thus a professional **ideology** (p. 84). In its most simple

Table 9.2 ■ Artistic and documentary conceptions of photography

Art photography	versus	Documentary photography
The photographer as seer		The photographer as witness
Photography as expression		Photography as reportage
Theories of imagination and conceptual truth		Theories of empirical truth
Affectivity		Information value
Symbolism		Realism

Source: adapted from Sekula (1975)

form it rests on two questionable assumptions: that the camera takes pictures and never lies, and that the camera faithfully records the world as it appears (Ruby, 1976). Against the first assumption it must be remembered that people, not cameras, take pictures and those pictures are always taken from some point of view that has an arbitrary component. Here 'arbitrary' does not mean happenchance; it means it could have been otherwise – another, different picture could easily have been made. The great French documentarist Henri Cartier-Bresson spoke of this as waiting for the 'decisive moment' to create his arresting pictures of Parisian street life. The second assumption also cannot be accepted without qualification. Photographs do not unambiguously and transparently record reality. The sense that we make of any photograph depends upon a variety of factors including our cultural and personal knowledge, visual literacy and the picture's place of publication and caption. Such criticisms lead to some further issues.

9.3.3 | Colin MacCabe: the classic realist text

In a much-quoted paper Colin MacCabe (1981) developed a controversial critique of the claims for **realism** (p. 61) in arts like film and photography. He argued that the dominant textual form in contemporary society is the classic realist text. It is important to note that MacCabe's argument is primarily about the *form* of the text. MacCabe's is not a referential argument which construes realism as correspondence to how things actually are in the world. Thus classic realist texts can range from Disney cartoons to the novels of Dickens, from *Neighbours* to *NYPD Blue* and from *Terminator 2* to 'classics' of British 'realist' cinema such as *Saturday Night and Sunday Morning.* He defines the classic realist text through four main features (Lovell, 1980).

First, the classic realist text consists of a hierarchy of **discourses** (p. 30). At the top of this hierarchy is a discourse that claims adequacy to the real. In the novel this may be the voice of the narrator, or the flow of the (constructed) narrative itself. In more visual forms of the classic realist text the truth will be revealed by what we see on the screen (Hill, 1986). When watching a television programme or a film, we expect the 'truth' to be revealed to us at some point. Furthermore, it is displayed *visually*, normally at the end of the narrative. Thus, at the conclusion of a detective story we expect to find out 'who dun it'. This will often be revealed to us by the central male hero, whose actions lead to the solution of the crime. In many respects the dominant discourse of the display of the truth and the depiction of reality is associated with male activity, which itself structures the narrative (Abercrombie and Longhurst, 1991).

Second, the classic realist text promotes relationships of identification, particularly between the hero and the reader or viewer of the text. As readers or viewers we tend to identify with the actions of the hero and his point of view in the narrative, often influencing us in **ideological** (p. 84) ways. The classic realist text does particular work on us as members of an audience, stitching us into the flow of the narrative, and its discourse of the revealing of truth. Thus, to simplify somewhat, in the Sherlock Holmes stories, truth is associated with the actions and knowledge of Holmes, who will reveal that truth to the reader. The actual narrator is Dr Watson, to whom things are communicated by Holmes, and who acts as a mediator to the audience. Watson may sometimes be critical of Holmes, especially when he acts particularly insensitively, but ultimately this discourse will be subsumed beneath that of the scientific revelation of the truth and the real state of affairs.

Third, and relatedly, the classic realist text is closed. It does not reveal a range of options on the truth or reality, then leaving the audience to choose between them. It offers the solution to the range of issues or enigmas raised during the course of the narrative. It is very rare for a popular film or novel to end without a resolution or a conclusion, which ties up all the loose ends. Indeed, it is possible to maintain that one of the pleasures involved in the consumption of the classic realist text is the resolution of the narrative's issues and its characters' fates.

Fourth, the reader of such texts is essentially passive. The truth or reality will be set out for him or her by the end. This means that when we read or watch classic realist texts we have relatively little work to do. We simply have to be receptive to the text, not actively engage with its presuppositions.

MacCabe is highly critical of the dominance of such classic realist texts and their effects. For MacCabe such texts are ideological, not in the sense that the characters may **represent** (p. 61) racist or sexist stereotypes, although they may indeed do this, but rather because the structure of the text suggests that contradictions or different points of view can be resolved. MacCabe argues that such texts cannot handle or deal with the very real contradictions that exist in a capitalist society without prioritising one particular version of the real. In the course of this process such texts render the reader passive, rather than encouraging them actively to seek out the truth or reality for themselves or in association with others. This is the case even with those texts that attempt to use the realist form to convey a radical or left-wing message. Again, according to MacCabe, a version of the real is displayed to the reader to accept, truth relatively unproblematic. This view gave rise to a debate around political practice and film or television making, which is often known as the *Days of Hope* debate (see Bennett *et al.*, 1981), where MacCabe's positions were disputed by those who saw potential in the realist form for the conveying of radical content, especially in a series such as *Days of*

Hope shown on British television, which dramatised the events of the General Strike of 1926. In turn, MacCabe disputes the realist claims of documentary film makers or photographers. MacCabe's essentially Brechtian position was a radical one which suggested that such attempts would be doomed to failure and that the clear alternative was to use more radical forms to disrupt the expectations associated with the classic realist text. MacCabe then suggests that dominant narratives induce passivity and what can be seen as essentially false pleasures.

9.3.4 | Laura Mulvey: the male gaze

MacCabe's description and critique of dominant, realist or narrative cinema chimes with Mulvey's pathbreaking work on the gaze in contemporary Hollywood cinema, as at the core of the classic realist text is the activity and the look of the male hero. Mulvey begins from within the framework of **psychoanalysis** (p. 8). In particular she explores the sexual aspects of visual pleasures that derive from the watching of narrative cinema of the dominant Hollywood type. She maintains that narrative cinema provides two main forms of pleasure: scopophilia and identification.

Scopophilia refers to the sexual pleasure derived from looking. In its extreme form this pleasure become voyeuristic – the 'perversion' of scopophilia is to become a 'peeping tom'. Scopophilic pleasure depends on a separation of the viewer from that which is being viewed. We are looking in upon a situation or a text. In general, we derive pleasure from 'using another person as an object of sexual stimulation through sight' (Mulvey 1981: 208).

In addition to these pleasures, Mulvey argues that the viewer of a film also derives pleasure from the process of identification. The looking at the screen leads to the identification of the spectator with what appears in front of them. This process of identification tends to break down the distance or separation that is inherent in the scopophilic process outlined above. The boundaries between the self and the film break down. The spectator almost becomes a part of the action in the film. Mulvey suggests therefore that these two processes are intertwined and paradoxical. This can be explained through Mulvey's main concern: the gendered nature of these processes.

Mulvey's contention here is that 'In a world ordered by sexual imbalance, pleasure in looking has been split between active/male and passive/female. The determining male gaze projects its phantasy on to the female figure which is styled accordingly' (1981: 209). Conventional Hollywood cinema displays women to be looked at by men. Men are active within the film itself and in their looking. Women are to be looked at. However, and here Mulvey returns to the paradox outlined above, the display of the woman on the screen tends to interrupt the narrative drive of the development of the film. If spectators become fixated on the image of the woman displayed before them, then they will not be integrated into the narrative flow of the film and will not be sewn into the dominant ideological frame in the way outlined by MacCabe. Mulvey argues that this paradox is resolved in particular ways by conventional cinema. As she says:

> The presence of woman is an indispensable element of spectacle in normal narrative film, yet her visual presence tends to work against the development of a story line, to

freeze the flow of the action in moments of erotic contemplation. This alien presence then has to be integrated into cohesion with the narrative.   (Mulvey, 1981: 209)

This is often done by positioning the woman as the object of the gaze within the narrative itself. Women characters are often looked at by the male characters in the course of the film. The female character may be a showgirl or a scantily dressed prostitute, for example. To use an example from television, the women police officers in *Miami Vice* often seemed to be working undercover as prostitutes, facilitating the display of their bodies for the male spectator. Male spectators derive pleasure from looking (in the scopophilic sense) and are integrated into the narrative through sharing and identifying with the look and the pleasure of the male characters in the narrative itself. The active hero in the film possesses the female character and identification occurs with his action: 'The male protagonist is free to command the stage, a stage of spatial illusion in which he articulates the look and creates the action' (Mulvey, 1981: 211). Through these processes the spectator becomes tied into the film.

Mulvey concludes by suggesting that there are three 'looks' associated with the cinema: first, 'that of the camera as it records the pro-filmic event' (that which is arranged in front of the camera); second, 'that of the audience as it watches the final product'; and, third, 'that of the characters at each other within the screen illusion' (1981: 214). In summary, Mulvey argues that 'the conventions of the narrative film deny the first two and subordinate them to the third' (1981: 214). Pleasure is derived from the male gaze at the female characters but this is incorporated into the narrative of the film itself and we are sewn in. We forget that we are watching a created product, that we are in a cinema and enter the world of the central (male) protagonist. Mulvey is exceptionally critical of this male gaze and of conventional and dominant Hollywood narrative cinema. She contends that 'women, whose image has been continually stolen and used for this [voyeuristic] end, cannot view the decline of the traditional film form with anything more than sentimental regret' (1981: 215). In the name of a more progressive film practice, she intends to destroy the pleasure in dominant cinema.

Mulvey's work is located within a psychoanalytic perspective which has been very influential in film studies. However, her work tends to neglect some issues which have subsequently been raised in both sociology and cultural studies. For example, it can be suggested that her work is over-general in that it neglects the more concrete ways in which different groups of people may react to film in particular ways according to gender, class, ethnicity and so on. Mulvey's focus is on how the cinema constructs male spectator positions. This gives us little inkling as to how audiences actually behave and the very specific pleasures that they derive from cinema. Likewise, she has very monolithic notions of male and female, ignoring the differences that exist here, to which cultural studies has increasingly drawn attention. However, one key merit of Mulvey's work has been to provoke debate on these matters. Thus, for example, there has been concern with the concept of female spectatorship (Stacey, 1994: 22) and the extent to which there is a female gaze. As Stacey (1994) suggests, one of the clear fault lines in these arguments has been between those who have adopted a 'film studies' approach and those operating in the domain of cultural studies. Film studies tends to emphasise the nature of the text and how it constructs subject or spectator positions for the viewer. It theoretically examines these issues with little regard for how people actually watch films in a cinema. Cultural studies shares the concern with the analysis of the text, but argues that how texts are produced and consumed are important theoretical and empirical issues. This has led to investigations of real audiences to identify their actual modes of looking and practices derived from cinema attendance (Stacey, 1994).

Despite these problems Mulvey's use of psychoanalysis represents an important influence on wider work which has taken up the idea of the gaze in very different contexts; an important example of this can be found in contemporary work on tourism and leisure. We shall address this in section 9.5. However, the extended consideration of the technologies of **realism** (p. 61) in this section has introduced some critical discussion of the dominance of forms of looking, realism and the visual in **modernity** (p. 400). This critical edge is also apparent in the work on the gaze by **Michel Foucault** (p. 28), which has been a key influence on contemporary discussions of surveillance.

9.4 | Foucault: the gaze and surveillance

In a number of important studies **Michel Foucault** (p. 28) (1926–84) developed a critique of the way in which the 'gaze' is implicated in the operation of power. Perhaps his most famous book, *Discipline and Punish* (1977), opens with a striking contrast between two forms of punishment. In the first from 1757 Damiens the regicide is tortured and his body literally ripped to pieces in a public spectacle. In Foucault's second example from eighty years later, young prisoners are subject to a regulated regime in which all their activities are structured by processes of inspection (see section 7.3.1).

Foucault's essential point here is not that somehow punishment has become less barbaric (although this might be the case). Rather, it is to identify how punishment has become less spectacular as a public ritual, moving away from destroying the body (see also Chapter 7), to become a process of inspection, classification and surveillance where the focus is on getting through the body to affect the soul. It is no accident then that the modern prison was known as the penitentiary or the reformatory.

The key principles of the modern prison are condensed in the English philosopher Jeremy Bentham's plans for the panopticon (see section 7.3.1). The basic idea here is that individual cells in the prison would be arranged around a central inspection/surveillance tower. This would mean that all the prisoners could potentially be inspected at any time chosen by the guards in the tower. Moreover, because the tower would be fitted with blinds the prisoners would not know when they were being inspected. They could be under constant surveillance or not studied at all. This leads to the internalisation and the normalisation of the idea of being under the gaze of the powerful. It becomes a part of the experience of the prison and punishment. While locked in their cells the prisoners would have time to reflect on their crimes and commit themselves to the process of reform, as the representation of the prisoner in Figure 9.1 shows.

The key points for our purposes here are that this panoptic mechanism constructs the powerless prisoner as a subject of the gaze of the powerful. There are no dark corners where he or she can shelter. Punishment is no longer a spectacle, but a form of inspection and surveillance. It is not difficult to see how much everyday life in modern societies approximates to Foucault's account. Thus, it is increasingly the case that as we shop in contemporary Western societies we are under the gaze of cameras which monitor and record our actions. Cameras may be located in police cars checking traffic or on the perimeters of more housing developments. Interestingly, surveillance cameras once oversaw only the most exclusive housing – now they are to be found on a wide variety of housing types of different values. Often, we cannot be sure if we are being watched or recorded at any one moment. Of course, for example, surveillance of crowds at football matches may be in the interests of safety, but it also has implications for civil liberties. It has been suggested that contemporary cities with their extended surveillance systems have become more prison-like. Society has become carcereal (Cohen, 1985). Ideas of the power of the gaze have been applied in diverse ways; perhaps one of the more surprising is in the analysis of tourism.

Figure 9.1 ▪ A prisoner in his cell, kneeling at prayer before the central inspection tower. (Source: Foucault, 1977.)

9.5 | Tourism: gazing and postmodernism

The author who has done most to put tourism on the agenda in cultural studies in recent times is John Urry. In his book *The Tourist Gaze* (1990a) and in a number of articles (for example, 1988, 1990b, 1992), Urry identifies a number of key aspects of contemporary tourism. He suggests that travel and tourism are central aspects of contemporary or modern social life. He is also concerned with potential changes in the nature of tourism in the most recent period, and especially as to whether a form of post-tourism is developing. This would be a core aspect of a **postmodern** (p. 400) society or culture. Such developments might also reflect a change from an industrial to a post-industrial society. Hence, Urry makes distinctions between **modern** (p. 400) and postmodern cultures, industrial and postindustrial societies, and mass tourism and post-tourism.

9.5.1 | The tourist gaze

Urry identifies a number of features of tourism in general, or what can be called mass tourism of the contemporary period. Urry (1990a: 2–4) identifies the following nine aspects which define tourism:

1. Separation of work and tourism, as a leisure activity, as different spheres of life.
2. Involves movement and a stay in a different place or places.
3. Places stayed in are different from places where the tourist normally lives and works, but the tourist will return to home and work.
4. Places visited are different from work.
5. A 'substantial' part of the population engages in tourism, and it is a social activity to be contrasted with more individual and instrumental travel.
6. Places visited are chosen because of the anticipation of pleasure and different experiences from those involved in normal, everyday experience.
7. The gaze of the tourist is to features which are different from those normally encountered. This implies greater sensitivity to the visual than normally occurs in everyday life. These features are then reproduced in photographs, postcards and so on.
8. This tourist gaze is constructed through signs. 'When tourists see two people kissing in Paris what they capture in the gaze is "timeless romantic Paris". When a small village in England is seen, what they gaze upon is the "real olde England"' (Urry, 1990a: 3).
9. Tourism generates an 'array of tourist professionals ... who attempt to reproduce ever-new objects of the tourist gaze' (Urry, 1990a: 3).

Such tourism, or *mass* tourism, developed in the late nineteenth century in the British practice of the mass movement of the working class of an industrial city to a particular seaside resort to which the city was connected by railway. Thus visitors to Morecambe on the north-west coast of England came from Bradford in Yorkshire and the industrial working class of Lancashire travelled to Blackpool. This activity took a mass form in that large numbers of people did it at the same time, as all the factories in a particular town would close for the same holiday period (a practice that still has residues in many northern towns and cities), and the activity would be organised so that people tended to do the same sorts of things and to gaze on the same sights. The decline of the seaside resort from the 1970s onwards (see Urry, 1990a: 32–9) has led to a greater range of tourist and leisure experiences, as well as the development of an extensive and increasingly global tourist industry.

A key aspect of Urry's work is his argument that the gaze is central to the tourist experience. Thus he maintains that the practices of looking, such as the taking of photographs and the purchasing of postcards, are at the core of the tourist activity. However, given its centrality the nature of the gaze is not systematically developed in Urry's book on the topic. However, he does suggest parallels between his notion of the gaze and that of the French theorist **Michel Foucault** (p. 28) introduced in the previous section, in that the gaze is 'socially organised and systematised' (1990a: 3). Despite this, he also maintains that, contrary to the ideas of Foucault, 'contemporary societies are developing less on the basis of surveillance and the normalisation of individuals, and more on the basis of the democratisation of the tourist gaze and the spectacle-isation of place' (1990a: 156). Thus, he argues that there are in particular two different forms of the gaze: the 'romantic' and the 'collective'. The romantic tourist gaze involves looking at what has been called 'undisturbed natural beauty' (Urry, 1990a: 45), the collective gaze involves 'the presence of large numbers of people', and it is the interaction between such large numbers that creates the atmosphere of the tourist place.

Urry (1992) subsequently revised some of these ideas on the gaze. In particular he reiterated his view that in emphasising the gaze he did not want to denigrate or play down other aspects of the tourist experience (smell, temperature and so on); rather, he argues that it is the visual that is dominant or *organises* this range of experience. More mundane activities like shopping or walking along a street become different because of the visual environment in which they are carried out. However, Urry admits that he did not discuss the precise nature of the gaze in enough detail in his book on the topic. He develops this in more detail, first by showing the way in which the concept of the gaze that he employs is derived from and continuous with the work of Foucault, and second by generating some ideal types of different forms of the tourist gaze which obtain in different contexts. This enables Urry to produce the fivefold categorisation of the gaze reproduced in Table 9.3.

In developing these categories, Urry draws upon the work of Sharratt (1989) and incorporates his discussion of different types of looking into his version of the gaze. However, as will be shown below, it is possible to use Sharratt's useful categorisations in other ways. The key aspect of Urry's work for the present discussion is this emphasis on the centrality of the gaze. However, in accord with the theme of historical change in visual culture in this chapter, it is also important to consider Urry's argument in this realm.

Table 9.3 ■ Forms of the tourist gaze

Romantic	Solitary
	Sustained immersion
	Gaze involving vision, awe, aura
Collective	Communal activity
	Series of brief encounters
	Gazing at the familiar
Spectatorial	Communal activity
	Series of brief encounters
	Glancing and collecting different signs
Environmental	Collective organisation
	Sustained and didactic
	Scanning to survey and inspect
Anthropological	Solitary
	Sustained immersion
	Scanning and active interpretation

Source: Urry (1992: 22)

9.5.2 | Postmodernism and post-tourism

Urry suggests that there is developing or has developed a form of post-tourism, which is engaged in by the post-tourist. The post-tourist 'does not have to leave his or her house in order to see many of the objects of the tourist gaze. Especially with TV and video everything can now be seen, noted, compared and contextualized' (1988: 37). Furthermore, 'the post-tourist is profoundly aware of change and delights in the multitude of choice' (1988: 38). In contrast to the situation where a whole town would go away to the same seaside town at the same time of the year, there is now great and increasing choice of tourist destinations and experiences. Finally, the post-tourist is involved in a game – the game of tourism. As Urry explains:

> the post-tourist is the person who knows that he or she is a tourist, that it is a game, or rather a whole series of games, with multiple texts and no single, authentic tourist experience. The post-tourist knows that he or she will have to queue time and time again, that there will be 'hassles' over foreign exchange, that the glossy brochure is a piece of pop culture, that the 'authentic' local entertainment is as socially contrived as is the 'ethnic' bar, and that the quaint 'fishing village' preserved in aspic could not survive without the income from tourism. (1988: 38)

Urry argues that due to social change towards **postmodernism** (p. 400), a post-tourism has developed. This social change is characterised by three general processes: first, a change in what we consume; second, change in the nature of our identities; and third, the development and increased influence of middle-class social groups. Concerning change in consumption, Urry follows the approach of the French sociologist and philosopher Jean Baudrillard, in arguing that we are living in an age where we consume signs and images rather than real things. These signs and images are copies of an original, but increasingly the idea of what the original actually was is lost. Everything is a copy of something that does not (or did not) exist, or a simulacrum. Urry gives a clear example of this from New Zealand:

> A popular nineteenth-century tourist attraction was a set of pink and white terraces rising up above Lake Rotomahana. These were destroyed by volcanic eruptions in 1886 although photographs of them have remained popular ever since. They are a well-known attraction even if they have not existed for a century. Now, however, there is a plan to recreate the physical attraction by running geothermal water over artificially built terraces in an entirely different location, but one close to existing tourist facilities. This set of what might be called themed terraces will look more authentic than the original which is only known about because of the hundred-year old photographic images.   (Urry, 1990a: 146–7)

Second, in accord with other writers on postmodernism, Urry maintains that our sense of self, or **identity** (p. 224), is shifting in contemporary society. We are much less rooted in time and space than were people in previous times. We are now familiar with many different representations of different cultures and places, due to their availability through the visual media, and the fact that people now travel more, and experience different things. So Urry suggests that we lose our sense of selfhood and became involved in play with different images and different experiences. Paradoxically, this can lead among some groups for the desire for the 'authentic' experience, or the natural, as in the popularity of hill walking among certain social groups.

Third, Urry links these postmodern developments to the influence of the service class (see also Lash and Urry, 1987). These are groups that 'neither own nor individually manage capital, and which cannot because of distinctions of taste be simply regarded as part of the working class' (1987: 40). The four features of the service class are set out in the extract from Urry (1988: 40–1) in Box 9.1.

Box *9.1*
Features of the service class

[T]hat set of places in the social division of labour (1) which do not principally involve the ownership of capital; (2) which are located within a set of interlocking social institutions that 'service' capital; (3) in which superior work and market situations are to be found particularly because of the existence of well-defined careers; and (4) in which entry is generally regulated by the differential possession of credentials which potentially serve to demarcate such a service class from the more general white-collar workers.

Urry (1988: 40–1)

While it may be suggested that the kind of postmodern tourist practices that Urry labels post-tourist may be confined to this group initially, his point is that because of the increased salience and influence of this group such practices are likely to become more widespread. In fact, one implication of Urry's more recent work with Scott Lash (Lash and Urry, 1994), where they play down the importance of class distinctions in an increasingly reflexive contemporary society, is to suggest that some of these practices have indeed moved out from the service class to other class fractions.

9.6 | The glimpse, the gaze, the scan and the glance

Other work has developed the idea of the gaze in rather different directions to those pursued by Urry. For example, in work on the differences between television and the cinema, John Ellis (1982) draws a clear distinction between the *gaze* which, following authors like MacCabe and Mulvey, he associates with forms of dominant cinema, and the *glance* which characterises the way that television is viewed. Television is a domestic medium (Morley, 1986) and due to its place in household routines is relatively rarely looked at in the way that films are in the cinema. When watching television we are often doing other things (ironing, playing with children, doing homework, reading the newspaper) and do not give the screen our full attention. It might be argued, therefore, that in contemporary culture we may be glancing as much as gazing. Such a point of view is elaborated by Bernard Sharratt (1989) who distinguishes between four modes of looking which exist in contemporary culture: the glimpse, the gaze, the scan and the glance.

The glimpse, according to Sharratt, is 'the elusively incomplete, though not necessarily fleeting, character of the visibility of the divine, of power, even of the sexual' (1989: 39). The glimpse offers us a partial view, perhaps of a representation that is potentially powerful, or something we desire. It is perhaps a characteristic of **power** (p. 94), that something is kept hidden, and therefore made mysterious and threatening.

The gaze is a more prolonged form of looking. According to Sharratt, it consists of three 'regimes'. The first, representation, is a regime similar to that identified by MacCabe in his examination of the classic realist text. The idea is that something can be represented in its key or representative forms which convey a sense of reality that is open to all. Reproduction implies that something can be completely reproduced, that a full picture can be given. However, there is a clear sense in which this form implies the artificial, as we are often being given copies of something, which suggests some degree of artifice in the reproduction. The third regime of the gaze is the spectatorial, which describes the way in which a spectator may be looking, or gazing, on an actual, rather than a reproduced, landscape.

Sharratt identifies senses of the scan, which are concerned with the operation of power in modern societies, in ways derived from the work of Foucault. These can be summarised in terms of 'surveillance', 'supervision', 'oversight' and 'inspection'. Thus in contemporary societies we are often under surveillance, through cameras in shops for example, which may or may not be recording our actions. Such surveillance may be used to supervise and order our behaviour, as when cameras are used in the process of crowd control. Furthermore, the scan involves notions of oversight and inspection, in the sense of being looked over and our behaviour or appearance inspected.

The glance implies a fleeting or rapid form of looking, where there is a 'rapidation of registration' and a postponement of the glimpse and the gaze: 'a perpetual procrastination (rather than look long at a landscape we take photos for a future scrutiny that never arises)' (Sharratt, 1989: 40).

Through these categories, we can both suggest forms of ways of looking which change historically and identify different ideal types of looking which may be mobilised in the actual analysis of forms of visual culture. Thus, there may be a shift from a dominance of the glimpse in premodern society, where power operated through mystery and keeping aspects of itself hidden. Tantalising glimpses would be given to awe or intrigue the population. Modern power relations are maintained by the forms of surveillance and inspection of the population described in the scan, and visual culture is also characterised by the development of forms of the gaze as in photography and the cinema described above. The glance implies a speed-up of life as images flash before us more rapidly. This is one aspect of what has been termed late or **postmodernity** (p. 400), where we are said to inhabit a media-saturated society. However, in addition to using Sharratt's categories in this way in terms of the historical theme of this chapter, they can also be used in terms of the second in the analysis of forms of visual culture. In particular, it is important to consider forms of looking that do not conform to the gaze as set out by such as Mulvey and Urry, as these may be characteristic of the way in which a number of forms of visual culture are actually appropriated. Thus, some of the analyses of advertising examined in Chapter 2 would seem to imply through their close attention to the advertisements themselves that they are appropriated through a concentrated gaze, when in fact they are more likely to be glanced at. This also raises the important issue of how visual representations are integrated into the relations of everyday interaction, to which issue we now turn.

9.7 | Visual interaction in public places

The figure of the *flâneur*, we have noted, took pleasure in witnessing the sights afforded by the public places and spaces of the modern city. What facilitates the activity of the *flâneur* is the anonymity of life in the public realm, a feature noted by **Simmel** (p. 368) and many other commentators. Simmel saw this anonymity and the accompanying reserve and blasé attitude as double edged: on the one hand it enlarges the scope of individual freedom beyond what was possible in small-scale rural society, but on the other it created conditions that seem to impoverish collective human existence.

This critical line is epitomised by books with titles like *The Fall of Public Man* (Sennett, 1977) and *The Lonely Crowd* (Reisman *et al.*, 1953). A social psychologist writing in this tradition, Stanley Milgram (1970), suggests that the city's large, dense and heterogenous population makes for 'stimulus overload' in the individual's experience. The 'urbanite' adapts to overload by choosing and prioritising. Since urbanites have many more contacts with people than rural-dwellers, they tend to keep these contacts brief and superficial (one filmic example is the splendid scene where Crocodile Dundee, fresh from the Australian Outback, endeavours to greet everyone he meets on a New York street). Urbanites minimise involvements with unacquainted persons by a range of measures including, for example, giving low priority to the requests or distress of others, assuming an unfriendly countenance when travelling on public transport, or by selecting who can approach them by telephone by going ex-directory or keeping the answerphone almost permanently turned on. These methods of dealing with overload can result in an attenuation or withdrawal of the common courtesies, like refusing to give up one's seat to an elderly person or failing to apologise to the person one has just collided with. At worst there is the phenomenon of 'bystander apathy': persons have been kidnapped, severely assaulted and even murdered in busy public places because no one would come to the victim's aid. Non-involvement becomes the shield that urbanites use to protect themselves from overload. But the preservation of privacy is something that also requires positive acts from others; they must act towards the self in the same way that self acts towards them for orderly life in public to be sustained. The general orderliness of public places is accomplished through the methods and strategies that people employ when walking down the street, asking directions, buying goods in a shop and so forth. In the accomplishment of this orderliness, ordinary practices of looking and making inferences on the basis of what is seen are central. The rest of this section considers how social organisation and cultural understandings figure in these ordinary looking and inference-making practices.

9.7.1 | Categoric knowing: appearential and spatial orders

Public places can be defined as those sites in a society that are freely accessible to persons (streets, stations and so on) and which can be contrasted with *private places* (such as homes and offices) where access is restricted and which may only be granted by invitation (Goffman, 1963a: 9; Lofland, 1973: 19). Obviously the distinction is not absolute; there are locations, like GPs' waiting rooms or restaurants, that have a hybrid status, semi-public places, and other places like airports which carefully demarcate public places from those that are restricted to various categories of person (people dropping off or collecting friends and relatives gather 'groundside', while passengers, airline personnel and security staff have access to 'airside'). In public places many of the people we encounter will be known to us only in *categoric* terms. We identify them as 'female', 'white', 'elderly', 'walking with a limp', categories that we can glean from visual cues, unlike those we know *personally*, that is those about whose biography we know something – great-aunt Maisie who's been finding it difficult to get around since her fall last year. Again, categoric and personal knowing are merely ends of a continuum.

The **modern** (p. 400) city differs from its pre-industrial counterpart in significant ways. According to Lyn Lofland (1973), public life in cities is made possible through the 'ordering' of urban populations by their appearance and by their spatial location. She suggests that within a city strangers 'know a great deal about one another simply by looking' (Lofland, 1973: 22, emphasis removed). Her thesis is that the pre-industrial city was dominated by appearential ordering: the distinctive costume and insignia worn by people gave visual evidence of social rank and occupation. The pre-industrial city was nowhere near as large as its modern equivalent and thus use of public space was mixed as prisons were built nearby palaces and rich and poor lived in the same parts of town. Status, legitimated by law and custom, was expressly symbolised in clothing which signifies the person's status as craftsperson, entertainer, priest, servant or trader. Public orderliness depends upon the personal appearance of the strangers reliably indexing their standing in society.

In contrast the modern city is dominated by spatial ordering. Considerably larger in area and population than its pre-industrial counterpart, it encompasses a wide range of specialised activities and an extensive division of labour. Activities that commonly occurred in public places, for example the education of children, the elimination of human wastes and the punishment of offenders, are now confined within walled spaces. Persons are sifted and sorted into discrete spaces as urban land use becomes specialised. Residential segregation emerges along class and ethnic lines. Distinct districts develop: working-class estates, middle-class suburbs, Chinatowns, ghettos and enclaves, Italian and gay 'villages', redeveloped docklands. There is also industrial and commercial segregation: industrial estates, malls and out-of-town shopping and entertainment complexes. And there is age segregation, especially at either end of the life cycle: colleges, schools and nurseries keep young people off the streets and away from workplaces for sizeable parts of the day while older people are to be found in homes, sheltered housing and retirement communities.

Moreover, as dress codes become more flexible, costume ceases to be a stable indicator of social status. People link their clothing choices to their activities rather than their status, often dressing up or down or using clothes to play with social conventions (see also Chapter 7). Where a person stands in the modern city matters more than what he or she wears:

> A homosexual male is a man in a homosexual bar and not necessarily a man in a pink ruffled shirt. A prostitute is a woman standing alone in the 'Tenderloin' and not necessarily a woman in a revealing costume. Elites are persons who can be found in the stores and restaurants which cater to their incredible buying power and not necessarily persons who wear silk. The poor are persons who live in a certain section of town and not necessarily the people who wear the most tattered clothes. ... A university professor is someone who stands facing the students in a university classroom. And the fact that he may look like his students, like a Wall Street lawyer, or like a skid row bum should not be allowed to obscure this simple truth.   (Lofland, 1973: 82–3)

In the modern city, 'who' you are is, for initial purposes at least, very much bound up with 'where' you are. The supplanting of the primacy of appearential ordering by spatial ordering in the modern city is no less a visual phenomenon, discernible to persons simply by looking. Lofland's appearential to spatial thesis articulates a very broad historical trend. She recognises that appearential considerations continue to be important in the modern city and that in given instances people will enhance the reliability of inferences about strangers by bringing to bear their categorical knowledge of places *in combination with* categorical knowledge of appearances. In order to further consider the complexities of such inference making on the basis of observable features of everyday life we need to consider some aspects of the work of Erving Goffman (1922–82), perhaps the pre-eminent scholar of face-to-face interaction, of what transpires when people are in one another's physical presence.

9.7.2 | Unfocused interaction, civil inattention and normal appearances

'Co-present' persons, simply by virtue of their capacity mutually to monitor each other's actions, generate an analytically distinguishable domain that Goffman (1983) calls 'the interaction order'. In other words, whenever we are in the actual presence of others our actions are at least in part shaped by rules and understandings deriving from the demands of interaction. Broadly speaking, these interactional demands or requirements boil down to two: the informational and the ritual (see Figure 9.2). When we interact we must acquire some information about the mood, intentions, trustworthiness, knowledgeability and so forth of others in order to achieve our practical purposes (answering a question, getting an appointment with the dentist, obtaining directions to the cinema that we're having trouble in finding). But we must attend to ritual concerns, that is we need to address the expression and control of our own feelings and those of others, showing respect towards ourself and consideration toward the other (for taking up their time with our queries, for example). Informational and ritual demands are interleaved in interesting ways in actual interaction.

Take the simple act of walking down a moderately busy street. This is an example of what Goffman calls *unfocused interaction* where people simply commingle, information about them becoming observable at a glance in virtue of 'sheer and mere copresence'. Although we may not talk to anyone, we are, none the less, interacting when we walk

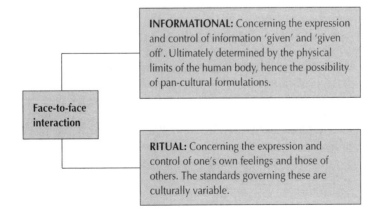

Face-to-face interaction

INFORMATIONAL: Concerning the expression and control of information 'given' and 'given off'. Ultimately determined by the physical limits of the human body, hence the possibility of pan-cultural formulations.

RITUAL: Concerning the expression and control of one's own feelings and those of others. The standards governing these are culturally variable.

Figure 9.2  Basic dimensions of face-to-face interaction.

down the street. We take care so as not to get in their way; we anticipate a way round persons with large shopping bags. We are oriented to the actions of those others. Without giving it much conscious thought we glance at the other, scan their appearance, then quickly look away, if need be adjusting our course. The other does the same. Each person thus succeeds in conveying to the other that neither is a threat. These brief actions – likened by Goffman to passing cars dipping their lights – are instances of the norm of 'civil inattention' (Goffman, 1963a: 83–8) at work. Note that civil inattention is not ignoring someone, giving them non-person treatment, nor is it incivil attention, as occurs when one person pointedly stares at another, e.g. the Al Pacino character in the shoe shop scene in *Sea of Love* (dir. Harold Becker, 1989). Civil inattention occurs everyday on countless occasions in cities throughout the world. It involves an informational element as we acquire some categoric knowledge of the other and it involves a ritual element because the act of turning away our glance as soon as it is given is an act of courtesy, a way of not further invading the privacy of the other. As Goffman says, civil inattention 'is perhaps the slightest of interpersonal rituals, yet one that constantly regulates the social intercourse of persons in our society' (1963a: 84). It is one essential prerequisite for trouble-free interaction in public, the cardinal norm through which civility is realised.

Yet interaction in public is not always free of troubles. Sometimes civil inattention can seem more honoured in the breach. As notorious cases like that of Rodney King and the Los Angeles police (Chapter 8) remind us, public places can be risky sites for the citizenry. But so too do more routine forms of public harassment, 'the abuses, harryings, and annoyances characteristic of public places and uniquely facilitated by communication in public' (Gardner, 1995: 4). Public harassment includes shouted remarks, gratuitous insults and innuendoes, staring, stalking and the like, which are most commonly (but not exclusively) targeted at women in public. The initiation of this intrusion is based on the observable characteristics of the person – their gender, ethnicity, sexual orientation, physical handicap and so forth.

The relationships or ties between co-present persons is a further observable feature of public places. Goffman distinguishes the 'anonymous relations' occurring between passers-by who know each other only in categoric terms from 'anchored relations', where an element of personal knowing exists. Goffman designates as a *tie-sign* that evidence of the relationship between co-present persons that can be discerned through their 'body placement, posture, gesture, and vocal expression' (1971: 195). Examples of tie-signs include hand-holding and kissing, sharing the same cup or the same bottle of sun-tan lotion, standing close to another or distinctly endeavouring to keep one's distance, wiping another's nose or feeding them with a spoon, addressing a person as 'sir' or 'madam' or replying to them with a term of endearment. Tie-signs such as these, when placed in the context of what we know and have witnessed, enable us to infer the likely anchored or personal relationship between persons: as intimates, servitor and client, parent and child, salesperson and customer, boss and employee, long-married spouses and so forth. While the public realm is sometimes characterised as a world of strangers, the unacquainted others we encounter are not wholly strange to us. We can readily interpret the tie-signs we witness to form an appraisal of the likely relationship between persons. To be sure, our appraisals are fallible (we all know the adage that appearances can be deceptive), but they are, none the less, adequate for many of our practical purposes. Moreover, these appraisals of relationship depend upon fitting the tie-sign to other features of the context such as time and place, appearance, activity, prior knowledge and so forth. Finally, while many tie-signs are accessible to us by merely looking, others depend upon the conversational fragments we hear ('Honey, where are my sunglasses?'). The observability of a relationship includes what is more broadly perceivable about it, not just what can be literally seen.

Especially in public places, then, human beings are what Harvey Sacks once called 'inference-making machines' (Sacks, 1992). As members of a society we acquire a body of common-sense cultural knowledge and practical skills which enable us to accomplish the ordinary tasks that face us in our everyday life. In going about our everyday business we will often adopt a stance of easy control which is only made possible because nothing out of the ordinary is happening. We check our immediate surrounds, our *Umwelt* (Goffman, 1971: 252–5), the sphere around us in which sources of alarm, of danger to ourselves reside, to confirm that all is well. The actual size of the individual's *Umwelt* will vary: on a crowded street this bubble of relevance will only span a metre or two; on an empty street at night we can become concerned at the approach of a stranger hundreds of metres away. In public places especially we will scan our immediate surrounds for signs of threat to our person, our property, our privacy and personal wellbeing. We have a well-developed sense of 'normal appearances', of the world around the individual looking just as we expect it should, portending no threatening or alarming features (Goffman, 1971: 239). As cultural beings interacting in public places we possess not only acquired knowledge but also practical, embodied skills, in short 'experience' in coping with the threats and opportunities that situations can present. One important dimension of experience concerns the looks of normal appearances.

Certain occupations which involve work on the city streets, such as the police, value such experience and describe it in craft-like terms. The policeman's practical problem in conducting work on the streets is to infer criminality from the appearances of persons (Sacks, 1972). The experience required to infer criminality correctly is acquired 'on the beat' by novices from more mature police officers. Part of this experience involves adopting a sceptical attitude to normal appearances, not treating appearances at their face value but rather scrutinising them for evidence of criminal activities that may be accomplished under their guise. An 'incongruity procedure' is employed by the officer in order to warrant further investigation. When something occurs that is at variance with normal appearances the officer has grounds to pursue inquiries. Officers are taught to see persons in behavioural terms, i.e. in terms of the activities in which they are engaged: 'the lovely young lady alighting from a cab is now observable as a call-girl arriving for a session' (Sacks, 1972: 285). The normality of normal appearances is practically defined as 'normal for the place at a time'; trucks that do not normally unload at midnight in this district become objects of suspicion to the officer. There is a 'normal ecology of territories'; persons who 'don't belong' in this place – e.g. the apparently poor in a wealthy neighbourhood – may be asked to justify their presence. People who observably treat the police's presence as anything other than normal – giving an officer a 'double look', for instance – may come under scrutiny. The routine uses of places and objects are seen in terms of favoured misuses: dustbins can contain dead babies, playgrounds attract child molesters, shops are regarded as venues for shoplifting. The police officer's street experience demands a studied attention to normal appearances and what they may conceal. The officer's safety may depend upon it: 'Where he is now is radically a matter of where he will have turned out to be. The corner he approaches may be the corner at which he will have been killed' (Sacks, 1972: 293). Police officers working the streets no doubt constitute a boundary case. Nevertheless, attention to normal appearances is the means whereby all users of public places endeavour to minimise their risks and maximise their wellbeing.

Of course it is possible to exaggerate the degree of risk, threat and incivility in urban public places and thereby to overlook the rich street life of wide boulevards, pavement cafés, parades, entertainments, sports and games and the like that it is possible to enjoy in many cities. Pleasure and conviviality are no less real features of the apprehension of city life. But both pleasure and risk in public places are underwritten by a taken-for-granted normative ordering, ensembles of cultural understandings that importantly depend upon the visual mediation of our socialised competence.

9.8 | Interpreting the built environment

In section 9.2.2 we identified the second strand in **Walter Benjamin**'s (p. 373) contribution to the study of visual culture as the examination of the city, and in particular the discussion of the social and cultural life of Paris in the nineteenth century. Paris has often been seen as the 'capital of the nineteenth century' in the sense that it represented and condensed the key developments of modernity. It was here that the shopping arcades and the *flâneur* originated. The key role of cities like Paris in the development of modern forms of life and visual culture is graphically captured in the work of Marshall Berman (1983).

9.8.1 | Marshall Berman: modernity, modernisation and modernism

Many of the key themes in Berman's work are summed up in the opening paragraph of his book which is reproduced in Box 9.2.

Berman used three key terms in his work (some of which we have also seen in the work of Urry considered above): **modernity** (p. 400), which is a form of social experience; modernisation, which is a social process; and modernism, which is a set of visions and values. Berman is essentially concerned with the relationship between modernisation and modernism, with the link between these two being the experience involved in modernity (Anderson, 1984). Berman sees three phases in modernity: first, from the start of the sixteenth century to the end of the eighteenth, when

---

Box **9.2**
The experience of modernity

There is a mode of vital experience – experience of space and time, of the self and others, of life's possibilities and perils – that is shared by men and women all over the world today. I will call this body of experience 'modernity'. To be modern is to find ourselves in an environment that promises us adventure, power, joy, growth, transformation of ourselves and the world – and, at the same time, that threatens to destroy everything we have, everything we know, everything we are. Modern environments and experiences cut across all boundaries of geography and ethnicity, of class and nationality, of religion and ideology: in this sense, modernity can be said to unite all mankind. But it is a paradoxical unity, a unity of disunity: it pours us all into a maelstrom of perpetual disintegration and renewal, of struggle and contradiction, of ambiguity and anguish. To be modern is to be part of a universe in which, as Marx said, 'all that is solid melts into air'.

Berman (1983: 15)

---

people are just beginning to experience modern life; they hardly know what has hit them. They grope, desperately but half blindly, for an adequate vocabulary; they have little or no sense of a modern public or community within which their trials and hopes can be shared.   (Berman, 1983: 16–17)

Modern life is new and there is the sense of being bowled over by these new developments. The second phase of modernity begins with the revolutionary wave of the 1780s and 1790s and lasts to the beginning of the twentieth century. Berman argues that after the French Revolution a modern public develops. People realise that they live in the modern age, but can remember what came before. Thus, the dualism of modernity, which is so important for Berman arises: the combination of the sense of adventure that is involved in modernity with the sense of loss and the feeling of insecurity. It is here that the great works of modernist literature and art arise as well as those forms of politics and writing that attempt to confront these dilemmas (notably Marxism).

Many of these changes are contained in Baudelaire's writings from Paris, which address the new forms of modern life in the arcades and the political insurrections of 1848, and in the subsequent redevelopment of Paris as boulevards were constructed in accord with the plans of Baron Haussmann. The boulevards destroyed old working-class neighbourhoods from where the earlier political protest had arisen, and were constructed to allow the clear and fast movement of troops to put down any future protest. These new roads are also the place of traffic and the dangerous bustle of modernity. 'Thus the life of the boulevards was also more risky and frightening for the multitudes of men and women who moved on foot' (Berman, 1983: 159).

The twentieth century is the third period of modernity. Here modernisation has become so generalised that it has taken in 'virtually the whole world'. Despite the fact that this is often cited as the period of the greatest achievement of modernism in the arts, which Berman recognises, he also feels that this is the period where modernism loses its way, as the sense of the duality of modernity is overcome. One course was to celebrate modernity as in the Italian futurists and those who would influence the look of cities and architecture for the rest of the twentieth century like Le Corbusier, who celebrates the power of the motor car and the rational redevelopment of the city (Berman, 1983: 166–7) in the direction that will point the way forward to the city of the tower block and the motorway. The other course was to denigrate modernity and seek a return to traditional forms of art and architecture.

Defining concept **9.1**

Modernity, modernism, postmodernity, postmodernism

These terms are often used in relatively loose and ill-defined ways, leading to much confusion and contestation. Any codification will itself be controversial. Modernity is best thought of as a form of society or experience. For Berman (1983) the key feature is its double-edged nature: change that disrupts the traditional is stimulating but frightening in that old certainties are lost. The sociologist Giddens (1990) argues that modern societies differ from traditional ones in pace and scope of social change, as well as in institutions, like the nation-state. Currently, the idea of modernity is resurgent in social science and the arts as attention has moved away from capitalism and patriarchy as structural concepts. Modernism is most frequently used to characterise a range of activities in the arts and culture (in the more narrow sense) which developed between 1890 and 1930. A key feature was the contestation of **realism** (p. 61) in **representation** (p. 61) and a related focus on form. The role of the artist was emphasised, as was the political nature of art.

Postmodernism is also often used in rather loose ways to refer to: a society or experience, particular forms of artistic activity, and a philosophical or theoretical approach. These should be separated analytically. Prefacing modern(ity, ism) with post- implies in some ways that the modern has been superseded, or that new activities are built upon the modern bases. Postmodernity might then refer to a society that still contains some modern aspects (it is not traditional) but which has added or developed a greater role for the mass media of communication (for example, in Baudrillard) or consumption (as in Featherstone, for instance). However, some authors reject this idea, suggesting that the best description is late modernity (Giddens, for example). As a form of artistic activity, postmodernism has been applied to diverse producers in different fields. Rap music or Talking Heads are examples from music. *Twin Peaks* was seen as a postmodernist television show. It can be suggested that such forms share some of the emphases of modernism, but inflect them in different directions. They are playful, refer to

→

other previous texts, break boundaries between high and popular culture and so on. A problem here is the attempt to apply an overarching term to diverse forms and types. This is particularly paradoxical when the nature of postmodernism as idea or philosophy is considered. A key suggestion here (associated with Lyotard) is that one of the characteristics of postmodernism is the impossibility of 'grand' or 'meta' narratives. Knowledge is both more local, contingent and relative. Postmodernist ideas in theory and philosophy often blur with those associated with **poststructuralism** (p. 24). Meaning is contested, as is the relation between words and things.

Debates over postmodernism were the storm centre of academic life in the social sciences and humanities in the 1980s. Some on the political left saw them as a new irrationalism which fitted well with the rightward drift of Western society and culture. Others emphasised the way in which these ideas allowed those previously marginalised (women, black people, homosexuals and so on) a place from which to speak and contest the domination of even leftist ideas and practices. This connects to contemporary notions of **identity** (p. 224) politics.

Further reading

Connor, S. (1989) *Postmodernist Culture*, Oxford: Blackwell.
Docherty, T. (ed.) (1993) *Postmodernism: A Reader*, Hemel Hempstead: Harvester Wheatsheaf.
Giddens, A. (1990) *The Consequences of Modernity*, Cambridge: Polity.

The work of critics like Benjamin and Berman suggests that it is possible to read cities as texts: to 'read' them as meaningful signs that are visually available to the citizenry. At least four aspects of cities as built environments can be interpreted in this fashion: buildings and architecture, features of the city, the city itself and the city (or landscape) as condensation of power. We illustrate these different aspects in the following four subsections (see also Chapters 4 and 6).

9.8.2 | Reading architecture

The sociologist Keith MacDonald (1989) has interpreted the features of particular buildings in London as representing the status claims and desires of professional groups. One way in which groups sought to enhance their prestige was in architectural display. The features examined are summarised by MacDonald (1989: 58) as follows:

A. SITE (1) Market Value
(2) Appropriateness
(3) Respectability and Fashion

B. BUILDING (1) Expenditure *per se*
– size
– appearance (materials, ornamentation, etc.)

(2) Expenditure – qualitative
     – wasted space
     – implications of leisure, scholarship, etc.
(3) Celebrity rating – evaluations of the buildings and their
     architects based on space devoted to them in a number of
     standard books on architecture

MacDonald examined three professions: accountancy, solicitors (as represented by the
Law Society) and physicians and surgeons (as represented by the Royal College of
Physicians and the Royal College of Surgeons). Accountants are the 'critical case' in that
they were not as successful in their drive for control over the regulation of their
profession as solicitors or the older established medical professions had been. He used
three methods to examine these cases: '(i) observation and photography; (ii) study of
works on architecture; (iii) examination of journals and documents which referred to
the construction and acquisition of the buildings' (1989: 59).

MacDonald argues that buildings such as the Chartered Accountants Hall (see
Figure 9.3) are clear attempts at symbolisation of the status of a profession. This is
demonstrated by the *site* of the buildings which were 'appropriate to their calling and

Figure 9.3 ■ The Chartered Accountants'
Hall. (Source: MacDonald, 1989: 62.)

are sought after and expensive' (1989: 75); the nature of the *buildings* themselves, which were imposing and clearly expensive; the *celebrity* of the buildings as indicated by their evaluation by architectural experts; and the *finance* raised to purchase them.

The purchase and use of such buildings is a form of conspicuous consumption which forms part of the strategic attempts of these professions to enhance their power. As MacDonald (1989: 77) concludes:

> Thus the professional bodies reviewed here, have (with the exception of the ACCA) erected or purchased imposing buildings (which were characteristically different from the office blocks of any period), in carefully chosen locations and furnished with paintings, panelling and *objets d'art et de vertu*, and devoted in part to 'gentlemanly' activities.

Jameson (1991) offers a rather different type of interpretation of a particular building in Box 9.3.

Box **9.3**
Jameson's analysis of the Bonaventure Hotel

Now before concluding, I want to sketch an analysis of a full-blown postmodern building – a work which is in many ways uncharacteristic of that postmodern architecture whose principal proponents are Robert Venturi, Charles Moore, Michael Graves, and, more recently, Frank Gehry, but which to my mind offers some very striking lessons about the originality of postmodernist space. Let me amplify the figure which has run through the preceding remarks and make it even more explicit: I am proposing the notion that we are here in the presence of something like a mutation in built space itself. My implication is that we ourselves, the human subjects who happen into this new space, have not kept pace with that evolution; there has been a mutation in the object unaccompanied as yet by any equivalent mutation in the subject. We do not yet possess the perceptual equipment to match this new hyperspace, as I will call it, in part because our perceptual habits were formed in that older kind of space I have called the space of high modernism. The newer architecture therefore – like many of the other cultural products I have evoked in the preceding remarks – stands as something like an imperative to grow new organs, to expand our sensorium and our body to some new, yet unimaginable, perhaps ultimately impossible, dimensions.

The building whose features I will very rapidly enumerate is the Westin Bonaventure Hotel, built in the new Los Angeles downtown by the architect and developer John Portman, whose other works include the various Hyatt Regencies, the Peachtree Center in Atlanta, and the Renaissance Center in Detroit. I have

➙

mentioned the populist aspect of the rhetorical defense of postmodernism against the elite (and Utopian) austerities of the great architectural modernisms: it is generally affirmed, in other words, that these newer buildings are popular works, on the one hand, and that they respect the vernacular of the American city fabric, on the other; that is to say, they no longer attempt, as did the masterworks and monuments of high modernism, to insert a different, a distinct, an elevated, a new Utopian language into the tawdry and commercial sign system of the surrounding city, but rather they seek to speak that very language, using its lexicon and syntax as that has been emblematically 'learned from Las Vegas'.

On the first of these counts Portman's Bonaventure fully confirms the claim: it is a popular building, visited with enthusiasm by locals and tourists alike (although Portman's other buildings are even more successful in this respect). The populist insertion into the city fabric is, however, another matter, and it is with this that we will begin. There are three entrances to the Bonaventure, one from Figueroa and the other two by way of elevated gardens on the other side of the hotel, which is built into the remaining slope of the former Bunker Hill. None of these is anything like the old hotel marquee, or the monumental porte cochere with which the sumptuous buildings of yesteryear were wont to stage your passage from city street to the interior. The entryways of the Bonaventure are, as it were, lateral and rather backdoor affairs: the gardens in the back admit you to the sixth floor of the towers, and even there you must walk down one flight to find the elevator by which you gain access to the lobby. Meanwhile, what one is still tempted to think of as the front entry, on Figueroa, admits you, baggage and all, onto the second-story shopping balcony, from which you must take an escalator down to the main registration desk. What I first want to suggest about these curiously unmarked ways in is that they seem to have been imposed by some new category of closure governing the inner space of the hotel itself (and this over and above the material constraints under which Portman had to work). I believe that, with a certain number of other characteristic postmodern buildings, such as the Beaubourg in Paris or the Eaton Centre in Toronto, the Bonaventure aspires to being a total space, a complete world, a kind of miniature city; to this new total space, meanwhile, corresponds a new collective practice, a new mode in which individuals move and congregate, something like the practice of a new and historically original kind of hypercrowd. In this sense, then, ideally the minicity of Portman's Bonaventure ought not to have entrances at all, since the entryway is always the seam that links the building to the rest of the city that surrounds it: for it does not wish to be a part of the city but rather its equivalent and replacement or substitute. That is obviously not possible, whence the downplaying of the entrance to its bare minimum. But this disjunction from the surrounding city is different from that of the monuments of the International Style, in which the act of disjunction was violent, visible, and had a very real symbolic significance – as in

→

Le Corbusier's great *pilotis*, whose gesture radically separates the new Utopian space of the modern from the degraded and fallen city fabric which it thereby explicitly repudiates (although the gamble of the modern was that this new Utopian space, in the virulence of its novum, would fan out and eventually transform its surroundings by the very power of its new spatial language). The Bonaventure, however, is content to 'let the fallen city fabric continue to be in its being' (to parody Heidegger); no further effects, no larger protopolitical Utopian transformation, is either expected or desired.

This diagnosis is confirmed by the great reflective glass skin of the Bonaventure, whose function I will now interpret rather differently than I did a moment ago when I saw the phenomenon of reflection generally as developing a thematics of reproductive technology (the two readings are, however, not incompatible). Now one would want rather to stress the way in which the glass skin repels the city outside, a repulsion for which we have analogies in those reflector sunglasses which make it impossible for your interlocutor to see your own eyes and thereby achieve a certain aggressivity toward and power over the Other. In a similar way, the glass skin achieves a peculiar and placeless dissociation of the Bonaventure from its neighborhood: it is not even an exterior, inasmuch as when you seek to look at the hotel's outer walls you cannot see the hotel itself but only the distorted images of everything that surrounds it.

Now consider the escalators and elevators. Given their very real pleasures in Portman, particularly the latter, which the artist has termed 'gigantic kinetic sculptures' and which certainly account for much of the spectacle and excitement of the hotel interior – particularly in the Hyatts, where like great Japanese lanterns or gondolas they ceaselessly rise and fall – given such a deliberate marking and foregrounding in their own right, I believe one has to see such 'people movers' (Portman's own term, adapted from Disney) as somewhat more significant than mere functions and engineering components. We know in any case that recent architectural theory has begun to borrow from narrative analysis in other fields and to attempt to see our physical trajectories through such buildings as virtual narratives or stories, as dynamic paths and narrative paradigms which we as visitors are asked to fulfill and to complete with our own bodies and movements. In the Bonaventure, however, we find a dialectical heightening of this process: it seems to me that the escalators and elevators here henceforth replace movement but also, and above all, designate themselves as now reflexive signs and emblems of movement proper (something which will become evident when we come to the question of what remains of older forms of movement in this building, most notably walking itself). Here the narrative stroll has been underscored, symbolized, reified, and replaced by a transportation machine which becomes the allegorical signifier of that older promenade we are no longer allowed to conduct on our own: and this is a dialectical intensification of the autoreferentiality of all

→

modern culture, which tends to turn upon itself and designate its own cultural productions as its content.

I am more at a loss when it comes to conveying the thing itself, the experience of space you undergo when you step off such allegorical devices into the lobby or atrium, with its great central columns surrounded by a miniature lake, the whole positioned between the four symmetrical residential towers with their elevators, and surrounded by rising balconies capped by a kind of greenhouse roof at the sixth level. I am tempted to say that such space makes it impossible for us to use the language of volume or volumes any longer, since these are impossible to seize. Hanging streamers indeed suffuse this empty space in such a way as to distract systematically and deliberately from whatever form it might be supposed to have, while a constant busyness gives the feeling that emptiness is here absolutely packed, that it is an element within which you yourself are immersed, without any of that distance that formerly enabled the perception of perspective or volume. You are in this hyperspace up to your eyes and your body; and if it seemed before that that suppression of depth I spoke of in postmodern painting or literature would necessarily be difficult to achieve in architecture itself, perhaps this bewildering immersion may now serve as the formal equivalent in the new medium.

Yet escalator and elevator are also in this context dialectical opposites; and we may suggest that the glorious movement of the elevator gondola is also a dialectical compensation for this filled space of the atrium – it gives us the chance at a radically different, but complementary, spatial experience: that of rapidly shooting up through the ceiling and outside, along one of the four symmetrical towers, with the referent, Los Angeles itself, spread out breathtakingly and even alarmingly before us. But even this vertical movement is contained: the elevator lifts you to one of those revolving cocktail lounges, in which, seated, you are again passively rotated about and offered a contemplative spectacle of the city itself, now transformed into its own images by the glass windows through which you view it.

We may conclude all this by returning to the central space of the lobby itself (with the passing observation that the hotel rooms are visibly marginalized: the corridors in the residential sections are low-ceilinged and dark, most depressingly functional, which one understands that the rooms are in the worst of taste). The descent is dramatic enough, plummeting back down through the roof to splash down in the lake. What happens when you get there is something else, which can only be characterized as milling confusion, something like the vengeance this space takes on those who still seek to walk through it. Given the absolute symmetry of the four towers, it is quite impossible to get your bearings in this lobby; recently, color coding and directional signals have been added in a pitiful and revealing, rather desperate, attempt to restore the coordinates of an older space. I will take as the most dramatic practical result of this spatial mutation the notorious

→

dilemma of the shopkeepers on the various balconies: it has been obvious since the opening of the hotel in 1977 that nobody could ever find any of these stores, and even if you once located the appropriate boutique, you would be most unlikely to be as fortunate a second time; as a consequence, the commercial tenants are in despair and all the merchandise is marked down to bargain prices. When you recall that Portman is a businessman as well as an architect and a millionaire developer, an artist who is at one and the same time a capitalist in his own right, one cannot but feel that here too something of a 'return of the repressed' is involved.

So I come finally to my principal point here, that this latest mutation in space – postmodern hyperspace – has finally been succeeded in transcending the capacities of the individual human body to locate itself, to organize its immediate surroundings perceptually, and cognitively to map its position in a mappable external world. It may now be suggested that this alarming disjunction point between the body and its built environment – which is to the initial bewilderment of the older modernism as the velocities of spacecraft to those of the automobile – can itself stand as the symbol and analogon of that even sharper dilemma which is the incapacity of our minds, at least at present, to map the great global multinational and decentered communicational network in which we find ourselves caught as individual subjects.

But as I am anxious that Portman's space not be perceived as something either exceptional or seemingly marginalized as leisure-specialized on the order of Disneyland, I will conclude by juxtaposing this complacent and entertaining (although bewildering) leisure-time space with its analogue in a very different area, namely, the space of postmodern warfare, in particular as Michael Herr evokes it in *Dispatches*, his great book on the experience of Vietnam. The extraordinary linguistic innovations of this work may still be considered postmodern, in the eclectic way in which its language impersonally fuses a whole range of contemporary collective idiolects, most notably rock language and black language: but the fusion is dictated by problems of content. This first terrible postmodernist war cannot be told in any of the traditional paradigms of the war novel or movie – indeed, that breakdown of all previous narrative paradigms is, along with the breakdown of any shared language through which a veteran might convey such experience, among the principle subjects of the book and may be said to open up the place of a whole new reflexivity. Benjamin's account of Baudelaire, and of the emergence of modernism from a new experience of city technology which transcends all the older habits of bodily perception, is both singularly relevant and singularly antiquated in the light of this new and virtually unimaginable quantum leap in the technological alienations:

> He was a moving-target-survivor subscriber, a true child of the war, because
> except for the rare times when you were pinned or stranded the system was
>
> →

geared to keep you mobile, if that was what you thought you wanted. As a technique for staying alive it seemed to make as much sense as anything, given naturally that you were there to begin with and wanted to see it close; it started out sound and straight but it formed a cone as it progressed, because the more you moved the more you saw, the more you saw the more besides death and mutilation you risked, and the more you risked of that the more you would have to let go of one day as a 'survivor.' Some of us moved around the war like crazy people until we couldn't see which way the run was taking us anymore, only the war all over its surface with occasional, unexpected penetration. As long as we could have choppers like taxis it took real exhaustion or depression near shock or a dozen pipes of opium to keep us even apparently quiet, we'd still be running around inside our skins like something was after us, ha ha, La Vida Loca. In the months after I got back the hundreds of helicopters I'd flown in began to draw together until they'd formed a collective meta-chopper, and in my mind it was the sexiest thing going; saver-destroyer, provider-waster, right hand–left hand, nimble, fluent, canny and human; hot steel, grease, jungle-saturated canvas webbing, sweat cooling and warming up again, cassette rock and roll in one ear and door-gun fire in the other, fuel, heat, vitality and death, death itself, hardly an intruder.

In this new machine, which does not, like the older modernist machinery of the locomotive or the airplane, represent motion, but which can only be represented *in motion*, something of the mystery of the new postmodernist space is concentrated.

Jameson (1991: 38–45)

For Jameson, the Bonaventure condenses some key aspects of postmodern culture and life. Jameson's focus on the idea of **postmodern** (p. 400) space and the experience of it is particularly important. For Jameson the confusion engendered by the Bonaventure is symbolic of wider confusions and our inability to locate ourselves in the complexity of the postmodern world. Such claims about postmodernism will be considered further in section 9.9; however, it may be illuminating to read this long extract carefully and to consider if these arguments might be applied more widely.

9.8.3 | Reading the landscape of taste

In 'Satellite dishes and the landscape of taste' Brunsdon (1991) examines the arguments over the siting of satellite dishes between 1989 and 1990 as reported in the British press. She suggests that this controversy raises a number of issues around class, status, national heritage and taste. Brunsdon says that these press reports identify two opposed forces: '"Anti-dishers" and "Dish-erectors"' (1991: 32). 'Anti-dishers' were professionals who represented groups, 'dish-erectors' were particular individuals. The 'anti-dishers' argued in a consistent and 'uniform' way, whereas 'dish-erectors' spoke on the basis of their own personal experience. Thus, 'anti-dishers' made 'no reference to television programmes' (1991: 34) as they spoke about the architecture disfigurement produced by the erection of the dish. They were knowledgeable about relevant planning legislation and consistently used evaluative phrases to suggest that dishes were 'eyesores' that were devaluing the environment in financial and status terms. Certain of the anti-dishers were concerned to suggest that the mounting of a dish would change the character of the environment for the worse. The suggestion is that the public environment would be contaminated or devalued by the dish. The dish-erectors made their case in more personal or individual terms. They wanted the greater choice or the potential variation in TV watching that a dish could bring and these concerns overrode concern about the environment. The debate around the siting of dishes raises issues of status and its display in consumption. This feature of the built environment also connects to issues of **power** (p. 94), in a way similar to the accounts provided by MacDonald and Jameson in the previous section.

9.8.4 | Reading cities: legibility and imageability

We have already shown how critics like **Benjamin** (p. 373) and Berman interpret a city like Paris. Other writers from different disciplinary backgrounds have carried out similar exercises in different ways and using different concepts. One influential case of this can be found in the work of Lynch (1960) which was used by Jameson (1991) in his work on postmodernism and **postmodernity** (p. 400).

Lynch analyses the nature and inhabitants' experience of three American cities: Boston, Jersey City and Los Angeles. At the heart of his analysis is the concept of *legibility* – 'the ease with which its parts can be recognized and can be organized into a coherent pattern' (1960: 2–3). Also of great importance is the idea of *imageability* – 'that quality in a physical object which gives it a high probability of evoking a strong image in any given observer' (1960: 9). From his three examples, Lynch classifies five different elements of the city which are important in the generation of the experience of the city: paths, edges, districts, nodes and landmarks. Definitions and examples of these are given in the extract from Lynch (1960) in Box 9.4.

Box **9.4**

Important elements of the city

The contents of the city images so far studied, which are referable to physical forms, can conveniently be classified into five types of elements: *paths, edges, districts, nodes, and landmarks.* These elements may be defined as follows:

1. Paths.   Paths are the channels along which the observer customarily, occasionally, or potentially moves. They may be streets, walkways, transit lines, canals, railroads. For many people, these are the predominant elements in their

→

image. People observe the city while moving through it, and along these paths the other environmental elements are arranged and related.

2. Edges.   Edges are the linear elements not used or considered as paths by the observer. They are the boundaries between two phases, linear breaks in continuity: shores, railroad cuts, edges of development, walls. They are lateral references rather than coordinate axes. Such edges may be barriers, more or less penetrable, which close one region off from another; or they may be seams, lines along which two regions are related and joined together. These edge elements, although probably not as dominant as paths, are for many people important organizing features, particularly in the role of holding together generalized areas, as in the outline of a city by water or wall.

3. Districts.   Districts are the medium-to-large sections of the city, conceived of as having two-dimensional extent, which the observer mentally enters 'inside of,' and which are recognizable as having some common, identifying character. Always identifiable from the inside, they are also used for exterior reference if visible from the outside. Most people structure their city to some extent in this way, with individual differences as to whether paths or districts are the dominant elements. It seems to depend not only upon the individual but also upon the given city.

4. Nodes.   Nodes are points, the strategic spots in a city into which an observer can enter, and which are the intensive foci to and from which he is traveling. They may be primarily junctions, places of a break in transportation, a crossing or convergence of paths, moments of shift from one structure to another. Or the nodes may be simply concentrations, which gain their importance from being the condensation of some use or physical character, as a street-corner hangout or an enclosed square. Some of these concentration nodes are the focus and epitome of a district, over which their influence radiates and of which they stand as a symbol. They may be called cores. Many nodes, of course, partake of the nature of both junctions and concentrations. The concept of node is related to the concept of path, since junctions are typically the convergence of paths, events on the journey. It is similarly related to the concept of district, since cores are typically the intensive foci of districts, their polarizing center. In any event, some nodal points are to be found in almost every image, and in certain cases they may be the dominant feature.

5. Landmarks.   Landmarks are another type of point-reference, but in this case the observer does not enter within them, they are external. They are usually a rather simply defined physical object: building, sign, store, or mountain. Their use involves the singling out of one element from a host of possibilities. Some landmarks are distant ones, typically seen from many angles and distances, over the tops of smaller elements, and used as radial references. They may be within the city or at such a distance that for all practical purposes they symbolize a constant

→

direction. Such are isolated towers, golden domes, great hills. Even a mobile point, like the sun, whose motion is sufficiently slow and regular, may be employed. Other landmarks are primarily local, being visible only in restricted localities and from certain approaches. These are the innumerable signs, store fronts, trees, doorknobs, and other urban detail, which fill in the image of most observers. They are frequently used clues of identity and even of structure, and seem to be increasingly relied upon as a journey becomes more and more familiar.

Lynch (1960: 46–8)

Lynch uses the identification and discussion of these elements to inform and argue for particular design strategies. However, it is important to recognise that these elements can also be used as a methodological base for the interpretation of the city in cultural studies. Another important aspect of Lynch's work is the emphasis that he places on the inhabitant's experience of the city. Lynch does not simply write as the interpreter or critic, but attempts to mobilise or tap what might be called the experience of the 'audience' for the city. However, it is important to remember that there may be many different audiences for the city is divided by class, gender, race and age and so on.

9.8.5 | Reading landscape and power

The examples examined in this section have raised the issue of the relationship between landscape and **power** (p. 94) (see also Chapter 4). For example, MacDonald argues that the offices of professional groups can be interpreted as part of the desire for professional enhancement and power and Brunsdon shows how conflicts over satellite dishes connect to and structure argument between different social groups over the meaning of the environment. Sharon Zukin (1991, 1992) has identified some of the general issues raised in this realm. She suggests that landscape gives a material form to relationships of power. Landscapes can then be interpreted to represent or symbolise the different contours of relationships of power at specific historical moments. Zukin is particularly concerned with the relationships of power that are characteristic of capitalism:

> Asymmetrical power in the visual sense suggests capitalists' great ability to draw from a potential repertoire of images, to develop a succession of real and symbolic landscapes that define every historical period, including postmodernity. This reverses Jameson's dictum that architecture is important to postmodernity because it is the symbol of capitalism. Rather, architecture is important because it is the capital of symbolism.
>
> (Zukin, 1992: 225)

A key aspect of Zukin's work is the emphasis that she places on the nature of the transformation of cities. She examines the nature of the process of *gentrification* which has transformed parts of older cities of modernity like London or New York (Zukin, 1989, 1995). Newer cities do not contain the sorts of buildings that can be transformed by this process. Such cities, like Los Angeles, which are emblematic of **postmodernity** (p. 400), are structured around entertainment – they are like a kind of Disney World. In this fashion Zukin raises some crucial issues concerning the contemporary transformation of power and visual culture in the city, which is the subject of the next section.

9.9 | Visual culture and postmodernity

In this book, and in this chapter, we have suggested that culture can be understood in two main ways: as text and as way of life. In keeping with this distinction, it is possible to argue that contemporary developments in culture can be divided into the movement towards the dominance of postmodernism as a textual form and **postmodernity** (p. 400) as a new way of life. Such an analytic distinction helps to organise a vast range of contemporary debates on contemporary culture.

Interpretations of postmodernism/ity can be summarised quite neatly in discussions of the city and its buildings. Thus in his discussion of the Bonaventure, Jameson examines the nature of this building, the experiences it provokes and its location in a particular city. Charles Jencks (1989), who is the most prominent writer on postmodernism in architecture, maintains that architectural postmodernism involves 'double coding'. He (1989: 7) suggests that postmodernism is

> fundamentally the eclectic mixture of any tradition with that of the immediate past: it is both the continuation of Modernism and its transcendence. Its best works are characteristically doubly-coded and ironic, making a feature of the wide choice, conflict and discontinuity of traditions, because this heterogeneity most captures our pluralism. Its hybrid style is opposed to the minimalism of Late-Modern ideology and all revivals which are based on an exclusive dogma or taste.

The following sections explore these issues in more detail.

9.9.1 | Postmodernism and capitalism: Fredric Jameson and David Harvey

In more critical discussions of postmodernism and postmodernity, such processes imply the loss of the sense of historical location, as features from many different historical periods and places are brought together, producing 'flattening' (Jameson, 1991) and 'time–space compression' (Harvey, 1990). This weakening of historicity is one of the four features of postmodernism identified by Jameson (1991: 6–25):

1. *Depthlessness.* The break-down of the depth models characteristic of pre-postmodern societies, such as those between the inside/outside, essence/appearance, authenticity/inauthenticity, signifier/signified, latent/manifest.

2. *Weakening of historicity.* We are no longer able to situate ourselves in historical time as

unfolding in a clear and coherent fashion. There has been a weakening of grand or meta-narratives. These developments are represented by the popularity of the 'nostalgia' film which incorporates a notion of 'pastness' or earlier films into an unlocated and vague present.

3. *New emotional tone.* The 'waning of affect' as we no longer seek the depths of human personality or feel separated from our essential self (as in the idea of alienation) but are 'burnt-out'.

4. *Pastiche.* Postmodern culture does not parody other culture with the intention of producing a particular effect but pastiches in a playful manner to no ultimate aim.

These transformations are also taking place in the wider culture of the contemporary period. It has been suggested that postmodernity consists of features that distinguish it from modernity such those detailed by David Harvey (1990) in Table 9.4.

The kind of changes identified by writers like Harvey and Jameson seem to be furthest advanced in the United States and especially in its cities. If Europe and Paris were the sites of the development of **modernity**, then **postmodernity** (p. 400) is centred in the United States and Los Angeles. The latter contains the predominant 'dream factory' of the late twentieth century – Hollywood – but is also at the core of contemporary communications and media developments in the wider sense. Los Angeles is also home to many aspects of US military power (Soja, 1989) and new forms of postmodern building like the Bonaventure. The home of the motor car has been central in the generation of new modes of social interaction, the accommodation of which has transformed other cities.

9.9.2 | Jean Baudrillard: simulacra and hyperreality

In this chapter we have tried to show the range of ways in which culture both as text and as way of life is visually available to its members. Seeing, we have suggested, is always cultured seeing and appearances are only real to us in so far as they have cultural significance. All cultures make some of their features visually available but the changes ushered in by modernity magnify this tendency. The writers discussed in the previous section suggest that contemporary shifts in culture and society are leading towards the development of new forms of visual culture of a postmodernist nature. While this is developed upon the foundations of modernity it can be seen to have certain distinctive features. Some of the shifts involved have been characterised by Baudrillard, whose work has already been considered in this chapter as influential on John Urry's analysis of the post-tourist.

Baudrillard criticises the classic **Marxist** (p. 97) ideas of the determination of the **ideological** (p. 84) or cultural superstructure by the economic base and of the distinction between use and exchange value. He suggests that these binary distinctions have been confused or blurred by the proliferation of images and the pronounced roles of the media in contemporary capitalist societies. Jameson's point that depth models are increasingly less central is similar. Moreover, Baudrillard develops an extended

Table 9.4 ■ Fordist modernity versus flexible postmodernity, or the interpenetration of opposed tendencies in capitalist society as a whole

Fordist modernity	Flexible postmodernity
economies of scale/master code/hierarchy homogeneity/detail division of labour	economies of scope/idiolect/anarchy diversity/social division of labour
paranoia/alienation/symptom public housing/monopoly capital	schizophrenia/decentring/desire homelessness/entrepreneurialism
purpose/design/mastery/determinacy production capital/universalism	play/chance/exhaustion/indeterminacy fictitious capital/localism
state power/trade unions state welfarism/metropolis	financial power/individualism neoconservatism/counter-urbanisation
ethics/money commodity God the Father/materiality	aesthetics/moneys of account The Holy Ghost/immateriality
production/originality/authority blue collar/avant-gardism interest group politics/semantics	reproduction/pastiche/eclecticism white collar/commercialism charismatic politics/rhetoric
centralisation/totalisation synthesis/collective bargaining	decentralisation/deconstruction antithesis/local contracts
operational management/master code phallic/single task/origin	strategic management/idiolect androgynous/multiple tasks/trace
metatheory/narrative/depth mass production/class politics technical–scientific rationality	language games/image/surface small-batch production/social movements/pluralistic otherness
utopia/redemptive art/concentration specialised work/collective consumption	heterotopias/spectacle/dispersal flexible worker/symbolic capital
function/representation/signified industry/protestant work ethic mechanical reproduction	fiction/self-reference/signifier services/temporary contract electronic reproduction
becoming/epistemology/regulation urban renewal/relative space	being/ontology/deregulation urban revitalisation/place
state interventionism/industrialisation internationalism/permanence/time	laissez-faire/deindustrialisation geopolitics/ephemerality/space

Source: Harvey (1990: 340–1)

critique of the relationship between the sign, as conceptualised within **semiotics** (p. 34) (see Chapter 2), and the referent. Baudrillard (1988: 170) argues that the sign, or the image, moves through the following four stages:

1. It is a reflection of a basic reality.
2. It masks and perverts a basic reality.
3. It masks the *absence* of a basic reality.
4. It bears no relation to any reality whatever: it is its own pure simulacrum.

In the first stage, images or language are seen to represent reality. Thus, for example, natural science suggests that it can capture the nature of the world in language which in many ways corresponds to that world or reflects it as if in a mirror. In the second stage, the sign or language conceals or misrepresents the nature of reality. This is the premise of Marxist theories of ideology (Connor, 1989: 55), where ideology or the 'false consciousness' of the workers serves to misrepresent or conceal the essentially exploitative nature of capitalist society. The image distorts reality in the manner of trick mirrors at a fairground. This situation has developed in the third phase where it is not something real that is masked but the absence of a real. This reaches its zenith in the final stage, where the sign bears no relation to reality at all.

Baudrillard's ideas can be illustrated through consideration of the example of the reporting and media coverage of an election campaign. In stage 1, the election is seen as an independently existing event which is reported in an *objective* way which reflects its *reality*. Certain 'quality' newspapers and public service broadcasting would probably want to argue that their coverage of an election still conforms to this model. The election would exist in this way without the reporting and the reporting does not affect its course. In the stage 2 model, the election is reported in a way that *constructs* it ideologically. For example, there is concealment of core issues and certain aspects are emphasised in a consistent fashion which reflect the interests of powerful groups. Marxists argue that the mass media do this systematically (see Chapter 2). In stage 3 the election is becoming a media event, for example aspects of actors' behaviour are tailored to the time scale of the media. Speeches are made to hit news bulletin deadlines for prime time and so forth. The election as a real event is becoming an absence. It is often suggested that this process began in Britain with the general election of 1959, which is seen as the first television election.

For Baudrillard the critical point is reached in stage 4. In terms of the election example, the media coverage *is* the election, which does not exist outside its coverage. The most important players are those who select the images and determine the sound bites. Hence, in the 1997 British general election campaign, the Labour Party 'spin doctors' made sure that no politician made a 'mistake' akin to Michael Foot's choice of coat at the Cenotaph discussed in Chapter 6. In this view it is impossible to conceive of the election outside the media circulation of images. The images are the election.

Baudrillard proposes that we live in a world of simulacra, in *hyperreality* where images desperately try to produce an effect of the real. This view is hugely controversial. For example, Baudrillard's claim that the Gulf War did not happen, seems to neglect the obvious fact that people died in it, or the claim that the election does not exist could seem to neglect the point that people do actually vote. However, the point that it is impossible to think or conceptualise these events outside the media images of them seems plausible. What is also true is that these events are now media events in the extensive nature of the coverage given to them. In the advanced Western world we are now accustomed to 24-hour television and radio news channels that will relay images instantaneously across the globe. In such a context the advancement of media technologies beyond the realms of photography and film is of great significance.

9.9.3 | Digitalisation and the future of representation

In particular, the so-called 'digital revolution' looks set to extend the realms of the hyperreal. Computer techniques which digitise photographic and film images permit an unprecedented enhancement and manipulation of the production of pictorial representations. Digitisation is a process through which a picture is divided in a grid into small picture elements ('pixels'). Each pixel is assigned a number from a code of colours or brightness. By changing the values of the pixels, or by adding or removing them, it becomes possible to change the photograph. As the popular press nowadays often shows us, persons who could not possibly have met can be depicted in a seamless photograph. Movies now contain shots constructed as simulations from angles that no human cameraperson would be capable of filming, affording perspectives that once could only be dreamt. The production of mass-mediated still and moving images is coming to be more a matter of computing proficiency than camera, darkroom or editing skills.

These changes strike at the heart of the notion of photographic causality and the easy conceptions of **realism** (p. 61) they support, severing the necessary tie between photographs and their referents. Digitisation finally puts an end to documentary's 'innocent arrogance of objective fact' by 'removing its claim on the real' (Winston, 1995: 259). When placed alongside such cognate developments as multimedia applications, the growth of the Internet, the emergence of large electronic data banks and virtual reality technologies, it seems that the 'post-photographic' age may have arrived. The broad shifts in the character of visual culture occasioned by these developments are summarised in Table 9.5.

Some consider the changes thus signalled to be as momentous as those postulated by Benjamin's classic essay on mechanical reproduction's implications for the work of art. Digitisation can promote the emergence of new forms of pictorial representation, for example the pop video which exemplifies such key **postmodern** (p. 400) themes as heterogeneity and fragmentation. While there is a basis for claiming that digitisation might provide new grounds for perception, claims about the death of photography

Table 9.5 ■ Types of society, modes of pictorial representation and their associated positions

Traditional society	Autographic (handmade) images	Worshippers
Modernity	Photographic images	Viewers
Postmodernity	Electronic images	Interactive users

need to be treated more circumspectly. Such claims rest on an over-simple techno-logical determinism and overlook the dependence of the new technologies on older skills, knowledges and ways of seeing. Continuities coexist with technologically driven ruptures. Moreover, the postmodern world is characteristically an increasingly inter-textual one where all kinds of borrowing and pastiche are permissible (Lister, 1997). So the more portentous claims about a post-photographic era are probably premature. As was suggested in the discussion of film and photography as technologies of realism (section 9.3 above), realism has always been properly understood in qualified terms. 'Seeing is believing' is an adage that has long been ironically framed. Digitisation now renders claims about, for example, documentary realism, as transparently **ideological** (p. 84) – it 'destroys the photographic image as evidence of anything except the process of digitisation' (Winston, 1995: 259). If this shifts attention away from the putatively distinctive characteristics of the photographic representation towards the reception and interpretation of these images, then this may be a step in the right direction. Or it may be seen as just another symptom of what Baudrillard has termed 'the triumph of signifying culture'. In these respects, as we have suggested in the course of this chapter, there are different visual regimes connected to forms of society and culture (pre-modern, modern and postmodern – that are themselves implicated in changing struggles over **power** (p. 94).

9.10 | Summary

We have organised this chapter around three main themes. First, we have shown how visual culture has changed in the shift from modernity to postmodernity. At the beginning of the chapter, we pointed to the significance of the 'classic' writings of Simmel and Benjamin on the visual cultures of modernity and developed this discussion through consideration of photography and film. In the closing sections of the chapter we examined the new visual representations of postmodernity. These shifts are intimately connected to the re-ordering of power relations. Second, we have explored a number of different ways in which visual culture can be studied, using ideas like the classic realist text, the male gaze, surveillance, unfocused interaction, civil inattention and so on. Finally, we have paid particular attention to the city, as a key site of social interaction and social transformation. Specifically, we have shown how a number of different dimensions of the city can be interpreted, using some of the ideas introduced in the chapter.

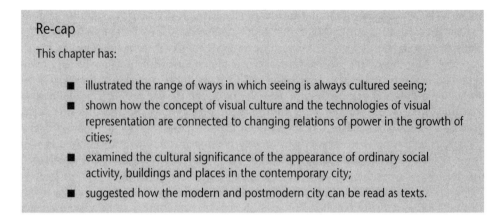

Re-cap

This chapter has:

- illustrated the range of ways in which seeing is always cultured seeing;
- shown how the concept of visual culture and the technologies of visual representation are connected to changing relations of power in the growth of cities;
- examined the cultural significance of the appearance of ordinary social activity, buildings and places in the contemporary city;
- suggested how the modern and postmodern city can be read as texts.

Further reading

The nature of photographic representation and how it implicates the viewer is critically examined in Susan Sontag's *On Photography* (1979). The arguments advanced in John Berger's *Ways of Seeing* (1972) caused a great deal of controversy when they were first made a quarter of a century ago and they still deserve careful consideration. A wide range of issues arising from the history, forms and technologies of photography are covered in contributions to Liz Wells's *Photography: A Critical Introduction* (1997). Chris Jenk's edited collection *Visual Culture* (1995) contains a number of papers that deal with aspects of the 'visual turn' in contemporary cultural theory. Ethnographic uses of photography are considered in Michael Ball and Greg Smith's *Analyzing Visual Data* (1992). A comprehensive method for explicating 'the grammar of visual design' is set out in Gunther Kress and Theo van Leeuwen's *Reading Images* (Routledge 1996).

Afterword

Our aim in writing this introductory text has been to stimulate an interest in the concepts, theories and analyses of cultural studies. We hope that this book will encourage you to want to find out more about cultural studies – the topics it addresses, the approaches it employs, the debates it has stimulated. Our objective has been to make accessible some of these topics, issues and debates. We are not in the business of establishing a canon. Cultural studies is, in a favourite metaphor, a contested terrain, riven with political dispute and interpretive disagreements. In this Afterword we want to briefly suggest some directions beyond this textbook to develop your understanding of cultural studies further.

The first thing you may wish to do is to consult the originals of those studies that have especially interested you. The Bibliography gives full references for all the sources mentioned in each chapter. If there is a particular source that you wish to follow up, it can be located in a good reference library. In addition we have drawn attention to a small selection of further reading at the end of each chapter. This Afterword describes: (a) periodical sources, (b) using the Internet and World Wide Web in cultural studies, and (c) some suggestions for doing projects in cultural studies.

Periodicals

There is a growing number of journals devoted to cultural studies or whose editorial policies are sympathetic to publishing work in this area. They include the following:

- *Australian Journal of Cultural Studies*
- *Cultural Studies*
- *Ecumene*
- *Gender, Place and Culture*
- *International Journal of Cultural Studies*

- *Media, Culture and Society*
- *New Formations*
- *Signs*

  Theory, Culture and Society

These journals publish articles, replies and shorter reports and interviews, and can usually be found in college and university libraries. Each has its own distinctive 'accent' and interests.

Internet and Web sources for cultural studies

The 'information superhighway' offers some unparalleled opportunities for further engagement with cultural studies. Among the sites worth visiting are the following:

- *Cultural Studies Central*
  URL: <http://home.earthlink.net/~markowitz/>
  According to its index page, 'Cultural Studies Central is a gathering spot and central clearinghouse where those of us who live and breathe Cultural Studies can go to learn more and do more.'
- *Cultural Studies Resources*
  URL: <http://atl46.atl.msu.edu/us.html>
  A site that 'provides links and information for doing US cultural studies projects'. Includes sections on media, music and sport.
- *CULTSTUD-L*
  URL: <http://www.cas.usf.edu/communication/rodman/cultstud/index.html>
  A discussion list established at the University of South Florida which now has a selection of essays and interviews available on its website.
- *The English Server*
  URL: <http://eng.hss.cmu.edu/>
  On its Cultural Theory page you can find a wide selection of original sources, discussions and bibliographies. The English Server has an excellent collection of links to other sites.
- *Sarah Zupko's Cultural Studies Center*
  URL: <http://www.mcs.net/~zupko/popcult.htm>
  Established in 1994, this site has a very extensive range of pages dealing with journals, articles, theorists and critics, news groups, conferences, book reviews, publishers and academic programmes.
- *The Institute: Sources in Sociology, Cultural Studies and Critical Theory*
  URL: <http://www.geocities.com/Athens/7364/Inst_CS_page.html>
  On-line essays, bibliographies, journals and links to other sites.
- *Voice of the Shuttle: Cultural Studies Page*
  URL: <http://humanitas.ucsb.edu/shuttle/cultural.html>

Includes an extensive listing of 'the intersection between cultural criticism/theory and selective resources in sociology, media studies, postcolonial studies, economics, literature, and other fields chosen to represent the alignments that now signify "culture" for the contemporary humanities'. Includes such special topics as body/corporeality theory, culture/canon wars and fashion. Lists journals, news groups and courses and programmes in cultural studies.

Each of these sites has hypertext links to related, often more specialised pages (such as those for Black Cultural Studies, Subaltern Studies or the Paul Gilroy page). Further sites can also be located by using a search engine such as AltaVista, HotBot, or Yahoo (URLs: <www.altavista.digital.com>, <www.hotbot.com> and <www.yahoo.com>). To avoid being overwhelmed with links to pages irrelevant to your interests, you may find it helpful to combine two or more key words – for example, 'power' and 'Foucault' – in your search (follow the guidance and suggestions supplied by the search engine). The same methods can also be used to locate websites that will supply information on substantive topics about which you wish to find out more.

Doing projects in cultural studies

The good news is that you do not need huge resources or expensive equipment. Some kinds of work in cultural studies require no more than a text (a magazine, a film, a CD, a book) and an analytical and critical inclination. For other kinds of work you may need to draw more extensively on established social science methods (interviews, ethnography, content analysis). Pertti Alasuutari presents a good guide to concepts and methods in *Researching Culture: Qualitative Method and Cultural Studies* (1995).

A useful exercise is to take a text and to interrogate it with ideas drawn from a particular theory or theorist. What insight might semiotics offer into the Spice Girls' dress sense? How would Walter Benjamin respond to the Internet? In what respects could the latest Rolling Stones tour be regarded as a postmodern phenomenon? What light could Georg Simmel cast on the attractions of shopping malls? How might Richard Hoggart rewrite *The Uses of Literacy* at the turn of the century? Attempting to apply the ideas of a theorist or perspective to a cultural phenomenon should give you a surer sense of its potential and shortcomings. What does the theory or theorist illuminate? What gets overlooked? How well does the evidence support a particular interpretation? Some careful thought needs to be given to the selection of the theory/theorist used to mobilise your analysis of any given phenomenon (which theory or theorist would *you* choose to analyse the Lottery?).

Proceeding in this manner can be a good way of writing a paper or doing a project in cultural studies. We hope that the ideas presented in this book have provided resources and suggested possibilities that will encourage you to take a critical and analytical look at the features of the cultures you encounter.

Bibliography

Abercrombie, N. (1996) *Television and Society*, Cambridge: Polity.

Abercrombie, N., Hill, S. and Turner, B.S. (1980) *The Dominant Ideology Thesis*, London: Allen & Unwin.

Abercrombie, N., Hill, S. and Turner, B.S. (1984) *The Penguin Dictionary of Sociology*, London: Allen Lane.

Abercrombie, N., Hill, S. and Turner, B.S. (eds) (1990) *Dominant Ideologies*, London: Unwin Hyman.

Abercrombie, N. and Longhurst, B. (1991) *Individualism, Collectivism and Gender in Popular Culture*, Salford Papers in Sociology, no. 12.

Abercrombie, N. and Longhurst, B. (1998) *Audiences: A Sociological Theory of Performance and Imagination*, London: Sage.

Abelove, H., Barale, M.A. and Halperin, D.M. (eds) (1993) *The Lesbian and Gay Studies Reader*, London: Routledge.

Abu-Lughod, J. (1989) *Before European Hegemony: The World System A.D. 1250–1350*, New York: Oxford University Press.

Achebe, C. (1988) *Hopes and Impediments*, London: Heinemann.

Acker, K. (1993) 'Against ordinary language: the language of the body', in A. and M. Kroker (eds) *The Last Sex: Feminism and Outlaw Bodies*, London: Macmillan, 20–7.

Adorno, T. (1967) *Prisms*, London: Neville Spearman.

Adorno, T.W. and Horkheimer, M. (1972) *Dialectic of Enlightenment*, New York: Continuum (orig. publ. in German, 1947).

Agnew, J. (1987) *Place and Politics: The Geographical Mediation of State and Society*, London: Allen & Unwin.

Agnew, J. and Duncan, J.S. (eds) (1989) *The Power of Place: Bringing Together Geographical and Sociological Imaginations*, London: Unwin Hyman.

Aizlewood, J. (ed.) (1994) *Love is the Drug*, London: Penguin.

Alasuutari, P. (1995) *Researching Culture: Qualitative Method and Cultural Studies*, London: Sage.

Alpers, S. (1983) *The Art of Describing: Dutch Art in the Seventeenth Century*, Chicago: University of Chicago Press.

Althusser, L. (1971) 'Ideology and ideological state apparatuses', in L. Althusser (ed.) *Lenin and Philosophy and Other Essays*, London: New Left Books, 121–76.

Amselle, J.-L. (1992) 'Tensions within culture', *Social Dynamics* 18(1), 42–65.

Anderson, B. (1991) *Imagined Communities: Reflections on the Origins and Spread of Nationalism*, London: Verso (orig. 1983).

Anderson, K. and Gale, F. (eds) (1992) *Inventing Places: Studies in Cultural Geography*, Melbourne: Longman Chesire.

Anderson, P. (1984) 'Modernity and revolution', *New Left Review* 144, March/April, 96–113.

Ang, I. (1985) *Watching 'Dallas': Soap Opera and the Melodramatic Imagination*, London: Methuen.

Anzaldúa, G. (1987) *Borderlands/La Frontera: The New Mestiza*, San Francisco: Ann Lute.

Appignanesi, L. and Maitland, S. (1989) *The Rushdie File*, London: Fourth Estate.

Ardener, E.W. (1974) 'Belief and the problem of women' in J.S. La Fontaine, *The Interpretation of Ritual*, Social Science paperback. London: Tavistock Publications (orig. 1972).

Ardener, S. (1975) (ed.) *Perceiving Women*, New York: Wiley.

Aries, P. (1962) *Centuries of Childhood*, London: Cape.

Armstrong, D. (1983) *Political Anatomy of the Body*, Cambridge: Cambridge University Press.

Ashcroft, B., Griffiths, G. and Tiffin, H. (1989) *The Empire Writes Back: Theory and Practice in Post-Colonial Literatures*, London: Routledge.

Assiter, A. and Carol, A. (eds) (1993) *Bad Girls and Dirty Pictures: The Challenge to Reclaim Feminism*, London: Pluto.

Aveni, A. (1990) *Empires of Time: Calendars, Clocks and Cultures*, London: I.B. Tauris.

Azaryahu, M. (1996) 'The power of commemorative street names', *Environment and Planning D: Society and Space* 14, 311–30.

Back, L. (1996) *New Ethnicities and Urban Culture: Racisms and Multiculture in Young Lives*, London: UCL Press.

Bacon-Smith, C. (1992) *Enterprising Women: Television Fandom and the Creation of Popular Myth*, Philadelphia: University of Pennsylvania Press.

Bakhtin, M.M. (1981) *The Dialogic Imagination*, Austin: University of Texas Press.

Bakhtin, M. (1984) *Rabelais and His World*, Bloomington, IN: Indiana University Press (orig. 1968).

Bakhtin, M.M. (1984) *Problems of Dostoevsky's Poetics*, Manchester: Manchester University Press.

Ball, M. and Smith, G. (1992) *Analyzing Visual Data*, Newbury Park, CA: Sage.

Balsamo, A. (1995) 'Forms of technological embodiment: reading the body in contemporary culture', *Body and Society* 1(3/4), November, 215–37.

Barber, B. and Lyle, S. (1952) ' "Fashion" in women's clothes and the American social system', *Social Forces* 31, 124–31.

Barker, M. (1992) 'Stuart Hall, *Policing the Crisis*', in M. Barker and A. Beezer (eds) *Reading into Cultural Studies*, London: Routledge.

Barker, F., Hulme, P. and Iverson, M. (1994) *Colonial Discourse/Postcolonial Theory*, Manchester: Manchester University Press.

Barnes, T.J. and Duncan, J.S. (eds) (1992) *Writing Worlds: Discourse, Text and Metaphor in the Representation of Landscape*, London: Routledge.

Barnouw, E. (1974) *Documentary: A History of Non-Fiction Film*, New York: Oxford University Press.

Barrell, J. (1980) *The Dark Side of the Landscape: The Rural Poor in English Painting 1730–1840*, Cambridge: Cambridge University Press.

Barthes, R. (1973) *Mythologies*, London: Paladin.

Barthes, R. (1976) *Mythologies*, St Albans: Paladin (orig. 1957).

Barthes, R. (1985) *The Fashion System*, London: Cape (orig. 1967).

Bartky, S. (1988) 'Foucault, femininity and the modernization of patriarchal power', in I. Diamond and L. Quinby (eds) *Feminism and Foucault: Reflections on Resistance*, Boston: Northeastern University Press, 61–86.

Baudrillard, J. (1988) 'Simulacra and simulations', in M. Poster (ed.) *Jean Baudrillard: Selected Writings*, Cambridge: Polity, 166–84.

Bauman, Z. (1989) *Modernity and the Holocaust*, Cambridge: Polity Press.

Baxandall, L. and Morawski, S. (eds) (1973) *Marx and Engels on Literature and Art*, New York: International General.

Baxter, P.T.W. (ed.) *When the Grass is Gone: Development Intervention in African Arid Lands*, Vddevalla: Nordiska Afrikaininstitutet.

Becker, H. (1963) *Outsiders: Studies in the Sociology of Deviance*, New York: The Free Press.

Benjamin, W. (1970) *Illuminations*, London: Cape.

Benjamin, W. (1973) *Charles Baudelaire: A Lyric Poet in the Era of High Capitalism*, translated by H. Zohn, London: New Left Books.

Benjamin, W. (1977) *Understanding Brecht*, London: New Left Books.

Benjamin, W. (1983) *Charles Baudelaire: A Lyric Poet in the Era of High Capitalism*, London: Verso.

Bennett, T., Martin, G., Mercer, C. and Woollacott, J. (eds) (1981) *Culture, Ideology and Social Process: A Reader*, Milton Keynes: Open University Press.

Benthall, J. (1975) 'A prospectus, as published in *Studio International*, July 1972', in J. Benthall and T. Polhemus (eds) *The Body as a Medium of Expression*, London: Allen Lane, 5–35.

Bereiter, C. and Englemann, S. (1966) 'Teaching disadvantaged children in the preschool', in N. Dittmar (1976) *Sociolinguistics: A Critical Survey of Theory and Application*, London: Edward Arnold.

Berger, J. (1972) *Ways of Seeing*, London: British Broadcasting Corporation and Harmondsworth: Penguin.

Berger, J. (1989) 'Appearances', in J. Berger and J. Mohr (eds) *Another Way of Telling*, Cambridge: Granta.

Berger, P. and Luckmann, T. (1966) *The Social Construction of Reality*, New York: Doubleday.

Berman, M. (1983) *All That Is Solid Melts Into Air: The Experience of Modernity*, London: Verso.

Bernstein, B. (1960) 'Language and social class', *British Journal of Sociology* 11, 271–6.

Bernstein, B. (1961) 'Social class and linguistic development: a theory of social learning', in N. Dittmar (1976) *Sociolinguistics: A Critical Survey of Theory and Application*, London: Edward Arnold.

Bhabha, H. (1990) 'The third space', interview with Jonathan Rutherford in J. Rutherford (ed.) *Identity: Community, Culture, Difference*, London: Lawrence & Wishart.

Bhabha, H. (1994) *The Location of Culture*, London: Routledge.

Bird, J., Curtis, B., Putnam, T., Robertson, G. and Tickner, L. (eds) (1993) *Mapping the Futures: Local Cultures, Global Change*, London: Routledge.

Black, M. (1972) *The Labyrinth of Language*, Harmondsworth: Penguin.

Bloch, M. (1991) 'Language, anthropology and cognitive science', *Man* 26(2) 183–98.

Bloch, E., Lukacs, G., Brecht, B., Benjamin, W. and Adorno, T.W. (1980) *Aesthetics and Politics: Debates between Bloch, Lukacs, Brecht, Benjamin, Adorno*, London: Verso.

Blumer, H. (1968) 'Fashion', in *Encyclopaedia of the Social Sciences*, vol. 4, ed. D.L. Sills, New York: Collier-Macmillan, 341–5.

Blunt, A. (1994) *Travel, Gender and Imperialism: Mary Kingsley and West Africa*, New York: Guilford Press.

Blunt, A. and Rose, G. (eds) (1994) *Writing Women and Space: Colonial and Postcolonial Geographies*, New York: Guilford Press.

Bock, G. (1989) 'Women's history and gender history: aspects of an international debate', *Gender and History* 1(1), Spring, 7–30.

Bordo, S. (1988) 'Anorexia nervosa: psychopathology as the crystallisation of culture', in I. Diamond and L. Quinby (eds) *Feminism and Foucault: Reflections on Resistance*, Boston: Northeastern University Press, 87–117.

Bourdieu, P. (1984) *Distinction: A Social Critique of the Judgement of Taste*, London: Routledge & Kegan Paul (orig. 1979).

Bourdieu, P. (1990) *In Other Words: Essays towards a reflexive sociology*, Cambridge: Polity.

Bourdieu, P., Boltanski, L., Castel, R. and Chamboredon, J.-C. (1990) *Photography: A Middle-Brow Art*, Cambridge: Polity.

Bourdieu, P. and Passeron, J.C. (1990) *Reproduction in Education, Culture and Society*, London: Sage.

Bowring, J. (ed.) (1843) *The Works of Jeremy Bentham*, IV, Edinburgh: William Tait.

Brah, A. (1996) *Cartographies of Diaspora: Contesting Identities*, London: Routledge.

Brannon, R. (1976) 'The male sex role: our culture's blueprint of manhood, and what it's done for us lately', in D. David and R. Brannon (eds) *The Forty-Nine Percent Majority: The Male Sex Role*, Reading, MA: Addison-Wesley.

Briggs, J. (1970) *Never in Anger*, Cambridge, MA: Harvard University Press.

Bristow, J. (1997) *Sexuality*, London: Routledge.

Brunsdon, C. (1991) 'Satellite dishes and landscapes of taste', *New Formations* 15, 23–42.

Reprinted in C. Brunsdon (1997) *Screen Tastes: From Soap Opera to Satellite Dishes*, London: Routledge, 148–64.

Buck-Morss, S. (1989) *The Dialectics of Seeing: Walter Benjamin and the Arcades Project*, Cambridge, MA: MIT Press.

Bukatman, S. (1993) *Terminal Identity: The Virtual Subject in Postmodern Science Fiction*, Durham and London: Duke University Press.

Burchill, J. (1986) *Girls on Film*, New York: Pantheon.

Butler, J. (1990) *Gender Trouble: Feminism and the Subversion of Identity*, London: Routledge.

Butler, J. (1993) *Bodies that Matter: On the Discursive Limits of 'Sex'*, New York: Routledge.

Caldwell, J.C. (1982) *Theory of Fertility Decline*, London: Academic Press.

Campbell, B. (1988) *Unofficial Secrets: Child Sexual Abuse – the Cleveland Case*, London: Virago.

Campbell, B. (1993) *Goliath: Britain's Dangerous Places*, London: Hutchinson.

Carby, H. (1982) 'White woman listen! Black feminism and the boundaries of black sisterhood', in Centre for Contemporary Cultural Studies, *The Empire Strikes Back: Race and Racism in 70s Britain*, London: Hutchinson.

Carlyle, T. (1971) *Selected Writings*, Harmondsworth: Penguin.

Carpentier, A. (1990) *The Kingdom of this World (El Reino de este Mundo)*, London: André Deutsch (orig. 1949).

Carr, E.H. (1964) *What is History?*, Harmondsworth: Penguin.

Carroll, J.B. (1956) *Language, Thought and Reality: Selected Writings of Benjamin Lee Whorf*, Cambridge, MA: MIT Press.

Carter, E., Donald, J. and Squires, J. (eds) (1993) *Space and Place: Theories of Identity and Location*, London: Lawrence & Wishart.

Centre for Contemporary Cultural Studies (1982) *The Empire Strikes Back: Race and Racism in 70s Britain*, London: Hutchinson.

Chrisman, L. and Williams, P. (eds) (1993) *Colonial Discourse and Post-Colonial Theory: A Reader*, Hemel Hempstead: Harvester.

Clark, T.J. (1985) *The Painting of Modern Life: Paris in the Art of Manet and his Followers*, London: Thames & Hudson.

Clarke, G. (1990) 'Defending ski-jumpers: a critique of theories of youth subcultures', in S. Frith and A. Goodwin (eds) *On Record: Rock, Pop, and the Written Word*, London: Routledge, 81–96.

Clarke, J., Hall, S., Jefferson, T. and Roberts, B. (1976) 'Subcultures, cultures and class: a theoretical overview', in S. Hall and T. Jefferson (eds) *Resistance through Rituals: Youth Subcultures in Post-war Britain*, London: Hutchinson, 9–79.

Clifford, J. (1988) 'On Orientalism', in J. Clifford (ed.) *The Predicament of Culture: Twentieth-Century Ethnography, Literature, and Art*, Cambridge, MA: Harvard University Press.

Clifford, J. (1992) 'Travelling cultures', in L. Grossberg, C. Nelson and P. Treicher (eds) *Cultural Studies*, London: Routledge, 96–116.

Cloke, P., Philo, C. and Sadler, D. (1991) *Approaching Human Geography: An Introduction to Contemporary Theoretical Debates*, London: Paul Chapman.

Cloward, R.A. and Ohlin, L.E. (1960) *Delinquency and Opportunity: A Theory of Delinquent Gangs*, Glencoe, IL: The Free Press.

Cohen, A. (1955) *Delinquent Boys: The Culture of the Gang*, Glencoe, IL: The Free Press.

Cohen, P. (1980) 'Subcultural conflict and working-class community', in S. Hall, D. Hobson, A. Lowe and P. Willis (eds), *Culture, Media, Language: Working Papers in Cultural Studies, 1972–79*, London: Hutchinson, 78–87.

Cohen, S. (1973) *Folk Devils and Moral Panics: The Creation of the Mods and Rockers*, St Albans: Paladin.

Cohen, S. (1985) *Visions of Social Control: Crime, Punishment and Classification*, Oxford: Blackwell.

Cohen, S. (1987) *Folk Devils and Moral Panics: The Creation of the Mods and Rockers*, new edn, Oxford: Blackwell (new edn first published by Martin Robertson, 1980).

Cohen, T. (1989) 'Pictorial and photographic representation', in E. Barnouw (ed.) *International Encyclopaedia of Communications*, New York: Oxford University Press in association with The Annenberg School of Communication, 453–8.

Colley, L. (1992) *Britons: Forging the Nation 1707–1837*, New Haven: Yale University Press.

Collier, J. and Yanagisako, S.J. (eds) (1987) *Gender and Kinship: Essays Towards a Unified Analysis*, Stanford: Stanford University Press.

Collins, R. (1980) 'Weber's last theory of capitalism: a systematization', *American Sociological Review* 45(6), 925–42.

Connell, R.W. (1987) *Gender and Power: Society, the Person and Sexual Politics*, Cambridge: Polity.

Connor, S. (1989) *Postmodernist Culture: An Introduction to Theories of the Contemporary*, Oxford: Blackwell.

Cooke, P. (1989) 'Nation, space, modernity', in R. Peet and N. Thrift (eds) *New Models in Geography: Volume 1*, London: Unwin Hyman, 267–91.

Corrigan, P. and Sayer, D. (1985) *The Great Arch: English State Formation as Cultural Revolution*, Oxford: Blackwell.

Cosgrove, D. (1983) 'Towards a radical cultural geography: problems of theory', *Antipode* 15, 1–11.

Cosgrove, D. (1994) 'Contested global visions: one-world, whole-earth, and the Apollo space photographs', *Annals of the Association of American Geographers* 84, 270–94.

Cosgrove, D. and Jackson, P. (1987) 'New directions in cultural geography', *Area* 19, 95–101.

Coulter, J. (1979) *The Social Construction of Mind*, London: Macmillan.

Cowie, C. and Lees, S. (1981) 'Slags or drags', *Feminist Review* 9, 17–31.

Cowie, E. (1993) '*Film noir* and women', in J. Copjec (ed.) *Shades of Noir: A Reader*, London: Verso, 121–65.

Cross, B. (1993) *It's Not About a Salary . . . Rap, Race and Resistance in Los Angeles*, London: Verso.

Crossley, N. (1995) 'Body techniques, agency and corporeality: on Goffman's *Relations in Public*', *Sociology* 29(1), February, 133–49.

Culler, J. (1983) *Barthes*, London: Fontana.

Cultural Trends 1990: 7, London: Policy Studies Institute.

Dandeker, C. (1990) *Surveillance, Power and Modernity: Bureaucracy and Discipline from 1700 to the Present Day*, Cambridge: Polity Press.

Daniels, S. (1993) *Fields of Vision: Landscape Imagery and National Identity in England and the United States*, Cambridge: Polity.

Davidson, A.I. (1986) 'Archaeology, genealogy, ethics', in P.C. Hoy (ed.) *Foucault: A Critical Reader*, Oxford: Blackwell.

Davis, F. (1992) *Fashion, Culture and Identity*, Chicago: University of Chicago Press.

Davis, K. and Moore, W. (1945) 'Some principles of stratification', *American Sociological Review* 10, 242–9.

Davis, M. (1990) *City of Quartz: Excavating the Future in Los Angeles*, London: Verso.

Davis, M. (1993a) 'Who killed LA? A political autopsy', *New Left Review* 197, 3–28.

Davis, M. (1993b) 'Who killed Los Angeles? Part Two: The verdict is given', *New Left Review* 199, 29–54.

Del Valle, T. (1993) (ed.) *Gendered Anthropology*, London: Routledge.

deWita, B. (1994) *French Bourgeois Culture*, Glasgow: Editions de la Maison des Sciences de l'Homme and Cambridge University Press (orig. 1988).

Diamond, E. (ed.) (1996) *Performance and Cultural Politics*, London: Routledge.

Dickens, C. (1970) *Dombey and Son*, Harmondsworth: Penguin (orig. 1848).

Dickens, C. (1969) *Hard Times*, Harmondsworth: Penguin (orig. 1854).

Disraeli, B. (1981) *Sybil*, Oxford: World's Classics (orig. 1845).

Dittmar, N. (1976) *Sociolinguistics: A Critical Survey of Theory and Application*, London: Edward Arnold.

Dobbins, B. (1994) *The Women: Photographs of the Top Female Bodybuilders*, foreword by A. Schwarzenegger, New York: Artisan.

Docherty, T. (ed.) (1993) *Postmodernism: A Reader*, Hemel Hempstead: Harvester Wheatsheaf.

Dollimore, J. (1991) *Sexual Dissidence: Augustine to Wilde, Freud to Foucault*, Oxford: Oxford University Press.

Douglas, M. (1966) *Purity and Danger: An Analysis of Concepts of Pollution and Taboo*, London: Routledge & Kegan Paul.

Downes, D. (1966) *The Delinquent Solution: A Study in Subcultural Theory*, London: Routledge & Kegan Paul.

Driver, F. (1992) 'Geography's empire: histories of geographical knowledge', *Environment and Planning D: Society and Space* 10, 23–40.

Duberman, M. (1991) 'Distance and desire: English boarding school friendships, 1870–1920' in M.B. Duberman, M. Vicinus and G. Chauncey Jr *Hidden from History: Reclaiming the Gay and Lesbian Past*, Harmondsworth: Penguin, 212–29.

du Gay, P. (1996) *Consumption and Identity at Work*, London: Sage.

Dumont, L. (1970) *Homo Hierarchicus: The Caste System and Its Implications*, London: Weidenfeld & Nicolson.

Duncan, J. and Ley, D. (eds) (1993) *Place/Culture/Representation*, London: Routledge.

Dworkin, A. (1983) *Pornography: Men Possessing Women*, London: The Women's Press.

Dyer, G. (1982) *Advertising as Communication*, London: Methuen.

Dyer, R. (1989) 'Don't look now', in A. McRobbie (ed.) *Zoot Suits and Second-Hand Dresses*, London: Macmillan (orig. 1983).

Eagleton, T. (1983) *Literary Theory: An Introduction*, Oxford: Blackwell.

Eagleton, T. (1991) *Ideology: An Introduction*, London: Verso.

Edgley, C. and Brissett, D. (1990) 'Health nazis and the cult of the perfect body: some polemical observations', *Symbolic Interaction* 13(2), 257–79.

Edley, N. and Wetherall, M. (1996) 'Masculinity, power and identity', in M. Mac An Ghaill (ed.) *Understanding Masculinities: Social Relations and Cultural Arenas*, Milton Keynes: Open University Press, 97–113.

Elias, N. (1978) *The Civilizing Process, Volume 1: The History of Manners*, Oxford: Blackwell (orig. 1939).

Elias, N. (1982) *The Civilizing Process, Volume 2: State Formation and Civilization*, Oxford: Blackwell.

Eliot, T.S. (1932) *Selected Essays*, London: Faber & Faber.

Ellis, J. (1982) *Visible Fictions*, London: Routledge (rev. edn, 1992).

Errington, F. and Gewertz, D.B. (1987) *Cultural Alternatives and a Feminist Anthropology: An Analysis of Culturally Constructed Gender Interests in Papua New Guinea*, Cambridge: Cambridge University Press.

Evans, M. (1991) *A Good School: Life at a Girls' Grammar School in the 1950s*, London: The Women's Press.

Evans-Pritchard, E.E. (1939) 'Nuer time-reckoning', *Africa* xii(2), April, 189–216.

Evans-Pritchard, E.E. (1960) *The Nuer*, Oxford: Oxford University Press (orig. 1940).

Ewing, W.A. (1994) *The Body: Photoworks of the Human Form*, London: Thames & Hudson.

Fanon, F. (1968) *Black Skin, White Masks*, London: MacGibbon & Kee.

Featherstone, M. (1990) 'Global culture: an introduction', *Theory, Culture and Society* 7, 1–14.

Featherstone, M. (1991) 'The body in consumer culture', in M. Featherstone, M. Hepworth and B.S. Turner (eds) *The Body: Social Process and Cultural Theory*, London: Sage, 170–96 (orig. 1982).

Featherstone, M. (1996) *Undoing Culture: Globalization, Postmodernism and Identity*, London: Sage.

Featherstone, M. and Burrows, R. (1995) 'Cultures of technological embodiment: an introduction', *Body and Society* 1(3–4), November, 1–19.

Feher, M. (1989) 'Introduction', in M. Feher with R. Naddaff and N. Tazi (eds) *Fragments for a History of the Human Body Vol. 1*, New York: Zone, 11–17.

Felski, R. (1995) *The Gender of Modernity*, Cambridge, MA: Harvard University Press.

Ferraro, G., Trevathan, W. and Levy, J. (1994) *Anthropology: An Applied Perspective*, Minneapolis/St Paul: West.

Fields, B.J. (1990) 'Slavery, race and ideology in the United States of America', *New Left Review* 181, 95–118.

Fine, G.A. and Kleinman, S. (1979) 'Rethinking subculture: an interactionist analysis', *American Journal of Sociology* 85(1), 1–20.

Firth, R. (1972) 'Verbal and bodily rituals of parting and greeting', in J.S. LaFontaine (ed.) *The Interpretation of Ritual*, London: Tavistock.

Fiske, J. (1987) *Television Culture*, London: Methuen.

Fiske, J. (1992) 'The cultural economy of fandom', in L. Lewis (ed.) *The Adoring Audience: Fan Culture and Popular Media*, London: Routledge.

Fiske, J. and Hartley, J. (1978) *Reading Television*, London: Methuen.

Fleming, J. (1992) *Never Give Up*, London: Penguin.

Foucault, M. (1970) *The Order of Things: An Archaeology of the Human Sciences*, London: Tavistock.

Foucault, M. (1973) *Madness and Civilization: A History of Insanity in the Age of Reason*, New York: Vintage.

Foucault, M. (1975) *The Birth of the Clinic: An Archaeology of Medical Perception*, New York: Vintage.

Foucault, M. (1977) *Discipline and Punish: The Birth of the Prison*, trans. Alan Sheridan, London: Allen Lane.

Foucault, M. (1980) *Power/Knowledge: Selected Interviews and Other Writings 1972–1977*, ed. Colin Gordon, Brighton: Harvester.

Foucault, M. (1984a) *The Foucault Reader*, ed. P. Rabinow, Harmondsworth: Penguin (first published 1978).

Foucault, M. (1984b) *The History of Sexuality, Vol 1*, Harmondsworth: Penguin.

Foucault, M. (1986) *The Use of Pleasure*, Harmondsworth: Penguin.

Foucault, M. (1990) *The Care of the Self*, Harmondsworth: Penguin.

Fox-Genovese, E. (1982) 'Placing women's history in history', *New Left Review* 133, May–June.

Frank, A.W. (1990) 'Bringing bodies back in: a decade review', *Theory, Culture and Society* 7(1), February, 131–62.

Frisby, D. (1981) *Sociological Impressionism: A Reassessment of the Social Theory of Georg Simmel*, London: Heinemann.

Frisby, D. (1985) *Fragments of Modernity: Theories of Modernity in the Work of Simmel, Kracauer and Benjamin*, Cambridge: Polity.

Frith, S. (1983) *Sound Effects: Youth, Leisure, and the Politics of Rock*, London: Constable.

Fryer, P. (1984) *Staying Power*, London: Pluto.

Fussell, S.W. (1991) *Muscle: Confessions of an Unlikely Bodybuilder*, New York: Poseidon.

Gadamer, H.-G. (1975) *Truth and Method*, London: Sheed & Ward.

Gaisford, J. (ed.) (1981) *Atlas of Man*, London: Marshall Cavendish.

Gallagher, C. (1985) *The Industrial Reformation in English Fiction*, Chicago: University of Chicago Press.

Gardner, C.B. (1995) *Passing By: Gender and Public Harassment*, Berkeley, CA: University of California Press.

Garfinkel, H. (1967) *Studies in Ethnomethodology*, Englewood Cliffs, NJ: Prentice Hall.

Geertz, C. (1983a) *Local Knowledge: Further Essays in Interpretive Anthropology*, New York: Basic Books.

Geertz, C. (1983b) 'Centers, kings and charisma: reflections on the symbolics of power', in *Local Knowledge: Further Essays in Interpretive Anthropology*, New York: Basic Books, 121–46.

Gelder, K. and Thornton, S. (1997) *The Subcultures Reader*, London: Routledge.

Gervais, D. (1993) *Literary Englands*, Cambridge: Cambridge University Press.

Gibson, W. (1986) *Neuromancer*, London: HarperCollins.

Gibson, W. (1993) *Burning Chrome*, London: HarperCollins.

Giddens, A. (1984) *The Constitution of Society*, Cambridge: Polity.

Giddens, A. (1985) *The Nation-State and Violence*, Cambridge: Polity.

Giddens, A. (1989) *Sociology*, Cambridge: Polity.

Giddens, A. (1990) *The Consequences of Modernity*, Cambridge: Polity.

Giddens, A. (1991) *Modernity and Self-identity: Self and Society in the Late-modern Age*, Cambridge: Polity.

Giddens, A. (1993) *Sociology*, 2nd edn, Cambridge: Polity.

Gilroy, P. (1987) *'There Ain't No Black in the Union Jack': The Cultural Politics of Race and Nation*, London: Hutchinson.

Gilroy, P. (1992) 'Cultural studies and ethnic absolutism', in L. Grossberg, C. Nelson and P. Treicher (eds) *Cultural Studies*, London: Routledge, 187–98.

Gilroy, P. (1993a) *Small Acts: Thoughts on the Politics of Black Cultures*, London: Serpent's Tail.

Gilroy, P. (1993b) *The Black Atlantic: Modernity and Double Consciousness*, London: Verso.

Gilroy, P. (1995) 'Sounds authentic: black music, authenticity and the challenge of a *changing* same', in S. Lemelle and R.D.G. Kelley (eds) *Imagining Home: Class, Culture and Nationalism in the African Diaspora*, London: Verso, 93–118.

Glaser, B. and Strauss, A. (1971) *Status Passage*, London: Routledge & Kegan Paul.

Glasgow University Media Group (1976) *Bad News*, London: Routledge & Kegan Paul.

Glasgow University Media Group (1980) *More Bad News*, London: Routledge & Kegan Paul.

Glassner, B. (1990) 'Fit for postmodern selfhood', in H. Becker and M. McCall (eds) *Symbolic Interaction and Cultural Studies*, Chicago and London: University of Chicago Press, 215–43.

Glyn, A. and Sutcliffe, B. (1992) 'Global but leaderless? The new capitalist order', *Socialist Register*, London: Merlin Press, 79–91.

Godlewska, A. (1995) 'Map, text and image. The mentality of enlightened conquerors: a new look at the *Description de l'Egypte'*, *Transactions of the Institute of British Geographers* 20, 5–28.

Goffman, E. (1963a) *Behavior in Public Places: Notes on the Social Organization of Gatherings*, New York: Free Press.

Goffman, E. (1963b) *Stigma: Notes on the Management of Spoiled Identity*, Englewood Cliffs, NJ: Prentice Hall.

Goffman, E. (1967) *Interaction Ritual*, Chicago: Aldine.

Goffman, E. (1971) *Relations in Public: Microstudies of the Public Order*, London: Allen Lane.

Goffman, E. (1977) 'The arrangement between the sexes', *Theory and Society* 4, 301–32.

Goffman, E. (1979) *Gender Advertisements*, Basingstoke and London: Macmillan.

Goffman, E. (1983) 'The interaction order', *American Sociological Review* 48, 1–17.

Gorham, D. (1978) 'The "Maiden Tribute of Modern Babylon" re-examined: child prostitution and the idea of childhood in late-Victorian England', *Victorian Studies* 21(3), Spring.

Gottdeiner, M. (1995) *Postmodern Semiotics*, Oxford: Blackwell.

Gramsci, A. (1971) *Selections from the Prison Notebooks*, London: Lawrence & Wishart.

Gramsci, A. (1985) *Selections from Cultural Writings*, London: Lawrence & Wishart.

Gray, C.H., Figueroa-Sarriera, H.J. and Mentor, S. (eds) (1995) *The Cyborg Handbook*, London: Routledge.

Greenblatt, S. (1988) *Shakespearean Negotiations*, Oxford: Clarendon.

Greenblatt, S. (1989) 'Cultural poetics', in A.H. Veeser (ed.) *The New Historicism*, London: Routledge.

Gregory, D. (1994) *Geographical Imaginations*, Oxford: Blackwell.

Gregory, D. (1995) 'Between the book and the lamp: imaginative geographies of Egypt, 1849–50', *Transactions of the Institute of British Geographers* 20, 29–57.

Grimshaw, A. (ed.) (1992) *The C.L.R. James Reader*, Oxford: Blackwell.

Grossberg, L. (1992) 'Is there a fan in the house? The affective sensibility of fandom', in L. Lewis (ed.) *The Adoring Audience: Fan Culture and Popular Media*, London: Routledge, 50–65.

Grossberg, L. and Nelson, C. (eds) (1988) *Marxism and the Interpretation of Culture*, Basingstoke: Macmillan.

Grossberg, L., Nelson, C. and Treicher, P. (eds) (1992) *Cultural Studies*, London: Routledge, 187–98.

Gruffudd, P. (1995) 'Remaking Wales: nation-building and the geographical imagination, 1925–50', *Political Geography* 14, 219–39.

Guthrie, S.R. and Castelnuovo, S. (1992) 'Elite women bodybuilders: models of resistance or compliance?', *Play & Culture* 5, 401–8.

Habermas, J. (1987) *The Philosophical Discourse of Modernity*, Cambridge, MA: MIT Press.

Halberstam, J. and Livingston, I. (eds) (1995) *Posthuman Bodies*, Bloomington and Indianapolis: Indiana University Press.

Halfacree, K. (1996) 'Out of place in the countryside: travellers and the "rural idyll"', *Antipode* 28, 42–72.

Hall, S. (1980) 'Encoding/decoding' in S. Hall, D. Hobson, A. Lowe and P. Willis (eds) *Culture, Media, Language: Working Papers in Cultural Studies, 1972–79*, London: Hutchinson.

Hall, S. (1991) 'The local and the global: globalization and ethnicity', in A. King (ed.) *Culture, Globalisation and the World System*, London: Macmillan, 19–39.

Hall, S. (1992) 'The question of cultural identity', in S. Hall, D. Held and T. McGrew (eds) *Modernity and its Futures*, Cambridge: Polity Press in association with Blackwell Publishers and The Open University, 273–325.

Hall, S. (1996) 'Introduction: who needs "identity"', in S. Hall and P. Du Gay (eds) *Questions of Cultural Identity*, London: Sage.

Hall, S., Critcher, C., Jefferson, T., Clarke, J. and Roberts, B. (1978) *Policing the Crisis: Mugging, the State and Law and Order*, London: Macmillan.

Hall, S. and du Gay, P. (eds) (1996) *Questions of Cultural Identity*, London: Sage.

Hall, S. and Jefferson, T. (eds) (1976) *Resistance through Rituals: Youth Subcultures in Post-war Britain*, London: Hutchinson.

Haraway, D. (1989) *Primate Visions: Gender, Race, and Nature in the World of Modern Science*, London: Routledge.

Haraway, D. (1991) *Simians, Cyborgs and Women: The Reinvention of Nature*, London: Free Association Books.

Haraway, D. (1997) *Modest_Witness@Second_Millenium. FemaleMan©_Meets_Oncomouse^{TM}: Feminism and Technoscience*, New York and London: Routledge.

Harding, S. (1991) *Whose Science? Whose Knowledge? Thinking from Women's Lives*, Milton Keynes: Open University Press.

Hargreaves, J. (1986) *Sport, Power and Culture*, Cambridge: Polity.

Harrington, C. Lee and Bielby, D.D. (1995) *Soap Fans: Pursuing Pleasure and Making Meaning in Everyday Life*, Philadelphia: Temple University Press.

Hart, N. (1976) *When Marriage Ends: A Study in Status Passage*, London: Tavistock.

Harvey, D. (1982) *The Limits to Capital*, Oxford: Basil Blackwell.

Harvey, D. (1985a) 'Monument and myth: the building of the Basilica of the Sacred Heart', in *Consciousness and the Urban Experience*, Oxford: Blackwell, 221–49.

Harvey, D. (1985b) 'Paris, 1850–1870', in *Consciousness and the Urban Experience*, Oxford: Blackwell, 63–220.

Harvey, D. (1988) *The Urban Experience*, Oxford: Basil Blackwell.

Harvey, D. (1990) *The Condition of Postmodernity*, Oxford: Blackwell.

Hawkes, Terence (1977) *Structuralism and Semiotics*, London: Methuen; rpt (1991), London: Routledge.

Hawkins, H. (1990) *Classics and Trash: Tradition and Taboos in High Literature and Popular Modern Genres*, Hemel Hempstead: Harvester Wheatsheaf.

Hayles, N.K. (1992) 'The materiality of informatics', *Configurations* 1, 147–70.

Hearn, J. (1996) 'Is masculinity dead? A critique of the concept of masculinity/masculinities', in M. Mac An Ghaill (ed.) *Understanding Masculinities: Social Relations and Cultural Arenas*, Milton Keynes: Open University Press, 202–17.

Hebdige, D. (1974) 'Aspects of style in the Deviant Subcultures of the 1960s' Unpublished MA Thesis, CCCS, Birmingham University. Available as CCCS Stenciled Papers, 20, 21, 24 and 25.

Hebdige, D. (1979) *Subculture: The Meaning of Style*, London: Methuen.

Hebdige, D. (1987) *Cut 'n' Mix: Culture, Identity and Caribbean Music*, London: Methuen.

Hebdige, D. (1988) 'Hiding in the light: Youth surveillance and display', in D. Hebdige, *Hiding in the Light: On Images and Things*, London: Comedia, publ. by Routledge.

Heffernan, M.J. (1991) 'The desert in French orientalist painting during the nineteenth century', *Landscape Research* 16, 37–42.

Heinemann, M. (1985) 'How Brecht read Shakespeare', in J. Dollimore and A. Sinfield (eds) *Political Shakespeare*, Manchester: Manchester University Press.

Held, D. (1980) *Introduction to Critical Theory*, London: Hutchinson.

Hepworth, M. and Featherstone, M. (1982) *Surviving Middle Age*, Oxford: Blackwell.

Hickerson, N.P. 'Linguistic anthropology' (1980) in Ferraro *et al.* (1994) *Anthropology: An Applied Perspective*, Minneapolis/St Paul: West.

Hill, J. (1986) *Sex, Class and Realism: British Cinema 1956–1963*, London: BFI.

Hobsbawm, E. (1994) *Age of Extremes: The Short Twentieth Century*, London: Michael Joseph.

Hobsbawm, E. (1996) 'Identity politics and the left', *New Left Review* 217, 38–47.

Hochschild, A. (1983) *The Managed Heart: Commercialization of Human Feeling*, Berkeley, CA: University of California Press.

Hoggart, R. (1958) *The Uses of Literacy*, Harmondsworth: Penguin (orig. 1957).

Hoggart, R. (1988) *A Local Habitation*, London: Chatto & Windus.

Hoggart, R. (1990) *A Sort of Clowning*, London: Chatto & Windus.

Hoggart, R. (1992) *An Imagined Life*, London: Chatto & Windus.

Hoggett, P. and Bishop, J. (1986) *Organizing Around Enthusiasms: Mutual Aid in Leisure*, London: Comedia.

Hollands, R.G. (1995) *Friday Night, Saturday Night: Youth Cultural Identification in the Post-industrial City*, Newcastle Upon Tyne: Department of Social Policy, University of Newcastle.

Hollis, M. and Lukes, S. (1982) 'Introduction' to M. Hollis and J. Lukes (eds) *Rationality and Relativism*, Oxford: Blackwell.

hooks, bell (1991) *Yearning: Race, Gender and Cultural Politics*, London: Turnaround.

Hornby, N. (1994) *Fever Pitch*, London: Gollancz.

Hornby, N. (1995) *High Fidelity*, London: Gollancz.

Inglis, Fred (1993) *Cultural Studies*, Oxford: Blackwell.

Jackson, P. (1980) 'A plea for cultural geography', *Area* 12, 110–13.

Jackson, P. (1989) *Maps of Meaning: An Introduction to Cultural Geography*, London: Unwin Hyman.

James, C.L.R. (1980) *The Black Jacobins*, London: Allison & Busby (orig. 1938).

James, C.L.R. (1984) *Selected Writings*, London: Allison & Busby.

Jameson, F. (1981) *The Political Unconscious: Narrative as Socially Symbolic Act*, London: Methuen.

Jameson, F. (1982) 'Progress versus utopia; or, can we imagine the future?', *Science Fiction Studies* 9, (2), July 147–58.

Jameson, F. (1991) *Postmodernism, or, the Cultural Logic of Late Capitalism*, London: Verso.

Jaquette, J. (1994) *The Women's Movement in Latin America: Participation and Democracy*, Oxford: Westview.

Jay, M. (1974) The Dialectical Imagination: *A History of the Frankfurt School and the Institute of Social Research 1923–1950*, London: Heinemann.

Jeater, D. (1992) 'Roast beef and reggae music: the passing of whiteness', *New Formations* (18), 107–121.

Jencks, C. (1989) *What is Postmodernism?*, London: Academy.

Jenkins, H. (1992) *Textual Poachers: Television Fans and Participatory Culture*, New York: Routledge.

Jenkins, R. (1994) *Pierre Bourdieu*, London: Routledge.

Jenkins, T. (1994) 'Fieldwork and the perception of everyday life', *Man* 29(2), 433–55.

Jenks, C. (1993) *Culture*, London: Routledge.

Jenks, C. (1995) 'Watching your step: the history and practice of the *flâneur*', in C. Jenks (ed.) *Visual Culture*, London: Routledge, 142–60.

Jenks, C. (ed.) (1995) *Visual Culture*, London: Routledge.

Jenson, J. (1992) 'Fandom as pathology: the consequences of characterization', in L. Lewis (ed.) *The Adoring Audience: Fan Culture and Popular Media*, London: Routledge, 9–29.

Johnson, N.C. (1995) 'The renaissance of nationalism', in R.J. Johnston, P.J. Taylor and M.J. Watts (eds) *Geographies of Global Change: Remapping the World in the Late Twentieth Century*, Oxford: Blackwell, 97–110.

Johnson, R. (1986) 'What is cultural studies anyway?', *Social Text* 6, 38–80.

Johnston, R.J., Gregory, D. and Smith, D.M. (eds) (1994) *The Dictionary of Human Geography*, 3rd edn, Oxford: Blackwell.

Joll, J. (1977) *Gramsci*, London: Fontana.

Jones, S. (1988) *Black Culture, White Youth: The Reggae Tradition from JA to UK*, Basingstoke: Macmillan.

Jordan, G. and Weedon, C. (1994) *Cultural Politics: Class, Gender, Race and the Postmodern World*, Oxford: Blackwell.

Kabbani, R. (1986) *Europe's Myths of Orient: Devise and Rule*, London: Macmillan.

Kaite, B. (1995) *Pornography and Difference*, Bloomington, IN: Indiana University Press.

Kamenka, E. (ed.) *The Portable Karl Marx*, Harmondsworth: Penguin.

Kaplan, C. (1983) 'Wild nights: pleasure/sexuality/feminism', in Tony Bennett *et al.* (eds) *Formations of Pleasure*, London: RKP, 15–35.

Kaye, H.J. and McClelland, K. (eds) (1990) *E.P. Thompson: Critical Perspectives*, Oxford: Polity Press.

Keat, R. and Urry, J. (1975) *Social Theory as Science*, London: Routledge & Kegan Paul.

Keith, M. (1990) 'Knowing your place: the imagined geographies of racial subordination', in C. Philo (ed.) *New Words, New Worlds: Reconceptualising Social and Cultural Geography*, Lampeter: SDUC, 178–92.

Keith, M. and Pile, S. (eds) (1993) *Place and the Politics of Identity*, London: Routledge.

Kern, S. (1983) *The Culture of Time and Space: 1880–1918*, London: Harvard.

Kinsman, P. (1995) 'Landscape, race and national identity: the photography of Ingrid Pollard', *Area* 27, 300–10.

Klein, A. (1994) *Little Big Men: Bodybuilding Subculture and Gender Construction*, Albany, NY: State University of New York Press.

Kristeva, J. (1982) *Powers of Horror: An Essay on Abjection*, New York: Columbia UP.

Kristeva, J. (1986) *The Kristeva Reader*, ed. Toril Moi, Oxford: Blackwell.

Kritzman, L.D. (ed.) (1988) *Michel Foucault: Politics, Philosophy, Culture. Interviews and Other Writings 1977–1984*, London: Routledge.

Kroker, A. and Kroker, M. (1988) *Body Invaders: Sexuality and the Postmodern Condition*, Basingstoke: Macmillan.

Krutnik, F. (1991) *In a Lonely Street: Film Noir, Genre, Masculinity*, London and New York: Routledge.

Labov, W. (1966) *The Social Stratification of English in New York City*, Washington DC: Georgetown University Press.

Labov, W. (1972a) *Sociolinguistic Patterns*, Philadelphia: University of Pennsylvania Press.

Labov, W. (1972b) 'The logic of nonstandard English', in *Language in the Inner City: Studies in the Black English Vernacular*, Oxford: Basil Blackwell, 201–40.

Labov, W. (1973) 'The logic of non-standard English', in N. Keddie (ed.) *Tinker, Tailor . . . The Myth of Cultural Deprivation*, Harmondsworth: Penguin.

Lakoff, R. (1975) *Language and Woman's Place*, New York: Harper & Row.

Landsberg, A. (1995) 'Prosthetic memory: *Total Recall* and *Blade Runner*', *Body and Society* 1(3–4), November, 175–89.

Larrain, J. (1979) *The Concept of Ideology*, London: Hutchinson.

Lasch, C. (1980) *The Culture of Narcissism*, London: Abacus.

Lash, S. and Urry, J. (1987) *The End of Organised Capitalism*, Cambridge: Polity.

Lash, S. and Urry, J. (1994) *Economies of Signs and Space*, London: Sage.

Latour, B. (1993) *We Have Never Been Modern*, Hemel Hempstead: Harvester Wheatsheaf.

Laver, J. (1946) *Letter to a Girl on the Future of Clothes*, London: Home and Van Thal.

Laver, J. (1950) *Dress: How and Why Fashions in Men's and Women's Clothes Have Changed During the Past Two Hundred Years*, London: Murray.

Leavis, F.R. (1962) *The Common Pursuit*, Harmondsworth: Penguin.

Leach, E. (1970) *Levi-Strauss*, London: Fontana.

Leach, S. (1975) 'Political ritual and social integration'. *Sociology* 9 (2), May, 289–308.

Leech, G., Deuchar, M. *et al.* (1982) *English Grammar for Today*, in B.V. Street (ed.) (1993) *Literacy in Theory and Practice*, Cambridge: Cambridge University Press.

Lefebvre, H. (1991) *The Production of Space*, Oxford: Blackwell.

Lefort, C. (1986) *The Political Forms of Modern Society: Bureaucracy, Democracy, Totalitarianism*, Cambridge: Polity.

Leighly, J. (1963) *Land and Life: A Selection from the Writings of Carl Ortwin Sauer*, Berkeley, CA: University of California.

Leslie, D.A. (1993) 'Femininity, post-Fordism, and the new traditionalism', *Environment and Planning D: Society and Space* 11, 689–708.

Lévi-Strauss, C. (1966) *The Savage Mind*, London: Weidenfeld & Nicolson.

Levitas, R. (1990) *The Concept of Utopia*, London: Philip Allan.

Lewis, L. (ed.) (1992) *The Adoring Audience: Fan Culture and Popular Media*, London: Routledge.

Lewis, O. (1961) *The Children of Sanchez*, New York: Random House.

Lewis, O. (1966) *La Vida*, New York: Random House.

Lewis, R. (1996) *Gendering Orientalism: Race, Femininity and Representation*, London: Routledge.

Ley, D. (1982) 'Rediscovering man's place', *Transactions of the Institute of British Geographers* 7, 248–53.

Linebaugh, P. (1982) 'All the Atlantic mountains shook', *Labour/Le Travailleur* 10, 87–121.

Linebaugh, P. and Rediker, M. (1990) 'The many-headed Hydra: sailors, slaves and the Atlantic working class in the eighteenth century', *Journal of Historical Sociology* 3, 225–52.

Linz, D. and Malamuth, N. (1993) *Pornography*, Newbury Park, CA, and London: Sage.

Lister, M. (1997) 'Photography in the age of electronic imaging', in L. Wells (ed.) *Photography: A Critical Introduction*, London: Routledge.

Lister, R. (ed.) (1996) *Charles Murray and the Underclass: The Developing Debate*, London: Institute for Economic Affairs Health and Welfare Unit/The Sunday Times.

Livingstone, D. (1995) 'The polity of nature: representation, virtue, strategy', *Ecumene* 2, 353–77.

Lodge, D. (1989) *Nice Work*, London: Penguin.

Lofland, L.H. (1973) *A World of Strangers: Order and Action in Urban Public Space*, New York: Basic.

Longhurst, B. (1995) *Popular Music and Society*, Cambridge: Polity.

Lovell, T. (1980) *Pictures of Reality: Aesthetics, Politics and Pleasure*, London: BFI.

Lowenthal, L. (1961) 'The idols of production and the idols of consumption', in *Literature, Popular Culture and Society*, Englewood Cliffs, NJ: Prentice Hall.

Luhmann, N. (1976) 'The future cannot begin: temporal structures in modern society', *Social Research* 43, 130–52.

Lukes, S. (1974) *Power: A Radical View*, Basingstoke: Macmillan.

Lukes, S. (1975) 'Political ritual and social integration', *Sociology* 9(2), May, 289–308.

Lukes, S. (ed.) (1986) *Power*, Oxford: Blackwell.

Lurie, A. (1992) *The Language of Clothes*, London: Bloomsbury.

Lury, C. (1993) *Cultural Rights: Technology, Legality and Personality*, London: Routledge.

Lynch, K. (1960) *The Image of the City*, Cambridge, MA: MIT Press.

MacCabe, C. (1981) 'Realism and the cinema: notes on some Brechtian theses', in T. Bennett, Boyd-Bowman, S., Mercer, C. and Woollacott, J. (eds) *Popular Television and Film*, London: BFI in association with The Open University Press, 216–35.

MacDonald, K.M. (1989) 'Building respectability', *Sociology* 23, 55–80.

Mansfield, A. and McGinn, B. (1993) 'Pumping irony: the muscular and the feminine', in S. Scott and D. Morgan (eds) *Body Matters: Essays on the Sociology of the Body*, London: Falmer, 49–68.

Martin, G. (1989) *Journeys Through the Labyrinth*, London: Verso.

Marx, K. (1951) 'The Eighteenth Brumaire of Louis Bonaparte' in Marx–Engels *Selected Works*, 1, London: Lawrence & Wishart.

Marx, K. and Engels, F. (1968) *The German Ideology*, Moscow: Progress (orig. 1846).

Marx, K. and Engels, F. (1967) *The Communist Manifesto*, Harmondsworth: Penguin (orig. 1848).

Massey, D. (1984) *Spatial Divisions of Labour: Social Structures and the Geography of Production*, London: Macmillan.

Massey, D. (1991) 'A global sense of place', *Marxism Today* June, 24–9.

Matless, D. (1995a) 'Culture run riot? Work in social and cultural geography, 1994', *Progress in Human Geography*, 19, 395–403.

Matless, D. (1995b) ' "The art of right living": landscape and citizenship, 1918–39', in S. Pile and N. Thrift (eds) *Mapping the Subject: Geographies of Cultural Transformation*, London: Routledge, 93–122.

Matless, D. (1996) 'New material? Work in social and cultural geography, 1995', *Progress in Human Geography* 20, 379–91.

Matza, D. (1964) *Delinquency and Drift*, New York: Wiley.

Mauss, M. (1979) 'Body techniques', in *Sociology and Psychology: Essays*, trans. B. Brewster, London: Routledge & Kegan Paul, 95–123.

May, J. (1996) 'Globalization and the politics of place: place and identity in an inner city London neighbourhood', *Transactions of the Institute of British Geographers* 21, 194–215.

Mayhew, H. (1968) *London Labour and the London Poor, Volumes 1–4*, New York and London: Dover (orig. 1851–2, 1862).

Mazrui, A.A. (1989) 'Moral dilemmas of the Satanic Verses', *The Black Scholar* 2(2), 19–32.

McCracken, S. (1997) 'Cyborg fictions: the cultural logic of posthumanism', *Socialist Register*, London: Merlin Press, 288–301.

McCrone, D. (1992) *Understanding Scotland: The Sociology of a Stateless Nation*, London: Routledge.

McDowell, L. (1994) 'The transformation of cultural geography', in D. Gregory, R. Martin and G. Smith (eds) *Human Geography: Society, Space and Social Science*, London: Macmillan.

McEwan, C. (1996) 'Paradise or pandemonium? West African landscapes in the travel accounts of Victorian women', *Journal of Historical Geography* 22, 68–83.

McLellan, D. (1975) *Marx*, London: Fontana.

McLellan, D. (ed.) (1977) *Karl Marx: Selected Writings*, Oxford: Oxford University Press.

McRobbie, A. (1978) 'Working class girls and the culture of femininity', in Women's Studies Group, Centre for Contemporary Cultural Studies, University of Birmingham, *Women Take Issue: Aspects of Women's Subordination*, London: Hutchinson, 96–108.

McRobbie, A. (1980) 'Settling accounts with subcultures: a feminist critique', *Screen Education* 34, 37–49.

McRobbie, A. (1984) 'Dance and social fantasy', in A. McRobbie and M. Nava (eds), *Gender and Generation*, Basingstoke: Mamillan, 130–61.

McRobbie, A. (ed.) (1989) *Zoot Suits and Second-hand Dresses: An Anthology of Fashion and Music*, Basingstoke: Macmillan.

McRobbie, A. (1991) '*Jackie* and *Just Seventeen*: girls' comics and magazines in the 1980s', in *Feminism and Youth Culture: From 'Jackie' to 'Just Seventeen'*, Basingstoke: Macmillan, 135–88.

McRobbie, A. (1991) *Feminism and Youth Culture: From 'Jackie' to 'Just Seventeen'*, Basingstoke: Macmillan.

McRobbie, A. (1993) 'Shut up and dance: youth culture and changing modes of femininity', *Cultural Studies* 7, 406–26.

McRobbie, A. (1994) 'The moral panic in the age of postmodern mass media', in *Postmodernism and Popular Culture*, London: Routledge, 198–219.

McRobbie, A. (1994) *Postmodernism and Popular Culture*, London: Routledge.

McRobbie, A. and Garber, J. (1976) 'Girls and subcultures: an exploration', in S. Hall and T. Jefferson (eds) *Resistance through Rituals: Youth Subcultures in Post-war Britain*, London: Hutchinson, 209–22.

Mead, G.H. (1934) *Mind, Self and Society: From the Standpoint of a Social Behaviorist*, Chicago: University of Chicago Press.

Mennell, S. (1989) *Norbert Elias: Civilization and the Human Self-Image*, Oxford: Blackwell.
Mennell, S. (1991) 'On the civilizing of appetite', in M. Featherstone, M. Hepworth and B.S. Turner (eds) *The Body: Social Process and Cultural Theory*, London: Sage (orig. 1987).

Meyer, A. (1960) *Caste and Kinship in Central India: A Village and Its Region*, London: Routledge & Kegan Paul.

Middleton, R. (1990) *Studying Popular Music*, Milton Keynes: Open University Press.

Miles, R. (1989) *Racism*, London: Routledge.

Milgram, S. (1970) 'The experience of living in cities', *Science* 167, 1461–8.

Miller, W.D. (1958) 'Lower class culture as a generating milieu of gang delinquency', *Journal of Social Issues* 15, 5–19.

Miner, H. (1956) 'Body ritual among the Nacirema', *The American Anthropologist* 58: 503–7.

Mitchell, D. (1995) 'There's no such thing as culture: towards a reconceptualisation of the idea of culture in geography', *Transactions of the Institute of British Geographers* 20, 102–16. See also the responses in *Transactions of the Institute of British Geographers* (1996), 21, 572–82.

Mitchell, J. (1984) *Women: The Longest Revolution, Essays in Feminism, Literature and Psychoanalysis*, London: Virago.

Mitchell, T. (1989) 'The world-as-exhibition', *Comparative Studies in Society and History* 31, 217–36.

Monaghan, L. (1997) 'Body-building ethnophysiology', paper presented to the Body Modification conference, Nottingham Trent University, June.

Moore, H. (1993) 'The differences within and the differences between', in T. del Valle, *Gendered Anthropology*, London and New York: Routledge/European Association of Social Anthropologists.

Moorhouse, H.F. (1991) *Driving Ambitions: An Analysis of the American Hotrod Enthusiasm*, Manchester: Manchester University Press.

Morgan, D. (1993) 'You too can have a body like mine: reflections on the male body and masculinities', in S. Scott and D. Morgan (eds) *Body Matters: Essays on the Sociology of the Body*, London: Falmer, 69–88.

Morgan, G. (1993) 'Frustrated development: local culture and politics in London's Docklands', *Environment and Planning D: Society and Space* 11, 523–41.

Morley, D. (1980) *The 'Nationwide' Audience*, London: British Film Institute.

Morley, D. (1986) *Family Television: Culture, Power and Domestic Leisure*, London: Comedia.

Morley, D. (1992) *Television, Audiences and Cultural Studies*, London: Routledge.

Morley, D. and Chen, K.-H. (eds) (1996) *Stuart Hall: Critical Dialogues in Cultural Studies*, London: Routledge.

Morley, D. and Robins, K. (1992) 'Techno-orientalism: futures, phobias and foreigners', *New Formations* 16, 136–56.

Morris, M.S. (1996) '"Tha'lt be like a blush-rose when tha' grows up, my little lass": English cultural and gendered identity in *The Secret Garden*', *Environment and Planning D: Society and Space* 14, 59–78.

Morris, W. (1986) *News from Nowhere in Three Works by William Morris*, London: Lawrence & Wishart (orig. 1891).

Morton, A.L. (1965) *The People's History of England*, London: Lawrence & Wishart.

Muggleton, D. (1997) 'The post-subculturalist', in S. Redhead with D. Wynne and J. O'Connor (eds) *The Clubcultures Reader: Readings in Popular Cultural Studies*, Oxford: Blackwell, 185–203.

Mulvey, L. (1981) 'Visual pleasure and narrative cinema', in T. Bennett *et al.* (eds) *Popular Television and Film*, London: British Film Institute, 206–15.

Munns, J. and Rajan, G. (eds) (1995) *A Cultural Studies Reader: History, Theory, Practice*, London and New York: Longman.

Myers, J. (1992) 'Nonmainstream body modification: genital piercing, branding, burning and cutting', *Journal of Contemporary Ethnography* 21(3), October, 267–306.

Myers, K. (1982) 'Towards a feminist erotica', *Camerawork* 24, March, 14–16, 19.

Nash, C. (1993) 'Remapping and renaming: new cartographies of identity, gender and landscape in Ireland', *Feminist Review* 44, 39–57.

Nash, C. (1996) 'Men again: Irish masculinity, nature and nationhood in the early twentieth century', *Ecumene* 3, 427–53.

Nicholson, L. (1995) 'Interpreting gender', in L. Nicholson and S. Seidman (eds) *Social Postmodernism*, Cambridge: Cambridge University Press.

Nixon, N. (1992) 'Cyberpunk: preparing the ground for revolution or keeping the boys satisfied?', *Science Fiction Studies* 19, 219–35.

Nochlin, L. (1991a) 'The imaginary Orient', in L. Nochlin (ed.) *The Politics of Vision: Essays on Nineteenth-Century Art and Society*, London: Thames & Hudson.

Nochlin, L. (1991b) *The Politics of Vision: Essays on Nineteenth-Century Art and Society*, London: Thames & Hudson.

Novack, C. (1993) 'Ballet, gender and cultural power', in H. Thomas (ed.) *Dance, Gender and Culture*, Basingstoke and London: Macmillan, 34–48.

Okely, J. (1983) *The Traveller-Gypsies*, Cambridge: Cambridge University Press.

Ó Tuathail, G. and Luke, T.W. (1994) 'Present at the (dis)integration: deterritorialisation and reterritorialisation in the new Wor(l)d order', *Annals of the Association of American Geographers* 84(3), 381–98.

Ó Tuathail, G. (1996) *Critical Geopolitics: The Politics of Writing Global Space*, London: Routledge.

Ó Tuathail, G. and Dalby, S. (1994) 'Critical geopolitics: unfolding spaces for thought in geography and global politics', *Environment and Planning D: Society and Space* 12(5), 513–14.

Ohrn, K. (1980) *Dorothea Lange and the Documentary Tradition*, Baton Rouge: Louisiana State University Press.

Ortner, S. (1974) 'Is female to male as nature is to culture?', in M. Rosaldo and L. Lamphere (eds) *Woman, Culture and Society*, Stanford: Stanford University Press.

Osborne, B.S. (1988) 'The iconography of nationhood in Canadian art', in D. Cosgrove and S. Daniels (eds) *The Iconography of Landscape*, Cambridge: Cambridge University Press, 162–78.

Osbourne, T. (1994) 'Bureaucracy as a vocation: governmentality and administration in nineteenth-century Britain', *Journal of Historical Sociology* 7(13), 289–313.

Painter, J. (1995) *Politics, Geography and 'Political Geography': A Critical Perspective*, London: Edward Arnold.

Parker, H. (1974) *View from the Boys: A Sociology of Down-town Adolescents*, London: David and Charles.

Parker, R. and Pollock, G. (1981) *Old Mistresses: Women, Art and Ideology*, London: Pandora.

Parker, R. and Pollock, G. (eds) (1987) *Framing Feminism: Art and the Women's Movement 1970–85*, London: Pandora.

Parkin, D. (1991) *Language is the Essence of Culture*, Group for Debates in Anthropological Theory, Manchester: Department of Social Anthropology, University of Manchester.

Parkin, F. (1973) *Class, Inequality and Political Order*, London: Paladin.

Parkin, F. (1982) *Max Weber*, Chichester: Ellis Horwood.

Parsons, T. (1952) *The Social System*, London: Routledge & Kegan Paul.

Passingham, R.E. (1982) *The Human Primate*, Oxford and San Francisco: W.H. Freeman.

Pateman, C. (1989) *The Disorder of Women: Democracy, Feminism and Political Theory*, Cambridge: Polity.

Patrick, J. (1973) *A Glasgow Gang Observed*, London: Eyre-Methuen.

Pearson, J. (1973) *The Profession of Violence*, London: Panther.

Pearson, R. (1992) 'Gender matters in development', in T. Allen and A. Thomas (eds) *Poverty and Development in the 1990s*, Oxford: OUP, 294.

Penley, C. (1992) 'Feminism, psychoanalysis, and the study of popular culture', in L. Grossberg, C. Nelson and P. Treichler (eds) *Cultural Studies*, London: Routledge.

Perraton, J., Goldblatt, D. and McGrew, A. (1997) 'The globalisation of economic activity', *New Political Economy* 2, 257–77.

Piercy, M. (1992) *Body of Glass*, Harmondsworth: Penguin (published in the USA by A.A. Knopf under the title *He, She and It*, 1991).

Polhemus, Ted (ed.) (1978) *Social Aspects of the Human Body*, Harmondsworth: Penguin.

Postman, N. (1986) *Amusing Ourselves to Death: Public Discourse in the Age of Showbusiness*, London: Heinemann.

Pred, A. (1984) 'Place as historically contingent process: structuration theory and the time geography of becoming places', *Annals of the Association of American Geographers* 74, 79–97.

Pred, A. (1989) 'The locally spoken word and local struggles', *Environment and Planning D: Society and Space* 7, 211–34.

Pred, A. (1990a) *Lost Words and Lost Worlds: Modernity and the Language of Everyday Life in Late Nineteenth-Century Stockholm*, Cambridge: Cambridge University Press.

Pred, A. (1990b) 'In other wor(l)ds: fragmented and integrated observations on gendered languages, gendered spaces and local transformation', *Antipode* 22, 33–52.

Pred, A. (1992a) 'Capitalisms, crises and cultures II: notes on local transformation and everyday cultural struggles', in A. Pred and M.J. Watts (eds) *Reworking Modernity: Capitalisms and Symbolic Dissent*, New Brunswick: Rutgers University Press, 106–17.

Pred, A. (1992b) 'Languages of everyday practice and resistance: Stockholm at the end of the nineteenth century', in A. Pred and M.J. Watts (eds) *Reworking Modernity: Capitalisms and Symbolic Dissent*, New Brunswick: Rutgers University Press, 118–54.

Price, M. and Lewis, M. (1993) 'The reinvention of cultural geography', *Annals of the Association of American Geographers* 83, 1–17. See also the replies and counter-replies in *AAAG* (1993), 83, 515–22.

Prior, L. (1988) 'The architecture of the hospital: a study of spatial organisation and medical knowledge', *British Journal of Sociology* 39, 86–113.

Pryce, K. (1979) *Endless Pressure*, Harmondsworth: Penguin.

Pulgram, E. (1954) 'Phoneme and grapheme', in B. Street (ed.) (1993) *Literacy in Theory and Practice*, Cambridge: Cambridge University Press.

Purvis, T. and Hunt, A. (1993) 'Discourse, ideology, discourse, ideology, discourse, ideology...', *British Journal of Sociology* 44, 473–99.

Rabinow, P. (ed.) (1984) *The Foucault Reader*, Harmondsworth: Penguin.

Radway, J.A. (1987) *Reading the Romance: Women, Patriarchy, and Popular Literature*, London: Verso.

Rao, R. (1938) *Kanthapura* in B. Ashcroft *et al.* (eds) (1989) *The Empire Writes Back: Theory and Practice in Post-colonial Literatures*, London: Routledge.

Redhead, S. (1990) *The End-of-the-Century Party: Youth and Pop towards 2000*, Manchester: Manchester University Press.

Redhead, S. (ed.) (1993) *Rave Off: Politics and Deviance in Contemporary Youth Culture*, Aldershot: Avebury.

Redhead, S. (1995) *Unpopular Cultures: The Birth of Law and Popular Culture*, Manchester: Manchester University Press.

Redhead, S. (1997) *Post-Fandom and the Millennial Blues*, London: Routledge.

Redhead, S. with Wynne, D. and O'Connor, J. (eds) (1997) *The Clubcultures Reader: Readings in Popular Cultural Studies*, Oxford: Blackwell.

Rediker, M. (1987) *Between the Devil and the Deep Blue Sea: Merchant Seamen, Pirates, and the Anglo-American Maritime World, 1700–1750*, Cambridge: Cambridge University Press.

Reed, A. (1987) *The Developing World*, London: Bell & Hyman.

Reisman, D. in collaboration with Denney, R. and Glazier, N. (1953) *The Lonely Crowd*, New Haven, CT: Yale University Press.

Relph, E. (1976) *Place and Placelessness*, London: Pion.

Richards, G.D.Api (1990*) Demons or Resistance: The Early History of Black People in Britain*, Revolutionary Education Development.

Rieff, D. (1992) *Los Angeles: Capital of the Third World*, London: Jonathan Cape.

Rietveld, H. (1993) 'Living the dream', in S. Redhead (ed.) *Rave Off: Politics and Deviance in Contemporary Youth Culture*, Aldershot: Avebury.

Rigby, P. (1985) *Persistent Pastoralists: Nomadic Societies in Transition*, London: Zed.

Robbins, D. (1991) *The Work of Pierre Bourdieu: Recognizing Society*, Milton Keynes: Open University Press.

Roberts, C. (ed.) (1994) *Idle Worship: How Pop Empowers the Weak, Rewards the Faithful and Succours the Needy*, London: HarperCollins.

Roper, M. (1994) *Masculinity and the British Organisation Man Since 1945*, Oxford: Oxford University Press.

Rose, G. (1988) 'Locality, politics and culture: Poplar in the 1920s', *Environment and Planning D: Society and Space* 6, 151–68.

Rose, G. (1993) *Feminism and Geography: The Limits of Geographical Knowledge*, Cambridge: Polity.

Rose, T. (1994) *Black Noise: Rap Music and Black Culture in Contemporary America*, Hanover: Wesleyan University Press, University Press of New England.

Ross, K. (1988) *The Emergence of Social Space: Rimbaud and the Paris Commune*, London: Macmillan.

Ruby, J. (1976) 'In a pic's eye: interpretive strategies for deriving meaning and significance from photographs', *Afterimage* 3(1), 5–7.

Runciman, W.G. (ed.) (1978) *Weber: Selections in Translation*, Cambridge: Cambridge University Press.

Rutter, M. and Madge, N. (1976) *Cycles of Disadvantage*, London: Heinemann.

Sacks, H. (1972) 'Notes on the police assessment of moral character', in D. Sudnow (ed.) *Studies in Social Interaction*, New York: Free Press.

Sacks, H. (1992) 'Lecture 14: The inference-making machine', in *Lectures on Conversation*, vol. 1, ed. G. Jefferson, Oxford: Blackwell, 113–25.

Said, E.W. (1978) *Orientalism*, Harmondsworth: Penguin.

Said, E.W. (1981) *Covering Islam: How the Media and the Experts Determine How We See the Rest of the World*, London: Routledge & Kegan Paul.

Said, E.W. (1993) *Culture and Imperialism*, London: Chatto & Windus.

Said, E.W. (1995) *The Politics of Dispossession*, London: Vintage.

Sapir, E. (1929) 'The status of linguistics as a science', *Language* 5, 207–14, cited in Ferraro, G. (1994) *Cultural Anthropology: An Applied Perspective*, Minneapolis/St Paul: West Publishing Co. 2nd edn.

Sapir, E. (1931) 'Fashion', in E.R.A. Seligman (ed.) *Encyclopaedia of the Social Sciences Volume 6*, New York: Macmillan, 139–44.

Sartre, J-P. (1983) *The Question of Method*, London: Methuen.

Sarup, M. (1996) *Identity, Culture and the Postmodern World*, Edinburgh: Edinburgh University Press.

Sauer, C.O. (1925) 'The morphology of landscape', repr. in J. Leighly (1963) *Land and*

Life: A Selection from the Writings of Carl Ortwin Sauer, Berkeley: University of California, 315–50.

Sauer, C.O. (1941) 'The personality of Mexico', repr. in J. Leighly (1963) *Land and Life: A Selection from the Writings of Carl Ortwin Sauer*, Berkeley: University of California, 104–17.

Savage, M. and Warde, A. (1993) *Urban Sociology, Capitalism and Modernity*, Basingstoke and London: Macmillan.

Savage, M. and Witz, A. (eds) (1992) *Gender and Bureaucracy*, Oxford: Blackwell.

Schama, S. (1995) *Landscape and Memory*, London: HarperCollins.

Schwartz, J.M. (1996) 'The Geography Lesson: photographs and the construction of imaginative geographies', *Journal of Historical Geography* 22, 16–45.

Scott, J.C. (1990) *Domination and the Arts of Resistance: Hidden Transcripts*, New Haven: Yale University Press.

Scott, J.W. (1986) 'Gender: a useful category of historical analysis', *American Historical Review* 91, 1053–1075.

Sedgwick, E.K. (1985) *Between Men*, Baltimore: Johns Hopkins University Press.

Sekula, A. (1975) 'On the invention of photographic meaning', *Artforum* 13, 36–45.

Semple, L. (1988) 'Women and erotica', *Spare Rib* 191, June, 6–10.

Senghor, L. (1993) 'Negritude', in L. Chrisman and P. Williams (eds) *Colonial Discourse and Post-Colonial Theory: A Reader*, Hemel Hempstead: Harvester.

Sennett, R. (1969) 'An introduction', in *Classic Essays on the Culture of Cities*, Englewood Cliffs, NJ: Prentice Hall, 3–19.

Sennett, R. (1977) *The Fall of Public Man*, Cambridge: Cambridge University Press.

Sharratt, B. (1989) 'Communications and image studies: notes after Raymond Williams', *Comparative Criticism* 11, 29–50.

Sherlock, J. (1993) 'Dance and the culture of the body', in S. Scott and D. Morgan (eds) *Body Matters: Essays on the Sociology of the Body*, London: Falmer, 35–48.

Shields, R. (1991) *Places on the Margin: Alternative Geographies of Modernity*, London: Routledge.

Shilling, C. (1993) *The Body and Social Theory*, London: Sage.

Shukman, A. (ed.) (1988) *Bakhtin School Papers*, Oxford: Russian Poetics in Translation.

Shurmer-Smith, P. and Hannam, K. (1994) *Worlds of Desire, Realms of Power: A Cultural Geography*, London: Edward Arnold.

Sidaway, J.D. (1997) 'The (re)making of the Western "geographical tradition": some missing links', *Area* 29, 72–80.

Simmel, G. (1950) *The Sociology of Georg Simmel*, ed. K.H. Wolff, Glencoe: Free Press.

Simmel, G. (1957) 'Fashion', *American Journal of Sociology*, 62(5), 541–58 (orig. 1904).

Simmel, G. (1969) 'Sociology of the senses: visual intereaction', in *Introduction to the Science of Sociology*, ed. R.E. Park and E.W. Burgess, Chicago: University of Chicago Press, 356–61 (orig. 1908).

Simmel, G. (1971) 'The metropolis and mental life' in *Georg Simmel on Individuality and Social Forms*, ed. D.N. Levine, Chicago: University of Chicago Press, 324–39 (orig. 1903).

Simmel, G. (1978) *The Philosophy of Money*, trans. T. Bottomore and D. Frisby, London: Routledge & Kegan Paul (orig. 1900).

Simmel, G. (1994) 'The sociology of the meal', *Food and Foodways* 5(4), 345–50 (orig. 1910).

Sinfield, A. (1994) *Cultural Politics, Queer Reading*, London: Routledge.

Smith, G. (1996) '*Gender Advertisements* revisited: a visual sociology classic?', *Electronic Journal of Sociology* 2(1).

Smith, L.S. (1978) 'Sexist assumptions and female delinquency: an empirical investigation', in C. Smart and B. Smart (eds) *Women, Sexuality and Social Control*, London: Routledge & Kegan Paul, 74–88.

Snead, J.A. (1984) 'Repetition as a figure of Black Culture' in H.L. Gates, Jr. (ed.) *Black Literature and Literary Theory*, London: Methuen.

Snyder, J. (1984) 'Documentary without ontology', *Studies in Visual Communication* 10(1), 78–95.

Snyder, J. and Allen, N.H. (1982 [orig. 1975]), 'Photography, vision and representation', in T. Barrow and S. Armitage, (eds) *Reading into Photography*, Albuquerque: University of New Mexico Press, 61–91 (orig. 1975).

Soja, E.W. (1989) *Postmodern Geographies: The Reassertion of Space in Critical Social Theory*, London: Verso.

Soja, E.W. (1996) *Thirdspace: Journeys to Los Angeles and Other Real-and-Imagined Places*, Oxford: Blackwell.

Sontag, S. (1979) *On Photography*, Harmondsworth: Penguin.

Sontag, S. (ed.) (1982) *A Barthes Reader*, London: Cape.

Sorokin, P.A. and Merton, R.K. (1937) 'Social time: a methodological and functional analysis', *The American Journal of Sociology* xlii(5), March, 615–29.

Spence, J. and Holland, P. (eds) (1991) *Family Snaps: The Meanings of Domestic Photography*, London: Virago.

Spencer, P. (1990) *Anthropology and the Riddle of the Sphinx: Paradoxes of Change in the Life Cycle*, ASA Monograph 28, London: Routledge.

Spender, D. (1982) *Invisible Women: The Schooling Scandal*, London: Writers & Readers.

Spivak, G.C. (1987) *In Other Worlds: Essays in Cultural Politics*, New York and London: Methuen.

Spivak, G.C. (1990) 'Reading The Satanic Verses', *Third Text* 11, Summer, 41–60.

Spivak, G.C. (1993) 'Can the subaltern speak?', in L. Chrisman and P. Williams (eds) *Colonial Discourse and Post-colonial Theory*, Hemel Hempstead: Harvester.

Sprinkler, M. (ed.) (1992) *Edward Said: A Critical Reader*, Cambridge, MA: Blackwell.

Stacey, J. (1994) *Star Gazing: Hollywood Cinema and Female Spectatorship*, London: Routledge.

Stallybrass, P. and White, A. (1986) *The Politics and Poetics of Transgression*, London: Methuen.

Stephens, G. (1992) 'Interracial dialogue in rap music: call-and-response in a multicultural style', *New Formations* 16, 62–79.

Storey, John (1993) *An Introductory Guide to Cultural Theory and Popular Culture*, Hemel Hempstead: Harvester Wheatsheaf.

Stott, W. (1973) *Documentary Expression and Thirties America*, New York: Oxford University Press.

Strathern, M. (1981) 'Culture in a netbag: the manufacture of a subdiscipline in anthropology', *Man(NS)* 16(4) 665–88.

Strathern, M. (1987) 'An awkward relationship: the case of feminism and anthropology', *Signs* 12(2) 277–95.

Strathern, M. (1988) *The Gender of the Gift*, Berkeley, CA: University of California Press, 280–93.

Street, B. (1993) *Literacy in Theory and Practice*, Cambridge: Cambridge University Press.

Tannen, D. (1990) *You Just Don't Understand: Women and Men in Conversation*, New York: Ballantine, 34–5.

Tannen, D. (ed.) (1993) *Gender and Conversational Interaction*, New York and Oxford: Oxford University Press.

Taylor, I. (1991) 'Moral panics, crime and urban policy in Manchester', *Sociology Review* 1(1), 28–32.

Tcherkezoff, S. (1993) 'The illusion of dualism in Samoa. "Brothers-and-sisters" are not "men-and- women"' in T. del Valle (ed.) *Gendered Anthropology*, European Association of Social Anthropologists, London and New York: Routledge.

Telles, J.L. (1986) 'Time, rank and social control', *Sociological Inquiry* 50(2), 171–83.

Theweleit, K. (1987) *Male Fantasies. Volume I: Woman, Floods, Bodies, History*, Cambridge: Polity.

Theweleit, K. (1989) *Male Fantasies, Volume 2. Male Bodies: Psychoanalysing the White Terror*, Minneapolis: University of Minnesota Press (orig. 1978).

Thompson, E.P. (1961) 'The long revolution', *New Left Review* 9, May–June, 24–33.

Thompson, E.P. (1965) 'The Peculiarities of the English' in R. Miliband and J. Saville (eds) *The Socialist Register 1965*, London: Merlin.

Thompson, E.P. (1968) *The Making of the English Working Class*, Harmondsworth: Penguin (orig. 1963).

Thompson, E.P. (1978) *The Poverty of Theory and Other Essays*, London: Merlin.

Thompson, E.P. (1991) *Customs in Common*, London: Merlin.

Thompson, J.B. (1984) *Studies in the Theory of Ideology*, Cambridge: Polity.

Thornton, S. (1994) 'Moral panic, the media and British rave culture', in A. Ross and T. Rose (eds) *Microphone Fiends: Youth Music and Youth Culture*, London: Routledge, 176–92.

Thornton, S. (1995) *Club Cultures: Music, Media and Subcultural Capital*, Cambridge: Polity.

Tosh, J. (1991) *The Pursuit of History* 2nd edn, London: Longman.

Tseëlon, E. (1995) *The Masque of Femininity: The Presentation of Woman in Everyday Life*, London: Sage.

Tuan, Yi-Fu (1974) 'Space and place: humanistic perspective', *Progress in Geography* 6, 211–52.

Tulloch, J. and Jenkins, H. (1995) *Science Fiction Audiences: Watching 'Doctor Who' and 'Star Trek'*, London: Routledge.

Turner, B.S. (1984) *The Body and Society: Explorations in Social Theory*, Oxford: Blackwell.

Turner, B.S. (1991) 'The discourse of diet', in M. Featherstone, M. Hepworth and B.S. Turner (eds) *The Body: Social Process and Cultural Theory*, London: Sage (orig. 1982).

Turner, B.S. (1992) *Regulating Bodies: Essays in Medical Sociology*, London: Routledge.

Turner, B.S. (1994) *Orientalism, Postmodernism and Globalism*, London: Routledge.

Turner, G. (1990) *British Cultural Studies: An Introduction*, London: Unwin Hyman.

Turner, V.W. (1967) *The Forest of Symbols*, Ithaca, NY: Cornell University Press.

Tyler, S.A. (1984) 'The vision quest in the West, or what the mind's eye sees', *Journal of Anthropological Research*, 40(1), 23–40.

Tylor, E. (1871) *Primitive Culture*, London: John Murray.

Urry, J. (1988) 'Cultural change and contemporary holiday-making', *Theory, Culture and Society* 5(1), 35–55.

Urry, J. (1990a) *The Tourist Gaze*, London: Sage.

Urry, J. (1990b) 'The "consumption" of tourism', *Sociology* 24(1), 23–35.

Urry, J. (1992) 'The tourist gaze and the environment', *Theory, Culture and Society* 9(3), 1–26.

Urry, J. (1995) *Consuming Spaces*, London: Routledge.

Valentine, C. (1968) *Culture and Poverty*, Chicago: University of Chicago Press.

van Gennep, A. (1960) *The Rites of Passage*, Chicago: University of Chicago Press (orig. 1908).

Veblen, T. (1934) *The Theory of the Leisure Class*, New York: Modern Library (orig. 1899).

Venturi, R., Scott Brown, D. and Izenour, S. (1977) *Learning From Las Vegas*, rev. edn, Cambridge, MA: MIT Press.

Volosinov, V.N. (1973) *Marxism and the Philosophy of Language*, London: Seminar Press (orig. 1929 and 1930).

Wacquant, L.J.D. (1995) 'Pugs at work: bodily capital and bodily labour among professional boxers', *Body & Society* 1(1), March, 65–94.

Walkowitz, J. (1992) *City of Dreadful Delight: Narratives of Sexual Danger in Late-Victorian London*, London: Virago.

Wallerstein, I.M. (1974) *The Modern World-System*, New York: Academic Press.

Walvin, J. (1982) *A Child's World: A Social History of English Childhood 1800–1914*, Harmondsworth: Penguin.

Walvin, J. (1997) *Fruits of Empire: Exotic Pleasures and British Taste, 1660–1800*, Basingstoke: Macmillan.

Ward, A.H. (1993) 'Dancing in the dark: rationalism and the neglect of social dance', in H. Thomas (ed.) *Dance, Gender and Culture*, Basingstoke and London: Macmillan, 16–33.

Warner, M. (1985) *Monuments and Maidens: The Allegory of the Female Form*, London: Picador.

Watt, I. (1963) *The Rise of the Novel: Studies in Defoe, Richardson and Fielding*, Harmondsworth: Penguin (orig. 1957).

Waylen, G. (1992) 'Rethinking women's political participation and protest: Chile 1970–1990', in *Political Studies* XL(2), June, 299–314.

Weber, E. (1976) *Peasants into Frenchmen: The Modernisation of Rural France, 1870–1914*, Stanford: Stanford University Press.

Weber, M. (1930) *The Protestant Ethic and the Spirit of Capitalism*, London: Allen & Unwin.

Weber, M. (1967) 'Bureaucracy', in H.H. Gerth and C. Wright Mills (eds) *From Max Weber: Essays in Sociology*, Routledge & Kegan Paul.

Weber, M. (1978) 'Classes, status groups and parties', in W.G. Runciman (ed.) *Max Weber: Selections in Translation*, Cambridge: Cambridge University Press, 43–56 (orig. 1922).

Weedon, C., Tolson, A. and Mort, F. (1980) 'Theories of language and subjectivity', in *Culture, Media, Language*, London: Unwin Hyman.

Weeks, J. (1981) *Sex, Politics and Society*, Essex: Longman.

Weiner, J. (1991) *Language is the Essence of Culture*, Group for Debates in Anthropological Theory, Department of Social Anthropology, University of Manchester.

Weinstein, D. and Weinstein, M. (1993) *Postmodern(ized) Simmel*, London: Routledge.

Wells, L. (ed.) (1997) *Photography: A Critical Introduction*, London: Routledge.

Wernick, A. (1991) *Promotional Culture: Advertising, Ideology and Symbolic Expression*, London: Sage.

West, C. and Fenstermaker, S. (1995) 'Doing difference', *Gender and Society* 9(1), 8–37.

Westerbeck, C. and Meyerowitz, J. (1994) *Bystander: A History of Street Photography*, London: Thames & Hudson.

Westwood, S. (1984) *All Day, Every Day: Factory and Family in the Making of Women's Lives*, London: Pluto.

Wetherell, M. and Potter, J. (1992) *Mapping the Language of Racism: Discourse and the Legitimation of Exploitation*, Hemel Hempstead: Harvester Wheatsheaf.

White, H. (1973) *Metahistory: The Historical Imagination in Nineteenth Century Europe*, Baltimore, MD and London: John Hopkins Press.

Widdicombe, S. and Wooffitt, R. (1995) *The Language of Youth Subcultures: Social Identity in Action*, Hemel Hempstead: Harvester Wheatsheaf.

Willet, J. (ed.) (1978) *Brecht on Theatre*, London: Methuen.

Williams, D. (1975) 'The brides of Christ', in S. Ardener (ed.) *Perceiving Women*, London: Dent.

Williams, L. (1990) *Hard Core: Power, Pleasure, and the 'Frenzy of the Visible'*, London: Pandora.

Williams, R. (1963) *Culture and Society 1780–1950*, Harmondsworth: Penguin (orig. 1958).

Williams, R. (1965) *The Long Revolution*, Harmondsworth: Penguin (orig. 1961).

Williams, R. (1973a) *The Country and the City*, rp 1993, London: Hogarth.

Williams, R. (1973b) 'Base and superstructure in Marxist cultural theory', *New Left Review*, 82, 3–16.

Williams, R. (1974) *Television: Technology and Cultural Form*, Glasgow: Fontana/Collins.

Williams, R. (1977) *Marxism and Literature*, Oxford: Oxford University Press.

Williams, R. (1983a) 'Culture', in D. McLellan (ed.) *Marx: The First Hundred Years*, London: Fontana, 15–55.

Williams, R. (1983b) *Keywords: A Vocabulary of Culture and Society*, London: Fontana, 2nd edn.

Williamson, J. (1978) *Decoding Advertisements: Ideology and Meaning in Advertising*, London: Marion Boyars.

Willis, P. (1977) *Learning to Labour: How Working Class Kids Get Working Class Jobs*, Farnborough: Saxon House.

Willis, P. (1978) *Profane Culture*, London: Routledge & Kegan Paul.

Willis, P. with Jones, S., Canaan, J. and Hurd, G. (1990) *Common Culture: Symbolic Work at Play in the Everyday Cultures of the Young*, Milton Keynes: Open University Press.

Wilson, E. (1985) *Adorned in Dreams: Fashion and Modernity*, London: Virago.

Wilson, E. (1992) 'The invisible flâneur', *New Left Review* 191, 90–110.

Wilson, W.J. (ed.) (1993) *The Ghetto Underclass: Social Science Perspectives*, Newbury Park: Sage.

Winston, B. (1995) *Claiming the Real: The Griersonian Documentary and its Legitimations*, London: British Film Institute.

Wittgenstein, L. (1981) *Tractatus logico-philosophicus*, London: Routledge & Kegan Paul (orig. 1921).

Witz, A. and Savage, M. (1992) 'The gender of organisations', in M. Savage and A. Witz (eds) *Gender and Bureaucracy*, Oxford: Blackwell, 3–62.

Wolfe, T. (1983) *From Bauhaus to Our House*, London: Abacus.

Wolff, J. (1981) *The Social Production of Art*, London: Macmillan.

Wolff, J. (1985) 'The invisible *flâneuse:* women and the literature of modernity', *Theory, Culture and Society* 2(3), 37–46.

Wolff, J. (1993) 'On the road again: metaphors of travel in cultural criticism', *Cultural Studies* 7, 224–39.

Woolf, V. (1964) *Mrs Dalloway*, Harmondsworth: Penguin.

Wright, W. (1975) *Sixguns and Society*, Berkeley, CA: University of California Press.

Yeoh, B.S.A. (1992) 'Street names in colonial Singapore', *The Geographical Review* 82, 312–22.

Young, I.M. (1980) 'Throwing like a girl: a phenomenology of feminine body comportent, motility and spatiality', *Human Studies* 3, 137–56; reprinted in I.M. Young (1990) *Throwing Like a Girl and Other Essays in Feminist Philosophy and Social Theory*, Bloomington, IN: Indiana University Press.

Young, M. (1991) *An Inside Job: Policing and Police Culture in Britain*, Oxford: Clarendon.

Zerubavel, E. (1979) *Patterns of Time in Hospital Life: A Sociological Perspective*, Chicago: Chicago University Press.

Zerubavel, E. (1982) *Hidden Rhythms: Schedules and Calendars in Social Life*, Chicago: Chicago University Press.

Zukin, S. (1989) *Loft Living: Culture and Capital in Urban Change*, New Brunswick, NJ: Rutgers University Press (2nd edn).

Zukin, S. (1991) *Landscapes of Power: From Detroit to Disney World*, Berkeley and Los Angeles: University of California Press.

Zukin, S. (1992) 'Postmodern urban landscapes: mapping culture and power', in S. Lash and J. Friedman (eds) *Modernity and Identity*, Oxford: Blackwell, 221–47.

Zukin, S. (1995) *The Cultures of Cities*, Oxford: Blackwell.

Index

.